Daniel Rock

Textile fabrics

a descriptive catalogue of the collection of church-vestments

Daniel Rock

Textile fabrics
a descriptive catalogue of the collection of church-vestments

ISBN/EAN: 9783742867209

Manufactured in Europe, USA, Canada, Australia, Japa

Cover: Foto ©ninafisch / pixelio.de

Manufactured and distributed by brebook publishing software (www.brebook.com)

Daniel Rock

Textile fabrics

SOUTH KENSINGTON MUSEUM.

TEXTILE FABRICS;

A DESCRIPTIVE CATALOGUE

Of the Collection of Church-veſtments, Dreſſes, Silk Stuffs,

Needlework and Tapeſtries, forming that

Section of the Muſeum.

BY THE VERY REV. DANIEL ROCK, D.D.

Publiſhed for the Science and Art Department of the

Committee of Council on Education.

LONDON:
CHAPMAN AND HALL, 193, PICCADILLY.
1870.

CONTENTS OF THE INTRODUCTION.

SECTION I.—TEXTILES.

HE Geography of the Raw Materials.
Wool, x.
Cotton, xiii.
Hemp, xiii.
Flax, xiii.
Silk, xvi.
Gold, xxv.
Cloth of Gold, xxv.
Tissue, xxxi.
Silver, xxxiii.
Wire-drawing, xxxiii.
Gold thread, xxxiv.

Silks had various Names:
Holosericum, xxxvii.
Subsericum, xxxvii.
Examitum, xxxvii.
Xamitum, xxxvii.
Samit, xxxvii.
Ciclatoun, xxxix.
Cendal, xl.
Taffeta, xli.
Sarcenet, xlii.
Satin, xlii.

Cadas, xliii.
Camoca, xliv.
Cloth of Tars, xliv.
Velvet, xlv.
Diaper, xlvi.
Chrysoclavus, xlix.
Stauracin, l.
Polystauron, l.
Gammadion, l.
De quadrapolo, li.
De octapolo, li.
De fundato, liii.
Stragulatæ, liv.
Imperial, lv.
Baudekin, lvi.
Cloth of Pall, lviii.
Lettered silks, lix.
The Eagle, lxi.

Styles of Silks.
Chinese, lxiii.
Persian, lxiii.
Byzantine, lxiv.
Oriental, lxv.
Syrian, lxv.
Saracenic, lxvi.
Moresco-Spanish, lxvi.

Contents of the Introduction.

Places weaving Textiles.

Sicily, lxvii.
Lucca, lxxi.
Genoa, lxxii.
Venice, lxxiii.
Florence, lxxv.
Milan, lxxvi.
Great Britain, lxxvi.
Ireland, lxxix.
Flanders, lxxix.
France, lxxx.
Cologne, lxxxi.
Acca or Acre, lxxxiii.
Buckram, lxxxv.
Burdalifaunder, lxxxv.
Fuftian, lxxxvi.
Muflin, lxxxvii.
Cloth of Arefte, lxxxvii.

Silks diftinguifhed through their Colours and fhades of Colour.

Cloth of Tars, lxxxix.
Indicus, or fky-blue, xc.
Murrey, xc.
Changeable, or fhot, xci.
Marble, xci.

Section II.—Embroidery.

Of the Egyptians, xcii.
Of the Ifraelites, xcii.
Of the Greeks and Latins, or Phrygionic, xciii.
Opus plumarium, or feather-ftitch, xcv.
Opus pulvinarium, or cufhion-ftyle, xcvi.
Opus pectineum, or comb-drawn, xcvi.
Opus Anglicum, or Englifh work, xcviii.

Opus confutum, or cut work, cii.
Acceffories of gold and filver, civ; glafs, cv; enamel, cv.
Diapering, cviii.
Thread embroidery, cix.
Quilting, cx.

Section III.—Tapestry.

Egyptian, cx.
Afiatic, cxi.
Englifh, cxi.
Flemifh, cxii.
Arras, cxii.
Saracenic, cxii.
Imitated Tapeftry—" ftayned cloth," cxiv.
Carpets, cxv.

Section IV.

Ufefulnefs of the Collection

To the Hiftorian, cxvi.
The mifcalled Bayeaux Tapeftry, cxvi.

Section V.—Liturgy.

Liturgical rarities, cxxiii.

Section VI.

Ufefulnefs of the Collection to
Artifts, cxxx.
Manufacturers, cxxx.

Section VII.

Symbolifm, cxxxv.
The Gammadion, cxxxvii.
Vow of the Swan, the Peacock, &c.. cxli.

Contents of the Introduction.

SECTION VIII.

Usefulness of the Collection
To Literature and Languages, clii.
The Cyrillian alphabet, clii.

SECTION IX.—HERALDRY.

Armorial bearings worked upon vestments, cliii.
The Scrope and Grofvenor claims for the bend *or* on a field *azure*, cliii.

Cafe of the Countefs of Salisbury, clv.
Cafe of the Earl of Surrey, clv.

SECTION X.—BOTANY AND ZOOLOGY.

The giraffe, clvi.
The pheafant, clvi.
The cheetah, clvi.
The hom, clvii.
The pine-apple, clix.
The artichoke, clix.
The paffion-flower, clx.

INTRODUCTION.

LIKE every other specific collection of art labour among the several such brought together within these splendid halls of the South Kensington Museum, this extensive one made from woven stuffs, tapestry, and needlework, is meant to have, like them, its own peculiar useful purposes. Here, at a glance, may be read the history of the loom of various times and in many lands. Here may be seen a proof of the onward march of trade and its consequent civilizing influences. Here we take a peep at the private female life in ages gone by, and learn how women, high-born and lowly, spent or rather ennobled many a day of life in needlework, not merely graceful but artistic. Here, in fine, in strict accordance with the intended industrial purposes of this public institution, artizans, designers, and workers in all kinds of embroidery, may gather many an useful lesson for their respective crafts, in the rare as well as beautiful samples set out before them.

The materials out of which the articles in this collection were woven, are severally wool, hemp, flax, cotton, silk, gold, and silver. The silken textures are in general wholly so; in many instances they are wrought up along with either cotton, or with flax; hence, in ancient documents, the distinction of "holosericum," all silk, and "subsericum," not all silk, or the warp—that is, the longitudinal threads—of cotton or flax, and the woof—that is the cross-threads of silk. Very seldom is the gold or the gilt silver woven into these textiles found upon them in a solid wire-drawn form, but almost always, after being flattened very thin, the precious metal was wound about a very small twist of cotton, or of flax, and thus became what we call gold thread. As a substitute for this, the Moors of Granada, and after them the Spaniards of that kingdom, employed strips of gilded parchment, as we shall have to notice.

Section I.—TEXTILES.

NDER its widest acceptation, the word "textile" means every kind of stuff, no matter its material, wrought in the loom. Hence, whether the threads be spun from the produce of the animal, vegetable, or the mineral kingdom—whether of sheep's wool, goats' hair, camels' wool, or camels' hair—whether of flax, hemp, mallow, Spanish broom, the filaments drawn out of the leaves of the yucca—Adam's needle—and other plants of the lily and asphodel tribes of flowers, the fibrous coating about pods, or cotton; whether of the mineral amianthus, of gold, silver, or of any other metal, it signifies nothing, the webs from such materials are textiles. Unlike to these are other appliances for garment-making in many countries; and of such materials, not the least curious, if not odd to our ideas, is paper, which is so much employed for the purpose by the Japanese.

At the outset of our subject a word or two may be of good use, upon

The Geography of the Raw Materials.

one or other of which we shall always find wrought up in the textiles in this collection. We will then begin with

WOOL.

After gleaning out of the writings of the ancients all they have said about the physical geography of the earth, as far as their knowledge of it went, and casting our eyes upon a map of the world as known of old, we shall see at once the materials which man had at hand, in every clime, for making his articles of dress.

In all the colder regions the well-furred skins of several families of beasts could, by the ready help of a thorn for a needle, and the animal's own sinews for thread, be fashioned, after a manner, into the requisites of dress.

Throughout by far the longest length and the widest breadth of the earth, sheep, at an early period, were bred, not so much for food as for raiment. At first, the locks of wool torn away from the animal's back by brambles, were gathered: afterwards shearing was thought of and followed in some countries, while in others the wool was not cut off, but plucked by the hand away from the living creature, as we learn from Pliny:[1] "Oves non ubique tondentur: durat quibusdam in locis vel-

---

[1] Lib. viii. c. 47.

lendi mos." Got in either method the fleeces were, from the earliest times, spun by women from the distaff. At last so wishful were the growers to improve the coats of their lambs that they clothed them in skins; a process which not only fined the staple of the wool, but kept it clean, and better fitted it for being washed and dyed, as we are told by many ancient writers, such as Horace and the great agricultural authority Varro. In uttering his wish for a sweet peaceful home in his old age, either at Tibur, or on the banks of the pleasant Gelæsus, thus sings the poet:

> Dulce pellitis ovibus Gelæsi
> Flumen.[1]

And what were these "oves pellitæ," or "tectæ" and "molles," as they were called, in contradistinction to "hirtæ," we understand from Varro, who says, "oves pellitæ; quæ propter lanæ bonitatem, ut sunt Tarentinæ et Atticæ, pellibus integuntur, ne lana inquinetur quo minus vel infici recte possit, vel lavari ac parari."[2]

This latter very ancient daily work followed by women of all degrees, spinning from off the distaff, was taught to our Anglo-Saxon sisters among all ranks of life, from the king's daughter downwards. In his life of Eadward the elder, A.D. 901, Malmesbury writes: "Filias suas ita instituerat ut literis omnes in infantia maxime vacarent, mox etiam colum et acum exercere consuescerent, ut his artibus pudice impubem virginitatem transigerent."[3] The same occupation is even now a female favourite in many countries on the Continent, particularly so all through Italy. Long ago it bestowed the name of spindle-tree on the Euonymus plant, on account of the good spindles which its wood affords, and originated the term "spinster," yet to be found in our law-books as meaning an unmarried woman even of the gentlest blood, while every now and then from the graves that held the ashes of our sisters of the British and the Anglo-Saxon epochs, are picked up the elaborately ornamented leaden whorls which they fastened at the lower end of their spindles to give them a due weight and steadiness as they twirled them round.

Beginning with the British islands on the west, and going eastward on a line running through the Mediterranean sea, and stretching itself out far into Asia, we find that the peoples who dwelt to the north of such a boundary wrought several of their garments out of sheep's wool, goats' hair, and beavers' fur, while those living to the south, including the

---

[1] Lyric. c. VI. vi. [2] De Re Rustica, ii. 2.
[3] Gesta Regum Anglorum, t. I. lib. ii. p. 198, ed. Hardy.

inhabitants of North Africa, Arabja, and Perfia, befides the above-named animal produce, employed for thefe purpofes, as well as tent-making, the wool and hair which their camels gave them: the Baptift's garment was of the very coarfeft kind.

Of the ufe of woollen ftuff, not woven but plaited, among the older ftock of the Britons, a curious inftance was very lately brought to light while cutting through an early Celtic grave-hill or barrow in Yorkfhire: the dead body had been wrapped, as was fhown by the few unrotted fhreds ftill cleaving to its bones, in a woollen fhroud of coarfe and loofe fabric wrought by the plaiting procefs without a loom.[1]

As time crept on, it brought along with it the loom, fafhioned though it was after its fimpleft form, to the far weft, and taught its ufe throughout the Britifh iflands. The art of dyeing very foon followed; and fo beautiful were the tints which our Britons knew how to give to their wools, that ftrangers, while they wondered at, were not a little jealous of the fplendour of thofe tones. From the heavy ftrefs laid upon the rule which taught that the official colour in their drefs affigned to each of the three ranks into which the bardic order was diftinguifhed, muft be of one fimple unbroken fhade, whether fpotlefs white, fymbolic of fun-light and holinefs, for the druid or prieft—whether fky-blue, emblem of peace, for the bard or poet—or green, the livery of the wood and field, for the Ovydd or teacher of natural hiftory and leech-craft, yet at the fame moment we know that party-coloured ftuffs were woven here, and after two forms: the poftulants afking leave to be admitted into bardifm might be recognized by the robe barred with ftripes of white, blue, and green, which they had to wear during all the term of their initiation. With regard to the bulk of our people, according to the Greek hiftorian of Rome—Dion Caffius, born A.D. 155—the garments worn by them were made of a texture wrought in a fquare pattern of feveral colours; and fpeaking of our brave-hearted Britifh queen, Boadicea, that fame writer tells us that fhe ufually had on, under her cloak, a motley tunic, χιτὼν παμποίκιλος, that is, checkered all over with many colours. This garment we are fairly warranted in deeming to have been a native ftuff, woven of worfted after a pattern in tints and defign exactly like one or other of the prefent Scotch plaids. Pliny, who feems to have gathered a great deal of his natural hiftory from fcraps of hearfay, moft likely included thefe ancient forts of Britifh textiles along with thofe from Gaul, when he wrote:—"Plurimis vero liciis texere quæ polymita appellant, Alexandria inftituit: fcutullis dividere, Gallia." But to weave with a

---

[1] Journal of the Archæological Inftitute, t. XXII. p. 254.

good number of threads, so as to work the cloths called polymita, was first taught in Alexandria; to divide by checks, in Gaul.[1]

The native botanical home of

COTTON

is in the East. India almost everywhere throughout her wide-spread countries, and many kingdoms of old, arrayed, as she still arrays herself, in cotton, which she gathered from a plant of the mallow family, that had its wild growth there; and in this same vegetable produce the lower orders of the people dwelling still further to the east were fain to clothe themselves.

HEMP,

a plant of the nettle tribe, and called by botanists "cannabis sativa," was of old well known in the far north of Germany, and all over the ancient Scandinavia. Full two thousand five hundred years ago, Herodotus[2] thus wrote of it: "Hemp grows in the country of the Scythians, which except in the thickness and height of the stalk, very much resembles flax; in the qualities mentioned, however, the hemp is much superior. It grows in a wild state, and is also cultivated. The Thracians make clothing of it very like linen cloth; nor could any person, without being very well acquainted with the substance, say whether this clothing is made of hemp or flax." From "cannabis," its name in Latin, have we taken our own word "canvas," to mean any texture woven of hempen thread.

FLAX

now follows. Who that has ever seen growing a patch of beautiless, sad-looking hemp, and as he wandered a few steps further, came upon a field of flax all in flower, with its gracefully-drooped head, strewing the breeze, as it strayed over it, with its frail, light-blue petals, could at first have thought that both these plants were about to yield such kindred helps for man in his wide variety of wants? Yet so it is. Besides many other countries, all over this our native land flax is to be found growing wild. Though every summer its handsome bloom must have caught the eye of our Celtic British forefathers, they were not aware for ages of the use of this plant for clothing purposes, else had they left behind them some shred of linen in one or other of their many graves; since, following, as they did, the usage of being buried in the best of the garments they were accustomed to, or most loved when alive, their bodies would have been found arrayed in some small article of linen texture, had they ever worn

---

[1] Plin. lib. viii.   [2] Herod. book iv. 74.

such. That at length they became acquainted with its usefulness, and learned to prepare and spin it, is certain; and in all likelihood the very name "lin-white thread," which those Celts gave it in its wrought shape, furnished the Greeks with their word λίνον, and the Latins their *linum*, for linen. The term "flax," which we still keep, from the Anglo-Saxon tongue, for the plant itself and its raw material, and the Celtic "linen," for the same vegetable produce when spun and woven into cloth, are words for things akin in our present language, which, as in many such like instances, show the footprints of those races that, one after another, have trod this land.

To the valley of the Nile must we go if we wish to learn the earliest history of the finest flaxen textiles. Time out of mind were the Egyptians famous as well for the growth of flax, as for the beautiful very fine linen they wove out of it, and which became to them a most profitable, because so widely sought for, article of commerce. Their own word, "byssus," for the plant itself, became among the Greeks, and afterwards among the Latin nations, the term for linens wrought in Egyptian looms. Long before the oldest book in the world was written, the tillers of the ground all over Egypt had been heedful in sowing their flax, and anxious about its harvest. It was one of their staple crops, and hence was it that, in punishment of their hard-hearted Pharaoh, the hail plague which, at the bidding of Moses, showered down from heaven, hurt throughout the land the flax just as it was getting ripe.[1] Though the Jordan grew flax upon its banks, and all over the land that would soon belong to Abraham's children, the women there, like Rahab, carefully dried it when pulled, and stacked it for future hackling upon the roofs of their houses;[2] still, it was from Egypt, as Solomon hints,[3] that the Jews had to draw their fine linen. At a later period, among the woes foretold to Egypt, the prophet Isaiah warns her that they shall be confounded who wrought (there) in combing and weaving fine linen.[4]

How far the reputation of Egyptian workmanship in the craft of the loom had spread abroad is shown us by the way in which, beside sacred, heathenish antiquity has spoken of it. Herodotus says:—"Amasis King of Egypt gave to the Minerva of Lindus, a linen corslet well worthy of inspection,"[5] and further on,[6] telling of another corslet which Amasis had sent the Lacedæmonians, observes that it was of linen, and had a vast number of figures of animals inwoven into its fabric, and was likewise embroidered with gold and tree-wool. What is more worthy

---

[1] Exodus ix. 31.   [2] Joshua ii. 6.   [3] Proverbs vii. 16.   [4] Isaiah xix. 9.
[5] Herodotus, b. ii. c. 182, Rawlinson's Translation, t. ii. p. 275.   [6] Ib. b. iii. c. 47.

of admiration in it is that each of the twifts, although of fine texture, contains within it 360 threads, all of them clearly vifible.[1] By thefe truftworthy evidences we clearly fee that in thofe early times, Egypt was not only widely known for its delicately woven byffus, but it fupplied all the neighbouring nations with the fineft fort of linens.

From written let us now go to material proofs at hand. During late years many mummies have been brought to this country from Egypt, and the narrow bandages with which they were found to have been fo admirably, even according to our modern requirements of chirurgical fitnefs, fo artiftically fwathed, have been unwrapped; and always have they been fo fine in their texture as to fully verify the praifes of old beftowed upon the beauty of the Egyptian loom-work. Moreover, from thofe who have taken a nearer and, fo to fay, a trade-like infight into fuch an article of manufacture, we learn that, "The fineft piece of mummy-cloth, fent to England by Mr. Salt, and now in the Britifh Mufeum, of linen, appears to be made of yarns of near 100 hanks in the pound, with 140 threads in an inch in the warp and about 64 in the woof."[2] Another piece of linen which the fame diftinguifhed traveller obtained at Thebes, has 152 threads in the warp, and 71 in the woof.[3]

Here ftarts up a curious queftion. Though, from all antiquity upwards till within fome few years back, the unbroken belief had been that fuch mummy-clothing was undoubtedly made of linen woven out of pure unmixed flax, fome writers led, or rather mifled, by a few ftray words in Herodotus about tree-wool, while fpeaking of the corflet of Amafis, quoted juft now, took at once the expreffion of that hiftorian to mean wool, and then fkipped to the concluſion that all Egyptian textiles wrought a thoufand years before were mixed with cotton. When, however, it be borne in mind that even feveral hundred years after the Greek hiftorian wrote, the common belief exifted that, like cotton, filk alfo was the growth of a tree, as we are told by Virgil:

> Quid nemora Æthiopum, molli canentia lana
> Velleraque ut foliis depectant tenuia Seres?[4]
>
> Soft wool from downy groves the Æthiop weaves,
> And Seres comb their filken fleece from leaves—

the εἰρίοισι ἀπὸ ξύλου of Herodotus may be underftood to mean filk, juft as well as cotton; nay, the rather fo, as it feems very likely that, at the

---

[1] Herodotus, t. ii. pp. 442-43.
[2] "Ancient Egypt," by Sir Gardiner Wilkinfon, t iii. p. 122.   [3] Ib. p. 125.
[4] Georg. lib. ii. 120-121.

time when Amafis lived, filk, in the fhape of thread, had found, through traders' hands, its way to the markets of Egypt, and muft have been thought a more fitting thing, from being a new as well as coftly material, to grace a royal gift to a religious fanctuary of high repute, than the lefs precious and more common cotton. While this queftion was agitated, fpecimens of mummy-cloth were fubmitted to the judgment of feveral perfons in the weaving trade deemed moft competent to fpeak upon the matter. Helped only by the fingers' feel and the naked eye, fome among them agreed that fuch textures were really woven of cotton. This opinion was but fhortlived. Other individuals, more philofophical, went to work on a better path. In the firft place, they clearly learned, through the microfcope, the exact and never-varying phyfical ftructure of both thefe vegetable fubftances. That of cotton they found in its ultimate fibre to be a tranfparent tube without joints, flattened fo that its inward furfaces are in contact along its axis, and alfo twifted fpirally round its axis; that of flax, a tranfparent tube, jointed like a cane, and not flattened or twifted fpirally.[1] Examined in the fame way, feveral old famples of byffus or mummy-bandages from Egypt in every one inftance were afcertained to be of fine unmixed flaxen linen. Ages before French Flanders had dreamed of weaving fine lawns, ages before one of her induftrial cities—Cambray—had fo far taken the lead as to be allowed to beftow her own name, in the fhape of "cambric," on the fineft kind that modern European ingenuity could produce, Egypt had known how to give to the world even a yet finer fort, and centuries after fhe had fallen away from her place among the kingdoms of the earth, her enthralled people ftill kept up their ancient fuperiority in fpinning and weaving their fine, fometimes tranfparent, byffus, of which a fpecimen or two may be feen in this collection.[2]

For many reafons the hiftory of

SILK

is not only curious, but highly interefting. In the early ages, its very exiftence was quite unknown, and when found out, the knowledge of it ftole forth from the far eaft, and ftraggled weftward very very flowly. For all that lengthened period during which their remarkable civilization lafted, the older Egyptians never once beheld filk: neither they, nor the Ifraelites, nor any other of the moft ancient kingdoms of the earth, knew of it in any fhape, either as a fimple twift, or as a woven ftuff. Not

---

[1] Thomfon in the Philofophical Magazine, 3rd feries, t. v. num. 29, Nov. 1834.
[2] No. 152.

Introduction. xvii

the smallest shred of silk has hitherto been found in the tombs, or amid the ruins of the Pharaonic period.

No where does Holy Writ, old or new, tell anything of silk but in one single place, the Apocalypse, xviii. 12. True it is that, in the English authorized version, we read of "silk" as if spoken of by Ezekiel, xvi. 10, 13; and again, in Proverbs, xxxi. 22; yet there can be no doubt, but that in both these passages, the word silk is wrong through the translators misunderstanding the original Hebrew משי (meschi). Of this word, Parkhurst says: "As a noun, משי, according to our translation (is) silk, but not so rendered in any of the ancient versions. *Silk* would indeed well enough answer the ideal meaning of the Hebrew word, from its being *drawn forth* from the bowels of the silk-worm, and that to a degree of fineness, so as to form very slender threads. But I meet with no evidence that the Israelites in very early times (and to these Ezekiel refers) had any knowledge of *silk*, much less of the manner in which it was formed; משי, therefore, I think, means some kind of *fine linen* or *cotton cloth*, so denominated from the *fineness* with which the threads whereof it consisted were *drawn out*. The Vulgate, by rendering it in the former passage, 'subtilibus' *fine*, as opposed to *coarse*, has nearly preserved the true idea of the Hebrew."[1] Braunius, too, no mean authority, after bestowing a great deal of study on the matter, gives it as his well-weighed judgment that, throughout the whole Hebrew Bible, no mention whatever can be found of silk, which was a material utterly unknown to the children of Israel.[2] Once only is silk spoken of in the New Testament, and then while St. John[3] is reckoning it up along with the gold, and silver, and precious stones, and pearls, and fine linen—byssus —and purple which, with many other costly freights merchants were wont to bring in ships to that mighty city which, in the Apostle's days, ruled over the kings of the earth.

Long after the days of Ezekiel was it that silk, in its raw form only, made up into hanks, first found its way to Egypt, western Asia, and eastern Europe.

To Aristotle do we owe the earliest notice, among the ancients, of the silk-worm, and although his account be incorrect, it has much value, since, along with his description, the celebrated Greek philosopher gives us information about the original importation of raw silk into the western world. Brought from China, through India, till it reached the Indus, the silk came by water across the Arabian Ocean, up the Red Sea, and

---

[1] Hebrew and English Lexicon. London, 1813, p. 415.
[2] De Vestitu Heb. Sac., lib. I. cap. viii. § 8.   [3] Apoc. xviii. 12.

thence over the Isthmus of Suez, or, perhaps, rather by the overland route, through Persia, to the small but commercial island of Cos (now Kos), lying off the coast of Asia Minor. Pamphile, daughter of Plates, is reported to have first woven it (silk) in Cos.[1] Here, by female hands, were wrought those light thin gauzes which became so fashionable among some high dames, but while so often spoken of by the poets of the Augustan period, were stigmatized by some among them, as well as by the heathen moralists of after ages, as anything but seemly for women's wear. Thus Tibullus says of this sort of clothing:

> Illa gerat vestes tenues, quas fœmina Coa
> Texuit, auratas difpofuitque vias.[2]
>
> She may thin garments wear, which female Coan hands
> Have woven, and in ftripes difpofed the golden bands.

Years afterwards, thus laments Seneca, the philofopher: "Video fericas veftes, fi veftes vocandæ funt, in quibus nihil eft, quo defendi aut corpus aut denique pudor poffit." I behold filken garments, if garments they can be called, which are a protection neither for the body nor for fhame.[3] And later ftill, and in the Chriftian era, an echo to the remarks of Seneca do we hear in the words of Solinus: " Hoc illud eft fericum in quo oftentare potius corpora quàm veftire, primò feminis, nunc etiam viris perfuafit luxuriæ libido."[4] This is filk, in which at firft women but now even men have been led, by their cravings after luxury, to fhow rather than to clothe their bodies.

While looking over fome precious early mediæval MS., often do we yet find that its beautifully limned and richly gilt illuminations, to keep them from harm, or being hurt through the rubbings of the next leaf, have faftened befide them a covering of the thinneft gauze, juft as we put in fheets of filver paper for that purpofe over engravings. The likelihood is that fome at leaft of thefe may be fhreds from fome of thofe thin tranflucent textiles which found fuch favour in the fafhionable world for fo long a time during the claffic period. To fome at leaft of our readers, the curious example of fuch gauzy interleafings in the manufcript of Theodulph, now at Puy en Velay, will occur.

Not only thefe tranfparent filken gauzes wrought in Cos, but far more tafty ftuffs, and flowered too, from Chinefe looms, found their way to Afia Minor and Italy. In telling of the barbarous nations then called the Seres, Dionyfius Periegetes writes that they comb the varioufly coloured flowers of the defert land to make precious figured garments,

---

[1] Hift. Anim. V. c. 19, p. 850, ed. Duval.   [2] Tibullus, l. ii. 6.
[3] De Beneficiis, l. vii. c.   [4] Solinus, c. 1.

resembling in colour the flowers of the meadow, and rivalling (in fineness) the work of spiders.[1]

As may be easily imagined, silken garments were brought, at an early period, to imperial Rome. Such, however, were the high prices asked for them, that few either would or could afford to buy these robes for their wives and daughters; since, at first, they were looked upon as quite unbecoming for men's wear; hence, by a law of the Roman senate under Tiberius, it was enacted: "Ne vestis serica vicos fœdaret." While noticing how womanish Caligula became in his dress, Suetonius remarks his silken attire: "Aliquando sericatus et cycladatus."[2] An exception was made by some emperors for very great occasions, and both Titus and Vespasian wore dresses of silk when they celebrated at Rome their triumph over Judæa. Of the emperors who adopted whole silk for their clothing, Heliogabalus was the first, and so fond was he of the material, that, in the event of wishing to hang himself, he had got for the occasion a rope, one strand of which was silk, and the other two dyed with purple and scarlet: "Paraverat funes, blatta et serico, et cocco intortos, quibus si necesse esset, laqueo vitam finiret."[3]

The abnegation of another Roman Emperor, Aurelian, both in respect of himself and his empress, is, however, very remarkable: "Vestem holosericam neque ipse in vestiario suo habuit neque alteri utendam dedit. Et cum ab eo uxor sua peteret, ut unico pallio blatteo serico uteretur, ille respondit absit, ut auro fila pensentur. Libra enim auri tunc libra serici fuit."[4] Aurelian neither had himself in his wardrobe a garment wholly silk, nor gave one to be worn by another. When his own wife begged him to allow her to have a single mantle of purple silk, he replied, "Far be it from us to allow thread to be reckoned worth its weight in gold." For then a pound of gold was the price of a pound of silk.

Here it ought to be mentioned that, for some time before this period a very broad distinction had been drawn, even in the sumptuary laws of the empire, between garments made wholly, and partially of silk; in the former, all the web, both woof and warp, is woven of nothing but silk; in the latter, the woof is of cotton or of thread, the warp only of silk. This difference in the texture is thus well set forth by Lampridius, in his life of Alexander Severus, of whom he says: he had few garments of silk—he never wore a tunic woven wholly of silk, and he never gave away cloth made of silk mixed with less valuable stuff. "Vestes sericas ipse raras habuit; holosericas nunquam induit subsericam nunquam donavit."[5]

---

[1] Quoted by Yates, Textrinum Antiquorum, p. 181. [2] Suetonius, c. 52.
[3] Lampridius, c. 26. [4] Vopiscus, c. 45. [5] Severus, c. 40.

Clothing made wholly or in part out of filk, became every year more and more fought for. So remunerative was the trade of weaving the raw material into its various forms, that, by the Juftinian pandects, the revifed code of laws for the Roman Empire, drawn up and publifhed A. D. 533—a monopoly in it was given to the court, and looms worked by women were fet up in the imperial palace. Thus Byzantium became, and long continued famous for the beauty of its filken ftuffs. Still, the raw filk itfelf had to be brought thither from abroad; but a remedy was very near at hand. Two Greek monks, while fpending many years among the Chinefe, had well learned the whole procefs of rearing the worm. They came home, and brought back with them a goodly number of eggs hidden in their walking-ftaves, likely made of that hollow tough fort of reed or tall grafs, the Arundo Donax; and, carrying them to Conftantinople, they prefented thefe eggs to the Emperor, who gladly received them. When hatched, the worms were diftributed all over Greece and Afia Minor, and very foon the weftern world reared its own filk. Not long afterwards, Perfia and India alfo became filk-growing countries. In fome places, at leaft in Greece, the weaving not only of the finer kinds of cloth, but of filk, got at laft into the hands of the Jews. Writing of his travels, A. D. 1161, Benjamin of Tudela tells us that the great city of Thebes contained about two thoufand Jewifh inhabitants. Thefe are the moft eminent manufacturers of filk and purple cloth in all Greece.[1]

Telling us how the fleet of our firft Richard coafted the fhores of Spain on its voyage to the Holy Land, Hoveden fays of Almeria and its filk factory: "Deinde per nobilem civitatem quæ dicitur Almaria ubi fit nobile fericum et delicatum quod dicitur fericum de Almaria."[2] So prized were thefe fine delicate textiles that they were paid as tribute to princes: "Infula de Maiore reddit ei (regi Arragoniæ) trecentos pannos fericos de Almaria per annum de tributo," &c.[3]

South Italy wrought rich filken ftuffs by the end of the eleventh century; for we are told by our countryman, Ordericus Vitalis, who died in the firft half of the twelfth century, that Mainerius, the abbot of his monaftery of St. Evroul, at Uzey, in Normandy, on coming home, brought with him from Apulia feveral large pieces of filk, and gave to the Church four of the fineft ones, with which four copes were made for the chanters: "De pallis quas ipfe de Apulia detulerat quatuor de pre-

---

[1] Early Travels in Paleftine, ed. T. Wright, p. 71.
[2] Rog. Hoveden, Ann. ed. Savile, Rer. Ang. Script., p. 382.
[3] Ib. p. 382, b.

ciosioris S. Ebrulfo obtulit ex quibus quatuor cappæ cantorum in eadem factæ funt ecclesia."[1]

From a feeling alive in every heart throughout the length and breadth of Chriftendom that the beft of all things ought to be given for the fervice of its religious rites, the garments of its celebrating prieſthood, from the far eaſt to the uttermoſt weſt, were, if not always, at leaſt very often wholly of filk—holofericus. To this fact we have pointed for the fake of remembering that were it not fo, we had been, at this day, without the power of being able to fee through the few but tattered ſhreds before us, what elegantly defigned and gorgeous ſtuffs the foreign mediæval loom could weave, and what beautiful embroidery our own countrywomen knew fo well how to work. Thefe fpecimens help us alfo to rightly underſtand the defcription of thofe fplendid veſtments and ritual appliances enumerated with fuch exactnefs in the old inventories of our venerable cathedrals and pariſh churches as well as the early wardrobe accompts of our kings, the wills and bequeſts of our dignified ecclefiaſtics and nobility, to fome of which documents we ſhall have to refer a little later.

In coming weſtward among us, all thefe fo much coveted ſtuffs brought along with them their own feveral names by which they were commonly known throughout the eaſt, whether Greece, Afia Minor, or Perfia. Hence when we read of Samit, ciclatoun, cendal, baudekin, and other fuch terms quite unknown to trade now-a-day, we ſhould bear in mind that notwithſtanding the wide variety of fpelling, or rather miſſpelling, each of thefe appellations has run through, we reach at laſt their true derivations, and fo happily get to know in what country and by whofe hands they were wrought.

As trade grew up, ſhe brought thefe fine filken textiles to our markets, and articles of drefs were made of filk for men's as well as women's wear among the wealthy. At what period the raw material came to be imported here, not fo much for embroidery as to be wrought in the loom, we do not exactly know; but from feveral fides we learn that our countrywomen of all degrees bufied themfelves in weaving. Among the home occupations of maidens dedicated to God, St. Aldhelm, at the end of the feventh century, feems to number: " Cortinarum five ſtragularum textura."[2] In the council at Clovefhoo, under Archbiſhop Cuthberht, A. D. 747, nuns are exhorted to fpend their time in reading or finging pfalms rather than weaving and knitting vainglorious garments of many

---

[1] Ordericus Vitalis, Ecc. Hift., l. v. p. 584.
[2] De Laudibus Virginitatis, Opp. ed. Giles, 15.

colours: "Magifque legendis libris vel canendis pfalmis, quam texendis et plectendis vario colore inanis gloriæ veftibus ftudeant operam dare."[1] By that curious old Englifh book, the "Ancren Riwle," written towards the end of the twelfth century, ankreffes are forbidden to make purfes to gain friends therewith, or blodbendes.[2] Were it not that the weaving efpecially of filk, was fo generally followed in the cloifter by Englifh women, it had been ufelefs to have fo ftrongly difcountenanced the practice.

Thofe "blodbendes," or narrow ftrips for winding round the arm after bleeding, are curioufly illuftrative of an old national cuftom for health-fake kept up in the remembrance of fome old folks ftill living, of periodical blood-letting. To his practices upon the heads and chins of people the barber at no remote period, added that of bleeding them; and the old Englifh barber furgeons held a high pofition among the gilds of London. To fhow where he lived each member of that brotherhood had hanging out from the walls of his houfe a long thin pole painted fpirally black and white, the white in token of the blodbende or bandage to be winded and kept about the patient's arm.

But on filk weaving by our women in fmall hand-looms, a very important witnefs, efpecially about feveral curious fpecimens in this collection, is John Garland, born at the beginning of the thirteenth century in London, where his namefakes and likely of his ftock, were and are known. Firft, a John Garland, A. D. 1170, held a prebend's ftall in St. Paul's Cathedral.[3] Another, A. D. 1211, was fheriff, at a later period.[4] A third, a wealthy draper of London, gave freely towards the building of a church in Somerfetfhire.[5] A fourth, who died A. D. 1461, lies buried in St. Sythe's;[6] and, at the prefent day, no fewer than twenty-two tradef-men of that name, of whom fix are merchants of high ftanding in the city, are mentioned in the London Poft Office Directory for this year 1868. We give thefe inftances as fome have tried to rob us of John Garland by faying he was not an Englifhman, though of himfelf he had faid: "Anglia cui mater fuerat, cui gallia nutrix," &c.

In a fort of very fhort dictionary, drawn up by that writer, and printed at the end of "Paris fous Philippe Le Bel," edited by M. H. Geraud, our countryman fays: "Textrices quæ texunt ferica texta projiciunt fila aurata officio cavillarum et percuciunt fubtemina cum linea (lignea?) fpata: de textis vero fiunt cingula et crinalia divitum mulierum et ftole facerdotum."[7] Though fhort, this paffage is curious and valuable. From

---

[1] Concil. Ecc. Brit. ed. Spelman, i, 256. [2] P. 421.
[3] Dugdale's St. Paul's, p. 264. [4] Liber de Antiq. Legibus, pp. 3, 223.
[5] Leland's Itinerary, t. 7, p. 99. [6] Stowe's Survey, B. iii. p. 31. [7] Ib. 607.

it we learn that, befides the ufual homely textiles, thofe more coftly cloth-of-gold webs were wrought by our women, and very likely, among their other productions—cingula—were thofe "blodbendes," the weaving of which had been forbidden to ankreffes and nuns; perhaps, too, of thofe narrow gold-wrought ribbons in this collection, pp. 24, 33, 38, 217, 218, 219, 221, &c., fome may have been fo employed by our high-born dames on occafion of their being bled, fince as late as the fixteenth century fome feafons were deemed fit, others quite unfitting for the operation. Hence, in his Richard II. act 1, fcene i. Shakefpeare makes the king to warn thofe wrath-kindled gentlemen, Bolingbroke and Norfolk:

> Our doctors fay this is no month to bleed.

And our moft popular books in olden time, one the Shepherd's Kalendar, fpeaking about the figns of the zodiack, tell us which of the twelve months are either good, evil, or indifferent for blood-letting.

John Garland's "cingula" may alfo mean thofe rich girdles or fafhes worn by our women round the waift, and of which we have one in this collection, No. 8571, p. 218. Of this fort, is that border—amber coloured filk and diapered—round a veftment found in a grave at Durham, and like "a thick lace, one inch and a quarter broad—evidently owing its origin, not to the needle, but to the loom," &c.[1] For the artift wifhful to be correct concerning the head-gear of ladies from Anglo-Saxon times till the end of the later Plantagenets, this collection can furnifh examples of thofe bands in thofe narrow textiles fpoken of by our John Garland. For an after-period thofe bands are fhown on the ftatuary, and amid the limning in illuminated MSS. of the thirteenth century; as inftances of the narrow girdle, may be viewed a lady's effigy, in Romney church, Hants; and that of Ann of Bohemia, in Weftminfter Abbey; both to be found in Hollis's Monumental Effigies of Great Britain; for the band about the head, the examples in the wood-cuts in Planchè's Britifh Coftumes, p. 116.

Of fuch head-bands we have one at number 8569, p. 217, and other three mentioned upon p. 221. They are, no doubt, the old fnôd of the Anglo-Saxon period. For high-born dames they were wrought of filk and gold; thofe of lower degree wore them of fimpler ftuff. The filken fnood, affected to the prefent hour by young unmarried women in Scotland, is a truthful witnefs to the fafhion in vogue during Anglo-Saxon and later times in this country.

With regard to what John Garland fays of ftoles fo made, there is one here, No. 1233, p. 24, quite entire.

---

[1] Raine's St. Cuthbert, p. 196.

From what has been here brought forward, it will be seen that of silk, whence it came or what was its kind, nothing was truly understood, even by the learned, for many ages. While, then, we smile at Virgil and the other ancients for thinking that silk was a sort of herbaceous fleece growing upon trees, let us not forget that not so many years ago our own Royal Society printed a paper in which it is set forth that the yet-called Barnacle Goose comes from a mussel-like bivalve shell, known as the "Anatifa," or Barnacle, an origin for the bird still believed in by some of our seafaring folks, and fostered after a manner by well-read people by the scientific nomenclature of the shell and the vernacular epithet for the goose. In the twelfth century, our countryman, Alexander Neckham, foster-brother to our Richard I., wrote of this marvel thus: " Ex lignis abiegnis salo diuturno tempore madefactis originem sumit avis quæ vulgo dicitur bernekke," &c.[1] Such, however, was the Cirencester Augustinian friar's knowledge of natural history, that, at least four hundred years ere the Royal Society had a being amongst us, he thus spurns the popular belief upon the subject:—

> Ligna novas abiegna salo madefacta, jubente
> Natura, volucres edere fama refert.
> Id viscosus agit humor, quod publica fama
> Asserit indignans philosophia negat.[2]

Of a truth the Record Commission is doing England good service by drawing out of darkness the works of our mediæval writers.

The breeding of the worm and the manufacture of its silk both spread themselves with steady though slow steps over most of those countries which skirt the shores of the Mediterranean; so that, by the tenth century, those processes had reached from the far east to the uttermost western limits of that same sea. Even then, and a long time after, the natural history of the silkworm became known but to a very few. Our aforesaid countryman, Alexander Neckham, made Abbot of Cirencester, A.D. 1213, was, it is likely, the first who, while he had learned, tried in his popular work, " De Natura Rerum," to help others to understand the habits of the insect: " Materiam vestium sericarum contexit vermis qui bombex dicitur. Foliis celsi, quæ vulgo morus dicitur, vescitur, et materiam serici digerit; postquam vero operari cœperit, escam renuit, labori deliciose diligentem operam impendens. Calathi parietes industrius textor circuit, lanam educens crocei coloris quæ nivei candoris efficitur per ablutionem, antequam tinctura artificialis superinduitur. Consummato

---

[1] De Natura Rerum, p. 99, published under the direction of the Master of the Rolls.
[2] Ib. p. 304.

Introduction.

autem opere nobilis textoris, thecam in opere proprio involutam centonis in modum fubintrat jamque fimilis papilioni, &c."[1]

Of thofe feveral raw materials that have, from the earlieft periods, been employed in weaving, though not in fuch frequency as filk, one is

Gold,

which, when judicioufly brought in, brings with it, not a barbaric, but artiftical richnefs.

The earlieft written notice we have about the employment of this precious metal in the loom, or of the way in which it was wrought for fuch a purpofe, we find fet forth in the Pentateuch, where Mofes tells us that he (Befeleel) made of violet and purple, fcarlet and fine linen, the veftments for Aaron to wear when he miniftered in the holy places. So he made an ephod of gold, violet, and purple, and fcarlet twice dyed, and fine twifted linen, with embroidered work; and he cut thin plates of gold and drew them fmall into ftrips, that they might be twifted with the woof of the aforefaid colours.[2] Inftead of "ftrip," the authorized verfion fays, "wire," another tranflation reads "thread;" but neither can be right, for both of thefe Englifh words mean a fomething round or twifted in the fhape given to the gold before being wove, whereas the metal muft have been worked in quite flat, as we learn from the text.

This brings us to a fhort notice of

Cloth of Gold, or Tissue.

The ufe of gold for weaving, both along with linen or quite by itfelf, exifted, it is likely, among the Egyptians, long before the days of Mofes. In either way of its being employed, the precious metal was at firft wrought in a flattened, never in a round or wire fhape. To this hour the Chinefe and the people of India work the gold into their ftuffs after the firft and ancient form. In this fafhion, to even now, the Italians love to weave their lama d'oro, or the more gliftening toca—thofe cloths of gold which, to all Afiatic and many European eyes, do not glare with too much garifhnefs, but fhine with a glow that befits the raiment of perfonages in high ftation.

Among the nations of ancient Afia, garments made of webs dyed with the coftly purple tint, and interwoven with gold, were on all grand occafions worn by kings and princes. So celebrated did the Medes and Perfians become in fuch works of the loom, that cloths of extraordinary

---

[1] Ed. T. Wright, p. 272. [2] Exodus xxxix. 1, 2, 3.

beauty got their several names from those peoples, and Medean, Lydian, and Persian textiles came to be everywhere sought for with eagerness.

Writing of the wars carried on in Asia and India by Alexander the Great, almost four centuries before the birth of Christ, Quintus Curtius often speaks about the purple and gold garments worn by the Persians and more eastern Asiatics. Among the many thousands of those who came forth from Damascus to the Greek general, Parmenio, many were so clad: "Vestes.... auro et purpura insignes induunt."[1] All over India the same fashion was followed in dress. When an Indian king, with his two grown-up sons, came to Alexander, all three were so arrayed: "Vestis erat auro purpuraque distincta, &c."[2] Princes and the high nobility, all over the East, are by Quintus Curtius called, "purpurati."[3] Not only garments but hangings were made of the same costly fabric. When Alexander wished to afford some ambassadors a splendid reception, the golden couches upon which they lay to eat their meat were screened all about with cloths of gold and purple: "Centum aurei lecti modicis intervallis positi erant: lectis circumdederat (rex Alexander) ælæa purpura auroque fulgentia, &c."[4] But these Indian guests themselves were not less gorgeously arrayed in their own national costume, as they came wearing linen (perhaps cotton) garments resplendent with gold and purple: "Lineæ vestes intexto auro purpuraque distinctæ, &c."[5]

The dress worn by Darius, as he went forth to do battle, is thus described by the same historian: The waist part of the royal purple tunic was wove in white, and upon his mantle of cloth of gold were figured two golden hawks as if pecking at one another with their beaks: "Purpureæ tunicæ medium album intextum erat: pallam auro distinctam aurei accipitres, velut rostris inter se concurrerent, adornabant."[6]

From the east this love for cloth of gold reached the southern end of Italy, called Magna Græcia, and thence soon got to Rome; where, even under its early kings and much later under its emperors, garments made of it were worn. Pliny, speaking of this rich textile, says:—Gold may be spun or woven like wool, without any wool being mixed with it. We are informed by Verrius, that Tarquinius Priscus rode in triumph in a tunic of gold; and we have seen Agrippina, the wife of the Emperor Claudius, when he exhibited the spectacle of a naval combat, sitting by him, covered with a robe made entirely of woven gold without any other

---

[1] Q. Curtii Rufi, lib. III. cap. xiii. 34, p. 26, ed Foss.
[2] Ib. lib. IX. cap. i. p. 217.   [3] Ib. lib. III. cap. ii. p. 4, cap. viii. p. 16.
[4] Ib. lib. IX. cap. vii. p. 233.   [5] Ib. cap. vii. p. 233.
[6] Ib. lib. III. cap. iii. p. 7.

material.¹ In fact, about the year 1840, the Marquis Campagna dug up, near Rome, two old graves, in one of which had been buried a Roman lady of high birth, inferred from the circumftance that all about her remains were found portions of fuch fine gold flat thread, once forming the burial garment with which fhe had been arrayed for her funeral : " Di due fepolcri Romani, del fecolo di Augufto fcoverti tra la via Latina e l'Appia, preffo la tomba degli Scipioni."

Now we get to the Chriftian epoch. When Pope Pafchal, A. D. 821, fought for the body of St. Cecily, who underwent martyrdom A. D. 230, the pontiff found, in the catacombs, the maiden bride whole, and dreffed in a garment wrought all of gold, with fome of her raiment drenched in blood lying at her feet: "Aureis illud (corpus) veftitum indumentis et linteamina martyris ipfius fanguine plena."² In making the foundations for the new St. Peter's at Rome, they came upon and looked into the marble farcophagus in which had been buried Probus Anicius, prefect of the Pretorian, and his wife, Proba Faltonia, each of whofe bodies was wrapped in a winding-fheet woven of pure gold ftrips.³ Maria Stilicho's daughter, was wedded to the Emperor Honorius, and died fometime about A. D. 400. When her grave was opened, A. D. 1544, the golden tiffues in which her body had been fhrouded were taken out and melted, when the yield of precious metal amounted to thirty-fix pounds.⁴ The late Father Marchi found, among the remains of St. Hyacinthus, martyr, feveral fragments of the fame kind of golden web, winding fheets of which were often given by the opulent for wrapping up the dead body of fome poor martyred Chriftian brother, as is fhown by the example fpecified in Boldetti's " Cimiteri de' fanti martiri di Roma."⁵

Childeric, the fecond and perhaps the moft renowned king of the Merovingean dynafty, died and was buried A. D. 485, at Tournai. In the year 1653 his grave was found out, and amid the earth about it fo many remains of pure gold ftrips were turned up, that there is every reafon for thinking that the Frankifh king was wrapped in a mantle of fuch golden ftuff for his burial.⁶ That the ftrips of pure gold out of which the burial cloak of Childeric was woven were not anywife round,

---

¹ Book XXXIII. c. 19. Dr. Boftock's Tranflation.
² Liber Pontificalis, t. ii. p. 332, ed. Vignolio, Romæ, 1752 ; Hierurgia, 2nd ed. p. 275.
³ Batelli, de Sarco. Marm. Probi Anicii et Probæ Faltoniæ in Temp. Vatic. Romæ. 1705.
⁴ Cancellieri, De Secretariis Bafil. Vatic. ii. 1000.
⁵ T. II. p. 22. ⁶ Cochet, Le Tombeau de Childeric Iʳ, p. 174.

but quite flat, we are warranted in thinking, from the fact that, while digging in a Merovingean burial ground at Envermeu, A.D. 1855, the diftinguifhed archæologift l'Abbe Cochet came upon the grave once filled, as it feemed, by a young lady whofe head had been wreathed with a fillet of pure golden web, the tiffue of which is thus defcribed: "Ces fils auffi brillants et auffi frais que s'ils fortaient de la main de l'ouvrier, n'étaient ni étirés ni cordés. Ils étaient plats et fe compofaient tout femplement de petites lanières d'or d'un millimètre de largeur, coupée à même une feuille d'or épaiffe de moins d'un dixième de millimètre. La longueur totale de quelques-uns atteignait parfois jufqu'à quinze ou dix-huit centimètres."[1]

Our own country can furnifh an example of this kind of golden textile. At Cheffel Down, in the Ifle of Wight, when Mr. Hillier was making fome refearches in an old Anglo-Saxon place of burial, the diggers found pieces of golden ftrips, thin, and quite flat, which are figured in M. l'abbé Cochet's learned book juft quoted.[2] Of fuch a rich texture muft have been the veftment covered with precious ftones, given to St. Peter's Church, at Rome, by Charles of France, in the middle of the ninth century: "Carolus rex fancto Apoftolo obtulit ex puriffimo auro, et gemmis conftructam veftem, &c."[3]

In the working of fuch webs and embroidery for ufe in the Church, a high-born Anglo-Saxon lady, Ælthelfwitha, with her waiting maids, fpent her life near Ely, where, "aurifrixoriæ et texturis fecretius cum puellulis vacabat, quæ de proprio fumptu, albam cafulam fuis manibus ipfa talis ingenii peritiffima fecit," &c.[4]

Such a weaving of pure gold was, here in England, followed certainly as late as the beginning of the tenth century; very likely much later. In the chapter library belonging to Durham Cathedral may be feen, along with feveral other very precious liturgical appliances, a ftole and maniple, which happily, for more reafons than one, bear thefe infcriptions: "Ælfflaed Fieri Precepit. Pio Epifcopo Frideftano." Queen to Alfred's fon and fucceffor, Edward the elder was our Ælfflaed who got this ftole and maniple made for a gift to Frideftan, confecrated bifhop of Winchefter A.D. 905. With thefe webs under his eye, Mr. Raine, in his "Saint Cuthbert,"[5] writes thus: In the firft, the ground work of the whole is woven exclufively with thread of gold. I do not mean by thread of gold, the filver-gilt wire frequently ufed in fuch matters,

---

[1] Cochet, Le Tombeau de Childeric Ier p. 175. [2] Ib. p. 176.
[3] Liber Pontificalis, l. iii., p. 201, ed. Vignolia.
[4] Liber Elienfis, ed. Stewart, p. 208. [5] P. 202.

but real gold thread, if I may fo term it, not round, but flat. This is the character of the whole web, with the exception of the figures, the undulating cloud-shaped pedestal upon which they stand, the inscriptions, and the foliage; for all of which, however surprising it may appear, vacant spaces have been left by the loom, and they themselves afterwards inserted with the needle. Further on, in his description of a girdle, the same writer tells us: Its breadth is exactly seven-eighths of an inch. It has evidently proceeded from the loom; and its two component parts are a flattish thread of pure gold, and a thread of scarlet silk, &c.[1] Let it be borne in mind that Winchester was then a royal city, and abounded, as it did afterwards, with able needle-women.

The employment, till a late period, of flattened gold in silk textiles is well shown by those fraudulent imitations, and substitution in its stead of gilt parchment, which we have pointed out among the specimens in this collection, as may be seen at Nos. 7095, p. 140; 8590, p. 224; 8601, p. 229; 8639, p. 244, &c.

That these Durham cloth-of-gold stuffs for vestments were home made—we mean wrought in Anglo-Saxondom—is likely, and by our women's hands, after the way we shall have to speak about further on.

This love for such glittering attire, not only for liturgical use but secular wear, lasted long in England. Such golden webs went here under different names; at first they were called "ciclatoun," "figlaton," or "fiklatoun," as the writer's fancy led him to spell the common Persian word for them at the time throughout the east.

By the old English ritual, plain cloth of gold was allowed, as now, to be taken for white, and worn in the Church's ceremonials as such, when that colour happened to be named for use by the rubric. Thus in the reign of Richard II., among the vestments at the Chapel of St. George, Windsor Castle, there was "unum vestimentum album bonum de panno adaurato pro principalibus festis B. Mariæ," &c.[2]

St. Paul's, London, had, at the end of the thirteenth century, two amices; one an old one, embroidered with solid gold wire: "Amictus breudatus de auro puro; amictus vetus breudatus cum auro puro.[3]

The use of golden stuffs not unlikely woven in England, but assuredly worn by royalty here, is curiously shown by the contrast between the living man clothed in woven gold, and the dead body, and its frightful state at burial, of Henry I., set forth by Roger Hoveden; who thus writes of that king: "vide... quomodo regis potentissimi corpus cujus cervix

---

[1] Mr. Raine, St. Cuthbert, p. 209.
[2] Dugdale's Mon. Angl. t. viii., p. 1363.   [3] Dugdale, p. 318.

diademite, auro et gemmis electiffimis quafi divino fplendore vernaverat
..: cujus reliqua fuperficies auro textile tota rutilaverat," &c.¹

Often was this fplendid web wrought fo thick and ftrong, that each ftring, whether it happened to be of hemp or of filk, in the warp, had in it fix threads, while the weft was of flat gold fhreds. Hence fuch a texture was called "famit," a word fhortened from its firft and old Byzantine name "exfamit," as we fhall have to notice further on. Among feveral other purchafes for the wardrobe of Edward I., in the year 1300, we find this entry: " Pro famitis pannis ad aurum tam in canabo quam in ferico," &c.² And fuch was the quantity kept there of this coftly cloth, that the nobles of that king were allowed to buy it out of the royal ftores; for inftance, four pieces at thirty fhillings each were fold to the Lord Robert de Clifford, and another piece at the fame price to Thomas de Cammill.³ Not only Afia Minor, but the Ifland of Cyprus, the City of Lucca, and Moorifh Spain, fent us thefe rich tiffues. The cloth of gold from Spain is incidentally fpoken of later in the Sherborn bequeft, p. lvi. Along with other things left behind him at Haverford caftle, by Richard II., were twenty-five cloths of gold of divers fuits, of which four came from Cyprus, the others from Lucca: " xxv. draps d or de diverfes fuytes dount iiii. de *Cipres* les autres de *Lukes*.⁴ How Edward IV. liked cloth-of-gold for his perfonal wear, may be gathered from his " Wardrobe Accounts," edited by Nicolas; and the lavifh ufe of this ftuff ordered by Richard III. for his own coronation, is recorded in the " Antiquarian Repertory."⁵ The robes to be worn by the unfortunate Edward V. at this fame function were cloth of gold tiffue. " Diverfe peces of cloth of gold " were bought by Henry VII., " of Lombardes."⁶

A "gowne of cloth-of-gold, furred with pawmpilyon, ayenft Corpus Xpi day," was brought from London to Richmond, to Elizabeth of York, afterwards Henry VII.'s queen, for her to wear as fhe walked in the proceffion on that great feftival.⁷ The affection fhown by Henry VIII., and all our nobility, men and women, of the time, for cloth of gold in their garments, was unmiftakingly fet forth in fo many of their likeneffes brought together in that very inftructive Exhibition of National Portraits in the year, A.D. 1866, in the South Kenfington Mufeum. This ftuff feems to have been coftly then, for Princefs, afterwards Queen

---

¹ Annalium, &c., p. 276, ed. Savile.
² Liber Quotidianus Garderobæ, p. 354.   ³ Ib., p. 6.
⁴ Ancient Kalendars, &c., ed. Palgrave, t. iii., 358.   ⁵ I. p. 43, &c.
⁶ Excerpta Hiftorica, p. 90.
⁷ Privy Purfe Expenfes of Elizabeth of York, p. 33, ed. Nicolas.

Introduction. xxxi

Mary, thirteen years before she came to the throne: " payed to Peycocke, of London, for xix yerds iii. q̃t of clothe of golde at xxxviij.s̃ the yerde, xxxvij *li*. x *s*. vj *d*."¹ And for "a yerde and d' q̃t of clothe of siluer xl *s*."²

Cloth of gold called

Tissue.

As between common silk and satin, there runs a broad difference, at least in look, one being dull, the other smooth and glossy, so there is a great distinction to be made among cloths of gold; some are, so to say, dead; others, brilliant and sparkling. When the gold is twisted into its silken filament, it takes the deadened look; when the flattened, filmy strip of metal is rolled about it so evenly as to bring its edges close to one another, it seems to be one unbroken wire of gold, sparkling and lustrous, like what is now known as "passing," and, during the middle ages, went by the term of Cyprus gold; and rich samits woven with it, were called damasks of Cyprus.

The very self-same things get for themselves other denominations as time goes on: such happened to cloths of gold. What the thirteenth century called, first, "ciclatoun," then "baudekin," afterward "nak," people, two hundred years later, chose to name "tissue," or the bright shimmering golden textile affected so much by our kings and queens in their dress, for the more solemn occasions of stately grandeur, as was just now mentioned. Up to this time, the very thin smooth paper made at first on purpose to be, when this rich stuff lay by, put between its folds to hinder it from fraying or tarnish, yet goes, though its original use is forgotten, by the name of tissue-paper.

The gorgeous and entire set of vestments presented to the altar at St. Alban's Abbey, by Margaret, Duchess of Clarence, A. D. 1429, and made of the cloth of gold commonly called "tyssewys," must have been as remarkable for the abundance and purity of the gold in its texture, as for the splendour of the precious stones set on it, as well as the exquisite beauty of its embroideries: "Obtulit etiam unum vestimentum integrum cum tribus capis choralibus de panno Tyssewys vulgariter nuncupato in quibus auri pretiosa nobilitas, gemmarum pulchritudo et curiosa manus artificis stuporem quendam inspectantibus oculis repræsentant."³ The large number of vestments made out of gold tissue, and of crimson, light blue, purple, green, and black, once belonging to York

---

¹ Privy Purse Expenses of Princess Mary, ed. Madden, p. 87.
² Ib. p. 86. ³ Mon. Anglic. II. 222.

Cathedral, are all duly regiftered in the valuable "Fabric Rolls" of that Church lately publifhed by the Surtees Society.[1]

Among thofe many rich and coftly veftments in Lincoln Cathedral, fome were made of this fparkling golden tiffue contra-diftinguifhed in its inventory, from the duller cloth of gold, thus : " Four good copes of blew tifhew with orphreys of red cloth of gold, wrought with branches and leaves of velvet ;"[2] "a chefable with two tunacles of blew tifhew having a precious orphrey of cloth of gold."[3]

To this day, in fome countries the official robes of certain dignitaries are wrought of this rich textile. Even now, thefe Roman princes, and the fenator whofe place on great feftivals when the Pope is prefent, is about the pontifical throne, are all arrayed in ftate garments made of cloth of gold.

Silken textures ornamented with defigns in copper gilt thread, were brought into market and honeftly fold for what they really were : of fuch inferior wares we find mention in the inventory of veftments at Winchefter Cathedral, drawn up by order of Henry VIII. where we read of " twenty-eight copys of white bawdkyne, woven with copper gold."[4] The fubftitution of gilt parchment for metal will be noticed further on, Section vi.

To imitate cloth of gold, the gilding of filk and fine canvas, like our gilding of wood and other fubftances, though not often, was fometimes reforted to for fplendour's fake on momentary occafions; fuch, for inftance, as fome ftately proceffion, or a folemn burial fervice. Mr. Raine tells us he got from a grave at Durham, among other textiles, " a robe of thinnifh filk ; the ground colour of the whole is amber ; and the ornamental parts were literally covered with *leaf gold*, of which there remained diftinct and very numerous portions."[5] In the churchyard of Cheam, Surrey, A. D. 1865, was found the fkeleton of a prieft buried there fome time during the fourteenth century ; around the waift was a flat girdle made of brown filk that had been gilt, and a fhred of it now lies before the writer.

In the " Romaunt of the Rofe," tranflated by Chaucer, Dame Gladneffe is thus defcribed :—

—in an over gilt famite
Clad fhe was.[6]

On a piece of German orphrey-web, in this collection, No. 1373, p. 80,

---

[1] Pp. 229, &c.   [2] Monafticon Anglicanum, ed. Dugdale, t. viii. p. 1282.
[3] Ib.   [4] Ib t. i. p. 202, new ed   [5] Saint. Cuthbert, by J. Raine, p. 194.
[6] Poems, ed. Nicolas, t. iv. p 27.

Introduction. xxxiii

and likely done at Cologne, in the fixteenth century, the gold is put by the gilding procefs.

In the year 1295, St. Paul's, London, had : " Cafula de panno inaurato fuper ferico," a chafuble of gilded filk ;[1] and it was lined with red cloth made at Ailefham,[2] or Elefham Priory in Lincolnfhire. It had, too, another chafuble, and altar frontals of gilded canvas : " cafula de panno inaurato in canabo, lineata carda Indici coloris cum panno confimili de Venetiis ad pendendum ante altare."[3] Venice feems to have been the place where thefe gilded filks and canvafes, like the leather and pretty paper of a later epoch, were wrought. As gold, fo too

Silver,

was hammered out into very thin fheets, which were cut into narrow long fhreds to be woven, unmixed with anything elfe, into a web for garments fitting for the wear of kings. Of this we have a ftriking illuftration in the "Acts," where St. Luke, fpeaking of Herod Agrippa, tells us that he prefented himfelf arrayed in kingly apparel, to the people, who to flatter him, fhouted that his was the voice, not of a man, but of a god; and forthwith he was fmitten by that loathfome difeafe—eaten up by worms—which fhortly killed him.[4] This royal robe, as Jofephus informs us, was a tunic all made of filver and wonderful in its texture. Appearing in this drefs at break of day in the theatre, the filver, lit up by the rays of the early morning's fun, gleamed fo brightly as to ftartle the beholders in fuch a manner that fome among them, by way of glozing, fhouted out that the king before them was a god.[5]

Intimately connected with the raw materials, and how they were wrought in the loom, is the queftion about the time when

Wire-Drawing

was found out. At what period, and among what people the art of working up pure gold, or gilded filver, into a long, round, hair-like thread —into what may be correctly called "wire"—began, is quite unknown. That with their mechanical ingenuity the ancient Egyptians bethought themfelves of fome method for the purpofe, is not unlikely. From Sir Gardiner Wilkinfon, we learn that at Thebes there was found the appearance of gold wire.[6] Of thofe remarkable pieces of Egyptian handicraft the corflets fent by King Amafis—one to Lindus, the fecond to Lacædemon—of which we have already fpoken (p. xiv.), we may fairly pre-

---

[1] Dugdale's St. Paul's, p. 335. [2] Ib. [3] Ib. [4] Acts. c. xii. vv. 21-23.
[5] Ant. l. xix. 8. [6] Ancient Egyptians, iii. 130.

fume that the work upon them done by the needle in gold, required by its minuteneſs that the precious metal ſhould be not flat, but in the ſhape of a real wire. By the delicate management of female fingers, the uſual narrow flat ſtrips might have been pinched or doubled up, ſo that the two edges ſhould meet, and then rubbed between men's harder hands, or better ſtill, between two pieces of ſmooth highly-poliſhed granite, would produce a golden wire of any required fineneſs. Belonging to the writer is an Egyptian gold ring, which was taken from off the finger of a mummy by a friend. The hoop is a plain, ſomewhat thick wire. On each ſide of its ſmall green-dyed ivory ſcarabee, to keep it in its place, are wound ſeveral rounds of rather fine wire. In Etruſcan and Greek jewellery, wire is often to be found; but in all inſtances it is ſo well ſhaped and ſo even, that no hammer could have hardly wrought it, and it muſt have been faſhioned by ſome rolling proceſs. All through the mediæval times the filigree work is often very fine and delicate. Likely is it that the embroidery which we thus read of in the deſcriptions of the veſtments belonging whilom to our old churches, for inſtance: "amictus breudatus cum auro puro"[1]—was worked with gold wire. To go back to Anglo-Saxon times in this country, ſuch gold wire would ſeem to have been well known and employed, ſince in Peterborough minſter there were two golden altar-cloths: "ii. gegylde peofad ſceatas;"[2] and at Ely Cathedral, among its old ritual ornaments, were, in the reign of William Rufus: "Duo cinguli, unus totus de auri filo, alter de pallio cujus pendentia" (the taſſels) "ſunt bene ornata de auri filo."[3]

The firſt idea of a wire-drawing machine dawned upon a workman's mind in the year 1360, at Nuremberg; and yet it was not until two hundred years after, A.D. 1560, that the method was brought to England. One ſample of a ſtuff with pure wire in it may be ſeen, p. 220, No. 8581, in this collection, as well as at No. 8228, p. 150.

Equally intereſting to our preſent ſubject is the proceſs of twining long narrow ſtrips of gold, or in its ſtead gilt ſilver, round a line of ſilk or flax, and thus producing

Gold Thread.

Probably its origin, as far as flax and not ſilk is concerned, as being the underlying ſubſtance, is much earlier than has been ſuppoſed; and when Attalus's name was beſtowed upon a new method of interweaving gold with wool or linen, it happened ſo not becauſe that Pargamanean king

---

[1] Church of our Fathers, i. 469. [2] Mon. Anglic. t. i. p. 382.
[3] Hiſt. Elien. lib. ii., c. 139, p. 283, ed. Steuart.

had been the first to think of twisting gold about a far less costly material, and thus, in fact, making gold thread such as we now have, but through his having suggested to the weaver the long-known golden thread as a woof into the textiles from his loom. From this point of view, we may easily believe what Pliny says: "Aurum intexere in eadem Asia invenit Attalus rex; unde nomen Attalicis."[1] In that same Asia King Attalus invented the method of using a woof of gold; from this circumstance the Attalic cloths got their name.

That, at least for working embroidery, ladies at an early Christian period used to spin their own gold thread, would seem from a passage in Claudian. Writing on the elevation to the consulate of the two brothers Probinus and Olybrius, at the end of the fourth century, the poet thus gracefully compliments their aged mother, Proba, who with her own hands had worked the purple and gold-embroidered robes, the "togæ pictæ," or "trabeæ," to be worn by her sons in their office:

> Lætatur veneranda parens, et pollice docto
> Jam parat auratas trabeas   *   *
> *   *   *   *   *   *
> Et longum tenues tractus producit in aurum
> Filaque concreto cogit squalere metallo.[2]

> The joyful mother plies her learned hands,
> And works all o'er the trabea golden bands,
> Draws the thin strips to all their length of gold,
> To make the metal meaner threads enfold.

A consular figure, arrayed in the purple trabea, profusely embroidered in gold, is shown in "The Church of our Fathers."[3]

That, in the thirteenth century our own ladies, like the Roman Proba, themselves used to make the gold thread needed for their own embroidery is certain; and the process which they followed is set forth as one of the items among the other costs for that magnificent frontal wrought A.D. 1271, for the high altar at Westminster Abbey. As that bill itself, to be seen on the Chancellor's Roll for the year 56 of Henry III., affords so many curious and available particulars about the whole subject in hand, we will give it here at full length for the sake of coming back hereafter to its several parts: "In xij. ulnis de canabo ad frontale magni altaris ecclesiæ (Westmonasterii) et cera ad eundem pannum ceranda, vs. vid. Et in vj marcis auri ad idem frontale, liij marcas. Et in operacione

---

[1] Lib. viii. c. 47.   [2] In Probini et Olybrii Consulatum, 177-182.   [3] T. ii. p. 131.

dicti auri, et seſſura (sciſſura?) et filatura ejuſdem, iiij *l.* xiij *s.* Et in ij libris ſerici albi et in duobus ſerici crocei ad idem opus, xxxv *s.* Et in perlis albis ponderis v marcarum, et dimidiæ ad idem opus lxx *li.* Et pro groſſis perlis ad borduram ejuſdem panni, ponderis ij marcarum, xiij *li.* dimidiam marcam. Et in una libra ſerici groſſi, x *s.* Et in ſtipendio quatuor mulierum operancium in predicto panno per iiij annos et iiij partes unius anni, xxxvi *li.* Et in Dccciij^{xx} vi eſtmalles ponderis liii *s.* ad borduram predictam. Et pro lxxvj aſmallis groſſis ponderis lxv *s.* ad idem frontale iiij^{xx} *li.* xvj *s.* Et pro Dl gernectis poſitis in predictis borduris, lxvi *s.* Et in caſtoniis auri ad dictas gernectas imponendas ponderis xij *s.* vj *d.*, cxij *s.* vj *d.* Et in pictura argenti poſita ſubtus predicta aſmalla, ij marcas. Et in vj ulnis cardonis de viridi, iij *s.*"[1] As the pound-weight now is widely different from the pound ſterling, ſo then the mark-weight of gold coſt nine marks of money. The " operacio auri" of the above document conſiſted in flattening out, by a broad-faced hammer like one ſuch as our gold-beaters ſtill uſe, the precious metal into a ſheet thin as our thinneſt paper. The " ſciſſura " was the cutting of it afterwards into long narrow ſtrips, the winding of which about the filaments of the yellow ſilk mentioned, is indicated by the word " filatura," and thus was made the gold thread of that coſtly frontal fraught with ſeed-pearls and other ſome, of a much larger ſize, and garnets, or rather carbuncles, and enamels, and which took four women three years and three-quarters to work. At the back it was lined with green frieze or baize—" cardo de viridi."

Such was the ſuperior quality of ſome gold thread that it was known to the mediæval world under the name of the place wherein it had been made. Thus we find a mention at one time of Cyprus gold thread— " veſtimentum embrowdatum cum aquilis de auro de Cipre ;"[2] later, of Venice gold thread —" for frenge of gold of Venys at vj *s.* the ounce ;"[3] " one cope of unwaterd camlet laid with ſtrokes of Venis gold."[4] What may have been their difference cannot now be pointed out: perhaps the Cyprian thread was ſo much eſteemed becauſe its ſomewhat broad ſhred of flat gold was wound about the hempen twiſt beneath it ſo nicely as to have the ſmooth unbroken look of gold wire; while the article from Venice ſhowed everywhere the twiſting of common thread.

As now, ſo of old,

---

[1] Rot. Cancel. 56 Henrici III. Compot. Will. de Glouc.
[2] Mon. Anglic. ii. 7.
[3] Wardrobe Accounts of King Edward IV. p. 117, ed. N. H. Nicolas.
[4] Mon. Anglic. ii. 167.

SILKS HAD VARIOUS NAMES
given them, meaning either their kind of texture and dreſſing, their colour and its ſeveral tints, the ſort of deſign or pattern woven on them, the country from which they were brought, or the uſe for which, on particular occaſions, they happened to be eſpecially ſet apart.

All of theſe deſignations are of foreign growth; ſome ſprang up in the ſeventh and following centuries at Byzantium, and, not to be found in claſſic writers, remain unknown to modern Greek ſcholars; ſome are half Greek, half Latin, jumbled together; other ſome, borrowed from the eaſt, are ſo ſhortened, ſo badly and variouſly ſpelt, that their Arabic or Perſian derivation can be hardly recognized at preſent. Yet, without ſome ſlight knowledge of them, we may not underſtand a great deal belonging to trade, and the manners of the times glanced at by our old writers; much leſs ſee the true meaning of many paſſages in our mediæval Engliſh poetry.

Among the terms ſignificative of the kind of web, or mode of getting up ſome ſorts of ſilk, we have

Holoſericum, the whole texture of which, as its Greek-Latin compound means to ſay, is warp and woof wholly pure ſilk: in a paſſage from Lampridius, quoted before, p. xix., we learn that ſo early as the reign of Alexander Severus, the difference between " veſtes holoſericæ," and " ſubſericæ," was ſtrongly marked, and from which we learn that

Subſericum implied that ſuch a texture was not entirely, but in part— likely its woof—of ſilk.

Although the warp only happened to be of ſilk, while the woof was of gold, ſtill the tiſſue was often called " holoſericum;" of the veſtments which Beda ſays[1] S. Gregory ſent over here to S. Auſtin, one is mentioned by a mediæval writer as " una caſula oloſerica purpurei coloris aurea textura"—a chaſuble all ſilk, of a purple colour, woven with gold.[2] Examples of " holoſericum " and " ſubſericum " abound in this collection.

Examitum, xamitum, or, as it is called in our old Engliſh documents ſo often, *ſamit*, is a word made up of two Greek ones, ἑξ, " ſix," and μίτοι, " threads," the number of the ſtrings in the warp of the texture. That ſtuffs woven ſo thick muſt have been of the beſt, is evident. Hence, to ſay of any ſilken tiſſue that it was "examitum," or "ſamit," meant that it was ſix-threaded, in conſequence coſtly and ſplendid. At the end of the thirteenth and beginning of the fourteenth centuries,

---

[1] Hiſt. Ecc. lib. i. c. 29.   [2] Bedæ Hiſt., ed. Smith, p. 691.

"examitum," as the writer still names the silk, was much used for vestments in Evesham abbey, as we gather from the " Chronicon" of that house, published lately for the Master of the Rolls.¹ About the same period, among the best copes, chasubles, and vestments in St. Paul's, London, many were made of " sametum ;" so Master Radulph de Baldock chose to call it in his visitation of that church as its dean, A. D. 1295.² As we observed just now, these rich silks, which were in all colours, with a warp so stiff, became richer still from having a woof of golden thread, or, as we should now say, being shot with gold. But years before, " examitum " was shortened into " samet ;" for among the nine gorgeous chasubles bequeathed to Durham cathedral by its bishop, Hugh Pudsey, A. D. 1195, there was the " prima de rubea samete nobiliter braudata cum laminis aureis et bizanciis et multis magnis perlis et lapidibus pretiosis."³ About a hundred years afterwards the employment of it, after its richest form, in our royal wardrobes, has been pointed out just now, p. xxviii., &c.

In that valuable inventory, lately published, of the rich vestments belonging to Exeter cathedral, A.D. 1277, of its numerous chasubles, dalmatics, tunicles, besides its seventy and more copes, the better part were made of this costly tissue here called " samitta ;" for example : " casula, tunica, dalmatica de samitta—par (vestimentorum) de rubea samitta cum avibus duo capita habentibus ;" " una capa samitta cum leonibus deauratis."⁴ In a later document, A. D. 1327, this precious silk is termed " samicta."⁵

Our minstrels did not forget to array their knights and ladies in this gay attire. When Sir Lancelot of the Lake brought back Gawain to King Arthur : —

> Launcelot and the queen were cledde
> In robes of a rich wede,
> Of samyte white, with silver shredde :
> * * * * *
> The other knights everichone,
> In samyte green of heathen land,
> And their kirtles, ride alone.⁶

In his " Romaunt of the Rose," Chaucer describes the dress of *Mirthe* thus :—

> Full yong he was, and merry of thought
> And in samette, with birdes wrought,

---

¹ Pp. 282-88.   ² Dugdale's St. Paul's, new ed. pp. 316, &c.
³ Wills and Inventories, part i. p. 3, published by the Surtees Society.
⁴ Lives of the Bishops of Exeter, and a History of the Cathedral, by Oliver, pp. 297, 298.   ⁵ Ibid. 313.   ⁶ Ellis's Metrical Romances, i. 360.

> And with gold beaten full fetoufly,
> His bodie was clad full richely.¹

Many of the beautifully figured damafks in this collection are what anciently were known as "famits;" and if they really be not "fix-thread," according to the Greek etymology of their name, it is becaufe, that at a very early period the ftuffs fo called ceafed to be woven of fuch a thicknefs.

Thofe ftrong filks of the prefent day with the thick thread called "organzine" for the woof, and a flightly thinner thread known by the technical name of "tram" for the warp, may be taken to reprefent the ancient "examits."

Juft as remarkable for the lightnefs of its texture, as happened to be "famit" on account of the thick fubftance of its web, yet quite as much fought after, was another kind of thin gloffy filken ftuff "wrought in the orient" by Paynim hands, and here called firft by its Perfian name which came with it, *ciclatoun*, that is, bright and fhining; but afterwards *ficklatoun*, *figlaton*, *cyclas*. Often a woof of golden thread lent it more glitter ftill; and it was ufed equally for ecclefiaftical veftments as for fecular articles of ftately drefs. In the "Inventory of St. Paul's Cathedral, London," A.D. 1295, there was a cope made of cloth of gold, called "ciclatoun:"—"capa de panno aureo qui vocatur ciclatoun."²

Among the booty carried off by the Englifh when they facked the camp of Saladin, in the Holy Land,

> King Richard took the pavillouns
> Of fendal, and of cyclatoun.
> They were fhape of caftels;
> Of gold and filver the pencels.³

In his "Rime of Sire Thopas," Chaucer fays of the doughty fwain,

> Of Brugges were his hofen broun
> His robe was of ciclatoun.⁴

Though fo light and thin, this cloak of "ciclatoun" was often embroidered in filk, and had fewn on it golden ornaments; for we read of a young maid who fat,

> In a robe ryght ryall bowne
> Of a red fyclatowne
> Be hur fader fyde;

---

¹ Poems, ed. Nicolas, t. iv. p. 26. ² Dugdale's St. Paul's, new ed. p. 318.
³ Ellis's Metrical Romances, t. ii. p. 253. ⁴ Poems, ed. Nicolas, t. iii. p. 83.

> A coronell on hur hedd fet,
> Hur clothys with beftes and byrdes wer bete
> All abowte for pryde.¹

When in the field, over their armour, whether of mail or plate, knights wore a long fleevelefs gown flit up almoft to the waift on both fides: fometimes of " famit," often of " cendal," oftener ftill of " ciclatourn," becaufe of its flowing fhowy texture was this garment made, and from a new and contracted way of calling it, the name of the gown, like the fhortened one for its ftuff, became known as " cyclas," nothing akin to the κυκλας—the full round article of drefs worn by the women of Greece and Rome. When, A.D. 1306, before fetting out to Scotland, Edward I. girded his fon, the prince of Wales, with fo much pomp, a knight, in Weftminfter Abbey; to the three hundred fons of the nobility whom the heir to the throne was afterward to dub knights in the fame church, the king made a moft fplendid gift of attire fitting for the ceremony, and among other textiles fent them were thefe "clycafes" wove of gold :—" Purpura, biffus, fyndones, cyclades auro textæ," &c. as we learn from Matthew Weftminfter, " Flores Hiftoriarum," p. 454. How very light and thin muft have been all fuch garments, we gather from the quiet wit of John of Salifbury while jeering the man who affected to perfpire in the depth of winter, though clad in nothing but his fine "cyclas:"—" dum omnia gelu conftricta rigent, tenui fudat in cylade."²

Not fo coftly, and even fomewhat thinner in texture, was a filken ftuff known as *cendal, cendallus, fandal, fandalin, cendatus, fyndon, fyndonus*, as the way of writing the word altered as time went on. When Sir Guy of Warwick was knighted,

> And with him twenty good gomes
> Knightes' and barons' fons,
> Of cloth of Tars and rich cendale
> Was the dobbing in each deal.³

The Roll of Caerlaverock tells us that among the grand array which met and joined Edward I. at Carlifle, A.D. 1300, on his road to invade Scotland, there was to be feen many a rich caparifon embroidered upon cendal and famit :—

> La ot meint riche guarnement
> Brodé fur fendaus e famis.⁴

And Lacy, Earl of Lincoln, leading the firft fquadron, hoifted his banner made of yellow cendal blazoned with a lion rampant purpre.⁵

---

¹ Ancient Englifh Met. Rom., ed. Ritfon, t. iii. pp. 8, 9.
² Polycraticus, lib. VIII. c. xii.   ³ Ellis's Met. Rom. i. 15.
⁴ Roll of Caerlaverock, ed. Wright, p. 1.   ⁵ Ibid. p. 2.

> Baner out de un cendal fafrin,
> O un lioun rampant purprin.

Moft, if not all the other flags were made of the fame cendal filk.

When the ftalworth knight of Southampton wifhed to keep himfelf unknown at a tournament, we thus read of him—

> Sir Bevis difguifed all his weed
> Of black cendal and of rede,
> Flourifhed with rofes of filver bright, &c.[1]

Of the ten beautiful filken albs which Hugh Pudfey left to Durham, two were made of famit, other two of cendal, or as the bifhop calls it, *fandal*: " Quæ dicuntur fandales."[2] Exeter cathedral had a red cope with a green lining of fandal : " Capa rubea cum linura viridi fandalis ;"[3] and a cape of fandaline : " Una capa de fandalin."[4] Chafubles, too, were, it is likely, for poorer churches, made of cendal or fandel ; Piers Ploughman fpeaks thus to the high dames of his day—

> And ye lovely ladies
> With youre long fyngres,
> That ye have filk and fandal
> To fowe, whan tyme is.
> Chefibles for chapeleyns,
> Chirches to honoure, &c.[5]

A ftronger kind of cendal was wrought and called, in the Latin inventories of the thirteenth and fourteenth centuries, cendatus afforciatus, and of fuch there was a cope at St. Paul's ;[6] while another cope of cloth of gold was lined with it,[7] as alfo a chafuble of red famit given by Bifhop Henry of Sandwich.

Syndonus or *Sindonis*, as it would feem, was a bettermoft fort of cendal. St. Paul's had a chafuble as well as a cope of this fabric : " Cafula de findone purpurea, linita cendata viridi ;[8] " capa de fyndono Hifpanico."[9]

Taffeta, it is likely, if not a thinner, was a lefs coftly filken ftuff than cendal ; which word, to this day, is ufed in the Spanifh language, and is defined to be a thin tranfparent textile of filk or linen : " Tela de feda ó lino muy delgada y trafparente."

As the Knights' flags :

> Ther gonfanens and ther penfelles
> Wer well wrought off grene fendels ;

---

[1] Ellis's Met. Rom. ii. 156. [2] Wills and Inventories, p. 3. [3] Oliver, p. 299.
[4] Ib. p. 315. [5] The Vifion, Paffus Sextus, t. i. p. 117, ed. Wright.
[6] P. 317. [7] P. 318. [8] P. 323.

as their long cyclafes which they wore over their armour were of cendal, fo too were of cendal, all blazoned with their armorial bearings, the houfing of the fteeds they ftrode. Of cendal, alfo, was the lining of the church's veftments, and the peaceful citizen's daily garments. Of his "Doctour of Phifike," Chaucer tells us :—

> In fanguin and in perfe he clad was alle
> Lined with taffata, and with fendalle.[1]

For the weaving of cendal, among the Europeans, Sicily was once celebrated, and a good example from others in this collection, is No. 8255, p. 163.

Sarcenet, during the fifteenth century took by degrees the place of cendal, at leaft here in England.

By fome improvement in their weaving of cendal, the Saracens, it is likely in the fouth of Spain, earned for this light web as they made it, or fold it, a good name in our markets, and it became much fought for here. Among other places, York Cathedral had feveral fets of curtains for its high altar, " de farcynet."[2] At firft we diftinguifhed this ftuff by calling it, from its makers, " faracenicum." But while Anglicifing, we fhortened that appellation into the diminutive "farcenet ;" and this word we keep to the prefent day, for the thin filk which of old was known among us as " cendal."

Satin, though far from being fo common as other filken textures, was not unknown to England, in the middle ages ; and of it thus fpeaks Chaucer, in his " Man of Lawes Tale :"

> In Surrie whilom dwelt a compagnie
> Of chapmen rich, and therto fad and trewe,
> That wide were fenten hir fpicerie,
> Clothes of gold, and fatins riche of hewe.[3]

But as Syria herfelf never grew the more precious kinds of fpices, fo we do not believe that fhe was the firft to hit upon the happy mechanical expedient of getting up a filken texture fo as to take, by the united action at the fame moment of ftrong heat and heavy preffure upon its face, that luftrous metallic fhine which we have in fatin. No. 702, p. 8, is a good example of late Chinefe manufacture, a procefs which this country is only now beginning to underftand and fuccefsfully employ.

When fatin firft appeared in trade, it was all about the fhores of the Mediterranean called "aceytuni." This term flipped through early Italian lips into "zetani ;" coming weftward this, in its turn, dropped its

---

[1] Prologue, Poems, ed. Nicolas, ii. 14.   [2] Fabric Rolls, &c. p. 227.
[3] Poems, ii. 137.

Introduction. xliii

"i," and smoothed itself into "satin," a word for this silk among us English as well as our neighbours in France, while in Italy it now goes by the name of "raso," and the Spaniards keep up its first designation in their dictionary.

In the earlier inventories of church vestments, no mention can be found of satin; and it is only among the various rich bequests (ed. Oliver) made to his cathedral at Exeter by Bishop Grandison, between A. D. 1327-69 that this fine silk is spoken of; though later, and especially in the royal wardrobe accompts (ed. Nicolas), it is perpetually specified. Hence we may fairly assume that till the beginning of the fourteenth century satin was unknown in England; afterwards it met much favour. Flags were made of it. On board the stately ship in which Beauchamp, Earl of Warwick, in the reign of Henry VI., sailed from England to France, there were flying "three penons of satten," besides " sixteen standards of worsted entailed with a bear and a chain," and a great streamer of forty yards in length and eight yards in breadth, with a great bear and griffin holding a ragged staff poudred full of ragged staffs.[1] Like other silken textiles, satin seems to have been, in some few instances, interwoven with flat gold thread, so as to make it a tissue: for example, Lincoln had of the gift of one of its bishops, eighteen copes of red tinsel sattin with orphreys of gold.[2]

Though not often, yet sometimes do we read of a silken stuff called, *cadas, carda, carduus*, and used for inferior purposes. The outside silk on the cocoon is of a poor quality compared with the inner filaments, from which it is kept quite apart in reeling, and set aside for other uses; this is *cadas* which the Promptorium Parvulorum defines, however, as " Bombicinium," or silk. St. Paul's, A. D. 1295, had " pannus rubeus diasperatus de Laret lineatus de carda Inda;"[3] and Exeter possessed another cloth for the purpose: "Cum carduis viridibus."[4] More frequently, instead of being spun it served as wadding in dress; on the barons at the siege of Caerlaverock, might be seen many a rich gambeson garnished with silk, cadas, and cotton:—

>Meint riche gamboison guarni
>De soi, de cadas e coton.[5]

One of the Lenten veils at St. Paul's, in the chapel of St. Faith, was of blue and yellow carde: "velum quadragesimale de carde croceo et indico."[6] The quantity of card purchased for the royal wardrobe,

---

[1] Baronage of England, Dugdale, i. 246.　　[3] Mon. Anglic. viii. 1282.
[2] P, 335.　　　　[4] Ed. Oliver, p. 317.　　[4] Roll. p. 30.
[6] St. Paul's ed. Dugdale, p. 336.

in the twenty-eighth year of Edward I.'s reign, A. D. 1299, is set forth in the Liber Quotidianus, &c.[1]

Chasubles made in the thirteenth century, and belonging to Hereford Cathedral, were lined with carda: " Unam casulam de rubeo sindone linita de carda crocea—tertiam casulam de serico de India linita de carda viridi," &c.[2]

Camoca, camoka, camak, camora (a misspelling), as the name is differently written, was a textile of which in England we hear nothing before the latter end of the fourteenth century. No sooner did it make its appearance than this camoca rose into great repute; the Church used it for her liturgical vestments, and royalty employed it for dress on grand occasions as well as in adorning palaces, especially in draping beds of state. In the year 1385, besides some smaller articles, the royal chapel in Windsor Castle had a whole set of vestments and other ornaments for the altar, of white camoca: " Unum vestimentum album de camoca," &c. . . . " Album de camoca, cum casula."[3] . . . " Duo quissini rubei de camoca."[4] To his cathedral of Durham, the learned Richard Bury left a beautifully embroidered whole set of vestments, A. D. 1345: " Unum vestimentum de alma camica (*sic*) subtiliter brudata," &c.[5]

Our princes must have arrayed themselves, on grand occasions, in camoca; for thus Herod, in one of the Coventry Misteries—the Adoration of the Magi—is made to boast of himself: " In kyrtyl of cammaka kynge am I cladde."[6] But it was in draping its state-beds that our ancient royalty showed its affection for camoca. To his confessor, Edward the Black Prince bequeaths " a large bed of red camora (*sic*) with our arms embroidered at each corner,"[7] and the prince's mother leaves to another son of hers, John Holland, " a bed of red camak."[8] Our nobles, too, had the same likings, for Edward Lord Despencer, A. D. 1375, wills to his wife, " my great bed of blue camaka, with griffins, also another bed of camaka, striped with white and black."[9] What may have been the real texture of this stuff, thought so magnificent, we do not positively know, but hazarding a guess, we think it to have been woven of fine camel's hair and silk, and of Asiatic workmanship.

From this mixed web pass we now to another, one even more precious, that is the *Cloth of Tars*, which we presume to have, in a manner, been

---

[1] P. 354.
[2] Roll of the Household Expenses of Swinford, Bishop of Hereford, t. ii. p. xxxvi. ed. Web. for the Camden Society.
[3] Mon. Anglic. ed. Dugdale, new edition, p. viii. 1363, *a*.   [4] Ib. p. 1366, *a*.
[5] Wills and Inventories, t. i. p. 25, published by the Surtees Society.
[6] Ed. Halliwell, p. 163.   [7] Nicolas's Testamenta Vetusta, t. i. p. 12.
[8] Ib. p. 14.   [9] Ib. p. 99.

the forerunner of the now so celebrated cashmere, and along with silk made of the downy wool of a family of goats reared in several parts of Asia, but especially in Tibet, as we shall try to show a little further on.

Velvet is a silken textile, the history of which has still to be written. Of the country whence it first came, or the people who were the earliest to hit upon the happy way of weaving it, we know nothing. The oldest piece we remember to have ever seen was in the beautiful crimson cope embroidered by English hands in the fourteenth century, now kept at the college of Mount St. Mary, Chesterfield, and exhibited here in the ever memorable year '62.

Our belief is, that to central Asia—perhaps China,—we are indebted for velvet as well as satin, and we think the earliest places in Europe to weave it was, first the south of Spain, and then Lucca.

In the earlier of those oldest inventories we have of church vestments, that of Exeter Cathedral, A. D. 1277, velvet is not spoken of; but in St. Paul's, London, A. D. 1295, there is some notice of velvet,[1] along with its kindred web, "fustian," for chasubles.[2] At Exeter, in the year 1327, velvet—and it was crimson—is for the first time there mentioned, but as in two pieces not made up, of which some yards had been then sold for vestment-making.[3] From the middle of the fourteenth century, velvet—mostly crimson—is of common occurrence.

The name itself of velvet, "velluto," seems to point out Italy as the market through which we got it from the East, for the word in Italian indicates something which is hairy or shaggy, like an animal's skin.

Fustian was known at the end of the thirteenth century. St. Paul's Cathedral had: "Una casula alba de fustian."[4] But in an English sermon preached at the beginning of this thirteenth century, great blame is found with the priest who had his chasuble made of middling fustian: "þe meshakele of medeme fustian."[5] As then wove, fustian, about which we have to say more, had a short nap on it, and one of the domestic uses to which, during the middle ages, it had been put, was for bed clothes, as thick undersheets. Lady Bargavenny bequeaths A. D. 1434, "A bed of gold of swans, two pair sheets of Raynes (fine linen, made at Rheims), a pair of fustians, six pair of other sheets, &c."[6] That this stuff may have hinted to the Italians the way of weaving silk in the same manner, and so of producing velvet, is not unlikely. Had the Egyptian Arabs been the first to push forward their own discovery of working cotton into fustian, and changing cotton for silk, and so brought forth velvet, it is probable some one would have told us; as it is, we

---

[1] P. 318.   [2] P. 323.   [3] Ed. Oliver, p. 317.   [4] Ed. Dugdale, p. 323.
[5] Reliquiæ Antiquæ, i. 129.   [6] Test. Vet. i. 227.

yield the merit to Afia—may be China. Other nations took up this manufacture, and the weaving of velvet was wonderfully improved. It became diapered, and upon a ground of filk or of gold, the pattern came out in a bold manner, with a raifed pile; and, at laft, that difficult and moft beautiful of all manners of diapering, or making the pattern to fhow itfelf in a double pile, one pile higher than the other and of the fame tint, now, as formerly, known as velvet upon velvet, was brought to its higheft perfection: and velvets in this fine ftyle were wrought in greateft excellence all over Italy and in Spain and Flanders. Our old inventories often fpecify thefe differences in the making of the web. York cathedral had "four copes of crimfon velvet plaine, with orphreys of clothe of goulde, for ftanders;"[1] and befides, "a greene cufhion of raifed velvet,"[2] poffeffed "a cope of purfhed velvet (redd)[3] "purfhed" meaning the velvet raifed in a network pattern.

Diaper was a filken fabric, held everywhere in high eftimation during many hundred years, both abroad and here in England. This we know from documents beginning with the eleventh century. What was its diftinctive characteriftic, and whence it drew its name, we have not been hitherto told, with anything like certainty. Several eminent men have difcuffed thefe points, but while hazarding his own conjecture, each of thefe writers has differed from the others. Till a better may be found, we fubmit our own folution.

The filk weavers of Afia had, of old, found out the way fo to gear their looms, and drefs their filk, or their threads of gold, that with a warp and woof, both precifely of the fame tone of colour they could give to the web an elegant defign, each part of which being managed in the weaving, as either to hide or to catch the light and fhine, looked to be feparated from or ftand well up above the feeming dufky ground below it: at times the defign was dulled, and the ground made gloffy. To indicate fuch a one-coloured, yet patterned filk, the Byzantine Greeks of the early middle ages bethought themfelves of the term διαϛπρον, diafpron, a word of their own coinage, and drawn from the old Greek verb, διαϛπαω, I feparate, but meant by them to fignify "what diftinguifhes or feparates itfelf from things about it," as every pattern muft do on a one-coloured filk. Along with this textile, the Latins took the name for it from the Greeks, and called it "diafper," which we Englifh have moulded into "diaper." In the year 1066, the Emprefs Agnes gave to Monte Caffino a diaper-chafuble of cloth of gold, "optulit planetam diafperam totam undique auro contextam.[4]

---

[1] Fabric Rolls, p. 309.   [2] Ib. p. 311.   [3] Ib. p. 310.
[4] Chron. S. Monaft. Caffin. Lib. iii. cap. 73, p. 450, ed. Muratori.

Introduction.

How a golden web may be fo wrought is exemplified, amid feveral other fpecimens in this collection, by the one under No. 1270, p. 38, done moſt likely by an Engliſh hand. At York Minſter, in the year 1862, was opened a tomb, very likely that of fome archbiſhop; and there was found, along with other textiles in filk, a few ſhreds of what had been a chafuble made of cloth of gold diapered all over with little croſſes, as we ourſelves beheld. It would ſeem, indeed, that cloth of gold was at moſt times diapered with a pattern, at leaſt in Chaucer's days, ſince he thus points to it on the houſing of his king's horſe:—

—— trapped in ſtele,
Covered with cloth of gold diapred wele.[1]

Our oldeſt Church inventories make frequent mention of fuch diapered filks for veſtments. In 1277, Exeter Cathedral had: "una (capa) de alba diapra cum noviluniis,"[2]—a cope of white diaper with half moons. It was the gift of Biſhop Bartholomew, A. D. 1161. Biſhop Brewer, A. D. 1224, beſtowed upon the Church a ſmall pall of red diaper: "parva palla de rubea diapra;" along with a chafuble, dalmatic and tunicle of white diaper: "cafula, &c. de alba diapra."[3] Among its vaſt collection of liturgical garments, A. D. 1295, old St. Paul's had a large number made of diaper, which was almoſt always white. Sometimes the pattern of the diapering is noticed; for inſtance, a chafuble of white diaper, with coupled parrots in places, among branches: "cafula de albo diafpro cum citaciis combinatis per loca in ramuſculis.[4] Again: "tunica et dalmatica de albo diafpro cum citacis viridibus in ramunculis,"[5] where we fee the white diaper having the parrots done in green. Probably the moſt remarkable and elaborate ſpecimen of diaper-weaving on record, is the one that Edmund, Earl of Cornwall gave, made up in "a cope of a certain diaper of Antioch colour, covered with trees and diapered birds, of which the heads, breaſts, and feet, as well as the flowers on the trees, are woven in gold thread: "Capa Domini Edmundi Comitis Cornubiæ de quodam diafpero Antioch coloris, tegulata cum arboribus et avibus diafperatis quarum capita, pectora et pedes, et flores in medio arborum funt de aurifilo contextæ.[6]

By degrees the word "diaper" became widened in its meaning. Not only all forts of textile, whether of filk, of linen, or of worſted, but the walls of a room were ſaid to be diapered when the felf-fame ornament was repeated and fprinkled well over it. Thus, to ſoothe his daughter's forrows, the King of Hungary promiſes her a chair or carriage, that—

---

[1] Knight's Tale, l. 2159-60.   [2] P. 297.   [3] P. 298.
[4] St. Paul's, ed. Dugdale, p. 323.   [5] Ib. p. 322.   [6] Ib. p. 318.

> Shal be coverd wyth velvette reede
> And clothes of fyne golde al about your heede,
> With damaſke whyte and azure blewe
> Well dyaperd with lylles newe.¹

Nay, the bow for arrows held by SWEET LOOKING is, in Chaucer's "Romaunt of the Roſe," deſcribed as—

> painted well, and thwitten
> And over all diapred and written, &c.²

Even now, our fine table linen we call "diaper," becauſe it is figured with flowers and fruits. Sometimes, with us, ſilks diapered were called "fygury:" una capa de fateyn fygury, cum ymagine B. M. V. in capucio.³

In their etymology of diaper, modern writers try to draw the word from Yprès, or d'Ypriès, becauſe that town in Belgium was once celebrated, not for ſilken ſtuffs, but for linen. Between the city and the name of "diaper" a kinſhip even of the very furtheſt ſort cannot be fairly ſet up. From the citations out of the Chronicle of Monte Caſſino we learn, that at the beginning of the eleventh century, the term in uſe there for a certain ſilken textile, brought thither from the eaſt, was "diaſperon." We find, too, how that great monaſtery was in continual communication with Conſtantinople, whither ſhe was in the habit of ſending her monks to buy art-works of price, and bring back with them workmen, for the purpoſe of embelliſhing her Church and its altars. Getting from South Italy to England, and our own records, we diſcover this ſame Greece-born phraſe, diaſpron, diaſper, given to precious ſilks uſed as veſtments during the twelfth and thirteenth centuries, in London and Exeter. By the latter end of the fourteenth century—Chaucer's time—the terms "diaſper," and "diaſperatus," among us, had ſlidden into "diaper," "diaperatus," Engliſhed, "diapered." Now, in this ſame fourteenth century, do we, for the firſt time, meet a mention of Yprès; and not alone, but along with Ghent, as famous for linen, if by that word we underſtand cloth; and even then our own Bath ſeems to have ſtood above thoſe Belgian cities in their textiles. Among Chaucer's pilgrims—

> A good wif was ther of beſide Bathe
> *   *   *   *   *
> Of cloth making ſhe hadde ſwiche an haunt
> She paſſed hem of Ipres and of Gaunt.⁴

Neither in this, nor any other ſubſequent notice of Yprès weaving, is there anything which can be twiſted into a warrant for thinking the

---

¹ Squire of Low Degree, ed. Ritſon.   ² "Romaunt of the Roſe." l. 900.
³ Fabric Rolls of York Cathedral, p. 230.   ⁴ The Prologue, 447.

distinctive mark to have been the first employment of pattern on its webs, or even its peculiar superiority in such a style of work. The important fact which we have just now verified that several ages had gone by between the period when, in Greece, in South Italy, and England, the common name for a certain kind of precious silk was "diaspron," "diasper," "diaper," and the day when, for the first time, Yprès, not alone, but in company with other neighbouring cities, started up into notice for its linens, quite overthrows the etymology thought of now-a-days for the word "diaper," and hastens us to the conclusion that this almost ante-mediæval term came to us from Greece, and not from Flanders.

Of the several oldest pieces in this collection, there are not a few which those good men who wrote out the valuable inventories of Exeter and St. Paul's, London, would have jotted down as "diasper," or "diaper." The shreds of creamy, white silk, number 1239, p. 26, fully illustrate the meaning of this term, and will repay minute inspection.

More ancient still are other terms which we are about to notice, such as "chrysoclavus," "stauraccin," "polystaurium," "gammadion," or "gammadiæ," "de quadruplo," "de octoplo," and "de fundato." First, textiles of silk and gold are, over and over again, enumerated as then commonly known under such names, in the so-called Anastasius Bibliothecarius, Liber Pontificalis seu de Gestis Romanorum Pontificum, the good edition of which, in three volumes, edited by Vignolius, ought to be in the hands of every student of early Christian art-work, and in particular of textiles and embroidery.

The *Chrysoclavus* or golden nail-head, was a remnant, which lingered a long time among the ornaments embroidered on ecclesiastical vestments, and robes for royal wear, of that once so coveted "latus clavus," or broad nail-head-like purple round patch worn upon the outward garment of the old Roman dignitaries, as we learn from Horace, while laughing at the silly official whom he saw at Fondi—

> Infani ridentes præmia scribæ,
> Prætextam et latum clavum.[1]

In the Court of Byzantium this device of dignity was elevated, from being purple on white, into gold upon purple. Hence came it that all rich purple silks, woven or embroidered, with the "clavus" done in gold, became known from their pattern as gold nail-headed, or chrysoclavus, a half Greek half Latin word, employed as often as an adjective

---
[1] Serm. lib. i. satir. v.

as a substantive; and silken textiles of Tyrian dye, sprinkled all over with large round spots, were once in great demand. Shortly after, A.D. 795, Pope Leo, among his several other gifts to the churches at Rome, bestowed a great number of altar frontals made of this purple and gold fabric, as we are told by Anastasius. To the altar of St. Paul's the pontiff sent " vestem super altare albam chrysoclavam;"[1] but to another " vestem chrysoclavam ex blattin Byzanteo."[2] Sometimes these " clavi" were made so large that upon their golden ground an event in the life of a saint, or the saint's head, was embroidered, and then the whole piece was called " figillata," or *sealed*.

Stauracin, or " stauracinus," taking its name from σταυρος, the Greek for " cross," was a silken stuff figured with small plain crosses, and therefore from their number sometimes further distinguished by the word signifying that meaning in Greek,

Polystauron. Of such a textile St. Leo gave presents to churches, as we learn from Anastasius, lib. Pont. ii. 265.

How much silken textiles figured with the cross were in request for church adornment we learn from Fortunatus, who, about the year 565, thus describes the hangings of an oratory in a church at Tours—

Pallia nam meruit, sunt quæ cruce textile pulchra,
* * * *
Serica qua niveis sunt agnava blattea telis,
Et textis crucibus magnificatur opus.[3]

Very often the crosses woven on these fabrics were of the simplest shape; oftener were they designed after an elaborate type with a symbolic meaning about it that afforded an especial name to the stuffs upon which they were figured, the first of which that claims our notice is denominated

Gammadion, or *Gammadiæ*, a word applied as often to the pattern upon silks as the figures wrought upon gold and silver for use in churches, we so repeatedly come upon in the " Liber Pontificalis."

In the Greek alphabet the capital letter of gamma takes the shape of an exact right angle thus, Γ. Being so, many writers have beheld in it an emblem of our Lord as our corner-stone. Following this idea artists at a very early period struck out a way of forming the cross after several shapes by various combinations with it of this letter Γ. Four of these gammas put so fall into the shape of the so-called Greek cross; and in this form it was woven upon the textiles denominated " stauracinæ;"

---

[1] Lib. Pon. ii. 257.   [2] Ibid. 258.   [3] Poematum, Liber II. iv.

Introduction.

or patterned with a crofs. Being one of the four fame-fhaped elements of the crofs's figure, the part was fignificant of the whole. Being, too, the emblem of our corner-ftone—our Lord, the gamma, or Γ, was fhown at one edge of the tunic on moft of the apoftles in ancient mofaics; wherein fometimes we find, in place of the gamma, our prefent capital H for the afpirate, with which for their fymbolic purpofe the early Chriftians chofe to utter, if not, write the facred name. This H is, however, only another combination of the four gammas in the crofs. Whatfoever, therefore, whether of filver or of filk, was found to be marked in thefe or other ways of putting the gammas together, or with only a fingle one, fuch articles were called "gammadion," or "gammadiæ;" but as often the fo-formed crofs was defignated as "gammaed," or "gammadia." St. Leo gave to the Church of S. Sufanna, at Rome, an altar-frontal, upon which there were four of fuch croffes made of purple filk fpeckled with gold fpots; "veftem de blatthin habentem ... tabulas chryfoclavas iiii cum gemmis ornatas, atque gammadias in ipfa vefte chryfoclavas iiii.[1]

Ancient ingenuity for throwing its favourite gamma into other combinations, and thus bringing forth other pretty but graceful patterns to be wrought on all forts of ecclefiaftical appliances, did not ftop here. In the "Liber Pontificalis" of Anaftafius, we meet not unfrequently with fuch paffages as thefe: "Cortinas miræ magnitudinis de palliis ftauracin feu quadrapolis;"[2] "vela . . . ex palliis quadrapolis feu ftauracin;"[3] "vela de octapolo."[4] The explanation of thefe two terms, "de quadrapolo," "de octapolo," has hitherto baffled all commentators of the text through their forgetfulnefs of comparing together the things themfelves and the written defcription of them. In thefe texts there is evidently meant a ftrong contraft between a fomething amounting to four, and to eight, in or upon thefe textiles. It cannot be to fay that one fabric was woven with four, the other with eight threads: had that been fo meant, then the fact would have been announced by words conftructed like "examitus," p. xxxvii. As the contraft is not in the texture, it muft then be fearched for in the pattern of thefe two ftuffs. Sure enough, there we find it, as "de quadrapolis" and "ftauracin" were, as we fee above, interchangeable terms; the firft, like the fecond fort of textile, was figured with croffes.

Given at the end of Du Cange's "Gloffary" is an engraving of a work of Greek art, plate IX. Here St. John Chryfoftom ftands between St. Nicholas and St. Bafil. All three are arrayed in their liturgical garments, which being figured with croffes, are of the textile called

---

[1] Lib. Pontif. ii. 243. [2] Ib. ii. 196. [3] Ib. ii. 198. [4] Ib. ii. 209.

of old "ftauracin;" but a marked difference in the way in which the croffes are put is difcernible. As a metropolitan St. John wears the faccos upon which the croffes are arranged thus ✛ ⊕ ✛ ⊕ ✛ ⊕ ✛ ⊕ St. Nicholas, and St. Bafil have chafubles which, though worked all over with croffes, made, as on St. John's faccos, with gammas, are furrounded with other gammas joined fo as to edge in the croffes, thus

As four gammas only are neceffary to form all the croffes upon St. John's veftment, therein we behold the textile called by Anaftafius, "Stauracin de quadruplo," or the ftuff figured with a crofs of four (gammas); while as eight of thefe Greek letters are required for the pattern on the chafubles, we have in them an example of the other "ftauracin de octaplo," or "octapulo," a fabric with a pattern compofed of eight gammas. But of all the fhapes fafhioned out of the repetition of the one fame element, the Greek letter Γ, by far the moft ancient, univerfal, and myftic, is that curious one particularized by many as the

Gammadion, or Filfot, a name by which, at one time in England, it was generally known. Several pieces in this collection exhibit on them fome modification of it, as Nos. 1261, p. 34; 1325, p. 60; 7052, p. 127; 829A, p. 174; 8305, p. 185; 8635, p. 242; 8652, p. 249. Its figure is made out of the ufual four gammas, fo that they fhould fall together thus ⌐⌐ : of its high antiquity and fymbolifm, we fpeak further on, fection VII.

Silks figured with a crofs, fome made with four, fome with eight Greek gammas, remained in Eaftern Church ufe all through the middle ages, as we may gather from feveral monuments of that period. Befides a good many other books, Gori's fine one, "Thefaurus Veterum Diptychorum" affords us feveral inftances.[1] The name alfo remained to fuch textiles as we know from the Greek canonift Balfamon, who, writing about the end of the twelfth century on epifcopal garments, calls the tunic, στιχάριον διὰ γαμμάτων or (with a pattern) of gammas—gammadion. How to this day the crofs made by four gammas is woven on Greek veftments, may be obferved in the plates we have given in "Hierurgia."[2] Two late fpecimens of "ftauracin" are in this collection under Nos. 7039, p. 123; 7048, p. 126; and 8250 A, p. 161.

---

[1] T. iii. p. 84.   [2] Pp. 445, 448, fecond edition.

Introduction. liii

Of filks patterned with the Greek crofs or "ftauracin," there are feveral examples in this collection; and though not of the remoteft period, are interefting; the one No. 8234, p. 154, wrought in Sicily as it is probable by the Greeks brought as prifoners from the Morea, in the twelfth century, is not without fome value. In the Chapter Library at Durham may be feen a valuable fample of Byzantine ftauracin "colours purple and crimfon; the only prominent ornament a crofs—often repeated, even upon the fmall portion which remains."[1] Thofe who have feen in St. Peter's facrifty at Rome, that beautiful light-blue dalmatic faid to have been worn by Charlemagne when he fang the Gofpel at high mafs, at the altar, vefted as a deacon, the day he was crowned emperor in that church by Pope Leo III. will remember how plentifully it is fprinkled with croffes between its exquifite embroideries, fo as to make the veftment a real "ftauracin." It has been well given by Sulpiz Boifferée in his "Kaifer Dalmatika in der St. Peterfkirche;" but far better by Dr. Bock in his fplendid work on the Coronation Robes of the German emperors.

Silks, from the pattern woven on them called *de fundato*, are frequently fpoken of by Anaftafius. From the texts themfelves of that writer, and paffages in other authors of his time, it would feem that the filks themfelves were dyed of the richeft purple, and figured with gold in the pattern of netting. As one of the meanings for the fubftantive "funda" is a fifherman's net, rich textiles fo figured in gold, were denominated from fuch a pattern "de fundato" or netted. To St. Peter's Church at Rome the pontiff, Leo III. gave "cortinam majorem Alexandrinam holofericam habentem in medio adjunctum fundatum, et in circuitu ornatum de fundato;"[2] and for the Church of St. Paul's, Leo provided "vela holoferica majora figillata habentia periclyfin et crucem tam de blattin feu de fundato."[3] From Fortunatus we gather that thofe coftly purple-dyed filks called "blatta," were always interwoven with gold:—

   Serica purpureis fternuntur vellera velis,
   Inlita blatta toris, aurumque intermicat oftro.[4]

This net-pattern lingered long, and, no doubt, we find it, under a new name, "laqueatus"—mefhed—as identified upon a cope made of baudekin, at St. Paul's, London, A.D. 1295: "Capa de baudekino cum pineis (fir-apples) in campis laqueatis.[5] Modifications of this very old pattern may be feen in this catalogue (pp. 35, 36, 154).

The Latin term "de fundato," for this net-pattern, fo unufual, has for many been quite a puzzle. Here, too, art works are our beft help to properly underftand the meaning of the word. The perfon of Con-

---

[1] Raine's St. Cuthbert, p. 196.   [2] Lib. Pontif. ii. 282.   [3] Ibid. 240.
[4] De Vita S. Martini lib. ii.   [5] Dugdale's St. Paul's, p. 318.

stantine the Great, given by Gori,[1] as well as that of a much later personage, shown us by Du Cange, at the end of his "Glossarium,"[2] shows the front of the imperial tunic, which was purple, to have been figured in gold with a netting-pattern, marked with pearls. Gori, moreover, presents us with a bishop whose chasuble is of the same design.[3] Further still, Paciaudi, in his "De Cultu S. Johannis Baptistæ,"[4] furnishes a better illustration, if possible, by an engraving of a diptych first published by him. Here St. Jacobus, or James, is arrayed in chasuble and pall of netting-patterned silk; and of the same-figured stuff is much of the trimming or ornamentation on the robes of the B. V. Mary, but on those more especially worn by the archangels, St. Michael and Gabriel. In the diapered pattern on some of the cloth of gold found lately in the grave of some archbishop of York, buried there about the end of the thirteenth century, is the same netting discernible.

Striped or *barred* silks—stragulatæ—got their especial name for such a simple pattern, and at one time were in much request. Frequent mention is made of them in the Exeter Inventories, of which the one taken, A. D. 1277, specifies, "Due palle de baudekyno—una stragulata;"[5] and A. D. 1327, the same cathedral had, "Unum filatorium de serico bonum stragulatum cum serico diversi coloris,"[6] a veil or scarf for the sub-deacon, made of silk striped in different colours. The illuminations on the MS. among the Harley collection at the British Museum, of the deposition of Richard II. published by the Society of Antiquaries, afford us instances of this textile. The young nobleman to the right sitting on the ground at the archbishop's sermon, is entirely, hood and all, arrayed in this striped silk,[7] and at the altar, where Northumberland is swearing on the Eucharist, the priest who is saying mass, wears a chasuble of the same stuff.[8] Old St. Paul's had copes like it: "Capæ factæ de uno panno serico veteri pro parte albi coloris, pro parte viridi;"[9] besides which, it had offertory-veils of the same pattern, one of them with its stripes paly red and green:—"Unum offertorium stragulatum, de rubeo et viridi;" and two others with their stripes bendy-wise: "Duo offertoria bendata de opere Saraceno."[10] York Cathedral also had two red palls paled with green and light blue: "Duæ pallæ rubiæ palyd cum viridi et blodio,"[11] so admirably edited for the Surtees Society, by Rev. Jas. Raine, jun. Under this kind of patterned silks must be put one the name for which has hitherto not been explained by our English antiquaries.

[1] T. iii. p. xx.
[2] T. viii. plate 5.
[3] Ib. p. 84.
[4] P. 389.
[5] Ed. Oliver, p. 298.
[6] Ib. p. 312.
[7] Plate v. p. 53.
[8] Plate xii. p. 141.
[9] Dugdale's St. Paul's, p. 318.
[10] Ib.
[11] York Fabric Rolls, p. 230.

At the end of the twelfth century there was brought to England, from Greece, a fort of precious filk named there *Imperial.*

Ralph, dean of St. Paul's cathedral, London, tells us, that William de Magna Villa, on coming home from his pilgrimage to the Holy Land, made prefents to feveral churches, A. D. 1178, of cloths which at Conftantinople were called imperial : " Pannos quos Conftantinopolis civitas vocat Imperiales, &c." [1] Relating the ftory of John's apparition, A. D. 1226, Roger Wendover, and after him Matt. Paris, tells us that the King ftood forth dreffed in royal robes made of the ftuff they call Imperial: " Aftitit rex in veftibus regalibus de panno fcilicet quem imperialem appellant." [2] In the Inventory of St. Paul's, London, drawn up A. D. 1295, four tunicles, veftments for fubdeacons and lower minifters about the altar, are mentioned as made of this imperial. No colour is fpecified, except in the one inftance of the filk being marbled ; and the patterns are noticed as of red and green, with lions wove in gold.[3] It feems not to have been thought good enough for the more important veftments, fuch as chafubles and copes. Were it not fpoken of thus by Wendover and Paris, as well as by a dean of St. Paul's, and mentioned once as ufed in a few liturgical garments for that cathedral, we had never heard a word about fuch a textile anywhere in England. Our belief is that it got its name neither from its colour—fuppofed royal purple—nor its coftlinefs, but through quite another reafon : woven at a workfhop kept up by the Byzantine emperors, juft like the Gobelins is to-day in Paris by the French, and bearing about it fome fmall, though noticeable mark, it took the defignation of "Imperial." That it was partly wrought with gold, we know ; but that its tint was always fome fhade of the imperial purple —hence its appellation—is a purely gratuitous affumption. Moreover, as Saracenic princes in general had wrought in their own palaces, at the tiraz there, thofe filks wanted by themfelves, their friends, and officers, and caufed them to be marked with fome adopted word or fentence ; fo, too, the rulers of Byzantium followed, it is likely the fame ufage, and put fome royal device or word, or name in Greek upon theirs, and hence fuch textiles took the name of Imperial. In France, this textile was in ufe as late as the fecond half of the fifteenth century, but looked upon as old. Here, at York, as late as the early part of the fixteenth, one of its deans beftowed on that cathedral "two (blue) copes of clothe imperialle." [4]

---

[1] Hift. Anglic. Script. X. t. i. p. 602, ed. Twyfden.
[2] Rog. de Wendover, Chronica, t. iv. p. 127, ed. Coxe.   [3] P. 322.
[4] Fabric Rolls, p. 310.

Baudekin

Was a coftly ftuff much employed and often fpoken of in our literature during many years of the mediæval period.

Ciclatoun, as we have elfewhere remarked, was the ufual term during centuries throughout Weftern Europe, by which thofe fhowy golden textiles were called. When, however, Bagdad, or Baldak, ftanding where once ftood the Babylon of old, took and held for no fhort length of time the lead all over Afia in weaving, every kind of fine filks and in efpecial golden ftuffs fhot, as now, in different colours, cloths of gold fo tinted became every where known more particularly among us Englifh as "baldakin," "baudekin," or "baudkyn," or filks from Baldak. At laft the earlier term "ciclatoun" dropped quite out of ufe. With this before him the reader will hereafter more readily underftand feveral otherwife puzzling paffages in many of our old writers in poetry and profe, as well as in the inventories of royal furniture and church veftments.

Our kings and our nobility affected much this rich ftuff for the garments worn by them on high occafions. When, A.D. 1247, girding in Weftminfter Abbey William de Valence his uterine brother, a knight, our Henry III. had on a robe of baudekin, or cloth-of-gold, likely fhot with crimfon filk: " Dominus Rex vefte deaurata facta de preciofiffimo Baldekino et coronula aurea, quæ vulgariter garlanda dicitur redimitus, fedens gloriofe in folio regio, fratrem fuum uterinum, baltheo militari gaudenter infignivit."[1] In the year 1259 the mafter of Sherborn Hofpital in the north, bequeathed to that houfe a cope made of cloth-of-gold, or "baudekin:"—" Capam de panno ad aurum fcilicet Baudekin cum veftimento plenario de panno Yfpaniæ ad aurum."[2]

But thefe Bagdad or Baldak filks, with a weft of gold known among us as "baudekins" were often wove very large in fize, and applied here in England to efpecial ritual purpofes. As a thanks-offering after a fafe return home from a journey, they were brought and given to the altar; at all the folemn burials of our kings and queens, and other great ones, each of the many mourners, when offertory time came, went to the illuminated hearfe,—one is figured in the "Church of Our Fathers,"[3] and ftrewed a baudekin of coftly texture over the coffin. Artifts or others who wifh to know the ceremonial for that occafion, will find it

---

[1] Matt. Paris, p. 249.
[2] Wills, &c. of the Northern Counties of England, Surtees Society, p. 6.
[3] Tom. ii. p. 501.

Introduction. lvii

set forth in the descriptions of many of our mediæval funerals. At the obsequies of Henry VII. in Westminster Abbey:—" Twoe herauds came to the Duke of Buck. and to the Earles and conveyed them into the Revestrie where they did receive certen Palles which everie of them did bringe solemply betwene theire hands and comminge in order one before another as they were in degree unto the said herse, thay kissed theire said palles and delivered them unto the said heraudes which laide them uppon the kyngs corps, in this manner: the palle which was first offered by the Duke of Buck. was laid on length on the said corps, and the residewe were laid acrosse, as thick as they might lie."[1] In the same church at the burial of Anne of Cleves, A.D. 1557, a like ceremonial of carrying cloth-of-gold palls to the hearse was followed.[2]

Among the many rich textiles belonging to St. Paul's, London, A.D. 1295, are mentioned: " Baudekynus purpureus cum columpnis et arcubus et hominibus equitantibus infra, de funere comitissæ Britanniæ. Item baudekynus purpureus cum columpnis et arcubus et Sampson fortis infra arcus, de dono Domini Henrici Regis. Duo baudekyni rubei cum sagittarijs infra rotas, de dono E. regis et reginæ venientium de Wallia, Unus Baudekynus rubei campi cum griffonibus, pro anima Alianoræ reginæ junioris,"[3] &c. At times these rich stuffs were cut up into chasubles: " Casula de baudekyno de opere Saracenico,"[4] as was the cloth-of-gold dress worn by one of our princesses at her betrothal : " Unam vestimentum rubeum de panno adaurato diversis avibus poudratum, in quo domina principessa fuit desponsata."[5] The word " baudekin" itself became at last narrowed in its meaning. So warm, so mellow, so fast were all the tones of crimson which the dyers of Bagdad knew how to give their silks, that without a thread of gold in them, the mere glowing tints of those plain crimson silken webs from Bagdad won for themselves the name of baudekins. Furthermore, when they quite ceased to be partly woven in gold, and from their consequent lower price and cheapness got into use for cloths of estate over royal thrones, on common occasions, the shortened form of such a regal emblem, the canopy hung over the high altar of a church, acquired, and yet keeps its appellation, at least in Italy, of " baldachino."

How very full in size, how costly in materials and embroidery, must have sometimes been the cloth of estate spread overhead and behind the throne of our kings, may be gathered from the " Privy Purse Expenses of Henry the Seventh," wherein this item comes: " To Antony

---

[1] Lelandi Collectanea, t. iv. p. 308.
[2] Excerpta Historica, p. 512.
[3] Dugdale's St. Paul's, pp. 328-9.
[4] Ibid. p. 331.
[5] Inventory of the Chapel, Windsor Castle, Mon. Ang. viii. 1363.

Corffe for a cloth of an eftate conteyning 47¼ yerds, £11 the yerd, £522 10s."[1]

About the feudal right, ftill kept up in Rome, to a cloth of eftate, among the continental nobility, we have fpoken, p. 107 of this catalogue, where a fragment of fuch a hanging is defcribed.

The cuftom itfelf is thus noticed by Chaucer:—

> Yet nere and nere forth in I gan me drefs
> Into an hall of noble apparaile,
> With arras fpred, and cloth of gold I geffe,
> And other filke of eafier availe :
> Under the cloth of their eftate fauns faile
> The king and quene there fat as I beheld.[2]

This fame rich golden ftuff afks for our notice under a third and even better known name, to be found all through our early literature as

CLOTH OF PALL.

The cloak (in Latin pallium, in Anglo-Saxon paell) of ftate for regal ceremonies and high occafions, worn alike by men as well as women, was always made of the moft gorgeous ftuff that could be found. From a very early period in the mediæval ages, golden webs fhot in filk with one or other of the various colours—occafionally blue, oftener crimfon—were fought out, as may be eafily imagined, for the purpofe, through fo many years, and everywhere, that at laft each fort of cloth of gold had given to it the name of "pall," no matter the immediate purpofe to which it might have to be applied, and after fo many fafhions. Veftments for church ufe and garments for knights and ladies were made of it. Old St. Paul's had chafubles and copes of cloth of pall : " Cafula de pal, capa chori de pal, &c."[3]

In worldly ufe, if the king's daughter was to have a

> Mantell of ryche degre
> Purple palle and armyne fre.[4]

So in the poem of Sir Ifumbras—

> The rich queen in hall was fet ;
> Knights her ferved, at hand and feet
> In rich robes of pall.[5]

---

[1] Excerpta Hiftorica, p. 121. [2] Poems, ed. Nicolas, t. vi. p. 134.
[3] Hift. ed. Dugdale, p. 336. [4] The Squire of Low Degree.
[5] Ellis's Metrical Romances, t. iii. p. 167.

For state receptions, our kings used to send out an order that the houses should be "curtained" all along the streets which the procession would have to take through London, "incortinaretur."[1] How this was done we learn from Chaucer in the "Knight's Tale,"[2]

> By ordinance, thurghout the cite large
> Hanged with cloth of gold, and not with sarge;

as well as from the "Life of Alexander:"—

> Al theo city was by-hong
> Of riche baudekyns and pellis (palls) among.[3]

Hence, when Elizabeth, our Henry VII.'s queen, "proceded from the Towre throwge the Citie of London (for her coronation) to Westminster, al the strets ther wich she shulde passe by, were clenly dressed and besene with clothes of Tappestreye and Arras. And some strets, as Cheepe, hangged with riche clothes of gold, velvetts, and silks, &c."[4] "As late as A.D. 1555, at Bow chyrche in London was hangyd with cloth of gold and with ryche hares (arras)."[5]

Those same feelings which quickened our doughty knights and highborn ladies to go and overspread the bier of each dead noble friend, with costly baudekins or cloths of gold, so the church whispered and she whispers us still to do, in due degree, the same to the coffin in which the poor man is being carried to the grave beneath a mantle of silk and velvet. The brother or the sister belonging to any of our old London gilds had over them, however lowly they might have been in life, one or other of those splendid hearse-cloths which we saw in this museum, among the loans, in the ever memorable year 1862.

This silken textile interwove with gold, first known as "ciclatoun," on account of its glitter, then as "baudekin," from the city where it was best made, came at last to be called by the name of "pall." Whether employed on jubilant occasions, for a joyful betrothal, or a stately coronation, or for a sorrowing funeral, it mattered not, it got the common term of "cloth of pall," which we yet keep up in that velvet covering for a coffin, a burial pall.

LETTERED SILKS

are of no uncommon occurrence, and some examples may be seen in this collection.

---

[1] Matt. Paris, p. 661.
[2] V. 2569-70.
[3] Warton's Hist. of English Poetry, t. ii. p. 8.
[4] Leland's Collectanea, t. iv. p. 220.
[5] Machyn's Diary, p. 102.

A celebrated Mohammedan writer, Ebn-Khaldoun, who died about the middle of the fifteenth century, while speaking of that spot in an Arab palace, the "Tiraz," so designated from the name itself of the rich silken stuffs therein woven, tells us that of the attributes of all Saracenic kings and sultans, and which became a particular usage for ruling dynasties, one was to have woven the name of the actual prince, or that special ensign chosen by his house, into the stuffs intended for their personal wear, whether wrought of silk, brocade, or even coarser kind of silk. While gearing his loom, the workman contrived that the letters of the title should come out either in threads of gold, or in silk of another colour from that of the ground. The royal apparel thus bore about it its own especial marks emblematic of the sultan's wardrobe, and so became the distinguishing ensigne of the prince himself, as well as for those personages around him, who were allowed, by their official rank in his court, to wear them, and those again upon whom he had condescended to bestow such garments as especial tokens of the imperial favour, like the modern pelisse of honour. Before the period of their having embraced Islamism the Kings of Persia used to have woven upon the stuffs wrought for their personal use, or as gifts to others, their own especial effigies or likeness, or at times the peculiar ensign of their royalty. On becoming Mussulmans, the rulers of that kingdom changed the custom, and instead of portraiture substituted their names, to which they added words sounding to their ears as foreboding good, or certain formulas of praise and benediction.[1] Wherever the Moslem ruled, there did he set up the same practice; and thus, whether in Asia, in Egypt, or other parts of Africa, or in Moorish Spain, the silken garments for royalty and its favoured ones, showed woven in them the prince's name, or at least his chosen badge. The silken garments wrought in Egypt for the far-famed Saladin, and worn by him as its Kalif, bore very conspicuously upon them the name of that conqueror.

In our old lists of church ornaments, frequent mention is found of vestments inscribed, like pieces here, with words in real or pretended Arabic; and when St. Paul's inventory more than once speaks of silken stuffs, "de opere Saraceno," we lean to the belief that, though not all, some at least of those textiles were so called from having Arabic characters woven on them. Such, too, were the letters on the red pall, figured with elephants and a bird, belonging to Exeter: "Palla rubea cum quibusdam literis et elephantis et quadam avi in superiori parte."[2]

---

[1] Silvestre De Sacy, Chrestomathie Arabe, t. ii. p. 287.   [2] Oliver, p. 298.

Later, our trade with the South of Spain and the Moors there, led us to call such words on woven stuffs Moorish, as we find in old documents, thus Joane Lady Bergavenny bequeaths (A. D. 1434) a "hullyng (hangings for a hall) of black, red, and green, with morys letters, &c."[1]

The weaving of letters in textiles is neither a Moorish, nor Saracenic invention; ages before, the ancient Parthians used to do so, as we learn from Pliny: "Parthi literas vestibus intexunt." A curious illustration of silken stuffs so frequently bearing letters, borrowed in general from some real or supposed oriental alphabet, is the custom which many of the illuminators had of figuring very often on frontals and altar canopies, made of silk, meaningless words; and the artists of Italy up to the middle of the sixteenth century did the same on the hems of the garments worn by great personages, in their paintings. On the inscribed textiles here, the real or pretended Arabic sentence is written twice on the same line, once forwards, once backwards.

THE EAGLE,

single and double-headed, may frequently be found in the patterns of old silks. In all ages certain birds of prey have been looked upon by heathens as ominous for good or evil. Of this our own country affords us a mournful example. Upon the standard which was carried at the head of the Danish masters of Northumbria was figured the raven, the bird of Odin. This banner had been woven and worked by the daughters of Regnar Lodbrok, in one noontide's while; and those heathens believed that if victory was to follow, the raven would seem to stand erect, and as if about to soar before the warriors, but if a defeat was impending, the raven hung his head and drooped his wings; as we are told by Asser: "Pagani acceperunt illud vexillum quod Reafan nominant: dicunt enim quod tres sorores Hungari et Habbæ filiæ videlicet Lodebrochi illud vexillum texuerunt et totum paraverunt illud uno meridiano tempore: dicunt etiam quod, in omni bello ubi præcederet idem signum, si victoriam adepturi essent, appereret in medio signi quasi corvus vivens volitans: sin vero vincendi in futuro fuissent, penderet directe nihil movens."[2] Another and a more important flag, that which Harold and his Anglo-Saxons fought under and lost at Hastings, is described by Malmesbury as having been embroidered in gold, with the figure of a man in the act of fighting, and studded with precious stones, all done in sumptuous art:

---

[1] Test. Vet. i. p. 228.   [2] Asserius, De Rebus Gestis Ælfredi, ed. Wise, p. 33.

"Quod (vexillum) erat in hominis pugnantis figura auro et lapidibus arte fumptuofa intextum."[1]

Still farther down in paft ages, known for its daring and its lofty flight, the eagle was held in high repute; throughout all the Eaft, where it became the emblem of lordly power and victory, often it is to be feen flying in triumph over the head of fome Affyrian conqueror, as may be witneffed in Layard's Work on Nineveh.[2] Homer calls it the bird of Jove. Upon the yoke in the war chariot of the Perfian king Darius fat perched an eagle as if outftretching his wings wrought all in gold: "Auream aquilam pinnas extendenti fimilem."[3] The fight of this bird in the air while a battle raged was, by the heathen looked upon as an omen boding victory to thofe on whofe fide it hovered. At the battle of Granicus thofe about Alexander faw or thought they faw fluttering juft above his head, quite heedlefs of the din, an eagle, to which Ariftander called the attention of the Macedonians as an unmiftakable earneft of fuccefs: "Qui circa Alexandrum erant, vidiffe fe crediderunt, paululum fuper caput regis placide volantem aquilam non gemitu morientium territam Ariftander . . . . . militibus in pugnam intentis avem monftrabat, haud dubium victoriæ aufpicium."[4] The Romans bore it on their ftandards; the Byzantine emperors kept it as their own device, and following the ancient traditions of the eaft, and heedlefs of their law that forbids the making of images, the Saracens, efpecially when they ruled in Egypt, had the eagle figured on feveral things about them, fometimes fingle at others double-headed, which latter was the fhape adopted by the emperors of Germany as their blazon; and in this form it is borne to this day by feveral reigning houfes. No wonder then that eagles of both fafhions are fo often to be obferved woven upon ancient and eaftern textiles.

Very likely, as yet left to fhow itfelf upon the walls of the citadel at Cairo, and thofe curious old glafs lamps hung up there and elfewhere in the mofques, the double-headed eagle with wings difplayed, which we find on royal Saracenic filks, was borrowed by the Paynim from the Crufaders, as it would feem, and felected for its enfign by the government of Egypt in the thirteenth century, which will eafily account for the prefence of that heraldic bird upon fo many fpecimens from Saracenic looms, to be found in this collection. The "tiraz," in fact, was for filk like the royal manufactory of Drefden and Sèvres china, or Gobelin's looms for tapeftry, and as the courts of France for its mark or enfign fixed upon the two LLs interlaced, and the houfe of Saxony the two fwords

---

[1] Will. Malmef. Gefta Regum Anglorum, t. ii. p. 415, ed. Duffus Hardy.
[2] Plates, 18, 20, 22.   [3] Quintus Curtius, Lib. iii. cap. iii. p. 7.
[4] Ibid. Lib. iv. cap. xv. p. 72.

placed faltire wife, fo at leaft for Saladin and Egypt, in the middle-ages the double-headed eagle with its wings outftretched, was the efpecial badge or enfign. In the fame manner the facred " horm," or tree of life, between the two rampant lions or cheethas may be the mark of Perfia.

As early as A.D. 1277 Exeter Cathedral reckoned among her veftments feveral fuch; for inftance, a cope of baudekin figured with fmall two-headed eagles: " Capa baudekyn cum parvis aquilis, ij capita habentibus;"[1] and our Henry III.'s brother, Richard the king of Germany, gave to the fame church a cope of black baudekin, with eagles in gold figured on it: " Una capa de baudek, nigra cum aquilis deauratis."[2] Many other inftances might be noticed all through England.

As in architecture, fculpture, and painting, ancient and modern, fo

IN WOVEN STUFFS THERE ARE STYLES NICELY DEFINED, AND EPOCHS EASILY DISCERNIBLE.

Hitherto no attempt has been anywhere made to diftribute olden filken textiles into various fchools, and as the prefent is the firft and only collection which has in any country been thrown open as yet to the public, the occafion feems a fitting one to warrant fuch an endeavour of claffification.

With no other than the fpecimens here before us, we think we fee them fall into thefe feveral groups—Chinefe, Perfian, Byzantine, Oriental or Indian, Syrian, Saracenic, Morefco-Spanifh, Sicilian, Italian, Flemifh, Britifh, and French.

Chinefe examples here are very few; but what they are, whether plain or figured, they are beautiful in their own way. From all that we know of the people, we are led to believe their own way two thoufand years ago is precifely theirs ftill, fo that the web wrought by them this year or two hundred years ago, like No. 1368, p. 75, would not differ hardly in a line from their textiles two thoufand years gone by, when Dionyfius Periegetes wrote that, the " Seres make precious figured garments, refembling in colour the flowers of the field, and rivalling in finenefs the work of fpiders." In the ftuffs, warp and woof are of filk, and both of the beft kinds.

Perfian textiles, even as we fee them in this collection, muft have been for many centuries juft as they were ever figured, and may be, even now, defcribed by the words of Quintus Curtius, with fome little allowance for thofe influences exercifed upon the mind of the weaver by his peculiar religious belief, which would not let the lowlieft workman forget the

---

[1] Oliver, p. 299. [2] Ibid.

"homa," or tree of life. When Marco Polo travelled through those parts, in the thirteenth century, and our countryman, Sir John Mandeville, a hundred years later, the old love for hunting wild beasts still lived, and the princes of the country were as fond as ever of training the cheetah, a kind of small lion or leopard, for the chase, as we have noticed, p. 178.

When the design is made up of various kinds of beasts and birds, real or imaginary, with the sporting cheetah nicely spotted among them; and the "homa" conspicuously set forth above all; sure may we be that the web was wrought by Persians, and on most occasions the textile will be found in all its parts to be woven from the richest materials.

As an illustration of the Persian type of style, No. 8233, p. 154, may be taken as a specimen.

For trade purposes, and to make the textile pass in the European market as from Persia, the manner of its loom was often copied by the Jewish and the Christian weavers in Syria, as we shall have to notice just now.

The Byzantine Greeks, for their textiles from the time when in the sixth century they began to weave home-grown silk, made for themselves a school of design which kept up in their drawing not a little of the beauty, breadth, and flowing outline which had outlived among them the days of heathenish art. Along with this a strong feeling of their Christianity showed itself as well in many of the subjects which they took out of holy writ, as in the smaller elements of ornamentation. Figures, whether of the human form or of beasts, are given in a much larger and bolder size than on any other ancient stuffs. Though there be very few known specimens from the old looms of Constantinople, the one here, No. 7036, p. 122, showing Samson wrestling with a lion, may serve as a type. In the year 1295 old St. Paul's Cathedral, here in London, would seem to have possessed several splendid vestments made of Byzantine silk, as we note in the samples to be named *infra* under the head of Damask.

The way in which those Greeks gave a pattern to the stuff intended more especially for liturgical purposes is pointed out while speaking about "Stauracin" and the "Gammadion," a form of the cross with which they powdered their silks; p. lii.

The world-wide fame of the Byzantine purple tint is attested by our Gerald Barry, whose words we quote further on. As a sample of the Byzantine loom in "diaspron," or diapering, we would refer to No. 1239, p. 26.

The specimens here from the Byzantine, and later Greek loom, are not to be taken as by any means appropriate samples of its general production. They are poor in both respects—material and, when figured, design—as may be seen at pp. 27, 28, 33, 36, 123, 124, 126, 219, &c. *Oriental* ancient silks and textiles have their own distinctive marks.

From Marco Polo, who wandered much over the far east, some time during the thirteenth century, we learn that the weaving there was done by women who wrought in silk and gold, after a noble manner, beasts and birds upon their webs:—"*Le loro donne lavorano tutte cose a seta e ad oro e a uccelli e a bestie nobilmente e lavorano di cortine ed altre cose molto ricamente.*"[1]

Out of the several specimens here from Tartary and India, during our mediæval period, we pick one or two which show well the meaning of those words uttered by that great Venetian traveller, while speaking about the textiles he saw in those countries. The dark purple piece of silk, figured in gold with birds and beasts, of the thirteenth century, No. 7086, p. 137, is good; but better still for our purpose is the shred, No. 7087, p. 138, of blue damask, with its birds, its animals, and flowers wrought in gold, and different coloured silks.

What India is, it has ever been, famous for its cloud-like transparent muslins, which since Marco Polo's days have kept till now even that oriental name, through being better than elsewhere woven at Mosul.

The *Syrian* school is well represented here by several fine pieces.

The whole sea-board of that part of Asia Minor, as well as far inland, was inhabited by a mixture of Jews, Christians, and Saracens; and each of these people were workers in silk. The reputation of the neighbouring Persia had of old stood high for the beauty and durability of her silken textiles, which made them to be sought for by the European traders. Persia's outlet to the west for her goods, lay through the great commercial ports on the coast of Syria. Setting, like Persia used to do, as it were, her own peculiar seal upon her figured webs, by mingling in her designs the mystic "homa," to the European mind this part of the pattern became, at first, a sort of assurance that those goods had been thrown off by Persian looms. By one of those tricks of imitation followed then, as well as now, the Syrian designers for the loom threw this "homa" into their patterns. This symbol of "the tree of life," had no doubt been a borrow by Zoroaster from Holy Writ.[2] Neither to the Christian's eye, nor to the Jew's, nor Moslem's, was there in it anything objectionable; all three, therefore, took it and made it a leading portion of design in the patterns of their silks; and hence is it that we meet it so often. Though

---

[1] I Viaggi di Marco Polo, ed. A. Bartoli, Firenze, 1865, p. 345.
[2] Genesis ii. 9.

done with perhaps a fraudulent intention of palming on the world Syrian for real Perfian filks, thofe Syrians ufually put into their own defigns a fomething which fpoke of their peculiar felves and their workmanfhip. Though there be feen the "homa," the "cheetah," and other elements of Perfian patterns, ftill the difcordant two-handled vafe, the badly imitated Arabic fentence, betray the textile to be not Perfian, but Syrian. No. 8359, p. 213, will readily exemplify our meaning. Furthermore, perhaps quite innocent of any knowledge about Perfia's firft belief, and her ufe of the "homa" in her old religious fervices, the Chriftian weavers of Syria, along with the Zorafterian fymbol, put the fign of the crofs by the fide of that "tree of life," as we find upon the piece of filk, No. 7094, p. 140. Another remarkable fpecimen of the Syrian loom is No. 7034, p. 122, whereon the Nineveh lions come forth fo confpicuoufly. As a good example of well-wrought "diafpron" or diaper, No. 8233, p. 154, may be mentioned, along with No. 7052, p. 127.

Saracenic weaving, as fhown by the defign upon the web, is exemplified in feveral fpecimens before us.

However much againft what looks like a heedleffnefs of the Koran's teachings, certain it is that the Saracens, thofe of the upper claffes in particular, felt no difficulty in wearing robes upon which animals and the likeneffes of other created things were woven; with the ftricteft of their princes, a double-headed eagle was a royal heraldic device, as we have fhown, p. lxiii. Stuffs, then, figured with birds and beafts, with trees and flowers, were not the lefs of Saracenic workmanfhip, and meant for Moflem wear. What, however, may be looked for upon real Saracenic textures is a pattern confifting of longitudinal ftripes of blue, red, green, and other colour; fome of them charged with animals, fmall in form, other fome written, in large Arabic letters, with a word or fentence, often a proverb, often a good wifh or fome wife faw.

As examples we would point to No. 8288, p. 178, and 7051, p. 127. For a fair fpecimen of diapering, No. 7050, p. 127, while No. 8639, p. 243, prefents us with a defign having in it, befides the crefcent moon, a proof that architectural forms were not forgotten by the weaver-draughtsman, in his fketches for the loom.

Later, in our chapter on Tapeftry, we fhall have occafion to fpeak about another fort of Saracenic work or tapeftry, of the kind called abroad, from the pofition of its frame, of the baffe-liffe.

Morefco–Spanifh, or Saracenic textiles, wrought in Spain, though partaking of the ftriped pattern, and bearing words in real or imitated Arabic, had fome diftinctions of their own. The defigns fhown upon thefe ftuffs are almoft always drawn out of ftrap-work, reticulations, or some combination or another of geometrical lines, amid which are occasionally to be found different forms of conventional flowers. Specimens are to be seen here at pp. 51, 55, 121, 124, 125, 186, 240, &c. Sometimes, but very rarely, the crescent moon is figured as in the curious piece, No. 8639, p. 243. The colours of these silks are usually either a fine crimson, or a deep blue with almost always a fine toned yellow as a ground. But one remarkable feature in these Moresco-Spanish textiles is the presence, when gold is brought in, of an ingenious though fraudulent imitation of the precious metal, for which shreds of gilded parchment cut up into narrow flat strips are substituted, and woven with the silk. This, when fresh, must have looked very bright, and have given the web all the appearance of those favourite stuffs called here in England "tissues," of which we have already spoken, p. xxiii.

We are not aware that this trick has ever been found out before, and it was only by the use of a highly magnifying glass that we penetrated the secret. Our suspicion was awakened by so often observing that the gold had become quite black. Examples of this gilt vellum may be seen here, at Nos. 7095, p. 140 ; 8590, p. 224 ; 8639, p. 244 ; &c.

When the Christian Spanish weavers lived beyond Saracenic control, they filled their designs with beasts, birds, and flowers; but even then the old Spanish fine tone of crimson is rather striking in their webs, as is evidenced in the beautiful piece of diaper, No. 1336, p. 64.

Spanish velvets—and they were mostly wrought in Andalusia—are remarkably fine and conspicuous both for their deep soft pile, and their glowing ruby tones ; but when woven after the manner of velvet upon velvet, are very precious : a good specimen of rich texture, and mellow colouring is furnished by the chasuble at No. 1375, p. 81.

The *Sicilian* school strongly marked the wide differences between itself and all the others which had lived before ; and the history of its loom is as interesting as it is varied.

The first to teach the natives of Sicily the use of cotton for their garments, and how to rear the silkworm and spin its silk, were, as it would seem, the Mahomedans, who, in coming over from Africa, brought along with them, besides the art of weaving silken textiles, a knowledge of the fauna of that vast continent—its giraffes, its antelopes, its gazelles, its lions, its elephants. These Mussulmans told them, too, of the parrots of India and the hunting sort of lion,—the cheetahs, that were found in Asia; and when the stuff had to be wrought for European wear, imaged both beast and bird upon the web, at the same time that they wove a word in Arabic, of greeting to be read among the flowers. Like all other Saracens, those in Sicily loved to mingle gold in their tissues ; and, to spare the silk, cotton thread was not unfrequently worked up in the warp. When, therefore, we meet with beasts taken from the fauna of Africa, such, especially, as the giraffe, and the several classes of the antelope family—in particular the gazelle—with, somewhere about, an Arabic motto—and part of the pattern wrought in gold, which, at first poor and thin, is now become black, as well as cotton in the warp, we may fairly take the specimen as a piece of Sicily's work in its first period of weaving, all so Saracenic to the eye. Even when that Moslem nation had been driven out by the Normans, if many of its people did not stay as workmen in silk at Palermo, yet they left their teachings in weaving and design behind them, and their practices were, years afterwards, still followed.

Now we reach Sicily's second epoch.

While at war with the Byzantines, in the twelfth century, Roger, King of Sicily, took Corinth, Thebes, and Athens, from each of which cities he led away captives all the men and women he could find who knew how to weave silks, and carried them to Palermo. To the Norman tiraz there, these Grecian new comers brought fresh designs, which were adopted sometimes wholly, at others but in part and mixed up with the older Saracenic style, for silks wrought under the Normano-Sicilian dynasty. In this second period of the island's loom we discover what traces the Byzantine school had impressed upon Sicilian silks, and helped so much to alter the type of their design. On one silk, a grotesque mask amid the graceful twinings of luxuriant foliage, such as might have been then found by them upon many a fragment of old Greek sculpture, was the pattern, as we witness, at No. 8241, p. 158; on another, a sovereign on horseback wearing the royal crown, and carrying as he rides a hawk upon his wrist—token both of the love for lordly sports at the period, and the feudalism all over Italy and Christendom, shown in the piece, No. 8589, p. 223; on a third, No. 8234, p. 154, is the Greek cross, along with a pattern much like the old netted or "de fundato" kind which we have described, p. liii.

But Sicily's third is quite her own peculiar style. At the end of the thirteenth and beginning of the fourteenth century, she struck out of herself into quite an unknown path for design. Without throwing aside the old elements employed till then especially, all over the east, and among the rest, by the Mahomedans, Sicily put along with them the emblem of Christianity, the cross, in various forms, on some occasions with the letter V. four times repeated, and so placed together as to fall into the shape of this symbol, like what we find at No. 1245, p. 28; in other instances the cross is floriated, as at No. 1293, p. 47.

From the far east to the uttermost western borders of the Mediterranen the weavers of every country had been in the habit of figuring upon their silks those beasts and birds they saw around them: the Tartar, the Indian, and the Persian gave us the parrot and the cheetah; the men of Africa the giraffe and the gazelle; the people of each continent the lions, the elephants, the eagles, and the other birds common to both. From the poetry and sculpture of the Greeks and Romans could the Sicilians have easily learned about the fabled griffin and the centaur; but it was left for their own wild imaginings to figure as they have, such an odd compound in one being as the animal—half elephant, half griffin—which we see in No. 1288, p. 45. Their daring flights of fancy in coupling the difficult with the beautiful, are curious; in one place, No. 1302, p. 50, large eagles are perched in pairs with a radiating sun between them, and beneath dogs, in pairs, running with heads turned back, &c.; in another, No. 1304, p. 51, running harts have caught one of their hind legs in a cord tied to their collar, and an eagle swoops down upon them; and the same animal, in another place, on the same piece has switched its tail into the last link of a chain fastened to its neck; on a third sample, No. 8588, p. 222, we behold figured, harts, the letter M floriated, winged lions, crosses floriated, crosses sprouting out on two sides with *fleurs-de-lis*, four-legged monsters, some like winged lions, some biting their tails. Exeter Cathedral had a cloth of gold purple cope, figured with "draconibus volantibus ac tenentibus caudas proprias in ore,"[1] doves in pairs upholding a cross, &c. Hardly elsewhere to be found are certain elements peculiar to the patterns upon silks from mediæval Sicily; such, for instance, as harts, and demi-dogs with very large wings, both animals having remarkably long manes streaming far behind them, No. 1279, p. 41; harts again, but lodged beneath green trees, in a park with paling about it, as in No. 1283, p. 43, and No. 8710, p. 269; that oft-recurring sun shedding its beams with eagles pecking at them, or gazing undazzled at the luminary, pp. 48, 50, 137, but sometimes stags, as at pp. 54, 239, carrying their well attired heads upturned to a large pencil of those sunbeams as they dart down upon them amid a shower of rain-drops. Of birds, the hawk, the eagle, double and single headed, the parrot, may be found on stuffs all over the east; not so, however, with the swan, yet this majestic creature was a favourite with Sicilians, and may be seen here often drawn with great gracefulness, as at Nos. 1277, p. 41; 1299, p. 49; 8264, p. 166; 8610, p. 232, &c.

The Sicilians showed their strong affection for certain plants and flowers. On a great many of the silks in this collection, from Paler-

---

[1] Oliver, p. 345.

mitan looms, we see figured upon a tawny coloured grounding, beautifully drawn foliage in green; which, on a nearer inspection, bears the likeness of parsley, so curled, crispy and serrated are its leaves. Besides their cherished parsley along with the vine-leaf for foliage, they had their especial favourite among flowers; and it is the centaurea cyanus, our corn blue-bottle, shown among others in No. 1283, &c. p. 43, No. 1291, p. 47, No. 1308, p. 53.

Another peculiarity of theirs is the introduction of the letter U, repeated so as at times to mark the feathering upon the tails of birds; at others, to fall into the shape of an O, as we pointed out at pp. 40, 225, 227, 228.

Whether it was that, like our own Richard I., crusaders in after times often made Sicily the halting spot on their way to the Holy Land, or that knights crowded there for other purposes, and thus dazzled the eyes of the islanders with the bravery of their armorial bearings, figured on their cyclases and pennons, their flags and shields, certain is it that these Sicilians were particularly given to introduce a deal of heraldic charges —wyverns, eagles, lions rampant, and griffins—into their designs; and the very numerous occasions in which such elements of blazoning come in, are very noticeable, so that one of the features belonging to the Sicilian loom in its third period, is that, bating tinctures, it is so decidedly heraldic.

Not the last among the peculiarities of the third period in the Sicilian school is the use, for many of its stuffs, of two certain colours— murrey, for the ground, and a bright green for the pattern. When the fawn-coloured ground is gracefully sprinkled with parsley leaves, and nicely trailed with branches of the vine, and shows beasts and birds disporting themselves between the boughs of lively joyous green; the effect is cheerful, as may be witnessed in those specimens No. 8594, p. 226, No. 8602, p. 229, No. 8607, p. 231, Nos. 8609, 8610, p. 232, all of which so admirably exemplify the style.

All their beauty and happiness of invention, set forth by bold, free, spirited drawing, were bestowed, if not thrown away, too often upon stuffs of a very poor inferior quality, in which the gold, if not actually base, was always scanty, and a good deal of cotton was sure to be found wrought up along with the silk.

Though Palermo was, without doubt, the great workshop for weaving Sicilian silks, that trade used to be carried on not only in other cities of the island, but reached towns like Reggio and other such in Magna Græcia, northward up to Naples. We think that, as far as the two Sicilies are concerned, the growth of the cotton plant always went along with the rearing of the filkworm. Of the main-land loom we would fpecify No. 8256, p. 163, No. 8634, p. 242, No. 8638, p. 243.

Till within a few years the royal manufactory at Sta. Leucia, near Naples, produced filks of remarkable richnefs; and the piece, likely from that city itfelf, No. 721, p. 13, does credit to its loom, as it wove in the feventeenth century. Northern Italy was not idle; and the looms which fhe fet up in feveral of her great cities, in Lucca, Florence, Genoa, Venice and Milan, earned apart for themfelves a good repute in fome particulars, and a wide trade for their gold and filver tiffues, their velvets, and their figured filken textiles. Yet, like as each of thefe free ftates had its own accent and provincialifms in fpeech, fo too had it a fomething often thrown into its defigns and ftyle of drawing which told of the place and province whence the textiles came.

Lucca at an early period made herfelf known in Europe for her textiles; but her draughtfmen, like thofe of Sicily, feem to have thought themfelves bound to follow the ftyle hitherto in ufe, brought by the Saracens, of figuring parrots and peacocks, gazelles, and even cheetahs, as we behold in the fpecimens here No. 8258, p. 163, and No. 8616, p. 234. But, at the fame time, along with thefe eaftern animals, fhe mixed up emblems of her own, fuch as angels clothed in white, like in the example the laft mentioned. She foon dropped what was oriental from her patterns, which fhe began to draw in a larger, bolder manner, as we obferve, under No. 8637, p. 243, and No. 8640, p. 244, and fhowing an inclination for light blue, as a colour.

As in other places abroad, fo at Lucca, cloths of gold and of filver were often wrought, and the Lucchefe cloths of this coftly fort were, here in England, during the fourteenth century, in particular requeft. In all likelihood they were, both of them, not of the deadened but fparkling kind, afterwards efpecially known as "tiffue." Exeter Cathedral, A.D., 1327, had a cope of filver tiffue, or cloth of Lucca:— "una capa alba de panno de Luk."[1] At a later date, belonging to the fame church, were two fine chafubles—one purple, the other red—of the fame glittering ftuff, "cafula de purpyll panno," &c.,[2] where we find it fpecified that not only was the textile of gold, but of that efpecial fort called tiffue. York cathedral was particularly furnifhed with a great many copes of tiffue fhot with every colour required by its ritual, and among them were—"a reade cope of clothe of tifhewe with orphry of pearl, a cope with orphrey, a cope of raifed clothe of goulde,"[3] making a diftinction between tiffue and the ordinary cloth of gold.

---

[1] Oliver, p. 315.   [2] P. 344.   [3] York Fabric Rolls, p. 308.

But at the court of our Edward II. its favour would seem to have been the highest. In the Wardrobe Accounts of that king, we see the golden tissue, or Lucca cloth, several times mentioned. Whether the ceremony happened to be sad or gay, this glistening web was used; palls made of Lucca cloth were, at masses for the dead, strewed over the corpse; at marriages the care-cloth was made of the same stuff; thus when Richard de Arundell and Isabella, Hugh le Despenser's daughter, had been wedded at the door of the royal chapel, the veil held spread out over their heads as they knelt inside the chancel during the nuptial mass, for the blessing, was of Lucca cloth.[1] Richard II.'s fondness for this cloth of gold was lately noticed, p. xxx.

Just about Edward II.'s time was it that velvet became known, and got into use amongst our churchmen for vestments, and our nobles for personal wear, and the likelihood is that Lucca was among the first places in Europe to weave it. The specimens here of this fine textile from Lucchese looms, though in comparison with those from Genoa, they be few and mostly after one manner—the raised or cut—still have now a certain historical value for the English workman: No. 1357, p. 72, with its olive green plain silken ground, and trailed all over with flowers and leaves in a somewhat deeper tone, and the earlier example, No. 8322, p. 192, with its ovals and feathering stopped with graceful cusps and artichokes, afford us good instances of what Lucca could produce in the way of artistic velvets.

Genoa, though in far off mediæval times not so conspicuous as she afterwards became for her textile industry, still must have from a remote period, encouraged within her walls, and over her narrow territory, the weaving of silken webs. Of these the earliest mention we anywhere find, is to be seen in the inventory of those costly vestments once belonging to our own St. Paul's Cathedral, London, in the year 1295: besides a cope of Genoa cloth, that church had, from the same place, a hanging patterned with wheels and two-headed birds.[2] Though this first description be scant, we read in it quite enough to gather that these Genoese cloths must have entirely resembled the textiles wrought at Lucca, but, in particular, in Sicily. Perhaps they had been carried by trade from Palermo to the north-west shores of Italy, whence they were brought in the same way to England, so that they may be deemed to have reached us not so much from the looms themselves of Genoa, as those of some other place, but through her then great port.

---

[1] Archæologia, t. xxvi. pp. 337, 344.
[2] Hist. of St. Paul's, ed. Dugdale, pp. 318, 329.

Introduction. lxxiii

Of Genoa's own weaving of beautiful velvets there can be no doubt, a reputation she keeps to the present day as far as plain velvet is concerned.

In this collection we have samples in every kind of Genoese velvets, from those with a smooth unbroken surface to the elaborately patterned ones—art-wrought velvets in fact—showing, together with wonderful skill in the weaving, much beauty of design. Among the plain velvets in which we have nothing but great softness and depth of pile, along with clear bright luminous tones of colour, No. 540, p. 3, is a very fair specimen for its delicious richness of pile; and No. 8334, p. 199, not merely for this property, but as well for its lightsome mellow deep tint of crimson.

Getting to what may be truly called art-velvets, we come to several specimens here. Some are raised or cut, the design being done in a pile standing well up by itself from out of a flat ground of silk, sometimes of the same, sometimes of another colour, and not unfrequently wrought in gold, as at pp. 18, 90, 107, 110, 263. Then we have at No. 7795, p. 145, an example of that precious kind—velvet upon velvet—in which the ground is velvet, and again of velvet is the pattern itself, but raised one pile higher and well above the other, so as to show its form and shape distinctly. Last of all we here find samples, as in No. 8323, p. 192, how the design was done in various coloured velvet. Such was a favourite in England, and called motley; in his will, A. D. 1415, Henry Lord Scrope bequeathed two vestments, one, motley velvet rubeo de auro; the other, motley velvet nigro, rubeo et viridi, &c.[1]

Venice does not seem to have been at any time, like Sicily and Lucca, smitten with the taste of imitating in her looms at home the patterns which she saw abroad upon textile fabrics, but appears to have borrowed from the Orientals only one kind of weaving cloth of gold: the yellow chasuble at Exeter Cathedral, A. D. 1327, figured with beasts, cum bestiis crocei coloris,[2] is the solitary instance we know, upon which she wove, like the east, animals upon silks. She, however, set up for herself a new branch of textiles, and wrought for church use certain square webs of a crimson ground on which she figured, in gold, or on yellow silk, subjects taken from the New Testament, or the persons of saints and angels. These square pieces were as they yet are, employed, when sewed together in squares as frontals to altars, but when longwise much more generally as orphreys to chasubles, copes and other vestments. Of such stuffs must have been those large orphreys upon a dalmatic and tunicle, at St. Paul's Cathedral, London, A. D. 1295.[3]

Though not of so early a date as the thirteenth century, there are in

---

[1] Rymer's Foedera, t. 9, p. 274.   [2] Oliver, p. 313.   [3] Ed. Dugdale, p. 321.

k

this collection specimens of this Venetian web belonging to the sixteenth, which are very fine, No. 5900, p. 112, represents the resurrection of our Lord; so does No. 8976, p. 271, while No. 8978, p. 272, presents us with the coronation of the Virgin, and No. 8976, the Virgin and the Child, as also No. 1335, p. 71. Far below in worth are the same kind of webs wrought at Cologne, as will be noticed just now.

Any one that has ever looked upon the woodcuts done at Venice in the sixteenth century, such as illustrate, for instance, the Roman Pontifical, published by Giunta, the " Rosario della G. V. Maria," by Varisco, and other such religious books from the Venetian press, will, at a glance, find on the webs before us from that state, the self same style and manner in drawing, the same broad, nay, majestic fold and fall of drapery, and in the human form the same plumpness, and not unfrequently with the facial line almost straight; and there, but more especially about the hands and feet, a somewhat naturalistic shape; so near is the likeness in design that one is led to think that the men who cut the blocks for the printers also worked for the weavers of Venice, and sketched out the drawings for their looms.

By the fifteenth century Venice knew how to produce good damasks in silk and gold, and of an historiated kind : if we had nothing more than the specimen, No. 1311, p. 54, where St. Mary of Egypt is so well represented, it would be quite enough for her to claim for herself such a distinction. That like her neighbours, Venice wrought in velvet, there can be little or no doubt, and if she it was who made those deep piled stuffs, sometimes raised, sometimes pile upon pile, in which her painters loved to dress the personages, men especially, in their pictures, then, of a truth, Venetian velvets were beautiful. Of this, any one may satisfy himself by one visit to our National Gallery. There, in the " Adoration of the Magi," painted by Paulo Veronese, A. D. 1573, the second of the wise men is clad in a robe all made of crimson velvet, cut or raised after a design quite in keeping with the style of the period.

No insignificant article of Venetian textile workmanship was her laces wrought in every variety—in gold, in silk, in thread. The portrait of a Doge usually shows us that dignitary clothed in his dress of state. His wide mantle, having such large golden buttons, is made of some rich dull silver cloth; and upon his head is that curiously Phrygian-shaped ducal cap bound round with broad gold lace diapered after some nice pattern, as we see in the bust portrait of Doge Loredano, painted by John Bellini, and now in our National Gallery. Not only was the gold in the thread particularly good, but the lace itself in great favour at our court during one time, where it used to be bought, not by yard measure, but by weight; a pounde and a half of gold of Venys was employed "aboutes the making of a lace and botons for the king's mantell of the garter."[1] " Frenge of Venys gold," appears twice, pp. 136, 163, in the wardrobe accounts of Edward IV.

Laces in worsted or in linen thread wrought by the bobbin at Venice; but more especially her point laces, or such as were done with the needle, always had, as indeed they still have, a great reputation: sewed to tablecovers, two specimens are found in this collection, described at p. 141.

Venetian linens, for fine towelling and napery in general, at one time were in favourite use in France during a part of the fifteenth century. In the " Ducs de Bourgogne," by Le Comte de Laborde,[2] more than once we meet with such an entry, as "une pièce de nappes, ouvraige de Venise," &c.

Florence, always so industrious and art-loving, got for its loom, about the middle of the fourteenth century, a place in the foremost rank amid the weavers of northern Italy. Specimens of her earliest handicraft are yet few—only two—here; but one sample of the able way in which she knew how to diaper, well shows her ability: No. 8563, p. 215, woven in the fifteenth century, will prove this with reference to her secular silks. The pieces described at pp. 202, 264, witness the boldness of her design during the sixteenth century. In her webs, expressly woven for churchuse, is it that she displays her great taste in design, and wonderful power— at least for that time, the fourteenth century—in gearing the loom: the violet silk damask, No. 1265, p. 36, and another like piece, No. 7072, p. 133, figured with angels swinging thuribles, or bearing crowns of thorns in the hands, or holding a cross, will warrant our remarks. The style of doing the face and hands in white of those otherwise yellow angels, is a peculiarity of the Tuscan loom.

The orphrey-webs of Florence are equally conspicuous for drawing and skill in weaving as her vestment textiles, and in beauty come up to those done at Venice, and far surpass anything of the kind ever wrought at Cologne; specimens of this sort of Florentine work may be seen at Nos. 4059, p. 89; 7080, p. 136; 7674, p. 142; 7791, p. 143; 197, p. 291. Along with these may be classed the hood of a cope, described at No. 8692, p. 260, as well as the apparels to the dalmatic and tunicle, p. 143, where the cherubic heads have white faces.

But it was of her velvets that Florence might be so warrantably proud. Our Henry VII. in his will, " Testamenta Vetusta,"[3] bequeathed " to

---

[1] Privy Purse Expenses of Elizabeth of York, p. 8.
[2] T. ii. Preuves, p. 107.   [3] Ed. Nicolas, t. i. p. 33.

God and St. Peter, and to the abbot and prior and convent of our monastery of Westminster, the whole suit of vestments to be made at Florence in Italy." Gorgeous and artistically designed was this textile, as we may yet see in one of these Westminster Abbey copes still in existence, and belonging to Stonyhurst college. The golden ground is trailed all over with leaf-bearing boughs of a bold type, in raised or cut ruby-toned velvet of a rich soft pile, which is freckled with gold thread sprouting up like loops. Though nothing so rich in material, nor so beauteous in pattern, there are here, pp. 144, 145, two specimens of Florentine cut, crimson velvet on a golden ground, quite like in sort to the royal vestments, and having too that strong peculiarity upon them—the little gold thread loop shooting out of the velvet pile. Though a full century later than the splendid cope at Stonyhurst, and the two pieces Nos. 7792, 7799, these illustrate the peculiar style of Tuscan velvets.

Among the truly prince-like gifts of vestments to Lincoln Cathedral, by John of Gaunt and his duchess, are many made of the richest crimson velvet of both sorts, that is, plain, and cut or raised to a pattern upon a ground of gold, as for instance :—two red copes, of the which one is red velvet set with white harts lying in colours, full of these letters S. S., with pendents silver and gilt, the harts having crowns upon their necks with chains silver and gilt ; and the other cope is of crimson velvet of precious cloth of gold, with images in the orphrey, &c.[1]

That peculiar sort of ornamentation—the little loop of gold thread standing well up, and in single spots—upon some velvets, seems at times to have been replaced, perhaps with the needle, by small dots of solid metal, gold or silver gilt, upon the pile ; of the gift of one of its bishops, John Grandisson, Exeter cathedral had a crimson velvet cope, the purple velvet orphrey to which was so wrought:—De purpyll velvete operata cum pynsheds de puro auro.[2]

Milan, though now-a-days she stands in such high repute for the richness and beauty of her silks of all sorts, was not, we believe, at any period during mediæval times, as famous for her velvets, her brocades, or cloths of gold, as for her well wrought admirably fashioned armour, so strong and trustworthy for the field—so furbished and exquisitely damascened for courtly service. Still, in the sixteenth century she earned a name for her rich cut velvets, as we may see in the specimen, No. 698, p. 7 ; her silken net-work, No. 8336, p. 200, which may have led the way to weaving silk stockings ; and her laces of the open tinsel kind once in such vogue for liturgical, as well as secular attire, as we have in No. 8331, p. 197.

Britain, from her earliest period, had textile fabrics varying in design

---

[1] Mon. Anglic. viii. 1281.   [2] Oliver, p. 345.

and material; of the colours in the woollen garments worn by each of the three several classes into which our Bardic order was apportioned. Of the checkered pattern in Boadicea's cloak we have spoken just now, p. xii.

Of the beauty and wide repute of English needlework, we shall have to speak when, a little further on, we reach the subject of embroidery.

From John Garland's words, which we gave at p. xxii, it would seem that all the lighter and more tasteful webs wrought here came from women's hands; and the loom, one of which must have been in almost every English nunnery and homestead, was of the simplest make.

In olden times, the Egyptians wove in an upright loom, and beginning at top so as to weave downwards, sat at their work. In Palestine the weaver had an upright loom too, but beginning at bottom and working upwards, was obliged to stand. During the mediæval period the loom, here at least, was horizontal, as is shown by the one figured in that gorgeously illuminated Bedford Book of Hours, fol. 32, at which the Blessed Virgin Mary is seated weaving curtains for the temple.

As samples of one of the several kinds of work wrought by our nuns and mynchens, as well as English ladies, we refer to Nos. 1233, p. 24, 1256, p. 33, 1270, p. 38, demonstrating the ability of their handicraft as well as elegance in design during the thirteenth century. For specimens of the commoner sorts of silken textiles and of wider breadth, which began to be woven in this country under Edward III., it would be as hard as hazardous to direct the reader. Very recent examples of all sorts—velvets among the rest—may be found in the Brooke collection. To some students the piece of Old English printed chintz, No. 1622, p. 84, will not be without an interest.

For the finer sort of linen napery, Eylisham or Ailesham in Lincolnshire was famous during the fourteenth century. Exeter cathedral, A.D. 1327, had "unum manutergium de Eylisham"—a hand towel of Ailesham cloth.[1]

Our coarser native textiles in wool, in thread or in both, woven together, forming a stuff called "burel," made of which St. Paul's London, A.D. 1295, had a light blue chasuble;[2] and Exeter cathedral, A.D. 1277, a long pall;[3] all sorts, in fine, of heavier work, were wrought in our monasteries for men. By their rule the Benedictine monks, and all their offsets, were bound to give a certain number of hours every week-day to hand work, either at home or in the field.[4]

---

[1] Oliver, p. 314.   [2] Dugdale's St. Paul's, p. 323.   [3] Oliver, p. 298.
[4] Reg. S. Ben. c. xlviii. De Opere Manuum quotidiano, p. 129; c. lvii. De Artificibus Monasterii, p. 131; ed. Brockie, t. i. "Lena" is the mediæval Latin for a bed coverlet.

Weeping over the wars and strife in England during the year 1265 and the woes of the people, our Matthew of Westminster sums up, among our losses, the fall in our trade of woollen stuffs, with which we used to supply the world. O Anglia olim gloriosa . . . . licet maris angustata littoribus . . tibi tamen per orbem benedixerunt omnium latera nationum de tuis ovium velleribus calefacta.¹

The weaving in this country of woollen cloth, as a staple branch of trade, is older than some are willing to believe. Of the monks at Bath abbey we are told by a late writer, "the shuttle and the loom employed their attention, (about the middle of the fourteenth century,) and under their active auspices the weaving of woollen cloth (which made its appearance in England about the year 1330, and received the sanction of an Act of Parliament in 1337) was introduced, established, and brought to such perfection at Bath as rendered this city one of the most considerable in the west of England for this manufacture."² Worcester cloth, which was of a fine quality, was so good, that by a chapter of the Benedictine Order, held A.D. 1422, at Westminster Abbey, it was forbidden to be worn by the monks, and declared smart enough for military men.³ Norwich, too, wove stuffs that were in demand for costly household furniture, for, A.D. 1394, Sir John Cobham bequeathed to his friends "a bed of Norwich stuff embroidered with butterflies."⁴ In one of the chapels at Durham Priory there were four blue cushions of Norwich work.⁵ Worsted, a town in Norfolk, by a new method of its own for the carding of the wool with combs of iron well heated, and then twisting the thread harder than usual in the spinning, enabled our weavers to produce a woollen stuff of a fine peculiar quality, to which the name itself of worsted was immediately given. Unto such a high repute did the new web grow that liturgical raiment and domestic furniture of the choicest sorts were made out of it; Exeter cathedral, among its chasubles, had several "de nigro worsted" in cloth of gold. Elizabeth de Bohun, A.D. 1356, bequeathed to her daughter the Countess of Arundel "a bed of red worsted embroidered;"⁶ and Joane Lady Bergavenny leaves to John of Ormond "a bed of cloth of gold with lebardes, with those cushions and tapettes of my best red worsted,"⁷ &c. Of the sixteen standards of worsted entailed with the bear and a chain which

---

¹ Flores Histor. p. 396. Frankfort, A.D. 1601.
² Monasticon Anglicanum, t. ii. p. 259.
³ Benedict. in Anglia, ed. Reyner, App. p. 165.
⁴ Testamenta Vetusta, ed. Nicolas, t. i. p. 136.
⁵ Hist. Dunelm. Scriptores Tres. Append. p. cclxxxvi.
⁶ Testamenta Vetusta, i. 61.   ⁷ Ibid. p. 227.

floated aloft in the ſhip of Beauchamp Earl of Warwick, we have ſpoken before (p. xliii.) In the "Fabric Rolls of York Minſter" veſtments made of worſted—there variouſly ſpelt "worſett,"[1] and "woryſt"[2]—are enumerated.

Iriſh cloth, white and red, in the reign of John, A.D. 1213, was much uſed in England; and in the houſehold expenſes of Swinford, biſhop of Hereford, A.D. 1290, an item occurs of Iriſh cloth for lining.[3]

But our weavers knew how to throw off from their looms, artiſtically deſigned and well-figured webs; in the "Wardrobe Accounts" of our Edward II. we read this item: "to a mercer of London for a green hanging of wool wove with figures of kings and earls upon it, for the king's ſervice in his hall on ſolemn feaſts at London."[4] Such "ſalles," as they were called in France, and "hullings," or rather "hallings," the name they went under here, were much valued abroad, and in common uſe at home: under the head of "Salles d'Angleterre," among the articles of coſtly furniture belonging to Charles V. of France, A.D. 1364, who began his reign ſome forty years after our Edward II.'s death, one ſet of ſuch hangings is thus put down: "une ſalle d'Angleterre vermeille brodée d'azur, et eſt la bordeure à vignettes et le dedens de lyons, d'aigles et de lyepars," quoted from the MS. No. 8356, in the Imperial Library, Paris, by Michel;[5] while here in England, Richard Earl of Arundel, A.D. 1392, willed to his dear wife "the hangings of the hall which was lately made in London, of blue tapeſtry with red roſes with the arms of my ſons,"[6] &c.; and Lady Bergavenny, after bequeathing her hullying of black, red, and green, to one friend, to another left her beſt ſtained hall.[7]

Flemiſh textiles, at leaſt of the leſs ambitious kinds, ſuch as napery and woollens, were much eſteemed centuries ago, and our countryman, Matthew of Weſtminſter, ſays of Flanders, that from the material—perhaps wool—which we ſent her, ſhe ſent us back thoſe precious garments ſhe wove.[8]

Though induſtrious everywhere within her limits, ſome of her towns ſtood foremoſt for certain kinds of ſtuff, and Bruges became in the latter end of the fifteenth century conſpicuous for its ſilken textiles. Here in England, the ſatins of Bruges were in great uſe for church garments; in Haconbie church, A.D. 1566, was "one white veſtmente of Bridges

---

[1] Pp. 301, 305.
[2] P. 302.
[3] Ed. Web. for the Camden Society, p. 193, t. i.
[4] Archæologia, t. xxvi. p. 344.
[5] Tom. i. p. 49.
[6] Teſt. Vetuſt. t. i. p. 130.
[7] Ibid. pp. 228, 229.
[8] Hiſt. p. 396, Frankfort, A.D. 1601.

fatten repte in peces and a clothe made thereof to hange before our pulpitt;"[1] and, A. D. 1520, York cathedral had " a veſtment of balkyn (baudekin) with a croſſe of green fatten in bryges."[2]

Her damaſk ſilks were equally in demand; and the ſpecimens here will intereſt the reader. Nos. 8318, p. 190, 8332, p. 197, ſhow the ability of the Bruges loom, while the then favourite pattern with the pomegranate in it, betrays the likings of the Spaniards, at that time the rulers of the country, for this token of their beloved Iſabella's reconquered Granada. No. 8319, p. 191, is another ſample of Flemiſh weaving, rich in its gold, and full of beauty in defign.

In her velvets, Flanders had no need to fear a compariſon with anything of the kind that Italy ever threw off from her looms, whether at Venice, Florence, or Genoa, as the ſamples we have here under Nos. 8673, p. 254, 8674, p. 255, 8704, p. 264, will prove. Nay, this laſt ſpecimen, with its cloth of gold ground, and its pattern in a dark blue deep-piled velvet, is not ſurpaſſed in gorgeouſneſs even by that ſplendid ſtuff from Florence yet to be ſeen in one of the copes for Weſtminſter Abbey given it by Henry VII.

Block-printed linen was, toward the end of the fourteenth century, another production of Flanders, of which pieces may be ſeen at Nos. 7022, p. 118, 7027, p. 120, 8303, p. 184, 8615, p. 234. Though to the eyes of many, theſe may look ſo poor, ſo mean; to men like the cotton-printers of Lancaſhire and other places they will have a ſtrong attraction; to the ſcholar they will be deeply intereſting as ſuggeſtive of the art of printing. Such ſpecimens are rare, but it is likely that England can ſhow, in the chapter library at Durham, the earlieſt ſample of the kind as yet known, in a fine ſheet wrapped about the body of ſome old biſhop diſcovered, along with ſeveral pieces of ancient ſilks, and ſtill more ancient Engliſh embroidery, in a grave opened by Mr. Raine, A. D. 1827, within that grand northern cathedral.

What Bruges was in ſilks and velvets Yprès, in the ſixteenth century, became for linen, and for many years Flemiſh linens had been in favourite uſe throughout England. Hardly a church of any ſize, ſcarcely a gentleman's houſe in this country, but uſed a quantity of towels and other napery that was made in Flanders, eſpecially at Yprès.[3] Of this textile inſtances may be ſeen at pp. 34, 73, 75, 124, 203, 205, 255, 263.

French ſilks, now in ſuch extenſive uſe, were until the end of the ſixteenth century not much cared for in France itſelf, and ſeldom heard

---

[1] Church Furniture, ed. Peacock, p. 94.
[2] Fabric Rolls, p. 302.
[3] Oliver's Exeter, p. 356.

of abroad. The reader, then, muſt not be aſtoniſhed at finding ſo few examples of the French loom, in a collection of ancient ſilken textiles.

France, as England, uſed of old to behold her women, old and young, rich and poor, while filling up their leiſure hours in-doors, at work on a ſmall loom, and weaving certain narrow webs, often of gold, and diapered with coloured ſilks, as we mentioned before (p. xxii.) Of ſuch French wrought ſtuffs belonging to the thirteenth century, ſome ſamples are deſcribed at pp. 29, 130, 131.

In damaſks, her earlieſt productions are of the ſixteenth century, and are deſcribed at pp. 13, 205, 206; and the laſt is a favourable example of what the loom then was in France; everything later is of that type ſo well known to everybody. In ſeveral of her textiles a leaning towards claſſiciſm in deſign is diſcernible.

Though ſo few, her cloths of gold, pp. 9, 15, are good, more eſpecially the fine one at p. 104.

Her velvets, too, pp. 14, 89, 106, are ſatisfactory.

Satins from France are not many here.

The curious and elaborately ornamented gloves, p. 105, which got into faſhion, eſpecially for ladies, at the end of the ſixteenth century, will be a welcome object for ſuch as are curious in the hiſtory of women's dreſs, in France and England.

Quilting, too, on coverlets, ſhown at pp. 13, 104, diſplays the taſte of our neighbours in ſuch ſtitchery, ſo much in uſe among them and ourſelves from the ſixteenth century.

Like Flanders, France knew how to weave fine linen, which here in England was much in uſe for eccleſiaſtical as well as houſehold purpoſes. Three new cloths of Rains (Rennes in Brittany) were, A.D. 1327, in uſe for the high altar in Exeter cathedral,[1] and many altar cloths of Paris linen. In the poem of the "Squier of Low Degree," the lady is told

> Your blankettes ſhal be of fuſtyane,
> Your ſhetes ſhal be of cloths of rayne;

and, A.D. 1434, Joane Lady Bergavenny deviſes in her will, "two pair ſheets of Raynes, a pair of fuſtians," &c.[2] For her Eaſter "Sepulchre" Exeter had a pair of this Rennes ſheeting; "par linthiaminum de Raynys pro ſepulchro."[3]

Cologne, the queen of the Rhine, became famous during the whole of the fifteenth and part of the ſixteenth century for a certain kind of eccle-

---

[1] Oliver, p. 314.　　[2] Teſt. Vet. i. 227.　　[3] Oliver, p. 340.

fiaftical textile which, from the very general ufe to which it has been applied, we have named "orphrey web." Since by far the greater part of this collection, as it now exifts, had been made in Germany, beginning with Cologne, it is, as might be expected, well fupplied with fpecimens of a fort of fluff, if not peculiar, at leaft abounding in that country. Thofe fame liturgical ornaments which Venice and Florence wove with fuch artiftic tafte for Italian church ufe, Cologne fucceeded in doing for Germany. Her productions, however, are every way far below in beauty Italy's like works. The Italian orphrey-webs are generally done in gold or yellow filk, upon a crimfon ground of filk. Florence's are often diftinguifhed from thofe of Venice by the introduction of white for the faces; Cologne's vary from both by introducing blue, while the material is almoft always very poor, and the weaving coarfe.

The earlieft fpecimen here of this Cologne orphrey-web is No. 8279, p. 174; but it is far furpaffed by many others, fuch as are, for inftance, to be found at pp. 61, 62, 63, 64, 69, 80, 82, 116, 117, 118, 119, 174, 175, 252, 253. Among thefe fome have noticeable peculiarities; No. 1329, p. 61, a good fpecimen, has the perfons of the faints fo woven that the heads, hands, and emblems are wrought with the needle; the fame, too, in Nos. 7023, p. 118, and 8667, p. 252; in No. 1373, though the golden ground looks very frefh and brilliant, the gilding procefs, as on wood, has been employed. Here in England this orphrey web was in church ufe and called "rebayn de Colayn."[1]

The piece of German napery at No. 8317, p. 190, of the beginning of the fifteenth century will be to thofe curious about houfehold linen, an acceptable fpecimen.

If by hazard while reading fome old inventory of church veftments the reader fhould ftumble upon fome entry mentioning a chafuble made of cloth of Cologne, let him underftand it to mean not a certain broad textile woven there, but merely a veftment compofed of feveral pieces of this kind of web fewed together, juft as was the frontal made out of pieces of woven Venice orphreys at No. 8976, p. 271.

THE COUNTRIES WHENCE SILKS CAME TO US are numerous; with confidence, however, we may fay, that till the middle of the fifteenth century, when we began to weave fome of them for ourfelves, the whole geography of filken textiles lay within the bafin of the Mediterranean to the weft, and the continent of Afia to the eaft.

Though mention is often made of tiffues coming from various places, thofe cities are always to be found upon the map we have juft marked

---

[1] Teftamenta Eborac, iii. 13.

out. Among thofe fpoken of *Antioch*, *Tarfus*, *Alexandria*, *Damafcus*, *Byzantium*, *Cyprus*, *Trip* or *Tripoli*, and *Bagdad*, are eafily recognized, as well as the later centres of trade and manufacture, Venice, Genoa and Lucca. To fix the localities of a few others would be but guefs-work.

At the beginning of the fourteenth century is mentioned occafionally a filk called "*Acca*," and, from the defcription of it, it muft have been a cloth of gold fhot with coloured filk, figured with animals: William de Clinton, Earl of Huntingdon, gave to St. Alban's monaftery a whole veftment of cloth of gold fhot with fky-blue, and called cloth of Acca; " unum veftimentum . . . de panno quem Accam dicimus; cujus campus eft aerius. In reliquis vero partibus refultat auri fulgor.[1] To fome it would look as if this ftuff took its name from having been brought to us through the port of Acre. We lean towards this belief on finding, on the authority of Macri, in his valuable Hierolexicon, Venice, 1735, pp. 5, 542, that fo ufed to be written the name of the ancient Ptolemais in Syria.

What in one age, and at a particular place, happened to be fo well made, and hence became fo eagerly fought for, at a later period, and in another place, got to be much better wrought and at a lower price. Time, indeed, changed the name of the market, but did not alter in any great degree either the quality of the material, or the ftyle of the defign wrought upon it. All over the kingdom of the Byzantine Greeks the loom had to change its gearing very little. The Saracenic loom, whether in Afia, Africa, or Spain, was alway Arabic, though Perfia could not forget her olden Zoroafterian traditions about the "hom" or tree of life feparating lions, and having all about lion-hunting cheetahs, and birds of various forts.

With regard to the whole of Afia, we learn that its many peoples, from the earlieft times, knew how not only to weave cloth of gold, but figure it too with birds and beafts. Almoft two thoufand years afterwards, Marco Polo, in the thirteenth century, found exactly the very fame kinds of textile known in the days of Darius ftill everywhere, from the fhores of the Mediterranean to far Cathay, in demand and woven. What he fays of Bagdad, he repeats in fewer words about many other cities.[2]

In finding their way to England thefe fabrics had given them not fo often the names of the places where they had been wrought, but, if not in all, at leaft in moft inftances, the names of the feaports in the Mediterranean where they had been fhipped.

---

[1] Mon. Anglic. ii. 221. [2] I Viaggi di Marco Polo, ed. A. Bartoli, Firenze, 1863.

For beautifully wrought and figured filk, of the few terms that ftill outlive the mediæval period, one is *Damafk*.

China, no doubt, was the firft country to ornament its filken webs with a pattern. India, Perfia and Syria, then Byzantine Greece, followed, but at long intervals between, in China's footfteps. Stuffs fo figured brought with them to the weft the name "diafpron" or diaper, beftowed upon them at Conftantinople. But about the twelfth century, fo very far did the city of Damafcus, even then long celebrated for its looms, outftrip all other places for beauty of defign, that her filken textiles were eagerly fought for everywhere, and thus, as often happens, traders faftened the name of Damafcen or Damafk upon every filken fabric richly wrought and curioufly defigned, no matter whether it came or not from Damafcus. After having been for ages the epithet betokening all that was rich and good in filk, "Samit" had to be forgotten, and Diaper, from being the very word fignificant of pattern, became a fecondary term defcriptive of merely a part in the elaborate defign on Damafk.

Baudekin, that fort of coftly cloth of gold fpoken of fo much during fo many years in Englifh literature, took, as we faid before, its famous name from Bagdad.

Many are the fpecimens in this collection furnifhing proofs of the ancient weavers' dexterity in their management of the loom, but efpecially of the artifts' tafte in fetting out fo many of their intricate and beautiful defigns.

What to fome will be happily curious is that we have this very day before our eyes pieces, in all likelihood, from the felf-fame web which furnifhed the material, centuries ago, for veftments and ornaments ufed of old in the cathedrals of England. Let any one turn to p. 122, and, after looking at number 7036, compare that filk with this item in the inventory of St. Paul's, London, A.D. 1225: "Item, Baudekynus rubeus cum Sampfone conftringente ora leonum," &c.[1] See alfo number 8589, and number 8235.

An identification between very many famples, brought together here, of ancient textiles in filk, and the defcriptions of fuch ftuffs afforded us in thofe valuable records—our old church inventories—might be carried on, if neceffary, to a very lengthened extent.

Dorneck was the name given to an inferior kind of damafk wrought of filk, wool, linen thread and gold, in Flanders. Towards the end of the fifteenth century, moftly at Tournay, which city, in Flemifh, was

---

[1] Dugdale's St. Paul's, p. 328.

often called Dorneck—a word variously spelt as Darnec, Darnak, Darnick, and sometimes even Darnefs.

The gild of the Blessed Virgin Mary at Boston had a care cloth of silke dornex and church furniture.¹ The "care cloth" was a sort of canopy held over the bride and bridegroom as they knelt for the nuptial blessing, according to the Salisbury rite, at the marriage mass. At Exeter it was used in chasubles for orphreys.² A specimen of Dornex may be seen, No. 7058, p. 129. See also York Fabric Rolls, pp. 291, 297, 298, 300, 305.

Buckram, a cotton textile, has a history and a reputation somewhat varied.

In our oldest inventories mention is often made of a "panus Tartaricus" or Tartary cloth, which was, if not always, at least often purple. Asia, especially in its eastern borders, became famous for the fine textiles it wove out of cotton, and dyed in every colour. Cities got for themselves a reputation for some especial excellence in their looms, and as Mosul had the name of Muslin from that place given to the fine and delicate cotton webs it wrought, so the term of buckram for another sort of cotton textile came from the city of Bokhara in Tartary where this cloth was made. All along the middle ages buckram was much esteemed for being costly and very fine, and consequently fit for use in church vestments, and for secular personal wear. John Grandison, consecrated bishop of Exeter, A.D. 1327, gave to his cathedral flags of white and red buckram;³ and among the five very rich veils for covering the moveable lectern in that church, three were lined with blue "bokeram."⁴ As late as the beginning of the sixteenth century this stuff was held good enough for lining to a black velvet gown for a queen, Elizabeth of York.⁵ The coarse thick fabric which now goes by the name was anything but the olden production known as "bokeram."

Burdalisaunder, Bordalisaunder, Bourde de Elisandre, with other varieties in spelling, is a term often to be met with in old wills and church inventories. In the year 1327 Exeter had a chasuble of Bourde de Elisandre of divers colours.⁶ It was wide enough for half a piece to form the adornment of a high altar.⁷

The difficulty of understanding what this textile was will vanish when we remember that in Arabic "bord" to this day means a striped cloth; and we know, both from travellers and the importation of the textile

---

¹ Peacock, p. 204.   ² Oliver, pp. 359, 365.   ³ Ib. p. 319.   ⁴ Ib. p. 329.
⁵ Her Privy Purse Expenses, ed. Nicolas, p. 22, &c.   ⁶ Oliver, p. 312.
⁷ Yorkshire Wills. Part i. p. 174.

itself, that many tribes in North and Eastern Africa weave stuffs for personal wear of a pattern consisting of white and black longitudinal stripes. St. Augustin too, living in North Africa near the modern Algiers, speaks of a stuff for clothing called " burda," in the end of the fourth and beginning of the fifth century. Burdalisaunder was a silken web in different coloured stripes, and specimens of this, at one time known as " stragulata" may be found here at pp. 21, 27, 33, 56, 57, 161, 225, 226, &c. Though made in so many places round the Mediterranean, this silk took its name, at least in England, from Alexandria, because it was to be had in that Egyptian city, always celebrated for its silks, either better made or at a much lower price than elsewhere.

In all likelihood the curtains for the tabernacle, as well as the girdles for Aaron and his sons, of fine linen and violet and purple, and scarlet twice dyed, were wrought with this very pattern, so that in the " stragulata " or " burd Aliscaunder " we behold the oldest known design for any textile.

Fustian, of which two of its forms we still have in velveteen and corduroy, was originally wove at Fustat, on the Nile, with a warp of linen thread and a woof of thick cotton, which was so twilled and cut that it showed on one side a thick but low pile; and the web so managed took its name of Fustian from that Egyptian city. At what period it was invented we do not rightly know, but we are well aware it must have been brought to this country before the Normans coming hither, for our Anglo-Saxon countryman, St. Stephen Harding, when a Cistercian abbot and an old man, *circ.* A.D. 1114, forbade chasubles in his church to be made of anything but fustian or plain linen : " neque casulas nisi de fustaneo vel lino sine pallio aureo vel argenteo," &c.[1] The austerity of his rule reached even the ornament of the church. From such a prohibition we are not to draw as a conclusion that fustian was at the time a mean material; quite the contrary, it was a seemly textile. Years afterwards, in the fourteenth century, Chaucer tells us of his knight :—

> Of fustian he wered a gepon.[2]

Fustian, so near akin to velvet, is more especially noticed along with what is said upon that fine textile.

In the fifteenth century Naples had a repute for weaving fustians, but our English churchwardens, not being learned in geography, made some laughable bad spelling of this, like some other continental stuffs : " Fuschan in appules," for fustian from Naples, is droll; yet droller still is

---

[1] Mon. Anglic. ed. Dugdale, v. 225.   [2] The Prologue, Poems, ed. Nicolas, ii. 3.

"muſtyrd devells," for a cloth made in France at a town called Muſtrevilliers.

Muſlin, as it is now throughout the world, ſo from the earlieſt antiquity has been everywhere in Aſia in favourite uſe, both as an article of dreſs and as furniture. Its cloud-like thinneſs, its lightneſs, were, as they ſtill are to ſome Aſiatics, not the only charms belonging to this ſtuff: it was eſteemed equally as much for the taſte in which ſtripes of gold had been woven in its warp. As we learn from the travels of Marco Polo, the further all wayfarers in Aſia wandered among its eaſtern nations, the higher they found the point of excellence which had been reached by thoſe people in weaving ſilk and gold into ſplendid fabrics. If the ſilkworm lived, nay, thrived there, the cotton plant was in its home, its birth-place, in thoſe regions. Where ſtood Nineveh Moſul ſtands now.

Like many cities of Middle Aſia, Moſul had earned for itſelf a reputation of old for the beauty of its gold-wrought ſilken textiles. Cotton grew all around in plenty; the inhabitants, eſpecially the women, being gifted with ſuch quick feeling of finger, could ſpin thread from this cotton of more than hair-like fineneſs. Cotton then took with them, on many occaſions, the place of ſilk in the loom; but gold was not forgotten in the texture. This new fabric, not only becauſe it was ſo much cheaper, but from its own peculiar beauty and comelineſs, won for itſelf a high place in common eſtimation. At once, and by the world's accord, on it was beſtowed as its diſtinctive name, the name of the place where it was wrought in ſuch perfection. Hence, whether wove with or without gold, we call to this day this cotton web Muſlin, from the Aſiatic city of Moſul.

Cloth of Areſte is another of thoſe terms for woven ſtuffs which ſtudents of textiles had never heard of were it not to be found in our old Engliſh deeds and inventories. The firſt time we meet it is in an order given, A.D. 1244, by Henry III. for finding two of theſe cloths of Areſte with which two copes had to be made for royal chapels: "Duos pannos del Areſte ad duas capas faciendas," &c.[1] Again it comes a few years later at St. Paul's, which cathedral, A.D. 1295, had, beſides a dalmatic and tunicle of this ſilk—"de ſerico albo diaſperato de Areſt,"[2] —as many as thirty and more hangings of this ſame texture.[3]

From the deſcription of theſe pieces we gather that this ſo-called cloth of Areſte muſt have been as beautiful as it was rich, being for the moſt

---

[1] Excerpta Hiſtorica, p. 404.
[2] St. Paul's Cathedral, ed. Dugdale, p. 322.   [3] Ibid. p. 329.

part cloth of gold figured elaborately, some with lions and double-headed eagles, others, for example, with the death and burial of our Lord— "campus aureus cum leonibus et aquilis bicapitibus de aurifilo contextis—campus rubeus cum historia Paffionis Domini et sepulturæ ejusdem." These designs speak of the looms at work in the middle ages on the eastern shore of the Mediterranean, and we are much strengthened in this thought by beholding how the death and burial of our Lord, like the sample here, number 8278, p. 170-1, are shown on a crimson ground, as we shall have to instance further on under Symbolism, § VI.

That this sort of stuff, wove of silk and gold, was of any kind of Arras, or made in that town, to our seeming is a very unhappy guess. Arras had not won for itself a reputation for its tapestry before the fourteenth century. Tapestry itself is too thick and heavy for use in vestments; yet this cloth of Areste was light enough for tunicles, and when worn out was sometimes condemned at St. Paul's to be put aside for lining other ritual garments—" ad armaturam faciendam."[1] The term "Areste" has little or nothing in it common to the word "Arras," as written either in French, or under its Latin appellation "Atrebatum."

Among the three meanings for the mediæval "Aresta," one is, any kind of covering. To us, then, it seems as if these cloths of Areste took their name not from the place whereat they had been wove, but from the use to which, if not always, for the most part, we put them— that of hangings about our churches, since in the St. Paul's inventory they are usually spoken of as such—" culcitræ pendules, panni penduli."[2] Moreover, tapestry, or Arras work, being thick and heavy, could never have been employed for such light use as that of apparels, nor would it have been diapered like silk, yet we find it to have been so fashioned and so used—" maniculariis apparatis quodam panno rubeo diasperato de Laret, &c."[3]

For not a few it would be hard to understand some at least among those epithets meant in bygone days to tell how

SILKS WERE DISTINGUISHED THROUGH THEIR COLOURS AND SHADES OF COLOUR.

To the inventories of vestments and church-stuffs of all sorts must we go to gather the information which we want about the textiles in use in this country at any particular period during by-gone days. The men

---

[1] St. Paul's Cathedral, ed. Dugdale, 329. [2] Ibid. p. 329. [3] Ibid. p. 335.

who had, in the thirteenth century, the drawing up of such lists, seem to have been gifted with a keen eye for the varieties of shade and tints in the colour of silks then before them. For instance, a chasuble at St. Paul's, London, A. D. 1295, is set down thus:—" De sameto purpureo aliquantulum sanguineo "—that is, made of samit (a thick silk) dyed in a purple somewhat bordering on a blood-red tone. Such language is unmistakable; not so, however, many other terms at the time in common use, and though well understood then, are now not so intelligible. We are told in the same inventory[1] several times of a " pannus Tarsicus," a Tarsus cloth, and of a " pannus Tarsici coloris," a Tarsus coloured cloth. What may have been the distinctive qualities of the stuffs woven at Tarsus, what the peculiar beauty in that tint to which that once so celebrated city had given its own name, we cannot say. We think, however, those Tarsus textiles were partly of silk, partly of fine goats' hair, and for this reason Varro tells[2]—" Tondentur (capræ) quod magnis villis sunt, in magna parte Phrygiæ; unde Cilicia, et cætera ejus generis ferri solent. Sed, quod primum ea tonsura in Cilicia sit instituta, nomen id Cilicas adjecisse dicunt." Goats are shorn in a great part of Phrygia, because there they have long shaggy hair. Cilicia (the Latin for hair cloths) and other things of the same sort, are usually brought from that country. For the reason that in Cilicia such a shearing of goats arose, they say that the name of Cilician was given to such stuffs woven of goats' hair. As Tarsus is, so always was it, the head city in all that part of Asia Minor known of old as Phrygia. Hence then we think that—

Cloth of Tarsus, of Tars, &c., was woven of fine goats' hair and silk. But this web was in several colours, and always looked upon as very costly.

The *Tarsus colour* itself was, as we take it, some shade of purple differing from, and perhaps to some eyes more beautiful than, the Tyrian dye. The people of Tarsus no doubt got from their murex, a shell-fish of the class mollusca and purpurifera family to be found on their coast, their dyeing matter; and when it is borne in mind what changes are wrought in the animal itself by the food it eats, and what strong effects are made by slight variations in climate, even atmosphere, upon materials for colouring in the moments of application, we may easily understand how the difference arose between the two tints of purple.

We are strengthened in our conjecture that not only was the cloth of Tarsus of a rare and costly kind, but its tint some shade of royal

---

[1] Pp. 322, 323. [2] De Re Rustica, lii. cap. xi.

purple, from the fact that while noticing the robes worn on a grand public occasion by a king, Chaucer thus sketches the prince:—

> The gret Emetrius, the king of Inde,
> Upon a stede bay, trapped in stele,
> Covered with cloth of gold diapred wele,
> Came riding like the god of armes Mars,
> His cote armure was of a cloth of Tars,
> Couched with perles, &c.[1]

Sky-blue was a liturgical colour everywhere in use for certain festivals throughout England, as we have shown in another place.[2] In the early inventories the name for that tint is "Indicus," "Indus," reminding us of our present *indigo*. In later lists it is called "Blodius," not sanguinary, but blue.

Murrey, or a reddish brown, is often specified; and a good specimen of the tint is given us, No. 709, p. 9. Old St. Paul's, London, had several pieces of baudekin of this colour: "baudekynus murretus cum griffonibus datus pro anima. Alphonsi filii regis E."[3]

Going far down, and much below the middle ages, Purple, in all its tones, and tints, and shades, was spoken of and looked upon as allowable to be worn in garments only to worshipful, ennobled, or royal personages. Whether it glowed with the brightness it seemed to have stolen from the rose, or wore its darkest tone it could borrow from the violet, whether it put on any one of those hundred shades to be found between those two extremes, it mattered not; it was gazed at with an admiring, a respectful eye. Eagerly sought out, and bought at high price, were those textiles that showed this colour, and had been dyed at Tyre, Antioch, Tarsus, Alexandria, Byzantium, or Naples. All these places were at one time or another, in days of old, famous for their looms, no less than their ability in the dyeing, especially of purple, among the nations living on the shores of the Mediterranean; and each of them had in its own tone a shade which distinguished it from that of all the others. What the tint of purple was which established this difference we cannot at this distance of time, and with our means of knowing, justly say. Of this, however, we are perfectly aware, that silks of purple usually bore their specific name from those above-named cities, as we perceive while reading the old inventories of our churches and cathedrals. Moreover, our native writers let us know that, if not always

---

[1] Knightes Tale, Poems, ed. Nicolas, ii. 64-5.
[2] Church of our Fathers, t. ii. p. 259.
[3] St. Paul's, ed. Dugdale, p. 328, &c.

Introduction. xci

from Greece, it was through that country that purple textiles were brought to England. Befides fpeaking of a converfation held about, befide other things, the produce of Greece in purple filks—" Græcorum purpuris, et pannis holofericis "—Gerald Barry gives us to underftand that in his days not only were our churches fumptuoufly hung with coftly palls and purple filks, but that thefe textiles were the work of Grecian looms—" rex (Willielmus Rufus) ecclefiam quandam (in nova forefta) intraret quam adeo pulchram et decentius ornatam auletis hiftoricis, et pretiofis Græcorum palliis, pannis holofericis et purpureis undique veftitam," &c.[1]

Silks woven of two colours, fo that one of them fhowed itfelf unmixed and quite diftinct on one fide, and the fecond appeared equally clean on the other—a thing fometimes now looked upon as a wonder in modern weaving—might occafionally be met with here at the mediæval period : Exeter Cathedral had, A. D. 1327 :—" Unus pannus fericus curtus rubei coloris interius et crocei coloris exterius."[2]

Shot, or, as they were then called, *changeable* filks, were fafhionable in England during the fixteenth century, for when the King's (Edward VI.) Lord of Mifrule rode forth with great pageantry, among other perfonages there came " afor xx. of ys confell on horfbake in gownes of chanabulle lynyd with blue taffata and capes of the fam, like fage (men); then cam my lord with a gowne of gold furyd," &c.[3] At York Cathedral, A. D. 1543, there was " a veftment of changeable filke,"[4] " befides one of changeable taffety for Good Friday."[5]

Marble filk had a weft of feveral colours fo put together and woven as to make the whole web look like marble, ftained with a variety of tints ; hence it got its name. In the year 1295 St. Paul's had " paruram de ferico marmoreo "[6]—an apparel of marble filk ; " tunica de quodam panno marmoreo fpiffo "[7]—a tunicle of a certain thick marble cloth ; " tunica de diafpro marmoreo fpiffo "[7]—a tunicle of thick diaper marble ; " cafula marmorei coloris "[8]—a chafuble of marble colour. During full three centuries this marble filk found great favour among us fince H. Machyn, in his very valuable and curious Diary tells his readers how " the old Qwyne of Schottes rod thrught London," and how " then cam the Lord Treforer with a C. gret horffe and ther cotes of marbull,"[9] &c., to meet her the 6th of November, A.D. 1551.[9]

---

[1] Giraldus Cambrenfis, De Inftructione Principum, pp. 168-173.
[2] Oliver, p. 316.
[3] Diary of Henry Machyn, ed. Nichols for the Camden Society, p. 13.
[4] Fabric Rolls, p. 301.   [5] Ibid. p. 311.   [6] Ibid. p. 320.
[7] Ibid. p. 322.   [8] Ibid. p. 323.   [9] Pp. 11, 12.

Section II.—EMBROIDERY.

THE art of working with the needle flowers, fruits, human and animal forms, or any fanciful defign, upon webs woven of filk, linen, cotton, wool, hemp, befides other kinds of ftuff, is fo old that it reaches far into the prehiftoric ages.

Thofe patterns, after fo many fafhions, which we fee figured upon the garments worn by men and women in Egyptian and Affyrian monuments, but efpecially on the burned-clay vafes made and painted by the Greeks during their moft archaic as well as later times, or we read about in the writings of that people, were not wrought in the loom, but done by the needle.

The old Egyptian loom—and that of the Jews muft have been like it—was, as we know from paintings, of the fimpleft fhape, and feems to have never been able to do anything more diverfified in the defigns of its patterns than ftraight lines in different colours, and at beft nothing higher in execution than checker-work: beyond this, all elfe was put in by hand with the needle. In Paris, at the Louvre, are feveral pieces of early Egyptian webs coloured, drawings of which have been publifhed by Sir Gardner Wilkinfon in his fhort work "The Egyptians in the time of the Pharaohs."[1] There are two pieces of the fame textile fcarlet, with one brede woven of narrow red ftripes on a broad yellow ftripe, the other border being a broad yellow ftripe edged by a narrow fcarlet one, both wrought up and down with needlework; the fecond piece of blue is figured all over in white embroidery with a pattern of netting, the mefhes of which fhut in irregular cubic fhapes, and in the lines of the reticulation the myftic "gammadion" or "fylfot" is feen. Of them Sir J. G. Wilkinfon fays:—"They are moftly cotton, and, though their date is uncertain, they fuffice to fhow that the manufacture was Egyptian; and the many dreffes painted on the monuments of the eighteenth dynafty fhow that the moft varied patterns were ufed by the Egyptians more than 3000 years ago, as they were at a later period by the Babylonians, who became noted for their needlework."[2] Other fpecimens of Egyptian embroidery were on thofe corflets fent to Grecian temples by Amafis, about which we have before fpoken (p. xiv.)

That the Ifraelites embroidered their garments, efpecially thofe worn

---

[1] P. 42. [2] Ibid. p. 41.

Introduction. xciii

in public worship, is clear from several passages in the Book of Exodus. The words "embroidery" and "embroidered" that come there so frequently in our English versions are not to be understood always to mean needlework, but on occasions the tasteful weaving in stripes of the gold, violet, and purple, and scarlet twice dyed, and fine twisted linen; the pomegranates at the bottom of Aaron's tunic between the golden bells, and wrought of four of these stuffs, were, it is likely, made out of such coloured shreds, and of that kind which is now called cut-work.

Picking up from Greek and Latin writers only, as was his wont, those scraps of which his Natural History is made, Pliny tells us, even in Homer, mention is made of embroidered cloths, which originated such as by the Romans are called "triumphal." To do this with the needle was found out by the Phrygians, hence such garments took the name Phrygionic: "Pictas vestes jam apud Homerum fuisse unde triumphales natæ. Acu facere id, Phryges invenerunt ideoque Phrygioniæ appellatæ sunt."[1] He might have added that the only word the Romans had to mean an embroiderer was "Phrygio," which arose from the same cause. Many passages in Virgil show that from Western Asia the Romans learned their knowledge of embroidery, and borrowed the employment of it on their garments of State; besides, "those art-wrought vests of splendid purple tint:"—"arte laboratæ vestes ostroque superbo,"[2] brought forth for the feast by the Sidonian Dido, the Phrygian Andromache bestows upon Ascanius, as a token of her own handicraft, garments shot with gold and pictured, as well as a Phrygian cloak, along with other woven stuffs—

> Fert picturatas auri subtemine vestes,
> Et Phrygiam Ascanio chlamydem, &c.[3]

and Æneas veils his head for prayer with the embroidered hem of his raiment—

> Et capita ante aras Phrygio velamur amictu.[4]

In Latin while an embroiderer was called a Phrygian, "Phrygio," needlework was denominated "Phrygium," or Phrygian stuff; hence, when, as often happened, the design was wrought in solid gold wire or golden thread, the embroidery so worked got named "auriphrygium." From this term comes our own old English word "orphrey." Though deformed after so many guises by the witless writers of many an inventory of church goods, or by the sorry cleric who in a moment of needful

---

[1] Lib. viii. c. 47. [2] Æneid i. 643. [3] Ibid. iii. 482. [4] Ibid. iii. 545.

haste had been called upon to draw up a will; other men, however small their learning, always spelled the word "orphrey," in English, and "auriphrygium," in Latin. In the Exeter inventory, given by Oliver, "cum orphrey de panno aureo, &c. cum orphrais, &c."[1] are found; and the cope bequeathed by Henry Lord de Scrope, A.D. 1415, had its "orphreis" "embraudata nobiliter cum imaginibus," &c.[2] The many beautiful orphreys on the Lincoln vestments are fully described in the "Monasticon Anglicanum:"[3] no one could be more earnest in commanding the use on vestments of the auriphrygium, or embroidered "orphrey" than St. Charles Borromeo.[4]

While Phrygia in general, Babylon in particular became celebrated for the beauty of its embroideries: "colores diversos picturæ intexere Babylon maxime celebravit et nomen imposuit;"[5] and those who have seen the sculptures in the British Museum brought from Nineveh, and described and figured by Layard, must have witnessed how lavishly the Assyrians must have adorned their dress with that sort of needlework for which one of their greatest cities was so famous.

Up to the first century of our era, the reputation which Babylon had won for her textiles and needlework still lived. Josephus, himself a Jew, who had often been to worship at Jerusalem, tells us that the veils of its Temple given by Herod were Babylonian, and of the outer one that writer says:—"there was a veil of equal largeness with the door. It was a Babylonian curtain, embroidered with blue and fine linen, and scarlet and purple, and of a texture that was wonderful."[6]

What the Jews did for the Temple we may be sure was done by Christians for the Church. The faithful, however, went even further, and wore garments figured all over with passages from Holy Writ wrought in embroidery. From a stirring sermon preached by St. Asterius, bishop of Amasia in Pontus, in the fourth century, we learn this. Taking for his text, "a certain rich man who was clothed in purple and fine linen," this father of the Church, while upbraiding the world for its follies in dress, lets us know that some people went about arrayed like painted walls, with beasts and flowers all over them; while others, pretending a more serious tone of thought, dressed in clothes figured with a sketch of all the doings and wonders of our Lord. "Strive," thunders forth St. Asterius, "to follow in your lives the teachings of the Gospel,

---

[1] Pp. 330, 335, 336.
[2] Rymer's Fœdera, t. ix. p. 272.
[3] T. viii. pp. 1290, new edition.
[4] Church of our Fathers, t. i. p. 453.
[5] Pliny, lib. viii. c. 47.
[6] Wars of the Jews, b. v. c. 5; Works translated by Weston, t. 4, p. 121.

rather than have the miracles of our Redeemer embroidered upon your outward dress."[1]

To have had so many subjects shown upon one garment, it is clear that each must have been done very small, and all wrought in outline; a style which is being brought back, with great effect, into ecclesiastical use.

Of the embroidery done by Christian ladies abroad during the Lower Roman Empire, we have already spoken, p. xxxv. Coming to our own land, and its mediæval times, we find how at the beginning of that period our Anglo-Saxon sisters knew so well to handle their needle. The many proofs of this we have brought forward in another place.[2]

The discriminating accuracy with which our old writers sought to follow while noting down the several kinds of textile gifts bestowed upon a church is as instructive as praiseworthy. Ingulph did not think it enough to say that abbot Egelric had given many hangings to the Church of Croyland, the great number of which were silken, but he must tell us, too, that some were ornamented with birds wrought in gold, and sewed on—in fact, of cut-work—other some with those birds woven into the stuff, other some quite plain:—" Dedit etiam multa pallia suspendenda in parietibus ad altaria sanctorum in festis, quorum plurima de serico erant, aureis volucribus quædam insita, quædam intexta, quædam plana."[3]

So also the care often taken by the writers of inventories, like him who wrote out the Exeter one, to mention how some of the vestments had nothing about them but true needlework, or, as they at times express it, " operata per totum opere acuali," may be witnessed in that useful work, " The Lives of the Bishops of Exeter," by Oliver.[4]

By the latter end of the thirteenth century embroidery, as well as its imitation, got for its several styles and various sorts of ornamentation mixed up with it a distinguishing and technical nomenclature; and the earliest document in which we meet with this set of terms is the inventory drawn up, A.D. 1295, of the vestments belonging to our London St. Paul's Cathedral: herein, the "opus plumarium,"[5] the "opus pectineum,"[6] the "opus pulvinarium,"[7] cut-work, "consutum de serico,"[8] " de serico consuto,"[9] may be severally found in Dugdale's " History of St. Paul's."

The "opus plumarium" was the then usual general term for what is now commonly called embroidery; and hence, in some old inventories,

---

[1] Ceillier, Hist. Gen. des Auteurs Sacrés et Ecclesiastiques, t. viii. p. 488.
[2] The Church of our Fathers, t. ii. p. 267, &c. &c.
[3] Ingulphi Hist. ed. Savile, p. 505, b.   [4] Pp. 336, 344, &c.
[5] P. 320.   [6] P. 316.   [7] P. 319.   [8] P. 320.   [9] P. 319.

we meet with such notices as this:—" capæ opere plumario factæ id est, brudatæ."

This term was given to embroidery needlework because the stitches were laid down never across but longwise, and so put together that they seemed to overlap one another like the feathers in the plumage of a bird. Not inaptly then was this style called "feather-stitch" work, in contradistinction to that done in cross and tent stitch, or the "cushion-style," as we shall, a little further on, have occasion to notice next.

Among the many specimens here done in feather-stitch, in all ages, we would especially instance No. 84, p. 3.

The "opus pulvinarium," or "cushion style," was that sort of embroidery like the present so-called Berlin-work. As now, so then it was done in the same stitchery, with pretty much the same materials, and put if not always, at least often, to the same purpose of being used for cushions, upon which to sit or to kneel in church, or uphold the massbook at the altar; hence its name of "cushion-style." In working it, silken thread is known to have been often used. Among other specimens, and in silk, the rare and beautiful liturgical cushion of a date corresponding to the London inventory, is to be seen here, No. 1324, p. 59. Being so well adapted for working heraldry, from an early period till now, this stitch has been mostly used for the purpose; and the emblazoned orphreys, like the narrow hem on the Syon cope, are wrought in it.

The oldest, the most elaborate, the best known sample in the world, and what to us is more interesting still from being in reality not French but English needlework, is the so-called, but misnamed, Bayeux tapestry, a shred of which is in this collection, No. 675, p. 6. Of all this more anon, § IV.

The "opus pectineum" was a kind of woven-work imitative of embroidery, and used as such, in truth, about which we have a description in the Dictionary of the Londoner, John Garland, who thus speaks of the process: "Textrices ducunt pectines cum trama quæ trahitur a spola et pano," &c.[1] From this use of a comb-like instrument—" pecten "— in the manufacture the work itself received the distinctive appellation of "pectineum," or comb-wrought. Before John Garland forsook England for France, to teach a school there, he must have often seen, while at home, his countrywomen sitting down to such an occupation; and the "amictus de dono dominæ Kathærinæ de Lovell de opere pectineo,"[2] may perhaps have been the doing of that same lady's own hands.

---

[1] Ed. H. Geraud, Paris sous Philippe le Bel. p. 607.
[2] Dugdale's Hist. of St. Paul's, p. 319.

Introduction.

Of such work as this "opus pectineum," or comb-drawn, wrought by English women here at home, we have several specimens in this collection, pp. 24, 33, 38, &c.

Foreign ones are plentifully represented in the many samples of such webs from Germany, especially from Cologne, pp. 61, 62, 63, &c.

Likely is it that Helifend, the bold young lady from the south of England, and one of the waiting maids to the English Maud, queen of David, king of Scotland, *circa* A. D. 1150, got, from her cunning in such work, the reputation of being so skilful in weaving and church-embroidery :—" operis texturæ scientia purpuraria nobilis extiterat, et aurifrixoria artificiofæ compositionis peroptima super omnes Angliæ mulieres tunc temporis principaliter enituerat."[1]

Our mediæval countrywomen were so quick at the needle that they could make their embroidery look as if it had been done in the loom—really woven. Not long ago, a shred of crimson cendal, figured in gold and silver thread with a knight on horseback, armed as of the latter time of Edward I., was shown us. At the moment we took the mounted warrior to have been, not hand-worked, but woven, so flat, so even was every thread. Looking at it however through a glass and turning it about, we found it to have been unmistakably embroidered by the finger in such a way that the stitches for laying down upon the surface, and not drawing through the gold threads and thus saving expense, were carried right into the canvas lining at the back of this thin silk. After this same manner was really done, to our thinking, all the design, both before and behind upon that fine English-wrought chasuble, No. 673, p. 5.

At the latter end of the thirteenth century our women struck out for themselves a new way of embroidery. Without leaving aside the old and usual "opus plumarium," or feather-stitch, they mixed it with a new style, both of needle-work and mechanism. So beautiful and telling was the novel method deemed abroad, that it won for itself from admiring Christendom the complimentary appellation of " opus Anglicum," or English work. In what its peculiarity consisted has long been a question and a puzzle among foreign archæological writers ; and a living one of eminence, the Canon Voifin, vicar general to the bishop of Tournai, while noticing a cope of English work given to that church, says :—" Il ferait curieux de favoir quelle broderie ou quel tiffu on designait fous le nom de *opus Anglicum*."[2]

---

[1] Reginaldi Dunelmensis Libellus, &c. Ed. Surtees Society, p. 152.
[2] Notice fur les Anciennes Tapisseries de la Cathedral de Tournai, p. 16.

But the reader may afk what is

The Opus Anglicum, or English Work,

about which one heard fo much of old ?

Happily, we have before us in the prefent collection, as well as elfewhere in this country, the means of helping our continental friends with an anfwer to their queftion.

Looking well into that very fine and invaluable piece of Englifh needlework, the Syon cope, No. 9182, p. 275, we find that for the human face, all over it, the firft ftitches were begun in the centre of the cheek, and worked in circular, not ftraight lines, into which, however, after the further fide had been made, they fell, and were fo carried on through the reft of the flefhes; in fome inftances, too, even all through the figure, draperies and all. But this was done in a fort of chain ftitch, and a newly practifed mechanical appliance was brought into ufe. After the whole figure had thus been wrought with this kind of chain ftitch in circles and ftraight lines, then with a little thin iron rod ending in a fmall bulb or fmooth knob flightly heated, were preffed down thofe middle fpots in the faces that had been worked in circular lines; as well, too, as that deep wide dimple in the throat, efpecially of an aged perfon. By the hollows thus laftingly funk, a play of light and fhadow is brought out, that, at a fhort diftance, lends to the portion fo treated a look of being done in low relief. Chain ftitch, then, worked in circular lines, and relief given to parts by hollows funk into the faces, and other portions of the perfons, conftitute the elements of the " opus Anglicum," or embroidery after the Englifh manner. How the chain-ftitch was worked into circles for the faces, and ftraight lines for the reft of the figures, is well fhown by a woodcut, after a portion of the Steeple Afton embroideries, given in the Archæological Journal, t. iv. p. 285.

Though, indeed, not merely the faces and the extremities, but the drefs too of the perfons figured, were fometimes wrought in chain-ftitch, and afterwards treated as we have juft defcribed, the more general practice was to work the draperies in our fo-called feather-ftitch, which ufed to be alfo employed for the grounding, but diapered after a pretty, though fimple, zig-zag defign, as we find in the Syon cope.

Apart from its ftitching in circles, and thofe hollows, there are elements in the defign for facred art-work almoft peculiar to mediæval England. Upon the rood loft in old Weftminfter Abbey, ftood hard by the crofs two fix-winged feraphim, each with his feet upon a wheel; fo, too, in the Syon cope, as well as in Englifh needlework on chafubles

Introduction. xcix

and copes, wrought even late in the fifteenth century. When, therefore, such angel-figures are found on embroideries, still to be seen in foreign hands, a presumption exists that the work is of English production.

How highly English embroideries were at one period appreciated by foreigners may be gathered from the especial notice taken of them abroad; and spoken of in continental documents. Matilda, the first Norman William's queen, stooped to the meanness of filching from the affrighted Anglo-Saxon monks of Abingdon their richest church vestments, and would not be put off with inferior ones.[1] Other instances we have given.[2] In his will, dated A.D. 1360, Cardinal Talairand, bishop of Albano, speaks of the English embroideries on a costly set of white vestments.[3] Ghini, by birth a Florentine, but, in the year 1343, bishop of Tournai, bequeathed to that cathedral an old English cope, as well as a beautiful corporal of English work—" cappam veterem cum imaginibus et frixio operis Anglicani. Item unum corporale de opere Anglicano pulchrum," &c.[4] Among the copes reserved for prelates' use in the chapel of Charles, Duke of Bourgogne, brother-in-law to our John Duke of Bedford, there was one of English work, very elaborately fraught with many figures, as appears from this description of it: " une chappe de brodeure d'or, façon d'Engleterre, à plusieurs histoires de N.D. et anges et autres ymages, estans en laceures escriptes, garnie d'un orfroir d'icelle façon fait à apostres, desquelles les manteulx sont tous couvers de perles, et leur diadesmes pourphiler de perles, estans en manière de tabernacles, faits de deux arbres, dont les tiges sont toutes couvertes de perles et à la dite chappe y a une bille des dites armes, garnie de perles comme la dessus dicte.[5]

Besides textiles, leather was at one time the material upon which our embroiderers exercised the needle; and the Exeter inventory, drawn up A.D. 1277, mentions, for its bier, a large pillow covered with leather figured with flowers: " magnum cervical co-opertum coreo cum floribus."[6]

While so coveted abroad, our English embroidery was highly prized and well paid for here at home. Henry III. had a chasuble embroidered by Mabilia of Bury St. Edmund's;[7] and Edward II. paid a hundred marks—a good round sum in those days—to Rose, the wife of John de Bureford, a citizen and mercer of London, for a choir-cope of her em-

---

[1] Chronicon Monasterii de Abingdon, p. 491.
[2] Church of our Fathers, t. iv. p. 271, &c.
[3] Texier, Dictionnaire, d'Orfeverie, p. 195.
[4] Voisin, Notice sur les Anciennes Tapisseries, p. 17.
[5] Les Ducs de Bourgogne, t. ii. p. 244, ed. Le Comte de Laborde.
[6] Ed. Oliver, p. 298.   [7] Issue Rolls, p. 25.

broidering, and which was to be sent to Rome for the Pope as an offering from the queen.[1]

Though English embroidery fell on a sudden from its high estate, it never died. All along through those years, wasted with the wars of the Roses, the work of the English needle was very poor, very coarse, and, so to say, ragged; as, for instance, the chasuble here, No. 4045, p. 88. Nothing whatsoever of the celebrated chain-stitch with dimpled faces in the figures can be found about it. Every part was done in the feather-stitch, slovenly put down, with some few exceptions, among which may be enumerated the three rich English copes with pointed hoods running, like one here, p. 207, through the orphreys, still to be seen in the Chapter Library at Durham, and other vestments of the period in private hands. During the early part of the seventeenth century our embroiderers again struck out for themselves a new style, which consisted in throwing up their figures a good height above the grounding. Of this raised work there is a fine specimen in the fourth of those Durham copes. It is said to have been wrought for and given by Charles I. to that cathedral. This red silk vestment is well sprinkled with bodiless cherubic heads crowned with rays and borne up by wings; while upon the hood is shown David, who is holding in one hand Goliath's severed head; and the whole is done in highly raised embroidery. Belonging to a few of our aristocracy are bibles of the large folio size, covered in rich white silk or satin, and embroidered with the royal arms done in bold raised-work. Each of such volumes is said to have been a gift from that prince to a forefather of the man who now owns it; and a very fine one we lately saw at Ham House.

This style of raised embroidery remained in use for many years; and even yet to be found are certain quaint old looking-glasses, the broad frames of which are overlaid with this kind of raised embroidery, sometimes setting forth, as in the specimen No. 892, p. 319, of the Brooke collection here, the story of Ahasuerus and Esther, or a passage in some courtship carried on after the manners of Arcadia.[2]

Occasionally on work of an earlier period, some element or another of this raised style may be found; for instance, in that fine Rhenish embroidery, Nos. 1194-5, p. 21, the bushiness of hair on all the angels' heads, is striking, but this is done with little locks of auburn coloured silk.

---

[1] Issue Rolls, p. 133.
[2] Archæological Journal, t. xviii. 191.

But a very few people, at the prefent moment, have the fainteft idea about the labour, the money, the length of time often beftowed of old upon embroideries which had been fketched as well as wrought by the hands of men, each in his own craft the ableft and moft cunning of that day. In behalf of this our own land, we may gather evidences ftrewed all over the prefent Introduction: as a proof of the felf-fame doings elfewhere, may be fet forth a remarkable paffage given, in his life of Antonio Pollaiuolo, by Vafari, where he fays: "For San Giovanni in Florence there were made certain very rich veftments after the defign of this mafter, namely, two dalmatics, a chafuble, and a cope, all of gold-wove velvet with pile upon pile—di broccato riccio fopra riccio—each woven of one entire piece and without feam, the bordering and ornaments being ftories from the life of St. John, embroidered with the moft fubtile maftery of that art by Paolo da Verona, a man moft eminent of his calling, and of incomparable ingenuity: the figures are no lefs ably executed with the needle than they would have been if Antonio had painted them with the pencil; and for this we are largely indebted to the one mafter for his defign, as well as to the other for his patience in embroidering it. This work took twenty-fix years for its completion, being wholly in clofe ftitch—quefti ricami fatti con punto ferrato—which, to fay nothing of its durability, makes the work appear as if it were a real picture limned with the pencil; but the excellent method of which is now all but loft, the cuftom being in thefe days to make the ftitches much wider—il punteggiare piu largo—whereby the work is rendered lefs durable and much lefs pleafing to the eye.[1] Thefe veftments may yet be feen framed and glazed in preffes around the facrifty of San Giovanni.[2] Antonio died A.D. 1498. The magnificent cope once belonging to Weftminfter Abbey, and now at Stonyhurft and exhibited here, A.D. 1862, is of one feamlefs piece of gorgeous gold tiffue figured with bold wide-fpreading foliage in crimfon velvet, pile upon pile, and dotted with fmall gold fpots; it came, it is likely, from the fame loom that threw off thefe San Giovanni veftments, at Florence."

---

[1] Vite de' piu Eccellenti Pittori, &c., di G. Vafari, Firenze, F. Le Monnier, 1849. t. v. pp. 101, 102; Englifh tranflation, by Mrs. Fofter, t. ii. p. 229.   [2] Ib.

Our Old English Opus Consutum, or Cut Work,

in French, "appliqué," is a term of rather wide meaning, as it takes in several sorts of decorative accompaniments to needlework.

When anything—flower, fruit, or figure—is wrought by itself upon a separate piece of silk or canvas, and afterwards sewed on to the vestment for church use, or article for domestic purpose, it comes to be known as "cut-work." Though often mixed with embroidery, and oftener still employed by itself upon liturgical garments; oftenest of all, it is to be found in bed-curtains, hangings for rooms and halls, hence called "hallings," and other items in household furniture.

Of cut-work in embroidery, those pieces of splendid Rhenish needle-work with the blazonment of Cleves, all sewed upon a ground of crimson silk, as we see, Nos. 1194-5, p. 21. The chasuble of crimson double-pile velvet, No. 78, p. 1, affords another good example. The niches in which the saints stand are loom-wrought, but those personages themselves are exquisitely done on separate pieces of fine canvass, and afterwards let into the unwoven spaces left open for them.

A Florentine piece of cut-work, No. 5788, p. 111, is alike remarkable for its great beauty, and the skill shown in bringing together so nicely, weaving and embroidery. Much of the architectural accessories is loom-wrought, while the extremities of the evangelists are all done by the needle; but the head, neck, and long beard are worked by themselves upon very fine linen, and afterwards put together after such a way that the full white beard overlaps the tunic. Another and a larger example, from Florence, of the same sort, is furnished us at No. 78, p. 1. Quite noteworthy too is the old and valuable vestment, No. 673, p. 5, in this regard, for parts of the web in the back orphrey were left open, in the looms for the heads, and extremities of the figures there, to be done afterwards in needlework. Such a method of weaving was practised in parts of Germany, and the web from the looms of Cologne, No. 1329, p. 61, exhibits an example.

Other methods were bade to come and yield a quicker help in this cut-work. To be more expeditious, all the figures were at once shaped out of woven silk, satin, velvet, linen, or woollen cloth as wanted, and sewed upon the grounding of the article. Upon the personages thus fashioned in silk, satin, or linen, the features of the face and the contours of the body were wrought by the needle in very narrow lines done in

Introduction. ciii

brown filk thread. At times, even thus much of embroidery was fet afide for the painting brufh, and inftances are to be found in which the fpaces left uncovered by the loom for the heads and extremities of the human figures, are filled in by lines from the brufh.

Often, too, the cut-work done in thefe ways is framed, as it were, with an edging, either in plain or gilt leather, hempen, or filken cord, exactly like the leadings of a ftained glafs window.

Belonging to ourfelves is an old Englifh chafuble, the broad crofs, at the back of which is figured with "The Refurrection of the Body." The dead are arifing from their graves, and each is wrought in fatin, upon which the features on the face, and the lineaments of the reft of the body, are fhown by thin lines worked with the needle in dark brown filk; and the edge, where each figure is fewed on the grounding, is covered with a narrow black filk cord, after much the fame fafhion as the lectern-veil here, No. 7468, p. 141, of filk and gold cut work. Inftances there are wherein, inftead of needlework, painting was reforted to; No. 8315, p. 189, fhows us a fine art-work in its way, upon which we fee the folds of the white linen garment worn by our Lord, marked by brown lines put in with the brufh, while the head and extremities, and the ground ftrewed with flowers, are wrought with the needle. No. 8687, p. 258, gives us a figure where the whole of the perfon, the flefhes and clothing, are done in woven filk cut out, fhaded and featured in colours by the brufh with fome little needlework here and there upon the garments. In that old fpecimen, No. 8713, p. 270, fuch parts of the defign as were meant to be white are left uncovered upon the linen, and the fhading is indicated by brown lines.

Perhaps in no collection open anywhere to public view could be found a piece of cut-work fo full of teaching about the procefs, and its eafy way of execution, as the one here, No. 1370, p. 76; to it we earneftly recommend the attention of fuch of our readers as may wifh to learn all about this method.

For the invention of cut-work or "di commeffo," as Vafari calls it, that writer tells us we are indebted to one of his Florentine countrymen: "It was by Sandro Botticelli that the method of preparing banners and ftandards in what is called cut-work, was invented; and this he did that the colours might not fink through, fhowing the tint of the cloth on each fide. The baldachino of Orfanmichele is by this mafter, and is fo treated," &c., and this work ferves to fhow how much more effectually that mode of proceeding preferves the cloth than do thofe mordants, which, corroding the furface, allow but a fhort life to the work; but as the mordants coft lefs, they are more frequently ufed in our day than the firft-mentioned method.[1]

However accurate fuch a ftatement may be regarding Italy in general, and Tufcany in particular, it is, neverthelefs, utterly untrue as applicable to the reft of the world. In this collection may be feen a valuable piece of this fame cut-work—or as Vafari would call it "di commeffo"—by French hands, fraught with a ftory out of our Englifh Romance, and done towards the end of the fourteenth century, No. 1370, p. 76. Now, as Botticelli was born A.D. 1457, and died A.D. 1515, he came into being almoft a whole century too late to have originated fuch a procefs of ornamental needlework, which was well known and practifed in thefe parts fo many years before the birth of that Florentine painter.

There are fome acceffories, in mediæval embroidery, which ought not to be overlooked here.

In fome few inftances,

GOLD, AND SILVER GILT,

in very many more, wrought after the smith's cunning into little ftar-like flowers—broader, bigger, and more craftily fafhioned than our modern fpangles—are to be found fewed upon the filks or amid the embroidery in the fpecimens before us, particularly thofe from Venice and its mainland provinces in Italy, and from Southern Germany. At No. 8274, pp. 168-9, we have a part of an orphrey embroidered on parchment, and having along with its coral, gold beads, and feed pearls, fmall boffes and ornaments in gilded filver ftars; it is Venetian, and of the fecond half of the twelfth century. No. 8307, pp. 185-6 is a linen amice, the filken apparel of which has fewed to it large fpangle-like plates in gilded filver ftruck with a variety of patterns, fhowing how the goldfmith's hand had been fought by the Germans of the fifteenth century to give beauty to this filken ftuff. The fine piece of ruby-tinted Genoa velvet, which was once the apparel for the lower hem of an alb, is fprinkled fomewhat thickly with fix-rayed ftars of gold and filver; but thofe made of the latter metal have turned almoft black: here we have a fample of Lombard tafte in this matter, of the ending of the fifteenth century. Silver-gilt fpangles wrought to figure fix-petalled flowers on a fine example of gold tiffue, under No. 8588, pp. 222-3, prefent us with a German craftfman's work, in the fourteenth century. No. 8612, p. 233, is not without its value in reference to Italian tafte. All over,

---

[1] Vite de piu Eccellenti Pittori, &c., di G. Vafari, t. v. p. 121; Englifh tranflation, t. ii. p. 239.

this curious now fragmental piece of silk damask, has at one time been thickly strewed with trefoils cut out of gilt metal, but very thin, and not sewed but glued on to the silk: many of these leaves have fallen off, and those remaining turned black.

From among these examples a few will show the reader how the goldsmith had been tasked to work upon them as jeweller also, and gem the liturgical garments to which these shreds belong, with real or imitated precious stones. In the orphrey upon the back of that very rich fine crimson velvet chasuble, No. 1375, pp. 81-2, the crossed nimb about our Lord's head is gemmed with stones set in silver gilt; and the sockets still left on the piece of crimson velvet, No. 8334, p. 199, unmistakably speak for themselves.

Besides precious stones, coral, and seed-pearls,

GLASS,

coloured and wrought into small beads and bugles, is another of those hard materials, the presence of which we find in this collection. As now, so far back during the mediæval period, the Venetians, at the island of Murano, wrought small glass beads and bugles of all colours, as well as pastes—smalti—in every tint for mosaics, and imitations of jewels. This art, which they had learned from the Greeks, they followed with signal success; and likely is it that from Venice came the several specimens of glass—blue, like lapis lazuli—which we still see on that beautiful frontal in Westminster Abbey,[1]—the work of our countryman Peter de Ispagna,[2] the member of an old Essex family. At No. 8276, pp. 168-9, is a piece of an orphrey for a chasuble, plentifully embroidered with glass beads and bugles, which shows how much such a style of ornament was used towards the latter end of the twelfth century, at least in Lower Germany, and some of the Italian provinces. Belonging to St. Paul's, London, A.D. 1295, among many other amices, there was one having glass stones upon it; "amictus . . . . ornatus lapidibus vitreis magnis et parvis per totum in capsis argenteis deauratis, &c."[3]

ENAMEL.

Another form of glass fastened by heat to gold and copper—enamel, the invention neither of Egypt, Greece, nor Italy, but of our own old Britons,[4] was extensively employed as an adornment upon textiles. Besides the examples we have given,[5] that gorgeous "chesable of red cloth

---

[1] Church of our Fathers, 1, p. 235.
[3] Dugdale's St. Paul's, p. 318.
[5] Church of our Fathers, t. i. p. 469.
[2] Monumenta Vetusta, vi. p. 26.
[4] Philostratus, Icon. L. 1. cap. 328.

of gold with orphreys before and behind set with pearls, blue, white and red, with plates of gold enamelled, wanting fifteen plates, &c."[1] bestowed by John of Gaunt's duchess of Lancaster, upon Lincoln Cathedral, is another instance to show how such a kind of rich ornamentation was sewed to garments, especially for church use, in such large quantities.

Here, in England, the old custom was to sew a great deal of goldsmith's work, for enrichment, upon articles meant for personal wear, as well as on ritual garments. When our first Edward's grave, in Westminster Abbey, was opened, A.D. 1774, on the body of the king, besides other silken robes, was seen, a stole-like band of rich white tissue put about the neck, and crossed upon his breast: it was studded with gilt quatrefoils in filigree work and embroidered with pearls. From the knees downwards the body was wrapped in a pall of cloth of gold. Concerning attire for liturgical use, the fact may be verified in those instances we have elsewhere given.[2] When Henry III., in the latter end of his reign, bestowed a frontal on the high altar in Westminster Abbey, besides carbuncles in golden settings, as we have just read, p. xxxvi, we may have observed that along with several larger pieces of enamel, there were as many as 866 smaller ones—the "esmaux de plique" of the French—all fastened on this liturgical embroidery.

A good instance of the appliance of figured solid gold or silver, upon church vestments, is the following one of a cope beaten all over with lions in silver, given by a well-wisher to Glastonbury Abbey:—"dederat unam capam rubeam cum leonibus laminis argenteis capæ infixis, &c."[3]

In the Norman-French, for so long a period in use at our Court, silken stuffs thus ornamented were said to be "batuz," or as we now say beaten with hammered-up gold. Among the liturgical furniture provided by Richard II. for the chapel in the castle of Haverford, were " ii rydell batuz"—two altar-curtains beaten (no doubt with ornaments in gilt silver.)[4]

For the secular employment of this same sort of decoration, we have several curious examples. Our ladies' dresses for grand occasions were so adorned, as we may see in the verses following:—

> In a robe ryght ryall bowne,
> Of a redd syclatowne,
> Be hur fadur syde;

---

[1] Dugdale's Mon. Anglic. t. VIII. p. 1281.
[2] Church of Our Fathers, i. 360, 362, 469, &c.
[3] Johannes Glastoniensis, p. 203.
[4] Kalendars of the Treasury, &c. ed Palgrave, t. iii. p. 359.

A coronell on hur hedd fett,
Hur clothys wyth beftes and byrdes wer bete,
All abowte for pryde.[1]

A.D. 1215 our King John fent an order to Reginald de Cornhull and William Cook to have made for him, befides five tunics, five banners with his arms upon them, well beaten in gold: "quinque banerias de armis noftris bene auro bacuatas" *(fic)*.[2] The *c* for *t* muft be a mifprint in the laft word.

An amice at St. Paul's had on it the figures of two bifhops and a king hammered up out of gilt filver: "amictus ornatus cum duobus magnis epifcopis et uno rege ftantibus argenteis deauratis."[3]

From the original bill for fitting out one of the fhips in which Beauchamp, Earl of Warwick, during the reign of Henry VI., went over to France, where he had been appointed to a high command, we gather hints which throw light upon this as well as feveral matters belonging to this Introduction. Among other items for the abovenamed equipage are thefe:—"Four hundred pencils (long narrow ftrips, may be of filk, ufed as flags), beat with the Raggedftaff in filver; the other pavys (one of two fhields, likely of wood, and faftened outfide the fhip at its bows), painted with black, and a Raggedftaff beat with filver occupying all the field; one coat (perhaps of filk, but no doubt blazoned with the Beauchamp's arms,) for my Lord's body, beat with fine gold; two coats (like the foregoing) for heralds, beat with demi gold; a great ftreamer for a fhip of forty yeards in length and eight yeards in breadth, with a great Bear and Griffin holding a Raggedftaff poudred full of Raggedftaffs; three penons (fmall flags) of fatten; fixteen ftandards of worfted entailed with the Bear and a chain."[4] The quatrefoils on the robe of our Firft Edward, the filver lions on the Glaftonbury cope, the beafts and birds on the lady's gown, the Bear, and Griffin, and Raggedftaff belonging to the Beauchamp's blazoning, and all fuch like enrichments—moftly heraldic —put upon filken ftuffs, were cut out of very thin plates of gold or filver, fo as to hang upon them lightly, and were hammered up to fhow in low relief the fafhion of the flower and the lineaments of the beaft or bird meant to be reprefented.

In fact, fuch a ftyle of ornamentation done in gold or filver, ftitched on filken ftuffs made up into liturgical garments, knights' coats of arms, ladies' dreffes, heralds' tabards, or flags and penoncels, was far more common once than is now thought. It had ftruck out for itfelf a tech-

---

[1] Ancient Englifh Metrical Romances, t. iii. pp. 8, 9.
[2] Clofe Rolls, ed. D. Hardy, p. 193.   [3] Dugdale, p. 318.
[4] Dugdale's Baronage of England, i. 246.

nical expreffion. In fpeaking of it men would either write or fay, "filk beaten with gold or filver," as the cafe might be—a meaning, by the way, for the word "beat," quite overlooked by our lexicographers; yet, making her will as late as the year 1538, Barbara Mafon bequeathed to a church "a veftment of grene fylke betyn with goold."[1]

The badge on the arm of the livery coat once commonly worn, and yet rowed for by the Thames watermen, as well as the armorials figured, before and behind, upon the fine old picturefque frocks of our buffetiers —the yeomen of the Royal guard, called in London "beefeaters,"— help to keep up the tradition of fuch a ftyle of ornament in drefs.

Spangles, when they happened to be ufed, were not like fuch as are now employed, but fafhioned after another and artiftic fhape, and put on in a different manner. Before me lies a fhred from the chafuble belonging to the fet of veftments wrought, it is faid, by Ifabella of Spain and her maids of honour, and worn the firft time high mafs was fung in Granada, after it had been taken by the Spaniards from the Moors. Upon this fhred are flowers, well thrown up in relief, done in fpangles on a crimfon velvet ground. Thefe fpangles—fome in gold, fome in filver—are, though fmall, in feveral fizes; all are voided—that is, hollow in the middle—with the circumference not flat, but convex, and are fewed on like tiles one overlapping the other, and thus produce a rich and pleafing effect. Our prefent fpangles, in the flat fhape, are quite modern.

Sadly overlooked, or but fcantily employed on modern embroideries, is the procefs of

DIAPERING,

after fo many graceful and ever-varying forms to be found almoft always upon mediæval works of the needle.

The garments worn by high perfonages in the embroidery, and meant to imitate a golden textile, were done in gold *paffing* fometimes by itfelf, fometimes with coloured filk thread laid down alternately afide it, fo as to lend a tinge of green, crimfon, pink, or blue, to the imagined tiffue of the robe, as if it were made of a golden ftuff fhot with the adopted tint.

For putting on this gold paffing, it was of courfe required to few it down. Now, from this very needful and mechanical requirement, thofe mediæval needlewomen fought and got an admirable as well as ingenious element of ornamentation, and fo truthful too. Of this our ladies at this day, feem, from their work, to have a very narrow, fhort idea.

---

[1] Bury Wills, p. 134.

Taking thin (ufually red) filk, and while faftening the golden or filver paffing, they dotted it all over in fmall ftitches fet exactly after a way that fhowed the one fame pattern. So teeming were their brains in this matter that hardly the fame defign in diapering is twice to be found upon the fame embroidered picture. With no other appliance they were thus enabled to lend to their draperies the appearance of having been, not wrought by the needle, but actually cut out of a piece of textile, and for which they have been fometimes miftaken.

Of the many famples here of this kind of diapering we felect one or two—Nos. 1194-5, p. 21, which is fo very fine, and of itfelf quite enough for fhowing what we wifh to point out, and to warrant our praifes of the method; No. 8837, p. 200, is another worth attention.

THREAD EMBROIDERY,

after feveral of its modes, is reprefented here; and though the fpecimens are not many, fome of them are fplendid.

By our Englifh women, hundreds of years gone by, among other applications of the needle, one was to darn upon linen netting or work thereon with other kinds of ftitchery, religious fubjects for Church-ufe; or flowers and animals for houfehold furniture.

In this country fuch a fort of embroidering was called net-work—filatorium—as we learn from the Exeter Inventory, where we read that its cathedral poffeffed, A.D. 1327, three pieces of it, for ufe at the altar—one in particular for throwing over the defk: "tria filatoria linea, unde unum pro defco."[1] From their liturgical ufe, as we have noticed, p. 212, they were more generally named lectern-veils, and as fuch are fpoken of, in the fame Devonfhire document: "i lectionale de panno lineo operato de opere acuali, &c."[2] Of thofe narrow, light, and moveable lecterns over which thefe linen embroideries were caft, Exeter had three —two of wood, another which folded up (fee p. 212 here,) of iron: "i defcus volubilis de ferro, pro Evangelio fupra legendo; ii alia lectrina lignea."[3]

Almoft every one of thefe thread embroideries were wrought during the fourteenth century, and feveral of them for the fervice of the fanctuary, either as reredos, frontal, or lectern-veil; and while thofe defcribed at pp. 19, 20, 31, 53, 60, 71, 99, 120, 242-3, 249, 261-7, deferve confideration, a more complete and an efpecial notice is due to thofe two very fine ones under Nos. 8358, p. 210, and 8618, p. 235. As

---

[1] Ed. Oliver, p. 312.   [2] Ib. p. 356.   [3] Ib. p. 329.

early as A. D. 1295, St. Paul's had a cushion covered with knotted thread: "pulvinar opertum de albo filo nodato."[1]

QUILTING,

too, must not be forgotten here; and a short look at Nos. 727, p. 14, and 786, p. 16, will be sufficient to make us understand how, in hands guided by taste, a work of real, though humble art, may be brought out and shewn upon any article, from a lady's skirt to a gentleman's daily skull-cap, by such a use of the needle.

Crochet, knitting done with linen thread, and in the convents throughout Flanders, as well as the thick kinds of lace wrought there upon the cushion with bobbins, came, under the name of nun's lace, to be everywhere much employed, from the sixteenth century and upwards, for bordering altar-cloths, albs, and every sort of towel required in the celebration of the liturgy. No. 1358, p. 72, is a good example.

SECTION III.—TAPESTRY.

THOUGH regarding actual time so very old, still in comparison with weaving and embroidery, the art of tapestry is, it would seem, the youngest of the three.

It is neither real weaving, nor true embroidery, but unites in its working those two processes into one. Though wrought in a loom and upon a warp stretched out along its frame, it has no woof thrown across those threads with a shuttle or any like appliance, but its weft is done with many short threads, all variously coloured, and put in by a kind of needle. It is not embroidery, though so very like it, for tapestry is not worked upon what is really a web—having both warp and woof— but upon a series of closely set fine strings.

From the way in which tapestry is spoken of in Holy Writ, we are sure the art must be very old; but if it did not take its first rise in Egypt, we are led by the same authority to conclude that it soon became much and successfully cultivated by the people of that land. The woman in Proverbs vii. 16, says:—"I have woven my bed with cords. I have covered it with painted tapestry, brought from Egypt." While, therefore, in those words we hear how it used to be employed as an article of household furniture among the Israelites, by them are we also told that the Egyptians were the makers.

---

[1] Dugdale, p. 316.

Like weaving and fine needlework, the art of tapeſtry came from Egypt and Aſia, weſtward; and in the days of Virgil our old Britiſh ſires were employed in the theatres at Rome as ſcene-ſhifters, where they had to take away thoſe tapeſtries on which they themſelves, as examples of imperial triumph, had been figured:—

Juvat . . .
Vel ſcena ut verſis diſcedat frontibus, utque
Purpurea intexti tollant aulæa Britanni.[1]

From Egypt through Weſtern Aſia the art of tapeſtry-making found its way to Europe, and at laſt to us; and among the other manual labours followed by their rule in religious houſes, this handicraft was one, and the monks became ſome of its beſt workmen. The altars and the walls of their churches were hung with ſuch an ornamentation. Matthew Paris tells us, that among other ornaments which, in the reign of Henry I, Abbot Geoffrey had made for his church of St. Alban's monaſtery, were three reredoſes, the firſt a large one wrought with the finding of England's protomartyr's body; the other two ſmaller-ones figured with the goſpel ſtory of the man who fell among thieves, the other with that of the prodigal ſon: "dedit quoque doſſale magnum in quo intexitur inventio Sancti Albani, cujus campus eſt aerius, et aliud minus ubi effigiatur Evangelium de ſauciato qui incidit in latrones, et tertium ubi hiſtoria de filio prodigo figuratur."[2] While in London, A.D. 1316, Simon Abbot, of Ramſey, bought for his monks' uſe looms, ſtaves, ſhuttles and a ſlay: "pro weblomes emptis xxˢ. Et pro ſtaves ad eaſdem vjᵈ. Item pro iiij ſhittles pro eodem opere ijˢ vjᵈ. Item in j. ſlay pro textoribus viijᵈ."[3]

What was done in one monaſtery was but the reflex of every other; hence, Giffard, one of the commiſſioners for the ſuppreſſion of the ſmaller houſes, in the reign of Henry VIII., thus writes to Cromwell, while ſpeaking of the monaſtery of Wolſtrope, in Lincolnſhire:—"Not one religious perſon there but that he can and doth uſe either imbrothering, writing books with very fair hand, making their own garments, carving, painting, or graving, &c."[4]

Pieces of Engliſh-made tapeſtry ſtill remain. That fine, though mutilated ſpecimen at St. Mary's Hall, Coventry, is one; a ſecond is the curious reredos for an altar, belonging to the London Vintners' Company; it is figured with St. Martin on horſeback cutting with his ſword

---

[1] Georg. L. iii. 24, &c.
[2] Vitæ S. Albani Abbatum, p. 40.   [3] Mon. Anglic. ii. p. 585.
[4] Collier, Eccleſiaſtical Hiſtory of Great Britain, ed. Lathbury, t. v. p. 3.

his cloak in two, that he might give one-half to a beggar man; and with St. Dunstan singing mass, and wrought by the monks of St. Alban's.

Though practised far and wide, the art of weaving tapestry became most successfully followed in many parts of France and throughout ancient Flanders where secular trade-gilds were formed for its especial manufacture, in many of its towns. Several of these cities won for themselves an especial fame; but so far, at last, did Arras outrun them all that arras-work came, in the end, to be the common word, both here and on the Continent, to mean all sorts of tapestry, whether wrought in England or abroad. Thus is it, we think, that those fine hangings for the choir of Canterbury Cathedral, now at Aix-en-Provence, though made at home, perhaps too by his own monks, and given to that church by Prior Goldston, A.D. 1595, are spoken of as, not indeed from Arras, but arras-work—"pannos pulcherrimos opere de aryſſe subtiliter intextos."[1]

Arras is but one among several other terms by which, during the middle ages, tapestry was called.

From the Saracens, it is likely Western Europe learned the art: at all events its earliest name in Christendom was Saracenic work—"opus Saracenicum"—and as our teachers, we too wrought in a low or horizontal loom. The artizans of France and Flanders were the first to bring forwards the upright or vertical frame, afterwards known abroad as " de haute lisse," in contradistinction to the low or horizontal frame called " de basse lisse." Those who went on with the latter unimproved loom, though thorough good Christians, came to be known, in the trade, as Saracens, for keeping to the method of their paynim teachers; and their produce, Saracenic. In year 1339 John de Croisettes, a Saracen-tapestry worker, living at Arras, sells to the Duke of Touraine a piece of gold Saracenic tapestry figured with the story of Charlemaine: " Jean de Croisettes, tapissier Sarrazinois demeurant à Arras, vend au Duc de Touraine un tapis Sarrazinois à or de l'histoire de Charlemaine."[2] Soon however the high frame put out of use the low one; and among the many pieces of tapestry belonging to Philippe Duke of Bourgogne and Brabant, very many are especially entered as of the high frame, and one of them is thus described:—" ung grant tapiz de haulte lice, ſauz or, de l'istoire du duc Guillaume de Normandie comment il conquiſt Engleterre."[3]

---

[1] Anglia Sacra, t. i. p. 148.
[2] Voisin, p. 4.   [3] Les Ducs de Bourgogne, par le Comte de Laboure, t. ii. p. 270.

With the upright, as with the flat frame, the workman went the same road to his labours; but, in either of these ways, had to grope in the dark a great deal on his path. In both, he was obliged to put in the threads on the back or wrong side of the piece following his sketch as best he could behind the strings or warp. As the face was downward in the flat frame he had no means of looking at it to correct a fault. In the upright frame he might go in front, and with his own doings in open view on one hand, and the original design full before him on the other, he could mend as he went on, step by step, the smallest mistake, were it but a single thread. Put side by side, when done, the pieces from the upright frame were, in beauty and perfection, far beyond those that had come from the flat one. In what that superiority consisted we do not know with certitude, for not one single flat sample, truly such, is recognizable from evidence within our reach.

To us it seems that the Saracenic work was in texture light and thin, so that it might be, as it often was, employed for making vestments themselves, or sewed instead of needlework embroidered on those liturgical appliances. In the inventory of St. Paul's, London, A.D. 1295, mention is made of it thus: "Duo amicti veteres quorum unus de opere Saraceno."[1] "Stola de opere Saraceno."[2] "Vestimentum de opere Saraceno."[3] "Tunica et Dalmatica de indico sendato afforciato cum bordura operis Saraceni."[4] "Quatuor offertoria de rubeo serico quorum duo habent extremitates de opere Saraceno."[5]

Of the tapestries in this collection, perhaps Nos. 1296, p. 296, and 1465, p. 298, may be of the so-called Saracenic kind, because wrought in the low flat loom, or, "de basse lisse," while all the rest are assuredly of the "dehaute lisse," or done in the upright frame.

When the illuminators of MSS. began—and it was mostly in Flanders—to put in golden shadings all over their painting, their fellow-countrymen, the tapestry-workers, did the same.

Such a manner, in consequence, cannot be relied on as any criterion whereby to judge of the exact place where any specimen of tapestry had been wrought, or to tell its precise age. To work figures on a golden ground, and to shade garments, buildings, and landscapes with gold, are two different things.

Upon several pieces here gold thread has been very plentifully used, but the metal is of so debased a quality that it has become almost black.

For Church decoration and household furniture the use of tapestry, both here and abroad, was—nay, on the Continent still is—very great.

---

[1] Dugdale, p. 319. [2] Ib. p. 319. [3] Ib. p. 320. [4] Ib. p. 322. [5] Ib. p. 324.

The many large pieces, moſtly of a ſcriptural character, provided by Cardinal Wolſey for his palace at Hampton Court, were very fine. The moſt beautiful collection in the world—the Arazzi—now in the Vatican at Rome, may be judged of by looking at a few of the original cartoons at preſent in the Muſeum, drawn and coloured by Raffael's own hand. Duke Coſimo tried to ſet up tapeſtry work at Florence, but did not ſucceed. Later, Rome produced ſome good things; among others, the fine copy of Da Vinci's Laſt Supper ſtill hung up on Maundy Thurſday. England herſelf made like attempts—firſt at Mortlake, then years afterwards in London, at Soho. Works from theſe two eſtabliſhments may be met with. At Northumberland Houſe there is a room all hung with large pieces of tapeſtry wrought at Soho, and for that place, in the year 1758. The deſigns were done by Franceſco Zuccherelli, and conſiſt of landſcapes compoſed of hills crowned here and there with the ſtanding ruins of temples, or ſtrewed with broken columns, among which are wandering and amuſing themſelves groups of country folks. Mortlake and Soho were failures. Not ſo the Gobelins at Paris, as may be obſerved in the beautifully executed ſpecimens in the Muſeum. As now, ſo in ages gone by, pieces of tapeſtry were laid down for carpeting.

In many of our old-faſhioned houſes—in the country in particular—good ſamples of Flemiſh tapeſtry may be found. Cloſe to London, Holland Houſe is adorned with ſome curious ſpecimens, eſpecially in the raiſed ſtyle.

Imitated tapeſtry—if paintings on canvas may be ſo called—exiſted here hundreds of years ago under the name of " ſtayned cloth," and the workers of it were embodied into a London civic gild. Of this " ſtayned cloth " we have lately found hangings upon the walls of a dining-room in one manſion; in another ornamenting, with great effect, the top of a ſtair-caſe.

At the beginning of the ſixteenth century Exeter Cathedral had ſeveral pieces of old painted or " ſtayned " cloth: " i pannus veteratus depictus cum ymaginibus Sancti Andree in medio et Petri et Pauli ex lateribus; i front ſtayned cum crucifixo, Maria et Johanne, Petro et Paulo; viij parvi panni linei ſtayned, &c." [1]

The very great uſe at that time of ſuch articles in houſehold furniture may be witneſſed in the will, A. D. 1503, of Katherine Lady Haſtings, who bequeaths, beſides ſeveral other ſuch pieces, " an old hangin of counterfeit arres of Knollys, which now hangeth in the hall, and all ſuch hangyings of old bawdekyn, or lynen paynted as now hang in the chappell." [2]

---

[1] Ed. Oliver, p. 359.   [2] Teſtamenta Vetuſta, ii. 453.

Carpets

are somewhat akin to tapestry, and though the use of them may perhaps be not so ancient, yet is very old. Here, again, to the people of Asia, must we look for the finest as well as earliest examples of this textile. Few are the mediæval specimens of it anywhere, and we are glad to recommend attention to two pieces of that period fortunately in the collection, No. 8649, p. 248, of the fourteenth century, and No. 8357, p. 209, of the sixteenth, both of Spanish make.

As even the antechambers of our royal palaces, so the chancels in most of our country parish churches used to be strewed with rushes. When, however, they could afford it, the authorities of our cathedrals, even in Anglo-Saxon times, sought to spread the sanctuary with carpets; and at last old tapestry came to be so employed, as now in Italy. Among such coverings for the floor before the altar, Exeter had a large piece of Arras cloth figured with the life of the Duke of Burgundy, the gift of one of its bishops, Edmund Lacy, A.D. 1420, besides two large carpets, one bestowed by Bishop Nevill, A.D. 1456, the other, of a chequered pattern, by Lady Elizabeth Courtney: "Carpet et panni coram altari sternendi—i pannus de Arys de historia Ducis Burgundie—i larga carpeta, &c."[1] In an earlier inventory, we find that among the "bancaria," or bench-coverings, in the choir of the same cathedral, A.D. 1327, one was a large piece of English-made tapestry, with a fretted pattern—"unum tapetum magnum Anglicanum frettatum."[2] And we think that as the Record Commission goes on under the Master of the Rolls, to print our ancient historians, evidences will turn up showing that the looms at work in all our great monasteries, among other webs, wrought carpets. From existing printed testimony we know that, in all likelihood, such must have been the practice at Croyland, where Abbot Egelric, the second of the name bestowed before the year 992, when he died, upon his church: "two large foot-cloths (so carpets were then called) woven with lions to be laid out before the high altar on great festivals, and two shorter ones trailed all over with flowers, for the feast days of the Apostles: "Dedit etiam duo magna pedalia leonibus intexta, ponenda ante magnum altare in festis principalibus et duo breviora floribus resperla pro festis Apostolorum."[3] The quantity of carpeting in our palaces may be seen by the way in which "my lady the queen's rooms were strewed with them 'when she took her chamber.'"[4]

---

[1] Ed. Oliver, p. 32.   [2] Ib. p. 317.   [3] Ingulphi Hist. ed. Savile, p. 505, b.
[4] Leland's Collectanea, t. iv. pp. 179, 186, &c.

Section IV.

WHILE telling of a coronation, a royal marriage, the queen's 'taking her chamber,' her after-churching, a baptism, a progress, or a funeral, the historian or the painter cannot bring before his own mind, much less set forth to ours, a fit idea of the circumstances in the splendour shown on any one of these imperial occasions, unless he can see old samples of those cloths of gold, figured velvets, curious embroidery, and silken stuffs, such as are gathered in this collection, and used to be worn of old for those functions.

Of the many valuable, though indirect uses to which this curious collection of textiles may, on occasions, be turned, a few there are to which we call particular attention, for the ready help it is likely to afford. In the first place, to

The Historian,

in some at least of his researches, as he not only writes of bloodshed and of wars, that make or unmake kings, but follows his countrymen in private life through their several ways onward to civilization and the cultivation of the arts of peace.

Besides a tiny shred (No. 675, p. 6) of the very needlework itself, we have here a coloured plaster-cast of one of the figures in the so-called Bayeux Tapestry, which, among some, it has of late been a fashion to look upon as a great historic document, because it was, they say, worked by no less a personage than William's own queen, Matilda, helped by her handmaids.

Its present and modern title is altogether a misnomer. It is needlework, and no tapestry. Not Normandy, but England, is most likely to have been the country; not Bayeux, but London, the place wherein it was wrought. Probabilities forbid us from believing that either Matilda herself, or her waiting ladies, ever did a stitch on this canvas; nay, it is likely she never as much as saw it.

Coarse white linen and common worsted would never have been the materials which any queen would have chosen for such a work by which her husband's great achievement was to be celebrated.

But three women are seen upon the work, and Matilda is not one or them. Surely the dullest courtier would never have forgotten such an opportunity for a compliment to his royal mistress by putting in her person.

A piece, nineteen inches broad and two hundred and twenty-six feet long, crowded with fighting men—some on foot, some on horseback—with buildings and castles, must have taken much time and busied many hands for its working. Yet of all this, nought has ever turned up in any notice of Matilda's life. She was not, like the Anglo-Saxon Margaret queen of Scotland, known to fill up her time amidſt her maids with needlework, nor ever ſtood out a parallel to an older Anglo-Saxon high-born lady, the noble Ælfleda, of whom we now ſpeak. Her huſband was the famous Northumbrian chieftain, Brithnoth, who had ſo often fought and ſo ſorely worſted the invading Danes, by whom he was at laſt ſlain. His loving wife and her women wrought his deeds of daring in needlework upon a curtain which ſhe gave to the minſter church at Ely, wherein the headleſs body of her Brithnoth lay buried: "cortinam geſtis viri ſui (Brithnothi) intextam atque depiĉtam in memoriam probitatis ejus, huic eccleſiæ (Elienſi) donavit (Ælfleda)."[1] Surely when Ælfleda's handiwork found a chronicler, that of a queen would never have gone without one. Moreover, had ſuch a piece any-wife or ever belonged to William's wife, we muſt think that, inſtead of being let to ſtray away to Bayeux, towards which place ſhe bore no particular affeĉtion, ſhe would have bequeathed it, like other things, to her beloved church at Caen. Yet in her will no notice of it comes, and the only mention of any needlework is of two Engliſh ſpecimens, one a chaſuble bought of Aldaret's wife at Wincheſter, and a veſtment then being wrought for her in England: "caſulam quam apud Winto-niam operatur uxor Aldereti... atque aliud veſtimentum quod operatur in Anglia," both of which ſhe leaves to the Church of the Holy Trinity at Caen.

But there is the tradition that it is Matilda's doing. True, but it is barely a hundred years old, and its firſt appearance was in the year 1730 or ſo: tradition ſo young goes then for nothing. Who then got it worked, and why did it find its way to Bayeaux?

Odo, biſhop of Bayeux, and own brother to William came himſelf, and, like other rich and powerful Norman Lords, brought vaſſals who fought at Haſtings. Of all the great chiefs, but one, at moſt but two, are pointed out by name on this piece. Odo, however, is figured in no leſs than three of its compartments; furthermore, three men quite unknown to fame, Turold, Vital, and Wadard, receive as many times as the biſhop this ſame honourable diſtinĉtion. Rich and influential in Normandy, Odo, after being made Earl of Kent by his viĉtorious brother, became richer and more influential in England; hence the three above-mentioned individuals, the prelate's feudatories, by their maſter's favour, got poſſeſſion of wide landed eſtates in many parts of England,

---

[1] Hiſtoria Elienſis, Lib. Secund. ed. Stewart, p. 183.

as appears from Domesday. Coming from Bayeux itself, and owing service to its bishop, through whom they had become rich lords in England, these three men may have very naturally wished to make a joint offering to the cathedral of their native city. Hence they had this piece of needlework done in London, and on it caused, neither Matilda nor any of the great chiefs of the Norman expedition, but instead, the bishop of Bayeux and themselves its citizens to be so conspicuously set forth upon what was meant to be, for Bayeux itself, a memorial of the part that the bishop and three men of Bayeux had taken in the Norman conquest of England.

On second thoughts, we look upon this curious piece as the work of the early part of the twelfth century, perhaps as an offering to the new church (the old one having been burned down by our Henry I. A.D. 1106) of Bayeux, as in measurement it exactly fits for hanging both sides of the present nave, its original as well as recent purpose.

In future, then, our writers may be led to use with caution this so-called Bayeux Tapestry, as a document cotemporaneous with the Norman conquest.

Though, in the reign of our Henry II. London was the head city of this kingdom, and the chief home of royalty, some reader may perhaps be startled on hearing that while its churches were 120, the inhabitants amounted only to the number of 40,000, as we learn from Peter, its then archdeacon: "nam quum sint in illa civitate (Londinensi) quadraginta millia hominum, atque centum et viginti ecclesiæ," &c.[1]—yet, at that very time, the capital of Sicily—Palermo—by itself was yielding to its king a yearly revenue quite equal in amount to the whole income of England's sovereign, as we are told by Gerald Barry the learned Welsh writer then living: "Urbs etenim una Siciliæ, Palernica scilicet, plus certi redditus regi Siculo singulis annis reddere solet, quam Anglorum regi nunc reddit Anglia tota."[2] This great wealth was gathered to Sicily by her trade in silken textiles, first with the Byzantines and the coasts of Asia Minor and Alexandria, where those stuffs were at the time wrought; and secondly, with Europe, and the products of her own looms somewhat later. Many of the pieces in this collection were woven at Palermo and other cities in that island. She herself was not the least consumer of her own industry, and of the profuse employment of silk for royal awnings, during the twelfth century in the kingdom of the two Sicilies. We have an example in the silken tent, made for queen Joan, and given her by

---

[1] Petri Blesensis Opera, ed. Giles, t. ii. p. 85.
[2] Geraldi Cambrensis De Instructione Principum, ed. J. S. Brewer, p. 168.

her husband king William, large enough to hold two hundred knights sitting down to dinner; and which, along with her chair of gold, and golden table twelve feet long and a foot and a-half wide, her brother, our Richard I. got back for his sister from Tancred: "Ipse (Richardus rex) enim a rege Tancredo exigebat—cathedram auream ad opus ejusdem Johannæ de consuetudine reginarum illius regni et ad opus sui ipsius mensam auream de longitudine duodecim pedum, et de latitudine unius pedis et semis et quoddam tentorium de serico magnum adeo quod ducenti milites in eo possint simul manducare."[1]

Among the old copes, dalmatics and chasubles which, one after the other, find their way at last to collections such as this, must the historian seek for what remains of those gorgeous robes worn at some interesting ceremony, or on some stirring occasion, by personages celebrated in our national annals. For example, along with the several gifts bestowed upon the church of Ely, by king Edgar, we find mentioned his mantle of costly purple and gold, of which was made a vestment: "Enimvero chlamydem suam de insigni purpura ad modum loricæ auro undique contextam illuc (ecclesiæ Eliensi) contulit rex Ædgarus."[2] Of a whole set of mass vestments at Windsor made out of the crimson and gold cloth powdered with birds, once the array worn by a royal princess when she was married, we have already spoken.

Queen Philippa gave to Symon, bishop of Ely, the gown she wore at her churching after the birth of her eldest son the Black Prince. The garment was of murrey-coloured velvet, powdered with golden squirrels, and so ample that it furnished forth three copes for choir use: "Contulit sibi (Symoni de Monte Acuto) Domina regina quandam robam preciosam cum omnibus garniamentis de velvet murreo squirrillis aureis pulverizato; qua induta erat in die Purificationis suæ post partum Principis excellentissimi Domini Edwardi filii sui primogeniti. De quibus garniamentis tres capæ efficiuntur," &c.[3] To St. Alban's Abbey was sent by Elizabeth Lady Beauchamp the splendid mantle made of cloth of gold lined with crimson velvet which Henry V. had on as he rode in state on horseback through London, the day before his coronation. Also another gown of green and gold velvet out of both of which vestments were made: "Elizabeth Beauchamp mulier nobilis . . . contulit monasterio S. Albani quandam togam pretiosissimam auro textam duplicatam cum panno de velvetto rubeo resperso cum rosis aureis quæ quondam

---

[1] Rog. Hoveden Annal. ed. Savile, p. 384, b.
[2] Hist. Elien. Lib. Secund. ed. Stewart, p. 160.
[3] Anglia Sacra, ed. Wharton, t. i. p. 650.

erat indumentum regis Henrici quinti dum regaliter equitaret per Londonias pridie ante coronationem suam. Item dedit et aliam gounam de viridi velvetto auro texto unde fieri possit integrum vestimentum quæ similiter fuit ejusdem regis."[1] Naturally wishful to know something about such costly stuffs, the historian will have to come hither, where he may find specimens in the gorgeous velvet and gold chasubles in this collection. Whilst here perchance his eye may wander toward such pieces as those Nos. 1310, p. 53, and 8624, p. 239, whereon he sees figured, stags with tall branching horns, couchant, chained, upturning their antlered heads to sunbeams darting down upon them amid a shower of rain; and beneath the stags are eagles; p. 239. This Sicilian textile, woven about the end of the fourteenth century, brings to his mind that bronze cumbent figure of a king in Westminster Abbey. It is of Richard II. made for him before his downfal, and by two coppersmiths of London, Nicholas Broker and Godfrey Prest. This effigy, once finely gilt, is as remarkable for its beautiful workmanship, as for the elaborate manner in which the cloak and kirtle worn by the king are diapered all over with the pattern (now hid under coats of dirt) on that silken stuff out of which those garments must have been cut for his personal wear while living; and it consists of a sprig of the Planta genesta, the humble broom plant—the haughty Plantagenets' device— along with a couchant hart chained and gazing straight forwards, and above it a cloud with rays darting up from behind. With Edward III. Richard's grandfather, "sunbeams issuing from a cloud" was a favourite cognizance. The white hart he got from the white hind, the cognizance of his mother Joan, the fair maid of Kent, and rendered remarkable by the unflinching steadfastness of the faithful Jenico in wearing it as his royal master's badge after Richard's downfal. Sometimes, did that king take as a device a white falcon, for, at a tournament held by him at Windsor, forty of his knights came clothed in green with a white falcon on the stuff. During a foppish reign, Richard was the greatest fop. When he sat to those two London citizens for his monument, which they so ably wrought, and which still is at Westminster, our own belief is that he wore a dress of silk which had been expressly woven for him at Palermo. We think, too, that the couple of specimens here, Nos. 1310, p. 53, and 8624, p. 239, were originally wrought in Sicily, after designs from England, and for the court of Richard: they quite answer the period, and show those favourite devices, the chained hart, sunbeams issuing from a cloud, the falcon or eagle—a group in itself quite peculiar to that

---

[1] Mon. Anglic. ed. Caley, t. ii. p. 223.

Introduction. cxxi

monarch. For the flight variations in thefe ftuffs from thofe upon the Weftminfter monument, we will account, a little further on, while treating the fubject of fymbolifm, Section VII.

The feemlinefs, not to fay comfort, of private life, was improved by the ufe, after feveral ways, of textiles. Let the hiftorian contraft the manners, even in a royal palace during the twelfth century, with thofe that are now followed in every tradefman's home. Then, rich barons and titled courtiers would fprawl amid the ftraw and rufhes, ftrewed in the houfes even of the king, upon the floor in every room, which, as Wendover fays : " junco folent domorum areæ operiri ; " [1] and, platting knots with the litter, fling them with a gibe at the man who had been flighted by the prince.[2] Not quite a hundred years later, when Eleanor of Caftile came to London for her marriage with our firft Edward, fhe found her lodgings furnifhed, under the directions of the Spanifh courtiers who had arrived before her, with hangings and curtains of filk around the walls, and carpets fpread upon the ground. This forrowed fome of our people; more of them giggled at the thought that fome of thefe coftly things were laid down to be walked upon, as we learn from Matthew Paris : " Cum veniffet illa nurus nobiliffima (Alienora) ad hofpitium fibi affignatum invenit illud . . . holofericis palliis et tapetiis, ad fimilitudinem templi appenfis; etiam pavimentum aulæis redimitum, Hifpanis, fecundum patriæ fuæ forte confuetudinem hoc procurantibus." [3] Now, our houfes have a carpet for every room as well as on its ftaircafe, and not a few of our fhops are carpeted throughout.

The Emperor Aurelian's wife once tried to coax out of her imperial hufband a filk cloak—only one filk cloak. "No," was the anfwer; " I could never think," faid that lord of the earth, " of buying fuch a thing; it fells for its weight in gold ;" as we fhowed before, p. xix. Now, however, little does the woman of the nineteenth century fufpect, when fhe goes forth pranked out in all her bravery of drefs, that an Egyptian Cleopatra equally with a Roman emprefs would have looked with a grudging eye upon her gay filk gown and fatin ribbons; or that, as late as three hundred years ago, even her filken hofe would have been an offering worthy of an Englifh queen's (Elizabeth's) acceptance. Little, too, does that tall young man who, as he ftands behind the lady's chariot going to a Drawing-room, ever and anon lets drop a ftealthy but complaifant look upon his own legs fhining in foft blufhing filk—ah ! little does he dream that in that old palace before

---

[1] T. iii. p. 109. [2] Vita S. Thomæ, auct. Eduardo Grim. ed. Giles, p. 47.
[3] Hift. Ang. in A.D. 1255, p. 612, col. b.

him there once dwelt a king (James I.) of Great Britain, who would have envied him his bright new stockings; and who, before he came to the throne of England, was fain to wear some borrowed ones, when in Scotland he had to receive an English ambassador. If we take this loan, for the nonce, from the Earl of Mar to his royal master, to have been as shapeless and befrilled as are the yellow pair (Blue Coat School boys' as yet) once Queen Elizabeth's, now among the curiosities at Hatfield; then were those stockings—the first woven in England, and presented by Lord Hunsdon—funny things, indeed.

Though so small a thing, there is in this collection a little cushion, No. 9047, p. 273, which bears in it much more than what shows itself at first, and is likely to awaken the curiosity of some who may have hereafter to write about the doings of our Court in the early part of the seventeenth century. This cushion is needle-wrought and figured all over with animals, armorial bearings, flowers, and love-knots, together with the letters I and R royally crowned with a strawberry leaf, and the strawberry fruit close by each of those capitals, as well as plentifully sprinkled all over the work.

In Scotland, several noble families, whether they spell their name FRASER or FRAZER, use as a canting charge—" arme che cantano "—of the Italians; the French " frasier," or strawberry, leafed, flowered, fructed proper; the buck too, figured here, comes in or about their armorial shields. Hence then we are fairly warranted in thinking that it was a Fraser's lady hand which wrought this small, but elaborate cushion, most likely as a gift, and with a strong meaning about it, to our King James I., whose unicorn is not forgotten here; and, in all probability, whilst she also wished to indicate that an S was the first letter in her own baptismal name. Siren too is another term for mermaid—that emblem so conspicuously figured by the lady's side. All this, with the love-knot so plentifully broadcast and interwoven after many ways, and sprinkled everywhere as such a favourite device, perhaps may help some future biographer of James to throw a light over a few hidden passages in the life of that sovereign.

Human hair, or something very like it, was put into the embroidery on parts of this small cushion. On the under side, to the left, stands a lady with her hair lying in rolls about her forehead. After looking well into them, through a glass, these rolls seem to be real human hair—may be the lady's own—it is yellow. Peering narrowly into those red roses close by, seeded and barbed, the seeded part or middle is found to be worked with two distinct sorts of human hair—one the very same as the golden hair on the lady's brow, the other of a light sandy shade: could this have been king James's? His son, Charles I., used, as it would seem, to send from his prison locks of his own hair to some few of the gentry favourable to his cause, so that the ladies of that house, while working his royal portraiture in coloured silks, might be able to do the head of hair on it, in the very hair itself of that sovereign. One or two of such wrought likenesses of king Charles were, not long ago, shown in the exhibition of miniatures which took place in this Museum.

For verifying passages in early as well as mediæval times, little does the historian think of finding in these specimens such a help for the purpose.

Quintus Curtius tells us, that, reaching India, the Greeks under Alexander found there a famous breed of dogs for lion-hunting more especially. On beholding a wild beast they hush their yelpings, and hold their prey by the teeth with so much stubbornness that sooner than let go their bite they would suffer one of their own limbs to be cut off: "Nobiles ad venandum canes in ea regione sunt: latratu abstinere dicuntur, quum viderunt feram, leonibus maxime, infesti," &c.[1] Such is the animal now known as the cheetah, which, as of old so all through the middle ages, up to the present time, has been trained everywhere in Persia and over India for hunting purposes; and called by our countryman, Sir John Mandeville, a "papyonn," as we have noticed in this catalogue, p. 178. This far-famed hunting-dog of Quintus Curtius, now known as the cheetah or hunting-lion, may be often met with on silken textiles here from Asiatic looms, especially in Nos. 7083, p. 136; 7086, p. 137; 8233, p. 154; 8288, p. 178.

Section V.—Liturgy.

FOR a sight of some liturgical appliances which, though once so common and everywhere employed have become rare from having one by one dropped into disuse, ritualists, foreign ones among the rest, will have to come hither. A few more of such articles, though still in common use, are remarkable for the antiquity or the costliness of those stuffs out of which they happen to be made.

For its age, and the beauty of its needle-work, the Syon cope is in itself a remarkable treasure, while its emblazoned orphreys, like the

---

[1] Lib. ix. cap. i. sect. 6.

vestments on the person of a Percy in Beverley minster, make it, at least according to present custom, singular. Several chasubles here so noteworthy for their gorgeousness, have their fellows equal in splendour, elsewhere ; but in this museum are a few articles which till now we might have sought for in vain throughout Christendom in any other private or public collection.

Such liturgical boxes as those two—No. 5958, p. 112, and No. 8327, p. 193—are of the kind known of old as the " capsella cum serico decenter ornata "—a little box beseemingly fitted up with silk—of the mediæval writers ; or the " capsula corporalium—the box in which are kept the corporals or square pieces of fine linen, a fine mediæval specimen of which is here, No. 8329, p. 195, of the rubrics which, to this day, require its employment for a particular service, during holy week. Like its use the name of this appliance is very old, and both are spoken of in those ancient " Ordines Romani," in the first of which, drawn up now more than a thousand years ago, it is directed : " tunc duo acolythi tenentes capsas cum Sanctis apertas, &c.;"[1] and again, in another " Ordo," written out some little time before A. D. 1143, a part of the rubric for Good Friday requires the Pope to go barefoot during the procession in which a cardinal carries the Host consecrated the day before, and preserved in the corporals' chest or box : " discalceatus (papa) pergit cum processione. . . . Quidam cardinalis honorifice portat corpus Domini præteriti diei confervatum, in capsula corpolarium."[2] About the mass of the presanctified, before the beginning of which this procession took as it yet takes place, we have said a few words at pp. 112, 113. What is meant by the word "corporal," we have explained, p. 194. Here in England, such small wooden boxes covered with silks and velvets richly embroidered, were once employed for the same liturgical uses. The Exeter inventories specify them thus : " unum repositorium ligneum pro corporalibus co-opertum cum saccis de serico ;"[3] " tria corporalia in casa lignea co-operta cum panno serico, operata cum diversis armis."[4]

Good Friday brings to mind a religious practice followed wherever the Greek ritual is observed, and the appliance for which, No. 8278, p. 170, we have there spoken of at such length as to save us here any further notice of this interesting kind of frontal, upon which is shown our dead Lord lying stretched out upon the sindon or winding-sheet. Of the Cyrillian character in which the Greek sentences upon it are written, we

---

[1] Ed. Mabillon, Museum Italicum, t. ii. p. 8.　　[2] Ib. p. 137.
[3] Oliver's Exeter Cathedral, p. 314.　　[4] Ib. p. 327.

shall have a more fitting opportunity for speaking a little further on. At Rome, in the Pope's chapel, the frontal set before the altar for the function of Maundy Thursday, is of gold cloth figured, amid other subjects suitable to the time, with our Lord lying dead between two angels who are upholding His head, as we learn from the industrious Cancellieri's description, in his " Settimana Santa nella cappella pontificia."[1]

In Greece may be still found several churches built with a dome, all around which is figured, in painting or in mosaics, what is there known as and called the " Divine Liturgy," after this manner. On the eastern side, and before an altar, but facing the west, stands our Lord, robed as a patriarch, about to offer up the mass. The rest of the round in the cupola is filled with a crowd of angels,—some arrayed in chasubles like priests, some as deacons, but each bearing in his hands either one of the several vestments or some liturgical vessel or appliance needed at the celebration of the sacred mysteries,—all walking, as it were, to the spot where stands the divine pontiff. But amid this angel-throng may be seen six of these winged ministers who are carrying between them a sindon exactly figured as is the one of which we are now speaking. How, according to the Greek ritual, this subject ought to be done, is given in the Painter's Guide, edited by Didron.[2] Though of yore as now a somewhat similar ceremonial was always observed according to the Latin rite, in carrying his vestments to a bishop when he pontificated, never in such a procession here, in the west, was any frontal or sindon borne, as in the east.

With regard to " red " as the mourning colour, in the sindon, our own old English use joined it with " black " upon vestments especially intended to be worn in services for the dead. For especial use on Good Friday Bishop Grandison gave to his cathedral (Exeter) a black silk chasuble, the red orphrey at the back of which had embroidered on it our Lord hanging upon a green cross : " j casula de nigro serico, pro Die Parafchive, cum j orfrey quasi rubii coloris, cum crucifixo pendente in viridi cruce, ex dono Johannis Grandissono ;"[3] and in the same document, among the black copes and chasubles, we find that they had their orphreys made of red : " cape nigre cum casulis—j casula de nigro velvete cum rubeo velvete in le orfrey. ij tuniculi ejusdem panni et secte. iij cape ejusdem panni et secte."[4]

At Lincoln cathedral there were " a chesable of black cloth of gold of bawdkin with a red orphrey, &c. ; a black cope of cloth of silver with

---

[1] P. 58.   [2] Manuel d'Iconographie Chretienne, pp. xxxvi. 229.
[3] Oliver, p. 344.   [4] Ib. p. 349.

an orphrey of red velvet broidered with flowers, &c.; a black cope of camlet broidered with flowers of woodbine with an orphrey of red cloth of gold," &c.; two copes of black satin with orphreys of red damask, broidered with flowers of gold, having, in the back, souls rising to their doom, &c., besides other vestments of the same kind.[1] Green, sometimes along with red, sometimes taking the latter's place in the orphreys, may be seen on some of our old vestments.

Those two pyx-cloths at No. 8342, p. 202, and No. 8691, p. 260, will have an interest for the student of mediæval liturgy as we have already pointed out, p. 202. While in Italy the custom, during the middle ages at least, never prevailed, here in England as well as all over France, and several countries on the Continent, it did, of keeping the Eucharist under one form, hung up over the high altar beneath a beautiful canopy within a pyx of gold, silver, ivory, or enamel, and mantled with a fine linen embroidered cloth or veil. At present this " velum pyidis " overspreading the ciborium or pyx in the tabernacle, is of silk.

In olden days the veil for the pyx was, here in England, beautifully embroidered with golden thread and coloured silks, and usually carried three crowns of gold or silver, as is shown in the woodcut, " Church of our Fathers,"[2] and often mentioned in many of our national documents which, without some such notice as this, could not be rightly understood. Among the things once belonging to Richard II. in Haverford castle and sent by the sheriff of Hereford to the exchequer, at the beginning of Henry IV.'s reign, are three crowns of gold, a gold cup, and one of the pyx-veils like these : " iij corones d'or pour le Corps Ihu Cryst. i coupe d'or pour le Corps Ihu Cryst. i towayll ove (avec) i longe parure de mesure la suyte."[3]

By different people, and at various periods, a variety of names was given to this fine linen covering. Describing in his will, one made in this country and so valuable for its English needlework, a bishop of Tournay (see before p. xcix) calls it a corporal : in the inventory of things taken from Dr. Caius, and in the college of his own founding at Cambridge, are : " corporas clothes, with the pix and 'sindon' and canopie," &c.[4] This variety in nomenclature doubtless led writers unacquainted with ritual matters to state that before Mary Queen of Scots bent her head upon the block, she had a " corporal," properly so

---

[1] Monasticon Anglicanum, t. viii. p. 1285, ed. Caley.   [2] T. iv. p. 206.
[3] The Ancient Kalendars and Inventories of His Majesty's Exchequer, t. iii. p. 361. ed. Palgrave.
[4] Munk's Roll of the Royal College of Physicians, t. i. p. 37.

called, bound over her eyes. What to our feeming this bandage really was, muſt have been a large piece of fine linen embroidered by her own hands—Mary wrought much with her needle, as fpecimens of her doing yet remain at Chatfworth, and at Greyſtock ſhow—meant for, perhaps too once ufed as a pyx-cloth, and not an altar corporal.

Whilſt thefe pages were going through the prefs, one of thefe old Engliſh pyx, or Corpus Chriſti cloths, was found at the bottom of a cheſt in Heſſett church, Suffolk. As it is a remarkable and unique fpecimen of the ingenious handicraft done by our mediæval countrywomen, we notice it. To make this pyx-cloth, a piece of thick linen, about two feet fquare, was chofen, and being marked off into fmall equal widths on all its four edges, the threads at every other fpace were, both in the warp and woof, pulled out. The checquers or fquares fo produced all over it were then drawn in by threads tied on the under fide, fo as to have the ſhape of ſtars, fo well and nicely given that, till this piece had been narrowly looked into, it was thought to be guipure lace. Of a textile fo admirably wrought, it is to be regretted that there is, as yet, no fample in this collection. This curious liturgical appliance is figured in the April number, for the year 1868, of the "Eccleſiologiſt," page 86.

For the feveral very curious forts of ornamental needlework about it, and the fomewhat intricate manner after which it is cut out, the old alb, No. 8710, p. 268, as well as the amice, No. 8307, p. 185, having both of them the apparels yet remaining fewed on to thefe church garments, muſt draw the attention of every inquirer after fuch rare exiſting famples of the kind.

Some very fine threaden cloths—now become rare—for liturgical purpofes, deferve attention. In the old inventories of church furniture in England, they are known under the name of "filatoria," about which we have fpoken juſt now, p. cix. At No. 4457, p. 99, is a towel which, it is likely, was fpread under the tapers for Candlemafs-day, and the twigs of the fallow, or willow (our fo-called palm), and flips of the box-tree, for Palm-Sunday, while they were being hallowed before diſtribution. For feveral lectern veils, we ſhall have to go to No. 7029, p. 120; No. 8358, p. 210; and No. 8693, p. 261.

Thofe two linen napkins, formerly kept hanging down from juſt below the crook on a paſtoral ſtaff or crozier are become fo exceſſively rare, that we unhefitatingly believe that none of our countrymen have ever been able to find, either in England or abroad, a fingle other fample; they are to be feen, No. 8279 A, p. 174, and No. 8662, p. 250.

Thofe who have ever witneſſed on a Sunday morning in any of the great churches at Paris, the bleſſing of the French " pain beni "—our old Engliſh " holy loaf "—the " eulogia " of antiquity—will call to mind how a fair white linen cloth, like the one here, No. 8698, p. 263, overſpread, and fell in graceful folds down from two ſides of the board upon which, borne on the ſhoulders of four youthful acolytes, a large round cake garniſhed with flowers and wax-tapers was carried through the chancel, and halting at the altar's foot got its bleſſing from the celebrant.

The rich crimſon velvet cope, No. 79, p. 2, has a fine hood figured with the coming down, after the uſual manner, of the Holy Ghoſt upon the infant church. No 8595, p. 226, preſents us with a ſhred merely of what muſt have been once a large hanging for the chancel walls, or perhaps one of the two curtains at the altar's ſides, having ſuch fragments of ſome Latin ſentences as theſe:—" et tui amoris in eis . . . tus. Re . . . le tuoru." The ſubject on the cope's hood tells of Penteсoſt Sunday; ſo too does the ſecond article, for thoſe broken ſentences are parts of particular words: " Veni Sancte Spiritus, reple tuorum corda fidelium: et tui amoris in eis ignem accende," to be found both in our own old Engliſh Saliſbury miſſal, and breviary, but in every like ſervice-book in uſe during the mediæval period throughout weſtern Chriſtendom. Be it kept in mind that both theſe liturgical appliances are red or crimſon; and as now, ſo heretofore, as well in old England, as elſewhere this very colour has been employed for the church's veſtments, thus to remind us of thoſe parted tongues, as it were, of fire that ſat upon every one of the Apoſtles.[1] We mention all this with a view to correct an error in lexicography. In our dictionaries we are told that " Whitſuntide " is a contracted form of White Sunday tide, ſo called from the white veſtments worn on that day by the candidates for baptiſm. Nothing of the ſort; but the word "wits," our intellect or underſtanding, is the root of the term, for a curious and valuable old Engliſh book of ſermons called " The Feſtival," tells us:—" This day is called Wytſonday by cauſe the Holy Ghooſt brought wytte and wyſdom in to Criſtis dyſcyples; and ſo by her preachyng after in to all Criſtendom."[2]

Somewhat akin to this ſubject, are thoſe ſeveral chriſtening cloaks here, pp. 8, 9, 10, 11. Not long ago the cuſtom was to carry to church for baptiſm the baby wrapped up in ſome ſuch a ſilken covering which was called a bearing-cloth. Of old, that uſed to be a conſpicuous article in all royal chriſtenings; and amongſt our gentry was looked upon as

---

[1] Acts ii. 1—11.   [2] In die Penthecoſtes, fol. xlvi. verſo

worthy enough of being made a teftamentary bequeft. At the chriftening of Arthur Prince of Wales, eldeft fon of Henry VII. " my Lady Cecill, the Queen's eldeft fifter, bare the prince wrapped in a Mantell of Cremefyn Clothe of Golde furred with Ermyn," &c.¹ Such ceremonial garments varied, according to the owner's pofition of life, in coftlinefs; hence Shakefpeare makes the fhepherd, in the " Winter's Tale," cry out, " Here's a fight for thee; look thee, a bearing cloth for a fquire's child!"² A well-to-do tradefman bequeathed, A. D. 1648, to his daughter Rofe his "beareing cloath fuch . . . linnen as is belonginge to infants at their tyme of baptifme."³

Very often in our old country houfes are found, thrown afide in fome antique cheft, certain fmall fquare pieces of nice embroidery, the former ufe for which nobody now knows, and about which one is afked. If their owners would look at thofe feveral cradle-quilts here—pp. 4, 13, 66, 67, 100, 103, 104, 110—they might find out fuch ancient houfehold ftuff was wrought for their forefathers' comfort and adornment, when mere babies. The evangelifts' emblems figured on feveral among thefe coverlets: fuch as No. 1344, p. 67, No. 4459, p. 100, No. 4644, p. 103, will call to mind thofe old nurfery-rhymes we referred to at p. 103. Of yore, not only little children, but grown-up, ay, aged men too loved to think about thofe verfes, when they went to fleep, for the inventory of furniture taken, A. D. 1446, in the Priory of Durham, tells us that in the upper chamber there was a bed-quilt embroidered with the four Evangelifts—one in each corner: "j culcitrum cum iiij or Evangeliftis in corneriis."⁴

The bag or purfe, No. 8313, p. 188, is of a kind which not only were ufed for thofe liturgical purpofes which we have already enumerated, but ferved for private devotional practices. In that very interefting will made by Henry, Lord de Scrope, A. D. 1415, among other pious bequefts, is the following one, of the little bag having in it a piece of our Lord's crofs, which he always wore about his neck;—" j burfa parva quæ femper pendet circa collum meum cum cruce Domini."⁵

The crimfon velvet mitre,—No. 4015, p. 85,—for the boy-bifhop, bairn-bifhop, or Nicholas-tide bifhop, as the little boy was feverally called in England, is a liturgical curiofity, as the ceremonies in which it was formerly worn are everywhere laid afide. Among the things given for the ufe of the chapel in the college—All Souls—of his founding at

---

¹ Leland's Collectanea, t. iv. pp. 205, 180, 181, 183.
² Act iii. fcene iii.   ³ Bury Wills, &c. p. 186.
⁴ Hift. Dunelm. Scriptores Tres, ed Surtees Society, p. cclxxxvii.
⁵ Rymer's Fœdera, t. ix. p. 278.

Oxford by Archbishop Chicheley, are a cope and mitre for this boy, there named the Nicholas-tide bishope:—" i cap. et mitre pro episcopo Nicholao."[1] To make good his election to such a dignity, at Eton College, a boy had to study hard and show at the examination for it, that he was the ablest there at his books: his success almost ennobled him among his schoolfellows:—"In die Sti Hugonis pontificis" (17 Nov.) "solebat Ætonæ fieri electio Episcopi Nihilensis, sed consuetudo obsolevit. Olim episcopus ille puerorum habebatur nobilis, in cujus electione, et literata et laudatissima exercitatio, ad ingeniorum vires et motos exercendos, Ætonæ celebris erat."[2] The colour, crimson, in this boy's mitre, was to distinguish it from that of bishops.

Of the episcopal bairn-cloth—the Gremiale of foreign liturgists—we have two specimens here,—Nos. 1031, 1032, pp. 19, 20. The rich one of crimson cloth of gold, once belonging to Bowet, Archbishop of York, who died A. D. 1423, brought more money than even a chasuble of the same stuff:—" Et de xxvjs. viijd. receptis pro j. bairnecloth de rubeo panno auri. Et de xxs. receptis pro j casula de rubeo beaudkyn, &c. Inventorium," &c.[3]

Old episcopal shoes are now become great liturgical rarities, but there is one here,—No. 1290, p. 46. At one time they were called " sandals ;" and among the episcopal ornaments that went by usage to Durham cathedral at the death of any of its bishops, were " mitra et baculum et sandalia et cætera episcopalia," of Hugh Pudsey, A. D. 1195.[4] Later was given them the name of " sabatines;" and Archbishop Bowet's inventory mentions two pairs :—" pro j pare de sabbatones, brouddird, et couch' cum perell'; pro j pare de sabbatones de albo panno auri," &c.[5]

Section VI.—Artists and Manufacturers

ILL, on many occasions, heartily rejoice to have, within easy reach, such an extensive, varied, and curious collection of textiles gathered from many lands, and wrought in different ages.

For the painter and the decorator it must have a peculiar value.

Until this collection of silken and other kinds of woven stuffs had been

---

[1] Collectanea Curiosa, ed. Gutch, t. ii. p 265.
[2] King's College, Cambridge, and Eton College Statutes, ed. Wright, p. 632.
[3] Test. Ebor. t. iii. p. 76, ed. Surtees Society.
[4] Wills of the Northern Counties, ed. Surtees Society, t. i. p. 3. [5] Ib. p. 76.

brought to England, and opened for the world's inspection and study, an artist had not, either in this country or abroad, any available means of being correctly true in the patterns of those silks and velvets with which he wished to array his personages, or of the hangings for garnishing the walls of the hall in which he laid the scene of his subject. In such a need, right glad was he if he might go to any small collection of scanty odds and ends belonging to a friend, or kept in private hands. So keenly was this want felt, that, but a few years ago, works of beautiful execution, but of costly price, were undertaken upon the dress of olden times, and mediæval furniture; yet those who got up such books could do nothing better than set out in drawings, as their authorities for both the branches of their subject, such few specimens as they could pick up figured in illuminated MSS. and the works of the early masters. Here, however, our own and foreign artists see before them, not copies, but those very self-same stuffs.

If we go to our National Gallery and look at the mediæval pictures there, taking note of the stuffs in which those old men who did them clothed their personages; if, then, we step hither, we shall be struck by the fact of seeing in these very textiles, duplicates, as far as pattern is sought, of those same painted garments. For example, in Orcagna's Coronation of the Blessed Virgin Mary, the blue silk diapered in gold, with flowers and birds, hung as a back ground; our Lord's white tunic diapered in gold with foliage; the mantle of His mother made of the same stuff; St. Stephen's dalmatic of green samit, diapered with golden foliage, are all quite Sicilian in design, and copied from those rich silks which came, at the middle of the fourteenth century, from the looms of Palermo. While standing before Jacopo di Casentino's St. John, our eye is drawn, on the instant, to the orphrey on that evangelist's chasuble, embroidered, after the Tuscan style, with barbed quatrefoils, shutting in the busts of Apostles. Isotta da Rimini, in her portrait by Pietro della Francesca, wears a gown made of velvet and gold, much like some cut velvets here.

In the patterns followed by the Sicilian looms, and those of Italy in general, may almost always be found the same especial elements. Of these, one is the artichoke in flower; and in F. Francia's painting of the Blessed Virgin Mary with our Lord in her arms, and saints standing about them,—No. 179,—St. Laurence's rich cloth of gold is diapered all over with the artichoke marked out in thin red lines. So, too, in the picture of V. Cappaccio, No. 750, the cloth-of-gold mantle worn by our Lord's mother, as well as the dress of the Doge, are both diapered with this favourite Italian vegetable. Often is this artichoke shut in by an oval, made sometimes of ogee arches, with their finials shooting forwards outside: thus is diapered the cloak of the Madonna, in Crivelli's Inthronement—No. 724. Much more frequently, however, this oval is put together out of architectural cusps—six or eight—turned inside, and their featherings sprouting out into a trefoil, as in our own Early English style. Such ovals round an artichoke are well shown in each of the four pictures by Melozzo da Forli, on the pede-cloth with which the steps in each of them are covered. Of such a patterned stuff here we select from several such, for the reader, Nos. 1352, p. 70; 1352 A, p. 70.

Stained and patterned papers for wall-hanging are even yet unknown but in a very few places on the Continent. The employment of them as furniture among ourselves is comparatively very modern, and came to England, it is likely, through our trade with China. Though in Italy the state apartment and the reception rooms of a palace are hung always with rich damasks, and often with fine tapestry, while some old examples of gilt and beautifully-wrought leather trailed all over with coloured flowers and leaves are still to be found, the rooms for domestic use have their whitewashed walls adorned at best with a coloured ornamentation, bestowed upon them by the cheap and ready process of stencilling.

From early times up to the middle of the sixteenth century, our cathedrals and parish churches, our castles, manorial houses, and granges, the dwellings of the wealthy everywhere, used to be ornamented with wall-painting done, not in "fresco," but in "secco;" that is, distemper. Upon high festivals the walls of the churches were overspread with tapestry and needle-work; so, too, those in the halls of the gentry, for some solemn ceremonial.

Our high-born ladies used to spend their leisure hours in working these "hallings," as they were called; and while Bradshaw, a monk of St. Werburgh's monastery at Chester, sings the praises of the patron-saint of his church, he gives us a charming picture of how a large hall was arrayed here in England with needlework, for a solemn feast some time about the latter end of the fifteenth century.

First of all, according to the then wont, when great folks were bidden to a feast:—

> All herbes and flowers, fragraunt, fayre and swete
> Were strawed in halles, and layd under theyr fete.
> Clothes of gold and arras were hanged in the hall
> Depaynted with pyctures and hystoryes manyfolde,
> Well wroughte and craftely.

The ſtory of Adam, Noe, and his ſhyppe; the twelve ſones of Jacob; the ten plages of Egypt, and—

> Duke Joſue was joyned after them in pyƈture,
> * * * * *
> Theyr noble aƈtes and tryumphes marcyall
> Freſhly were browdred in theſe clothes royall.
> * * * * *
> But over the hye deſſe in pryncypall place
> Where the ſayd thre Kynges ſat crowned all
> The beſt hallynge hanged as reaſon was,
> Whereon were wrought the ix orders angelicall,
> Dyvyded in thre ierarchyſes, not ceſſynge to call,
> *Sanƈus, Sanƈus, Sanƈus,* bleſſed be the Trynite,
> *Dominus Deus Sabaoth,* thre perſons in one deyte.[1]

The tapeſtries here will afford much help to the artiſt if he have to paint a dining room with feſtive doings going on, any time during the latter portion of the mediæval period; but ſuch "hallings" are by no means ſcarce. Not ſo, however, ſuch pieces of room hangings as he may find here at No. 1370, p. 76; No. 1297, p. 296; No. 1465 p. 298. Their fellows are nowhere elſe to be met with.

At a certain period, gloves were a much more ornamented and decorative article of dreſs than now; and, when meant for ladies' wear, a ſomewhat laſting perfume was beſtowed upon them. Among the new year's day preſents to Tudor Queen Mary, ſome years before ſhe came to the throne, was "a payr of gloves embrawret with gold."[2] A year afterwards, "x payr of Spanyneſhe gloves from a Duches in Spayne," came to her;[3] and but a month before, Mrs. Whellers had ſent to her highneſs "a pair of ſwete gloves." Shakeſpeare, true to manners of his days, after making the pretended pedler, Autolycus, thus chant the praiſes of his—

> Laura, as white as driven ſnow;
> Cyprus, black as e'er was crow;
> Gloves, as ſweet as damaſk roſes;

puts this into Mopſa, the ſhepherdeſs', mouth, as ſhe ſpeaks to her ſwain:—"Come, you promiſed me a tawdry lace, and a pair of ſweet gloves."[4] Here, in this collection, we may find a pair of ſuch gloves, No. 4665, p. 105. What, though the fragrance that once, no doubt, hung about them, be all gone, yet their ſhape and embroideries will render them a valuable item to the artiſt for ſome painting.

Manufacturers and maſter-weavers of every kind of textile, as well as

---

[1] Warton's Hiſtory of Engliſh Poetry, ed. 1840, t. ii. p. 375, &c.
[2] Privy Purſe Expenſes of the Princeſs Mary, ed. Madden, p. 144. [3] Ib. p. 164.
[4] "A Winter's Tale," act iv. ſcene iii.

their workmen, may gather some useful hints for their trade, by a look at the various specimens set out here before them.

They will, no doubt, congratulate themselves, as they fairly may, that their better knowledge of chemistry enables them to give to silk, wool, and cotton, tints and tones of tints, and shades, nay, entire colours quite unknown to the olden times, even to their elders of a few years ago: our new-found chemicals are carrying the dyeing art to a high point of beauty and perfection.

Among the several boasts of the present age one is, that of making machinery, as a working power in delicate operations, so true, as if it had been quickened with a life and will and power all its own: mechanism applied to weaving is, at least for the speed of plain work, most marvellous; and the improvements of the morrow over those of yesterday make the wonder grow. But, though having such appliances at hand, let an able well-taught designer for silken stuffs come hither, along with a skilled weaver, from Coventry, Glasgow, or Manchester, and the two will say, that for truthfulness and beauty in the drawing of the patterns, and their good renderings in the weaving, nothing of the present day is better, while much is often not so good. Yet these old stuffs before our eyes were wrought in looms so clumsy, and awkward, and helpless, that a weaver of the present day laughs at them in scorn. The man, however, who should happen to be asked to make the working drawings for several of such textiles, would fain acknowledge that he had been taught much by their study, and must strive hard before he might surpass many of them in the often crowded, yet generally clear combination of parts borrowed from beasts, birds, and flowers, all rendered with beauty and fittingness.

What has been, may be done again. We know better how to dye; we have more handy mechanism. Let, then, all those who belong anywise to the weaving trade and come hither, go home resolved to stand for the future behind no nation, either of past or present time, in the ability of weaving not only useful, but beautiful and artistic textiles.

Before leaving the South Kensington Museum the master weaver may, if he wishes, convince himself that the so-called tricks of the trade are not evils of this age's growth, but, it is likely, older than history herself. For mediæval instances of fraud in his own line of business, he will find not a few among the silks from Syria, Palermo, and the South of Spain.

What we said just now about Lettered Silks, p. lix. should be borne here in mind. With the Saracens, wherever they spread themselves, the usage was to weave upon their textiles, very often, either the title of the prince who was to wear them or give them away, or some short form of prayer or benediction. By Christian eyes, such Arabic words were looked upon as the true unerring sign that the stuffs that showed them came from Saracenic looms—the best of those times—or, in other terms, were the trade-mark of the Moslem. The Christian and Jewish weavers in many parts of the East, to make their own webs pass as Saracenic goods, wrought the Paynim trade-mark, as then understood, upon them. The forgery is clumsy: the letters are poor imitations of the Arabic character, and the pretended word runs, as it should, first correctly, or from right to left, then wrong or backward from left to right, just as if this part of the pattern—and it is nothing more—had been intended, like every other element in it, to confront itself by immediate repetition on the self-same line. Our young folks who sometimes amuse themselves by writing a name on paper, and while the ink is wet fold the sheet so that the word is shown again as if written backwards, get such a kind of scroll.

In many Oriental silk textiles the warp is either of hemp, flax, or cotton; but this is so easily discoverable that it could hardly have been done for fraud' sake. There is however a Saracenic trick, learned from that people, and afterwards practised by the Spaniards of the South, for imitating a woof of gold. It is rather ingenious, and we presume unknown among collectors and writers until now.

For the purpose, the finer sort of parchment was sought out, sometimes as thin as that now rare kind of vellum called, among manuscript collectors, "uterine." Such skins were well gilt and then cut into very narrow shreds, which were afterwards, instead of gold, woven, as the woof to the silken warp, to show those portions of the pattern which should be wrought in golden thread. But as these strips of gilded parchment were flat, they necessarily gave the stuffs in which they came all the look of being that costly and much used web called by us in the fifteenth century "tyssewys," as we have before noticed, p. xxxi. Specimens of such a fraudulent textile are to be seen here, Nos. 7067, p. 132; 7095, p. 140; 8590, p. 224; 8601, p. 229; 8639, p. 243, &c.

Section VII.—SYMBOLISM.

METAPHOR or figurative speech is the utterance to the understanding through the ear of words which have other and further meanings in them than their first one. Symbolism is the bringing to our thoughts, through the eye, some natural object, some human personage, some art-wrought figure,

which is meant to set forth a some one, or a something else besides itself.

The use of both arose among men when they first began to dwell on earth and live together. Through symbolism, and the phonetic system, Egypt struck out for herself her three alphabets—the hieroglyphic or picture writing; the hieratic or priestly characters, or shortened form of the hieroglyphics; and the enchorial or people's alphabet, a further abridgment still. The Hebrew letters are the conventional symbols of things in nature or art; and even yet, each keeps the name of the object which at first it represented; as "aleph" or "ox," "beth" or "house," "gimel" or "camel," &c.

Holy Writ is full of symbolism; and from the moment that we begin to read those words—"I will set my bow in the clouds, and it shall be the sign of a covenant,"[1] till we reach the last chapter in the New Testament, we shall, all throughout, come upon many most beautiful and appropriate examples. The blood sprinkled upon the door posts of the Israelites; the brazen serpent in the wilderness; that sign—that mystic and saving sign (Tau) of Ezekiel, were, each and every one of them symbols.

Being given to understand that things which happened to the Jews were so many symbols for us, the early Christian Church figured on the walls of the catacombs many passages from ancient Jewish history as applicable to itself, while its writers bestowed much attention on the study of symbolism. S. Melito, bishop of Sardes, A.D. 170, drew out of scripture a great many texts which would bear a symbolical meaning, and gave to his work the name of "The Key." Almost quite forgotten, and well nigh lost, this valuable book, after long and unwearied labour, was at last found and printed by Dom (now Cardinal) Pitra in his Spicilegium Solesmense, t. ii. Among other works from the pen of St. Epiphanius, born A.D. 310, we have his annotations on a book, then old, and called "The Physiologist," and a work of his own—a treatise on the twelve stones worn by Aaron,[2] in both of which, the Saint speaks much about symbolism. But the fourth century witnessed the production of the two great works on Scriptural Symbolism; that of St. Basil in his homilies on the six days' creation;[3] which sermons in Greek were styled by their writer "Hexæmeron;" and the other by St. Ambrose, in Latin, longer and more elaborated, on the same subject and bearing the same title. A love for such a study grew up with the church's growth everywhere, from the far east to the utmost west, amid

---

[1] Gen. ix. 13.   [2] Exod. xxviii.   [3] Gen. i.

Greeks as well as Latins, all of whom beheld, in their feveral liturgies, many illuftrations of the fyftem. It was not confined to clerics, but laymen warmly followed it. The artift, whether he had to fet forth his work in painting or mofaic; the architects, whether they were entrufted with the raifing of a church, or building a royal palace, nay a dwelling-houfe, were, each of them, but too glad to avail themfelves, under clerical guidance, of fuch a powerful help for beautiful variety and happy illuftration as was afforded them by Chriftian Symbolifm. So fyftema-tized at laft became this fubject that by the eleventh century we find it feparated into three branches—beafts, birds, and ftones—and works were written upon each. Thofe upon beafts were, as they ftill are, known by the title of "Beftiaria," or books on beafts; "Volucraria," on birds, and "Lapideria," on ftones. About the fame period, as an offfet from fymbolifm, heraldry fprang up; whether the crufaders were the firft to bethink themfelves of fuch a method for perfonal recognition and dif-tinction; or whether they borrowed the idea from the peoples in the eaft, and while adopting, much improved upon it, matters not; heraldry grew out of fymbolifm. Very foon it was made to tell about fecular as well as facred things; and poets, nay political partizans were quick in their learning of its language. The weaver too of filken webs was often bade, while gearing his loom, to be directed by its teaching, as feveral fpecimens in this collection will teftify. That fome of the patterns, made up of beafts and birds, upon filken ftuffs from Sicilian, or Italian looms and here before us, were fketched by a partizan pencil and advifedly meant to carry about them an hiftoric, if not political fignifi-cation, we do not for a moment doubt. Several inftances of facred fymbolifm here, have been fpecified, and fome explanation of it given.

The "gammadion," or the crofs made thus ⌐⌐ a figure which, as we faid before, is to be feen traced upon the earlieft heathenifh art-works, as well as the lateft mediæval ones for Chriftian ufe, may be often found wrought on textiles here.

Knowing, as we do, that the firft time this fymbol fhows itfelf to our eyes, is in the pattern figured on a web of the Pharaonic period, it is to the early hiftory of Egypt we ought to go, if we wifh to learn its origin and meaning.

The moft aftounding event of the world's annals was the going out of Ifrael from Egypt. The blood of the lamb flain and facrificed the evening before, and put upon both the door-pofts, as well as fprinkled at the threshold of the house wherein any Hebrew dwelt—a sign of safety from all harm and death to man and beast, within its walls, on that awful night when throughout all Egypt the first-born of everything else was killed—must have caught the sight of every wonder-stricken Egyptian father and mother who, while weeping over their loss, heard that death had not gone in to do the work of slaughter where the blood had signed the gates of every Israelite.

Among the Hebrew traditions, handed down to us by the Rabbins, one is that the mark made by the Israelites upon their door-posts with the blood of the sacrificed lamb, the night before starting out of Egypt, was fashioned like the letter Tau made after its olden form, that is, in the shape of a cross, thus +.

What is still more curious, we are told that the lamb itself was spitted as if it had been meant to bear about its body, an unmistakable likeness to a kind of crucifixion. Treating of the passover, the Talmud says:—The ram or kid was roasted in an oven whole, with two spits made of pomegranate wood thrust through it, the one lengthwise, the other transversely (crossing the longitudinal one near the fore-legs) thus forming a cross.[1] Precisely the same thing is said by St. Justin, martyr, born A.D. 103, in his Dialogue with Tryphon the Jew. This very mode of roasting is expressed in Arabic by the verb "to crucify;" according to Jahn, in his "Biblical Antiquities," § 142, as quoted by Kitto, under the word Passover.[2]

From the words of St. Jerome, it would seem that that learned hebraist, well knowing, as he did, the traditions of the rabbins of his day, had understood from them that the mark of the lamb's blood sprinkled on the doors of the Israelites going out of Egypt, had been so made as to take the shape of a cross.

Deeply smitten as the whole of Egypt must have been at the woe that befel them and theirs, the night before the great exode of the Israelites from among them, those Egyptians could not help seeing how all the Hebrews, their children, and their flocks had gone forth scatheless out of that death-stricken land. At peep of dawn, the blood upon the door-posts of every house where an Israelite had lately dwelt, told the secret; for the destroyer had not been there. From that hour, a Tau was thought by them to be the symbol of health and safety, of happiness, and future life. St. Epiphanius, born A.D. 310, in Palestine, for many years Archbishop of Salamis in Cyprus, and a great traveller in Egypt, tells us, that being mindful of that day on which the Israelites who had besmeared

---

[1] Pesachim, c. 3.   [2] T. ii. p. 477 of the "Cyclopædia of Biblical Literature."

the door-pofts of their houfes with the blood of the lamb, had been fpared the angel's death-ftroke, the Egyptian people were accuftomed, at every vernal equinox—their new year—to daub, with red paint, their doors, their trees, and animals, the while they cried out that, " once at this time fire blighted every thing ; " againft fuch a plague, they think that the remedy is a fpell in the colour of blood : " Egyptios memores illius diei quo a cæde angeli liberati funt Ifraelitæ qui agni fanguine poftes domorum illinierant, folitos effe, intrante æquinoctio vernanti, accipere rubricam et illinere omnes arbores domofque clamantes ' quia in tempore hoc ignis vaftavit omnia' contra quam luem remedium putant ignis colorem fanguineum rubricæ."[1]

While they found blood upon the departed and unharmed Ifraelites' door-pofts, the forrowing Egyptians muft have feen that it had been fprinkled there, not at hazard, but with the ftudied purpofe of making therewith the Egyptian letter Tau, as it ufed to be fafhioned at the time. But what was then its common fhape ? That the old Tau was a crofs, we are told by written authority, and learn from monumental evidence. Learned as he was in all the wifdom of the Egyptians, Mofes, no doubt, wrote with the letters of their alphabet. Now, the oldeft fhape of the Tau in the Hebrew alphabet, and ftill kept up among the Samaritans in St. Jerome's days, was in the form of a crofs : " Antiquis Hebræorum literis, quibus ufque hodie Samaritæ utuntur, extrema Tau crucis habet fimilitudinem, quæ in Chriftianorum frontibus pingitur et frequentius manus infcriptione fignatur."[2] For monumental teftimony we refer the reader to the proofs we have given, at large, in " Hierurgia," pp. 352-355, fecond edition. Strengthening our idea that the lamb's blood had been put on the door-poft in the fhape of a crofs, and that hence the old Egyptians had borrowed it as a fpell againft evil hap, and a fymbol of a life hereafter, is a paffage fet forth, firft by Rufinus, A. D. 397, and then by Socrates, A. D. 440 :—" On demolifhing at Alexandria a temple dedicated to Serapis, were obferved feveral ftones fculptured with letters called hieroglyphics, which fhowed the figure of a crofs. Certain Gentile inhabitants of the city who had lately been converted to the Chriftian faith, initiated in the method of interpreting thefe enigmatic characters, declared that the figure of the crofs was confidered as the fymbol of future life."[3] We know that, while the old Tau kept the fhape of a crofs, it took at leaft three modifications of that form on thofe monuments which, up to this time, have been brought to light: others

---

[1] Hærefes, xviii.
[2] Hier. in cap. ix. Ezech.
[3] Hift Eccles. lib. v. c. 17.

may turn up with that letter traced exactly like the so-called " gammadion" found upon an Egyptian stuff of such an early date. Most probably this was the very shape, but with shorter arms, of the letter found traced upon the door-posts.

The recurrence of the gammadion upon Christian monuments is curious. We find it shown upon the tunic of a gravedigger in the catacombs; it comes in among the ornamentation wrought upon the gold and parcel-gilt altar-frontal dome by our Anglo-Saxon countryman Walwin for the Ambrosian basilican church at Milan; it is seen upon the narrow border round some embroidery of the twelfth century, lately found within a shrine in Belgium, and figured by that untiring archæologist the Canon Voisin of Tournay ; and upon a piece of English needlework of the latter half of the same twelfth century—the mitre of our St. Thomas, figured by Shaw, and still kept at Sens cathedral. As a favourite element in the pattern worked upon our ecclesiastical embroideries, this "gammadion" is as conspicuously shown upon the apparel round the shoulders, and on the one in front of his alb, in the effigy of Bishop Edington, at Winchester cathedral, as upon the vestments of a priest in a grave-brass at Shottesbrook church, Berks, given by Waller in his fine work.

Always keeping up its heathenish signification of a "future life," Christianity widened the meaning of this symbol, and made it teach the doctrine of the Atonement through the death of our Lord upon a cross. Furthermore, it set forth that He is our corner-stone. About the thirteenth century, it was taken to be an apt memorial of His five wounds ; and remembering the stigmata or five impressions in the hands, feet, and side of St. Francis of Assisi, this gammadion became the favourite device of such as bore that famous saint's name, and was called in England, after its partial likeness to the ensigne of the Isle of Man—three feet—a fylfot.[1]

To the symbolic meaning affixed unto some animals, we have pointed in the catalogue, wherein, at p. 156, the reader will find that Christ, as God, is typified under the figure of a lion, under that again of the unicorn, as God-man. Man's soul, at pp. 237, 311, is figured as the hare; mischief and lubricity are, at p. 311, shadowed forth in the likeness of the monkey.

Birds often come in here as symbols; and of course we behold the lordly eagle very frequently. Bearing in mind how struggled the two great factions of the Guelphs whose armorial arms were " un' Aquila con

---

[1] M. S. Harley, 874, p. 190.

Introduction. cxli

un Drago fotto i piedi "—an eagle with a dragon under its feet—and the Ghibellini, we do not wonder at finding the noble bird, fometimes fingle, fometimes double-headed, fo frequently figured on filks woven in Sicily, or on the Italian peninfula, triumphing over his enemy, the dragon or Ghibelline ftretched down before him. About the emblematic eagle of claffic times we have already fpoken.

If the Roman Quintus Curtius, like the Greeks before him, was in amazement at certain birds in India, fo quick in mimicking the human voice: "aves ad imitandum humanæ vocis fonum dociles,"[1] we naturally expect to find the parrot figured, as we do here, upon ftuffs from Afia, or imitations of fuch webs.

Famous, in eaftern ftory, are thofe knowing birds—and they were parrots—that, on coming home at evening, ufed to whifper unto Æthiopia's queen (whom Englifhmen not till the fixteenth century began to call Sheba, but all the world befides called and yet calls Saba) each word and doing, that day, of the far-off Solomon, or brought round their necks letters from him. Out of this Talmudic fable grew the method with artifts during the fifteenth century of figuring one of the wife men as very fwarthy—an Æthiopian—under the name of Balthafar, taking as their warrant, a work called "Collectaneæ," erroneoufly affigned to our own Beda; and becaufe our Salifbury books for the liturgy, fang, as all the old liturgies yet fing, on the feaft of the Ephipany:—"All fhall come from Saba"—the name of the country as well as of that queen who once governed it—"bringing gold and frankincenfe," &c. thofe mediæval artifts deemed it proper to fhow fomewhere about the wife men, parrots, as fure to have been brought among the other gifts, efpecially from the land of Saba. Upon a cope, belonging now to Mount St. Mary's, Chefterfield, made of very rich crimfon velvet, there is beautifully embroidered by Englifh hands, the arrival at Bethlehem of the three wife men. In the orphrey, on that part juft above the hood, are figured in their proper colours two parrots, as thofe may remember who faw it in the Exhibition here of 1862; on textiles before us this bird is often fhown. The appearance of the parrot on the veftments at old St. Paul's is very frequent.[2]

But of the feathered tribe which we meet with figured on thefe textiles, there are three that merit an efpecial mention through the important part they were made to take, whilom in England at many a high feftival and regal celebration—we mean the fo called "*Vow of the Swan, the Peacock and the Pheafant.*" From the graceful eafe—the almoft royal

---

[1] Lib. viii. cap. 9.   [2] Dugdale, p. 317.

dignity with which it walks the waters, the fwan with its plumage fpotlefs and white as driven fnow, has everywhere been looked upon with admiring eyes; and its flefh while yet a cygnet ufed to be efteemed a dainty for a royal board, on fome extraordinary occafions. To make it the fymbol of majeftic beauty in a woman, it had fometimes given it a female's head. Among the gifts beftowed on his fon, Richard II. by the Black Prince, in his will were bed-hangings embroidered with white fwans having women's heads. To raife this bird ftill higher, in ecclefiaftical fymbolifm, it is put forth to indicate a ftainlefs, more than royal purity; and as fuch, is often linked with and figured under the Bleffed Virgin Mary, as is fhown upon an enamelled morfe given in the "Church of our Fathers."[1]

Befides all this, the fwan owns a curious legend of its own, fet forth by fome raving troubadour in the wildeft dream that minftrel ever dreamed. "The life and myraculous hyftory of the moft noble and illuftryous Helyas, knight of the fwanne, and the birth of y* excellent knight Godfrey of Boulyon," &c., was once a book in great favour throughout Europe; and was "newly tranflated and printed by Robert Copland, out of Frenfshe in to Englifshe at thinftigacion of y* Puyffaunt and Illuftryous Prynce Lorde Edwarde Duke of Buckyngham—of whom lynyally is dyfcended my fayde lorde."[2]

While our noble countryman boafted of an offspring from this fabled fwan, fo did the greateft houfes abroad. In private hands in England is a precious ivory cafket wrought on its five panels, before us in photography, with this hiftory of the fwan. Helyas's fhield and flag are enfigned with St. George's crofs; the armour tells of England and its military appliances, about the end of the fourteenth century; and the whole feems the work of Englifh hands. At the great exhibition of loans in this mufeum, A. D. 1862, one of the many fine textiles then fhown was a fine but cut-down chafuble of blue Sicilian filk, upon which was, curioufly enough for what we have faid about the birds before which the "Vow" was made, figured, amid other fowls the pheafant. The handfome orphreys upon this veftment were wrought in this country, and good fpecimens they are of Englifh needlework during the fourteenth century. Thefe orphreys, before and behind, are embroidered on a bright red filk ground, with golden flower and leafbearing branches, fo trailed as, in their twinings, to form Stafford knots in places, and to embower fhields of arms each fupported by gold fwans

---

[1] T. ii. p. 41.
[2] Typographical Antiquities of Great Britain, ed. Dibdin, t. iii. pp. 152-3.

all once ducally gorged. From thefe and other bearings on it, this chafuble would feem to have been worked for the Staffords, Dukes of Buckingham. At Corby Caftle there is an altar frontal of crimfon velvet made for and figured with the great Buckingham and his Duchefs both on their knees at the foot of a crucifix. Amid a fprinkling of the Stafford knot, for the Duke (Henry VIII. beheaded him) was Earl of Stafford, the fwan is fhown, and the Lord Stafford of Coffey, in whofe veins the blood of the old Buckingham ftill runs, gives a filver fwan as one of his armorial fupporters. At Lincoln cathedral there were :—A cope of red cloth of gold with fwans of gold ;[1] and a cope of purple velvet having a good orphrey fet with fwans.[2]

In mediæval fymbolifm, as read by Englifhmen, the fwan was deemed not only a royal bird, but, more than that, one of the tokens of royal prowefs. Hence we may eafily underftand why our great warrior king, Edward I., as he fat feafting in Weftminfter Hall, amid all the chivalry, old and young of the kingdom, on fuch a memorable day, fhould have had brought before him the two fwans in their golden cages :—" tunc allati funt in pompatica gloria duo cygni vel olores, ante regem, phalerati retibus aureis, vel fiftulis deauratis, defiderabile fpectaculum, intuentibus. Quibus vifis, rex votum vovit Deo cœli et cygnis, fe proficifci in Scotiam," &c.[3] And then folemnly made the " Vow of the Swan," as we defcribed, p. 287 of the Catalogue.

In the pride of place, on fuch occafions, abreaft with the fwan ftood the peacock, " with his angel fethers bright ;" and was at all times and everywhere looked upon as the emblem of beauty. Not a formal banquet was ever given, at one period, without this bird being among the difhes ; in fact, the principal one. To prepare it for the table, it had been killed and fkinned with ftudious care. When roafted, it was fewed up in its fkin after fuch an artiftic way that its crefted head and azure neck were kept, as in nature, quite upright ; and its fan-like tail out-fpread ; and then, put in a fitting pofition on a large broad filver difh parcel gilt, ufed to be brought into the hall with much folemnity.

On the laft day of a tournament, its gay feftivities ended in a more than ufual fumptuous banqueting. The large baronial hall was hung all over with hangings, fometimes figured with a romance, fometimes with fcenes fuch as we read of in " The Flower and the Leaf;" and becaufe trees abounded on them, were known as tapeftry of " verd." At top of and all along the travers ran the minftrel-gallery, and thither—

---

[1] Mon. Anglic. t. viii. p. 1282. [2] Ibid.
[3] Flores Hiftoriarum, per Matt. Weftmonaft. Collectæ, p. 454.

> Come firſt all in their clokes white,
> A company, that ware for their delite,
> Chapelets freſh of okes ſeriall,
> Newly ſprong, and trumpets they were all.
> On every trumpe hanging a broad banere
> Of fine tartarium were full richely bete,
> Every trumpet his lordes armes bare,
> About their neckes with great pearles ſete
> Collers brode, for coſt they would not lete, &c.[1]

From among thoſe high-born damoſels who had crowded thither, one was choſen as the queen of beauty. When all the gueſts had gathered in that dining-hall, and been marſhalled in their places by the herald, and the almoner had ſaid grace, and ſet the " grete almes diſhe of ſilver and overgilt, made in manner of a ſhippe full of men of armes feyghtyng upon the ſhippe ſyde weyng in all lxvii lb ix unc̄ of troye,"[2] at the high board under the dais, a bold fanfar was flouriſhed upon ſilver trumpets, from which drooped ſilken flags embroidered with the blazon of that caſtle's lord, or—

> Of gold ful riche, in which ther was ybete

ſome quaint device. Then a burſt of muſic from the minſtrel-gallery aroſe as came in the queen of beauty. Her kirtle was of ciclatoun, cloth of pall, or ſparkling tiſſue :—

> To don honour (to that day)
> Yclothed was ſhe freſhe for to deviſe.
> Hire yelwe here was broided in a treſſe,
> Behind hire back a yerde long I geſſe ;
> And in the gardin at the ſonne upriſt,
> She walketh up and doun wher as her liſt.
> She gathereth floures, partie white and red,
> To make a ſotel gerlond for hire hed.[3]

One at each ſide of her, walked two of the youngeſt bachelors in chivalry. Theſe youths did not wear their harneſs, but came arrayed in gay attire, having on white hoods, perhaps embroidered with dancing men in blue habits, like the one given by Edward III. to the Lord Grey of Rotherfield, to be worn at a tournament ; or looking,[4] each of them, like the " yonge Squier," of whom Chaucer ſaid :—

> Embrouded was he, as it were a mede,
> Alle ful of freſhe floures, white and red.[5]

---

[1] Chaucer, The Flower and the Leaf, v. 207, &c.
[2] Antient Kalendars of the Exchequers, ed. Palgrave, ii. p. 184.
[3] Chaucer, The Knightes Tale, v. 1050.   [4] Dugdale's Baronage, i. 723.
[5] The Prologue, v. 79.

Treading out sweetness from the bay leaves strewed among the rushes on the floor, and with step as stately as the peacock's own, the queen of beauty for the nonce, bearing in both her hands the splendid charger with the bird—the symbol of herself—slowly paced the hall. Halting on a sudden, she set it down before the knight who, by general accord, had borne him best throughout that tournament; such was the ladies' token of their praises. To carve well at table was one of the accomplishments of ancient chivalry; and our own King Arthur was so able in that gentle craft, that on one occasion he is said to have cut up a peacock so cleverly that every one among the one hundred and fifty guests had a morsel of the fowl. To show himself as good a knight at a feast as at a passage of arms, the lady bade him carve the bird. What the lances of his antagonists could not do, this meed of praise from the ladies did—it overcame him. With deference, he humbly pleaded that many a doughty knight there present was more worthy of the honour: all his words were wasted. The queen of beauty would brook no gainsaying to her behest. He therefore bowed obedience, and she went away. Ere applying himself to his devoir, outstretching his right hand on high above the dish before him, amid the deepest silence, and in a ringing voice, so as to be well heard by all that noble presence, the knight vowed his vow of the peacock. Almost always this vow was half religious, half military; and he who took it bound himself to go on pilgrimage to the Holy Land, and, on his road thither or homeward, to join, as he might, any crusade against the Paynim.

Hardly had the words of such a plight been uttered, when other knights started up at every table, and bound themselves by his or some like vow.

The dinner done, the feast was not quite over. Plucking from its tail the best and brightest of the peacock's feathers, the beauty-queen wove them into a diadem; the minstrel who had long distinguished himself, was summoned by a pursuivant and brought before her; and she crowned him as he knelt lowly down. Ever afterwards, at festival or tournament, this music king wore this crown about his hat as blithely as did the knight his lady's glove or favour on his helmet, at a joust. Such was—

> Vowis of Pecok, with all ther proude chere.

Sometimes a pheasant, on account of its next beautiful plumage, used to be employed, instead of the larger, grander peacock.

With these facts set before him, any visitor to this collection will take a much more lively interest in so precious a piece of English embroidery as is the Syon cope, for while looking at it in admiration of the art-work shown in such a splendid church vestment, he finds, where he never thought of coming on, a curious record of our ancient national manners.

Besides all that has been said in reference to this cope, at pp. 289-90 of the Catalogue, we would remind our reader that at easy distances from Coventry might be found such lordly castles as those of Warwick, Kenilworth, Chartley, Minster Lovel, Tamworth. The holding of a tournament within their spacious walls, or in the fields beside them, was, we may be certain, of frequent occurrence at some one or other of them. The tilting was followed by the banquet and the "vow;" and the vow by its fulfilment from those barons bold, who bore in their own day the stirring names of Beauchamp, Warwick, Ferrers, Geneville, or Mortimer. Of one or other of them might be said:—

> At Alisandre he was whan it was wonne.
> Ful often time he hadde the bord begonne
> No cristen man so ofte of his degre.
> In Gernade at the siege eke hadde he be
> Of Algesir, and ridden in Belmarie.
> At mortal batailles hadde he ben fiftene,
> And foughten for our faith at Tramissene
> In listes thries, and ay slain his fo.[1]

At Warwick itself, and again at Temple Balsall, not far off, the Knights Templars held a preceptory, and, as it is likely, aggregated to the Coventry gild, had their badge—the Holy Lamb—figured on its vestment. Proud of all its brotherhood, proud of those high lords who had gone on pilgrimage to the Holy Land, figured by the Star of Bethlehem, and had done battle with the Moslem, according to the vow signified by the swan and peacock, the Coventry gild caused to be embroidered on the orphrey of their fine old cope, the several armorial bearings of those among their brotherhood who had swelled the fame of England abroad; and by putting those symbols—the swan and the peacock, the star and crescent—close by their blazons, meant to remind the world of those festive doings which led each of them to work such deeds of hardihood.

In the fourteenth century a fashion grew up here in England of figuring symbolism—heraldic and religious—upon the articles of dress, as we gather from specimens here, as well as from other sources. The ostrich feather, first assumed by our Black Prince, was a favourite device with his son Richard II. for his flags and personal garments. This is well shown in the illumination given, p. 31, of the "Deposition of

---

[1] Chaucer, The Prologue, vv. 51, &c.

Richard II.," published by the Antiquarian Society. That king's mother had bequeathed to him a new bed of red velvet, embroidered with oftrich feathers of filver, and heads of leopards of gold, with boughs and leaves iffuing out of their mouths.¹ Through family feeling, not merely the white fwan, but this cognizance of the Yorkifts—the oftrich feather—was fometimes figured on orphreys for church copes and chafubles, fince in the Exeter, A. D. 1506, we find mentioned a cope, " le orfrey de rubeo damafco operato de opere acuali cum rofis aureis ac oftryge fethers infertis in rofis," &c. ;² and again, " le orfrey de blodio ferico operata de opere acuali cum cignis albis et oftryge fethers—i cafula de blodio ferico operata opere acuali cum oftryge fethers fericis, le orfrey de rubeo ferico operato cum oftryge fethers aureis."³ Lincoln Cathedral, too, had a cope of red damafk, with oftriges feathers of filver.⁴ This fomewhat odd element of defign for a textile is to be found on one here, No. 7058, p. 129.

To eyes like our own, accuftomed to fee nowhere but in Englifh heraldry, and Englifh devices, harts figured as lodged beneath green trees in a park as in Nos. 1283-4, p. 43, or ftags couchant, with a chain about the neck, as at pp. 53, 239, and in both famples gazing upward to the fun behind a cloud, it would appear that they were but varieties of the pattern fketched for the filken ftuffs worn by Richard II., and admirably fhown on that valuable, yet hitherto overlooked fpecimen of Englifh mediæval workmanfhip in copper and engraving ftill to be found in Weftminfter Abbey, as we before obferved,⁵ and the fymbolifm of which we now explain. The pattern of the filken textile worn by the king confifts of but three elements—the broom-pod, the fun's rays darting upwards from behind a cloud, and a ftag lying down on the grafs, looking right forward, with about its neck a royal crown, down from which falls a long chain. The broom tells, of courfe, that Richard was a Plantagenet. His grandfather's favourite cognizance was that of funbeams iffuing from clouds; his mother's—Joan, the fair maid of Kent—the white hart. The latter two were evidently meant to bring to mind the words of the Pfalmift, who fays :—" The heavens fhow forth the glory of God. He hath fet His tabernacle in the fun. The Lord is my light, and His throne as the fun." The white hind brings to our thoughts how the hart panting for the water-fountains, is likened to the foul that pants after God. This fymbolifm is unfolded into a wider breadth upon the defign for the ftuffs here, No. 1310, p. 53; No.

---

¹ Teftamenta Vetufta, i. 14. ² Ed. Oliver, p. 347. ³ Ibid. p. 365.
⁴ Mon. Anglic. t. viii. p. 1282, ed. Caley. ⁵ P. cxx.

8624, p. 239. Here, inſtead of the ſunbeams ſhooting upwards, as if to light the·whole heavens, they dart downward, as if for the individual ſtag with upturned gaze, amid a gentle ſhower of rain; as if to ſay that if man look heavenward by prayer, light will be ſent down to him, and helping grace, like rain, like the ſhower upon the graſs to ſlake his ghoſtly thirſt.

About the time of Richard II. the white hart ſeems to have been a favourite element in ornamental needlework here in England, for Lincoln cathedral had " a red velvet cope ſet with white harts lying, colours (with collars?) full of theſe letters S S . . . the harts having crowns upon their necks with chains, ſilver and gilt," &c.[1] So thoroughly national at the time was this emblem that we believe every piece of ſilken textile to be found here or elſewhere had its deſign ſketched in this country and ſent to Palermo to be woven there in ſtuffs for the uſe of the Engliſh court. When his order had been done, the weaver having his loom geared at our king's expenſe, threw off a certain quantity of the ſame pattern for home uſe or his trade with Germany; and hence we ſee ſuch a beautiful variation figured on the apparels upon the old alb, No. 8710, p. 268 of the catalogue. The eagle ſhown all in gold, with a crown not on but above its head, may refer to one of Richard's anceſtors, the King of the Romans, who never reigned as ſuch. The hart, collared and lodged in its park, is Richard's own emblem. That dog, collared and courant, has a ſtory of its own in Richard's eventful life. Dogs when petted and great favourites, were always arrayed in ornamented collars; hence we muſt not be ſurpriſed to find put down among the things of value kept in the Treaſury of the Exchequer:—" ii grehondes colers of ſilk enbrouded with lettres of gold and garnyſſed with ſilver and overgilt."[2] Telling of Richard's capture in Flint caſtle by the Earl of Derby, ſoon afterwards Henry IV., Froiſſart ſays:— " King Richard had a greyhound called Math, beautiful beyond meaſure who would not notice nor follow any one but the king. Whenever the king rode abroad the greyhound was looſed by the perſon who had him in charge, and ran inſtantly to careſs him, by placing his two fore feet on his ſhoulders. It fell out that as the king and the Duke of Lancaſter were converſing in the court of the caſtle, their horſes being ready for them to mount, the greyhound was untied, but inſtead of running as uſual to the king, he left him, and leaped to the Duke of Lancaſter's ſhoulders, paying him every court, and careſſing him as he was formerly

---

[1] Mon Anglic. t. viii. p. 1281, ed. Caley.
[2] Antient Kalendars and Inventories, ed. Palgrave, t. ii. p. 252.

used to caress the king. The duke asked the king, 'What does this mean?' 'Cousin,' replied the king, 'it means a great deal for you, and very little for me. This greyhound fondles and pays his court to you this day as King of England.'"[1] That such a pet as Math once so given to fawn upon his royal master should, with other emblematic animals, have been figured in the pattern on a textile meant for its master's wear, or that of his court, seems very likely: and thus the piece before us possesses a more than ordinary interest.

Respecting ecclesiastical symbolism, we have to observe that with regard to the subjects figured upon these liturgical embroideries, we may see at a glance, that the one untiring wish, both of the designer and of those who had to wear those vestments, was to set before the people's eyes and to bring as often as possible to their mind the divinity of Christ, strongly and unmistakably, along with the grand doctrine of the Atonement. Whether it be cope, or chasuble, or reredos, or altar-frontal such a teaching is put forth upon it. Beginning with the divinity of our Saviour's manhood, sometimes we have shown us how, with such lowly reverence, Gabriel spoke his message to the Blessed Virgin Mary with the mystic three-flowered lily standing up between them; or the Nativity with the shepherds or the wise men kneeling in adoration to acknowledge the divinity of our Lord even as a child just born; then some event in His life, His passion, His scourging at the pillar, the bearing of His cross, His being crowned with thorns, always His crucifixion, often above that, His upraised person like a king enthroned and crowning her of whom He had taken flesh; while everywhere about the vestment are represented apostles, martyrs, and saints all nimbed with glory, and among them, winged seraphim standing upon wheels, signifying that heaven is now thrown open to fallen but redeemed man, who, by the atonement wrought for him by our Divine Redeemer, is made to become the fellow-companion of angels and cherubim. To this same end, the black vestments worn at the services for the dead were, according to the old English rite, marked; the chasubles on the back with a green cross upon a red ground, the copes with a red orphrey at their sides, to remind those present that while they mourned their departed friend, they must believe that his soul could never enter heaven unless made clean and regenerated by the atoning blood shed for it on the cross.

At his dubbing, "unto a knight is given a sword, which is made in the semblance of the cross, for to signify how our Lord God vanquished in the cross the death of human lineage, to the which he was judged for

---

[1] Froissart's Chronicles, by Johnes, t. ii. chap. cxiii p. 692.

the sin of our first father Adam." This we are told in the "Order of Chivalry," translated by Caxton.¹ While stretched wounded and dying on the battle-field, some friendly hand would stick a sword into the ground before the expiring knight, that as in its handle he beheld this symbol of the cross, he might forgive him who had struck him down, as he hoped forgiveness for himself, through the atonement paid for him on the cross at Calvary.

The ages of chivalry were times of poetry, and we therefore feel no surprise on finding that each young knight was taught to learn that belonging to every article of his armour, to every colour of his silken array, there was a symbolism which he ought to know. All these emblematic significations are set forth in the "Order of Chivalry," which we just now quoted. The work is very rare, but the chapter on this subject is given by Ames in his "Typographical Antiquities of Great Britain;"² as well as in "Lancelot du Lac" modernized and printed in the "Bibliothèque Bleu," pp. 11, 12. In that black silk chasuble with a red orphrey upon which our Lord is figured hanging upon a green cross —"cum crucifixo pendente in viridi cruce,"³ it was for a particular reason that the colour of this wood for the cross is specified: as green is the tint of dress put on by the new-born budding year, which thus foretells of flowers and fruits in after months, so was this same colour the symbol of regeneration for mankind, and the promise of paradise hereafter. For such a symbolic reason is it that, upon the wall painting lately brought again to light in West Somerton Church, Norfolk, our uprisen Lord is shown stepping out of the grave, mantled in green, with the banner of the resurrection in His left hand, and giving a blessing with His upraised right. At all times, and in every land, the "Language of Flowers" has been cultivated, and those who now make it their study will find much to their purpose in Chaucer, especially in his "Flower and the Leaf." There speaking of "Diane, goddesse of chastite," the poet says:—

> And for because that she a maiden is,
> In her hond the braunch she beareth this,
> That agnus castus men call properly;
> . . . . . .
> And tho that weare chapelets on their hede
> Of fresh woodbind, be such as never were
> Of love untrue in word, thought ne dede,
> But aye stedfast, &c.⁴

---

[1] Typographical Antiquities, ed. Dibdin, t. i. p. 234.   [2] Ibid.
[3] Oliver, p. 134.   [4] Works, ed. Nicolas, t. vi. p. 259.

Were it not for this symbolism for the woodbine, we had been quite unable to understand why in our old testamentary bequests, the flower should have been so especially mentioned as we find in the will of Joan Lady Bergavenny who, A. D. 1434, leaves to one of her friends, a "bed of silk, black and red, embroidered with woodbined flowers of silver," &c.[1] Besides its symbolism of those colours—black and red—for which we have but this moment given the reasons, p. cxlix., the funeral cope which we noticed before, p. cxxvi., showed a symbolism of flowers in the woodbine wrought upon it. Sure may we be that the donor's wish—perhaps the fingers of a weeping widow had worked it for Lincoln Cathedral—was to tell for her in after days the unfaltering love she ever bore towards her husband, and to say so every time this vestment happened to be worn at the services founded for him. May be that quaint old likeness of Anne Vavasour, exhibited here A.D. 1868 among the "National Portraits," and numbered 680, p. 138 of the Catalogue, had its background trailed all over with branches of the woodbine in leaf, at the particular behest of a fond spouse Sir H. Lee, and so managed that the plant's only cyme of flower should hang just below her bosom. By Shakespeare floral symbolism was well understood; and he often shows his knowledge of it in " A Winter's Tale," act iv. scene iii. He gives us several meanings of flower-speech, and when he makes (Henry VIII. act iv. scene ii.) Queen Katherine say to Griffith " Farewell—when I am dead—strew me over with maiden flowers, that all the world may know I was a chaste wife to my grave," he tells of an olden custom still kept up among us, and more fully carried out in Wales and the Western parts of England, where the grave of a dear departed one is weekly dressed by loving hands with the prettiest flowers that may be had. The symbolism of colours is learnedly treated by Portal in his "Couleurs Symboliques."

The readers of those valuable inventories of the chasubles, copes, and other liturgical silk garments which belonged to Exeter cathedral and that of London, about the middle of the thirteenth century, will not fail to observe that some of them bore, amongst other animals, the horse, and fish of different sorts, nay, porpoises figured on them : " una capa de palla cum porphesiis et leonibus deauratis,"[2] " due cape de palla cum equis et avibus,"[3] " unum pulvinar breudatum avibus, piscibus et bestiis,"[4] " capa de quodam panno Tarsico, viridis coloris cum pluribus piscibus et rosis aurifilo contextis."[5] Even here, under No. 8229, p. 151, we have

---

[1] Test. Vet. i. 228.   [2] Oliver's Exeter, p. 199.   [3] Ibid.
[4] St. Paul's, p. 316.   [5] Ibid. p. 318.

from the East a small shred of crimson silk, which shows on it a flat-shaped fish. If to some minds it be a subject of wonderment that, amid flowers and fruits, not only birds and beasts—elephants included—but such odd things as fish, even the porpoise, are to be found represented upon textiles chosen for the service of the altar, they should learn that all such stuffs were gladly put to this very use for the symbolism they carried, by accident, about them. Then, as now, the clergy had to say, and the people to listen daily to that canticle: " O all ye works of the Lord, bless ye the Lord; O ye angels of the Lord, O ye whales, and all that move in the waters, O ye fowls of the air, O all ye beasts and cattle, bless ye the Lord and magnify Him for ever!" Not merely churchmen, but the lay folks, deemed it but fitting that while the prayer above was being offered up, an emphasis should be given to its words by the very garment worn by the celebrant as he uttered them.

Section VIII.—LITERATURE AND LANGUAGES.

FOR those who bestow their attention upon Literature and Languages, this collection must have, at times, an especial value, whichever way their choice may lead them, whether towards subjects of biblical, classic or mediæval study: proofs of this, we think, may be gathered, up and down the whole of this "Introduction." With regard to our own country, we deem it quite impossible for any one among us to properly know the doings, in private and in public, throughout this land in by-gone days, or to take in all the beauty of many a passage in our prose writers, much less understand several particulars in the poetry of the middle ages, without an acquaintance, such as may be made here, with the textiles and needlework of that period.

To the student of languages, it may seem, at first sight, that he will have nothing to learn by coming hither. When he looks at those two very curious and interesting pieces, Nos. 1297, p. 296; 1465, p. 298, and has read the scrolls traced upon them, he may perhaps, if he be in search of the older forms of German speech, have to change his mind : of the words, so often to be met with here, in real or pretended Arabic, we say nothing. To almost every one among our English students of languages there is one inscription done in needlework quite unreadable. At No. 8278, p. 170, going round the four sides of this liturgical appliance, are sentences in Greek, borrowed from the ritual, but hidden to the Greek scholar's eye, under the so-called Cyrillian character.

Toward the second half of the ninth century, a monk, known in his cloister under the name of Conſtantine, but afterwards, when a biſhop, as Cyrillus, became earneſtly wiſhful of bringing all the many tribes of the Sclavonic race to a knowledge of Chriſtianity; and warming in the heart of his brother Methodius a like hope, they both bethought themſelves, the ſooner to ſucceed, of inventing an alphabet which ſhould be better adapted for that purpoſe than either the Greek or the Latin one; and becauſe its invention is owing, for the greater part, to St. Cyril, it immediately took, and ſtill keeps, its name from him, and is now denominated Cyrillian. Of this invention we are told by Pope John VIII. to whom the two brothers had gone together, to aſk authority and cravè his bleſſing for their undertaking: " Letteras Sclavonicas, a Conſtantino quodam philoſopho repertas, quibus Deo laudes debitæ reſonant. Ep. ad Svaplukum, apud Dobrowſky, Inſtitutiones Linguæ Slavicæ." This great and ſucceſsful miſſionary took not any Gothic, but a Greek model for his letters, as is ſhown by Dobrowſky. The Sclaves who follow the Greek rite, uſe the Cyrillian letters in their liturgical books, while thoſe of the ſame people who uſe the Latin rite employ, in their ſervice, the Glagolitic alphabet, which was drawn up in the thirteenth century. The probability is that this latter—a modification of the Cyrillian, is no older than that period, and is not from the hand, as ſuppoſed by ſome, of St. Jerom.

A ſhort time ago, the Sclaves celebrated with great ſplendour the thouſandth anniverſary of St. Cyril, to whom they owe their Chriſtianity and their alphabet; and among the beautiful wall paintings lately brought to light in the lower church of St. Clement at Rome, by the zealous labours of Father Malooly, an Iriſh Dominican, the tranſlation of St. Cyril's body from the Vatican, to that church, is figured.

Section IX.—HERALDRY,

AND how the appearance of it, real or imagined, under any ſhape, and upon veſtments, was made available, after different ways, in our law-courts, aſk for and ſhall have a paſſing notice.

At the end of the fourteenth century, there aroſe, between the noble houſes of Scrope and Groſvenor, a difference about the legal right of bearing on their reſpective ſhields the bend *or* on a field *azure;* and the ſuit was carried to the Court of Honour which ſat at Weſtminſter, and commiſſioners were ſent about the country for the purpoſe of gathering evidence.

Besides a numerous body of the nobility, several distinguished churchmen were examined; and their depositions are curious. John, Abbot of St. Agatha, in Richmondshire, said the arms (*Azure*, a bend *or*, the bearing of the Scrope family who contended against its assumption by the Grosvenors) were on a corporas case belonging to the church of his monastery, of which the Scropes were deemed the second founders.¹ John de Cloworthe, sub-prior of Wartre, exhibited before the commissioners an amice embroidered on red velvet with leopards and griffons *or*, between which are sewn in silk, in three pieces, three escochens with the entire arms of Sir Richard Scrope therein, viz.—*azure* a bend *or*.² William, Prior of Lanercost, said they had in their church the same arms embroidered on the morse of a cope.³ Sir Simon, parson of Wensley (whose fine grave brass may be seen in the "Church of Our Fathers,"⁴ placed before the commissioners an albe with flaps, upon which were embroidered the arms of the Scropes entire, &c.⁵ The Scropes were the patrons of that living. Thomas de Cotyngham, prior of the Abbey of St. Mary, York, said that they had vestments with the Scrope arms upon them.⁶ Sir John de Manfeld, parson of the Church of St. Mary sur Rychille, in York, said that in the church were diverse vestments on which were sewn, in silk, the entire arms of Scrope.⁷ Sir Bertram Mountboucher said that these arms of the Scropes were to be seen on vestments, &c., in the abbey and churches where Sir R. Scrope was born.⁸ Not the least remarkable individual who bore evidence on the subject was the poet Chaucer, who was produced on behalf of Sir Richard Scrope. When asked whether the arms *azure*, a bend *or*, belonged, or ought to belong to the said Sir Richard? said yes, for he saw him so armed in France, &c., and that all his time he had seen the said arms in banners, glass, paintings and vestments, and commonly called the Arms of Scrope.⁹ For the better understanding of all these evidences the reader should look at No. 8307, p. 185, an amice with its old apparel still on it. The "flaps" of an alb are now called apparels; and an old one, with these ornaments upon it, both at the cuffs as well as before and behind, is in this collection, No. 8710, p. 268 of the Catalogue. The two fine old English apparels here, No. 8128, p. 146, show how shields with heraldry could be put along with Scriptural subjects in these embroideries. The monumental effigy of a priest

---

¹ Scrope and Grosvenor Rolls, ed. Sir H Nicolas, t. ii. p. 275.
² Ibid. p. 278.   ³ Ibid. p. 279.   ⁴ T. i. p. 325.
⁵ Scrope and Grosvenor Rolls, ed. Sir H. Nicolas, t. ii. p 330.
⁶ Ibid. p. 344.   ⁷ Ibid. p. 346.   ⁸ Ibid. p. 384.   ⁹ Ibid. p. 411.

Introduction. clv

—a Percy by birth—in Beverley Minster, exhibits how these apparels, on an amice, were sometimes wrought with armorial bearings. Of "corporas cases," there are several here, and pointed out at pp. 112, 144, 145, and 194 of the Catalogue.

Margaret, Countess of Salisbury, the last of the Plantagenets, and mother of Lord Montague and Cardinal Pole, was, like her son the peer, beheaded, and at the age of seventy, by their kinsman Henry VIII. This fact is recorded by Collier;[1] but Miss A. Strickland mentions it more at length in these words:—Cromwell produced in the House of Lords, May 10th, by way of evidence against the aged Countess of Salisbury, a vestment (a chasuble no doubt) of white silk that had been found in her wardrobe, embroidered in front with the arms of England, surrounded with a wreath of pansies and marigolds, and on the back the representation of the host with the five wounds of our Lord, and the name of Jesus written in the midst. The peers permitted the unprincipled minister to persuade them that this was a treasonable ensign, and as the Countess had corresponded with her absent son (Cardinal Pole) she was for no other crime attainted of high treason, and condemned to death without the privilege of being heard in her own defence.[2] The arms of England, amid the quarterings of some great families, are even now to be found upon vestments; a beautiful one was exhibited here, A.D. 1862, and described in the Loan Catalogue, p. 266; another fine one is at present at Abergavenny. With regard to the representation of the "Host with the five wounds of our Lord," &c. this is of very common occurrence in ecclesiastical embroidery; and in this very collection, on the back orphrey to the splendid chasuble, No. 8704, p. 264 of this Catalogue, we find embroidered the crucifixion, and a shield *gules*, with a chalice *or* and a host *argent* at top, done in Flanders full half a century before the "Pilgrimage of Grace" in our northern counties had adopted such a common device upon their banner when the people there arose up against Henry VIII.

To a Surrey, for winning the day at Flodden Field, King Henry VIII. gave the tressured lion of the royal arms of Scotland to be borne upon the Howard bend as arms of augmentation. In after years, the same Henry VIII. cut off a Surrey's head because he bore, as his House had borne from the time of one of their forefathers, Thomas de Brotherton, Edward I.'s son, the arms of the Confessor, the use of which had been confirmed to it by Richard II. If, like Scrope, Surrey had bethought himself of vestments, even of the few we have with the royal arms upon

---

[1] Eccles. Hist. t. v. p. 51, ed. Lathbury. [2] Queens of England, iii. p. 68.

them, and assumed by other English noblemen, perhaps those liturgic embroideries might have stood him in some good stead to save his life. Had the poor aged Countess of Salisbury been heard, she might have shamed ner kinsman the king not to take her life for using upon her church furniture emblems, then as now, employed upon such appliances throughout all Christendom.

For the genealogist, the lawyer, the herald, the historian, such of these old liturgical garments as, like the Syon cope, bear armorial shields embroidered upon them, will have a peculiar value, and a more than ordinary interest. Those emblazonries not only recall the names of men bound up for ever with this land's history, but may again serve, as they once before have served, to furnish the lost link in a broken pedigree, or unravel an entangled point before a law tribunal.

Section X.—BOTANY AND ZOOLOGY.

BY all those for whom, among other allurements drawing them on in their studies of Botany and Zoology, one is the gratification they feel in learning how many of the subjects belonging to these two sections of the natural sciences were known, and how they used to be depicted during the middle ages, this large collection of textiles figured so often with birds, beasts and flowers, will be heartily welcomed.

Our Zoological Society prides itself, and in justice, with treating the Londoners with the first sight of a live giraffe; but here its members themselves may behold, Nos. 8591-91A, p. 224; 8599, p. 228, the earliest known portrait of that curious quadruped sketched upon Sicilian silks of the fourteenth century.

We once listened to a discussion between English sportsmen about the travels of the pheasant from its native home by the banks of the river Phasis at Colchis, and the time when it reached this island. Both parties agreed in believing its coming hither to have been somewhat late. Be that as it may, our country gentlemen will see their favourite bird figured here, No. 1325, p. 60.

About the far-famed hunting cheetahs of India, we have heard, and still hear much; and on pieces of silk from eastern looms, in this collection, they are often to be seen figured.

With regard to the way in which all kinds of fowl, as well as animals are represented on these stuffs, there is one thing which we think will strike most observers who compare the drawing of them here with that of the fame objects among the illuminations in old MSS. The birds and beafts on the textiles are always very much better rendered than in the wood-cuts to be found in our old black-letter books, from Caxton's days upwards, efpecially in fuch works as that of Æfop and the reft. Figures of animals and of birds in manufcripts are hardly better, as we may fee in the prints of our own Sir John Maundevile's Travels, and the French " Beftiaire d'Amour," par R. de Fournival, lately edited by C. Hippeau. Scarcely better does their defign fare in illuminated MSS. Belonging to the Duke of Northumberland, and now in the library at Alnwick caftle is the fineft Salifbury miffal we have ever beheld. This tall thick folio volume was, fome time during the end of the fourteenth century, begun to be written and illuminated by a Benedictine monk—one John Whas—who carried on this gorgeous book as far as page 661. From the two Leonine verfes which we read there, it would feem that this labour of love carried on for years at early morn in the fcriptorium belonging to Sherbourne Abbey, Dorfetfhire, had broken, as well it might, the health of the monk artift, of whom it is faid:—

"Librum fcribendo Ion Whas monachus laborabat;
Et mane furgendo multum corpus macerabat."

Among his other taftes, this Benedictine had that for Natural Hiftory, and in the beautifully illuminated Kalendar at the beginning of this full miffal, almoft every month is pointed out by the prefence of fome bird, or fifh, or flower, peculiar to that feafon, with its name beneath it,—for inftance, " Ys is a throftle," &c. However much the thrufh's fong may have cheered him at his work at Spring-tide peep of day, Whas did not draw his bird with half the individuality and truthfulnefs which we find in birds of all forts that are figured upon Sicilian ftuffs woven at the very period when the Englifh Benedictine was at work within the cloifters of his houfe in Dorfetfhire—a fact which may lead the ornithologift to look with more complacency upon thofe textiles here patterned with Italian birds.

For Botany, it has not gone fo well; yet, notwithftanding this drawback, there are to be feen figured upon thefe textiles plants and trees which, though ftrangers to this land and to Europe, and their forms no doubt, oddly and clumfily reprefented, yet, as they keep about them the fame character, we may fafely believe to have a true type in nature, which at laft by their help we fhall be able to find out. Such is the famous "homa," or "hom,"—the facred tree—among the ancient followers of Zoroafter, as well as the later Perfians. It is to be feen figured on many filks in this collection of real or imitated Perfian textiles, woven at various periods during the middle ages.

From the earliest antiquity a tradition came down throughout middle Asia, of some holy tree—perhaps the tree of life spoken of as growing in Paradise.—Gen. ii. 9. Some such a tree is very often to be seen sculptured on Assyrian monuments; and, by the place which it holds there, must have been held in peculiar, nay religious veneration. Upon those important remains from Nineveh, now in the British Museum, and figured in Mr. Layard's fine work, it appears as the object of homage for the two men symbolized as sacerdotal or as kingly personages, between whom it invariably stands. It is to be found equally figured upon the small bucket meant for religious rites,[1] as embroidered upon the upper sleeve of the monarch's tunic.[2] From Fergusson's "Palaces of Nineveh, and Persepolis restored," we learn that it was frequently to be found sculptured as an architectural ornament. When seen done in needlework upon dresses, the two animals—sometimes winged bulls, sometimes gazelles—which its umbel of seven flowers is separating, are shown with bended knees, as if in worship of it. Always this plant is represented as a shrub, sometimes bearing a series of umbels with seven flowers sprouting, each at the end of a tangled bough; sometimes as a stunted tree with branches growing all the way up right out of a thick trunk with ovated leaves; but the height never looks beyond that of a good sized man. Never for one moment can it be taken as any conventionalism for a tree, since it is as distinct an imitation of a particular plant, as is the figure of the palm which occurs along with it. To us, it has every look of belonging to the family of Asclepiadeæ, or one of its near kindred.

The few Parsees still to be found in East India, are the only followers of Persia's olden religious practices; and in his "Essays on the sacred writings, language, and religion of the Parsees," Haug tells us,[3] that those people yet hold a certain plant—the Homa, or hom?—to be sacred, and from it squeeze a juice to be used by them in their religious services. To our seeming, those buckets in the left hand of many an Assyrian figure were for holding this same liquor.

Can the "hom" of the old Persians be the same as the famous Sidral Almuntaha which bears as many leaves inscribed with names as there are men living on the earth? At each birth a fresh leaf bearing the name of the newly born bursts out, and, when any one has reached the end of his life, the leaf withers and falls off.[4]

---

[1] Layard's Discoveries at Nineveh, abridged, p. 46.   [2] Ibid. p. 245.
[3] Pp. 132, 239.
[4] The Bible, the Koran, and the Talmud, or Biblical Legends of Mussulmans compiled, &c., by Dr. G. Weil, pp. 183, 184.

Though unable to identify among the plants of Asia, which was the "hom" or tree of life, held so sacred by the Assyrians and later Persians, we know enough about that king of fruits—the "pine-apple"—as to correct a great mistake into which those have fallen who hitherto have had to write about the patterns figured on ancient or mediæval textiles. In their descriptions, we are perpetually told of the pine-apple appearing there; and at a period when the Ananas, so far from having been even once beheld in the old world, had never been dreamed of. Among the Peruvians our pine-apple, the "Nanas," was first found and seen by Europeans. Hardly more than two hundred years ago was a single fruit of it brought to any place in the old world. A little over a century has it been cultivated here in England; and, as far as our memory goes, a pine-apple, fifty years ago, had never been planted in any part of Italy or Sicily, nor so much as seen. Writing, October 17, 1716, from Blankenburg, and telling her friend all about a royal dinner at which she had just been, Lady Mary Wortley Montague says:—"What I thought worth all the rest (were) two ripe Ananasses, which, to my taste, are a fruit perfectly delicious. You know they are naturally the growth of Brazil, and I could not imagine how they came here, but by enchantment. Upon enquiry, I learned that they have brought their stoves to such perfection, &c. I am surprised we do not practise in England so useful an invention."[1] As turnips grow in England, so do artichokes all over middle and south Italy, as well as Sicily, large fields are full of them. Put side by side with the pine-apple, and its narrow stiff leaves, the artichoke in bloom amid its graceful foliage, shows well; and every artistic eye will see that the Sicilian weaver, so fond of flowers and nice foliage for his patterns, must have chosen his own vegetable, unfolding its beauties to him at every step he took, and not a fruit of which he had never heard, and which he had never looked upon.

In his description of fruits or flowers woven on a textile, let not the youthful or unwary writer be led astray by older men with a reputation howsoever high for learning other than botanical. Some years ago we were reading with great delight a tale about some things that happened in the third century, and near Carthage. Though avowedly a fiction, most of its incidents were facts, so admirably put together that they seemed to have been drawn by the pen of one who had lived upon the spot. But taking one of his personages to a walk amid the hills running down to the shores of North Africa, the writer leads him through a narrow glen tangled over head, and shaded with sweet smelling creepers and

---

[1] Letters, t. i. p. 105, London, 1763.

climbers, among which he fees the paffion-flower in full bloom. Now, as every fpecies—fave one from China of late introduction—that we have of this genus of plants, came to the old world from the new one, to fpeak of them as growing wild in Africa, quite fourteen hundred years before they could have been feen there, and America was known, is fpoiling a picture otherwife beautifully fketched.

With fome, there perhaps may be a wifh to know what was the origin of this collection.

As is fet forth, in the "Church of Our Fathers,"[1] fome thirty years ago there began to grow up, amid a few, a ftrong defire to behold a better tafte in the building of churches, and the defign of every ecclefiaftical acceffory. Our common fympathies on all thefe points brought together the late Mr. A. Welby Pugin, and him who writes thefe lines, and they became warm friends. What were the refults to Pugin through our intercourfe he himfelf has acknowledged in his "Principles of Pointed or Chriftian Architecture," p. 67. To think of anything and do it, were, with Pugin, two confecutive actions which followed one another fpeedily. While at Birmingham Hardman was working in metal, after drawings by Pugin, and putting together a ftained-glafs window from one of his cartoons, a loom at Manchefter, which had been geared after his idea, was throwing off textiles for church ufe, and orphreys, broad and narrow, were being wove in London: the mediæval court at Hyde Park, in the year 1851, was the gem of our firft Exhibition. Going back, a German lady took from England a cope made of the textiles that had been defigned by Pugin. This veftment got into the hands of Dr. Bock, whofe feelings were, as they ftill are, akin to our own in a love for all the beauties of the mediæval period. While fo glad of his new gift, it fet this worthy canon of Aix-la-Chapelle thinking that other and better patterns were to be feen upon ftuffs of an old and good period, could they be but found. He gave himfelf to the fearch, and took along with him, over the length and breadth of Europe, that energy and fpeed for which he is fo confpicuous; and the gatherings from his many journeys, put together, made up the bulk of a moft cúrious and valuable collection—the only one of its kind —which has found an abiding home in England, at the South Kenfington Mufeum. Thus have thefe beautiful art-works of the loom become, after a manner, a recompenfe moft gratefully received, to the native

---

[1] T. i. pp. 348, &c.

Introduction. clxi

land of those men whose action, some thirty years ago, indirectly originated their being brought together.

Before laying down his pen, the writer of this Catalogue must put on record his grateful remembrances of the kindness shown so readily by M. Octave Delepierre, Secretary of Legation and Consul-General for Belgium, in rendering those inscriptions of old German upon that curious piece of hanging, No. 1297, p. 296, as well as upon another piece of the same kind, No. 1465, p. 298. For the like help afforded about the same, together with those several long inscriptions upon No. 4456, p. 92, the writer is equally indebted to Dr. Appell; and, without the ready courtesy of the Rev. Eugene Popoff, the writer could not have been able to have given the Greek readings, hidden under Cyrillian characters, worked by the needle all around the Ruthenic Sindon, No. 8278, p. 170.

17, Essex Villas,
Kensington

A DESCRIPTIVE CATALOGUE

OF THE COLLECTION OF CHURCH VESTMENTS, DRESSES,

SILK STUFFS, NEEDLEWORK, AND TAPESTRIES

IN THE SOUTH KENSINGTON MUSEUM.

CONTENTS OF THE BOOK.

Part the First.

	Page
CHURCH-VESTMENTS, SILK-STUFFS, NEEDLEWORK AND DRESSES	1

Part the Second.

TAPESTRY	294

The Brooke Collection.

NEEDLEWORK AND DRESSES	312

Lent by Her Majesty, and by the Board of Works.

TAPESTRY	324

INDEX I. Alphabetical	339
INDEX II. Geography of Textiles	355

ILLUSTRATIONS.

No.		Page
84.	HOOD OF A COPE. Embroidered (Coloured plate). *Flemish*, 16th century . . . *Frontispiece*	3
1269.	SILK AND GOLD DAMASK. *Sicilian*, 14th century .	37
1362.	SILK DAMASK. (Coloured plate.) *North Italian, 16th century*	74
1376.	PART OF THE ORPHREY OF A CHASUBLE. *German, 15th century*	82
1376.	PART OF THE ORPHREY OF THE SAME CHASUBLE *German, 15th century*	82
4068.	STRIP OF RAISED VELVET. (Coloured plate.) *North Italian, 16th century*	90
7004.	SILK DAMASK. *Italian, late 16th century* .	113
7039.	SILK DAMASK. *Byzantine, 14th century* . .	123
7043.	SILK DAMASK. *Sicilian, 15th century* . .	125
7795.	SILK DAMASK (BACK OF A BURSE). *Italian, 16th century*	145
8264.	SILK AND GOLD TISSUE. *Sicilian, early 14th century*	166
8265.	LINEN AND SILK TEXTILE. *Spanish, late 14th century*	166
8331.	LACE EMBROIDERY. *Milanese, late 16th century* .	197
8605.	SILK DAMASK. *Italian, 14th century* .	230
8607.	SILK DAMASK. *Sicilian, 14th century*	231

clxviii   *Illustrations.*

No.		Page
8626.	Silk Damask. *Italian, end of* 14th *century*	239
8667.	Silk and Gold Embroidery. Portion of an Orphrey. (Coloured plate.) *German,* 15th *century*	252
8702.	Silk and Linen Damask. *Florentine,* 16th *century*	264
8704.	Part of the Orphrey of a Chasuble. *Flemish, very late* 15th *century*	264
9182.	Part of the Orphrey of the Syon Monastery Cope. *English,* 13th *century*	275

PART THE FIRST.

Church-veſtments, Silk-ſtuffs, Needlework, and Dreſſes.

64.

CHINESE Mandarin's Tunic of Ceremony embroidered in various coloured flos-filks and gold upon an orange-red ſatin. Chineſe. 4 feet high by 6 feet round; modern.

Sprawling all in gold and lively colours, both before and behind, upon this rich garment of ſtate, is figured, with all its hideouſneſs, the imperial five-clawed dragon, before which, according to the royal fancies of that land, the lion turns pale and the tiger is ſtruck with dumbneſs. In the ornamentation the light blue quantity of ſilk is very conſpicuous, more eſpecially upon the broad lower hem of this robe.

78.

CHASUBLE of crimſon velvet, with both orphreys embroidered; the velvet, pile upon pile, and figured with large and ſmall flowers in gold and colour, and other ſmaller flowers in green and white; the orphreys figured with the Apoſtles and the Annunciation. Florentine, late 15th century. 4 feet 3½ inches by 2 feet 5½ inches.

Like moſt other chaſubles, this has been narrowed, at no late period, acroſs the ſhoulders. The velvet is very ſoft and rich, and of that peculiar kind that shows a double pile or the pattern in velvet upon velvet, now so seldom to be found. On the back orphrey, which is quite straight, is shown St. Peter with his keys; St. Paul with a sword; St. John blessing with one hand, and holding a chalice, out of which comes a serpent, in the other; St. James with a pilgrim's hat and staff: on the front orphrey the Annunciation, and St. Simon holding a club, but his person so placed, that, by separating the archangel Gabriel from the Blessed Virgin Mary, a tau-cross is made upon the breast; St. Bartholomew with a knife, and St. James the Less with the fuller's bat. For their greater part, the Gothic niches in which these figures stand, are loom-wrought; but these personages themselves are done on separate pieces of fine canvas and are applied over spaces left uncovered for them. Another curious thing is that in these applied figures the golden parts of the draperies are woven, and the spaces for the heads and hands left bare to be filled in by hand; and most exquisitely are they wrought, for some of them are truly beautiful as works of art.

79.

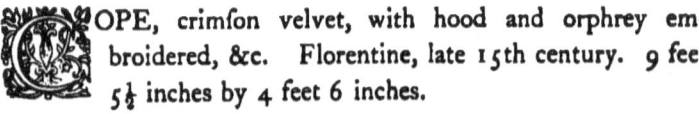
OPE, crimson velvet, with hood and orphrey embroidered, &c. Florentine, late 15th century. 9 feet 5½ inches by 4 feet 6 inches.

This fine cope is of the same set a part of which was the beautiful chasuble No. 78, and, while made of precisely the same costly materials, is wrought with equal care and art. Its large fine hood is figured with the coming down of the Holy Ghost upon the infant Church, represented by the Blessed Virgin Mary amid the Apostles, and not merely this subject itself, but the crimson colour of the velvet would lead us to think that the whole set of vestments was intended for use on Witsunday. On the orphrey, on the right hand, the first saint is St. John the Baptist, with the Holy Lamb; then, Pope St. Gregory the Great; afterwards, an archbishop, may be St. Antoninus; after him a layman-saint with an arrow, and seemingly clad in armour, perhaps St. Sebastian; on the left side, St. George with banner and shield; under him St. Jerome, below whom, a bishop; and lowermost of all St. Onuphrius, hermit, holding in one hand a cross on a staff, in the other a walkingstick, and quite naked, saving his loins, round which he wears a wreath of leaves. All these subjects are admirably treated, and the heads done with the delicacy and truth of miniatures.

84.

OOD of a Cope, figured with the Adoration of the Wife Men. Flemish, 16th century. 1 foot 8¼ inches wide, 1 foot 4¼ inches deep.

This is one of the best preserved and the most beautiful works of the period in the collection, and is remarkable for the goodness of the gold, which is so plentifully bestowed upon it. It is somewhat large, and the three long hooks by which it used to hang are still attached, while its fine green and yellow silk fringe is a pleasing specimen of such a kind of decoration.

540.

PURSE in crimson velvet, embroidered with comic masks, and mounted in chased steel damascened in gold. Attached is a crimson Band with a Buckle of cut and gilt steel. Milanese, 16th century. 11½ inches by 11 inches.

The rich crimson velvet is Genoese; the frame, an art work of the Milan school, is figured with two monsters' heads, and two medallions, one containing a naked youth seated, the other a nude female figure standing. On the front of the bag are applied two embroideries in gold and coloured silk, one an owl's head, the other that of a full-faced grotesque satyr; on the back is another satyr's side-face. At one time, such bags or ornamental purses, under the name of "gibecières" in France and England, but known in Italy as "borsa," were articles of dress worn by most people; and "the varlet with the velvet pouch" will not be forgotten by those who have read Walter Scott's novel of "Quentin Durward." The expressions, in English of "cut-purse," in Italian "taglia borse," for a pickpocket, are well illustrated by this gay personal appendage.

623.

IECE of Edging; ground, purple thread-net; pattern, bunches of flowers, of two sorts alternated, in various coloured flos-silks. Italian, 18th century. 5 feet 5 inches by 5 inches.

Intended for a border to a dress or to a bed-quilt, and no attention shown to the botanical exactness of the flowers, most of which are seemingly tulips. A large coverlet is edged with a broad piece of needlework, after this manner, in the collection.

624.

PIECE of Edging; ground, purple thread-net; pattern, large flowers, mostly the same, embroidered in various coloured flos-silks, within scrolls and foliage. Italian, 18th century. 8 feet 3 inches by 11 inches.

Probably by the same hand as the foregoing piece, and equally careless of botanical exactness in the flowers.

625.

CUSHION-COVER, oblong, centre in striped cherry-coloured silk, the border of open work embroidered in various coloured flos-silks upon a net of purple thread. Italian, 18th century. 2 feet 6 inches by 2 feet.

The only difference in the way of the stitchery is that the geometrical pattern shows the same on both sides.

626.

QUILT for a Bed; ground, an amber-coloured cotton, figured with a net-work of ovals and squares in diapered raised crimson velvet, the ovals filled in with a floriation of crimson and green raised velvet; the squares, with a small vase having a flower-bearing tree, crimson raised velvet. This is the centre, which is bordered by a like kind of stuff 11 inches deep; the ground, primrose yellow; the pattern, ovals, enclosing a foliage bearing crimson and amber-tinted flowers, and placed amid boughs bearing the same coloured flowers; on both edges this border has three stripes—two crimson raised velvet, the

Needlework, and Dresses.

third and broader one a pattern in shades of purple—all on a light yellow ground ; at the ends of the quilt hangs a long partycoloured fringe of linen thread ; the lining of it is fine Chinese silk of a bright amber, figured with sprigs of crimson flowers, shaded yellow and white. Genoese, 17th century. 5 feet 11 inches by 3 feet 10½ inches.

627.

QUILT for a Bed ; ground, brown canvas; pattern, all embroidered scales or scollops jagged like a saw, and overlapping each other in lines, some blue and green shaded white or yellow, some amber. The border is a broad scroll of large flowers, among which one at each corner, the fleur-de-lis, is conspicuous. This again has a scollop edging of flowers separated by what seem two Cs interlaced. French, 17th century. 7 feet 8 inches by 5 feet 8 inches.

673.

CHASUBLE of green silk, figured with animals and scrolls in gold, with an embroidered orphrey at back, and a plain orphrey in front. Sicilian, early 13th century. 3 feet 9¾ inches by 2 feet 2 inches.

This very valuable chasuble is very important for the beauty of its stuff; but by no means to be taken as a sample in width of the fine old majestic garment of that name, as it has been sadly cut down from its former large shape, and that, too, at no very distant period. Though now almost blue, its original colour was green. The warp is cotton, the woof silk, and that somewhat sparingly put in ; the design showing heraldic animals, amid gracefully twining branches all in gold and woven, is remarkably good and free. The front piece is closely resembling the back, but, on a near and keen examination, may be found to differ in its design from the part behind; on this we see that it must have consisted of a lioncel passant gardant, langued, and a griffin ; on that on the part in front, a lioncel passant, and a lioncel passant regardant. When the chafuble was in its firft old fulnefs, the defign on both parts came out in all its minutenefs; now, it is fo broken as not to be difcernible at firft. In front the orphrey is very narrow, and of a fort of open lacework in green and gold; on the back the orphrey is very broad, 1 foot 1¼ inches, and figured with the Crucifixion, the Bleffed Virgin Mary ftanding on our Lord's right hand, St. John the Evangelift on His left; below, the Bleffed Virgin Mary crowned as a queen and feated on a royal throne, with our Lord as a child fitting on her lap; lower ftill, St. Peter with two keys—one filver, the other gold—in his left hand, and a book in the right; and St. Paul holding a drawn fword in his right, and a book in his left; and, laft of all, the ftoning of St. Stephen. All the fubjects are large, and within quatrefoils; as much of the body of our Lord as is uncovered on the Crofs, and the heads, hands, and feet in the other figures, as well as thofe parts of the draperies not gold, are wrought by needle, while the golden garments of the perfonages are woven in the loom.

This very interefting chafuble has a hiftory belonging to it, given in " The Gentleman's Magazine," t. lvi. pp. 298, 473, 584, by which we are taught to believe that it has always been in England; belonging once to it were a ftole and maniple, upon which latter appliance were four armorial fhields, which would lead to the idea that it had been expreffly made for the chapel of Margaret de Clare, Countefs of Cornwall, who is known to have been alive A.D. 1294. That time quite tallies with the ftyle of the ftuff of which this chafuble is made; and though now fo worn and cut away, it is one of the moft curious in this or any other country, and particularly valuable to an Englifh collection.

675.

PIECE of the Bayeux Tapeftry; ground, white linen; defign, two narrow bands in green edged with crimfon (now much faded) with a very thin undulating fcroll in faded crimfon, and green between them. Englifh, 11th century. 3¼ inches by 2½ inches.

Though done in worfted, and fuch a tiny fragment of that great but debated hiftorical work, it is fo far a valuable fpecimen as it fhows the fort of material as well as ftyle and form of ftitch in which the whole was wrought. In the " Vetufta Monimenta," publifhed by the Society

Needlework, and Dresses.

of Antiquaries, plate 17, shows, in large, a portion of this embroidery where the piece before us is figured; and, from the writing under it, we learn that it was brought away from Bayeux by Mrs. Stothard, when her husband was occupied in making drawings of that interesting record. There is not the slightest reason for believing that this embroidery was the work of Matilda, or any of her ladies of honour, or waiting maids; but all the probabilities are that it was done by English hands, may be in London by order, and at the cost, of one or other of three knights from Bayeux, who came over with William, on whom he bestowed much land in England, as we have already shown in the Introduction to this Catalogue, § 4.

698.

DOOR-CURTAIN, ground, yellow and gold; pattern, in rich raised green velvet, two small eagles with wings displayed, and between them a large vase, out of which issues a conventional flower showing the pomegranate, surmounted by a modification of the same fruit amid wide-spreading foliations. Milanese, 16th century. 8 feet 8 inches by 6 feet 6 inches.

Though the golden threads of the ground in this magnificent stuff are much tarnished, still this piece is very fine, and may have been part of some household furniture wrought at the order of the Emperor Charles V, whose German eagle is so conspicuous in the design, while the pomegranate brings to mind Spain and Granada.

699.

PIECE of Embroidery; ground, a brown fine linen, backed with strong canvas; pattern, female figures, monkeys, flowers, shells, &c. in coloured worsteds. French, late 17th century. 8 feet 9 inches by 8 feet 3 inches.

This large work is admirably done, and a fine specimen both of the taste with which the colours are matched, and the stitchery executed; and it may have been intended as the hanging for the wall of a small room.

700.

LADY'S Dress, white silk; embroidered with flowers in coloured silks and gold and silver threads. Chinese, 18th century. 4 feet 2½ inches.

Worked by order, very probably of some European dame, at Macao or Canton, and exactly like No. 713 in design and execution. The gold and silver, as in that, so in this specimen, are much tarnished.

701.

LADY'S Dress, sky-blue satin; brocaded with white flowers, in small bunches. French, late 18th century. 4 feet 7 inches.

702.

CHRISTENING Cloak of green satin, lined with rose-coloured satin. Chinese. 5 feet 8½ inches by 3 feet 6¾ inches.

A fine specimen, in every respect, of Chinese manufacture; the satin itself is of the finest, softest kind; whether we look at the green or the light rose-colour, nothing can surpass either of them in tone and clearness. Few European dyers could give those tints.

In its present form this piece constituted an article to be found, and even yet seen, in very many families in Italy, Germany, and France, and was employed for christening occasions, when the nurse or midwife wore it over her shoulders, like a mantle, for muffling up the new-born babe, as she carried it, in state, to church for baptism. In this, as in other specimens of the Museum, there was a running string at top by which it might be drawn tight to the neck. Those who have lived abroad for even a short time must have observed how the nurse took care to let a little of this sort of scarf hang out of the carriage-window as she rode with baby to church. The christening cloth or cloak was, not long since, in use among ourselves.

703.

HRISTENING Cloak of bright red satin. Italian, 18th century. 5 feet by 5 feet 11 inches.

The material is rich, and of a colour rather affected for the purpose in Italy.

704.

HRISTENING Cloth or Cloak of murrey-coloured velvet. Italian, 17th century. 8 feet by 5 feet 5 inches.

The pile is soft and rich, and its colour, once such a favourite in the by-gone days of England, of a delicious mellow tone. Like Nos. 702 and 703, it robed the nurse as she went to the baptismal font with the new-born child, and has the string round the neck by which it could be drawn, like a mantle, about her shoulders.

705.

ADY'S Dress of brocaded satin; ground, dull red; pattern, slips of yellow flowers and green leaves. Italian, late 18th century. 4 feet 10½ inches.

The satin is rich, but the tinsel, in white silver, tawdry.

706.

KIRT of a Lady's Dress of brocaded silk; ground, white; pattern, bunches of flowers in pink, blue, yellow, and purple, amid a diapering of interlaced strap-design in white floss-silk. French, 18th century. 3 feet 3 inches.

Good in material, but in pattern like many of the stuffs which came from the looms of the period at Lyons.

707.

HRISTENING Scarf of white brocaded silk. Lucca, 17th century. 5 feet square.

Of a fine material and pleasing design.

708.

IECE of green Silk Brocade; pattern, lyres, flowers, ribbons with tassels. French, 18th century. 5 feet 6 inches by 1 foot 8 inches.

709.

KIRT of a Lady's Dress; ground, bright yellow, barred white; pattern, a brocade in small flowers in gold, green, and red sparingly sprinkled about. Italian, 18th century. 7 feet 8 inches by 3 feet 4 inches.

A pleasing specimen of the time.

710.

IECE of White Silk, brocaded with flowers in white floss-silk, and in silver, between bands consisting of three narrow slips in white. French, 17th century. 5 feet by 4 feet 6 inches.

When the silver was bright and untarnished, the pattern, so quiet in itself, must have had a pleasing effect.

711.

HRISTENING Scarf of silk damask; ground, light blue; pattern, flowers in pink, white, and yellow. Levant, 18th century. 5 feet 5 inches by 5 feet.

Garish in look, still it has a value as a specimen of the loom in the eastern parts of the Mediterranean; the blue diapering on the blue ground shows, in the architectural design, a Saracenic influence.

712.

IECE of Damaſk Silk; ground, crimſon; pattern, flowers and vaſes in white and green. Italian, 17th century. 8 feet 9 inches by 1 foot 9 inches.

Rich in ſubſtance, and intended for hangings in ſtate rooms.

713.

KIRT of a Lady's Dreſs; white ſilk embroidered with flowers in coloured ſilks, and gold and ſilver. Chineſe, 18th century. 3 feet.

Though well done, and by a Chineſe hand, very likely at Canton or Macao, for ſome European lady, it is far behind, in beauty, the Chineſe piece No. 792.

714.

HRISTENING Cloak of yellow ſilk damaſk; pattern, bunches of flowers. Lucca, 17th century. 7 feet 10 inches by 5 feet.

Like other ſuch cloaks, or ſcarves, it has its running ſtring, and is of a fine rich texture.

715.

IECE of Silk Damaſk; ground, dove-coloured white; pattern, large foliage in pale green. Italian, 18th century. 4 feet 8 inches by 3 feet 8 inches.

A fine material, and the bold deſign well brought out.

716.

HRISTENING Cloak of pink ſatin damaſk. Italian, 18th century. 4 feet 8 inches by 4 feet 6 inches.

The little ſprigs of fruits and flowers are well arranged; and the pomegranate is diſcernible among them.

717.

IECE of Silk Brocade; ground, stone-white chequered silk; pattern, deep blue garlands and bunches of flowers, both dotted with smaller flowers in silver. Italian, 17th century. 3 feet 8 inches by 3 feet.

718.

IECE of Embroidered Silk; ground, sky-blue; pattern, leaves, flowers, and fruit, in white silk. Italian, 18th century. 3 feet 8 inches by 3 feet.

The embroidery is admirably done, and the pomegranate is there among the fruit.

719.

OOR-CURTAIN, crimson worsted velvet; pattern, flowers and foliage. Italian, 17th century. 10 feet 3 inches by 4 feet 3 inches.

A very fine and rich specimen of its kind, and most likely wrought at Genoa.

720.

IECE of Silk; ground, white; pattern, flowers and foliage, embroidered in gold thread and coloured silks. Chinese, 18th century. 3 feet 2½ inches by 1 foot 6½ inches.

Another specimen of Chinese work done for Europeans, and most likely after an European design; in character resembling other examples in this collection from the same part of the world.

Needlework, and Dresses.

721.

PIECE of Silk; ground, white; pattern, flowers and pomegranates embroidered in gold and coloured silks. Neapolitan, 17th century. 3 feet 3 inches by 1 foot 5 inches.

The design is rich, the flowers well-raised, and the gold unsparingly employed.

722.

CRADLE-COVERLET; white satin quilted, after a design of fruits, and branches of leaves upon a chequer pattern. French, 18th century. 3 feet 2¼ inches by 3 feet.

Among the fruits the symbolic pomegranate is not forgotten, perhaps as expressive of the wish that the young mother to whom this quilt may have been given by a lady friend, might have a numerous offspring, hinted at by the many pips in the fruit.

723.

DOOR-CURTAIN of silk damask; ground, crimson; pattern, scrolls in gold foliage, and flowers in coloured silks. Italian, early 17th century. 6 feet 7 inches by 3 feet 5 inches.

This is a fine rich stuff; it is lined with purple satin, and must have been very effective when in use.

724.

CHASUBLE of woven silk; ground, white; pattern, floral scrolls in green, and lined pink; the cross at the back and the two stripes in front in gold lace of an open design. French, 18th century. 4 feet 2 inches by 2 feet 5 inches.

The open-worked lace is good of its kind.

725.

ALTAR-FRONTAL of crimson velvet, ornamented on three sides with a scroll ornamentation in gold, and applied; and with seven armorial bearings all the same. French, 17th century. 6 feet 1 inch by 2 feet 6½ inches.

The armorial shield, as it stands at present, is—*azure* a cross ankred *sable* between two fleur-de-lis *argent*. On looking narrowly at the azure velvet on which these charges are worked, it is evident that something has been picked out, and, in its place, the sable-cross has been afterwards wrought in, thus explaining the anomaly of colour upon colour not in the original bearing. The applied ornaments in gold are in flowers and narrow gold lace, and of a rich and effective manner.

726.

CRADLE-COVERLET of white satin; embroidered in white, with a roving border of flowers, and fringed. French, 18th century. 3 feet 5½ inches by 2 feet 8 inches.

Rich in its material, and nicely wrought.

727.

SKIRT of a Lady's Dress; sky-blue satin, quilted round the lower border with a scroll of large palmate leaves, and bunches of flowers, with an edging of fruits, in which the pomegranate may be seen. Italian, 18th century. 8 feet 9 inches by 3 feet.

The pattern in which the quilting comes out is very tasteful; and the body of this skirt has an ornamentation in quilting of a cinquefoil shape, and made to lap one over the other in the manner of tiles.

Needlework, and Dresses.

728.

IECE of Silk Damask; ground, bright yellow silk ribbed; pattern, white plumes twined with brown ribbons, and bunches of white flowers. Lucca, 17th century. 8 feet 10 inches by 7 feet.

Of rich material and wrought for household use.

729.

OOR-CURTAIN of yellow silk damask; pattern, strap-work and conventional foliage. Italian, 17th century. 7 feet 2 inches by 5 feet.

A bold design, and wrought in a good material.

730.

OPE of brocaded silk; ground, orange-red; pattern, foliage, and bunches of flowers amid white garlands, in coloured silks. French, 18th century. 10 feet 10 inches by 5 feet 6 inches.

The hood and morse are of the same stuff, which was evidently meant to be for secular, not liturgical, use.

731.

OOR-CURTAIN of crimson damask silk; pattern, a large broad conventional floriation. Italian, 17th century. 10 feet by 8 feet 10 inches.

732.

CURTAIN of pale sea-green damask; pattern, large leaves and flowers. Italian. 17 feet 8 inches by 13 feet 7 inches.

The satiny ground throws up the design in its dull tone extremely well; and the whole is edged with a border of narrow pale yellow lace, figured with small green sprigs.

750.

TABLE-COVER; ground, fine ribbed cream-coloured linen; pattern, flowers, butterflies, and birds, embroidered in various-coloured flos-silks. Indian, 17th century. 7 feet by 5 feet 6 inches; fringe 3 inches deep.

The curiosity of this piece is that, like many such works of the needle from India, the embroidery shows the same on both sides; and there is evidently a Gothic feeling in the edgings on the borders of the inner square.

786.

SCULL-CAP of white satin; quilted after an elaborate running design. English, 17th century. 10¼ inches diameter.

Tradition tells us that this scull-cap belonged to our King Charles the First, and says, moreover, that, at his beheading, it was worn by that unfortunate King. The style of design would not, as far as art-worth can speak, invalidate such a history of this royal ownership. Its lining is now quite gone.

792.

PIECE of Chinese Embroidery; ground, greyish white satin; pattern, girls, flowers, birds, fruits, and insects in various-coloured flos and thread silks, and gold. 11 feet by 1 foot 7 inches.

Justly may we look upon this specimen as one among the best and most beautiful embroideries wrought by the Chinese needle known, not merely in this country, but in any part of Europe. Putting aside the utter want of perspective, and other Chinese defective notions of art, it is impossible not to admire the skilful way in which the whole of the piece before us is executed. In the female figures there seems to be much truthfulness with regard to the costume and manners of that country; and the sharp talon-like length of finger-nails affected by the ladies there is conspicuously shown in almost every hand. The birds, the insects, the flowers are all admirably done; and the tones of colour are

Needlework, and Dresses.

so soft and well assorted, and there is such a thorough Chinese taste displayed in the choice of tints—tints almost unknown to European dyers—that the eye is instantly pleased with the production. The embroidery itself is almost entirely well raised.

839.

IECE of Velvet Hanging; ground, crimson velvet; pattern, large conventional flowers and branches in yellow applied silk. Italian, 17th century. 6 feet 4 inches by 1 foot 8 inches.

This piece is rather a curiosity for the way in which its design is done. On the plain length of velvet a pattern was cut, and the void spaces were filled in with yellow silk, and the edges covered with a rather broad and flat cording, and the whole—that is, velvet and silk—gummed on to a lining of strong canvas, having the cord only stitched to it.

840.

IECE of Applied Work; ground, crimson velvet; pattern, large conventional flowers in yellow satin. Italian, 17th century. 2 feet 6 inches by 2 feet 3 inches.

Here the same system is followed, but the ground is yellow satin uncut, the crimson velvet being cut out so as to make it look the ground, and the real ground the design, both are, as above, gummed on coarse canvas.

841.

IECE of Velvet Hanging; ground, yellow silk; pattern, scrolls and flowers in applied crimson velvet. Italian, 17th century. 6 feet 4 inches by 1 foot 9 inches.

Executed exactly as No. 840. In all likelihood these three pieces served as hangings to be put at open windows on festival days—a custom yet followed in Italy.

842.

IECE of Raised Velvet; ground, pale yellow silk; pattern, in raised velvet, a fan-like floriation in crimson and green. Florentine, 16th century. 3 feet 2 inches by 2 feet 1 inch.

A specimen of rich household decoration.

843.

AISED Velvet; ground, creamy white satin; pattern, the artichoke amid wide-spreading ramifications in crimson raised velvet. Genoese, 17th century. 2 feet 1 inch by 1 foot 8¼ inches.

Intended for household furniture. When hung upon the walls of a large room this stuff must have had a fine effect.

882.

KIRT of Female Attire; ground, coarse white linen; pattern, a broad band of blue worsted, figured with flowers and animals in white thread, and the broad edging of crochet work. German, 17th century. 3 feet 8¼ inches by 2 feet 8 inches deep.

This piece of embroidery must have been for secular personal use, and not for any ecclesiastical employment, and very likely was part of the holyday dress of some country girl in Germany or Switzerland. The blue embroidery, though of a bold well-raised character, is coarse; so, too, is the lace below it.

1029.

AN Algerine Embroidered Scarf; ground, very thin canvas; pattern, a modification of the artichoke form, and ramifications in various-coloured flos-silks, and parted by short bands of brace-like work in white flos-silk. 2 feet 3¾ inches by 1 foot 3¾ inches.

Neither old, nor remarkable as an art-work.

1030.

ABLE-COVER of linen, embroidered in white thread, with flowers, vases, trophies, and monograms. French, 18th century. 4 feet 4 inches by 3 feet 10 inches.

This beautifully-executed piece of needlework is richly deserving a notice from those who admire well-finished stitchery, which is here seen to advantage. In the centre is a basket with wide-spreading flowers, upon each side of which is a military trophy consisting of cannon-balls, kettle-drums, other drums, knights' tilting-lances, halberts, swords, cannon, trumpets, all gracefully heaped together and upholding a herald's tabard blazoned with a leopard rampant, by the side of which, and drooping above, are two flags, one showing the three fleurs-de-lis of France, and the other with a charge that is indistinct; and the whole is surmounted by a full-faced barred helmet wreathed with a ducal coronet, out of which arises a plume of ostrich feathers; on the other sides are two elegantly-shaped vases full of flowers. At each of the four corners of this inner square is the monogram A. M. V. P. T. between boughs, and surmounted by a ducal coronet; and at every corner of the border below is a flaming heart pierced by two arrows, while all about are eagles with wings displayed and heads regardant, seemingly heraldic.

1031.

IECE of Silk Brocade; ground, white; pattern, large red flowers seeded yellow, and foliage mostly light green. Lyons, 18th century. 2 feet 10 inches by 1 foot 9 inches.

A specimen of one of those large showy flowered tissues in such favour all over Europe during the last century, as well as in the earlier portion of the present one, for church use. The example before us, in all probability, served as a bishop's lap-cloth at solemn high mass; for which rite, see " The Church of our Fathers," i. 409.

1032.

PIECE of Silk and Silver Brocade; ground, a brown olive; pattern, large flowers, some lilac, but mostly bright crimson, intermixed with much silver ornamentation. Lyons, 18th century. 2 feet 8¼ inches, by 1 foot 8¼ inches.

Another specimen of the same taste as No. 1031, but even more garish. Like it, it seems to have served the purpose of a liturgical lap-cloth, or, as it used to be called, a barm-cloth.

1033.

LECTERN-VEIL; ground, yellow satin; pattern, conventional flowers in applied velvet in blue, green, and crimson. Italian, early 17th century. 6 feet 6 inches by 1 foot 8 inches.

In fact the whole of this liturgical veil for the deacon's book-stand is of the so-called " applied style;" that is, of pieces of satin and of velvet cut out to the required shape, and sewed on the canvas ground, and the edges bordered with a cord of silk, mostly white; and altogether it has a rich appearance.

1035.

BED-COVERLET; ground, white thread net; pattern, flowers in white thread. Spanish, 17th century. 6 feet 5 inches by 5 feet 3¼ inches.

This specimen of netting and crochet needlework displays much taste in its design of flowers, among which the rose and the pomegranate are very conspicuous. It was wrought in four strips joined together by narrow linen bands, and the whole edged with a shallow fringe.

Needlework, and Dresses.

1037, 1037 A.

IECES of Stuff for Silk Sashes; pattern, perpendicular bars, some whity-brown figured with gold and silver flowers, some plain olive green, and bordered on both edges of the stuff with bands of whity-brown ornamented with sprigs of gold flowers. Oriental, 16th century. 2 feet 4¼ inches, by 11 inches.

The trimming and cross, done in tinsel, show that its last European use was for the church; in the East, such silken stuffs, in long lengths, are worn about the waist by men and women as a sash or girdle.

1038.

HASUBLE-BACK; ground, green satin; design, scrolls in raised red silk thread. 18th century. Satin, French. 3 feet 8 inches by 2 feet 2 inches.

Very likely the satin formed some part of a lady's gown, and for its richness was given to the church for making vestments. As a ritual garment it could not have looked well, nor is its gaudy red embroidery in good taste for any ecclesiastical purpose.

1039.

AISTCOAT-PATTERN, embroidered and spangled. Second half of the 18th century. French. 10 inches by 7¼ inches.

Of such stuffs were gentlemen's vests made in Paris under Louis XV, and in London at the beginning of George III.'s reign.

1194, 1195.

RPHREYS for a Chasuble; ground, crimson silk; design, an angel-choir in two rows amid wreaths, of which the flowers are silver and the leaves gold, some shaded green; on the back orphrey are two heraldic bearings. German, very late 15th century.

This beautifully-wrought specimen of Rhenish needlework, most likely done at Cologne, confists of twenty-six small figures of winged angels robed in various liturgical vestments, and playing musical instruments of all sorts—some wind, some stringed. Of these celestial beings several wear copes over their white albs; others have over their albs narrow stoles, in some instances crossed upon the breast as priests, but mostly belt-wise as deacons: other some are arrayed in the sub-deacon's tunicle, and the deacon's dalmatic: thus vested they hold the instrument which each is playing; and no one but a German would have thought of putting into angels' hands such a thing as the long coarse aurochs' horn wherewith to breathe out heavenly music. On the front orphrey are ten of such angels; on the one made in the shape of a cross, for the back of the chasuble, there are sixteen. At both ends of the short beam or transom of this cross we find admirably-executed armorial bearings. The first blazon—that to the left—shows a shield *gules* an inescutcheon *argent*, over all an escarbuncle of eight rays *or*, for CLEVES.; dimidiated by, *or* a fess checky *argent* and *gules*, for MARCK; surmounted by a helmet *argent* crested with a buffalo's head cabosed *gules*, having the shut-down bars of the helmet's visor thrust out through the mouth of the animal, which is crowned ducally *or* the attire *argent* passing up within the crown; and the mantlings *gules*. As if for supporters, this shield has holding it two angels, one in a tunicle, the other in a cope. The second shield—that on the right hand,—shows *gules* an inescutcheon *argent*, over all, an escarbuncle of eight rays *or*, crested and supported as the one to the left, thus giving, undimidiated, the blazon of the then sovereign ducal house of CLEVES.

All these ornaments, armorial bearings, angels, flowers, and foliage, are not worked into, but wrought each piece separately, and afterwards sewed on the crimson silk ground, which is the original one; they are "cut work." The angels' figures are beautifully done, and their liturgic garments richly formed in gold, as are the leaves and stems of the wreaths bearing large silver flowers. From its heraldry we may fairly assume that the chasuble, from which these handsome orphreys were stripped, belonged to the domestic chapel in the palace of the Dukes of Cleves, and had been made for one of those sovereigns whose wife was of the then princely stirring house of De la Marck.

As was observed, while describing the beautiful Syon Cope, No. 9182, the nine choirs of angels separated into three hierarchies is indicated here also; and the distinction marked by the garments which they are made to wear in these embroideries; some are clothed in copes, others in tunicles, the remainder, besides their narrow stoles, in long-flowing white albs only—that emblem of spotless holiness in which all of them are garmented, as with a robe of light. The bufhinefs of the auburn hair on all of them is remarkable, and done in little locks of filk.

For a ftudent of mediæval mufic, this angel-choir will have an efpecial intereft; but, to our thinking, neither this, nor any other production of the fubject, whether wrought in fculpture, painting, or needlework, hitherto found out on the Continent, at all comes up in beauty, gracefulnefs, or value, to our own lovely minftrel-gallery in Exeter Cathedral, or the far more fplendid and truly noble angel-choir fculptured in the fpandrils of the triforium arches in the matchlefs prefbytery at Lincoln Minfter. A caft of the Exeter minftrel-gallery is put up here on the weftern wall of the north court, and among the cafts lent by the Architectural Society are thofe of the angels in Lincoln.

Of the mufical inftruments themfelves, we fee feveral in thefe two pieces of cut-work. Beginning with the back orphrey, marked No. 1194 at top, the firft of the two angels is playing with the fingers of both hands an inftrument now indifcernible; the fecond, the lute; below them one is beating a tabour with a ftick; the other is turning the handle of the gita, our hurdy-gurdy. After thefe we have an angel blowing a fhort horn, while his fellow angel ftrikes the pfaltery. Then an angel robed as a deacon in alb, and ftole worn like a belt falling from his right fhoulder to under his left arm, founding the fiftrum or Jew's harp, and his companion fingers with his right hand a one-ftringed inftrument or ancient monochord. In the laft couple, one with a large bow is playing the viol, a long narrow inftrument with feveral filver ftrings.

On the orphrey,—made in the fhape of a crofs and worn on the back of the chafuble, No. 1195,—the firft angel plays the pan-pipes; the fecond, a gittern, or the modern guitar; the next two fhow one angel, as a deacon in dalmatic, jingling an inftrument which he holds by two ftraps, hung all round with little round ball-like bells; and his companion, robed in alb and ftole croffed at the breaft like a prieft, ringing two large hand-bells; lower down, of the two angels both vefted as deacons, one blowing a large, long curved-horn, like that of the aurochs, the other, the fhalmes or double-reeded pipe. Below thefe, one in alb and ftole, belt-wife as a deacon, blows a cornamufe or bag-pipe; the other, as deacon, the aurochs' horn. Then a deacon angel has a trumpet; his fellow, a prieft in alb and croffed ftole, is playing a triangle; laft of all, one plays a tabour, the other the monochord. So note-worthy are thefe admirable embroideries, that they merit particular attention.

1233.

STOLE; ground, very pale yellow filk; defign, an interlacing ftrap-work in the greater part; for the expanding ends, a diamond in gold thread, with a fringe of filk knots alternately crimfon and green; the lining, thin crimfon filk. Englifh or French, 13th century. 9 feet 9 inches by 1¾ inches in the narrow parts, and 2¼ inches in the expanded ends.

Another of thofe fpecimens of weaving in fmall looms worked by young women in London and Paris, during the 13th century, which we have met in this collection. As the expanded ends are formed of fmall pieces of gold web they were wrought apart, and afterwards fewed on to the crimfon filk ground. The defign of the narrow part has all along its length, at its two edges, a pair of very fmall lines, now brown, enclofing a dented ornament. As a liturgical appliance, this ftole, for its perfect ftate of prefervation, is valuable; Dr. Bock fays that a ftole called St. Bernhard's, now in the church of our Lady at Treves, as well as another curious one in the former cathedral at Afchaffenburg, are in length and breadth, juft like this.

1234.

ISSUE of Silk and Cotton; the warp, cotton; the woof, filk; ground, green; defign, fo imperfect that it can hardly be made out, but apparently a monfter bird in yellow, lined and dotted in crimfon; ftanding on a border of a yellow ground marked with croffes and mullets of four points. Syrian, late 12th century. 6¼ inches by 4¼ inches.

When perfect this ftuff muft have been fomewhat garifh, from its colours being fo bright and not well contrafted.

1235.

ISSUE of Silk and Cotton; the warp, filks of different colours; the woof, fawn-coloured fine cotton; defign, ftripes, the broader ones charged with wild beafts, eagles, and a monster animal having a human head; the narrow bands showing a pretended Arabic inscription. Syrian, 13th century. 13 inches by 2 inches.

So very torn and worn away is this piece that the whole of its elaborate design cannot be made out; but enough is discernible to prove an Asiatic influence. The monster, with the human face staring at us, calls to mind the Nineveh sculptures in the British Museum.

1236.

SILK Damask; ground, crimson silk; pattern, in gold thread, two very large lions, and two pairs, one of very small birds, the other of equally small dragons, and an ornament not unlike a hand looking-glass. Oriental, 14th century. 2 feet 5¼ inches by 2 feet ¼ inch.

A piece of this same stuff is described under No. 7034 in this catalogue; and Dr. Bock, in his useful work, "Geschichte der Liturgischen Gewänder des Mittelalters," t. i. plate iv. has figured it.

1237.

TISSUE of Silk; ground, dull reddish deep purple; design, a lozenged diapering. South Italian, 13th century. 6½ inches by 5½ inches.

So thin is this web that we may presume it was meant as a stuff for lining garments of a richer texture.

1238.

PIECE of Linen, or the finest byssus of antiquity. Egyptian. 5½ inches by 3 inches.

Whether this very curious example of that rare and fine tissue known in classic times, and later, as byssus, was of mediæval production in Egypt, or found in one of the ancient tombs of that land, would be hard to determine. Another equally fine and no lefs valuable fpecimen may be feen in this collection, No. 8230.

From Dr. Bock we learn that the fudary of our Lord, given to the Abbey of Cornelimünfter, near Aix-la-Chapelle, by the Emperor Louis the Pious, circa A.D. 820, was much like the prefent example.

1239.

PIECE of Silk Damafk; ground, creamy white; defign, broad-banded lozenges, enclofing a two-headed difplayed eagle, and a pair of birds addorfed, each within an oval. Greek, 11th century. $10\frac{1}{4}$ inches by $7\frac{1}{4}$ inches.

It is faid to have been a fragment of the imperial tunic belonging to Henry II, Emperor of Germany; and not unlikely. If wrought for the occafion, and a gift from his imperial brother-Emperors of Conftantinople, Bafil and Conftantine, worthy was it for their fending and of his acceptance, fince the filk is rich, the texture thick, and the defign in accordance with the enfigns of German royalty. In fhreds, and ragged as it is, we may prize it as a valuable piece.

1240.

PIECE of Silk and Cotton Damafk; ground, a yellowifh green; defign, large elliptical fpaces filled in with Saracenic figurations. The warp is of green cotton, the woof, of pale yellow filk. South of Spain, 14th century. $16\frac{1}{4}$ inches by $4\frac{3}{4}$ inches.

This ftrong ftuff moft likely came from the looms of Granada.

1240 A.

PIECE of Silk and Cotton. Another piece of the fame texture.

1241.

SILK and Cotton Damask; ground, blue; design, circles filled in with conventional ornamentation in crimson (now faded). Greek, 13th century. 15¼ inches by 7¼ inches.

In some very small parts of the pattern, at first sight, indications appear of four-footed animals, but the outlines are a fortuitous combination. This stuff is poor in material, and the design not very artistic.

1242.

SILK and Cotton Damask; ground, light green; design, a Saracenic pattern formed by lines in long lozenges. South of Spain, 14th century. 9¾ inches by 7 inches.

Much like in tint and style of pattern the fine specimen at No. 1240. In both the Moslem's sacred colour of green may be noticed, and the two pieces may have been woven at Granada.

1243.

DAMASK, silk and linen; ground, crimson and yellow stripes; design, on the crimson stripes, circles enclosing a lion rampant, and six-petaled flowers, in yellow; on the yellow, one stripe with flowers in white silk, the other with flowers in gold, now faded black. Syrian, 14th century. 7¼ inches by 6¼ inches.

The quality of this damask is coarse, from the great quantity of thread of a thick size wrought up in it. The design has no particular merit.

1244—1244 C.

PIECES of Damask; ground, gold; design, in crimson silk, broad round hoops, marked with a golden floriation, and enclosing a lion passant, the spaces between the hoops filled in with a floriated square topped by fleur-de-lis. Sicilian, 14th century. Each piece about 4¼ inches square.

When whole the design of this rich stuff must have been effective, and the fragments we here have prove it to have been sketched in a bold free style. Unfortunately, so bad was the gold that, in places, it has turned green. The warp is of a thick linen thread, but, though it gives a strength to the texture, is not to be perceived upon its face.

1245.

PIECE of Silk and Gold Damask; ground, crimson silk; design, a network formed by cords twined into circles enclosing four V's, put so as to form a cross, and the meshes filled in alternately with a flower and a leaf, each surrounded by a line like an eight-petaled floriation, all in gold thick thread. Sicilian, 14th century. 5 inches by 4¾ inches.

The way in which the pattern affects the form of a cross in its design is remarkable.

1246.

SILK Damask; ground, brick-red; design, within broad-banded squares, ornamented with stars and flowers, a large double-headed eagle with wings displayed. Greek, 13th century. 12¼ inches by 8 inches.

Being so very thin in texture, it is not surprising that this stuff is in such a tattered condition. When new, it must have been meant, not for personal wear, but rather for church purposes, or household use, as the hanging of walls. Its design is not happy, and the ornamentation about the eagle thick and heavy.

1247.

NARROW Web for Orphreys; ground, a broad stripe of crimson silk between two narrow ones of green; design, a succession of oblong six-sided spaces in gold, filled in with a sort of floriated cross having sprouting from both ends of the upright beam, stalks bending inwards and ending in a fleur-de-lis, all in red filk. French, 13th century. 3¼ inches by 1⅞ inches.

Of this kind of textile, wrought by women in a fmall loom, we have before us in this collection feveral fpecimens; and what was done by poor females at the time in England and France, it is likely was performed by induftrious women elfewhere. The fleur-de-lis upon this fragment leads us to think of France; but Dr. Bock informs us that laces much like this in pattern were obferved upon the royal robes in which two princes of the imperial houfe of the Hohenftaufen were clad for their burial, when their graves were opened in the cathedral of Palermo.

1248.

IECE of Silk and Gold Brocade; ground, blue filk; defign, a broad border with large pretended Arabic letters, and a griffin(?) fegreant, both in gold. Sicilian, early 13th century. 8¼ inches by 4⅞ inches.

The heraldic monfter-bird here, fuppofed to be a griffin, is drawn and executed in a very fpirited manner.

1249.

INEN, embroidered, in gold and filk, with the figure of a king. German, late 12th century. Diameter 6¾ inches.

The figure of this grim-bearded perfonage is carefully worked, and the gold employed is good though thin. Upon his head he wears a crown, fuch as are figured upon the monuments of the time; the face is badly drawn, but the ermine lining of his mantle is carefully reprefented.

1250.

N Orphrey; ground, gold; defign, various fubjects from Holy Writ, with borders; the whole length figured with monfters, floriations, and an infcription. French, 13th century. 4 feet 2 inches by 7 inches.

In all probability this orphrey belonged to the back of a chafuble, and, as fuch, the fubjects figured in it would find an appropriate place there; but it ought to be obferved that, in reality, it is made up of four portions, the two narrow bands, befides the long and the fhort lengths of the middle or broad parts which they border. At top we have the Crucifixion, wherein each of our Lord's feet is faftened by its own feparate nail. On one fide of His head is the fun, on the other the moon; St. Mary and St. John are ftanding on the ground befide Him; and, at the crofs's foot, looks out a head, that of Adam, which, whether from accident or defign, has very much the fhape of a lion's with a fhaggy mane; one of the fymbols belonging to our Lord is a lion, in token of the refurrection. Some way down a female, crowned and wimpled, bears in both her hands, which are muffled in a veil, a golden-covered cup,—very likely Mary Magdalen, with her veffel full of coftly fpikenard for anointing our Saviour's feet againft the day of His burying. Oppofite to her is St. Michael, fpearing Satan, an emblem of the great atonement, as is fhown under No. 9182, while defcribing the Syon Cope. Lower down we have the three women or, as they are fometimes called, Maries, with their fweet fpices, and the angel telling them of the uprifing of our Redeemer. Lower yet, our Lord's Afcenfion is reprefented by fhowing Him feated in majefty with both His arms outftretched, within an almond-fhaped glory. On the fecond or fhorter length, and, as far as the Gofpel hiftory is concerned, out of its due place, we behold the Annunciation, and a little under that fubject a row of four nimbed and feemingly winged heads, like thofe of the cherubim, may be fymbols of the four evangelifts. At each fide of thefe fubjects runs a border of gold wrought with lions crowned, and imaginary winged monfter-animals feparated by graceful floriations; and on one of thefe borders, at the lower end, is worked this infcription—" Odilia me fecit," in nicely fhaped letters. This female name was common in Auvergne, where St. Odilo, the fixth abbot of Cluni, was born, a fon of the noble houfe of Mercœur, and, to our thinking, it is very likely this Odilia was a daughter of one of the lords of that once great family in the South of France.

So worn away is this curious orphrey that often the feveral fubjects figured on in the loom, and not by the needle, can be hardly made out till held in various lights.

1251.

RINTED Silk Taffeta; ground, very light purple; defign, a fcroll, block-printed in deeper purple, and edged black. Sicilian, 13th century. 8¾ inches by 6 inches.

The boughs, fprouting into a fort of trefoil, are gracefully twined with a bold free hand; and the fcroll reminds us of much of the like fort of ornament found, in this country, on various art-works of its time. As an early fpecimen of block-printing upon filk, it is valuable and rare.

1252.

ART of an Altar-Frontal, embroidered, in coloured threads, upon coarfe canvas; defign, within a medallion, the ground, light blue and broad border, fawn-colour, a figure, feated, holding in his left-hand a ftaff, and having on his knee an open book infcribed,—" Ego fum Liber Vite." The figure is clothed in a girded white tunic, and a mantle now fawn-coloured; but the head is fo damaged that the perfonage cannot be recognized; the probability is that it reprefents our Lord in majefty, having the ftaff of a crofs in one hand and giving His bleffing with the other. German, early 12th century, 12¾ inches by 10 inches.

1252A.

ART of an Altar-Frontal; defign, the bufts of two winged and nimbed angels, within round arches, bearing between them a white fcroll with thefe words—" Deus Sabaoth." This was a portion of the frontal mentioned above. German, early 12th century. 17 incnes by 7¼ inches. In both pieces the parts now fawn-coloured have faded into fuch from crimfon.

1253.

SILK Damask; ground, fawn-colour; design, in light green, a sprinkling of fleur-de-lis amid griffins, in pairs, rampant, regardant. Sicilian, 14th century. 10 inches by 8 inches.

The pattern is not of that spirited character found on many of the earlier specimens of the Sicilian loom; the griffins, especially, are weakly drawn. The fleur-de-lis would signify that it was wrought for some French family or follower of the house of Anjou.

1254.

SILK Damask; ground, crimson; design, a diapering of birds pecking at a cone-like ornament ending in a fleur-de-lis, all in yellow. Sicilian, 14th century. 5 inches by 4 inches.

A very thin stuff with a pattern of a small but pretty design. What the birds are with their long square tails is hard to guess; so, too, with respect to the ornament between them, like a fir-cone purfled at its sides with crockets, and made to end in a flower, which may have some reference to the French family of Anjou, once reigning in Sicily. The stuff itself is poor and may have been woven for linings to richer silks.

1255.

SHRED of Silk Damask; ground crimson; design, seemingly horsemen separated by a large circular ornament in one row, and the gable of a building in the other, in yellow and blue. Greek, 12th century. 8 inches by 6¼ inches.

Though this stuff be thin and poor, the design, could it be well seen, would be curious. The circle seems a leafless but branchy tree, with a low wall round it; and the gable is full of low pillared arches with voids for windows in them.

1256.

FRAGMENTS of Narrow Orphrey Web; ground, crimson; design, in gold ramified scrolls, with beasts and birds. English or French, 13th century. 10¼ inches by 3 inches.

This very handsome piece is another specimen of the small loom worked by young women, as before noticed; and may have served either for sacred or secular use. The band is parted into spaces by a thin chevron, and each division so made is filled in with tiny but gracefully-twined boughs, among which some times we have a pair of birds, at others a pair of collared dogs; at top another arrangement took place, but no more of it remains than the body of a lion.

1257.

SILK and Thread Tissue; ground, stripes of red, green, and yellow; design, rows of circles, large and small, with a conventional flower between, the large circles red, the small ones merely outlined in white. Greek, 13th century. 8¼ inches by 6 inches.

Even when new it must have been flimsy, and could have served but for a lining. Of exactly the same design, but done in other and fewer colours, a specimen now at Paris is figured in the "Mélanges d'Archéologie," tome iii. plate 15.

1258.

SILK and Cotton Damask; ground, yellow; design, a net-work with six-sided meshes, each filled in with flowers and foliage in deep dull purple. Italian, late 13th century. 14 inches by 10 inches.

The well-turned and graceful foliation to be seen in architectural scroll-work, on monuments raised at the period, enters largely into the design; and for its pattern, though poor for the quantity of its silk, this specimen is very good.

1259.

PIECE of a Napkin; ground, nicely diapered in lozenges, all white; defign, horizontal dark brown ftripes, with a lined pattern in white upon them. Flemifh, 16th century. 24 inches by 13 inches.

Moft likely Yprès fent forth this pleafing example of fine towel linen.

1260.

EMBROIDERY for liturgical ufe; ground, dark blue filk; defign, our Lord, as the "Man of Sorrows," within a quatrefoil flowered at the barbs in gold thread fewed on with crimfon filk. Italian, 15th century. 6 inches fquare.

The figure of our Redeemer, wrought upon linen with white filk, much of which is worn away, is holding His wounded hands crofs-wife, and a fcourge under each arm. From His brows, wreathed with thorns, trickle long drops of blood; and the whole, with the large bleeding gaping wound in His fide, ftrikingly reminds us of the wood-cut to be found at the beginning of our Salifbury Grails, or choir-books, with thofe anthems fung at high mafs, called graduals. In England fuch reprefentations were ufually known under the name of "S. Gregory's Pity," as may be feen in "The Church of our Fathers," t. i. p. 53. This embroidery is figured by Dr. Bock, in his "Gefchichte der Liturgifchen Gewänder des Mittelalters," I. Band, II. Lieferung, pl. 14.

1261.

THE Embroidered Apparel for an Amice; ground, crimfon flos-filk, now faded; defign, large and fmall fquares, green, blue, and purple, filled in with gold, and modifications of the gammadion, in white or crimfon filks. German, 14th century. 14 inches by 5¼ inches.

This apparel is made out of three pieces, and ftiffened with parchment; and is bordered by a narrow but effective lace of a green ground, bearing circles of white and red, parted by yellow. The brown canvas upon which it is worked is very fine of its kind; and the gold, which is of a good quality, is of narrow tinsel strips. From age, or use, the design is worn away from a great portion of the ground, and the pattern was a favourite one for liturgical appliances up to the 16th century.

1262.

MANIPLE; embroidered, in various-coloured silk, upon brown canvas; design, a net-work in bright crimson, the lozenge-shaped meshes of which, braced together by a fret, are filled in with a ground alternately yellow charged with modifications of the gammadion in blue, and green, with the same figure in white voided crimson. The extremities are cloth of gold, both edged with a parti-coloured fringe, and one figured with a lion in gold on a crimson field. German, 14th century. 3 feet 11 inches by 3 inches.

1263.

NAPKIN of linen embroidered in white thread; ground, plain white linen; design, a conventional rectangular floriation, filled in with other floriations, and in the middle an eight-petaled flower, and in the square intervening spaces outside a fleur-de-lis shooting out of each corner, all in white broad thread. German, late 14th century. 23 inches by 13¼ inches.

Like many other examples of the kind, the present one can show its elaborate and beautifully-executed design only by being held up to the light, when it comes forth in perfection.

1264.

SILK Damask; ground, crimson; design, a network in broad bands of yellow silk and gold wrought like twisted cords, and the meshes, which are wreathed inside with a green garland bearing green and white flowers, filled in

36 Church-veſtments, Silk-ſtuffs,

with a conventional artichoke in yellow ſilk mixed with gold thread, and edged with a green and white border. Spaniſh, early 16th century. 17 inches by 15¼ inches.

As a furniture-ſtuff, this muſt have been very effective; and from the under ſide being thickly plaſtered with ſtrong glue, the laſt ſervice of the preſent piece would ſeem to have been for the decoration of the wall of ſome room.

1265.

SILK Damaſk; ground, deep blue, or violet; deſign, a ſprinkling of ſmall ſtars and rows of large angels, ſome iſſuing from clouds and ſwinging thuribles in the left hand, others kneeling in worſhip with uplifted hands, bearing crowns of thorns, and the laſt row kneeling and holding up before them a croſs of the Latin ſhape. Florentine, late 14th century. 21¼ inches by 13 inches.

From its form this piece ſeems to have been cut off from a chaſuble; and the ſtuff itſelf, it is likely, was woven expreſsly for the purple veſtments worn in Lent, and more particularly during Paſſion time. At No. 7072 another portion of the ſame damaſk is deſcribed.

1266.

TRIANGULAR Piece of Yellow Silk; ground, light yellow; deſign, a netting filled in with eight-petaled roſes and circles encloſing other flowers, all in white. Greek, 14th century. 9½ inches.

Lined as it is with ſtout blue canvas, this piece may have been in liturgical uſe, and, in all likelihood, ſerved as the hood to ſome boy-biſhop's cope.

About the boy-biſhop himſelf and his functions, according to our old Saliſbury Rite, ſee "Church of Our Fathers," t. iv. p. 215.

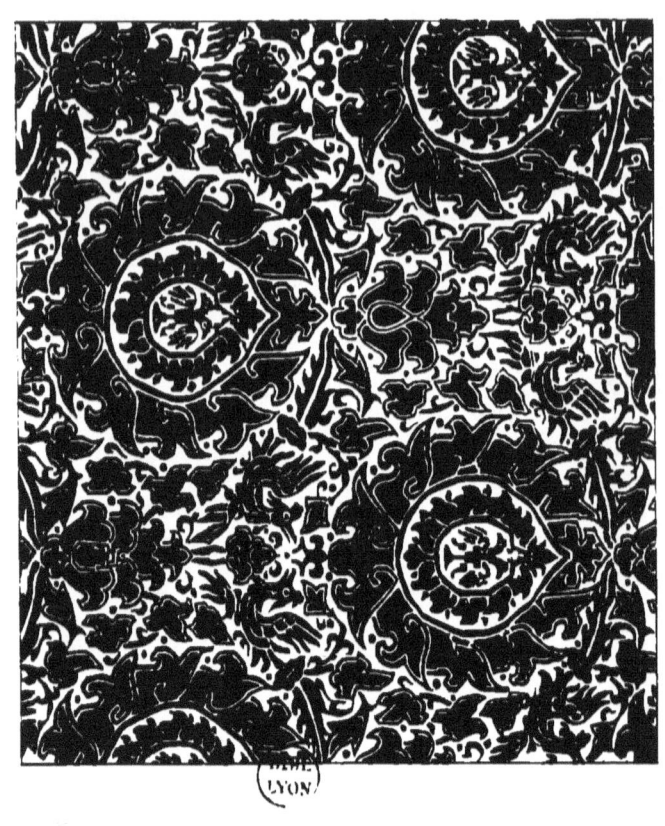

SILK GIT AMA K
XII M ...

Needlework, and Dresses.

1267.

TISSUE, silk upon linen; ground, white; design, broad circles filled in with floriated ornamentation, bearing in the middle a five-petaled purple flower. Italian, early 14th century. 7 inches by 3 inches.

1267 A.

ANOTHER Piece of the same Tissue. 12¼ inches by 2¼ inches.

The thread in the warp of this stuff is more than usually thick; and so sparingly is the silk employed on its pattern, that in its best days it could have looked but poor.

1268.

SILK and Cotton Damask; ground, yellow silk mixed with cotton; design, a sprinkling of eight-rayed voided stars, in dusky purple. Italian, 14th century. 5 inches by 2¼ inches.

A thin stuff for linings.

1269.

SILK and Gold Damask; ground, light fawn-colour in silk; design, a large conventional flower enclosing another flower of the same character, which is filled in with a double-headed eagle displayed, and the spaces between the large flowers diapered with foliage shooting from a sort of fir-cone, at the top of which are birds in pairs hovering over the plant and having a long feather drooping from the head, all in gold thread. Sicilian, early 14th century. 10¾ inches by 9¾ inches.

Though not so spirited in the drawing of its pattern, and the gold so poor and bad that it has become almost lost to the eye, this stuff is a valuable item in the collection. The eagle, with its double head, and wings diſplayed, would lead to the belief that it had been wrought to the order of ſome emperor of Germany, or for ſome Sicilian nobleman who cheriſhed a love for the houſe of Hohenſtaufen.

1270.

PART of a Maniple; ground, cloth of gold; deſign, in needlework, St. Blaſe and St. Stephen. Engliſh or French, 13th century. 12 inches by 6¼ inches.

Both with regard to its golden cloth, and the figures upon it, this piece is very valuable. The ſtuff is of that kind which our countryman, John Garland, tells us was wrought by young women at his time, and ſhows, in its grounding, a pretty zig-zag pattern. The two kneeling figures, though done in mere outline of the ſcantieſt ſort, diſplay an eaſe and gracefulneſs peculiar to the ſculpture and illuminations in England and France of that period. St. Blaſe is ſhown us veſted in his chaſuble and mitre—low in form—with a very long grey beard, and holding a comb in one hand—the inſtrument of his martyrdom; St. Stephen is robed as a deacon, and kneeling amid a ſhower of large round ſtones, pelted at him on all ſides.

1271.

SILK and Gold Damaſk; ground, light green ſilk; deſign, griffins paſſant and fleur-de-lis in one row, fleur-de-lis and ſlipped vine-leaves ariſing from two tendrils formed like the letter C, and put back to back, all in gold. Sicilian, 14th century. 12 inches by 7¼ inches.

The whole of this pattern is thrown off with great freedom, and an heraldic eye will ſee the boldneſs of the griffins. The vine-leaves are as criſpy as any ever ſeen upon ſuch ſtuffs, and the whole does credit to the royal looms of Palermo, where it was probably wrought at the command of the prince, for himſelf, or as a gift to ſome French royalty. An exactly ſimilar ſtuff to this may be found at No. 7061; and it is ſaid that the robes now ſhown at Neuburg, near Vienna, are traditionally believed to have been worn, at his marriage, by Leopold the Holy.

Needlework, and Dresses.

1272.

SILK and Cotton Stuff; ground, light purple cotton; design, small but thick foliage, interspersed with birds of various kinds, in pairs and face to face, in amber-coloured silk. Sicilian, 14th century. 9¾ inches by 7 inches.

Though so small in its elements, this is a pleasing design, and extremely well drawn, like all those from Palermo.

1273.

SILK and Cotton Damask; ground, of cotton, a light orange; design, within a ten-cusped circle, and divided by the thin trunk of a tree, two cocks, face to face, all in gold thread, upon a purplish crimson ground, and between the circles an ornamentation in which a small crown tipped with fleur-de-lis, over a lion passant gardant, is very frequent in gold. Sicilian, late 14th century. 10¾ inches by 3 inches.

Though such a mere rag, this piece is so far valuable, as it shows that France then got her silken stuffs from Sicily, and, in this instance, perhaps sent her own design with her Gallic cock, and her fleur-de-lis mingled so plentifully in it. How or why the lion is there cannot be explained.

1274.

SILK Damask; ground, fawn colour; design, parrots, and giraffes in pairs, amid floriated ornamentation, all, excepting the parts done in gold, of the tint of the ground. Sicilian, 13th century. 20¾ inches by 10¾ inches.

Upon an egg-shaped figure, nicely filled in with graceful floriated ornaments, stand two parrots, breast to breast, but with heads averted, which (as well as their pinion-joints, marked by a broad circle crowded with little rings on their wings, and legs and claws) are wrought in threads of gold, all now so tarnished as to look as if first worked in some dull purple silk. Their long broad perpendicular tails have the feathers shown by

U shaped lines, looking much like the kind of ornamentation noticed under Nos. 8591, 8596, 8599. Below, and back to back, or—as some may choose to see them—affronted, and biting the stems of the foliage, are two giraffes, with one leg raised—may be better described as tripping. They are specked all over with quatrefoil spots, and have head and hoofs done in gold, now faded to black. This stuff is as beautiful in design as substantial in its material, being all of good fine silk; though so poor and sparing was the gold upon the thread, that it has quite faded. From the curve at the upper end, this piece seems to have been cut out of an old chasuble.

1275.

SILK Damask (made up of four pieces); ground, brown, once purple; design, in gold thread and coloured silks, griffins, eagles, and flowers. Sicilian, early 13th century. 19½ inches by 19¾ inches.

At top we have a row of griffins looking to the east, mostly wrought in gold, but relieved on coloured silks, and having at the pinion-joints of the wing that singular circle, filled in with a small design; then a row of conventional flowers in red, crimson, green, and white, and, last of all, a row of eagles at rest, done mostly in gold, slightly shaded with green, and looking west. The beasts and birds are admirably drawn, and when the stuff was new it must have been very fine and effective, though now the gold looks shabby.

1276.

STOLE, of silk and gold damask; ground, purple silk; design, mostly in gold, pricked out with green silk, a floriated oval, filled in with a pair of young parded leopards, addorsed regardant, and wyverns regardant in couples. Sicilian, late 13th century. 8 feet 4 inches by 3 inches, not including the expanded ends.

This is a magnificent stuff; but the stole itself could have been made out of it only in the middle of the 17th century.

1277.

THE Hood of a Cope; filk and gold; ground, fawn-coloured filk; defign, bands, in gold thread, alternately broad, figured with harts couchant, and flowers with an oblique pencil of rays darting down; and narrow, marked with raylefs flowers. Underlying the latter gold band is a very broad one of filk, figured in green, with collared dogs running at fpeed towards a fmall fwan, with fprigs of flowers, green and white, between them. Sicilian, late 13th century. 14¼ inches by 13¼ inches.

The very pointed fhape of this hood is fomewhat unufual in the form of this part of a cope, as made during mediæval times, in England. The ftuff is of a fpirited defign, and fhows a curious element in its pattern, in thofe golden flowers with their pencils of rays.

1278.

SILK and Cotton Damafk; ground, black; defign, a lion rampant amid trees, all in light green. Sicilian, 14th century. 15 inches by 7¾ inches.

Very few examples occur with ground coloured black, yet the bright green of the defign goes well upon its fombre grounding. The animal and alfo the leaves and trees around him are all admirably and fpiritedly drawn, and one regrets that a pattern of fuch merit fhould have been loft upon fuch poor materials.

1279.

SILK and Gold Damafk; ground, bright green filk; defign, in gold, conventional artichokes, large and fmall, and harts, and demi-dogs with very large wings, both animals having remarkably long manes ftreaming far behind them. Sicilian, 14th century. 27 inches by 14 inches.

This beautifully and richly wrought ftuff, with its fantaftic defign drawn with such spirit, must have been, when seen in a large piece, very pleasing. Its last use was in a chasuble of rather modern cut, to judge from its present shape.

1280.

SMALL Bag to hold relics; ground, gold; design, all embroidered by needle, white rabbits (?) segreant, peacocks in couples, face to face, with the rabbits between them, two hearts and rows of black or purple spots, like women's heads, one in the middle surrounded by a wreath of eight crimson stars, with small green flower-bearing trees, and the whole field sprinkled with letters, now, from the ill condition of the embroidery, not to be read. German, 16th century. 4⅜ inches square.

1281.

PART of a Liturgical Ornament; silk upon linen; ground, crimson, faded; design, in yellow flos-silk, beasts and birds. Syrian, late 13th century. 2 feet 6 inches by 7¼ inches.

It does not seem to have last served as either stole or maniple, but, apparently, was part of an altar curtain of which two were hung, one at each side of the sacred table. Lions and dogs seated and eagles perched amid flowers and foliage form the pattern, which is not as well figured as those usually are which came from the eastern shores of the Mediterranean.

1282.

SILK and Cotton Damask; ground, green; design, large ovals filled in with foliation, enclosed with a net-work of garlands, the fruits of which might be mistaken for half-moons. North Italy, 14th century. 13¼ inches by 7½ inches.

On better material, for the quantity of its silk is small, and in happier colours, this stuff might have been very pretty.

1283.

ILK Damafk; ground, amber yellow; defign, a hart, in gold, lodged beneath green trees in a park, the paling of which is light green, with a bunch of the corn-flower, centaurea, before it. Sicilian, 14th century. 7¼ inches by 5¼ inches.

1283 A.

ILK Damafk; ground, amber yellow; defign, the fun in its fplendour, an eagle in gold, a green tree. Sicilian, 14th century. 7¼ inches by 5½ inches.

1284.

ILK Damafk; ground, amber yellow; defign, a hart, in gold, lodged beneath green trees in a park, the paling of which is light green, with a bunch of the corn-flower before it. Sicilian, 14th century. 7 inches by 6¼ inches.

1284 A.

SILK Damafk; ground, amber yellow; defign, a running hart, in gold, amid foliage. Sicilian, 14th century. 8 inches by 4¼ inches.

The laft four pieces are, in fact, but fragments of the fame ftuff, and when put together make up its original pattern, and beautiful it muft have feemed when beheld as a whole; the bird and animals are done with much freedom and fpirit; fo likewife the foliage: but two of the portions, by being more expofed to the light, are much faded, in fuch a manner that the green in them has almoft fled. As ufual, fo poor was the golden thread that the bird and animals now look almoft black, but here and there, with a good glafs, fhimmerings of gold may be found upon them. To fome eyes the fun may look like a rofe furrounded by rays. At one time or another an unfeeling hand has moft plentifully fprinkled all thefe four pieces with flowers made from gilt paper ftamped out, and pafted on the ftaff with ftiff glue. The filk, efpecially the yellow, of this tiffue was mixed with very fine threads of cotton.

1285.

ONE of the Ends of a Stole, embroidered in beads; ground, dark blue; design, very likely the head of an apostle, in various coloured and gold beads. Venetian, late 12th century.

So like both in design, execution, and materials to the portion of an orphrey, No. 8274, that it would seem this piece was not only worked by the self-same hand, but formed a part of the self-same set of vestments. The places, now bare, in the nimb and neck, were, no doubt, once filled in with fine seed-pearls that have been wantonly picked out. The other end of the same stole to which this belonged is the following.

1286.

EXACTLY like the foregoing; but if in its fellow piece seed-pearls are not to be seen, here they are left in part of the nimb, but especially over the left eye. Of the large piece with the head of the Blessed Virgin Mary, we have spoken at length, No. 8274.

1287.

SILK and Cotton Damask; ground, light yellow silk; design, a reticulation of vine-branches bearing grapes and leaves, and enclosing butterflies, an armorial shield having a royal crown over it, all in light purple cotton. Sicilian, early 14th century. 17¼ inches by 15¼ inches.

The design in all its elements is so like many other specimens wrought by the looms of Palermo at the period, that we are warranted to presume it came from that great mart of silken stuffs during the middle ages. So thin in its texture, it must have been meant for the lining of a heavier material. Père Martin has figured, in his very valuable " Mélanges d'Archéologie," t. iv. plate xxii, a piece of silk, now in the Museum of the Louvre, almoſt the ſame in pattern, but differing much in colour, from the ſpecimen before us. In the ſpecimen at Paris little dogs and dragons, both in pairs, come in, but here they are wanting; ſo that we may learn that, to give variety to the pattern, parts were changed. Upon the ſhield there is a charge not unlike a ſtar, rather oblong, of ſix points.

1288.

DAMASK, ſilk and cotton; ground, deep bluiſh green; deſign, pairs of monſters, half griffin, half elephant, in gold, a conventional flower in light green, encloſing a pair of wings in gold, and pairs of birds amid foliation, with ſhort ſentences of imitated Arabic here and there. Sicilian, early 14th century. 14 inches by 11 inches.

This is a fine and noteworthy production of the Palermitan loom, and ſhows in its pattern much fancy and great freedom of drawing; for whether we look at thoſe very ſingular griffin elephants, ſitting in pairs —and gazing at one another, or the two birds of the hoopoe family, with a long feather on the head, or the two gold wings conjoined and erect, ſo heraldically tricked, with that well-deviſed flower ending in a honeyſuckle ſcroll, an ornament ſprinkled all about, we cannot but be pleaſed with the whole arrangement. The combination of elephant and griffin in ornamentation is almoſt, perhaps quite, unique. The pretended Arabic points to a locality where once Saracenic workmen laboured, and left behind them their traditions of excellency of handicraft. In Dr. Bock's "Geſchichte der Liturgiſchen Gewänder des Mittelalters," 4 Lieferung, pl. ix. may be ſeen this curious ſtuff figured.

1289.

PART of a Maniple, ſilk damaſk; ground, fawn-coloured; deſign, an ovate foliation amid monſter beaſts and birds, all in light blue ſilk, excepting the heads of the birds; the feet and heads of the animals done in gold. Sicilian, late 13th century. $13\frac{1}{4}$ inches by 7 inches.

1289 A.

PART of a Maniple, silk damask; ground, fawn-coloured; design, an ovate foliation amid small lions and large monster beasts and birds, in light blue silk, excepting the small lions all in gold, and the heads and claws of the others in the same metal. Sicilian, late 13th century. 21¼ inches by 6¼ inches.

The two articles were evidently parts of the same maniple; a liturgical appliance of such narrow dimensions that we cannot make out the entire composition of the very fine and admirably drawn design upon the stuff, out of which it was cut originally. From what is before us we perceive that there were a pair of small lions, face to face, all in gold, a pair of wyverns segreant in green, a pair of griffins passant, with heads of gold, and a pair of other large animals, antelopes, with their horned heads and cloven hoofs in the same metal; slight indications of the fleur-de-lis here and there occur.

1290.

A BISHOP'S Liturgical Shoe, of silk and gold damask; ground, crimson silk; design, eagles, in couples, at rest, in gold, amid foliations in green silk; a small piece on the left side of the heel is of another rich stuff in gold and light green. Italian stuff, 14th century. 11¼ inches.

Such old episcopal liturgic shoes are now great rarities; and a specimen once belonging to one of our English worthies, Waneflete, is given in the "Church of our Fathers," t. ii. p. 250; it is of rich silk velvet, wrought with flowers, and still kept at Magdalen College, Oxford, built and endowed by that good bishop of Winchester. In the present example we have, in its thin leather sole for the right foot, a proof that making shoes right and left was well known then.

1291.

SILK and Gold Damask; ground (now very faded), crimson silk; design, animals, all in gold, and flowers in gold, pricked out, some in green, others in purple silk. Sicilian, 14th century. 14¾ inches by 8¾ inches.

The animals are large antelopes couchant, and smaller ones in the like posture, within flowers, along with large oddly-shaped wyverns with the head bent down; the flowers are roses, and a modification of the centaurea, or corn-flower. Though the gold be tarnished, the pattern is still rich.

1292.

TAFFETA, silk and cotton; ground, dull crimson cotton; design, reticulated foliage with a conventional artichoke in the meshes, all in pale blue. Spanish, 15th century. 7¼ inches by 6¾ inches.

1292 A.

TAFFETA, silk and cotton; ground, dull crimson cotton; design, reticulated foliage with a conventional artichoke in the meshes, all in pale blue. Spanish, 15th century. 5¼ inches by 5¼ inches.

As poor in material as in design, and evidently manufactured for linings to silks of richer substances.

1293.

SILK and Cotton Damask; ground, bright crimson silk; design, floriated circles filled in with a pair of griffins rampant, addorsed, regardant, and the spaces between the circles ornamented with a floriated cross, all in yellow cotton. Sicilian, 14th century. 9¼ inches by 7 inches.

A good design bestowed upon somewhat poor materials. At first the yellow parts of the pattern had their cotton thread covered with gold, but of such a debased quality and so sparingly, too, that it has almost all disappeared, and, where seen, has tarnished to a dusky black.

1294.

SILK Damask; ground, purple; design, large fan-like leaves, between small fruits of the pomegranate, in dead purple. Spanish, late 15th century.

Upon this specimen there was sewed an inscription, now so broken as not to make sense, and from the style of letter, of the floriated form, done in red and gold thread upon purple canvas, as is all the scroll-work about it, some German hand must have wrought it.

1295.

TISSUE of Cotton Warp and Silk and Gold Woof; ground, now yellow; design, eagles in pairs, divided by rayed orbs, amid foliage all in gold. Sicilian, middle 14th century. 6¼ inches by 5¼ inches.

The eagles are about to take wing, and are pecking at the rays of, seemingly, the sun which separates them. The foliage is much like, in form, that which so often occurs on works from the looms of Palermo; and, in all likelihood, the ground, now yellow, was once of a fawn-colour. Though good in design, this stuff is made of poor materials, the silk in it is small, and the gold of such a base quality that it has become a dusky brown.

1296.

TISSUE of Flaxen Thread Warp and Silk and Gold Woof; ground, fawn-coloured; design, eagles in pairs affronted, with a pencil of sun-rays darting down upon their heads, and resting amid flowers all in gold. Sicilian, middle 14th century. 8 inches by 4¼ inches.

What we said of No. 1295 is equally applicable to this specimen, in which, however, may be seen, the corn-flower, centaurea, so often met with in Palermitan textures of the time.

1297.

SILK Damask; ground, light green; design, within a heart-shaped figure, a large vine-leaf, at which two very small hoopoes, one at each side, are pecking; outside the ovals, from which large bunches of small-fruited grapes are hanging, runs a scroll with little vine-leaves, all now of a fawn-colour, but at first in a rosy crimson hue. Italian, late 14th century. 15 inches by $5\frac{1}{4}$ inches.

The design for this tasteful stuff was thrown off by an easy flowing hand; and Dr. Bock has given a good plate, in his "Dessinateur des Etoffes," 3 Livraison, of a silk almost the very same, the differences being some very slight variations in parts of its colours.

1298, 1298 A.

SILK Damask; ground, purple; design, amid foliage and small geometrical figures, birds in pairs, all in rosy red, and beasts in gold. Sicilian, 14th century. $9\frac{1}{4}$ inches by $3\frac{3}{4}$ inches, and $4\frac{1}{2}$ inches by 4 inches.

Putting these two pieces together we make out this beautiful, elaborate, though small pattern. What the birds may be is hard to guess, but the beasts seem lionesses, with bushy tails, and bold spirited griffins. Dr. Bock has figured this stuff in the before-mentioned large work.

1299.

DAMASK, gold, silk, and thread; ground, dull purple; design, two broad horizontal bands, the first charged with a hound, green, collared, armed, and langued white, lying down with head upturned to a large swan in gold, with foliage all about them; on the second, a dog chasing a hart, both in gold, and between two cable ornaments in gold, and two scrolls of roving foliage, in light green pricked with white. Sicilian, late 14th century. 18 inches by 12 inches.

The beautiful and boldly-drawn pattern of these beasts and birds in pairs, and succeeding each other, is not duly honoured by the materials used in it; the quantity of thread is large, and the gold of the poorest sort.

1300.

SILK Damask; ground, blue; design, in yellow, a network done in ovate geometrical scrolls, and the meshes filled in with geometrical lozenges, and others showing an ornamentation of singular occurrence, somewhat like the heraldic nebule. Lucca, early 15th century. $10\frac{1}{2}$ inches by $7\frac{1}{4}$ inches.

After a pattern that seldom is to be found on mediæval stuffs.

1301.

SILK and Gold Damask; ground, bright crimson silk; design, in gold, fruit of the pomegranate, mingled with flowers and leaves of another plant. South of Spain, 15th century. 9 inches by $8\frac{3}{4}$ inches.

At a distance this stuff must have shown well, but its materials are not of the first class; though lively in tone, the silk is poor, and its gold made of that thin gilt parchment cut into flat shreds, like other examples here—Nos. 8590, 8601, 8639, &c.

1302.

SILK and Gold Damask; ground, fawn-coloured faded from crimson, in silk; design, large eagles perched in pairs, with a radiating sun between them, and beneath the rays dogs in pairs, running with heads turned back and looking on the foliage separating them, all in gold. Sicilian, 14th century. 17 inches by 8¼ inches.

The fine and spirited pattern of this piece is now very indistinct, owing to the bad colour of the ground, which has so much faded, and the inferior quality of the gold upon the thread.

1303.

SILK Damask; ground, a rose-coloured tint; pattern, in a dull tone of the same, broad strap-work, in reticulations enclosing a circular conventional floriation. Moresco-Spanish, 14th century. 6 inches by 5½ inches.

The tone of the colour has changed from its first brightness, and the stuff is of a very thin texture.

1304.

SILK and Gold Damask; ground, crimson silk much faded; design, harts collared and flying eagles amid foliage, all in gold. Sicilian, 14th century. 2 feet 8 inches by 1 foot.

In this spirited pattern the running harts in the upper row have caught one of their hind-legs in the cord tied to their collar, and an eagle swoops down upon them; in the second row, the same animal has switched its tail into the last link of the chain fastened to its collar, and an eagle seems flying at its head, as it screams with gaping beak. The last use of this specimen of so magnificent a stuff appears to have been as part of a curtain (with its 15th century poor parti-coloured thread fringe) for hanging at the sides of an altar.

1305.

EMBROIDERED Lappet of a Mitre; ground, linen; design, beneath a tall niche, a female in various coloured silks and gold; and under her, within a lower-headed niche, a male figure after the same style. German, late 14th century. 17¼ inches by 3 inches.

The high-peaked canopy, with its crocketing and finial well formed and once all covered with gold, holds a female figure, crowned like a queen, with the banner of the Refurrection in one hand and a chalice, having on it the facred hoft, in the other, which may be taken for the perfon of the Church, while the majeftic prophet beneath her feems to be Malachi holding a long unfolded fcroll fignificative of thofe words of his relating to the facrifice in the New Law. In the embroidery of the figures this piece very much refembles the ftyle of needlework in the part of an orphrey, No. 1313. In his "Gefchichte der Liturgifchen Gewänder des Mittelalters," 2 Lieferung, pl. xii. Dr. Bock has given figures of this curious lappet.

1306, 1306 A.

SILK Damafk; ground, fawn-coloured; defign, amid funbeams, raindrops, and foliage, large birds clutching in their talons a fcroll charged with a capital letter R thrice repeated, all in light green. Sicilian, late 14th century. 13 inches by 6¼ inches; and 8 inches by 3¾ inches.

The defign of this ftuff is rather curious from the infcribed fcroll, the letter R of which is very Italian.

1307.

SILK and Gold Damafk; ground, fawn-colour; defign, amid a conventional foliation fhooting out in places with large fan-like flowers in gold, braces of fmall birds on the wing and pairs of running dogs with two antelopes, couchant, biting a bough, both in gold. Sicilian, 14th century. 12¼ inches by 8¼ inches.

A very good defign well drawn, but unfortunately not quite perfect in the fpecimen, the golden parts of which are much tarnifhed.

1308.

SILK Damafk; ground, rofy fawn-coloured; defign, within a wreath made up moftly of myrtle-leaves and trefoils, a lion's head cabofed, above which is a bunch

of vine-leaves fhutting in a blue corn-flower, and at each fide, in white, a word in imitated Arabic; excepting the blue centaurea and two white flowers in the wreath, all the reft is in light green. Sicilian, 14th century. 22 inches by 10¾ inches.

This well-varied pattern is nicely drawn, and fhows the traditions of the Saracenic workmen who once flourifhed at Palermo.

1309.

EMBROIDERY of Thread upon Linen; defign, in raifed ftitchery, the hunting of the unicorn. German, late 14th century. 26¼ inches by 13¼ inches.

This fine piece of needlework fhows us a foreft where a groom is holding three horfes, on two of which the high-peaked faddles are well given; running towards him are two hunting dogs, collared. In the midft of the wood fits a virgin with her long hair falling down her back, and on her lap an unicorn is refting his fore-feet; behind this group is coming a man with a ftick upon his fhoulder, from which hangs, by its coupled hind-legs, a dead hare. Not only the lady, but the men wear fhoes with remarkably long toes, and the gracefulnefs with which the foliage is everywhere twined fpeaks of the period as marked in the architectural decoration of the period here in England. In another number (8618) the fame fubject is noticed as fignificative of the Incarnation, and fully explained. No doubt, like the other piece of fine Rhenifh needlework, this alfo formed but a part of a large cloth to hang behind an altar as a reredos. Thofe very long-toed fhoes brought into fafhion here by Ann of Bohemia, our Richard II.'s queen, were called " cracowes."

1310.

ANIPLE of Crimfon and Gold Damafk; ground, bright crimfon; defign, ftags and funbeams. Sicilian, late 14th century. 3 feet 7½ inches by 4 inches.

Under No. 8624 there is a fpecimen of filk damafk, without gold in it, of a pattern fo like this that, were the prefent piece perfect in its defign, we might prefume both had come from the fame loom, and differed only in materials. In that, as in this, we have a couple of stags well attired, with their heads upturned to a large pencil of sunbeams darting down upon them amid a shower of raindrops.

1311.

SILK and Gold Damask; ground, deep violet; design, St. Mary of Egypt, with her own hair falling all over her, as her only garment, on her knees before an altar on which stands a cross; behind her, a tree, upon which hovers a bird with a long bough in its beak; and high up over against her an arm coming from a cloud with the hand in benediction, and rays darting from the fingers, between two stars, one of eight, the other of six points, all mostly in gold. Venetian, 15th century. 12 inches by 11½ inches.

The materials and the weaving of this valuable tissue are both good, and figure a saint once in great repute in Oriental Christendom as well as among those Europeans who traded with the East, as an example of true repentance. A part of the design is, so to say, ante-dated, and to understand the whole of it we ought to know something of the life of this second Magdalen.

In the latter half of the fourth century St. Mary of Egypt, then a girl of twelve, fled to Alexandria, where she led an abandoned life.

It chanced that she went in a certain ship full of pilgrims to Jerusalem, where, on the feast of the Elevation of the Cross, she was hindered by a miracle from entering the church. Then, coming to herself, she made a vow of penance, and withdrew to the desert beyond the Jordan. There she lived unseen for forty years, till all her garments fell away and she had nothing wherewith to clothe herself but her own long hair.

On the stuff before us the anachronism of its design will be soon perceived from this rapid sketch of St. Mary's life. Instead of being, as she must have been, arrayed in the female fashion of the time when she went to Jerusalem, the great penitent is represented so far quite naked that her own long tresses, falling all around her, are her only mantle—just as she used to be more than forty years afterwards. But yet the design well unfolds her story; the hand darting rays of light signifies the revelation given her from heaven, and the bleffing that followed it; while the two ftars tell of Jerufalem, as alfo does the elaborately-fafhioned crofs that is ftanding on the altar, the frontal to which, in the upper border, feems ornamented in purple, with an infcription, now unreadable, but the laft letters of which look as if they are R L I. The bird, perhaps a dove, has no part in the faint's hiftory, but is a fancy of the artift. In Dr. Bock's "Gefchichte der Liturgifchen Gewänder des Mittelalters," 1 Band, 1 Lieferung, pl. xi. is a figure of this ftuff.

1312.

SILK Damafk; ground, crimfon; defign, a complication of geometric lines and figures in yellow, blue, green and white. Morefque, 15th century. 22½ inches by 18¼ inches.

Thofe who know the ornamentation on the burned clay tiles and the gilt plafter ceilings in the Alhambra at Granada will recognize the fame feeling and ftyle in this fhowy ftuff, the filk of which is fo good, and the colours, particularly the crimfon, fo warm.

1313.

PART of an Orphrey; ground, deep crimfon fatin, edged with a narrow green band; defign, three apoftolic figures beneath Gothic canopies, all wrought in gold thread and coloured filks upon canvas and applied. German, early 15th century. 30 inches by 7¼ inches.

Each figure is nicely worked; and the firft, beginning at the top, holding a fword erect in his right hand, is St. James the Greater; beneath him, with a halbert, St. Matthew; and laft of all, holding in one hand a book, in the other a fword, St. Paul. The flowery crocketing running up the arches of the niches is particularly good.

1314.

SILK Damask; ground, crimson (now faded); design, two golden lions with their fore-paws resting on a white scroll, looking down upon an orb darting straight down its rays upon the heads of two perched eagles, amid foliation, all in green. Italian, late 14th century. 26 inches by 9¾ inches.

A fine design, and sketched with great freedom; but the silk and gold employed in it are not of the best.

1315.

SILK Taffeta; ground, brown; design, broad bands made up of eight red-edged orange stripes within two white ones. Egyptian, 10th century. 26 inches by 9¾ inches.

1316.

SILK Taffeta; ground, purple; design, narrow stripes made up of white purple and green lines. Egyptian, 10th century. 24 inches by 3½ inches.

These scarce examples of Oriental ability in the production of very thin substances for personal adornment and dress, under such a sun as even the north of Africa has, were originally wrought for ordinary, not religious use. They were brought to Europe as precious stuffs, and given as such to the Church and used for casting over the tombs of the saints, as palls, or as linings for thicker silken vestments. That these or any of the following specimens of gauze or taffeta were ever put to the purpose of making stockings, or rather leggings like boots, still worn by bishops on solemn occasions during the celebrations of the liturgy, cannot for a moment be thought of. Such appliances are, and always were, made either of velvet or strong cloth of gold or silver.

1317.

SILK Gauze; ground, light green; design, broad bands composed of white, black, and orange stripes. Egyptian, 10th century. 13 inches by 4 inches.

1318.

TAFFETA, Silk and Cotton; ground and design, broad stripes of crimson, green, crimson and orange, separated by narrow lines of white; the warp is of brown fine cotton. Egyptian, 10th century. 12 inches by 2½ inches.

Of such stuffs the Orientals make their girdles to this day; and for such a purpose we presume this taffeta was woven at Cairo and for Moslem use, as the green of the so-called prophet is one among its colours.

1319.

ILK Gauze; ground, a light green. Egyptian, 10th century. 10 inches by 3½ inches.

Though without any pattern, such a specimen is very valuable for letting us see the delicate texture which the Saracens, like the ancient Egyptians, knew how to give to the works of the loom. This, like No. 1317, if ever used for church purposes, could only have been employed for spreading over shrines, or the lining of vestments; specimens like these are sometimes found between the leaves in illuminated MSS, to protect the paintings.

1320.

SILK and Gold Damask; ground, crimson (now faded) silk; design, lions in pairs addorsed, regardant, each with a swan swung upon its back, and held by the neck in its mouth, bounding from out a small space surrounded

I

by a low circular paling, and amid two large conventional floriations; at the top of one of these are two squirrels sitting upright, or sejant, all in gold. Italian, late 14th century. 17½ inches by 10¾ inches.

Unfortunately this curious well-figured and interesting design is somewhat wasted upon materials so faded, as scarcely to show it now. The foliation is rather thick and heavy. In Dr. Bock's work, "Geschichte der Liturgischen Gewänder des Mittelalters," 1 Band, 1 Lieferung, pl. xiv. may be found this stuff, nicely figured.

1321.

SMALL Piece of Embroidery; background, canvas diapered with lozenges in brown thread; foreground, once partly strewed with streaks of gold; design, two men bearded and clad in long garments, seemingly personages of the Old Law, talking to each other. Florentine, 15th century.

With quite an Italian and Florentine character about them, these two figures, both worked in silk, have no great merit; though there are some good folds in the brown mantle, shot with green, of the hooded individual standing on the left-hand. That it has been cut away from some larger piece is evident, but what the original served for, whether a sacred or secular purpose, it is impossible now to say.

1322.

STOLE; ground, light blue silk; design, a thin bough roving along the stole's whole length in an undulating line, and sprouting out into fan-like leaves, and small flowers, and in a white raised cord, narrowly edged with crimson silk and gold thread. At one expanded end is the Holy Lamb upon a golden ground; at the other, the dove, emblem of the Holy Ghost, alighting upon flowers. German, 15th century. 8 feet 6¼ inches by 3¾ inches.

Though the work upon this stole is rather coarse, still from its raised style it must have been effective; but its chief value is from having been a liturgic ornament. The diapering at the end figured with the Holy Lamb, done upon a yellow canvas ground, with its thin golden threads worked into three circles, with their radiations not straight but wavy, is remarkable, and may be found upon another work wrought by a German needle in this collection. Not only the Lamb and the Dove, but the floriation, are thrown up into a sort of low relief.

1323.

EMBROIDERED Linen; design, barbed quatrefoils filled in with armorial birds and beasts, and the spaces between wrought with vine-leaves. German, 15th century. 16 inches by 11¾ inches.

This is but a piece of a much larger work, the pattern of which, in its entire form, can only be guessed at from a few remains. One quatrefoil is occupied by a pair of eagles (as they seem to be) addorsed regardant; and the two legs of another three-toed creature remaining near them prove that other things besides the eagles were figured. The whole is coarsely done in coarse materials, and, in workmanship, far below very many specimens here. It appears to have served for household not for church use.

1324.

EMBROIDERED Cushion for the missal at the altar; ground, crimson silk; design, our Infant Lord in the arms of the Blessed Virgin Mary, with St. Joseph and four angels worshipping, on the upper side, in various-coloured silk; on the under side, a reticulation filled in with a pair of birds and a flowering plant alternately. German, late 13th century. 19 inches by 13 inches.

Such cushions, and of so remote a period, are great liturgical curiosities, and, fortunately, the present one is in very good preservation, and quite a work of art. Throned within a Gothic building, rather than beneath a canopy, sits the mother of the Divine Babe, who is outstretching His little hands towards the lily-branch which the approaching St. Joseph is holding in one hand, while in the other he carries a basket of doves. Outside, and on the green sward, are kneeling four angels robed as deacons, three of whom bear lily flowers, a fourth the liturgical fan; the whole is encircled by a garland of lilies. The under-side is worked with white doves in pairs, and a green tree blooming with red flowers; and though much of the needlework is gone, this cushion is a good example for such an appliance. Dr. Bock has figured it in his "Geschichte der Liturgischen Gewänder des Mittelalters," 1 Band, 2 Lieferung, p. xiii.

1325.

PART of an Altar-cloth; ground, linen; design, amid foliage sparingly heightened with yellow silk, birds, and beasts, and one end figured with the gammadion. German, 14th century. 6 feet 4¼ inches by 2 feet 2½ inches.

This altar-cloth, now shortened and without one of its ends figured with the gammadion, is made up of two different pieces, of which one showing two large-headed pheasants, put one above the other, amid foliage plentifully flowered with the fleur-de-lis and roses, is quite perfect in its pattern; but the other, marked with alternate griffins and lions, has been cut in two so as to give us but the hinder half of each animal, amid a foliage of oak-leaves. The whole design, however, is boldly drawn and spiritedly executed.

1326.

DAMASK, silk and cotton; ground, green; design, large and small conventional artichokes, in gold and yellow silk, amid garlands in white silk. Italian, 15th century. 2 feet 10 inches by 1 foot 3¼ inches.

Though much cotton is mixed up with the silk, and its gold was of an inferior quality, still the crowded and elaborate design of its pattern makes this stuff very pleasing.

1327.

SILK Net; green. Turkish, 16th century (?). 11¼ inches by 4½ inches.

Such productions of the loom are used among the Moslem inhabitants of the East in various ways, for concealing their females when they go abroad in carriages, &c.

1328.

LINEN Diaper. Flemish, 15th century. 2¾ inches square.

Very likely from the looms of Yprès, then famous for its napery, and which gave its name, "d'ypres," to this sort of wrought linen.

1329.

PART of an Orphrey Web; ground, crimson silk; design, straight branches bearing flowers and boughs, in gold thread; and amid them St. Dorothy and St. Stephen. German, 15th century. 23 inches by 2¾ inches.

St. Dorothy is figured holding in her right hand a golden chalice-like cup filled with flowers, and in her left, a tall green branch blooming with white roses; St. Stephen carries a palm-branch, emblem of his martyrdom. Both saints are standing upon green turf sprinkled with crimson daisies, and beneath each is the saint's name, written in gold. Though the persons of the saints are woven, the heads, hands, and emblems are wrought with the needle. The dalmatic of the proto-martyr is nicely shown, in light green, with its orphreys in gold. This piece is a favourable specimen of its kind, and very likely was produced at Cologne.

1330.

FRONTLET to an Altar-cloth; ground, diapered white linen; design, embroidery of two large flower-bearing trees, with an uncharged shield between them, and under them inscriptions. German, 16th century. 15¾ inches by 5 inches.

So very like the piece No. 8864 that it would seem to have been wrought by the same hand. To the left we read—" Spes unica, stabat mater;" to the right—" Mater dolorosa juxta crucem," &c.

1331.

WEB for Orphreys; ground, crimson silk; design, two boughs with leaves and flowers twined in an oval form, all in gold thread. German, late 15th century. 10 inches by 4¼ inches.

Graceful in its design, but poor in both its silk and gold, the latter having become almost black.

1332.

PIECE of Raised Velvet, brocaded in gold; ground, dark blue; design, a diapering in cut velvet on the blue ground, and large leaves and small artichokes in gold. Italian, early 16th century. 16¼ inches by 15¾ inches.

This nicely diapered velvet, of a good pile and sprinkled with a gold brocade, may have been wrought either at Lucca or Genoa. Unfortunately, the gold thread was of an inferior quality.

1333.

SILK and Gold Damask; ground, crimson silk; design, broad garlands twined into a net-work, the almost round meshes of which are filled in with a conventional artichoke wreathed with corn-flowers, all in pure good gold, upon a ground fpecked with gold. Spanifh, late 15th century. 22¼ inches by 9 inches.

This is a fine rich fpecimen of an article of the Spanifh loom, very likely from Almeria; its crimfon tone is frefh and warm, while its gold is as bright now as when firft woven into its prefent graceful pattern.

1334.

WEB for Orphreys; ground, gold thread; defign, two branches twined into large oval fpaces, and bearing leaves and red and white flowers, having, in one fpace, the name Gumprecht and a fhield, applied, *or*, a fpread-eagle *fable*, langued and armed *gules*, (may be for Brandenburg); and under this, in the web itfelf, another fhield *or*, a lion rampant *gules*, armed langued and crowned *or*, and double tailed, feemingly for Bohemia. German, 15th century. 16 inches by 5½ inches.

Though of poor materials, this piece is interefting from fhowing a name and armorial bearings.

1335.

WEB for Orphreys; ground, fawn-coloured filk; defign, almoft all in gold, fitting on a throne beneath a Gothic canopy the Bleffed Virgin Mary, crowned and nimbed, with our Lord as a child upon her lap, alternating with a circle bearing within it the facred monogram (worked the wrong way) done in blue filk, furrounded by golden rays. German, middle of 15th century. 11¼ inches by 4½ inches.

The defign of this orphrey-web is good, but the gold fo amalgamated with copper that it has become quite brown. Though the monogram is that ufually feen in the hands of St. Bernardinus of Sienna, and the drawing of the group of the Bleffed Virgin Mary and the facred Child is fomewhat Italian, this was not the work of any Italians loom; for in no part of Italy would the monogram have had given it letters of fuch a German type.

1336.

SILK Damaſk; ground and pattern in rich crimſon; deſign, eight-cuſped ovals, each cuſp tipped not with a flower, but tendrils; the ovals encloſe a conventional artichoke purfled with flowers; and the ſpaces between the ovals are filled in with ſmall artichokes in bloom. Spaniſh, 15th century. 20 inches by 14¾ inches.

This is a fine ſpecimen both for the richneſs of its ſilk and the warm and mellow tint of its ground, upon which the pattern comes out in a duller tone. Further on we ſhall meet with another ſtuff, No. 1345, which muſt have proceeded from the ſame loom, and ſhows in its deſign many elements of the one in this. Either Granada or Almeria produced this fine piece, which affords us, in the brilliancy of its colour, an apt ſample of our old poet Chaucer's dreſs for one of his characters, of whom he tells us,—

"In ſanguin and in perſe he clad was alle;"

and helps us to underſtand Spenſer's alluſion to the young maiden's bluſhes:—

"How the red roſes fluſh up in her cheekes
. . . . . with goodly vermill ſtayne,
Like crimſon dyde in grayne."

1337.

WEB for Orphreys; ground, crimſon ſilk; deſign, in gold thread, a ſtraight branch of a tree bearing pairs of boughs with flowers, alternating with other boughs with ſprigs of leaves. German, early 16th century. 14¾ inches by 2½ inches.

The warp of this web is thick linen thread, and where the woof of crimſon ſilk is worn away, this thread, as if part of the deſign, ſhows itſelf; and, as the gold is poor and ſparingly put on, the ſpecimen now looks ſhabby. Like many other ſamples of the kind, woven, probably, at Cologne, this was intended as the narrow orphrey on liturgical garments.

1338.

AN Apparel to an Alb; ground, strong linen; design, within twining boughs bearing flowers and leaves, a dove and a lamb, all in various-coloured silks and outlined in narrow strips of leather. Spanish, early 15th century. 13 inches square.

That the last liturgic use of this piece was as an apparel to an alb there can be little doubt, though, in all likelihood, it may have been cut off a larger piece of needlework wrought for the front border of an altar-cloth. The outline in leather is rather singular; though now black, it was once gilt, like those strips we see cut into very narrow shreds, and worked up, instead of gold thread, into silken stuffs from the looms of Almeria or Granada, specimens of which are in this collection. As an art-production of the needle, this is but a poor one.

1339.

RAISED Gold Brocaded Velvet; ground, green silk; design, within an oval in crimson raised velvet of a floriated pattern, dotted with flowers and grapes in white, a large trefoil on raised crimson velvet, bearing inside an artichoke in green and gold, springing from a white flower. Italian, 16th century. 11¾ inches by 8 inches.

This tasteful and pleasing design is wrought in rich materials; and large state-chairs are yet to be seen in the palaces of Rome covered with such beautiful and costly velvets.

1340.

SILK and Gold Damask; ground, blue silk; design, ogee arches, over the finial of each a large conventional flower, and within and without the arches a slip of the mulberry-leaf and fruit, all in bright gold. Lucca, 16th century. 3 feet 5 inches by 2 feet 4 inches.

This fine rich stuff must have been most effective for wall-hangings. The blue silk ground is tastefully diapered in bright and dull shades of the silk itself; and in the fine gold design the artichoke is judiciously brought in upon the ogee arches. When nicely managed, nothing is better than a ground in one shade and a design in a deeper tone of the same colour.

1341.

SILK and Gold Damask; ground, fawn-coloured silk; design, pomegranates piled together in threes, all gold, and flowers in silk alternately crimson and green. Spanish, 16th century. 16¾ inches by 12 inches.

The rich ground of this fine stuff has a well-designed and rather raised diapering of geometrical scroll-work; the pomegranates are wrought in pure gold thread, and the tones of the flowers are bright.

1342.

WORSTED Work; ground, black; design, flowers. German, 16th century. 21¼ inches square.

Very likely this was part of a carpet, embroidered by hand, for covering the top of the higher step at the altar, called by some a pedecloth; the ground is of a black worsted warp, with a woof of thick brown thread. The flowers are mostly crimson-shaded pink, some are, or were, partly white, and seem to be made for sorts of the pentstemon, digitalis, and fritillaria; a butterfly, too, is not forgotten.

1343.

CRADLE-QUILT, linen, embroidered in coloured silks with flowers and names. German, late 15th century. 3 feet 4¼ inches by 1 foot 8¼ inches.

At each of its four corners, as well as in the middle, is wrought a large bunch of our " meadow pink;" between the flowers are worked these names,—" Jhesus, Maria, Johanes, Jaspar, Baltasar, Maria,

Melchior, Johanes." From the names affigned to the three wife men, whofe relics are enfhrined in the cathedral at Cologne, being fo confpicuoufly wrought upon this piece, we may prefume that the needlework was done in that great German city. By wear, the greens of the leaves have turned brown, and the pink of the flowers become pale. Thofe pieces of printed linen with which the holes in two places are mended will not be without an intereft for thofe who are curious in tracing out the origin of fuch manufactures. Other examples of thefe cradle-quilts are in this collection.

1344.

CRADLE-QUILT, linen, embroidered in coloured filks; defign, within a broad border of fcroll-work in fimple lines, the emblems of the four Evangelifts, one at each corner; of the Crucifixion, with the Bleffed Virgin Mary on the right, and St. John to the left, only a fmall part of the young apoftle's figure is to be found at prefent. German, early 16th century. 2 feet 6 inches by 2 feet 2 inches.

Though in mere outline, the whole defign was well drawn, and the emblems at the corners have great freedom about them. On the popular ufe of the evangelifts' emblems upon fuch baby's furniture, fome obfervations are given on another good fample, No. 4644, in this collection. A cradle-quilt like the prefent one occurs at No. 4459.

1345.

SILK Damafk; ground and pattern in reddifh crimfon; defign, eight-cufped ovals,—each cufp tipped with a flower, ending in a fleur-de-lis above a crown, at top, and enclofing a conventional artichoke purfled with flowers. Spanifh, 15th century. 14 inches by 13 inches.

- From its prefent fhape, this piece was evidently laft in ufe as the hood to a liturgical cope.

1346.

PART of an Embroidered Orphrey; ground (now faded), crimson silk; design, a green silk bough so twined as to end in a long pinnatified leaf or flower, now white but once gold, with little rounds of gold sprouting from parts of the outside branches. German, 16th century. 16¾ inches by 3 inches.

A specimen as meagre in design as it is poor in materials.

1347.

PART of an Embroidered Orphrey; ground, crimson silk; design, a green silk bough, &c. German, 16th century. 17¼ inches by 5 inches.

In all likelihood a part of the broader orphrey wrought for the same vestment as the one just before mentioned.

1348.

WEB for Orphreys; ground, gold thread; design, the fleur-de-lis composed into a geometric pattern, outlined in dark brown silk. German, late 15th century. 14¼ inches by 4¼ inches.

Both the brown colour and the design are somewhat rare, as found upon ecclesiastical appliances. Here, as elsewhere, the gold is so poor that it is hardly discernible. Under the canvas lining is a piece of parchment, on which is written some theological matter.

1349.

WEB for Orphreys; ground, cloth of gold pricked with crimson; design, the names—" Jhesus," " Maria," done in blue silk, between two trees, one bearing heads of crimson fruit, the other lilies, parti-coloured white with crimfon; and the green fward, from which both fpring, covered with full-blown daifies in one inftance, with unexpanded daifies in the other. German, late 15th century. 17½ inches by 4½ inches.

Like feveral other fpecimens in the collection, and moft probably woven to be the orphreys fewed, before and behind, in a horizontal ftripe, upon the dalmatics and tunicles for high mafs. The ftudent of fymbolifm will not fail to fee in the tree to the right hand the myftic vine, bearing bunches of crimfon grapes; while, to the left, the tree covered with parti-coloured lilies—white for purity, red for a bleeding-heart—is referrible to the Bleffed Virgin Mary, whofe heart, as fhe ftood at the foot of the crofs, underwent all the pains of martyrdom foretold her by Simeon when he faid,—"And thine own foul a fword fhall pierce," *Luke* ii. 35.

1350.

WEB for Orphreys; ground, narrow blue fpaces alternating with wider crimfon ones; defign, the name of "Jhefus," in gold upon the blue, between two borders checkered crimfon blue and yellow, the crimfon fpaces charged with a floriation, alternately gold and yellow; the next blue fpace infcribed with the name "Maria" in gold. In the names, as well as the floriation, the metal has become tarnifhed fo as to look a dull brown. German, late 15th century. 19 inches by 2¼ inches.

Of fuch webs there are feveral fpecimens in the collection; and their ufe was to ornament liturgical veftments, in thofe long perpendicular lines found upon tunicles and dalmatics.

1351.

PIECE of Raifed Velvet; ground, crimfon; defign, a conventional artichoke, wreathed with fmall flowers in green and yellow within a garland of the fame colours. Italian, 16th century. 11½ inches by 11 inches.

1351 A.

IECE of Raised Velvet. A part of the same stuff. Italian, 16th century. 9¾ inches by 1¾ inches.

1351 B.

IECE of Raised Velvet. A part of the same stuff. Italian, 16th century. 12¼ inches by 1¾ inches.

These three pieces are portions of a material made of excellent rich silk, and of good tones in colour.

1352.

IECE of Raised Velvet, brocaded in gold; ground, crimson; design, an oval with cusps inside and enclosing a large artichoke, the whole wreathed with a garland, and in gold. Italian, 16th century. 2 feet 3¾ inches by 8¼ inches.

This magnificent stuff is rendered still more valuable, as a specimen, from having much of its design of that rare kind of velvet upon velvet, or one pile put over, in design, another but lower pile. The state-rooms of a palace could alone have been hung with such sumptuous wall-coverings. Perhaps church vestments and hangings about the altar may have been sometimes made of such a heavy material.

1352 A.

IECE of Raised Velvet, brocaded in gold; ground, crimson; design, a cusped oval enclosing a conventional artichoke, and the whole wreathed with a broad garland, all in gold. Italian, 16th century. 18 inches by 7 inches.

This differs both in design and quality from the former, having no pile upon pile in it.

1352 B.

PIECE of Raised Velvet, brocaded in gold; ground, crimson; design, not very clear: though, from what can be observed, it is the same with No. 1352.

1353.

WEB for Orphreys; ground, crimson silk; design, in yellow silk and gold thread, between two floriated borders, a series of foliated scrolls, with the open round spaces filled in with the Blessed Virgin holding our Lord as a naked child in her arms, and a saint-bishop wearing his mitre and cope, giving his blessing with one hand, and holding his pastoral staff in the other. Venetian, 16th century. 25 inches by 8¼ inches.

The materials are good, excepting the gold thread, which has turned black, though the large quantity of rich yellow silk used along with it somewhat hides its tarnish. In gearing his loom the weaver has made the mistake of showing the bishop as bestowing his benediction with his left, instead of his right hand.

1354.

EMBROIDERED Linen; ground, very fine linen; design, separated by a saltire or St. Andrew's cross, lozenges filled in with a Greek cross, and half lozenges, the whole ornamented with circles enclosing other small crosses. Italian, 16th century. 10¼ inches by 3¼ inches.

This elaborate design is as delicately worked as it is beautiful in pattern.

1355.

SILK Damaſk; ground, ſea-green; deſign, in the ſame tint, a conventional foliation of the pomegranate, ſurrounding a wide broad-banded oval filled in with a large fruit of the ſame kind. Spaniſh, early 16th century. 33 inches by 12½ inches.

In the beauty of its deſign, the rich ſoftneſs of its ſilk, and its grateful tone, this is a pleaſing ſpecimen of the loom from the ſouth of Spain.

1356.

PIECE of Raiſed Velvet; black; deſign, foliated branches joined at intervals by royal crowns alternating with vaſes, and large artichokes in the intervening ſpaces. Italian, late 15th century. 25¼ inches by 21¾ inches.

This truly beautiful velvet was, no doubt, meant for perſonal attire.

1357.

RAISED Velvet; ground, olive-green ſilk; deſign, ſlips with flowers and leaves of a ſomewhat deeper tone, and outlined in a lighter coloured raiſed velvet. Lucca, 16th century. 8⅞ inches by 8¼ inches.

This nicely-wrought ſtuff of pleaſing pattern muſt have been made for perſonal attire.

1358.

LINEN Crochet Work; deſign, ſaltires, between croſſes formed of leaves, and a modification of the Greek meander. Flemiſh, 16th century. 21 inches by 7½ inches.

The convents in France, but more particularly in Flanders, were at all times famous for this kind of work; hence it is often called nun's lace, becaufe wrought by them for trimming altar-cloths and albs. The prefent one is a good fpecimen of a geometrical pattern, and the two borders are neatly done by the needle upon linen. In all likelihood this piece was the hem of an altar-cloth.

1359.

LINEN Damafk; defign, fcrolls and foliage, with a deep border fhowing ducal coronets, armorial fhields, and the letters L and K. Flemifh, early 17th century. 28¼ inches by 11¼ inches.

An elaborate fpecimen of the way they geared their looms in Flanders, and more efpecially at Yprès, where moft likely, this fine damafk was woven. The fhield is party per pale, 1ft, two chevronels embattled; 2nd, three turreted towers, two and one. Seemingly this piece of Flemifh napery was made for fome nobleman whofe wife was, or claimed to be, of the ancient blood of the royal houfe of Caftile.

1360.

SILK Damafk; ground, crimfon; defign, bunches of flowers, artichokes, and pomegranates, in yellow. Spanifh, 16th century. 20 inches by 11¾ inches.

A rich ftuff, whether colour or material be confidered; and quite agreeing with other fpecimens in the love of the fouthern Spanifh loom for the pomegranate, the emblem of Granada, where probably it was wrought.

1361.

SILK Damafk; ground, dull violet; defign, within reticulated fquares, a conventional bunch of flowers much in the honeyfuckle fhape, in white and yellow. Italian, 16th century. 6 inches by 7¾ inches.

Though the filk is good, the weaving is rather coarfe and rough.

1362.

ILK Damask; ground, bright crimson; design, a conventional floriation in various-coloured silks. North Italian, 16th century. 9¼ inches by 6¾ inches.

So thick is this somewhat showy stuff, that it must have been meant for furniture purposes.

1363.

SILK Damask; ground, reddish purple; design, slips of three kinds of flower-bearing plants, one of which is the pomegranate. Spanish, late 15th century. 10¾ inches by 6⅞ inches.

From the south of Spain, and bearing a token, if not of the city, at least of the kingdom of Granada.

1364.

DAMASK, linen woof, silken warp; ground, yellow; design, a conventional floriation, showing a strong likeness to the whole plant of the artichoke, in white linen. Italian, 16th century. 10 inches by 9¼ inches.

A poor stuff in respect to materials, colour, and design; which latter is the best element in it. Intended for household decorative purposes.

1365.

DAMASK, silk woof, linen warp; ground, light red, now faded; design, vases filled with flowers, in yellow silk. Italian, late 16th century. 24 inches by 22 inches.

SILK DAMASK

Crimson ground with large branching pattern in coloured silk
Italian 16th century.

No doubt this stuff was meant for hangings in a palace or dwelling-house; and among the flowers may be seen the bignonia or trumpet-flower, and the pomegranate opening and about to shed its seed.

1366.

LINEN Diaper; design, square made out of four leaves. Flemish, late 16th century. 20 inches by 9 inches.

The pattern, though so simple, is very pleasing, and the stuff itself speaks of Ypres as being the place of its origin.

1367.

SILK Taffeta; ground, purple; design, amid boughs, a pair of birds, with an artichoke between them, all in orange-yellow. Sicilian, 14th century. $9\frac{3}{4}$ inches square.

This light thin stuff, quiet in its tones and simple in its pattern, must have been wrought for lining robes of rich stuffs.

1368.

SILK Damask; ground, white satin; design, amid flowers, among which the chrysanthemum is very conspicuous, a group, consisting of a man inside a low fence looking upwards upon a blue lion and a golden tiger, seemingly at play, side by side, one of which is about to be struck by a long spear held by a man standing above, within a walled building. Just over him stands another man with a short mace in one hand, in the other a small bottle, out of which comes a large bough of the pomegranate tree in leaf, flower, and fruit. Chinese, 16th century. 2 feet $6\frac{3}{4}$ inches by $10\frac{3}{4}$ inches.

For the soft warm tints of its several coloured flos-silks, the pureness of the gold thread upon the human faces, the animals and the flowers, the correctness of the drawing, and the well-arranged freedom of the whole pattern, there are few pieces that come up to this in the whole collection. In all likelihood it was brought from China, perhaps made up as a liturgical chasuble, by some Portuguese missionary priest, in the latter portion of the 16th or beginning of the 17th century.

1369.

ALMATIC; ground, blue silk; design, narrow bands charged with circles enclosing a word in imitated Arabic, and coventional flowers separating two hounds couchant, gardant, each within his own circle, all in gold, and a large conventional floriation, at the foot of which are two cheetahs collared, courant, face to face, all in white silk, slightly specked with crimson, and between this group two eagles, in white silk, flying down upon two small hounds, sejant, gardant, both in gold. The orphreys, broad and narrow, are embroidered with heraldic shields set upon a golden ground. Sicilian, 14th century. 3 feet 5½ inches by (across the sleeves) 4 feet 2¾ inches.

Some ruthless hand has cut away from the back a large square piece of this vestment; and, to adopt it to modern fashion, its sleeves have been slit up at the under side. The armorial bearings are, on one shield, a chief *or*, *gules*, three stars, two, and one *argent*; on the other, *purpure*, two arrows in saltire *or*.

The cheetahs are well marked by the round spots upon them; and when new, this stuff, with its pattern so boldly figured, must have been pleasing.

1370.

IECE of Cut-work, for wall hanging; ground, square of blue and red, with the upper border blue, the side one red; design, at top, knights and ladies talking, and each within a separate arch; in the body of the piece, the history of some dragon-slayer, figured in two horizontal rows of compartments, every one of which is contained within an archway with a head compofed of three trefoil arches in a ftraight line, and refting on trefoil-brackets, and having, all through, birds and flowers in the fpandrils. French, late 14th century. 7 feet 11 inches by 3 feet 4 inches.

Though now fo rough and tattered this almoft unique piece of " cut-work" (which French people would call appliqué, but better defcribed by the Englifh words), of fo large a fize, is valuable for its ufe in fhowing how, with cheap materials and a little knowledge of drawing, a very pleafing, not to fay ufeful, article of decoration may be made, either for church appliance or houfehold furniture.

Unfortunately the heads of the perfonages in the upper row are all cut away, but lower down we plainly fee the hiftory meant to be reprefented. Upon the firft pane, to the left, we have a regal throne, upon which are fitting, evidently in earneft talk, a king, crowned and fceptred, and a knight, each belted with a fplendid military girdle falling low down around the hips. Behind the knight ftands his 'fquire. In the next pane the enthroned king is giving his orders to the ftanding knight, toward whom his 'fquire is bringing his fword, his fhield, (*argent* a fefs *azure*, furmounted by a demi-ox *azure*,) and a bafcinet mantled and crefted with the head of the fame demi-ox or aurochs and its tall horns. After this we behold the knight with lance and fhield, and his 'fquire on horfeback riding forth from the caftle, at the gate of which ftands the king, outftretching his hand and bidding farewell to the knight, who is turning about to acknowledge the good-bye. Going firft upon the road, the knight, followed by the 'fquire, feems afking the way to the dragon's lair, from a gentleman whom they meet. The monfter is then found in a wood, and the knight is tilting his fpear into its fire-red maw. The next pane carrying on the romance is the firft to the left in the fecond or lower feries. Here the knight is unhorfed, and his good grey fteed is lying on the field; but the knight himfelf, wielding his fword in both hands, is about to fmite the dragon breathing long flames of fire towards him. Afterwards he catches hold of his fiery tongue, and is cutting it off. It would look as if the dragon, though wounded to the lofs of its tongue, had not been worfted; for in the following compartment we behold the fame knight all unarmed, but well mounted, galloping forth from a caftle gate with a hound and fome fort of bird, both with ftrings to them, by his horfe's fide, and having found the dragon again, appears holding an argument with the beaft that, for anfwer, fhows the fiery ftump of his tongue in his gaping mouth. But the dragon will not give himself up and be led away captive. Now, however, comes the grand fight. In a forest, with a bird perched on high upon one of the trees, the knight, dismounted from his horse, cuts off the head of the dragon, which, to the last, is careful to show his much shortened yet still fiery tongue to his victor. Now have we the last passage but one in the story. Upon his bended knee the triumphant knight is presenting the open-mouthed, tongueless, cut-off dragon's head to the king and queen, both throned and royally arrayed, the princess, their daughter, standing by her mother's side. The young maiden, no doubt, is the victor's prize; but now—and it is the last chapter—the knight and lady, dressed in the weeds of daily life and walking forth upon the flowery turf, seem happy with one another as man and wife. The two panes at this part, and serving as a border, seem out of place, and neither has a connection with the other; in the first, just outside a castle wall, rides a crowned king followed by a horseman, evidently of low degree; and a column separates him from a large bed, lying upon which we observe the upper part of a female figure, the head resting upon a rich cushion; next to this, but put in anglewise to fill up the space, we have a crowned lady and a girdled knight, sitting beneath a tree, each with a little dog beside them.

The costume of both men and women in this curious piece of cut-work is that of the end of the 14th century. The parti-coloured dress of the men, their long pointed shoes, and the broad girdles, worn so low upon their hips by the king and knight, as well as the bascinet and helmet of the latter, with the horses' trappings, all speak of that period; nor should we forget the sort of peaked head-dress, as well as the way in which the front hair of the ladies is thrown up into thick short curls. All the human figures, all the beasts, as well as the architecture, are outlined in thin leather or parchment once gilt, but now turned quite black. With the same leather, too, were studded the belts of the king and knight, and the spangles and golden enrichments of the ladies' dress were of the same material. Saving here and there a few stitches of silk, everything else was of worsted, and that none of the finest texture. With such small means a good art-work was produced, as we see before us. The way in which each figure over the whole of this curious piece of cut-work is outlined by the leather edging strongly reminds us of the leadings in stained glass; in fact, both the one and the other are wrought after the same manner, and the principal difference between the window and the woollen hanging is the employment of an opaque instead of a transparent material. If the personages are dressed sometimes in blue, at others in crimson, it will be found that these colours alternate with the alternating tints of the panes upon which they are sewed.

So often do the passages in the romance here figured correspond with certain parts in the wild legend of our own far-famed "Sir Guy of Warwick," that, at first sight, one might be led to think that as his renowned story was carried all through Christendom, we had before us his mighty feats and triumph over the dragon in Northumberland, set forth in this handiwork of some lady-reader of his story.

1371.

WORSTED Work; ground, green; design, conventional flowers in yellow, with, at one end, a border of foliated boughs, the leaves of which are partly green, partly red, and an edging of a band made up of white, green, yellow, scarlet straight lines on the inner side; on three sides there is a narrow listing of bluish-green lace. German, 15th century. 4 feet 3¼ inches by 1 foot 10 inches.

In all probability this was intended and used as a carpet for some small altar-step. It is worked upon coarse canvas.

1372.

PIECE of Needlework; pattern, upon bell-shaped spaces of silver thread, flowers mostly white and shaded yellow, divided by a sort of imperial high-peaked cap of blue shaded white, arising out of a royal crown. 17th century. 12¾ inches by 7¼ inches.

1372 A.

BORDER to an Altar-cloth, embroidered; ground, crimson silk; design, animals and birds amid branching foliage and fleurs-de-lis, well raised in white and gold; the upper part linen, wrought into lozenges alternately crimson and yellow, braced together by a fret, and filled in with narrow bars faltire wife. German, 15th century. 3 feet 10¼ inches by 11½ inches.

Among the animals is the fymbolic lamb and flag, with a chalice underneath its head. From the exact fimilarity of ftyle in the ornamentation and needlework, there can be no doubt but the fame hand which wrought the ftole, No. 1322, worked this piece, and probably both formed a portion of the fame fet of ornaments for the chantry chapel of fome fmall family.

1373.

COPE; ground, green raifed-velvet; defign, amid leaves of a heart-fhape or cordate, freckled with a kind of check, large conventional artichokes. The orphreys are of web, figured, on a golden ground, with faints, infcription, and flower-bearing trees; the hood is ornamented with applied cut-work and needle embroidery, and the morfe is of plain velvet. The raifed velvet is Italian, 16th century; the orphrey web, German, 16th century; the embroidery of the hood, 16th century. 9 feet 2 inches by 3 feet 11¼ inches.

The raifed velvet, though now fo torn and ftitched together, is of a very fine pile, and pleafing elaborate defign. The hood is figured with the Annunciation, and the faces are applied pieces of white filk with the features and hair brought out by the needle in coloured filks; the other parts of the embroidery are coarfe but effective. On the orphreys are fhown, on one fide, St. Peter and St. Katherine, on the other, St. Paul and St. Barbara. The ground for the name of the laft faint looks very bright and frefh in its gold; but the gold is, fo to fay, a fraud. It is put, by the common gilding procefs, upon the web after being woven, and not twined about the thread itfelf. The fringe all round the lower part is rather unufual.

1374.

APPLIED Embroidery; ground, green silk; pattern, a flower-vase between two horns of plenty with flowers coming out of them, and separated by a conventional floral ornament, mostly done in amber-coloured cord. French, late 17th century. 2 feet 3 inches by 6¾ inches.

Tame in its design, and easy in its execution.

1374 A. '64.

CHASUBLE of Silk Damask; ground, purple; design, a quatrefoil within another charged with a cross-like floriation, having a square white-lined centre, surmounted by two eagles with wings displayed and upholding in their beaks a royal crown, all in green. Italian, early 15th century. 4 feet 6 inches by 2 feet 7 inches.

By some unfeeling hand a large piece was, not long ago, cut out from the front of this fine old ample chasuble; and, very likely, the specimen of the same stuff, No. 7057, is that very portion.

1375. '64.

CHASUBLE; ground, very rich velvet; design, in the middle of a large five-petaled flower, a pomegranate, and another pomegranate in the spaces between these flowers. The orphreys are, before and behind, of rich diapered cloth of gold, the one behind of the Y form, figured in embroidery with the Crucifixion; the one before on a piece of velvet of a different diapering from the back, with the Blessed Virgin Mary and our Lord, as a child, in her arms; and below, the figure of Religion. Spanish, late 15th century. 3 feet 2 inches by 2 feet 4¾ inches.

This chafuble muft have been truly grand and majeftic when new, and feen in all its fumptuous fulnefs, for it has been fadly cut away about the fhoulders. It muft, originally, have meafured, on that part, at leaft fome inches beyond four feet. The Y crofs orphrey on the back is figured with the crucifixion, done after a large and effective manner, for the perfon of our Redeemer meafures more than 1 foot 9 inches in length, and His, as well as all the other faces are thrown up in low relief. At the ends of the tranfom of the crofs are four winged angels—two at each fide, of whom one is catching, in a golden chalice, the facred blood fpirting from the wounds in the hands, the other flying down in forrow from the clouds. High above the crofs are two angels with peacock-feather wings, fwinging two golden thuribles, which are in low relief; and between thefe angelic fpirits, a golden eagle in high relief, with wings difplayed, armed and beaked *gules* and holding in his once crimfon talons a fcroll which, from the letters obfervable, may have been infcribed with the motto, "(Refpice) in fi(nem)." The front of the chafuble is made of a piece of velvet of another and much broader defign—a large flower of five petals and two ftipulæ—but equally remarkable for its deep mellow ruby tone and foft deep pile. Its orphrey of fine diapered gold-thread embroidery, but much worn away through being long rubbed by its wearers againft the altar, is worked with the Bleffed Virgin Mary carrying in her arms our Saviour, as a naked child, careffing His mother's face; and, lower down, with a female figure crowned and nimbed, bearing in her right hand a golden chalice, at the top of which is a large euchariftic particle marked with a crofs-crofflet; this is the emblem of the Church. Both figures are large and of a telling effect; and, like the other figures, have more of a naturaliftic than ideal type of beauty about them.

1376.

CHASUBLE; ground, raifed crimfon velvet with concentric circles in cloth of gold, within garlands of which the leaves are green, the flowers gold. The orphreys are woven in coloured filks on cloth of gold, with infcriptions. The velvet, Florentine, late 15th century; the orphrey web, German, late 15th century. 3 feet 10¾ inches by 2 feet 10¼ inches.

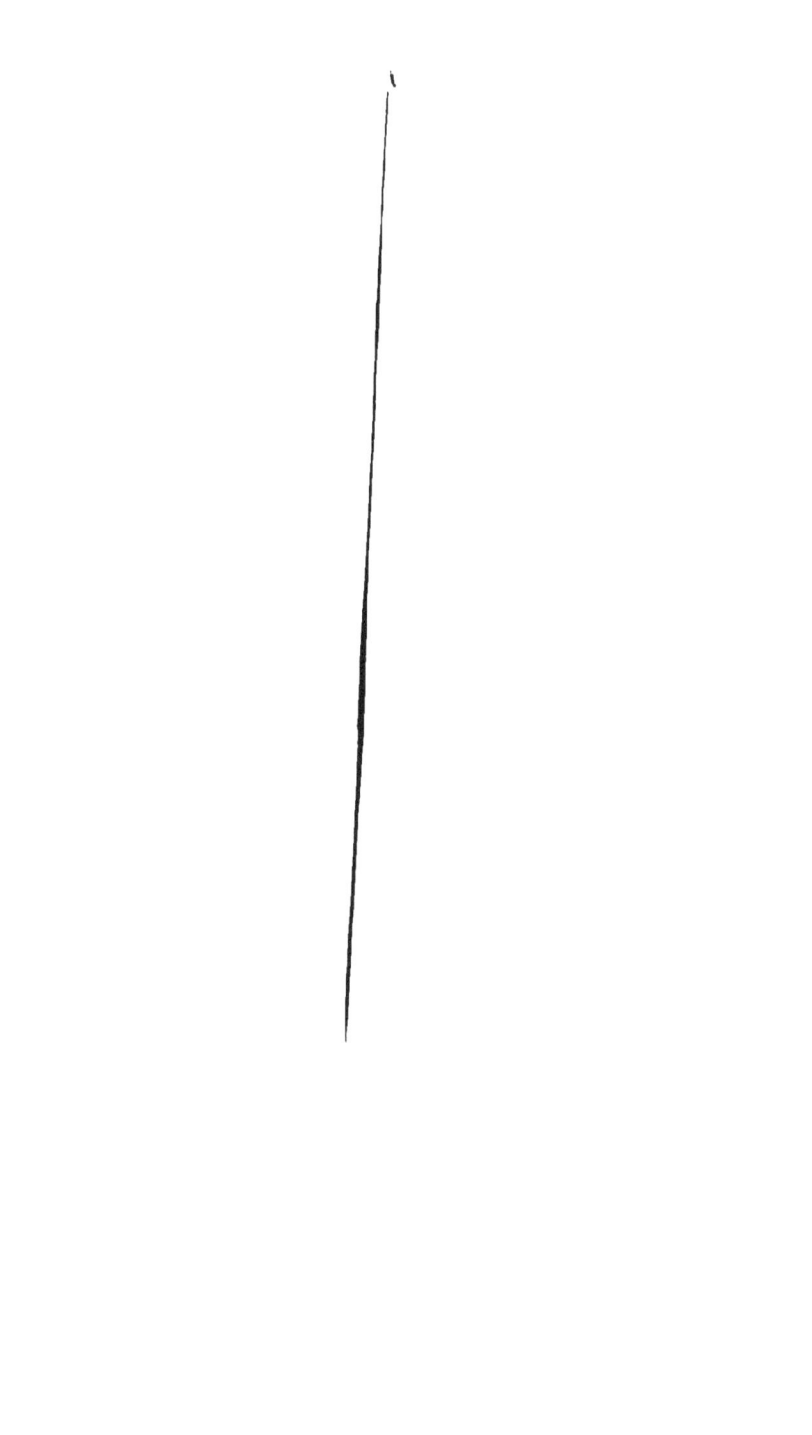

PART OF THE ORPHREY OF A CHASUBLE.
German 15th century

The very rich stuff of this vestment far surpasses in splendour the orphreys, which ought to have been better. On the one behind, we have the Crucifixion with the words below, in blue silk, "O Crux Ave." Further down an angel is holding a sheet figured with all the instruments of the Passion. After the word Maria, a second angel is shown with another sheet falling from his hands and figured with the Holy Lamb, having, beneath it, the words "Ecce Agnus Dei;" then a third angel, with the word, but belonging to another piece, "Johan." On the orphrey in front a fourth angel is displaying a chalice surmounted by a cross and standing within a fenced garden, and beneath the sheet the word "Maria." Lower down a fifth angel is showing the column and two bundles of rods, with "Jhesus." Last of all there is an angel with a napkin marked with the crown of green thorns and two reeds placed saltire-wise, and the word "Maria."

1375.

SADDLE-BAG of Persian carpeting; ground, deep crimson; pattern, stripes in various colours running up the warp. Persian. 3 feet 4 inches by 1 foot 5 inches.

The warp and weft are of a strong coarse texture, and not only at the corners but upon each pouch there are tassels.

1376.

TRAVELLING-BAG, of the same stuff, but varying in pattern. Persian. 1 foot 8 inches by 1 foot 7 inches.

1378.

BAG of woven worsted; ground, deep crimson; pattern, narrow stripes figured with diversified squares in different colours. Persian. 1 foot $3\frac{3}{4}$ inches by 1 foot $2\frac{1}{4}$ inches.

From the string of worsted lace attached to the side it would seem that this bag was meant to be slung across the person of the wearer. None of these three articles are very old.

1379.

BAG of woven silk and worsted; ground, deep crimson worsted; pattern, horizontal bands in silk figured, in places, with four-legged beasts, white, yellow, red, and green, and with vertical bands figured with a green net-work filled in with what look like birds, crimson, separated by a tree. Persian. 11¾ inches by 10 inches.

Most Persian in look is this bag, which, from the thick cord attached to it, seems to have been for carrying in the hand. It is lined with brown linen, and has two strings for drawing the mouth close up. The two birds repeated so often on the lower part, and separated by what looks like a tree, may be an ornament traditionally handed down from the times when the Persian sacred "hom" was usual in the patterns of that country. No great antiquity can be claimed by the textile before us.

1547, 1548.

TWO Escutcheons of the Arms of France, surmounted by a royal crown, and encircled with the collars of two orders—one St. Michael, the other the Holy Ghost—embroidered upon a black ground, in gold and silver, and the proper blazon colours. French, 17th century.

All well and heraldically done.

1622.

IECE of Printed Chintz. Old English, presented by F. Fellingham, Esq.

2864A.

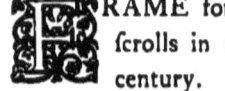RAME for enamels; ground, purple velvet; pattern, scrolls in raised gold embroidery. French, late 17th century. 8 inches by 7 inches.

The velvet is put on pasteboard. In the centre, left uncovered, a larger enamel must have been let in; upon the four small circular and unembroidered spaces of the velvet, lesser enamels, or precious stones, were sewed.

2865.

FRAME for enamels; ground, crimson velvet; pattern, scrolls in raised gold embroidery. French, late 17th century. 8 inches by 7 inches.

Though differing in its colour, this is evidently the fellow to the one just mentioned.

4015.

MITRE; crimson and gold velvet. Florentine, 15th century. 1 foot 10½ inches by 11 inches.

This liturgical curiosity is of that low graceful shape which we find in most mitres before the 16th century; in all probability this one was made not for real episcopal use, but to be employed in the service of the so-called boy-bishop who used, for centuries, to be chosen every year from among the boys who served in the cathedral, or the great churches of towns, at Christmas-tide, as well in England as all over Christendom; (see " Church of our Fathers," t. iv. p. 215). As the rubrical colour for episcopal mitres is white, or of cloth of gold, a crimson mitre is of great rarity. The one before us is made of those rich stuffs for which Florence was so famous, as may be instanced in the gorgeous vestments given to Westminster Abbey by our Henry VII. The mitre itself is of crimson velvet, freckled with gold threads, raised in a rich pile upon a golden ground, with green fringed lappets; but the "titulus," or upright stripe before and behind, along with the " corona," or circular band, are all of a kind of lace or woven texture of raised velvet, green, white, and crimson, after a pretty design, upon a golden ground. The mitre is lined throughout with light-blue silk.

4016.

BED-QUILT; ground, cherry-coloured satin; pattern, birds amid flowers and foliage, in the centre a double-headed eagle, displayed. East Indian (?), early 17th century. 8 feet 6 inches by 6 feet 10 inches.

The satin is poor, and its colour faded; but the embroidery, with which it is plentifully overspread, is of a rich, though not tasty, kind. Birds of extraordinary, and, no doubt, fanciful plumage are everywhere flitting about it, among flowers as unusual as themselves; but the glowing tones of the many-coloured silks in which they are wrought must strike every one's eye. From the double-headed eagle, done in gold, with wings blue, yellow, and green, displayed, it would appear that this quilt was wrought for some (perhaps imperial) house in Europe.

4018.

STATE-CAP, of crimson velvet turned up with white satin, which is faced with crimson velvet, and all embroidered in gold and silver threads. German (?), late 17th century. 14¼ inches by 10 inches.

By a very modern hand the words "King Charles" are written upon the green silk lining; what Charles, however, is not mentioned. There is much about the shape of the cap itself, and especially in the design of its embroidery, to induce the belief that it was wrought and fashioned by a German hand, and for German and not English use. In a piece of tapestry once belonging to the famous Bayard, and now in the Imperial Library at Paris, the same form of high-crowned crimson velvet cap is worn by Pyrrhus while he is being knighted, as may be seen, plate 42, in Shaw's "Dresses and Decorations of the Middle Ages," t. ii, borrowed from Jubinal's fine work on "Early Tapestries."

4024.

ALTAR-FRONTAL; ground, crimson satin; subjects, five apostles, each under a Gothic canopy, with bunches of flowers between them wrought in coloured silks and gold thread. Italian, late 15th century. 7 feet 3 inches by 2 feet.

Beginning at the left-hand we have St. Paul holding a sword, then St. James the Greater with the pilgrim-staff; in the middle, St. Thomas holding in one hand a spear, and giving his blessing with the right, St. Andrew with a cross of large size leaning against his shoulder; and, last of all, St. John with an eagle at his feet. The figures are better done than the niches about them, which are very heavy and bad in taste, as are the bunches of flowers. The whole is applied, and upon a more modern piece of crimson satin. The back is lined with leaves of a printed book relating to the Abbey of Vallombrosa, near Florence.

Hanging behind this frontal, and put together as a background to it, are Numbers:—

4513—4516.

FRINGED Panels of Domestic Furniture; ground, deep maroon velvet; pattern, a small arabesque within a square of the same design, in cloth of gold edged with gold cord. Italian, 16th century. Nos. 4513 and 4515, each 4 feet 6 inches by 1 foot 4 inches; Nos. 4514 and 4516, each 3 feet 7 inches by 1 foot 4 inches.

Bedsteads in Italy are so large that these pieces look far too small to have ever been applied to such a purpose as bed-furniture. They were, probably, the hangings for the head of a canopy in the throne-room of a palace during the year of mourning for the death of its prince.

4045.

CHASUBLE; the ground, tawny-coloured velvet; pattern, angels and flowers in coloured flos-filks and gold thread, the orphreys before and behind figured with saints. English, 15th century. 7 feet by 3 feet.

Though the needlework upon this chafuble is effective at a diftance, like much of the embroidery of the time, both in this country and abroad, it is found to be very rude and coarfe when feen near. The ftyle of the whole ornamentation is fo very Englifh that there is no miftaking it. The back orphrey is in the fhape of a crofs; and on it, and figured at top, Melchifedek with three loaves in his hand; beneath him, the prophet Malachi, on the left of whom we have Abraham with a large broad facrificial knife in his hand, on the right, King David and his harp; thefe three form the tranfom of the crofs. Going downward, we fee St. John the Evangelift with the chalice; below this apoftle, David again; and, laft of all, half the perfon of fome faint. On the front orphrey are given St. James the Greater, and two prophets of the Old Law. This chafuble, with its ftole and maniple, is faid to have been found at Bath, hidden behind the wainfcot of a houfe there. Certain it is that the chafuble has been much cut down. The original fize was far larger.

4046, 4046 A.

STOLE and Maniple; ground, tawny-coloured velvet, embroidered with flowers in gold and coloured filks. Englifh, 15th century. Stole, 8 feet 6 inches by 2¾ inches; maniple, 3 feet 3 inches by 2¾ inches.

The embroidery is quite of the ftyle of the period, and in character with that ufually found upon the commoner clafs of Englifh veftments, done in flos-filk and gold thread, after a large defign. The velvet is Italian, and this tone of colour feems to have been then in favour.

4059.

PIECE of Woven Orphrey; ground, crimſon ſilk; ſubject, the Aſſumption of the Bleſſed Virgin Mary, in yellow ſilk. Florentine, 15th century. 2 feet 9 inches by 8¾ inches.

This favourite ſubject of all art-ſchools in the mediæval period is treated here much after other examples in this collection, as No. 8977, &c, but with ſome variations, and better deſign and drawing. The Eternal Father, with glory round Him, and two cherubim, is putting a crown upon the head of St. Mary, who is ſeated upon ſun-beams ſurrounded by angels, while ſhe drops her girdle to St. Thomas as he kneels at her late grave, now filled with new-blown lilies, and bearing on its front the words "Aſſunta eſt." "Aſſunta" for "Aſſumpta" is the weaver's own blunder. Dr. Bock gives a plate of it in his "Geſchichte des Liturgiſchen Gewänder des Mittelalters," 1 Band, 2 Lieferung, pl. xvi.

4061.

PIECE of Raiſed Velvet; ground, pale yellow ſilk; pattern, in raiſed velvet, a large oblong ſquare, having within a border of corn-flowers a large ſtar-like inflorescence, and each ſquare ſeparated by a border or band charged with liliaceous flowers, in crimſon raiſed velvet, in part upon a ſilver ground, now blackened, ſurrounded by an ornament in amber-ſtreaked green in raiſed velvet. Italian, late 16th century. 4 feet by 1 foot 1 inch.

Another of the ſeveral ſpecimens of the rich raiſed velvet for furniſhing purpoſes.

4062.

PURSE in Green Velvet, embroidered with gold and ſilver threads, and at bottom emblazoned with a ducal crown and two ſhields of arms. French, 18th century. 4¼ inches in diameter, 3 inches high.

Though so small, this little purse is tastefully and richly wrought, and has nicely worked double strings, with gold-covered knobs at their ends for drawing its mouth close, and two other like knobs for opening it. At bottom it is very richly ornamented with a golden mantle, upon which are two shields, the one on the man's side is *azure* two lions passant gardant, royally crowned *or*; that on the woman's side, *azure* a chevron *or*, between two four-petaled and barbed flowers, in chief, and a double transomed cross in base *argent*; over both shields is a ducal coronet. No doubt this purse, which is lined with white kid-leather, was one of those still used by ladies in France, and held in their hands as they stand at the doors or go about the church at service-time to collect the alms of the congregation, for the poor or other pious purposes; this one may have belonged to an heiress married to a duke.

4068.

STRIP of Raised Velvet; ground, silver and white silk; pattern, a large crimson and green flower seeded gold, alternating with a floriation having flowers of crimson, tawny, and purple on green stems. North Italy, 16th century.

This fine specimen of raised velvet is of a deep pile and rich mellow colouring. The silver threads of the ground have become quite dimmed, while the gold in the flower is fresh and glowing. Seemingly, this piece last served as the hanging of a bed.

4069.

PIECE of Raised Velvet on a gold ground; pattern, large conventional flowers and ears of corn issuing out of a ducal coronet. Genoese, early 17th century. 8 feet by 4 feet.

The gold of the ground is now so tarnished, and was, at first, so sparingly used that now it is almost invisible; but the pile of the velvet is deep and the pattern bold. Doubtless this stuff was for household decoration.

4070.

PIECE of Silk Brocade; purple; pattern, in gold and silver, a large vafe out of which fpring two ramifications and two eagles, one on each fide, alternating with a floriation bearing at top a pomegranate feeded; in the narrow border at top and bottom the fleur-de-lis is the chief ornament, while the taffeled fringe, defigned at bottom, fhows that this texture muft have been intended as a hanging for a frieze. Lyons, late 16th century. 12 feet by 1 foot 10 inches.

The occurrence of birds or animals of any fort in ftuffs of the period is unufual; and, in all likelihood, the laft ufe of this piece was as a hanging in fome large hall.

4209, 4210.

PIECES of White Brocaded Silk. Lyons, 18th century. 1 foot 4 inches by 11 inches.

The manufacture of this ftuff is rather remarkable, not fo much for that fatin look, produced by flos-filk, in fome parts of its defign of flower-bearing branches, as by the way in which portions of it are thrown up in little feed-pearls.

4216.

PIECE of Needlework figured with a female faint at her prayers before a picture of our Saviour, and a crowd of men ftanding behind her near a belfry, in which are fwinging two bells. Italian, early 15th century. 1 foot 4¼ inches by 11¼ inches.

By the coftume this work would feem to have been done in Tufcany, and it fhows the bed-room of fome faintly noble dame, wimpled and clad in a crimfon mantle embroidered with gold. At the foot of her bed there is, wrought and diapered in gold, a praying defk on which lies open a book in filver having a large M in red marked on its firft page; above is a picture of our Redeemer, known by His croffed glory, in the act of giving His blessing, before whom the saint is praying. At her knees are two green snakes, and above her two angels are carrying her soul, under her human form, up to heaven. Behind her, and close to a belfry, where the bells are swinging and the ropes of which are hanging down, is a group of men, one a tonsured cleric, seemingly, from his dalmatic, a deacon, with both hands upraised in surprise; near him other clerics tonsured, two of whom are reading with amazement out of a book held by a noble layman. This work contains allusions to several events in the life of St. Frances, widow, known in Italy, as Santa Francesca Romana; but a very remarkable one is here especially sketched forth. She is said to have often beheld the presence of her guardian angel, clothed as a deacon, watching over her. Such was the obedience and condescension yielded by her to her husband that, though wrapped in prayer, or busied in any spiritual exercise, if called by him or anywise needed by the lowliest servant in her family, she hastened to obey at the moment. It is told of her, that one day, being asked for as many as four times in succession, just as she was, each time, beginning the same verse again, of a psalm in the Office of the Blessed Virgin, on coming back for the fifth time she found that verse written all in gold. Here then we have the loving husband showing this prayer-book, with its golden letters, to a crowd of friends, among whom is his wife's angel hidden under a deacon's dalmatic; while the saint herself is at her devotions, foreseeing in vision the evils that are to befall Italy, through civil strife, shown by those serpents and the swinging bells betokening alarm and fright.

4456.

TABLE-COVER; ground, coarse canvas; design, armorial bearings, symbolical subjects, fruits, and animals, besides five long inscriptions in German, dated A.D. 1585. German. 6 feet by 6 feet 6 inches.

The whole of this large undertaking was worked by some well-born German mother as an heirloom to her offspring. At the right hand corner, done upon a separate piece of finer canvas and afterwards applied to the ground, is a shield of arms, *sable*, three lions rampant *or* armed and langued *gules* two and one between a fess *argent*; at another corner, but worked upon the canvas ground itself, a shield, *gules* three bars dancetté *argent*; upon a third shield, *argent*, a fess dancetté *sable*; on the laſt corner ſhield, quarterly *or* and *gules*, a feſs *argent*; upon a ſmaller ſhield in the middle of the border, *sable* a pair of wings expanded *argent*; on the border oppoſite, party per feſs *sable* and *or*, two creſcents *argent*; in the centre of the next border, *gules* two bars (perhaps) *sable* charged, the upper one with three, the lower with one, bezants or plates; and laſt of all, upon the other border, *or*, a lion rampant, *gules* with chief vair, *sable*, and *or*. Repeated at various places are a vaſe ſurmounted by a croſs with two birds, half-ſerpent, half-dove, ſipping out of the veſſel; and below this group another, conſiſting of two ſtags well "attired," each with one hoof upon the brim of a fountain out of which they are about to drink. This latter ſymbol is evidently a reference to the Pſalmiſt's hart that panteth after the fountains of water, while the former one is a repreſentation of the union of the ſerpent's wiſdom with the ſimplicity of the dove. In many ancient monuments the upper half of the bird is that of a dove, the lower ends in a ſnake-like ſhape with an eye ſhown at the extremity of the tail. There are five long rhythmical inſcriptions on this cloth; in German, one at every corner, and the longeſt of all in the middle; conſidering the period at which they were written, theſe doggerel verſes are very poor, and run nearly as follows:—

"ALS . MAN . ZALT . FUNFZEHN . HUNDERT . JAHR .
DARZU . NOCH . ACHTZIG . UND . FUNF . ZWAR .
HAT . DER . EDEL . UND . VEST . HEINRICH .
VON . GEISPITZHEIM . DIE . TUGENTREICH .
ANNA . BLICKIN . ZUM . GMAL . ERKORN .
WELCHE . VON . LIGTENBERG . GEBORN .
BEID . ALTES . ADELICHS . GESCHLECHT .
ZUSAMMEN . SICH . VERMEHLT . RECHT .
DAMIT . NUHN . IN . IHREM . EHESTANDT .
VLEISIG . HAUSHALTUNG . WURDT . ERKANDT .
HAT . SIE . IHREM . TUNCKERN . ZU . EHRN .
DEN . HAUSRAHT . WOLLEN . ZIRN . UND . MEHRN .
DARUMB . MIT . IHRER . EIGNEN . HANDT .
DIES . UND . NOCH . VIEL . ZIERLICHS . GEWANDT .
ZU . IHRER . GEDACHTNIS . GEMACHT .
MIT . BEIDER . NECHSTEN . ANGHEN . ACHT .
MIT . GOTT . IHRH . TUNCKERN . D . KINDER . ZART .
AUCH . SIE . ERHALTE . BEI . WOHLFAHRTH .
DARNEBEN . VERLEIHEN . GEDULT .
DAS . WIR . BEZAHLN . DER . NATUR . SCHULT .

NACH . VOLLPRACHTEM . LANGEN . LEBEN .
UNS . ALLEN . DIE . EWIG . FREUD . GEBEN .
AMEN .
OBGMELTER . HEINRICH . DICHTET . MICH .

" When one wrote the year Fifteen hundred and Eighty five, the noble and true Henry von Geiſpitzheim had choſen for his ſpouſe the virtuous Anna Blickin von Lichtenberg. Both of them were of ancient noble deſcent. And ſhe, to honour the eſquire, her huſband, wiſhed to adorn and increaſe the houſe furniture, and there has worked with her own hand this and ſtill many other pretty cloths, to her memory. Praying that God may preſerve the eſquire, and the tender children, and herſelf alſo, and that they may pay the debt of nature at the end of a long life, and eternal joy may be granted them.
Amen.
The aforeſaid Henry has compoſed me (i. e. the doggerel verſes)."

"NUN . FOLGET . AUCH . BEI . DIE . ZEIT . UND . JAHR .
DARIN . ICH . ZUR . WELT . GEPOHREN . WAR .
DES . WEN . MEIN . DREI . DOCHTERLEIN .
AUCH . SONN . ZUR . WELT . GEPOHREN . SEIN .
ALS . MAN . ZALTT . FUNFF . ZEHEN . HUNDERT . LII .
ERFREUWET . MEIN . MUTTER . MEIN . GESCHREI .
AN . DEM . JAR . ACHTZIG . FUNFF . HER . NACH .
ICH . MEINEM . JUNCKERN . EIN . DOCHTER . PRACHT .
EMILIA . CATHARIENA . IST . IHR . NAHM .
VON . JUGENT . GERECHT . UND . LOBESAM .
ZWEI . JHAR . DAR . NACH . IM . JANNER . HART .
MICH . GOT . WIEDERUM . ERFREUET . HAT .
MIT . EINER . DOCHTER . ZART . UND . FEIN .
SIE . DRINCKT . WASER . UND . KEINEN . WEIN .
MAGDALENA . ELISABETH . GENNANT .
JHREM . VATER . WERTH . GAR . WOHL . BEKANNT .
NACH . GEHENTS . JHAR . ACHTZIG . ACHT .
MEINEN . SON . REICHART . AN . DAS . LICHT . GEPRACHT
DAS . WAR . DEM . VATER . GROSSE . FREUWDT .
GOT . SEI . GELOBT . IN . EWIGKEIT .
DAS . VOLGT . JAHR . ACHTZIG . UND . NEUN .
BRACHT . ICH . ZUR . WELT . DIE . ZWILING . MEIN .
HANS . CASPARN . ERST . DRAUFF . EMICHEN . BALDT .
DAS . SICH . ERFREUDT . DER . VATER . ALT .

DAS . GESCHACH . DEN . IZ . HORNUNGS . DAG .
GOTS . ALLMACHT . NOCH . VIEL . MEHR . VERMAG .
ZU . LETZ . IM . JAHR . NEUNTZIG . UND . DREI .
ANNA . MARGARETHA . KAM . AUCH . HERBEI .
DEN . ZWOLFFTEN . FEBRUARIUS .
DAMIT . ICH . DISSE . SACH . BESCHLUSZ .
O . IHR . HERTZ . LIEBE . KINDTER . MEIN .
ICH . LASZ . EUCH . MIR . BEFOHLEN . SEIN .
BEHTET . ALLENS . MORGENS . OHN . UNDER . LASZ .
IN . FROLIGKEIT . HALT . GNAE . MASZ .
ACH . IHR . HERTZ . LIEBE . KINDTER . MEIN .
MACHT . EUCH . MIT . GOTTES . WORT . GEMEIN .
SO . WIRT . EUCH . GOT . DER . HER . ERHALTEN .
DAS . IHR . EWEREM . VATER . NOCH . MIT . EHRN . [some letters wanting]
DISEN . SPRUCH . MERCKT . EBEN .
SO . WIRT . EUCH . GOT . GLICK . UND . SGEN . GEBN .

"Now follows here my own birthday. When one wrote 1552 my mother's heart was gladdened by my firſt cry. In the year 1585 I gave birth myſelf to a daughter. Her name is Emilia Catharina, and ſhe has been a proper and praiſeworthy child. Two years later, in a cold January, has God again gratified me with a daughter tender and fine, ſhe drinks water and no wine, her name is Magdalena Elizabeth. In 1588 my ſon Richard came into this world, whoſe birth gave great pleaſure to his father. In the following year, in February, I gave birth to my twins, Hans Caſpar and Emich (Erich ?). At laſt, in 1593, on the 12th of February, my daughter Anna Margaretha was born.—O you truly beloved children, I commend myſelf to your memory. Do not forget your prayers in the morning. And be temperate in your pleaſures. And make yourſelves acquainted with the Word of God. Then God will preſerve you, and will grant you happineſs and bliſs."

" DISZ . HAB . ICH . EUCH . LIEBE . KINDER . MEIN .
IN . REIMEN . BRINGEN . LASZEN . FEIN .
AUFF . DAS . IR . WUST . EUWERS . ALTERS . ZEIT .
DURCH . DIESE . MEINER . HANDT . ARBEIT .
WELCHS . ICH . EUCH . ZUR . GEDECHTNIS . LAS .
UND . BITT . EUCH . FREUNDLICH . ALLER . MASS .
SEIDT . UFFRICHTIG . IN . ALLEN . SACHEN .
DAS . WIRT . EUCH . GOSZ . UND . HERLICH . MACHN .

THUT . IEDEM . EHR . NACH . SEINEM . STANDT .
DAS . WIRT . EUCH . RUMLICH . MACHEN . BEKANDT .
UND . IHR . HERTZ . LIEBE . SONE . MEIN .
WOLT . EUCH . HUTEN . VOR . VERIGEM (Feurigem) . WEIN .
DRINCKT . DEN . WEIN . MIT . BESCHEIDENHEIT .
DA . SICHS . GEBURTT . DAS . PEHUT . VOR . LEIDT .
UND . IHR . HERTZ . LIEBE . DOCHTER . MEIN .
LAST . EUCH . ALLE . TUGENT . BETOLEN . SEIN .
BEWART . EUHER . EHR . HAPT . EUHR . GUT . ACHT .
BEDENCKT . ZU . VOR . JDE . SACH .
DAN . VOR . GETHAN . UND . NACH . BEDRACHT .
HAT . MANCHEN . WEIT . ZURUCK . GEBRACHT .
DAS . MITELL . DIS . ALLES . ZU . GEPEN .
IST . DIE . FORCHT . GOTTES . MERCKT . MICH . EBEN .
GOTTS . FORCHT . BRINGT . WEISHEIT . UND . VERSTANT .
DAR . DORCH . GESEGNET . WIRDT . DAS . LANDT .
GOTS . FORCHT . MACHT . REICH . BRINGT . FRED . U . MUHT .
ERFRISCHT . DAS . LEBEN . UND . DAS . BLUT .
GOTES . FORCHT . BEHUTT . VOR . ALLEM . LEIDT .
UND . IST . EIN . WEG . ZUR . SELIGKEIT .
GOTTES . FORCHT . IST . DAS . RECHT . FUNDAMENT .
DARUFF . DES . MENSCHEN . GLICK . BEWENDT .
UND . IST . EIN . HAUPTMITTEL . ALLER . DUGENT .
WER . SICH . DER . ANIMPT . IN . DER . JUGENT .
DEM . GEHT . SEIN . ALTER . AN . MIT . EHREN .
UND . SEIN . GLICK . WIRD . SICH . TAGLICH . MEHREN .
DAR . DURCH . DER . MENSCH . ZUM . SELIG . ENDT .
LETZLICH . GELANGT . ACH . HER . UNS . SENDT .
DEIN . HEILIGER . GEIST . DER . UNS . THUT . EINFREN .
ZU . SOLCHER . FORCHT . DIE . WOL . EUCH . RIHREN .
EWER . HERTZ . UND . SIN . IHR . SOLICH . FORCHT .
ERGREIFFEN . KONT . UND . GOT . GEHRCHT .
AMEN . DAS . WERDT . WARH . G . GOTT . DIE . ERH .

"This, O my dear children, has at my wish been put into rhymes, in order that you may know your age by this work of my own hand, which I leave to you as a memorial. I beseech you to be sincere in all matters; that will make you great and glorious. Honour everybody according to his station; it will make you honourably known. You, my truly beloved sons, beware of fiery wine, and drink with moderation; that will preserve you from evil. And you, my truly beloved daughters, let me recommend you to be virtuous. Preferve and guard your honour; and reflect before you do anything; for many have been led into evil by acting firft and reflecting afterwards. The way to get to this end is the fear of God, mark me well! The fear of God brings wifdom and underftanding. The fear of God makes rich, and gives joy and courage, refrefhes life and blood. The fear of God protects us from all evil; and is the way to the ftate of blifs. The fear of God is the foundation on which the happinefs of man refts; and is the chief way to all virtues. He who feeks it in his youth will live with honour till his old age; and his happinefs will daily increafe.

"Amen. Give to God all honour."

"ALS . MAN . ZALT . FUFZEHN . HUNDERT . JAHR .
UND . NEUNTZIG . NEUN . DARZU . JST . WAR .
DEN . ERSTEN . APRIL . NACH . MITNACHT .
GLEICH . UMB . EIN . UHR . OFFT . ICHS . BETRACHT .
DER . ALLERLIEBSTE . JUNCKER . MEIN .
GENANDT . HEINRICH . VON . GEISPITZHEIM .
ZU . DIR . O . GOTT . AUS . DIESER . WELT .
ERFORDERT . WIRT . ALS . DIRS . GEFELLT .
SEIN . ALTER . WAR . SECHZIG . UND . ACHT .
DIE . WASSER . SUCHT . IHN . UMGEPRACHT .
DEN . WOLLEST . O . GOTT . GNED . GEBEN .
SEIN . PFLEGEN . NACH . DEM . WILLEN . DEIN .
JCH . SEIN . BETRUEBTE . NACHGELASSEN . ANN .
BLICKIN . VON . LIECHTENPERG . GENANDT .
HAB . MIT . NICHT . UNDER . LASSEN . WOLLEN .
SONDERN . EIN . SOLICHES . HIE . MELDEN . SOLLEN .
IN . DIESEM . TUCH . MIT . MEINER . HANDT .
DAMIT . ES . WERD . MEINEN . KINDERN . BEKANDT .
DIESES . MEIN . GROSSES . LEID .
WELCHES . MIR . VON . GOTT . WARD . BEREIT .

"When one wrote the year Fifteen hundred and ninety-nine, on the firft of April after midnight, juft at one o'clock—often I think of it—my truly beloved hufband, the Squire Henry von Geifpitzheim, was called to Thee, O God! from this world, according to Thy will. His age was fixty and eight years. The dropfy has killed him. To him grant, O God! Thy mercy, after Thy will. I, his afflicted Anna Blickin von Liechtenperg who was left behind, have related it with my hand in this cloth, that it might be known to my children—this my great forrow, which God has fent me."

"DEN . FUNFFTEN . AUGUST . BALDT . HERNACH .
WIEDERUM . SICH . FUGT . EIN . LEIDIG . SACH .
MEIN . JUNGSTER . SON . EIMCH . EIN . ZWILLING .
VON . DIESER . WELT . ABSCHIEDT . GAB . GEHLINGS .
DARDURCH . WARDT . MIR . MEIN . LEID . GEMERT .
UND . ALLE . HOFFNUNG . UMBGEKERTH .
ACH . GÖTT . LAS . DICHS . MIENER . ERBARMEN .
UND . KOM . ZU . TROST . UND . HILFF . MIR . ARMEN .
HILF . TREUWER . GOT . UND . STEH . BEI . MICH .
TROST . MICH . MIT . DEINEM . GEIST . GNEDIGGLICH .
UND . BEHUT . MIR . MEIN . LIEBE . KINDT .
SO . BISZ . NOCH . GESUND . UEBRIG . SINT .
UND . SCHAFF . O . GOT . DAS . WIR . ZUGLICH .
DICH . SCHAU . DEN . IM . HIMMEL . EWIGLICH .
DARZU . HILFF . UNS . GNEDIGKLICH .
ACH . HER . VER . GIEB . ALL . UNSER . SCHULT .
HILFF . DAS . WARTEN . MIT . GEDULT .
BIES . UNSER . STUNTLIN . NACHT . HERBEI .
AUCH . UNSER . GLAUBE . STETZ . WACKER . SEI .
DEIN . WORT . ZU . DRAUWEN . TESTIGKLICH .
BIS . WIR . ENDT . SCHLAFFEN . SELIGKLICH ."

"On the fifth of Auguft foon afterwards another forrowful event happened. My youngeft fon Eimah (Erich?), one of my twins, fuddenly departed from this world; and therefore my forrow was increafed, and all hope overthrown. O God! have mercy upon me, and come to comfort and help me, poor one. Help, true God! and affift me, comfort me with Thy Spirit, and protect me and my dear children who are ftill left in good health. And grant, O God! that we then may behold Thee in Heaven eternally. O Lord! forgive us our trefpaffes, help that we may wait with patience until our laft hour may come; and alfo that our faith may be true, to believe in Thy Word fteadfaftly until we fink into the flumber of death."

4457.

TABLE-COVER of white linen, figured in thread, with the "Agnus Dei," or "Holy Lamb," in the middle, and the symbolic animals of the four Evangelists, one at each corner. German, late 16th century. 6 feet 3 inches by 5 feet 8 inches.

For its sort and time there is nothing superior to this fine piece of needlework. About the evangelic emblems, as well as the Lamb in the centre, there is a freedom and boldness of design only equalled by the beauty and nicety of execution, making the piece altogether quite an art-work. The little dogs chasing the young harts, as well as the rampant unicorns, but especially the bird of the stork-kind preening its feathers, and the stag looking back at the hound behind, all so admirably placed amid the branches so gracefully twining over the whole field, show a master's spirited hand in their design. Unfortunately, however, none of its beauty can be seen unless, like a piece of stained glass, it be hung up to the light. Its use was most likely liturgic, and occasions for it not unfrequently occur in the year's ritual round; and on Candlemas-day and Palm Sunday it might becomingly have been spread over the temporary table on the south side of the altar, upon which were put, for the especial occasion, the tapers for the one service, and the palm-branches for the other, during the ceremony of blessing them before their distribution.

4458.

LINEN Napkin; the four corners embroidered in crimson thread. German, 17th century. 3 feet by 2 feet 6¼ inches.

The design consists of a stag at rest couchant, and an imaginary figure, half a winged human form, half a two-legged serpent, separated by a flower of the centaurea kind. This is repeated on the other side of the square, up the middle of which runs an ornamentation made out of a love-knot, surmounted by a heart, sprouting out of which is a stalk bearing a four-petaled flower, and then a stem with the usual corn-flower at the end of it. To all appearance, this linen napkin was for household use,

4459.

LINEN Cradle-Coverlet; ground, fine white linen; pattern, the Crucifixion, with Saints and the Evangelists' emblems, all outlined in various-coloured silk-thread; dated 1590. German. 6 feet by 6 feet 6 inches.

This piece of needlework is figured with the Crucifixion in the middle, and shows us, on one side, the Blessed Virgin Mary and St. Christopher; on the other, St. John and the Blessed Virgin Mary holding our Lord in her arms, and, at her feet, a youthful virgin-saint, most likely St. Catherine of Sienna. From the cross itself flowers are in some places sprouting out, and three angels are catching, in chalices, the sacred blood that is gushing from the wounds on the body of our Lord. At each corner is an evangelist's symbol, and the whole is framed in a broad border in crimson and white silk, edged by crochet-work, and at the corners are the letters A. H. A. R. Though the figures are in mere outline they are well designed, but poorly, feebly executed by the needle. Another specimen of a cradle-quilt, much like this, is No. 1344, and under No. 4644 notice is taken of feeling for the employment of the four Evangelists' symbols at the corners of this nursery furniture.

4460.

LINEN Napkin; embroidered at one end with two wreaths of flowers above a narrow floral border; it is edged with lace, and bears the date 1672, and the initials A. M. W. German, 3 feet 6 inches by 1 foot 6 inches.

Probably meant to hang in the sacristy for the priest to wipe his fingers on after washing the tips of them, before vesting for mass.

4461.

LINEN Table-Cover; pattern, a wide floriation done in white and yellow threads; in the centre, a ftag couchant within a wreath. German, late 16th century. 5 feet 4 inches by 4 inches.

Free in defign and eafy of execution.

4462.

EMBROIDERY on Silk Net; ground, crimfon; pattern, branches twined into ovals, and bearing flowers and foliage, in various-coloured filks, and heightened, in places, with gold and filver thread. Italian, late 17th century. 2 feet 8 inches by 9 inches.

A very pleafing and exceedingly well-wrought fpecimen of its ftyle. Like in manner, but much better done than the examples at Nos. 623, 624. No doubt it was meant for female adornment.

4522.

ALTAR-FRONTAL; embroidered in the middle with nine reprefentations of the birth, &c. of our Lord; and four paffages from the Saints' lives on each fide, all in gold and various-coloured filks, upon fine linen. Italian, 14th century. 4 feet 3 inches by 1 foot 8 inches.

This frontal is faid to have been brought from Orvieto; but in it there is nothing about the celebrated relic kept in the very beautiful and fplendid fhrine in that fine cathedral. So very worn is this piece of embroidery, that feveral panels of it are quite indiftinct. It may be, however, diftinguifhed into three parts—the centre and the two fides. In the firft we have, in nine compartments, the Annunciation, the Nativity, the coming of the Wife Men, the Bleffed Virgin Mary, with St. Jofeph, going to the temple and carrying in a bafket her pair of turtle-doves, which she is giving to Simeon; the Last Supper; our Lord being taken in the garden; the Crucifixion; the burial; the Resurrection of our Saviour; on the right side, the legend of St. Christopher, mixed up with that of St. Julian Hospitaler; on the left are passages from the life of St. Ubaldo, bishop of Gubbio in the middle of the 12th century. In the first square is the saint mildly forgiving the master-mason who carried the new walls of the city across a vineyard belonging to St. Ubaldo, and, when reproved about the wrong thus done to private property, knocked down the saint; in the second we behold the saint at the bedside of a converted sinner, whose soul, just breathed forth, an angel is about to waft to heaven; in the third we have before us the saint himself, upon his dying bed, surrounded by friends, one of whom—a lady—is throwing up both her arms in great affright at the sudden appearance of a possessed man who has cast himself upon his knees at the bedfoot, and, with one hand outstretched upon the bed, is freed from the evil spirit, which is flying off over head in shape of a devil-imp; in the last the saint is being drawn in an open bier, by two oxen, to church for burial, followed by a crowd, among whom is his deacon.

From the subjects on this much-decayed frontal, figured, as it is, with the life of St. Ubaldo, known for his love of the poor, his kindness to wayfarers and pilgrims, and his healing of the sick, as well as with the legends of St. Julian and St. Christopher, remarkable for the same virtues, we may infer that this ecclesiastical appliance hung at the altar of some poor house or hospital, in by-gone days, at Orvieto.

4643.

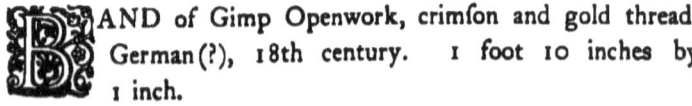
AND of Gimp Openwork, crimson and gold thread. German (?), 18th century. 1 foot 10 inches by 1 inch.

Evidently for ladies' use, but how employed is not so clear; from a little steel ring sewed to it, perhaps it may have been worn hanging from the hair behind the neck.

4644.

RADLE-QUILT; ground, green satin, embroidered with armorial bearings, the four Evangelists, and flowers, all in coloured silks, and dated 1612. German. 2 feet 5 inches by 1 foot 9 inches.

Within a narrow wreath of leaves and flowers there are two shields, of which the first bears *gules* a wheel *or*, surmounted by a closed helmet, having its mantlings of *or* and gules, and on a wreath *gules* a wheel *or* as a crest; the second, *azure*, a cross couped *argent* between a faced crescent and a ducal coronet, both *or*, and all placed in pile, surmounted by a closed helmet having its mantlings of *or* and *azure*, and on a wreath *or*, a demy bear proper with a cross *argent* on its breast, crowned with a ducal coronet *or*, and holding in its paws a faced crescent *or*. At each of the four corners is the emblem of an evangelist with his name, and shown as a human personage nimbed and coming out of a flower, with his appropriate emblem upholding an open volume which he has in his hands, thus calling to mind those nursery rhymes:—

"Matthew, Mark, Luke, and John,
Guard the bed I lie upon," &c;

which seem to be as well known in Germany as they were, and yet are, in England. See "Church of Our Fathers," t. iii. p. 230.

4645.

RADLE-QUILT; centre, crimson silk, embroidered with flowers in coloured silk, mostly outlined with gold thread, and here and there sprinkled with gold ornamentations, and surrounded by a broad satin quilting edged with a gold lace-like border. German, late 17th century. 2 feet 7 inches by 2 feet 2 inches.

The cradle-cloths, or quilts, are of common occurrence, and afford occasions for much elegance of design.

4646.

CRADLE-QUILT; ground, brown filk; pattern, a wreath of green leaves encircling two armorial fhields, and filled in with flowers outfide the fpandrils; the whole furrounded by a border of flowers, all in various-coloured flos-filk. German, late 16th century. 3 feet by 2 feet 5 inches.

Of the two fhields the firft is party per fefs *azure* and *fable*, a griffin rampant *or* holding three ears of wheat; the fhield itfelf furmounted by a helmet clofed, having green mantlings and crefted with a ducal coronet out of which iffues a demi-griffin rampant holding three ears of wheat *or*. The fecond fhield is party per fefs *fable* and *or*, a lion rampant *or* noued, and langued *gules*, counterchanged *or* and *fable*, furmounted by a clofed helmet with green mantlings, and crefted with a demy-lion rampant *or*, langued *gules* iffuing from a wreath *fable* and *or* (now faded). By means of a long flit with hooks and eyes to it a blanket might be introduced to make this coverlet warmer.

4647.

SATIN Bed-quilt; the middle a filk brocade diapered with a large floriation within a broad wreath-like band, all bright amber upon a crimfon ground; the broad border is of crimfon fatin, quilted, after an elaborate pattern fhown by a cording of blue and gold. French, 17th century. 6 feet by 5 feet 6 inches.

4648.

SATIN Bed-quilt; the middle, filk brocade diapered with a fomewhat fmall floriation, in bright amber and white upon a crimfon ground. The wide border, in crimfon fatin of rich material and brilliant tone, is quilted after an agreeable defign with yellow cord. French, 17th century. 7 feet 10 inches by 5 feet 4 inches.

4649.

LITURGICAL Scarf; ground, white silk; pattern, bunches of leaves and flowers, in various-coloured silk thread. French, 18th century. 11 feet 5 inches by 1 foot 4 inches.

Such scarves are used for throwing on the lectern, and to be worn by the sub-deacon at high mass; and, from its appearance, this one must have seen much service. All its flowers, as well as its two edgings, are worked in braid, nicely sewed on and admirably done.

4661.

LONG Piece of Silk Brocade; ground, light maroon; pattern, creamy white scrolls, dotted with blue flowerets, and placed so as to form a wavy line all up the warp amid bunches of red and blue flowers and leaves. Lyons, late 17th century. 8 feet 6 inches by 1 foot 7 inches.

The colours are faded somewhat, and though showy, this stuff is not so glaring in its design as were the silks that came, at a later period, from the same looms.

If used in the liturgy, it must have been for covering the moveable lectern for holding the Book of the Gospels, out of which the deacon at high mass chants the gospel of the day. It might, too, have served as a veil for the sub-deacon for muffling his hands while he held the paten after the offertory.

4665.

PAIR of Lady's Gloves of kid leather, with richly embroidered cuffs. French, late 17th century. 13 inches by 7½ inches.

The hands are of a light olive tone, and embroidered on the under seams in gold; the cuffs are deep, and embroidered in gold and silver after a rich design upon crimson silk, and are united by the novelty of a gusset formed of three pieces of broad crimson ribbon.

4666.

URSE in gold tiffue, embroidered with flowers in pots, and bound with ribbons in filver and colours. French, 18th century. 5 inches by 4½ inches.

Some of the flowers are fpringing up from filver bafkets; others are tied up with filver ribbons, and the whole pleafingly done.

4667.

URSE in gold and filver embroidery, with gilt clafp. Englifh, 19th century. 4½ inches by 4 inches.

The defign of this is pretty, and confifts of fmall gold and filver difks wrought in thread, and linked together by a ftrong green filk netting.

4894.

ELVET Hanging; ground, black; pattern, a frieze made up of a flower-bearing vafe between two broad horns of plenty, full of fruits, and two imaginary heraldic monfters, one on each fide, like fupporters, fafhioned as red-tongued eagles, with wings difplayed in the head, but having a taillefs haunch, and cloven-footed legs of an ox; the fimbriations are edged with green fringe, and the fpaces filled with a conventional floriation; and the greater parts done in yellow fatin, fmaller parts in other coloured fatins, all edged with gold cording and filver thread, and applied to the ground of black velvet. French, early 17th century. 25 inches by 12 inches.

The whole of this curious piece is defigned with great boldnefs and fpirit, and moft accurately wrought.

5662.

FOUR Pieces of Raised Velvet, sewed into one large square; ground, yellow and crimson silk; pattern, a bold floriation in raised crimson velvet. Genoese, 16th century.

A fine specimen of the Genoese loom, showing a well-managed design composed of a modification of the artichoke, mixed with pomegranates, ears of corn (rather an unusual ornament), roses, and large liliacious flowers. Not unlikely this stuff was ordered by some Spanish nobleman for hangings in the state halls of his palace. Such stuffs are sometimes to be seen on the canopy in the throne-room of some Roman princely house, whose owners have the old feudal right to the cloth of estate.

5663.

SET of Bed Hangings complete, in green cut velvet raised upon a yellow satin ground, diapered in gold. Genoese, 16th century.

The foliated scroll pattern of this truly rich stuff is executed in a bold and telling manner; and the amber satin ground is marked with a small but pleasing kind of diaper, which is done in gold thread. To give a greater effect to the velvet, which is deep in its pile, a cord of green and gold stands stitched to it as an edging.

5664, 5664 A.

TWO Pieces of Embroidery; ground, light purple, thin net lined with blue canvas; pattern, nosegays of white and red flowers and large green branches tied up in bunches, with white and with yellow ribbons alternately; the narrow borders, which are slightly scolloped, are figured with sprigs of roses; and the whole is done in bright-coloured untwisted silks, and has throughout a lining of thin white silk.

French, late 16th century. 10 feet 9¼ inches by 2 feet 9¼ inches.

Each piece confifts of two lengths of the fame embroidery fewed together all along the middle; and ferved for fome houfehold decoration.

5665.

EMBROIDERED Table-cover; ground, green cloth; pattern, within a large garland of fruits and flowers, feparated into four parts by as many cherubic heads, two armorial fhields and a fcroll bearing the date 1598, and the four fides bordered with an entablature filled in with animals, fruits, flowers, and architectural tablets having about them ornaments of the ftrap-like form, and each charged with a female face. South Germany, 16th century. 5 feet 7 inches by 5 feet 3 inches.

The defign of the embroidery, done in various-coloured worfteds, is admirable, and quite in accordance with the beft types of that period; nor ought we to overlook the artiftic manner in which the colours are everywhere about it fo well contrafted. The animals are feveral, not forgetting the unicorn and monkey; though, from the frequency of the Alpine deer kind, it looks as if this fine piece of work had been fketched and executed by thofe familiar with the Alps. The fhields are, firft, barry of fix *argent* and *azure*, with mantlings about a helmet clofed and crefted with a demi-bloodhound collared and langued, and, from the neck downward, barry like the fhield; fecond, quarterly 1 and 4 *or* charged with a pair of pincers *fable*; 2 and 3 *fable*, a lion rampant *or*, and mantlings about a helmet clofed and crefted with a demi-lion rampant *or*, upon a wreath *fable* and *argent*. The filver has now become quite black.

5666.

TABLE-COVER; ground, dark green ferge; pattern, embroidered in filk and thread, the four feafons and their occupations, &c, and in the centre the Annunciation. German, early 17th century. 5 feet 3 inches by 4 feet 6 inches.

This piece, though much resembling the foregoing, No. 5665, is far below it as an art-work, and, by its style, betrays itself as the production of another period. Within a wreath, the Annunciation is figured, after the usual manner, but without gracefulness, in the middle of the cloth; at one corner Winter is shown, by men in a yard chopping up and stacking wood; then, by the inside of a room where a woman is warming herself before one of those large blind stoves still found in Germany, and a bearded man, seated in a large chair, doing the same at a brazier near his feet, while outside the house a couple are riding on a sledge drawn by a gaily caparisoned horse. At the corner opposite we have Spring—a farm-house, with its beehives, and a dame coming out with a jug of milk to a woman who is churning, near whom is a hedger at his work, and other men pruning, grafting, and sowing. For Summer, two gentlemen are snaring birds with a net; a woman and a man, each with a sickle in hand, are in a cornfield; two people are bathing in a duck-pond before a farm-house, on the roof of which is a nest with two storks sitting, one of which has caught a snake; and in a meadow hard by a man is mowing and a woman making hay. For Autumn, we see a vineyard where one man is gathering grapes and another carrying them in a long basket on his shoulders; and near, a man with a nimb, or glory, about his head, and lying on the ground with one leg outstretched, which a dog is licking above the thigh—perhaps the shepherd St. Rock, and, while a gentleman is walking past behind him, a girl, with a basket of fruit upon her head, is coming towards the spot. Between the seasons, and within circular garlands, are subjects akin to these parts of the year; in a boat, upon the water, a young couple are beginning the voyage of life together; a lady on a grey horse is, with hawk on hand, disporting herself in the flowery fields; a young lady is caressing a lamb with one hand and carries a basket of young birds in the other; last of all, another lady is kneeling at her prayers, with a book open before her on a table overspread with a nicely worked cloth. A deep gold fringe runs all round the four sides of this table-cover.

5670—5676.

SEVEN Chair-feat Covers; ground, yellow fatin; pattern, birds, flowers, and a mafk of an animal, all embroidered in various-coloured flos-filk. French, late 17th century. 2 feet 6 inches by 2 feet.

The fatin is rich, and all the embroideries done in a bold effective manner; in fome of thefe pieces the beak of each green parrot holds a ftrawberry or arbutus-fruit; and the lily and fleur-de-lis here and there betray a French feeling. It fhould be noticed, too, that much botanical knowledge is fhown in the figuration of the flowers, which are more pleafing and effective from being thus done correctly.

5677.

TWO Pieces of Raifed Silk Brocade; ground, yellow; pattern, the artichoke amid ftrap-work ornamentation, all of a large bold character, in raifed crimfon. Italian, 16th century. 10 feet 1 inch by 4 feet 2 inches.

A rich ftuff, and made up for houfehold decoration, perhaps for the throne-room of fome palace.

5678.

CRADLE-COVERLET, green filk, brocaded in gold and filver; pattern, imitation of Oriental defign in gold and filver flowers, after a large form, lined in red. French, 18th century. 3 feet 6 inches fquare.

A fpecimen of a rich and telling, though not artiftic, ftuff.

5723.

PIECE of Raifed Velvet; green, on a light amber-coloured ground. Genoefe, late 16th century. 7 feet 10 inches by 1 foot 8 inches.

The pattern, rich in its texture and pleasing in its colours, consists of large stalks of flowers springing out of royal open crowns, all in a fine pile of green velvet, and, no doubt, was meant for palatial furniture.

5728.

MISSAL-CUSHION; ground, white satin; pattern, flowers and fruit embroidered in coloured silks, amid an ornamentation of net-work, partly in gold; it has four tassels of green silk and gold thread. French, 17th century. 1 foot 5 inches by 10 inches.

One of those cushions once so generally used for supporting the Missal at the altar. It is figured only on the upper side, and underneath is lined with a silk diapered in a pleasing pattern, in amber-colour. Its tassels are rather large and made of several coloured silk threads and gold.

5788.

FIGURE of St. Mark, seated; embroidered, in part by the hand, in part woven. Florentine, early 16th century. 1 foot 3 inches by 8¼ inches.

Beneath a circular-headed niche, with all its accessories in the style of the revival of classic architecture, sits St. Mark, known as such by the lions at his side. Within his right arm the Evangelist holds a large cross; and on his lap lies an open book, both pages of which are written with the words:—" Gloria in excelsis Deo, et in tea." Much of the architecture, as well as of the drapery of this personage, is loom-wrought, assisted in places by needle-embroidery. The head, the hands, the feet, are all done by the needle; but the head, neck, and beard are worked upon very fine linen by themselves, and afterwards applied, and in such a manner that the long white beard overlaps the tunic. His chair, instead of legs, is upheld upon the backs of two lions lying on the ground. The head is done with all the fineness and delicacy of a miniature on ivory, and the way in which the massive folds of his full wide garments are thrown over his knees is noteworthy and majestic.

112   *Church-vestments, Silk-stuffs,*

5900.

SILK Damask Orphrey Web; ground, crimson; pattern, the Resurrection. Venetian, 16th century. 1 foot 4 inches by 8¾ inches.

One of those numerous examples of woven orphrey-work for vestments such as copes and chasubles. Our Lord is figured as uprising from the grave, treading upon clouds, giving, with His right hand, a blessing to the world, and holding the triumphal banner in the left. Glory streams from His person, and a wreath of Cherubim surrounds Him; while, from the top part of this piece, we know that two Roman soldiers were sitting on the ground by the side of the sepulchre, which they were charged to guard.

5958.

BOX for keeping the linen corporals used at mass, in the vestry. It is covered with fine linen, of a creamy brown tint, embroidered with crimson silk and gold. Inside it is lined, in part green, on the lid crimson, where a very rude print of the Crucifixion, daubed with colour, has been let in. German, 17th century. 8½ inches by 7½ inches, 1¾ inches deep.

Such boxes seem to have been much used, at one time, throughout Germany, for keeping, after service, the blessed pieces of square fine linen called corporals, and upon which, at mass, the host and chalice are placed.

Before being employed all the year round as the daily repository for laying up the corporals after the morning's masses, this sacred appliance, overlaid with such rich embroidery, and fitly ornamented with the illumination of the Crucifixion inside its lid, would seem to have been originally made and especially set aside for an use assigned it by those ancient rubrics, which we have noticed in our Introduction, § 5. As such, it is, like No. 8327 further on, a great liturgical rarity, now seldom to be found anywhere, and merits a place among other such curious objects which give a value to this collection.

At the mass on Maundy Thursday, besides the host received by the officiating priest, another host is and always has been consecrated by him for the morrow's (Good Friday's) celebration; and because no consecration of the Holy Eucharist, either in the Latin or in the Greek part of the Church, ever did nor does take place on Good Friday, the service on that day is by the West called the " Mass of the Pre-sanctified," by the East, " Λειτουργία τῶν προηγιασμένων."

Folded up in a corporal (a square piece of fine linen), the additional host consecrated on Maunday Thursday was put into this receptacle or " capsula corporalium " of the old rubrics, and afterwards carried in solemn procession to its temporary resting-place, known in England as the sepulchre, and there, amid many lights, flowers, and costly hangings of silk and palls of gold and silver tissue, was watched by the people the rest of that afternoon, and all the following night, till the morning of the next day, when, with another solemn procession, it was borne back to the high altar for the Good Friday's celebration.

6998.

IECE of Green Satin; pattern, an arabesque stenciled in light yellow, and finished by touches done by hand. Italian, very late 18th century. 3 feet 1¼ inches by 1 foot 6¼ inches. (Presented by Mr. J. Webb).

This piece may have been part of a frieze, round the head of a bed; and have had a good effect at that height, though, in a manner, an artistic cheat, pretending to be either wrought in the loom or done by the needle. The design, in its imitative classicism, is bold and free, and the touches of the pencil effective. To this day stencil ornamentation upon house-walls is very much employed in Italy, where papering for rooms is seldom used even as yet, and not long ago was in many places almost unknown.

7004.

IECE of Silk Damask; ground, crimson; pattern, wheat-ears, flowers, and conventional foliage in gold, shaded white. Italian, late 16th century. 11 inches by 10¾ inches.

A pleasing design, but the gold is very scant.

7005.

WOOLLEN and Thread Stuff; ground, white; pattern, sprigs of artichokes and pomegranates. Spanish, 16th century. 11 inches by 7½ inches.

The warp is white linen thread, rather fine; and the weft of thick blue wool; and, altogether, it is a pleasing production, and the design nicely managed.

7006.

SATIN Brocade; ground, bright green satin; pattern, sprigs of gold flowers. Genoese, late 16th century. 7½ inches by 6¼ inches.

The flowers upon this rich and showy stuff are the lily, the pomegranate, and the artichoke in sprigs, each after a conventional form; and the gold in the thread is of the best, as it shows as bright now as almost on the first day of its being woven in the satin, which so seldom happens.

7007.

SILK Diaper; ground, creamy white; pattern, small bunches of leaves, flowers, and fruit, in white, green, and brown silk. Spanish, 16th century. 4¾ inches by 3¼ inches.

Though the warp is woollen, the silk in the weft is rich and the pattern after a pretty design, where the pomegranate comes in often.

7008.

PIECE of Silk Damask of the very lightest olive-green; pattern, a diaper of large sprigs of flowers. Italian, late 16th century. 1 foot 2¼ inches by 9¼ inches.

Pleasing in its quiet tone, and good design.

Needlework, and Dresses. 115

7009.

AMASKED Silk; ground, light red, with lines of gold; pattern, leaves and flowers in deeper red. Sicilian, late 14th century. 10 inches by 6¼ inches.

Very like several other specimens in this collection from the looms of Sicily, Palermo especially, in the pattern of its diapering, usually in green upon a tawny ground.

7010.

ILK Damask; ground, crimson; pattern, bunches of flowers of the pink and lily kinds, mingled with slips of the pomegranate. Spanish, 15th century. 12 inches by 10 inches.

The colour has much faded; but the design of the pattern, which is a crowded one, is very pretty; and the stuff seems to have been for personal wear.

7011.

ATIN Damask; ground, green; pattern, an acorn and an artichoke united upon one small sprig, in yellow silk. Genoese, 16th century. 8 inches by 3½ inches.

Though small, this is a pretty design; and, perhaps, the great family of Della Rovere belonging to the Genoese republic may have suggested the acorn, "rovere" being the Italian word for one of the kinds of oak.

7012.

ATIN Damask; the diapering is a sprig fashioned like the artichoke, and, in all likelihood, was outlined in pale pink. Italian, late 16th century. 1 foot 4½ inches by 9¼ inches.

A texture for personal attire which must have looked well.

7013.

ILK Damaſk; ground, crimſon; pattern, a large artichoke flower bearing, in the middle, a fleur-de-lis. Genoeſe, late 16th century.

The deſign in the pattern is rather ſingular; and may have been meant for ſome noble, if not royal French family, connected with a houſe of the ſame pretenſions in Spain.

7014.

ILK Brocade; ground, dull purple ſilk; pattern, flowers in gold, partially relieved in white ſilk. Spaniſh, late 16th century. 10 inches by 6 inches.

The flowers are moſtly after a conventional form, though traces of the pomegranate may be ſeen; the gold thread is thin and ſcantily employed, and always along with broad yellow ſilk. With ſomewhat poor materials, a ſtuff rather effective in deſign is brought out.

7015.

ILK Web, on linen warp; ground, deep crimſon; pattern, a quatrefoil with flowers at the tips of the barbs or angles at the corners, in gold thread, and filled in with a four-petaled flower in gold upon a green ground. German, 15th century. 14½ inches by 4½ inches.

Intended as orphreys of a narrow form; but made of poor materials, for the gold is ſo ſcant that it has almoſt entirely diſappeared.

7016.

END of a Maniple; pattern, lozenges, green charged with a yellow croſs, and red charged with a white croſs of web; the end, linen embroidered with a faint holding a ſcroll, and fringed with long ſtrips of flos-ſilk, green blue white and crimſon. German, early 15th century. 15¼ inches by 3 inches.

Needlework, and Dresses.

As this piece is put the wrong side out in the frame, the figure of the saint cannot be identified, nor the word on the scroll read.

7017.

LINEN Web; ground, crimson and green; pattern, on the crimson square, a device in white; on the green, two narrow bands chequered crimson, white, and green, with an inscription (now illegible) between them. German, 15th century. 16 inches by 2½ inches.

Poor in every respect, and the small band of gold is almost black.

7018.

ORPHREY Web; ground, gold; pattern, a flower-bearing tree in green, red, and white; and the sacred Name in blue silk. German, 15th century. 13½ inches by 3¼ inches.

The same stuff occurs at other numbers in this collection.

7019.

ORPHREY Band; ground, gold thread; pattern, flowers in various-coloured silks. Flemish, 16th century. 19¼ inches by 2¾ inches.

The whole of this pretty piece is done with the needle, upon coarse canvas, and, no doubt, ornamented either a chasuble, dalmatic, or some liturgical vestment.

7020.

CRIMSON and Gold Damask; ground, crimson; pattern, a diaper of animals in gold. Italian, 15th century. 14¾ inches by 4 inches.

Exactly like another piece in this collection; a winged gaping serpent, with a royal crown just above but not upon its head, occupies the loweſt part of the deſign; over it is the heraldic nebulée or clouds darting forth rays all about them, and above all, a hart, collared, and with head regardant lies lodged within a paliſade or paled park.

7021.

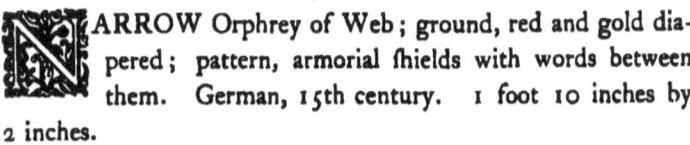ARROW Orphrey of Web; ground, red and gold diapered; pattern, armorial ſhields with words between them. German, 15th century. 1 foot 10 inches by 2 inches.

One of the ſhields is *azure*, two arrows *argent* in ſaltire; the other ſhield is *argent*, three eſtoils, two and one, *azure*; and on a chief *or*, two animals (indiſcernible) *ſable*: the words between the ſhields are ſo worn away as not to be readable.

7022.

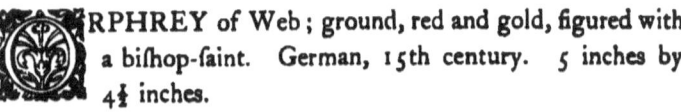INEN, block-printed; ground, white; pattern, two eagles or hawks creſted, amid floriations of the artichoke form, and a border of roving foliage; all in deep dull purple. Flemiſh, late 14th century. 1 foot 8 inches by 6¾ inches.

The deſign is good, and evidently ſuggeſted by the patterns on ſilks from the ſouth of Europe. Further on, we have another piece, No. 8303.

7023.

RPHREY of Web; ground, red and gold, figured with a biſhop-ſaint. German, 15th century. 5 inches by 4¼ inches.

The ſpaces for the head and hands are left uncovered by the loom, ſo that they may be, as they are here, filled in by the needle. In one hand the biſhop, who wears a red mitre—an anomaly—and a cope with a quatrefoil morſe to it, holds a church, in the other a paſtoral ſtaff.

7024.

EMBROIDERY, in coloured filks upon fine linen damafk. Flemifh, 16th century. 10 inches by 2½ inches.

The fine linen upon which the embroidery is done, is diapered with a lozenge pattern: on one fide of a large flower-bearing tree are the words:—" Jhefu Xpi," and the other, " O crux Ave," on each fide of the tree is a fhield unemblazoned but furrounded by a garland of flowers. Moft likely this piece ferved to cover the top of the devotional table in a lady's bed-room.

7025.

EMBROIDERY, in coloured filks upon white linen; pattern, fymbols of the Paffion, flowers, and birds, with faints' names. German, 17th century. 20¾ inches by 6 inches.

Within a green circle, overfhadowed on four fides by ftems bearing flowers, ftands a low column with ropes about it and a fcourge at one fide, and divided by it is the word Martinus, in red filk; amid the flower-bearing wide-fpread branches of a tree are the names Urfula, Auguftinus; within another circle like the firft we fee the crofs with the fponge at the end of a reed, and the lance, having the name of Barbara in blue and crimfon; and, laft of all, another tree with the names Laurentius—Katerina. It is edged with a border of rofes and daifies, and has a parti-coloured filk fringe. No doubt this piece ferved as the ornament of a lady's praying-defk in her private room, and bore the names of thofe for whom fhe wifhed more efpecially to pray.

7026.

ORPHREY of Web; ground, gold; pattern, two ftems intertwined and bearing leaves and flowers, in crimfon filk. German, 15th century. 9 inches by 2¾ inches.

7027.

LINEN, block-printed; ground, white; pattern, crested birds and foliage, just like another piece, No. 8615, in this collection. Flemish, late 14th century. 14 inches by 2¾ inches.

7028.

SMALL Piece of Orphrey; ground, yellow silk stitchery upon canvas, embroidered, within barbed quatrefoils in cords of gold, and upon a gold diapered ground, with the busts of two Evangelists in coloured silks, and the whole bordered by an edging of gold stalks, with trefoils. Italian, the middle of the 15th century. 10 inches by 5¼ inches.

The quatrefoils are linked together by a kind of fretty knot, as well as the lengths in the two narrow edgings on the border by a less intricate one, all of which looks very like Florentine work. Most likely this orphrey served for the side of a cope.

7029.

PIECE of a Liturgical Cloth, embroidered in white thread, very slightly shaded here and there in crimson silk, upon linen, with a quatrefoil at top enclosing the Annunciation and four angels, one at each corner swinging a thurible, and lower down, with St. Peter and St. Paul, St. James the Less and St. Matthias, St. James the Greater and St. Andrew; amid the leaf-bearing boughs, roving all over the cloth, may be seen an occasional lion's head cabossed and langued *gules*. German, late 14th century. 2 feet 9½ inches by 1 foot 10¼ inches.

This is but a small piece of one of those long coverings or veils for the lectern, of which such fine examples are in this collection.

The lion's head cabossed would seem to be an armorial ensign of the family to which the lady who worked the cloth belonged, although such an ornament does sometimes appear, without any heraldic meaning, upon monuments of the period. In the execution of its stitchery the specimen before us is far below others of the same class.

7030.

PIECE of a Stole or Maniple; ground, crimson silk (much faded); and embroidered with green stems twining up and bearing small round flowers in gold, and large oak leaves in white. Italian, 16th century. 13¾ inches by 3 inches.

The leaves, now so white, were originally of gold, but of so poor a quality that the metal is almost worn off the threads.

7031.

SILK Ribbon; ground, green and gold; pattern, squares and lozenges on one bar, spiral narrow bands on another, the bars alternating. Italian, early 17th century. 8 inches by 8¼ inches.

Both silk and gold are good in this simple pattern.

7032.

SILK Damask; ground, crimson; pattern, a square enclosing a floriation; both in bright yellow. Spanish, 15th century. 8 inches by 4½ inches.

Designed on Moorish principles, and coarse in its workmanship.

7033.

SILK Texture; ground, yellow; pattern, net-work, with flowers and mullets, all in dark blue. Sicilian, late 14th century. 10 inches by 3½ inches.

Of a simple design and poor in texture, and probably meant as the lining for a richer kind of stuff.

R

7034.

SILK Damask; ground, crimson silk; pattern, in gold thread, two very large lions, and two pairs, one of very small birds, the other of equally small dragons, and an ornament like a hand looking-glass. Oriental, 14th century. 2 feet 4 inches by 2 feet.

The large lions, which strongly resemble, in their fore-legs, the Nineveh ones in the BritishMuseum, are placed addorsed regardant and looking upon two very small birds, while between their heads stands what seems like a looking-glass, upon a stem or handle; at the feet of these huge beasts are two little long-tailed, open-mouthed, two-legged dragons. The whole of this design now appears to be in coarse yellow thread, which once was covered with gold, but so sparingly and with such poor metal that not a speck of it can now be detected anywhere in this large specimen. The probability is that this stuff was wrought in some part of Syria, for the European market; at the lions' necks are broad collars bearing two lines or sentences in imitated Arabic characters. Copes and chasubles for church use during the Middle Ages were often made of silks like this. Dr. Bock has figured this very piece in his "Geschichte der Liturgischen Gewänder des Mittelalters," t. i. pl. iv.

7035.

SILK and Linen Texture; ground, crimson; pattern, star-like flowers. Spanish, 15th century. 5¾ inches by 2⅞ inches.

Poor in design as well as material.

7036.

SILK Diapered, with a man wrestling with a lion repeated; ground, crimson, the diaper in various colours, and the waving borders in creamy white, edged black, and charged with crimson squares, and fruits crimson and deep green. Byzantine, 12th century. 15¾ inches by 12¼ inches.

SILK FABRIC
Byzantine — 4th century.

Needlework, and Dresses.

This is one among the known early productions of the loom, and therefore very valuable. The lion and man seem to be meant for Samson's victory over that animal, though, for the sake of a pattern, the same two figures are repeated in such a way that they are in pairs and confronted. Samson's dress is after the classic form, and he wears sandals, while a long narrow green scarf, fringed yellow, flutters from off his shoulder behind him; and the tawny lion's mane is shown to fall in white and black locks, but in such a way that, at first sight, the black shading might be mistaken for the letters of some word. This stuff is figured by Dr. Bock in his "Geschichte der Liturgischen Gewänder des Mittelalters," t. i. pl. ii.

7037.

SILK and Linen Damask; ground, pale dull yellow-coloured linen; pattern, circles enclosing tawny foliation, in the midst of which is a purple cinquefoil, and the spandrils outside filled in with other foliations in the same tawny tone. Byzantine, 14th century. 13½ inches by 13 inches.

Of poor stuff, but of a rather pleasing design.

7038.

SILK Texture; ground, crimson; pattern, geometrical figures, mostly in bright yellow, filled in with smaller like figures in blue, green, and white. Moorish, 15th century. 1 foot 10¾ inches by 1 foot 2¼ inches.

Most likely this garish and rather staring silk was woven either at Tangier or Tetuan, and found its way to Europe through some of the ports on the southern coast of Spain.

7039.

SILK Damask; ground, purple; pattern, lozenges, with so-called loveknots, one on each side, enclosing a flower and a lozenge chequered with Greek crosses alternately, all in yellow. Byzantine, 14th century. 8¼ inches by 4 inches.

Though poor in material this silk is so far interesting as it gives a link in that long chain of traditional feeling for showing the cross about stuffs, meant, as most likely this was, for ritual uses, and known among both the Latins and the Greeks as " stauracina." To this day the same custom is followed in the East of having the cross marked upon the textiles employed in liturgical garments.

7040.

WHITE Linen, diapered with a small lozenge pattern, and a border of one broad and two narrow bands in black thread. Flemish, 15th century. 12 inches by 11¼ inches.

A good example of Flemish napery with the diaper well shown.

7041.

SILK and Linen Texture; ground, blue; pattern, a large petaled flower within a park fencing, upon the palings of which are perched two birds, and another somewhat like flower enclosed in the same way with two quadrupeds rampant on the palings. Italian, 15th century. 16 inches by 12¾ inches.

The birds seem to be meant for doves; and the animals for dogs. In design, but not in richness of material, this specimen is much like No. 7020.

7042.

SILK Damask; ground, deep blue; pattern, floriated lozenges, enclosing chequered lozenges in deep yellow. South of Spain, 14th century. 12 inches by 7¾ inches.

A tissue showing a Saracenic feeling.

SILK DAMASK
Sicilian — 12th century

7043.

ILK Damask; ground, tawny; pattern, a cone-shaped floriation amid foliage and flowers. Sicilian, 15th century. 13½ inches by 13 inches.

Both around the cone, as well as athwart the flowers, there are attempts at Arabic sentences, but in letters so badly done as easily to show the attempted cheat.

7044.

ILK Damask; ground, deep blue; pattern, six-sided panels filled in with conventional floriations, all in orange yellow. Spanish moresque, 15th century. 7 inches by 3¼ inches.

If not designed and wrought by Moorish hands, its Spanish weaver worked after Saracenic feelings in the forms of its ornamentation.

7045.

ILK Damask; ground, amber, diapered in small lozenges; pattern, parrots in pairs outlined in blue and crimson, both which colours are almost faded, and having a border consisting of narrow parallel lines, some dark blue with white scrolls, others of gold thread, with deep blue scrolls. Oriental, late 12th century. 9 inches by 5¾ inches.

7045 A.

SILK Border, torn off from the foregoing number. Both the one and the other are valuable proofs of the care taken by the Greek weavers, in the Greek islands, Greece proper, and in Syria, to give an elaborate design to the grounds of their silks.

7046.

SILK Brocade; ground, deep crimfon; pattern, a diapering, in the fame colour, of heart-fhaped fhields charged with a fanciful floriation, amid wavy fcrolls bearing flowers upon them. South of Spain, 14th century. 6¼ inches by 4¼ inches.

The fine rich tone of colour, fo fixed that it is yet unfaded, is remarkable.

7047.

SILK Crape, deep crimfon, thickly diapered with leaves upon the ftems. Syrian. 8¼ inches by 5¾ inches.

Not only the mellow tone, but the pretty though fmall pattern is very pleafing.

7048.

SILK and Cotton Texture; ground, white cotton; pattern, lozenges filled up with a broken fret of T-fhaped lines and dots, and a crofs in the middle; and with fimilar markings in the intervening fpaces. Byzantine, 14th century. 14 inches by 5 inches.

Though of fuch poor materials this fpecimen is rather interefting from its defign where the narrow-lined lozenges with their T's and fhort intervening lines are all in green filk, now much faded; and the crofs, known as of the Greek form, with thofe little dots are in crimfon filk. Moft likely it was woven in one of the iflands of the Archipelago, and for liturgical ufe, fuch as the broad flat girdle ftill employed in the Oriental rituals.

7049.

SILK Damafk; ground, fawn-colour; defign, parrots and giraffes in pairs amid floriated ornamentation, all, excepting the portions done in gold, of the fame tint with the ground. Sicilian, 13th century. 15 inches by 8 inches.

Like the specimen under No. 1274, where it is fully described.

7050.

SILK Damask; all creamy white; pattern, net-work, the oval meshes of which show floriations in thin lines upon a satiny ground. Syrian, 13th century. 11¼ inches by 6 inches.

This fine rich textile is, in all probability, the production of a Saracenic loom, and from the eastern part of the Mediterranean.

7051.

SILK Tissue; ground, amber; pattern, a reticulation, each six-sided mesh filled in with alternate flowers and leaves, with here and there a circle enclosing a pair of parrots, addorsed, regardant; and between them a lace sort of column having, at top, a crescent all in dark blue. Oriental, late 12th century. 12¼ inches by 6¼ inches.

A good specimen, when fresh and new, of the eastern loom.

7052.

WHITE Silk Damask, diapered with a chequer charged with lozenges, bearing the Greek gammadion, and sprinkled with larger flowers. Oriental, 14th century. 7¼ inches by 5¼ inches.

The pattern of this curious stuff is very small; and from the presence of the gammadion upon it, we may presume it was originally wrought for Greek liturgical use, somewhere on the coast of Syria.

7053.

SILK Damask; green; the pattern, an oval, enclosing an artichoke, and the spaces between filled in with foliations and pomegranates. Spanish, 16th century. 23 inches by 12½ inches.

Beautiful in tone of colour, and of a pleasing design, well shown by a shining satiny look of the silk; this is a specimen of a rich stuff.

7054.

DIAPERED Silk; ground, yellow; pattern, a large conventional foliation, in rows, alternating with rows of armorial shields, all in blue. Spanish, early 17th century. 20 inches by 17 inches.

A very effective design for household use: the shield is a pale, the crest a barred closed helmet topped by a demy wyvern.

7055.

SILK Diaper; ground, gold; pattern, flowers and fruits in crimson, slightly shaded in blue and green silk. Spanish, 16th century. 12½ inches by 8½ inches.

Though the gold on the ground be so sparingly put in, this stuff has a rich look, and the occurrence of the pomegranate points to Granada as the place of manufacture of this and other tissues of such patterns.

7056.

SILK Tissue, now deep amber, once bright crimson, diapered with a modification of the meander, and over that sprigs of flowers. Oriental, 13th century. 8 inches by 4½ inches.

To see the raised diapering of this piece requires a near inspection, but when detected, it is found to be of a pleasing type.

7057.

SILK Damaſk; ground, purple; pattern, a quatrefoil, within another, charged with a croſs-like floriation, with a ſquare white centre, ſurmounted by two eagles with wings diſplayed, upholding in their beaks a royal crown, all in green. Italian, early 15th century. 14 inches by 11½ inches.

Though the ſilk be poor the deſign is in good character, and the ſtuff would ſeem to have been wrought either at Florence or Lucca, for ſome princely German houſe.

7058.

PIECE of Silk Damaſk; ground, red and gold; pattern, a pair of oſtrich feathers, ſpringing from a conventional flower, and drooping over an artichoke-like floriation, of a tint once light green, and ſhaded dull white. Spaniſh, 15th century. 14¾ inches by 7¼ inches.

A curious mixture of ſilk, wool, linen thread and gold very ſparingly employed. The oſtrich feather is ſo unuſual an element of ornamental deſign, eſpecially in woven ſtuffs, that we may deem it a kind of remembrance of the Black Prince who fought for a Spaniſh king, Don Pedro the Cruel, at the battle of Navaretta, or Najarra, if not having a ſignificance of the marriage of Catherine of Arragon, firſt with our Prince Arthur, eldeſt ſon of Henry VII, and after his death, with his younger brother, Henry VIII, each of whom was in his time Prince of Wales, whoſe badge became one or more oſtrich feathers. In old Engliſh church inventories drawn up towards the middle and the end of the 15th century, mention is often found of veſtments made of a Flemiſh ſtuff, called Dorneck, from the name in Flanders for the city of Tournay, where it was made, but ſpelt in Engliſh various ways, as Darnec, Darnak, Darnick, and even Darnep. Such an inferior kind of tiſſue woven of thin ſilk mixed with wool and linen thread, was in great demand, for every-day wear in poor churches in this country. Though not wrought at Tournay, the preſent ſpecimen affords a good example of that ſort of ſtuff called Dorneck, which, very probably, was introduced into Flanders from Spain. Besides the present textile, another, figured in the " Mélanges d'Archéologie," t. iii. pt. xxxiii. furnishes an additional instance in which the ostrich feather is brought into the design.

7059.

REEN Silk Damask; pattern, floriations and short lengths of narrow bands arranged zig-zag. Italian, 17th century. 8 inches by 6¼ inches.

An extraordinary but not pleasing pattern.

7060.

ILK and Linen Damask; ground, creamy white; pattern, in light brown, once pink, a conventional artichoke. Italian, 16th century. 1 foot 5 inches by 9¼ inches.

The warp is thread, but still the texture looks well.

7061.

ILK and Gold Damask; ground, light green silk; pattern, large vine leaves and stars, with a border of griffins and fleur-de-lis, in gold. Sicilian, 14th century. 10¼ inches square.

This beautiful stuff was, in all likelihood, woven at the royal manufactory at Palermo, and meant as a gift to some high personage who came from the blood royal of France. The griffins, affronted or combatant, are drawn with much freedom and spirit, and though the gold be dull, the pattern still looks rich.

7062.

OLD Web, diapered with animals in green silk. French, late 13th century. 14¼ inches by 2¼ inches.

Probably wrought in a small frame, at home, by some young woman, and for personal adornment. So much is it worn away, that the green beardless lion, with a circle of crimson, can be well seen only in one instance. A narrow short piece of edging lace, of the same make and time, but of a simple interlacing strap-pattern, is pinned to this specimen.

7063.

GREEN and Fawn-coloured Silk Diaper; pattern, squares, green, filled in with leaves fawn-coloured, and beasts and birds, green. Sicilian, late 13th century. 8 inches by 3¼ inches.

Another of those specimens, perhaps of the Palermitan loom: all the animals look heraldic, and are lions, griffins, wyverns, and parrots. The stuff itself is not of the richest.

7064.

GOLD Lace, so worn by use that the floriation on the oblong diaper is obliterated. French, 13th century. 9 inches by 1¼ inches.

7064 A.

GOLD Lace; pattern, interlacing strap-work. French, 13th century. 7 inches by 1½ inches.

Equally serviceable for personal or ecclesiastical use.

7065.

BLACK Silk Damask; figured with a tower surrounded by water, over which are two bridges; in the lower court are two men, each with an eagle perched upon his hand; from out the third story of the tower springs a tree, bearing artichoke floriations. Italian, 15th century. 11 inches by 8 inches.

Another piece of this identical damask occurs at No. 8612, but there the design is by no means so clear as in the piece before us.

7066.

GREEN Silk; pattern, a lozenge reticulation, each mesh filled in with four very small voided lozenges placed crosswise, in pale yellow. Oriental, 14th century. 5¼ inches by 4¼ inches.

7067.

SILK and Gold Damask; ground, green silk; pattern, conventional floriation, with a circular form of the artichoke. Spanish, early 15th century. 1 foot 3¼ inches by 4 inches.

One of those samples of that poor texture which came from the Spanish loom, with the sham gold, which we have before observed in other examples, of thin parchment gilt with a much debased gold.

7068.

SILK Damask; straw-colour; pattern, lozenge-shaped net-work, each mesh enclosing a flower. Spanish, 15th century. 13¾ inches by 12 inches.

So worn is this piece that it is with difficulty that its simple design can be made out.

7069.

SILK Damask; straw-colour; pattern, an imaginary eagle-like bird, enclosed by a garland full of ivy leaves. Sicilian, 14th century. 7¾ inches by 6 inches.

The ground is completely filled in with the well-designed and pretty diapering; but damp has sadly spoiled the specimen.

Needlework, and Dresses.

7070.

ILK Damask; ground, purple; pattern, heraldic figures, birds, and oval floriations, in gold thread. Oriental, 14th century. 16 inches by 9 inches.

On an oval, floriated all round, and enclosing two lionesses addorsed rampant regardant, are two wyvern-like eagles with curious feathered tails, regardant; below, are two cockatoos addorsed regardant, all in gold. The oval floriation is outlined with green. When new, this stuff must have had a brave appearance, and shows a Persian tradition about it.

7071.

INEN, embroidered in silk; ground, fine linen; pattern, a zigzag, alternating in light blue and brown. German, 15th century. 14 inches by 3¼ inches.

The zigzag may be termed dancette, and all over is parted into lozenges, each lozenge charged with a cross made of mascles, and the spaces between the brown and the blue zigzags, filled in with others of a light brown coloured diapering.

7072.

ILK Damask; ground, violet or deep purple; pattern, angels with thuribles, and emblems of the Passion, in yellow and white. Florentine, late 14th century. 18¼ inches by 15¼ inches.

This truly artistic and well-executed stuff displays a row of angels in girded albs, all flying one way, as with the left hand they swing thuribles, and another row kneeling, each with a crown of thorns in his hands, alternating, with a second set of angels, in another row, each bearing before him a cross. All the angels are done in yellow, but with face and hands white, and the whole ground is strewed with stars. It is likely that this fine stuff was woven expressly for the purple vestments worn in Passion time, at the end of Lent.

7073.

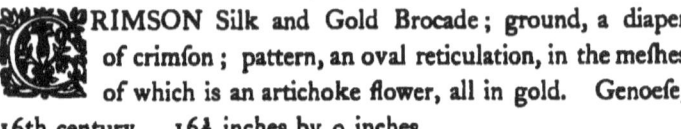RIMSON Silk and Gold Brocade; ground, a diaper of crimson; pattern, an oval reticulation, in the meshes of which is an artichoke flower, all in gold. Genoese, 16th century. 16¼ inches by 9 inches.

The design of this rich stuff is well managed, and the diapering in dull silk upon a satin ground throws out the gold brocading admirably; the meshes which enclose the flowers are themselves formed of garlands.

7074.

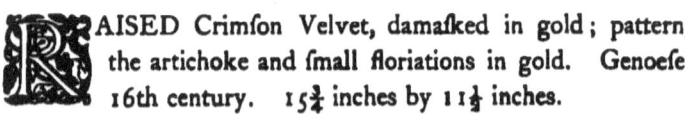AISED Crimson Velvet, damasked in gold; pattern, the artichoke and small floriations in gold. Genoese, 16th century. 15¾ inches by 11½ inches.

A specimen of what, in its prime, must have been a fine stuff for household decoration, though of such a nature as to have freely allowed it to be employed for ecclesiastical purposes. It has seen rough service, so that its pile is in places thread-bare, and its gold almost worn away.

7075.

AISED Velvet on Gold Ground; pattern, a very large rose with broad border in raised crimson velvet, filled in with a bush of pomegranates, in very thin lines of raised crimson velvet; the rest of the ground is diapered all over with the pomegranate tree in very thin outline. Genoese, early 16th century. 2 feet 9 inches by 2 feet.

The gold thread was so poor that the precious metal has almost entirely disappeared; but when all was new, this stuff must have looked particularly grand. The large red rose, and the pomegranate, make it seem as if it had been wrought, in the first instance, for either our Henry the Seventh, or Henry the Eighth, after the English marriage of Catherine of Arragon.

7076.

AISED Velvet and Gold; pattern, conventional flowers in gold, upon tawny-coloured velvet. Genoese, late 15th century. 12 inches by 8 inches.

The gold of the design is, in parts, nicely diapered; and the gold thread itself thin, and now rather tarnished.

7077.

AISED Crimson Velvet; pattern, an artichoke amid flowers. Genoese, late 15th century. 16½ inches by 11½ inches.

The pile is rich; and when it is borne in mind how the Emperor Charles V. honoured Andrea Dorea, it is not surprising that his countrymen had a partiality for the Spanish emblem of their great captain's admirer.

7078.

AISED Blue Velvet; ground, deep blue; pattern, within an outlined seven-petaled floriation in silk, an artichoke, with sprigs of flowers shooting out of it. Genoese, late 15th century. 17¼ inches by 10¼ inches.

Though much worn by hard usage, this stuff is of a pleasing effect, owing to its agreeable design, which not unfrequently occurs perfect, and consists of a kind of circle in narrow lines, somewhat in the shape of a flower, but having at the tips of its prominent feathering cusps of florets.

7079.

IGURED Blue Velvet; embroidered in gold thread, with cinquefoils, enclosing a floriation of the artichoke form, with smaller ones around it. Spanish, 15th century. 15 inches by 9¾ inches.

By the shape of this piece it must have been cut off from the end of a chasuble. Though the velvet is rich, the embroidery is poor, done as it is in thin outline, but still of a good form.

7080.

ORPHREY Web, silk and gold; ground, crimson; pattern, on a gold diapering, conventional floriations and scrolls, in one of which is the bust of St. Peter, with his key in one hand and a book in the other. Florentine, late 15th century. 21 inches by 8 inches.

Like many other samples, this rich web of crimson silk and fine gold thread was wrought for those kinds of broad orphreys needed for chasubles and copes; and sometimes worked up into altar-frontals.

7081.

SILK Damask; ground, yellow; pattern, net-work, the meshes, which are looped to each other, filled in with a conventional floriated ornament, all in green. Italian, 16th century. 16¼ inches by 10¾ inches.

Intended for household adornment. This stuff must have had an agreeable effect, though the green has somewhat faded.

7082.

SILK Damask; ground, yellowish pale green; pattern, a diapering of very small leaves and flowers. Oriental, 13th century. 6¼ inches by 5¼ inches.

Just like No. 7056, and needing the same near inspection to find out its small but well-managed delicate design.

7083.

SILK and Linen Texture; ground, yellow; pattern, amid foliage, two cheetahs, face to face, all blue, but spotted yellow. Syrian, 14th century. 7¼ inches by 6¼ inches.

At the same time that the warp is of linen, the woof of silk is thin; and a bold design is almost wasted upon poor materials. The specimen, however, is so far valuable, as it shows us how, for ages, a Persian feeling went along with the workmen on the eastern shores of the Levant.

7084.

SILK Damask; ground, tawny; pattern, birds, flowers, and heart-shaped figures, encircled with imitated Arabic letters, all mostly in green, very partially shaded white. Sicilian, 14th century. 19¼ inches by 5¼ inches.

Above a heart-shaped ornament, bordered by a sham inscription in Arabic, and surrounded by a wreath, are two birds of the hoopoe kind, and beneath, two other birds, like eagles; and this design is placed amid the oval spaces made by garlands of flowers. All the component elements of the pattern are in small, though well-drawn figures.

7085.

SILK and Gold Damask; ground, tawny; pattern, fruit, beasts, and birds. Sicilian, 14th century. 22¼ inches by 10 inches.

This rich stuff has an elaborate pattern, consisting of three pieces of fruit, like oranges or apples, with a small pencil of sun-rays darting from them above, out of which springs a little bunch of trefoils, which separate two lions, in gold, that are looking down, and with open langued mouths; below is another and larger pencil of beams, shining upon two perched eagles, with wings half spread out for flight. Between such groups is a large flower like an artichoke, with two blue flowers, like the centaurea, at the stalk itself; above which is, as it were, the feathering of an arch with a bunch of three white flowers, for its cusp. With the exception of the lions and flowers, the rest of the pattern is in green.

7086.

SILK and Gold Brocade; ground, dark purple; pattern, all in gold, floriations, birds and beasts. Oriental, 13th century. 18¼ inches by 7 inches.

When new, this rich stuff must have been very effective, either for liturgical use or personal wear. There is a broad border, formed by the shallow sections of circles, inscribed with imitated Arabic characters. Out of the points or featherings made by the junctions of the circular

T

sections spring forth bunches of wheat-ears, separating two collared cheetahs with heads reversed; and from other featherings, a large oval well-filled floriation, upon the branches of which are perched two crested birds, may be hoopoes, at which the cheetahs seem to be gazing. Over the wheat-ears, drops are falling from a pencil of sunbeams above them; below are two flowers in silk, once crimson.

7087.

SILK Damask; ground, blue; pattern, birds, animals, and flowers, in gold, and different coloured silks. Oriental, late 13th century. 17¼ inches by 7¼ inches.

So fragmentary is this specimen, that it is rather hard to find out the whole of the design, which was seemingly composed of white cheetahs collared red, in pairs; above which sit two little dogs, in gold, looking at one another; and just over them a pair of white eagles, small too, on the wing, and holding a white flower between them. Running across the pattern was a band, in gold, charged with circles enclosing a sitting dog, a rosette, a circle having an imitated Arabic sentence over it.

7088.

PART of a Stole, or of a Maniple; silk brocade; ground, light crimson; pattern, floriations in green, with lions rampant in gold. Sicilian, late 14th century. 20¼ inches by 3 inches.

The parti-coloured fringe to this liturgical appliance is of poor linen thread not corresponding to the richness of the stuff.

7089.

SILK and Gold Damask; ground, gold; pattern, branches of foliation, in yellow silk. Oriental, 15th century. 17½ inches by 3½ inches.

Though rather rich in material, the design is so obscure as hardly to be observable.

7090.

SILK Damask; ground, purple; pattern, a diaper of parrots, and floriations, in bright greenish yellow. Oriental, 14th century. 11 inches by 4¼ inches.

Though of a poor silk, the design is pretty, and tells of the coast of Syria, where many of the looms were kept at work for European use.

7091.

SILK and Gold Damask; ground, purple; pattern, fleurs-de-lis in gold. Sicilian, late 14th century. 4 inches square.

Done, as was often the case, for French royalty, or some one of French princely blood, at Palermo, and sent to France. The stuff is rich, and well sprinkled with the royal golden flower.

7092.

SILK Damask; ground, amber (once crimson); pattern, a diaper of flowers and leaves, in yellow. Sicilian, late 14th century. 9 inches by 5¼ inches broad.

Of a quiet and pleasing kind of design, showing something like a couple of letters in the hearts of two of its flowers.

7093.

EMBROIDERY in silk upon linen; pattern, men blue, women white, standing in a row hand in hand; the spaces filled up with lozenges in white. The women upon a green, the men upon a white ground. German, 16th century. 8¾ inches by 6¼ inches.

So very worn away is the needle-work, that it is very hard to see the design, which, when discovered, looks to be very stiff, poor, and angular.

7094.

SILK Damaſk; ground, ſtraw-colour; pattern, net-work of lozenges and quatrefoils, filled in each with a croſs pommée, amid which are large circles containing a pair of parrots, all in raiſed ſatin. Oriental, 13th century. 8¾ inches by 7¾ inches.

This fine textile was, in all likelihood, woven by Chriſtian hands ſomewhere upon the Syrian coaſt, and while a religious charaƈter was given it both by the croſſes and the emblematic parrots, a Perſian influence by the uſe of the olden traditional tree between the parrots, or the Perſians' ſacred " hom," was allowed to remain upon the deſigner's mind without his own knowledge of its being there, or of its ſymbolic meaning in reference to Perſia's ancient heathen worſhip.

7095.

BLUE Linen, wrought with gilt thin parchment; pattern, an oval, filled in with another oval, ſurrounded by ſix-petaled flowers, all in outline; this piece is put upon another of a different deſign, of which the pattern is an eagle on the wing. Spaniſh, 14th century. 7¼ inches by 4¼ inches.

This is another ſpecimen of gilt parchment being uſed inſtead of gold thread.

7099.

FOOT-CLOTH; ground, green worſted; pattern, birds and flowers. German, 16th century. 4 feet 7 inches by 2 feet 7 inches.

In all likelihood, this piece of needlework ſerved the purpoſe of a rug or foot-cloth, or, may be, as the cloth covering for the ſeat of a carriage. It is worked in thick worſted upon a wide-meſhed thread net, and after a ſomewhat ſtiff deſign.

7218.

ABLE-COVER, in green filk, with wide border of Italian point lace. Venetian, late 16th century. 5 feet 6 inches by 3 feet 2 inches.

The pattern of the lace is very bold and well executed, and confifts of a large foliage-fcroll of the claffic type, ending in a lion's head, fo cherifhed by the Venetians, as the emblem of the Republic's patron-faint, St. Mark. The poor thin filk is not worthy of its fine trimming.

7219.

ABLE-COVER, in light blue filk, with wide border of Italian point lace. Venetian, late 16th century. 6 feet 5 inches by 4 feet.

The pattern of the lace, like the foregoing fpecimen, is after a claffic form, confifting of two horns of plenty amid foliage and fcroll-work; in both pieces we fee the effect of that fchool which brought forth a Palladio.

7468.

 LECTERN Veil of filk and gold cut-work; ground, crimfon filk; defign, of cut-work in cloth of gold and white and blue filk, ramifications ending in bunches of white grapes, horns of plenty holding fruit, and ears of wheat. French, 17th century. 9 feet by 1 foot 9¼ inches.

Such veils are thrown over a light moveable ftand upon which the book of the Gofpels and Epiftles is put at high mafs, for the deacon's ufe as he fings the Gofpel of the day. The cut-work is well-defigned, and fewed on with an edging of blue cord in fome places, of yellow in others. The cloth of gold was fo poor that now it looks at a fhort diftance like mere yellow filk.

7674.

MISSAL Cushion; ground, red silk; pattern, two angels standing face to face and holding between them a cross, all in gold, excepting the angels' faces and hands, which are white; there are four tassels, one at each corner, crimson and gold. Florentine, early 15th century. 1 foot 3 inches by 1 foot.

The covering for this cushion is made of orphrey web, the gold of which is very much faded; and, like other specimens from the same looms, shows the nudes of the figures in a pinkish white. The use of such cushions for upholding the missal upon the altar is even now kept up in some places. According to the rubric of the Roman Missal, wherein, at the beginning among the " rubricæ generales," cap. xx. it is directed that there should be " in cornu epistolæ (altaris) cussinus supponendus missali."

7788.

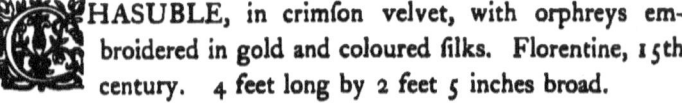

CHASUBLE, in crimson velvet, with orphreys embroidered in gold and coloured silks. Florentine, 15th century. 4 feet long by 2 feet 5 inches broad.

This garment has been much cut down, and so worn that, in parts, its rich and curious orphreys are so damaged as to be unintelligible. Over the breast and on the front orphrey is embroidered the Crucifixion, but after a somewhat unusual manner, inasmuch as, besides our Lord on the Cross, with His mother and St. John the Evangelist standing by; two other saints are introduced, St. Jerome on one side, St. Lucy on the other, kneeling on the ground at the foot of the Cross, possibly the patrons, one of the lady, the other of the gentleman, at whose cost this vestment was wrought. Under this is St. Christina defending Christianity against the heathens; her arraignment, for her belief, before one of Dioclesian's officials; her body bound naked, and scourged at a pillar. On the back orphrey, the same martyr on her knees by the side of another governor, her own pagan father, and praying that the idol, held to her for worship by him, may be broken; the saint maintaining her faith to those who came to argue with her before the window of the prison, wherein she is shut up naked in a cauldron, with flames under it, and praying with one of the men who are feeding the fire with bundles of wood, on his knees, as if converted by her words; then, the faint ftanding at a table, around which are three men; and below all, a piece fo worn and cut, as to be unintelligible. Upon the laft fquare but one is a fhield *argent*, a bend *azure*, charged with a crefcent *or*, two ftars *or*, and another crefcent *or*, probably the blazon of the Pandolfini family, to whofe domeftic chapel at Florence this veftment is faid to have belonged.

7789, 7790.

ALMATIC, and Tunicle, in crimfon velvet, with apparels of woven ftuff in gold and crimfon filk, figured with cherubic heads. Florentine, 15th century.

The velvet is of a rich pile, and the tone of colour warm. The orphreys, or rather apparels, are all of the fame texture, woven of a red ground, and figured in gold with cherubic heads, having white faces; the lace alfo is red, and gold; but in both the gold is quite faded. The fleeves are fomewhat fhort, but the garment itfelf is full and majeftic. Doubtlefs the dalmatic and tunicle formed a part of a full fet of veftments, to which the fine and curioufly embroidered chafuble, No. 7788, belonged; and their apparels, or fquare orphreys, above and below, before and behind, are in defign and execution alike to feveral others from the looms of Florence, which we have found among various other remains of liturgic garments in this collection.

7791.

IECE of Woven Orphrey; ground, crimfon filk; defign, in gold, an altar, with an angel on each fide clafping a column, and above, other two angels worfhipping; and upon the ftep leading to the altar, the words " fanctus, fanctus." Florentine, early 16th century. 9 feet 7 inches by 9 inches.

The defign is evidently meant to exprefs the tabernacle at the altar, where the blefled facrament is kept in church, for adminiftration to the fick, &c, and, like all fimilar textiles, was made of fuch a length as to be applicable to copes, chafubles, and other ritual ufes.

7792.

VEIL for the subdeacon, of raised velvet and gold; ground, gold; pattern, a broad scroll, showing, amid foliation, a conventional artichoke in raised crimson velvet. Florentine, late 16th century. 14 feet 4 inches by 1 foot 10 inches.

The bright yellow ground is more of silk than gold thread, and the velvet design, deep in its rich pile and glowing in its ruby tint, is dotted with the usual gold thread loops; at each end is a golden fringe; both edges are bordered with poor gold open lace; and still attached to it are the two short yellow silk strings for tying it in front, when put about the shoulders of the subdeacon at the offertory, when the paten is given him to hold at high mass.

7793.

HOOD of a Cope; ground, mostly gold, and a small part, silver; figured with two adoring angels; the centre piece gone, and in its place a saint standing, and done in woven work. Flemish, 15th century; the inserted saint, Florentine, 15th century. 1 foot $4\frac{1}{4}$ inches by 1 foot $4\frac{1}{2}$ inches.

The figures of the angels in worship are nicely done in flos-silk; and perhaps the original lost figure was that of our Lord, or of the B. V. Mary. The lay saint now inserted, bare-headed, and leaning on his sword, wearing a green tunic, and a blue mantle sprinkled with trefoils in red and gold, perhaps meant for fleurs-de-lis, seems to be intended for St. Louis of France. The broad green silk fringe, and the pointed shape of the hood will not escape notice; and behind may yet be seen the eyes by which this hood was hung upon the cope. The poor shabby silver tinsel round this king is an addition quite modern.

7794.

BURSE for Corporals; ground, crimson satin; pattern, foliations and flowers in coloured silks and gold, with a phœnix rising from the flames in the middle. German, late 17th century. 11 inches by $10\frac{3}{4}$ inches.

SILK DAMASK.

7795.

BURSE for Corporals; ground, crimson velvet; pattern, velvet upon velvet, lined at back with silk; ground, amber, figured with a modification of the artichoke, in deep crimson. Italian, 16th century. $10\frac{3}{4}$ inches by 10 inches.

Though probably this burse, like the one above, may have come from a church in Germany, its beautiful materials are of Italian manufacture; the fine deep piled velvet upon velvet, from Genoa, the well-designed and pleasing silk at back, from Lucca, and many years, may be a half century, older than the velvet, make this small liturgical article very noteworthy on account of its materials.

7799.

VEIL of raised crimson velvet; ground, yellow silk and gold thread; pattern, large floriations all in crimson velvet, freckled with little golden loops. Florentine, 17th century. 11 feet $2\frac{1}{2}$ inches by 1 foot 10 inches.

One of those magnificent textures of cut velvet, with a fine rich pile, sent forth by the looms of Tuscany. Its use may have been both for a veil to the lectern for the Gospel, and to be worn by the subdeacon at high mass; the two strings, attached to it still, evidently show its application to the latter purpose. A heavy gold fringe borders its two ends, the scolloped shape of which is rather unusual.

7813.

FRONT Orphrey of a Chasuble, embroidered with figures in niches. Italian, late 15th century. 3 feet 1 inch by 7 inches; at the cross, $1\frac{1}{4}$ inches.

The first figure is that of our Lord giving His blessing, and of a very youthful countenance; next, seemingly the figure of St. Peter; then St. John the Evangelist. All these are done in coloured silks, upon a ground of gold, and within niches; but are sadly worn. The two angels at our Lord's head are the best in preservation; but the whole is rather poor in execution. As a border, there are two strips figured with silver crosses upon grounds of different coloured silks.

7813 A.

ART of an Orphrey, embroidered with figures of the Apostles. Italian, late 15th century. 4 feet by 7¼ inches.

Of the five personages, only the second, St. Paul, can be identified by his symbol of a sword. All are wrought upon a golden diaper, and standing within niches; but though the features are strongly marked in brown silk lines, as a specimen it is not remarkably good; and, most likely, served as the orphrey to some vestment, a chasuble, the orphrey of which for the front was the piece numbered 7813.

7833.

IECE of Applied Embroidery, upon silk of a creamy white, an ornamentation in crimson velvet and cloth of gold, scolloped and tasseled. Italian, early 17th century.

Rich of its kind, and probably a part of household furniture.

7900.

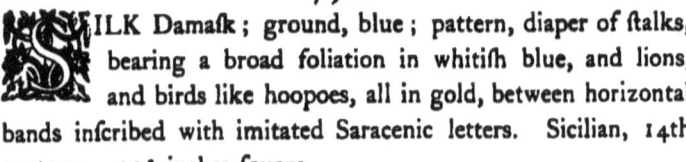ILK Damask; ground, blue; pattern, diaper of stalks, bearing a broad foliation in whitish blue, and lions, and birds like hoopoes, all in gold, between horizontal bands inscribed with imitated Saracenic letters. Sicilian, 14th century. 10¾ inches square.

A beautiful design; and in the bands, at each end of the imitated word in Saracenic characters, are those knots that are found on Italian textiles. So poor was the gold on the thread, that it is sadly tarnished.

8128.

PPARELS to an Alb; figured with the birth of the B. V. Mary, in the upper one; and in the lower, the birth of our Lord; with two armorial shields alternating between the spandrils of the canopies. English needlework, on crimson velvet, and in coloured silks and gold thread, done in the latter half of the 14th century. Each piece 2 feet 8¼ inches by 10½ inches. Presented by Ralf Oakden, Esq.

In many respects these two apparels, seemingly for the lower adornment of the liturgical alb, one before, the other behind, are very valuable; besides the subjects they represent, they afford illustrations of the style of needlework, architecture, costume, and heraldry of their time.

In the upper apparel, we have the birth and childhood of the mother of our Lord, as it is found in one of the apocryphal books of the New Testament, entitled,—" Evangelium de Nativitate S. Mariae," which the Latins got from the Greeks, as early, it would seem, as the second or third age of the Church. Though of no authority, this book was in especial favour with our countrymen, and it was not unfrequently noticed in their writings; hence, no doubt, the upper apparel was suggested by that pseudo-gospel. In its first compartment, we behold a middle-aged lady, richly clad, having a mantle of gold, lined with vair or costly fur, about her shoulders, seated on a cushioned stool with a lectern, or reading-desk before her, and upon it an open book of the Psalms, with the beginning of the fiftieth written on its silver pages,—" Miserere mei, Deus," &c, and outstretching her hands towards an angel coming down from the clouds, and as he hails her with one hand, holds, unrolled, before her eyes, a scroll bearing these words:—" Occurre viro ad portam." This female is Ann, wife of Joachim, and mother of Mary; and the whole is thus set forth in the Codex Apocryphus Novi Testamenti; where the angel, who appeared to her while she was at prayer, is said to have spoken these words:—" Ne timeas, Anna, neque phantasma esse putes . . . . Itaque surge, ascende Hierusalem, et cum perveneris ad portam quæ aurea, pro eo quod deaurata est, vocatur, ibi pro signo virum tuum obvium habebis," &c.—*Evangelium de Nativitate S. Mariae*, c. iv. in Cod. Apocry. ed. Thilo, pp. 324, 325. This passage is thus rendered in that rare old English black-letter book of sermons called " The Festival," which was so often printed by Caxton, Wynkyn de Worde, and other early printers in London:—" Anne was sory and prayed to God and sayde, Lorde, that me is woo. I am bareyne, and I may have noo frute . . . . and I knowe not whyther he (Joachim my husband) is gone. Lorde have mercy on me. Whene as she prayed thus an angell come downe and comforted her, and sayd: Anne, be of gode comfort, for thou shalt have a childe in thyne olde age, there was never none lyke, ne never shall be . . . . and whan he (Joachim) come nye home, the angell come to Anne, and bade her goo to the gate that was called the golden gate, and abide her huſbonde there tyll he come. Thene was ſhe glad .... and went to the gate and there ſhe mete with Joachim, and ſayd, Lord, I thanke thee, for I was a wedow and now I am a wyfe, I was bareyne and now I ſhall bear a childe .... and whan ſhe (the child) was borne, ſhe was called Mary."—*The Feſtival*, fol. lxvi. In the ſecond compartment we have a further illuſtration of the foregoing text in the repreſentation of the golden gate at Jeruſalem, and Anna and Joachim greeting one another as they meet there. In the third, there is the lying-in of Anna, who from her own bed is ſwathing her new-born child, whom the Almighty's right hand coming from heaven is bleſſing. In the fourth is Anna bringing her little girl Mary, when three years old, as an offering to God, in the temple, before the High Prieſt. In the fifth and laſt compartment of this upper row of niches, we ſee Anna teaching her daughter, the B. V. Mary, to read the Pſalter. In the firſt compartment in the lower apparel, or on the ſecond row, the angel Gabriel, winged and barefoot, is repreſented ſtanding before the B. V. Mary, whom with his right he is bleſſing, while in his left he holds out before her a ſcroll on which are the words :—" Ave Maria gracia." She outſtretches her hands, and gently bending her head forwards, ſeems to bow aſſent ; between them is the lily-pot, and, as it ſhould, holds but one flower-ſtem, with three, and only three, full-blown lilies (" Church of our Fathers," t. iii. p. 247); above, is the Holy Ghoſt, figured as a white dove, coming down upon the Virgin. To this follows St. Elizabeth's viſit to the B. V. Mary, or the Salutation, as it is often called in this country. Then we have the Nativity, after the uſual manner, with the ox and aſs worſhipping at the crib wherein our Lord is lying in ſwaddling clothes ; and St. Joſeph is figured wearing gloves. Filling the next niche, we behold the angel coming from the ſkies, with a ſcroll in his hands inſcribed,— " Gloria in excelſis Deo," to the ſhepherds, one of whom is playing on a bag-pipe with one hand, as with the other he is ringing a bell, which draws the attention of his dog that ſits before him with upturned head and gaping mouth. In the laſt compartment we have the three wiſe men, clothed and crowned as kings, going to Bethlehem with their gifts, but none of them is a negro. Of the two ſhields hung alternately between every ſpandril, one is,—barry of ten *argent* and *gules*, which was the blazon of Thornell de Suffolk ; and the other,—*azure* three cinquefoils *argent*, that of the family of Fitton, according to a MS. ordinary of arms, drawn up by Robert Glover, ſome time Somerſet herald. In the ſubject of the ſhepherds, the ground is ſo plentifully ſprinkled with growing daiſies, that it ſeems as if it were done on purpoſe to tell us that she whose hands had wrought the work was called Margaret; as the flower was in French designated " La Marguerite," it became the symbol of that saint's name, and not unfrequently was the chosen emblem of the females who bore it.

8226.

GOLD Embroidery on purple silk over a white cotton ground, with figures of our Saviour and of the apostles St. Peter, St. Simon, and St. Philip. Sicilian work, done about the end of the 12th century. 14¾ inches by 7 inches.

This piece of needlework with its figures, as well as its architectural accessories, wrought in gold thread, though rude in its execution, is not without an interest. In it the liturgical student will find the half of an apparel (for it has been unfeelingly cut in half at some remote time) for the lower hem in front of the linen garment known as the alb. Originally it must have consisted of seven figures; one of our Lord, in the middle, sitting upon a throne in majesty with the A on the one side and the Ω on the other side of His nimbed head, and His right hand uplifted in the act of bestowing His benediction. To the left must have been three apostles; to the right are still to be seen the other three, nearest our Saviour, St. Peter, holding in his left hand a double-warded key, next to him St. Simon, with his right hand in the act of blessing, and holding in his left a saw fashioned not like ours, but as that instrument is still made in Italy, and last of all St. Philip, but without any symbol. What look like half-moons with a little dot in the inside, and having a cross between them, are nothing more than the word "Sanctus," thus contracted with the letter S written as the Greek sigma formed like our C, a common practice in Italy during the middle ages, as may be seen in the inscriptions given by writers on Palæography.

Our Lord is seated within an elongated trefoil, and, at each corner at the outward sides, is shown one of His emblems, better known as the Evangelists' symbols hinted at by the prophet Ezekiel, i. 10: of these, two are very discernible, the winged human bust, commonly called St. Matthew's emblem, at top, and the nimbed and winged horned ox or calf for St. Luke. The Apostles all stand within round-headed arches, the spandrils of which are filled in with a kind of diaper ornamentation.

8227.

IECE of Crimson Silk, with pattern woven in gold thread. Sicilian, early 13th century. 10¼ inches by 7 inches.

This rich sample of the looms of Palermo betrays the architectural influences which acted upon the designers of such stuffs, by the introduction of that ramified ornamentation with its graceful bendings, that is so marked a character in the buildings of England and France at the close of the 12th and opening of the 13th century. The fleur-de-lis is rather an accidental than intentional adaptation, years before the French occupation of Sicily.

8228.

IECE of Purple Silk Embroidery in gold and silver; pattern of interlaced dragons, human figures, and birds. North German, 12th century. 8¼ inches by 7¼ inches.

This small sample of needlework is as remarkable for the way in which it is wrought, as for the wild Scandinavian mythology which is figured on it.

The usual process for the application of gold and silver in textiles and embroidery is to twine the precious metal about cotton thread, and thus weave it in with the shuttle or stitch it on by the needle. Here, however, the silver, in part white in its original condition, in part gilt, is laid on in the form of a very thin but solid wire, unmixed with cotton, and the effect is very rich and brilliant.

In the middle of this piece are shown two monsters interlacing one another; within the upper coil which they make with their snake-like lengths, stands a human figure which, from its dress, looks that of a man who with each outstretched hand, seems fondling the serpent-heads of these two monsters; that at the other end terminates in the upper portion of an imaginary dragon with wings on its shoulders, its paws well armed with claws, and a wolfish head largely horned, and jaws widely yawning, as eager to swallow its prey. To our thinking, we have shown to us here the Scandinavian personification of evil in the human figure of the bad god Loki (the embroidery of whose face is worn away) and his wicked offspring, the Midgard serpent, the wolf Fenrir, and Hela or Death, who may be identified in that female figure seated within the smaller lower coil made by the twining serpents. Amid some leaf-bearing branches to the right is perceived a man as if running away affrighted; to the left we behold Thor himself, mallet in hand, about to deal a heavy blow upon the scaly length of this Midgard serpent. About the same time this embroidery was worked the bishop's crozier began to end in the serpent's head. A good figure of this piece is given by Dr. Bock, in his "Geschichte der Liturgischen Gewänder des Mittelalters," 1 Band, 2 Lieferung, pt. vi.

8229.

PIECE of Crimson Silk, with interlacing pattern woven in gold; the centre occupied with representations of flat-shaped fish, and, as we learn from Dr. Bock, like to an imperial robe at Vienna, made A.D. 1133. Oriental. 11 inches by 5 inches.

Though of a very tame design and rather striking for the sparing way in which the dim gold is rolled about its thread, still it is not fair to judge of what this stuff might have once been when new, fresh from the loom and unfaded. If, in the first half of the 12th century, silks so wrought with the representation of fishes were deemed worthy of being put into use for state garments of a German Emperor; a short hundred years later, they were for their symbolism thought even more fitting to be employed for making the chasubles and copes worn at divine service in the cathedral of London. From the inventory drawn up, A. D. 1295, of the altar vestments belonging to old St. Paul's, we learn that among them there were:—"Capa magistri Johannis de S. Claro, de quodam panno Tarsico, viridis coloris, cum plurimis piscibus et rosis de aurifilo, contexitis." Dugdale's "History of St. Paul's," new ed. p. 318. "Item casula de panno Tarsico indici coloris cum pisculis et rosulis aureis, &c." Ib. p. 323. In all likelihood, the fish here shown was meant for what we oddly call "John Dory," a corruption of the Italian "Gianitore," or gate-keeper, the name of this fish in some parts of Italy, in reference to St. Peter, who is deemed to have found the tribute-money in the mouth of this fish, hence denominated St. Peter's fish.

8230.

IECE of so-called Bissus, of a yellowish white, with squares formed by intersecting bars of dark brown. 11¼ inches by 8¼ inches.

Though so unattractive to the eye, this fragment of one of the most delicate sorts of textile manufacture is one among the most curious and interesting specimens of this valuable collection. Unfortunately, Dr. Bock does not furnish us with any clue to its history, nor tell us where he found it. The large whitish squares measure 4¼ inches by 3¼ inches, and those deep brown bars that enclose them are a quarter of an inch broad, and meant evidently to have not a straight but wavy form. Another piece of this curious textile may be seen under No. 1238.

8231.

IECE of Yellow Silk, with a diapering of an artichoke shape marked with lines like letters. Moresco-Spanish, 14th century. 6 inches by 3 inches.

The texture of this silk is rather thick; and though resembling Arabic letters, the marks in the diapering are not alphabetical characters, but attempts to imitate them.

8231 A.

IECE of Dark Blue Purple Stuff, partly silk, partly cotton, double-dyed, with a diapering of small hexagons. Oriental. 5 inches by 2½ inches.

This somewhat strong texture seems to have come from Syria and to be of the 14th century.

8232.

IECE of Silk and Gold Embroidery. German, 8¼ inches by 3 inches.

It is said that an imperial tunic, now kept in the Maximilian Museum at Munich, once belonged to the Emperor Henry II, and was spoken of as such in a list of the treasures of Bamberg Cathedral in the 12th century. From the border of this tunic the piece before us is reported to have been cut off.

That in the 12th century Bamberg Cathedral had the imperial (probably the coronation) tunic of its builder and great benefactor, and as such reckoned it among its precious things, was but natural; it, however, by no means follows that this is the garment now at Munich and brought from Bamberg six hundred years after its reputed owner's death, and put into the museum in his palace by the Elector Maximilian, A.D. 1607. Keeping in mind that the Emperor Henry II. was crowned at the very beginning of the 11th century, about the year 1002, and seeing in the piece before us the style of the end of the 12th century—with thus a period of almost two hundred years between the two epochs—we cannot recognize this specimen to have ever formed a portion of the real tunic of the above-named German emperor. Besides its style, its materials forbid us to accept it as such. Its design is set forth in cording of a coarse thread roughly put together; the spaces between are filled in with shreds of red silken gold tissue, and of gold stuff sewed on to very coarse canvas. That, in this condition, it had been much used, and needed mending through long wear, is evident from other pieces of a gold and velvet texture of the 14th century being let in here and there over the frayed portions, thus showing a second example of what is called "applied." Like Germany, England, too, has made its mistakes on such matters, for we are told that " as the kings of England are invested with the crown of St. Edward, their queens are crowned with that of St. Edgitha, which is named in honour of the Confessor's consort."—Taylor's " Glory of Regality," p. 63. In the inventory, drawn up in the year 1649, " of that part of the Regalia which are now removed from Westminster to the Tower Jewel House," we find entered " Queen Edith's crowne, King Alfred's crowne," &c.—Taylor's " Glory of Regality," p. 313. The likelihood is that, in the 17th century, these supposed Anglo-Saxon crowns were not 200 years old.

8233.

PIECE of White Silk, with rich pattern of circles enclosing leopards and griffins, and a diaper of scrolls and birds. Oriental, 13th century. 1 foot 11 inches by 9 inches.

Like the piece immediately preceding, this too comes to us with an account that it once formed a part of the white silk imperial tunic belonging to the same holy Emperor Henry II, and was cut off from that garment now preserved in the Maximilian Museum in the royal palace at Munich. That it could have been wrought so early as the beginning of the 11th century, that is, about the year 1002, we are hindered from believing by the style of the ornamentation of this very rich stuff. As a specimen of the Arabic loom in the 13th century it is most valuable, and looks as if its designer had in his mind Persian traditions controlled by Arabic ideas while he drew its pattern. A remembrance of the celebrated Persian *Hom*, or sacred tree, which separates both the griffins, the leopards, and the birds—seemingly peacocks in one place, long-tailed parrots in another—was clearly before him. The griffins are addorsed regardant and sketched with spirit; so too are the leopards, which are collared, and like the " papyonns," or present East Indian " cheetahs," of which mention is made at No. 8288. Altogether this pattern, which is thrown off with so much freedom, is among the most pleasing and effective in the collection, and the thickness of its silken texture renders it remarkable.

8234.

PIECE of Purple Silk, double-dyed, the pattern formed of squares filled in with a Greek cross amid conventional ornaments. Sicilian, 12th century. 7¼ inches by 9 inches.

The warp is of linen thread, the woof of silk, and as the two materials have not taken the dye in the same degree, the ground is of quite another tone from the pattern, which is, in a manner, fortunate, as thus a better effect is produced.

Needlework, and Dreſſes.

Not for a moment can we look upon this piece as a ſpecimen of real imperial purple wrought at Byzantium for royal uſe, and ſo highly ſpoken of by Anaſtaſius Bibliothecarius, and called by him "blatthin," with the diſtinguiſhing adjunct of "holoſericus," or made entirely of ſilk, and ſometimes noticing it as "porphyreticum," while enumerating the gifts of rich ſilks beſtowed upon the churches at Rome by pontifical and imperial benefactors.

8235.

IECE of Yellow Silk, with pattern of circles encloſing griffins, the interſpaces filled in with hawks. Byzantine, 11th century. 12 inches by 10¼ inches.

This well woven and thickly bodied ſtuff ſhows its Byzantine origin in that ſtyle of ornamentation ſeen in the circles ſo characteriſtic of a Greek hand, as may be found in the Byzantine MSS. of the period. What makes this ſpecimen ſomewhat remarkable, is the rare occurrence of finding the birds and animals figured in lines of ſilver thread. Dr. Bock tells us that the chaſuble of Biſhop Bernward, who died in the 11th century, is decorated with a ſimilar deſign.

8236.

IECE of Silk, Tyrian purple, diapered with palmette pattern. Oriental, 11th century. 1 foot 4 inches by 8¼ inches.

The hundreds of years that have paſſed over this remnant of the Eaſtern looms have ſtolen from it that brightneſs of tone which once, no doubt, ſhone about its ſurface.

8237.

ORTION of Silk Border, crimſon wrought in gold, with circles containing groteſque animals. Italian (?), middle of the 13th century. 1 foot 5½ inches by 3½ inches.

This well filled piece contains birds and beaſts, among the latter two dogs addorſed, embroidered with circles, upon plain red ſilk. By the ornamentation, the embroidery muſt be about the middle of the 13th century, and is of that general character which hinders national identification, though there can be no doubt it muſt have been wrought by ſome hand in Weſtern Europe.

8238.

THREE Pieces of Silk, diſcoloured to dull olive, diapered with a cloſely foliated pattern. Sicilian, 13th century. Reſpectively 6 inches by 4 inches, 4½ inches by 4 inches, and 6 inches by 3 inches.

The deſign of the pattern is very elaborate and worthy of attention for the taſteful way in which it is arranged.

8238 A.

PIECE of Silk, with lilac pattern, encloſing groteſque animals. Sicilian, 13th century. 3¾ inches by 1¼ inches.

There is no reaſon for aſſuming that this piece of woven ſtuff formed the orphrey of a ſtole or any other liturgical ornament. It is, however, a fine ſpecimen in its kind, and is one of the very many proofs to be found among the textiles and embroideries in the Muſeum, of the influence exerciſed by heraldry upon the looms of Weſtern Europe. The beaſts and birds are evidently heraldic, and are heraldically placed, eſpecially the beaſts, which are ſtatant regardant.

8239.

MANIPLE in Crimſon Silk, embroidered in colours and gold with emblematical animals. The ends contain within circles, one the lion, ſymbolical of Chriſt, the other the initial M, but of much later work. The ſilk, Oriental; the embroidery, German, early 14th century. 3 feet 8 inches by 7 inches.

This valuable ſpecimen of mediæval church-embroidery is very curious, inaſmuch as it contains three diſtinct periods of work; the middle part of the earlieſt portion of the 14th century, embroidered with ſo many fantaſtic figures; the lion paſſant with the human head, at the left end, of the beginning of the 13th; and the green letter M, poorly worked on the red garment laid bare at the right end by the loſs of the circular piece of embroidery once ſewed on there, no doubt in the ſtyle and of the ſame period of the human-faced lion, of the latter part of the 15th century.

The whole of the middle piece is of needlework, and figured with ſixteen figures, four-legged beaſts in the body, and human in the heads, all of which are ſeen, by the hair, to be female. All are ſtatant gardant or ſtanding and looking full in the face of the ſpectator. Eight of them are playing muſical inſtruments, moſt of which are ſtringed and harp-ſhaped, one a clarionet-like pipe, another caſtanets, and two cymbals, and are human down to the waiſt; the other eight ſeem meant for queens wearing crowns, and having the hair very full, but reaching no further than the ſhoulders, while the minſtrel females ſhow a long braid of dark brown hair falling all down the back. The queens have wings, and are human only in head and neck; the muſical figures are wingleſs, and human as far as the waiſt. All theſe monſters diſplay large tails, which end in an open-mouthed head like that of a fox, and are all noued. Each of theſe figures ſtands within a ſquare, which is ſtudded at each corner with the curious four-pointed love-knot, and in the ornamentation of its ſides the creſcent is very conſpicuous; beſides which, upon the bodies of theſe figures themſelves numerous ring-like ſpots are ſtudiouſly marked, as if to ſhow that the four-legged animal was a leopard. Groteſques like thoſe in this curious piece of embroidery abound in the MSS. of the 14th century; and thoſe cut in ſtone on the north and ſouth walls outſide Adderbury Church, Oxon, bear a ſtrong likeneſs to them. Theſe fictitious creatures, made up of a woman, a leopard—the beaſt of prey, a fox—the emblem of craftineſs and ſly cunning, wielding too the power of wealth and authority, ſhown in thoſe regal heads, and bringing thoſe ſiren influences of muſic, love, and revelry into action, lead to the belief that under ſuch imagery there was once hidden a ſymbolic meaning, which ſtill remains to be found out, and this embroidery may yield ſome help in ſuch an intereſting ſtudy.

All the figures are wrought on fine canvas in gold thread, and ſhaded with ſilk thread in various colours, the ground being filled in, in ſhort ſtitch, with a bright-toned crimſon ſilk that has kept its colour admirably. The narrow tape with a gold ornament upon a crimſon ground, that encloſes the ſquare at each end of this liturgical appliance, is very good, and perhaps of the 13th century, as well as the many-coloured fringe of the 15th. There is no doubt this maniple, for such it is, was made out of scraps of secular adornments of various dates; and gives us remarkable examples of embroidery and weaving at various periods. One end of it is figured in Dr. Bock's "Geschichte der Liturgischen Gewänder des Mittelalters," 1 Band, 2 Lieferung, part vi.

8240, 8240 A.

TWO Pieces of Silk Border; red purple, embroidered with monsters, birds, and scroll patterns. To No. 8240 is attached a portion of edging, embroidered in gold, with the rude figure of a saint, on a blue-purple ground. Sicilian, 13th century. 8240, 1 foot 3¼ inches by 5 inches; 8240A, 1 foot 11 inches by 2 inches.

Among the animals figured on these pieces may be discerned a wolf passant, the fabulous heraldic wyvern, an eagle displayed, and a stag. The figure, however, of the saint, done in gold now much faded, is of the 12th century.

8241.

PIECE of Tapestry, the warp cotton, the woof partly wool, partly silk; in the centre, a grotesque mask, connecting scroll-patterns in blue, bordered with Tyrian purple. Sicilian, late 12th century. 1 foot 2¾ inches by 6 inches.

This is a rare as well as valuable specimen of its kind, and deserves attention, not only for the graceful twinings of its foliage, but the happy contrast of its colours.

8242.

PORTION of Gold Embroidery, on red-purple silk, over a dark blue cotton ground, figure of St. Andrew within an arch. German work, 12th ceutury. 9¾ inches by 5¼ inches.

8243.

PIECE of Silk, dark Tyrian purple ground, with dark olive pattern of angular figures, and circles enclosing crosses, composed of four heart-shaped ornaments. Byzantine, beginning of the 12th century. 6 inches by 6 inches.

8243 A.

PIECE of Silk Border, ground alternately lilac, purple, and yellowish, with figures of animals within the spaces of the patterns; edging, green. Sicilian, 13th century. 3¼ inches by 1 inch.

Though small, this is a beautiful sample of textile excellence; on it various animals are figured, of which one is the heraldic wyvern.

8244, 8244 A.

TWO Pieces of Crimson, embroidered, in gold, with a scroll-pattern. Sicilian, 13th century. 8244, 6⅜ inches by 2½ inches; 8244 A, 6¼ inches by 2¼ inches.

8245.

PIECE of Silk Tissue; the ground of pale purple, woven in a diaper with stripes of yellow and blue; the pattern formed of parrots perched in pairs. Sicilian, 12th century. 1 foot 6¼ inches by 10 inches.

It is said that St. Bernard, abbot of Clairvaux, when his grave was opened, was found vested in a chasuble made of a stuff much like this.

8245 A.

PIECE of Tissue, like the foregoing (No. 8245), with a centre stripe woven with gold thread and dark blue, and two side-stripes with figures of parrots. Sicilian, early 13th century.

Though seemingly so slight and insignificant, these two pieces will richly repay a close examination, exhibiting, as they do, great beauty of design.

8246.

IECE of Border, of silk and gold thread, pale purple ground, with pattern of animals and flower (?) ornament. Sicilian (?). 10¼ inches by 1¼ inches.

From age, the design of the pattern is so very indistinct that it becomes almost a puzzle to make it out.

8247.

HREE Pieces of Silk, orange-red ground, with yellow pattern, apparently composed in part of grotesque animals. Oriental, 13th century. 6 inches by 4¼ inches; 3 inches by 2¼ inches; 4¼ inches by 2 inches.

This last piece shows signs of having been waxed, and probably is the fragment of a cere-cloth for the altar, to be placed immediately on the stone table, and under the linen cloths.

8248.

IECE of Tissue, woven of silk and linen; ground, Tyrian purple, with a Romanesque pattern in white. Moresco-Spanish, 13th century.

The design of this specimen is very effective; and, as the materials of this stuff are poor and somewhat coarse, we may perceive that, even upon things meant for ordinary use, the mediæval artisans bestowed much care in the arrangement and sketching of their patterns.

8249.

IECE of Silk; purple ground, and yellowish pattern in lozenge forms, intersected by interlaced knots. Byzantine, end of the 12th century. 6¼ inches by 5 inches.

The knots in this piece are somewhat like those to be found upon Anglo-Saxon work, in stone, and in silver and other metals; and the lozenges powdered with Greek crosses, and stopped at each of the four corners of the lozenge by a three-petaled flower ornament—not, however, a fleur-de-lis,—make this piece of stuff remarkable.

8250.

IECE of Broad Border of Gold Tissue, portion of a vestment. Sicilian, 13th century. 6 inches by 5 inches.

This was once part of the orphrey of some liturgical garment, and is figured with lions rampant combatant, and foliage in which a crofs flory may be discovered.

8250A.

IECE of Silk; green ground, with a stripe diapered in silver. Byzantine, end of 12th century. 4¾ inches by 2 inches.

The design of the stripe not only shows the St. Andrew's crofs, or saltire, but, in its variety of combination, displays other forms of the crofs, that make this stuff one of the kind known among Greek writers as " stauracinus" and " polystauria," and spoken of as such by Anastasius Bibliothecarius in very many parts of his valuable work.

8251.

ORTION of a Maniple, linen web with an interlaced diamond-shaped diapering, in silk. 12th century. Byzantine. 1 foot 9 inches by 2¾ inches.

This curious remnant of textiles, wrought on purpose for liturgical use, shows in places another combination of lines, or rather of a digamma, so as to form a sort of crofs: and stuffs so diapered were called by Greek, and after them by Latin, Christian writers, " gammadia." It was a pattern taken up by the Sicilian and South Italian looms, whence it spread so far north as England, where it may be found marked amid the ornaments designed upon church vestments figured in many graven brasses. From us it got the new name of " filfod " through the idea of " full foot," which by some English mediæval writers was looked upon as an heraldic charge, and is now called " cramponnée." During the 13th century, in this country, ribbon-like textiles, for the express purpose of making stoles and maniples to be worn at the altar, were extensively wrought, and constituted one of the articles of trade in London, for a distinguished citizen of hers, John de Garlandia, or Garland, tells us:—" De textis vero fiunt cingula, et crinalia divitum mulierum et ftole(ae) facerdotum." Thefe " priefts' ftoles," in all likelihood, were figured with the gammadion or filfod pattern; and, perhaps, many of them which are to be found in foreign facrifties to this day came from London.

The piece before us is figured in Dr. Bock's " Gefchichte de Liturgifchen Gewänder des Mittelalters," 4 Lieferung, pt. iii. fig. 3.

8252.

IECE of Silk and Gold Tiffue, lilac-purple with fleur-de-lis diapering in gold. South Italian, end of 14th century. 5 inches by 4½ inches.

This ftuff feems to have been made exprefsly for French royalty, perhaps fome member of the houfe of Anjou.

8253.

IECE of Dark Blue Silk, with pattern in yellow, confifting of centre ornaments furrounded by four crowned birds like parrots. South Italian, 14th century. 9 inches by 7 inches.

8254.

IECE of Silk Net, embroidered with crofslets and triangular ornaments charged with chevrons in lilac and green. North Italian, 14th century. 7 inches by 5 inches.

This is a good fpecimen of a kind of cobweb weaving, or "opus araneum," for which Lombardy, efpecially its capital, Milan, earned fuch a reputation at one time.

8255.

IECE of Silk, crimson ground, with pattern in violet and green, consisting partly of wyverns. Sicilian, end of 13th century. 10 inches by 5 inches.

Another good specimen of the Sicilian loom, and very likely one of those "cendals" for which Palermo was once so famous.

8256.

IECE of Silk, pink-buff colour, with pattern, in green, of vine-leaves and grapes. South Italian, middle of 14th century. 8 inches by 5½ inches.

The design of this silk is remarkably elegant, and exemplifies the ability of the weaver-draughtsmen of those times.

8257.

IECE of Crimson Silk, damasked with a pattern in which occur leopards and eagles pouncing upon antelopes. Sicilian, end of 13th century.

The design of this piece of what must have been such a beautiful stuff is very skilfully imagined, and the whole carried out in a spirited manner. The leopards are collared, and from the presence of, as well as mode of action in, the eagles stooping on their prey, a thought may cross the mind that some political or partisan meaning is hidden under these heraldic animals.

8258.

IECE of Silk; ground, lilac-purple; pattern, in bright yellow, composed of stags, parrots, and peacocks, amid foliage. Italian, 14th century. 10 inches by 4½ inches.

A pretty design, in cheerful colours, and a pleasing example probably of the Lucca loom towards the close of the 14th century.

8259.

PIECE of Tissue, with hemp warp and silk woof; ground, dark blue; pattern, yellowish, representing a tree imparked, with eagles, and leopards having tails noued or tied in a knot. Italian, early 15th century. 1 foot 7 inches by 1 foot.

Though somewhat elaborate, the design of this piece is rather heavy.

8260.

PIECE of Silk and Gold Tissue, lilac-purple ground, with a green pattern, showing eagles statant regardant, with wings displayed. Sicilian, 14th century. 7 inches by 4¾ inches.

The design is very good.

8260 A.

PIECE of Silk, lilac-purple ground with green pattern, and gold woven border, exhibiting an antelope courant regardant. Sicilian, early 14th century. 6¼ inches by 3¼ inches.

Good in design.

8260 B, C.

TWO Pieces of Silk, green ground and lilac-purple pattern, with dragons and cranes. Sicilian, early 14th century. 4¼ inches by 4 inches; and 4¼ inches by 2¼ inches.

A pleasing design.

8261.

PORTION of an Orphrey embroidered in silk and gold, with figures of two Apostles beneath crocketed canopies. German, early 14th century.

8262.

PIECE of Silk, rose-coloured ground, with pattern of eagles rising from trees, both green, and wild beasts spotted (perhaps leopards) in gold, and lodged in a park, paled green. South Italian, 14th century. 2 feet by 10¾ inches.

8263.

PIECE of Silk, rose-coloured ground, pattern in green and gold, of two female demi-figures addorsed, gathering date-fruit with one hand, with the other patting a dog rampant and collared with bells, and other two female demi-figures holding, with one hand, a frond of the palm-tree out of which they are issuing, and with the other hand clutching the manes of lions rampant regardant and tails noued. Sicilian, 14th century. 1 foot 9 inches by 1 foot 2 inches.

> This valuable and important piece displays an intricate yet well-managed and tastefully arranged pattern. One must be struck with the peculiar style of assortment of pink and green in its colours, the somewhat sameness in the subjects, and the artistic and heraldic way in which these silks (very likely wrought at Palermo) are woven. Dr. Bock has given a fine large plate of this stuff in his "Dessinateur pour Etoffes," &c. Paris, Morel.

8264.

PIECE of Silk and Gold Tissue; the ground black, with pattern, in gold, of a rayed star, with eagles statant and swans naiant (swimming) upon water on a foliated scroll. Sicilian, early 14th century. 1 foot 2 inches by 1 foot 1¼ inches.

The design of this piece is as easy and flowing as it is bold; and the specimen affords us a very choice example of fine manufacture.

8265.

PIECE of Linen and Silk Textile; the ground, dark blue; the pattern, yellow, consisting of arcades beneath which are rows of parrots and hawks alternately, both gardant, and perched upon a vine; the initial M surmounted by a crown or fleur-de-lis in gold thread is inserted in the alternate range of arches. Southern Spanish, late 14th century. 1 foot 6 inches by 10 inches.

As a specimen of the Andalusian loom, and wrought by Christian hands, perhaps at Granada, while that part of Spain was under Moorish rule, this piece has a peculiar interest about it.

8266.

MANIPLE, embroidered in silk, inscribed in Gothic letters with "Gratia + plena + Dom . . ." German, end of 14th century. 3 feet 10 inches by 2 inches.

8267.

PIECE of Tissue, of cotton warp, of silk and gold woof, with pattern of birds and stags amid foliated ornamentation. Spanish, 14th century.

8268.

PIECE of Silk and Gold Tiffue; the ground, lilac-purple; the pattern in gold, fymmetrically arranged and partly compofed of birds, upon which hounds are fpringing. Sicilian, 14th century. 2 feet 3¼ inches by 11 inches.

A very effective and well-executed defign.

8269.

PIECE of Silk; ground, blue, diapered in yellow with mullets of eight points and eight-petaled flowers, within lozenges. Sicilian, early 15th century. 6 inches by 4¼ inches.

8269 A.

PIECE of Silk and Cotton Border; ground, crimfon, now much faded; pattern, a diaper of the fleur-de-lis within a lozenge, both yellow; the ftuff which it edged has a deep blue ground powdered with fleurs-de-lis, and eight-petaled flowers within lozenges, both yellow. South Italian, late 13th century. 4 inches by 2¾ inches.

Though from its pattern we may affume that this ftuff was made for the requirement of the Sicilian Anjou family or one of its adherents, the poornefs of its materials forbids us from thinking it could have ferved for any other than common ufe.

8270.

PIECE of Silk and Gold Tiffue; pattern, confifting of diaper and leaves interfpered with fmall circles, within each of which is a conventional flower expanded. South Italian, 14th century. 11 inches by 10 inches.

8271.

IECE of Silk, with portions of the pattern in gold; ground, green, on which are parrots (?) and little dogs, amid a sprinkling of quatrefoils. Sicilian, beginning of 14th century. 10½ inches by 4 inches.

8272.

IECE of Silk and Gold Tissue; ground, green; the pattern in gold seems to have been divided by bars, and consists of an interlaced knot, on which rest birds. Southern Spanish, early 14th century. 8¼ inches by 4¼ inches.

The knots in this piece are somewhat like our own Bouchier one; but the four ends of the English badge are not shown in this Andalusian ornament, perhaps meant to be really an heraldic charge peculiar to Spanish blazon.

8273.

IECE of Silk; ground, lilac-purple; pattern, yellow, diapered with crescents, within the horns of which are two very small wyverns addorsed. Sicilian, late 13th century. 7¼ inches by 4½ inches.

The design is so indistinct that it requires time to unpuzzle it.

8274.

ORTION of an Orphrey, embroidered on parchment with glass, coral, gold beads, and seed pearls, having also small bosses and ornaments in silver-gilt. The ground is dark blue, on which is figured the B. V. Mary nimbed and crowned within an oblong aureole terminated by scrolls ending in trefoils and cinquefoils. Venetian, late 12th century.

That this curious and elaborate piece of bead embroidery muſt have been part of an orphrey for a chaſuble, and not a maniple, is evident from the pointed ſhape in which it ends. From its ſtyle, and the quantity of very ſmall beads and bugles which we ſee upon it, it would ſeem to have been wrought either at Venice itſelf, in ſome of its mainland dependencies, or in Lower Styria. Then, as now, the Venetian iſland of Murano wrought and carried on a large trade in beads of all kinds; and the ſilverſmith's craft was in high repute at Venice. Finding, then, this remnant of a liturgical veſtment ſo plentifully adorned with beads, bugles, and coral, beſides being ſo dotted with little ſpecks of gold, and ſprinkled with ſo many ſmall but nicely worked ſilver-gilt ſtars, we are warranted in taking this embroidery to have been wrought ſomewhere in North Eaſt Italy or South Weſt Germany, upon the borders of the Adriatic. Thoſe fond of eccleſiaſtical ſymboliſm will look upon this old piece of needlework with no ſmall intereſt, and obſerve that it was by intention that the ground was blue. It is figured in Dr. Bock's "Geſchichte der Liturgiſchen Gewänder Mittelalters," 1 Band, 2 Lieferung, pt. x. s. 275.

8275.

PIECE of Linen Tiſſue, with pattern woven in gold; the deſign conſiſts of bands curving to a ſomewhat lozenge form and incloſing an ornament compoſed of interſecting circles with a three-pointed or petaled kind of conventional flower (not a fleur-de-lis) radiating from the centre. Sicilian, 14th century. 5 inches by 4¼ inches.

8276.

PIECE of Silk; ground, pinkiſh purple; pattern in dark blue, or rather green, divided by four-ſided compartments and formed of conventional flowers and ſalamanders, the borders of a running deſign. Sicilian, 14th century. 10¼ inches by 6 inches.

Moſt likely woven at Palermo, but no good ſample of dyeing, as the colours have evidently changed; what is now a pinkiſh purple hue was of a light cheerful crimſon tone, and the dark blue pattern muſt have originally been a warm green.

8277.

PIECE of Crimſon Silk and Gold Tiſſue; the pattern, in gold, of conventional ornaments and circles containing birds and animals; the border conſiſts of a repetition of a wyvern, an eagle diſplayed, and an elephant and caſtle. Italian, early 14th century. 11 inches by 4 inches.

This fine coſtly ſpecimen of old ſilken ſtuff cannot fail in drawing to itſelf a particular attention from the heedful obſerver, by its gracefully elaborate deſign, ſo well carried out and done in ſuch rich materials, but more eſpecially by the ſymbols figured on it.

Though now unable to read or underſtand the meaning of all thoſe emblematic hints ſo indiſtinctly uttered in its curious border, made up, as it is, of a wyvern, a ſtork embowed and ſtatant on an elephant and caſtle, and a diſplayed eagle, we hopefully think that, at no far-off day, the key to it all will be found; then, perhaps, the piece before us, and many other ſuch textiles in this very collection, may turn out to be no little help to ſome future writer while unravelling ſeveral entanglements in mediæval hiſtory.

Not for a ſingle moment can we admit that through theſe heraldic beaſts and birds the ſlighteſt reference was intended to be made to the four elements; heaven or the air, earth or its productions, fire and water, were quite otherwiſe ſymbolized by artiſts during the middle ages, as we may ſee in the nielli on a ſuper-altar deſcribed and figured in the "Church of Our Fathers," t. i. p. 257.

8278.

A SINDON or kind of Frontal, of Crimſon Silk, on a linen or canvas lining, embroidered in ſilk and ſilver thread, with a large figure of our Lord dead, two ſtanding angels, and, at each of its four corners, a half-length

Needlework, and Dresses.

figure of an evangelift; the whole enclofed in a border infcribed with Sclavonic characters. Ruthenic work, middle of 17th century. 4 feet 6¼ inches by 2 feet 10 inches.

In the centre of this curious ecclefiaftical embroidery (for fpreading outfide the chancel, at the end of Holy Week, among the Greek,) our dead Lord, with the ufual infcription, I C, X C, over Him, is figured lying full length, ftretched out, as it were, upon a flab of ftone which a fheet overfpreads. His arms are at His fides as far as the elbows, where they bend fo that His hands may be folded downward crofs-wife upon His ftomach, from which, to His knees, His loins are wrapped in a very full-folded cloth done in filver thread, but now nearly black from age. His fkin is quite white, His hair and beard of a light brown colour, and His right fide, His hands and feet are marked each with a blood-red wound; and the embroidery of His perfon is fo managed as to difplay, in fomewhat high relief, the hollows and elevations of the body's furface; all around and beneath His head goes a nimbus marked infide with a crofs very flightly pattee, the whole nicely diapered and once bright filver, but now quite black. Two nimbed angels, beardlefs and, in look, quite youthful, are ftanding, one at His head, the other at His feet, each, like the other, vefted, as is the deacon at the prefent day, for mafs, according to the Greek and Oriental rites; they wear the "chitonion" or alb, over that the "ftoicharion" or dalmatic, and from the right—though it fhould have been from the left—fhoulder falls the "orarion" or ftole, upon which the Greek word "agios," or holy, is repeated, juft as a Greek deacon is fhown in "Hierurgia," p. 345; in his right hand each holds extended over our Lord, exactly as Greek deacons now do, at the altar, after the confecration of the Holy Euchariſt, a long wand, at the end of which is a large round fix-petaled flower-like ornament, having within it a cherub's fix-winged face; this is the holy fan, concerning which fee the "Church of our Fathers," iv. 197; and each has his left hand fo raifed up under his chin as to feemingly afford a reft for it. At each of the four corners of the frontal is the buft of an evangelift with a nimb about his head; in the upper left, "Agios o Theologos," for fo the Greeks ftill call St. John the Evangelift: in the lower left, St. Luke; in the upper right, St. Matthew; in the lower right, St. Mark; each is bearded, and the hair, whether on the head or chin, is fhown in blue and white as of an aged man. While the heads and faces of all four evangelifts are red, with the features diftinguifhed by white lines, the angels have white faces and their hair is deep red with ftrokes in white to indicate the curly wavings of their locks. There are two croffes, rather pattee, done in filver thread, meafuring 2½ inches, one above, the other below our Lord, in the middle of the ground, which is crimfon, and wrought all over with gracefully twined flower-bearing branches; and each evangelift is fhut in by a quarter-circle border charmingly worked with a wreath of leaves quite characteriftic of our 13th century work. All the draperies, infcriptions, and ornamentation, now looking fo black, were originally wrought in filver thread that is thus tarnifhed by age.

Among the liturgical rarities in this extenfive and precious collection of needlework, not the leaft is the prefent Ruffo-Greek " findon," or ritual winding-fheet, ufed in a portion of the Eaftern Church fervice on the Great Friday and Great Saturday, as the Orientals call our Good Friday and Holy Saturday.

The colour itfelf—purplifh crimfon—of the filk ground upon which our Lord's dead body lies, as it were, outftretched upon the winding-fheet in the grave, is not without a fymbolic meaning, for amongft the Greeks, up to a late period, of fuch a tint were invariably the garments and the ftuffs employed on every occafion any wife connected with the dead, though now, like the Latins, the Mufcovites at leaft ufe black for all fuch functions.

All around the four borders of this findon are wrought in golden thread, now much tarnifhed, fentences of Greek, but written, as the practice is among the Sclaves, in the Cyrillian character, thus named from St. Cyrill, the monk, who invented that alphabet a thoufand years ago, as one of the helps for himfelf and his brother St. Methodius, in teaching Chriftianity to the many tribes of the widely-fpread Sclavonian people, as we noticed in our Introduction, § 5.

Beginning at the right-hand fide, from that portion of the filk being fomewhat torn, the words are not quite whole, but thofe that can be read, fay thus:—" Pray for the fervant of God, Nicolaus . . . . and his children. Amen ;" here, no doubt, we have the donor's name, and the exact time itfelf of this pious gift was put down, but owing to the ftuff being, at this place too, worn away, the date is fome-what obliterated, but feems to be the year 1645.

All the other fentences are borrowed from the Greek ritual-book known as the 'Ωρολόγιον, or Horologium, in the fervice for the afternoon on Good Friday and Holy Saturday. Along the lower border runs this " troparion," or verficle:—'Ο εὐσχήμων Ἰωσὴφ ἀπὸ τοῦ ξύλου καθελὼν τὸ ἄχραντόν σου Σῶμα, σινδόνι καθαρᾷ εἰλήσας καὶ ἀρώμασιν ἐν μνήματι καινῷ κηδεύσας ἀπέθετο. "The comely Jofeph (of Arimathea) having taken down from the wood (of the crofs) the fpotlefs body of Thee (O Jefus), and having wrapped it up in a clean winding-sheet together with aromatics, taking upon himself to afford it a becoming burial, laid it in a new grave." Upon the left hand side comes this versicle:—Ταῖς μυροφόροις γυναιξὶ παρὰ τὸ μνῆμα ἐπιστάς, ὁ Ἄγγελος ἐβόα: Τὰ μύρα τοῖς θνητοῖς ὑπάρχει ἁρμόδια, Χριστὸς δὲ διαφθορᾶς ἐδείχθη ἀλλότριος—Τροπάρια τοῦ Τριαδίου. Τῷ ἁγίῳ καὶ μεγάλῳ Σαββάτῳ. "Seeing at the grave the women who were carrying perfumes, the Angel cried out, ' The ointments fitting (to be used in the burial) for mortal beings are lying here, but Christ, having undergone death, has shown Himself (again) after another form.' "

According to the rite followed by the Russians and Greeks, on the afternoon of Good Friday, as well as that of Holy Saturday, a sindon or liturgical winding-sheet, figured just like the one before us, is brought into the middle of the church, and placed outside the sanctuary, so that it may be easily venerated by all the people in turn. First come the clergy, making, as they slowly advance, many low and solemn bows, and bendings of the whole person. Reaching the sindon, each one kisses with great devotion the forehead of our Lord, and the place of the wounds in His side, His hands, and feet. Then follow the congregation, every one approaching in the same reverential manner, and going through the same ceremonial like the clergy; all this while are being sung, along with other versicles, the ones embroidered round this piece of needlework. But this is not all, at least in some provinces where the Greek ritual obtains. As soon as it is dark on Good Friday evening, upon a funeral bier is laid the figure of our Lord, either wrought in low relief, painted on wood or canvas, or shown in needlework like this sindon. Lifted up and borne forwards, it is surrounded by a crowd carrying lights. Then follow the priests vested in chasubles and the rest of the garments proper for mass; after them walk the lower clergy, and the lay-folks of the place come last. Then the procession goes all through and about the streets of the town, singing the cxviiith Psalm, the "Beati immaculati in via," &c. of the Vulgate, or cxixth of the authorized version, between each verse of which is chanted a versicle from the Horologium. Everywhere the populace bow down as the bier comes by, and many times it halts that they may kiss the figure of our dead Saviour, whose image is overspread by the flowers sprinkled upon it as it is carried past, and afterwards these same flowers are eagerly sought for by the crowd, who set much store by them as the bringers of health to their bodies and a blessing on their homesteads all the after year. Now it should be observed that, even in the present piece, what is the real sindon or white linen winding-sheet shown open and spread out quite flat beneath our Lord's body, is put upon a mourning pall of red silk, which is worked all over with flowers, doubtless in allusion to this very custom of showering down upon it flowers as it is carried by.

Very like, in part, to the Greek ceremony, is the Latin rite still followed on Good Friday of kissing the crucifix as it lies upon a cushion on the steps going up to the altar, and known of old in England as creeping to the cross, the ritual for which among the Anglo-Saxons, as well as later, according to the use of Salisbury, may be seen in the "Church of Our Fathers," t. iv. pp. 88, 241. Those who have travelled in the East, or in countries where the Greek rite is followed, may have observed that, almost always, the cupola of the larger churches is painted with the celebration of the Divine Liturgy; and among the crowd of personages therein shown are usually six angels reverently bearing one of these so-figured sindons, as was noticed in the Introduction, § 5.

8279.

PORTION of an Orphrey for a Chasuble; border woven in silk, with a various-coloured diapering. German, late 14th century. 3 feet.

Such textiles (for they are not embroideries) as these were evidently wrought to serve as the orphreys for liturgical garments of a less costly character, and made, as this example is, out of thread as well as silk, fashioned after a simple type of pattern.

8279 A.

LINEN Napkin, for a Crozier; of very fine linen, and various embroideries. German, late 14th century. 2 feet 10 inches by 6 feet.

Such napkins are very great liturgical curiosities, as the present one, and another in this collection, are the only specimens known in this country; and perhaps such another could not be found on any part of the Continent, the employment of them having been for a very long time everywhere left off. Its top, like a high circular-headed cap, 4¼ inches by 4 inches, is marked with a diapering, on one side *lozengy*, on the other *checky*, ground crimson, and filled in with the gammadion or filfot in one form or another. On the lozenges this gammadion is parti-coloured, green, yellow, white, purple; in the checks, all green, yellow, white, and purple. Curiously enough, the piece of vellum used as a stiffening for this cap is a piece of an old manuscript about some loan, and bears the date of the year 1256. The slit up the middle of the linen, 11 inches long, is bordered on both edges with a linen woven lace, 1¼ inches broad, embroidered on one side of the slit with L, one of the forms of the gammadion; on the other with the saltire, or St. Andrew's cross; the gammadion and saltire are wrought in purple, green, crimson (faded), or yellow, each of one colour, and not mixed, as in one part of the cap. These two edgings brought together, and thus running up for the space of 6 inches, are stopped by a piece of woven silk lace, 3¼ inches by 2 inches, and figured with the filfot or gammadion. The linen is very fine, and of that kind which, in the middle ages, was called " bissus;" tent-like in shape, and closed, it hung in full folds. Its gold and silken cords, of various colours, as well as those large well-platted knobs of silk and gold by which it was strung to the upper part of the crozier, are all quite perfect; and an account of this ornament is given in the " Church of Our Fathers," t. ii. p. 210. Dr. Bock has given a figure of the present one in his " Geschichte der Liturgischen Gewänder des Mittelalters," 4 Lieferung, pl. xiv. fig. i; and another specimen will be found here, No. 8662.

8280.

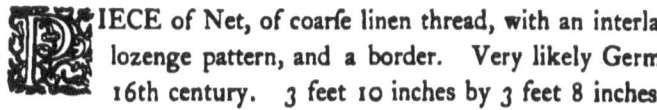IECE of Net, of coarse linen thread, with an interlaced lozenge pattern, and a border. Very likely German, 16th century. 3 feet 10 inches by 3 feet 8 inches.

Those who amuse themselves by netting will find in this specimen a good example to follow, both in design and accurate execution. It must have been wrought for domestic, and not for Church use.

8281.

ORTION of an Orphrey, in red and purple silk, figured in gold, with a fleur-de-lis, inscriptions, and armorial bearings. German, late 15th century. 12¾ inches by 2¾ inches.

This piece is woven throughout, and the letters, as well as the heraldry, are the work, not of the needle, but of the shuttle. On a field *gules* is shown a fleur-de-lis *argent*, which device, not being upon a shield, may have been meant for a badge. On a field *or* is a crofs *purpure*, and over it, another crofs of the field. Though the words given may possibly be intended to read "Pete allia (alia)," there are difficulties in so taking them. It is imagined that these heraldic bearings refer to the archiepiscopal sees and chapters of Cologne and Treves.

8282.

PIECE of Silken and Linen Texture. Upon a yellow thread ground are figured, in green silk, trees, from the lower right side of which darts down a pencil of sunbeams, and just over these rays stand birds like cockatoos or hoopoes, and six-petaled flowers and eagles stooping, both once in gold, now dimmed; the flowers and eagles well raised above the rest of the design. Made in North Italy, during the middle of the 14th century.

When bright and fresh, this stuff must have been very effective; and a play of light could not fail in well showing off its golden eagles and flowers, that are made to stand out somewhat boldly amid the green foliage of the trees.

8283.

PIECE of Lilac-purple Silk, with a delicate diapering of vine-branches and birds. Italian, late 14th century.

Though everything is small in the design of this piece, it is remarkably pleasing. The way in which the boughs are twined is quite graceful, and the foliage very good.

8284.

PIECE of Light Crimson Silk and Gold Tissue. This small bit of a large pattern shows a crested bird plucking a bell-shaped flower. Italian, early 15th century.

Unfortunately this scrap is so small as not to exhibit enough of the original defign to let us know what it was; but, to judge by the ends of fome wings, we have before us fufficient to fee that, when entire, it muft have confifted of large birds, and have been bold and telling.

8285.

PIECE of Light Crimfon Silk and Gold Tiffue; the pattern is a diapering, all in gold, formed of a tree with a lionefs fejant regardant beneath it, and a bird alighting on a flower, the centre of which is fpotted with ftamens of blue filk. North Italian, beginning of the 15th century.

This fpecimen is valuable both for its rich materials and the effective way in which the defign is brought out.

8286.

PIECE of Dark Purple Silk and Silver Tiffue, relieved with crimfon thrown up in very fmall portions. The pattern is a bold diapering of grotefque animals and birds, together with infcriptions affecting to be in Arabic. Very likely from the South of Spain, at the beginning of the 15th century. 24 inches by 19 inches.

Alike confpicuous for the richnefs of materials, as for the exuberance in its defign, this fpecimen deferves particular attention. Spotted leopards and fhaggy-haired dogs, all collared, and feparated by bundles of wheat ears; birds of prey looking from out the foliage, hoopoes pecking at a human face, dragon-like fnakes gracefully convoluted amid a Moorifh kind of ornamentation, and imitated Arabic letters ftrung together without a meaning, fhow that the hand of the Chriftian workman was guided fomewhat by Saracenic teachings, or wrought under the fet purpofe of paffing off his work as of Oriental produce. But in this, as in fo many other examples, a ftrong liking for heraldry is difplayed by thofe pairs of wings conjoined and elevated, in the one inftance eagle's, in the other wyvern's.

8287.

PIECE of Silk and Gold Tissue, on a red ground; a design in green, relieved by bands of scroll-pattern, with an eagle's head and neck in gold and flowers in white and dark purple. Sicilian, 15th century. 12¼ inches by 12 inches.

When new this tissue must have been very showy, but now the whole of its pattern is somewhat difficult to trace out. The way in which the large eagle's head and neck are given, resting upon a broad-scrolled bar, is rather singular; so, too, is the lifting or border, on one side charged with a small but rich ornamentation, amid which may be detected some eaglets.

8288.

PIECE of Silk and Gold Tissue, the ground of which is gold banded with patterns in blue, red, and green, divided by narrowed stripes of black; on one golden band is an Arabic word repeated all through the design. Syrian. 16½ inches by 16 inches.

The value of this fine rich specimen will be instantly appreciated when it is borne in mind that it is one of the few known examples of real Saracenic weaving which we have.

Its ornamentation has about it, in the checkered and circular portions of its design, much of that feeling which shows itself in Saracenic architecture; and those who remember the court of lions, in the Alhambra at Granada, will not be surprised at seeing animals figured upon this piece of stuff so freely.

The broad bands are separated by very narrow black ones, on which are shown, in gold, short lengths of thick foliage like strawberry-leaves, and an animal, which, from the tuft of hair on its ears, seems a lynx, chased by the hunting-leopard, of which our celebrated travelling countryman, Sir John Mandeville, in his "Voiage," written in the reign of Edward III, speaks thus: "In Cipre men hunten with Papyonns that ben lyche Lepardes, and thei taken wylde bestes righte welle and thei ben somedelle more than Lyonns; and thei taken more

Needlework, and Dresses.

fcharpely the beftes and more delyverly than don houndes." Ed. Halliwell, p. 29. This fort of leopard, the claws of which are not, like the reft of its kind, retractile, is, to this day, employed in Afia, more efpecially in the Eaft Indies, like dogs for hunting, and known by the name of "Cheetah."

Each of thefe lengths is ftudded with thofe knots, found fo often upon eaftern wares of all forts, and formed by narrow ribbons interlacing one another at right angles fo as to produce fquares or checks; thefe knots are alternately large—of three rows of checks, and fmall—of two rows. Upon one of the large bands, gold in its ground, is, all along it, woven a fentence in Arabic letters in dufky white, of which tint is the circular ornament which everywhere ftands between this writing; very likely thefe characters, as well as the dividing flower, were once of a crimfon colour, which is now faded. The infcribed fentence itfelf being figured without the diftinctive points, may be underftood various ways. That it is fome well-known Oriental faying or proverb is very likely, and, to hazard a guefs, reads thus: "Injury, hurt, reception,"—meaning, perhaps, that the individual who has done you, behind your back, all the harm he can, may, when next he meets you, utter the greetings and put on all the looks of friendfhip. Such was its meaning, as read by the late lamented Oriental fcholar, Dr. Cureton.

Upon the next broad band, on a ground once crimfon, are figured, in gold, the before-mentioned "papyonns," or hunting-leopards, collared and in a fitting pofition under foliage, fwans fwimming, and an animal of the gazelle or antelope genus, heraldically lodged regardant, with a flower-bearing ftem in its mouth, and another animal not eafily identified. The remaining two broad bands, one blue, the other green, are figured, in gold, with fquares filled up by checks of an Oriental character, alternating with quatrefoils fprouting all over into flowers.

8289.

IECE of Silk and Gold Tiffue; the ground, lilac; the pattern, green and white, of flowers, beneath which couch two animals, and under them ftand two eagles. Italian or Sicilian, late 14th century. 15¼ inches by 15¼ inches.

One of thofe well-balanced defigns thrown off fo freely by the looms of Italy and Sicily during the whole of the 14th century. What thofe two animals collared, couchant and addorsed regardant, may be meant for it is hard to imagine. Rays, like those from the sun, dart down beneath these dog-like creatures, and looking upward to those beams stand two eagles. Some of the flowers and the two animals are wrought in gold.

8290.

IECE of Silk; ground, dark blue; pattern, yellow, in zigzag arabesque. Moorish work of the South of Spain, 14th century. 12½ inches by 8¼ inches.

Though of such simple elements in its design, this Moresco stuff is not unpleasing.

8291, 8291 A.

WO Pieces of Silk and Gold Tissue, having a pattern in bands diapered with arabesques, birds, and animals. Syrian, 14th century. 5 inches by 4 inches, and 5 inches by 3¼ inches.

Although but mere rags, these two specimens are interesting. They tell, of their country and time, by the management of their design, and have a near relationship to the specimen No. 8288.

8292.

IECE of Silk; ground, red with pattern, in violet, of vine-leaves, conventional foliage, and animals. Sicilian, early 14th century. 12½ inches by 6 inches.

This very pretty produce of the Italian loom, like No. 8283, commends itself to our admiration by the graceful manner in which the design is carried out. Though small in its parts, the pattern is attractive. Those stags, tripping and showing heads well attired, are not uncommon, about the period, upon stuffs, but those wild boars—like the deer, in pairs—segeant face to face, are somewhat new.

8293.

PIECE of Linen embroidered in red silk, with an open diaper of crosslets leaving circular and lozenge spaces, the former now empty, the latter ornamented with cross-crosslets in yellow, purple, and green silk. Late 14th century. 15 inches by 12¼ inches.

In all likelihood the round spaces were filled in with heraldic animals, and the piece served as the apparel to an alb, resembling the one shown on the fine Wensley brass, figured by the brothers Waller, and also given in the "Church of our Fathers," t. i. p. 325.

8294.

PIECE of Silk and Gold Tissue, the ground red with a pattern in green and white, forming a large lozenge, enclosing, in one instance, a bunch of foliage and two eagles, in the other, a bough and two dogs. South Italian, late 14th century. 21½ inches by 11¼ inches.

In this rich pattern there are certain portions that, at first sight, might be taken for attempts to represent Oriental letters; they are, however, no forms of any alphabet, and, least of all, bear any likeness to the Cufic.

8295.

PIECE of Silk and Cotton Tissue; ground, deep red mixed with green, blue, white, and gold; the pattern consists of loosely branched stems with large flower-heads, and monsters alternately blue and gold, bearing in their hands a white flower. Italian, late 14th century. 27¼ inches by 9¾ inches.

The so-called sphinxes in this piece are those monster figures often found in art-work during the middle ages, and are formed of a female head and waift joined on to the body of a lionefs paffant cowed, that is, with its tail hanging down between its legs. In this fpecimen may be detected an early form of the artichoke pattern, which afterwards became fuch a favourite.

8296.

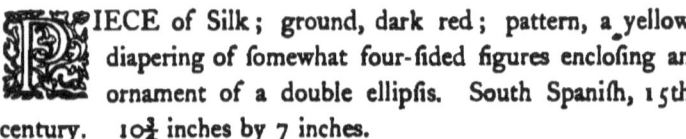IECE of Silk; ground, dark red; pattern, a yellow diapering of fomewhat four-fided figures enclofing an ornament of a double ellipfis. South Spanifh, 15th century. 10¾ inches by 7 inches.

8297.

IECE of Crimfon Silk; pattern, in green, of open arabefque fpread in wide divifions. Southern Spain, late 14th century. 18 inches by 7 inches.

The defign of this valuable piece is very good, and muft have had a pleafing effect. From the way in which the crofs is introduced by combinations of the ornamentation and flight attempts at fhowing the letter M for Maria—the Bleffed Virgin Mary, it would feem that it was the work of a Chriftian hand well practifed in the Saracenic ftyle of pattern-drawing.

8298.

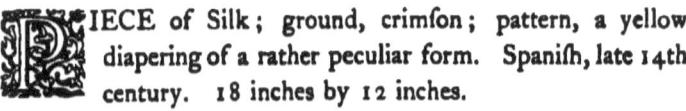IECE of Silk; ground, crimfon; pattern, a yellow diapering of a rather peculiar form. Spanifh, late 14th century. 18 inches by 12 inches.

Rich in its tones, this fpecimen may have been defigned under the influence of Moorifh teachings; it is, however, very agreeable.

8299.

IECE of Silk Tiffue; the pattern, a large raifed diaper, which confifts of a centre, in red filk, reprefenting the web of the geometric fpider, with the infect refting in the middle, enclofed within the branches of a conventional tree, in silver thread. Italian, early 15th century. 12 inches by 6 inches.

Though the silk ground of this elegant stuff must have been once of a bright crimson tinge, almost the whole of the colour has flown; and the silver thread, of which the beautifully arranged tree is formed, has become so tarnished as to look as if it had been from first a dull olive-green. Such events give a warning to manufacturers about the quality of their dyes, and the purity as well as sort of the metals they may choose to employ. The manner in which the tree and its graceful branches are made to stand well out and above the red grounding is remarkably good; and, altogether, the pattern, composed as it is of a spider in its web, hanging so nicely between the outspread limbs of the tree, is as singular as it is pleasing. Of old, a Lombard family bore, as its blazon, a spider in its web.

8300.

IECE of very rich Crimson Silk and gold Tissue; the large pattern represents a palm-tree rising from a close palisade, within which is a lion seated; from one side shoots a slender branch, to which clings a bird. Italian, late 14th century. 31 inches by 14 inches.

A fine bold pattern, but the gold so tarnished that it looks as if the threads had always been brown. The down-bent eagles, and the shaggy-maned lion couchant regardant at the foot of a palm-tree in a park palisaded, make this heraldic design very pleasing.

8301.

ORTION of Linen; border, probably of an altar-cloth, stamped in red and yellow with a geometric pattern composed of circles and leaves. Flemish, 15th century.

The design and colouring of this old piece of printed cloth are so very like those employed upon the glazed paving tiles of the mediæval period, that the idea of the potter's work immediately suggests itself; though of such poor material, it is a valuable link in the history of textiles.

8302.

PIECE of Purple Silk and Gold Tissue; the pattern is formed of angels holding a monstrance, beneath which is a six-winged cherub's head. Florentine, 14th century. 18 inches by 16 inches.

This is one of the most elaborate and remarkable specimens of the mediæval weavers' works, and shows how well, even with their appliances, they could gear their looms. The faces of the six-winged cherubic heads, as well as the hands and faces of the seraphim, vested in long albs, were originally shaded by needle-work, most of which is now gone. The Umbrian school of design to be seen in the gracefully floating forms of the angels, is very discernible. This rich stuff must have been purposely designed and woven for especial liturgical use at the great Festival of Corpus Christi, and its solemn processions. It may have been employed for hanging the chancel walls, or for altar-curtains; but most likely it overspread the long wooden framework or portable table upon which stood, and was thus carried all about the town by two or four deacons, the Blessed Sacrament enclosed in a tall heavy gold or silver vessel like the one shown in this textile, and called a "monstrance," because, instead of shutting up from public gaze, it displayed the consecrated host as it was borne about among the people. Dr. Bock has figured this stuff in his "Geschichte der Liturgischen Gewänder des Mittelalters."

8303.

PIECE of Linen; pattern, stamped in black with a central stem of conventional branches and flowers, at either side of which are hawks crested, regardant; at one side is a running border of detached portions of scroll-foliage. Flemish, very late 14th century. 13 inches by 6¾ inches.

Any specimen of such printed linen has now become somewhat a rarity, though there are other pieces here, Nos. 7022, 8615.

8304.

LINEN Towel, for use at the altar, with deep border embroidered in various coloured silk, with a geometrical pattern interspersed with small figures of birds. Beginning of 15th century. 3 feet by 1 foot 1 inch.

8305.

A DIACONAL Stole, embroidered in linen thread and various-coloured silk, with a pattern somewhat like the "gammadion" ornaments, the ends of gold tissue, fringed with silk and linen. German, 14th century. 8 feet 8 inches by 2¾ inches.

For the distinction of the priest's and the deacon's stole, and the manner in which either wears it in the celebration of the liturgy, see Hierurgia, p. 434, 2nd edition.

8306.

PIECE of Dark-brown raised Velvet and Gold Tissue; portion of the robe in which the Emperor Charles IV. was buried at Prague, as it is said. Italian, 14th century. 7 inches by 6¼ inches.

8307.

LINEN Amice, with its "apparel" of crimson silk, to which are sewed small ornaments in silver and silver-gilt. German, 15th century. 4 feet 2 inches by 1 foot 11 inches.

The example of linen in this amice will, for the student of mediæval antiquities and manufactures, be of great service, showing, as it does, what we are to understand was the kind of stuff meant by canvas in old accounts which speak of that material so often as bought for making albs, surplices, and other linen garments used in the ceremonial of the Church. The crimson ornament of silk sprinkled with large spangle-like plates of silver gilt, and struck with a variety of patterns, is another of various instances to show how the goldsmith's craft in the middle ages was brought into play for ornaments upon silk and other textiles; and the liturgical student will be glad to see in this specimen an instance, now so very rare, of an old amice, with its strings, but more especially its apparel, in its place; about which see " Church of our Fathers," t. i. 463.

8308.

IECE of Embroidery in Silk, on linen ground; the subject, partly needlework, and partly sketched in, represents the Adoration of the three Kings. German, 14th century. 12 inches square.

Though in the style of that period, it is roughly done, and by no means a good example.

8309.

IECE of Silk and Gold Tissue; the ground, lilac-blue; the pattern, in gold, represents the Annunciation. Florentine, late 14th century. 17¾ inches by 12 inches.

This is another of those many beautiful and artistic exemplars of the loom given to the world, but more especially for the use of the Church, by North Italy, during the 14th and 15th centuries. The treatment of the subject figured on this fragment—the Annunciation—is quite typical, in its drawing and invention, of the feelings which spread themselves all over the sweet gentle Umbrian school of painting, from the days of its great teacher the graceful Giotto. The lover, too, of ecclesiastical symbolism will, in this small piece, find much to draw his attention to it: the dove, emblem of the Holy Ghost, is in one place flying down from heaven with an olive-branch, and hovers over the head of the Blessed Virgin Mary; in another place, it stands at rest behind her, and bearing in its beak a lily-like flower; the angel Gabriel, clothed in a full, wide-flowing alb, carrying in his left hand a wand

—the herald's fign—tipped with a fleur-de-lis, to fhow not only that he was fent from God, but for an efpecial purpofe, is on his bended knee before the mother of our Lord, while, with his right hand uplifted in the act of bleffing according to the Latin rite, he utters the words of his celeftial meffage. The colour, too, of the ground—lilac-blue, emblematic of what is heavenly—muft not be overlooked.

8310.

FRAGMENT of a Veftment for Church ufe; embroidered in filk and gold, on a dark blue linen ground, with figures of the Bleffed Virgin Mary, and Infant, our Saviour, and St. John. German, 15th century. 3 feet 6 inches by 10 inches.

This fine example of the German needle, in its defign and treatment, calls to mind the remarkably painted folding altar-piece by Mafter Stephen Sothener, A. D. 1410, in the chapel of St. Agnes, at the eaft end of Cologne Cathedral.

8311.

THE Apparel for an Amice; the ground, crimfon, embroidered in filk; the centre pattern is edged at both fides with infcriptions done in letters of the mediæval form. German, 15th century. 15¼ inches by 3¾ inches.

This apparel for an amice is embroidered in fampler-ftitch and ftyle with the names of St. Odilia and St. Kylianus, and the firft line of the hymn in honour of the Bleffed Virgin Mary, " Ave Regina celorum," as well as the infcription " Mater Regis," having, except in one inftance, a crowned head between each word in the lettering. St. Kilian or Kuln was an Irifhman born of a noble houfe: with two companions, he went to Germany to preach to the unbelieving Franconians, and being made bifhop by Pope Conon, he fixed his fee at Wurtzburg, where he was martyred, A. D. 688. Dr. Bock has figured it in his " Gefchiĉte der Liturgifchen Gewänder des Mittelalters," iv Lieferung, pl. iii. fig. 4.

8312.

PIECE of Raised Velvet; ground, crimson; pattern, flowers and foliage in green, white, and purple. North Italian, middle of 15th century. Attached is a piece of dark blue plush lining of the same date and country. 14¼ inches by 13¼ inches.

As a specimen of a pattern in raised velvet upon a plain silk ground, this fragment is valuable; and the occurrence of roses, both white and red, seeded and barbed, would, at first sight, lead to the thought that its designer had in his mind some recollection of the English Yorkist and Lancastrian strife-stirring and direful badges; but it must have been woven some years before the war of the Roses raged in all its wildness through the length and breadth of this land.

8313.

PURSE with cords; white lattice-work on crimson ground, with crimson and yellow pattern in the spaces, four of which on each side are ornamented with gold thread. German, latter half of the 14th century. 5¼ inches by 5 inches.

Not only is this little bag nicely embroidered, but it has a lining of crimson sarcenet, and is supplied with platted silken strings of several colours for drawing its mouth close, as well as another silk string made after the same fashion, for carrying it in the hand. In church inventories of the period mention is often found of silk bags holding relics, and from Dr. Bock we learn that in the sacristy of St. Gereon's, at Cologne, may yet be seen just such another bag, which served, if it does not still serve, as a sort of reliquary. For taking to the sick and dying, the holy Eucharist shut up in a small silver or ivory box, such little bags were and yet are employed, but then they were borne slung round the neck of the priest, which in this instance could not be done, as the cord is too short. Bags for prayer-books are often figured, but this one is too small for such a purpose; its most probable use was that of a reliquary.

8314.

PIECE of Velvet; ground of crimſon, bordered with green, brown, white, and purple, and ſtriped with bands of gold thread, probably for ſecular uſe. Spaniſh, beginning of the 16th century. 13½ inches by 5 inches.

The pile of this velvet is good, but ſo bad was the gold, that it has turned black.

8315.

TWO Pieces of Embroidery, in ſilk and gold thread upon white linen; the one ſhows our Saviour bearing His croſs; the other, an inſcription with the date 1442. Theſe pieces have been mounted on a piece of crimſon damaſk of a much later date. The embroideries, German, middle of 15th century; the crimſon ſilk, Lyons, late 17th century. 6 inches ſquare.

To all appearance, this figure of our Lord carrying His croſs to Calvary, as well as the inſcription above it, formed part of the orphrey of a chaſuble, and to preſerve it, was mounted upon the crimſon ſilk which is ſtiffened by a thin board; and from the black loop at top it ſeems it was hung as a devotional picture upon the wall, moſt likely, of a private oratory or bedroom. As a work of art, the figure of our Lord is beautiful. The head, hands, and feet, as well as the croſſed nimbus in gold, the croſs, and the ground ſtrewed with flowers, are worked with the needle; while the folds of the white linen garment are all, with but a very few ſtrokes, marked by brown lines put in with the bruſh. The inſcription, quite a ſeparate piece, done in gold upon thin brown ſilk lined with canvas, reads thus:—Wyderoyd Paſtor S. Jac(obi) Colon(ienſis). 1442.

In its original ſtate it muſt have been, as now, "applied," and not wrought upon the veſtment itſelf, and affords a good hint to thoſe who are ſtriving to bring back the uſe of ſuch a mode of embroidery in cut work.

8316.

PIECE of Silk Embroidery on green silk ground. The pattern is in branches decorated with glass beads, and gilt spangles, flowers in white and red silk, and leaves in red and yellow. German, middle of 15th century. 6 inches square.

Remarkable for the freedom of its design and beautiful regularity of its stitches. The thin green sarcenet upon which the embroidery was originally made is nearly all gone, and scarcely anything like a grounding is to be seen beside the thick blue canvas, which is backed by a lining of the same material, but white. Those small opaque white beads, in all likelihood, came from Venice, where Murano, to this day, is the great manufactory for Africa of the same sort of ornament.

8317.

NAPKIN, or Towel, in White Linen Diaper, with patterns woven in blue and brown. German, beginning of the 15th century. 19½ inches by 9 inches.

Though not conspicuous for the richness of its material, this linen textile is somewhat a curiosity, as such specimens have now become rare; and it shows how, even in towels, the ornamentation of colour, as well as the pattern in warp and weft, were attended to in the mediæval period.

8318.

PIECE of Silk Damask, green, with pattern of pomegranates, crowns, and wreaths of flowers. Flemish, middle of 16th century.

The tastefully-arranged design of this silk would seem to have been a favourite, as we shall again meet it in other specimens, especially at No. 8332.

8319.

IECE of Silk Damaſk, ſlate blue ground, with winding borders of cinnamon colour, encloſing pomegranates wrought in gold thread and white ſilk. Flemiſh, middle of 16th century. 2 feet 6¼ inches by 2 feet.

Though elaborate in deſign and rich in gold, this piece is not happy in its colours. Its uſe muſt have been for the court and palace, but not for the church, and the whole is loom-wrought, and nothing about it done by the needle.

8320.

RPHREY, woven of crimſon wool and white linen thread. The pattern is of flowers and leaves on a trellis of branches, in which appear the names of " Jheſus," " Maria." German, end of 15th century. 2 feet 8¼ inches by 2¾ inches.

In this textile the warp is of white ſtrong linen thread, the woof of crimſon wool; and ſtuffs of ſuch cheap materials were wrought to ſerve as orphreys to tunicles and dalmatics worn by deacon and ſub-deacon at high maſs, and in proceſſions, as well as for trimming other adornments for church uſe; the liturgical girdle neither is, nor ever was made, according to the Latin rite, of ſo broad a width, nor after ſuch a faſhion; in the Greek ritual, broad girdles are in uſe.

The weavers of laces for carriage-trimming, or the adornment of ſtate liveries, will in this ſpecimen ſee that, more than three hundred years ago, their craft was practiſed in Germany; and Cologne appears to have been the centre of ſuch a loom production.

8321.

IECE of Satin Damaſk, ground of golden yellow, covered with a rich pattern in roſe-colour. French(?), middle of the 16th century. 2 feet 10¼ inches by 11 inches.

In this ſpecimen we obſerve how the deſigns for textiles were gradually loſing the conventional forms of the mediæval period.

8322.

IECE of Velvet, dark blue, figured with a pomegranate kind of pattern. Italian, end of the 15th century. 17¾ inches by 14½ inches.

Lucca seems to be the place where this specimen of a deep-piled and prettily designed velvet was produced; and a mediæval conventionality hung about the pencil of its designer, as we may observe in the scrolls or featherings stopped with graceful cusps which go round and shut in those modifications of the so-called pine, really an artichoke, and the pomegranate pattern.

Though equally employed for secular as well as sacred purposes, such velvets, in their latter use, are often found in the remains of copes, chasubles, &c. and altar-frontals.

8323.

ORTION of a Chasuble, in figured velvet; the ground, purple, with a pomegranate pattern in yellow, green, and white, with a broad yellow scroll. Genoese, middle of 16th century. 2 feet 3¼ inches by 1 foot 9 inches.

Genoa had earned for itself a notoriety, about this period, for its velvets, wrought in several colours, and the present piece seems no bad specimen of the style. By the warp of cotton and the thin low pile of its silken woof we learn that Genoese velvets varied much in the richness of their materials, and, in consequence, in their cost. This piece was once in a chasuble, as we may see by the bend, to fit the neck, in the upper part.

8324.

IECE of Silk and Linen Tissue; pattern, white crosses on ground of crimson, barred with purple, yellow, and green. German, 16th century. 4 inches square.

This specimen of German trimming, like the one No. 8320, seems to have been made at Cologne, and for the same ecclesiastical uses.

8325.

PIECE of Silk-Velvet Damask; green, with pattern of large and small pomegranates in gold. Lucca, latter half of the 15th century. 3 feet 10 inches by 11¼ inches.

Among the remarkable specimens of velvet in this collection, not the least conspicuous is the present one, being velvet upon velvet, that is, having, in a portion of it, a pattern in a higher pile than the pile of the ground. By looking narrowly at the larger pomegranate in golden thread within its heart-shaped oval, with featherings bounded by trefoiled cusps, the eye will catch an undulating pattern rising slightly above the rest of the pile; such examples, as distinguished from what is called cut or raised velvet, are very rare. The tone, too, of the fine green, as well as the goodness of the gold, in the ornamentation, enhance the value of this piece, which was once the back part of a chasuble.

8326.

PIECE of Silk Damask; white, with the rose and pomegranate pattern woven in gold thread. Spanish, latter half of the 15th century.

This piece, from the looms of Spain, for the beauty of design and the thick richness of its silk, is somewhat remarkable.

8327.

BOX covered with crimson raised velvet, having, round the lid, a many-coloured cotton fringe. It holds two liturgical pallæ, both of fine linen and figured—one mounted on pasteboard and measuring 7¼ inches by 7¼ inches, with an altar and two figures; the other, with the Crucifixion and St. Mary and St. John, measuring 9⅜ inches by 9¾ inches. Inside the lid of this box is an illuminated border of flowers, and the central defign is effaced. Velvet, Italian, 16th century; all the paintings very late 15th century, and German. Box, 10 inches by 9¼ inches.

As a cafe for holding "corporals" and "palls," this box is a curiofity, in its way, of rare occurrence. It muft be carefully diftinguifhed from a fquare fort of cafe for the "corporal," and called the "burfe." The corporal is a large fquare piece of fine linen; and at one time the chalice at mafs not only ftood upon it but was covered too by its inward border; but for a long period, the ufage has been and is to put upon the chalice, inftead of any part of the corporal, a much fmaller feparate fquare piece of fine linen, often ftiffened, the better to ferve its purpofe, with card-board, like this example; fuch is a pall, and the one before us is figured, we may fay illuminated, with what ufed to be called, in England, St. Gregory's Pity; "Church of our Fathers," i. 53. Upon an altar, around which are the inftruments of the Paffion, and on one fide St. Peter, known by the key in his hand, and on the other the cock on the column, crowing, ftands our Lord all bleeding, with the blood trickling into a chalice between His feet. At the foot of the altar kneels, vefted for mafs, St. Gregory the Great, behind whom we fee, holding a book in both hands, St. Jerome, robed as a cardinal; the whole is framed in a floriated border. The other, and unftiffened "pall," is illuminated with the Crucifixion after the ufual conventional manner, in all refpects, that prevailed at the time it was done, that is, fomewhere about the year 1490. As fpecimens on linen thefe two palls are rather rare. The border of flowers, on vellum, attached to the infide of the lid, is a free, well-coloured, and pleafing example of the Flemifh fchool late in the 15th century. The raifed velvet is of a rich crimfon tone, and from Lucca or Genoa.

Though, in later times, employed as an ordinary cafe for the cleanly keeping after fervice of the corporals or pieces of fine linen, always fpread out in the middle of the altar-ftone for the hoft and chalice to reft upon, at mafs, its firft ufe feems to have been for refervation of the Bleffed Sacrament confecrated on Maundy-Thurfday to ferve at the celebration of the divine office on Good Friday morning, as we have fully fet forth in the Introduction § 5, and again while defcribing a fimilar box, No. 5958.

In the prefent fpecimen all that remains of the vellum illumination, once upon the infide of the lid, is a wreath of painted flowers, within which ftood the miffing Crucifixion. The abfence of that fcene is, however, well fupplied by the other kind of art-work wrought in colours of the fame fubject; done, too, after a broad bold manner, upon a fquare piece of very fine linen, which, as it is moveable, ferves now as a lining for the lower infide of this cafe.

Such ecclefiaftical appliances are rare, fo much fo, that, befides the two in this collection, none is known to be in this country; while very few, even on the Continent, are to be feen at the prefent day.

8328.

AMICE of Linen; with its apparel of crimfon velvet, on which are three hexagonal rofes woven in gold. Spanifh, middle of the 15th century. 3 feet 9 inches by 1 foot 9 inches.

The velvet of the apparel is of a fine rich pile, and the tone of colour light ruby. The flowers, feeded and barbed, are not put in by the needle but woven. Such a liturgical appliance is not now often to be met with in its original ftate; but, in this inftance, it ought to be noticed, that while the amice itfelf—that is, the linen portion of this veftment—is remarkable for its large fize, the velvet apparel fewed on it is broader and fhorter than thofe which we find figured on Englifh ecclefiaftical monuments during the mediæval period. The narrow green ferret which hems the apparel is ufually found employed as a binding in crimfon liturgical garments anciently made in Flanders. Though the velvet was woven in Spain, this linen amice feems to have once belonged to fome Flemifh facrifty: at one period the connection between the two countries was drawn very clofe.

8329.

LINEN Cloth or Corporal, with an edge on all its four fides; 2¼ inches broad, embroidered in blue, white, and yellow filks. German, late 15th century. 22 inches by 21 inches.

To the ftudent of ecclefiaftical antiquities this liturgical appliance will be a great curiofity, from its being fo much larger than the corporals now in ufe; but its fize may be eafily accounted for. From being put over the altar-cloth, on the middle of the table of the altar, fo that the priest, at mass, might place the host and chalice immediately upon it before and after the consecration of the Eucharist, it got, and still keeps the name of "corporale," about which the reader may consult "Hierurgia," p. 74, 2nd edition.

The embroidery, seemingly of a vine, is somewhat remarkable from being, like Indian needlework, the same on both sides, and was so done for a purpose to be noticed below. Its greater size may be easily explained. During the middle ages, as in England, so in Germany, the usage was to cover the chalice on the altar, not with a little square piece of linen called a "palla," two specimens of which are mentioned, No. 8327, but with the corporal itself, as shown in those illuminations copied and given as a frontispiece to the fourth volume of the "Church of our Fathers." To draw up for this purpose the inner edge of the corporal, it was made, as needed, larger than the one now in use. Moreover, as the under side of the embroidery would thus be turned upwards and conspicuously shown, even on the consecrated chalice, to a great extent; and as anything frayed and ragged—and this single embroidery always is on the under side—would, at such a time, in such a place, have been most unseemly; to hinder this disrespect the embroidery was made double, that is, as perfect on the one side as on the other, giving the design clear and accurate on both, so that whichever part happened to be turned upwards it looked becoming.

8330.

IECE of Silk Damask; green, with pattern of crowns connected by wavy ribbons, in each space is a rose. North Italian, 15th century. 22 inches by 21 inches.

This fine and valuable piece of damask exhibits a very effective design, which is thoroughly heraldic in all its elements. Of these, the first are roselettes—single roses having five petals each—seeded and barbed, and every petal folds inward very appropriately; all about each roselette roves a bordure nebulé, significative in heraldry of a cloud-wreath, above which and just over the flower rests an open crown, the hoop of which is studded with jewels, and bears on the upper rim two balls—pearls—on pyramidal points, and three fleurs-de-lis. To take these roselettes for the Tudor flower would be a great mistake, as it was not thought of at the period when this stuff was manufactured, besides which, it is never shown as a roselette or single rose, but as a very

LACE EMBROIDERY
Maltese — 18th century

double one. It is not unlikely that this damask was, in the first instance, ordered from Italy, if not by our Edward IV, at least by one of the Yorkist party after the Lancastrian defeat at Mortimer's Cross: the crown with its fringe of clouds seems to point to the curious appearance in the heavens that day. When once his loom was geared the Lombard weaver would not hesitate to work off stuffs after the same pattern ordered by his English customer and sell them in the Italian markets.

8331.

IECE of Lace in Open Work. The pattern, oblong and octagonal spaces framed in gold thread, and containing stars in silver and flowers in gold, upon a black silk ground. Milanese, end of the 16th century. 14¼ inches by 4¼ inches.

During a long time Milan, the capital of rich and manufacturing Lombardy, stood conspicuous among its neighbouring cities for the production of its gold thread, and beautifully wrought laces in that material; and the specimen before us is a pleasing example of this far-famed Milanese handicraft. To all appearance, it once served as the apparel to an amice to be used in religious services for the dead. It seems the work of the loom; and the piece of stout black silk under it was meant, though quite apart from it, to be, as it were, a grounding to throw up more effectively its gold and silver ornamentation.

8332.

IECE of Silk, formerly crimson, but much faded, with elaborate pattern of pomegranates, crowns and wreaths of flowers. Flemish, middle of the 16th century. 19 inches by 17¼ inches.

In this piece, though so faded, we have a good specimen of the Bruges loom about the second half of the 16th century, and seemingly from the same workshop which sent forth No. 8318.

8333.

HOOD of a Cope, with figures embroidered on a very rich ground of red and gold velvet. Velvet, Florentine; the embroidery Flemish, late 15th century. 16 inches by 15½ inches.

About this period, Florence was noted for its truly rich and beautiful crimson velvets of a deep pile and artistically flowered in gold, and profusely sprigged, or rather dotted, with small loops of golden thread standing well up from the velvet ground; and in this production of Florentine contrivance we have a good example of its speciality.

The needlework is a very favourable specimen of Flemish embroidery, and the management of the three subjects shows that the hand that wrought them was quickened with a feeling love for the school of Hans Memling, who has made Bruges to be the pilgrimage of many an admirer of the beautiful in Christian art. The holy woman, who, according to the old tradition, gave a napkin to our Lord on His way to Calvary, is figured, at top, holding, outstretched before her to our view, this linen cloth showing shadowed on it the head of our Redeemer crowned with thorns and trickling with blood: the Saint became known as St. Veronica, and the handkerchief itself as the "Varnicle." Just below, we have the Blessed Virgin Mary seated and holding on her knees the infant Saviour, before whom kneels St. Bernard, the famous abbot of Clairvaux, in the white Cistercian habit which he had received from our fellow-countryman, St. Stephen Harding, the founder of the Cistercian Order, about the year 1114. The group itself is an early example of a once favourite subject in St. Bernard's life, thus referred to by Mrs. Jameson, in one of her charming books:—
"It was said of him (St. Bernard) that when he was writing his famous homilies on 'The Song of Songs which is Solomon's,' the Holy Virgin herself condescended to appear to him, and moistened his lips with the milk from her bosom; so that ever afterwards his eloquence, whether in speaking or in writing, was persuasive, irresistible, supernatural." (Legends of the Monastic Orders, p. 142). Lower still, St. Bernard, with his abbot's pastoral staff, cast upon the ground by his side, is praying, on bended knees, before a crucifix, from off of which our Redeemer has loosened Himself to fall into the arms of the saint, who was so fond of meditating on all the throes of our Lord upon the cross.

8334.

PIECE of Crimson Velvet, spangled with gold and silver stars, and embroidered with leaves and flowers in gold thread, once dotted with precious stones. North Italian, end of the 15th century. 14¼ inches by 5¼ inches.

The Genoese velvet of this piece is of a very deep ruby tone, deeper than usual; but the way in which it is ornamented should not be passed over by those who wish to learn one among the very effective styles of embroidering. The design consists chiefly of branches gracefully bent in all directions and sprouting out, here and there, with leaves and variously fashioned flowers which, from one example that still holds its tiny round-headed piece of coloured glass set in a silver gilt socket, bore in them mock precious stones, and perhaps seed-pearls. These branches themselves are made of common hempen string, edged on both sides with a thread of gold of a smaller bulk, and the flowers are heightened to good effect by the bright red stitches of the crimson silk with which the gold that forms them is sewed in; and the whole of the design appears to have been worked, first upon a strong canvas, from which it was afterwards cut and appliqué upon its velvet ground. All the space between the boughs is sprinkled rather thickly with six-rayed stars of gold and silver, but the latter ones have turned almost black. This piece was once the apparel for the lower border of an alb.

8335.

PIECE of Silk Damask; upon a light blue ground, an elaborate pattern of pomegranates and flowers in pale yellow. Flemish, end of the 16th century. 24¼ inches by 21 inches.

Like, in many respects, to another piece of the looms of ancient Bruges, it shows that the Flemings were unfortunate in their mode of dyeing, for this, as well as No. 8332, has faded much in colour, but the pattern is very rich and graceful. This textile is figured by Dr. Bock, in his "History of Liturgical Robes," vol. i.

8336.

IECE of Silk Net-Work, formerly crimson. The design is evidently circular, and consists of a lozenge filled in with two other very much smaller lozenges touching each other lengthwise. Milanese, end of the 16th century.

This curious little piece of frame-work seems to be another specimen of the lace of Milan, concerning which a notice has been given under No. 8331. Some would take it to be crochet, but it looks as if it came from a loom. To our thinking, it was either the heel or the toe part of a silk stocking. Though of a much finer texture, it much resembles, in pattern, the yellow silk pair of stockings belonging now to the Marquis of Salisbury, but once presented by Lord Hunsdon to Queen Elizabeth, and said to be the first ever made in England.

8837.

IECE of Crimson Raised Velvet, with pattern of pomegranates, flowers and scrolls embroidered in gold thread and coloured silks. Genoese, beginning of the 16th century.

This piece affords a very instructive instance of how velvet textiles were not unfrequently treated. The pattern was first wrought in the weaving, and made the fabric what is now known as cut or raised velvet. Then those parts left bare of the silken pile were filled in by hand-embroidery, done in gold, silver, and silks of various colours, as the fancy of the individual might like, and produced a mixed work similar to the one before us. The velvet itself of this specimen is poor in colour and thin in substance, but the gold thread is of the finest, and admirably put together; and those little specks of the crimson silk employed in sewing it on, help, in no small manner, to heighten its brilliancy and effect.

8338.

PART of an Orphrey; ground, gold thread, with ornamentation, in filk, of a rofette, a tree with flowers, and the infcriptions—" Ave Regina Celorum," and " Jhefus." Cologne work, late 15th century. 22½ inches by 3¾ inches.

Much, in ftyle, like No. 8320.

8338 A.

PART of an Orphrey, woven in filk upon linen; ground, red; pattern, in gold thread upon blue filk. Cologne work, 15th century. 15½ inches by 4¼ inches.

This and the piece immediately preceding afford us one of the peculiarities of the German loom, and, in all likelihood, were woven at Cologne, the great manufacturing centre of Germany in the middle ages. Such webs were wrought for the orphreys of chafubles, copes, and dalmatics, &c. The defign is ftiff, and wanting in much of the elegance to be found in earlier works of the loom, and, from its famplerlike look, might, at firft fight, be taken for needlework.

8339.

PIECE of Silk and Linen Damafk; pattern, rich, broad and flowing, in crimfon, on a gold ground. Genoefe, late 16th century. 2 feet 4 inches by 1 foot 11⅓ inches.

This gives us a fine fpecimen of Italian weaving in the middle or latter portion of the 16th century. So rich, and fo folid in materials, it is as bold as it is, at firft fight, attractive in its defign, and fhows indications of that ftrap-fhaped ornamentation which foon afterwards became fo confpicuous in all cut-work, efpecially fo in bookbindings, all over Weftern Europe. Such ftuffs were moftly ufed for hangings on the walls of ftate-rooms and the backs of the ftalls in churches, as well as for curtains at the fides of altars.

D D

8340.

PIECE of Silk Damask; pattern, of the 16th century revival character, in crimson upon a yellow ground; probably a border to some other stuff. Florentine, end of the 16th century. 10½ inches by 5½ inches.

8341.

PIECE of Linen and Woollen Damask, white and green; the pattern, birds, oak-leaves, and acorns. North Italian, end of the 16th century. 7 inches by 5 inches.

Though made out of such humble materials as linen-thread and worsted, this charming little piece of stuff cannot fail in drawing upon itself the eye of the observer, by the beauty and elegance which it has about it.

8342.

LINEN Napkin, or rather Sindon or Pyx-cloth, the borders embroidered with coloured silks and silver-thread. Perhaps Flemish, 16th century. 18¼ inches by 16¼ inches.

In more senses than one this small linen cloth is of great value, being, in the first place, a liturgical appliance of the mediæval period, now unused in this form, certainly unique in this country, and hardly ever to be met with on the continent, either in private hands or public collections. According to ancient English custom, the pyx containing particles of the Blessed Eucharist for giving, at all hours of day or night, the Holy Communion to the dying, and kept hanging up over the high altar of every church in this land, was overspread with one of such fine linen and embroidered veils, as may be seen in an illumination from the "Life of St. Edmund, King and Martyr," in the Harley Collection, British Museum, and engraved in the "Church of our Fathers," t. iv. p. 206.

The readers of English history will, no doubt, feel an interest in this specimen, when they learn that, with such a linen napkin, Mary

Queen of Scots had her face muffled juft before fhe laid her head upon the block: " Then the maid, Kennedy, took a handkerchief, edged with gold, in which the Euchariſt had formerly been encloſed, and faſtened it over her eyes." " Pict. Hiſt. of England, ed. Knight," t. ii. p. 671. Knight is wrong in ſaying that the Holy Euchariſt had ever been immediately encloſed in this cloth, which is only the veil that uſed to be caſt over the pyx or ſmall veſſel in which the conſecrated hoſts were kept, as we obſerved in the introduction, § 5.

8343.

PIECE of Linen Damaſk; pattern, of the pomegranate type, with a border of an armorial ſhield repeated, and the initials C. L. An edging of lace is attached to one end. Flemiſh, middle of the 16th century. 17¾ inches by 13 inches.

The ſhield is party per pale; in the firſt, two bars counter-embattled; in the ſecond, a chevron charged with three eſcallop ſhells.

Moſt likely this ſmall piece of Flemiſh napery ſerved as the fingercloth or little napkin with which, when ſaying maſs, the prieſt dried the tips of his fingers after waſhing them, the while he ſaid that prayer, " Munda me, Domine," &c. in the Saliſbury Miſſal; " Church of our Fathers," t. iv. p. 150. By the rubrics of the Roman Miſſal, the prieſt was, and yet is, directed to ſay, at the ritual waſhing of his hands, that portion of the 25th Pſalm, which begins, verſe 6, " Lavabo manus meas," &c. " Hierurgia," p. 21; hence theſe ſmall liturgical towels got, and ſtill keep, the name of Lavabo cloths or Lavaboes, eſpecially in all thoſe countries where the Roman Miſſal is in uſe.

8344.

PIECE of Silk Damaſk; ground, blue and yellow; pattern, a large conventional flower, with heraldic ſhields, helmets, and creſts. Italian, late 16th century. 1 foot 8¼ inches by 13 inches.

The ſhields ſhow a pale; the helmets are given ſidewiſe with the beaver cloſed; and the creſts, a demi-wyvern ſegeant, but with no wreath under it, doubtleſs to ſhow the armorial bearings of the eſquire or gentleman of blood, as, according to the readings of English blasonry, he could have been of no higher degree, for whom this stuff had been woven.

8345.

FRAGMENT of an Ecclesiastical Vestment; ground, cloth of gold, diapered with an elaborate flower-pattern. French, middle of the 16th century. 2 feet 1¼ inches by 1 foot 9 inches.

This valuable specimen of cloth of gold is figured, in small red lines, with a free and well-designed pattern, and shows us how much above modern French and Italian toca and lama d'oro were those fine old cloth of gold stuffs which, in the 16th century, became so variously employed for secular purposes. Let the reader imagine a vast round royal tent of such a textile with the banner of a king fluttering over it, and then he may well conceive why the meadow upon which it stood was called "the field of the cloth of gold."

8346.

PIECE of Silk and Linen Damask, green and yellow; pattern, a small conventional flower, probably a furniture stuff. Italian, late 16th century. 10 inches by 7¼ inches.

8347.

PIECE of Silk Damask, blue and yellow; pattern of flowers. French, late 16th century. 8 inches square.

In the design of the pattern there is evidently a wish to indicate the national fleur-de-lis.

8348.

PORTION of a Housing or Saddle-cloth, grey velvet, embroidered with interlaced patterns in silver and gold thread. In one corner is an armorial shield in silver and coloured silks. Spanish, middle of the 16th century. 1 foot 8¼ inches by 6½ inches.

Very probably the blazon of the shield on this curious horse-furniture may be the canting arms of its primitive owner; and it is *argent*, a hoopoe *gules* on a mount *vert*.

8349.

IECE of Silk Damask; green, with the pomegranate pattern. French, end of the 16th century. 2 feet 7 inches by 1 foot 7 inches.

8350.

EMBROIDERED Girdle; pattern, rectangular, in gold and silver threads and crimson silk; there are long gold tassels at the ends. French, late 16th century. 6 feet 3 inches by $\frac{7}{8}$ inch.

Most likely a liturgical girdle, for the use of which see " Hierurgia," p. 426, 2nd edition, and " Church of our Fathers," t. i. p. 448. Such ecclesiastical appliances are now become great rarities, and though this one is very modern, it is not less valuable on that account. The only other good example known in England is the very fine and ancient one kept, in Durham Cathedral Library, among the remains of those rich old vestments found upon the body of a bishop mistaken, by Mr. Raine, for that of St. Cuthbert. Flat girdles, whenever used in the Latin rite, were narrow; while those of the Greek and Oriental liturgies are much broader.

8351.

INEN Cloth; pattern, a white diaper lozenge. Flemish, end of the 16th century. Shape, oval, diameters 22 inches and 17 inches.

Though of so simple a pattern the design is pleasing, and well brought out.

8352.

IECE of Silk Damaſk, ſky-blue and white; pattern, interſecting ribbons with flowers in the ſpaces. French, late 16th century. 9¾ inches by 4¼ inches.

A very agreeable ſpecimen of the taſte of the period and country, as well as grateful to the eye for the combination and management of its two colours in ſuch a way that neither overmatches the other—a beauty often forgotten by the deſigners of textiles, but to be found in ſeveral other examples of the mediæval loom in this collection.

8353.

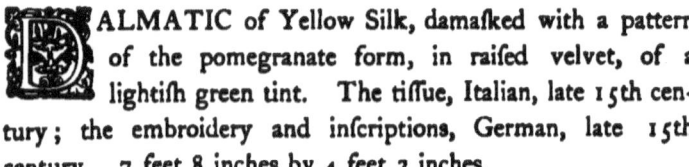ALMATIC of Yellow Silk, damaſked with a pattern of the pomegranate form, in raiſed velvet, of a lightiſh green tint. The tiſſue, Italian, late 15th century; the embroidery and inſcriptions, German, late 15th century. 7 feet 8 inches by 4 feet 3 inches.

This fine dalmatic—for the liturgical uſe of which the reader may conſult the "Church of our Fathers," t. i. p. 375—is rather curious for the way in which the two very ſingular taſſels hanging on the back from the ſhoulders are ornamented. Theſe uſual appendages are in this inſtance made of remarkably long (15 inches) flakes of white, red, and deep-brown ſilken thread, and, inſtead of ſilk nobs at the end of the cords, have large round balls of rock cryſtal. The orphreys, or ſtripes, down both ſides, before and behind, are 2¼ inches broad, woven in gold and charged with ſquares of flower-bearing trees, and inſcribed in blue with "Jheſus," "Maria." The fringes on the two lower borders of the dalmatic, 3¼ inches deep, are alternately red, green, white, and blue, and thoſe on the ſides and around the ſleeves are much narrower. The ſleeves themſelves from being 18 inches wide at the ſhoulder become as narrow as 12 inches towards the wriſt. The two apparels on the upper part, before and behind, are woven in gold, and meaſure 16¼ inches in length, and 5¼ inches in breadth; the one on the back juſt under the neck is figured with three golden-grounded ſquares, the centre one ornamented with a crimſon quatrefoil, barbed, and encloſing a various-coloured conventional flower; the other two, with a green

Needlework, and Dresses. 207

tree bloffomed with red flowers: the apparel acrofs the breaft is infcribed with the names, in large blue letters, of "Jhefus," "Maria." Half way down the back hangs, tranfverfely, a fhield of arms quarterly, one and four *gules*, two bars *argent*, between feven fleurs-de-lis, *or*, three, two, and two; two and three, *fable* two bars, *argent*: as a creft, a full-forward open-faced helmet, with fix bars all gold, furmounted by a pair of horns barred *fable* and *argent*, with mantlings of the fame. This blazon, according to Englifh heraldry, would indicate that the giver of this fplendid veftment—and very likely it was only one of a large fet—could boaft, by fhowing the golden five-barred fullforward helmet, of royal blood in his pedigree, and was not lower than a Duke in title. Dr. Bock has figured this finely-preferved dalmatic in his "Gefchichte des Liturgifchen Gewänder des Mittelalters," 4 Lieferung, pt. vii. fig. 1.

8354.

COPE of Crimfon Raifed Velvet; pattern of the focalled pomegranate defign. The orphreys and hood embroidered on a golden ground; the latter with the death of the Bleffed Virgin Mary; the former, with various faints. Velvet, Spanifh, the embroidery, German, both of the end of the 15th century. 10 feet 8 inches by 5 feet 8 inches.

The velvet, both for its ruby tone and richnefs of pile, is remarkable, while its defign of the pattern is efficiently fhown.

The hood which, it fhould be obferved by thofe curious in liturgical garments, runs right through the orphreys quite up to the neck, is an elaborate and well-wrought piece of needle-work; and ftrongly reminds one of the picture of the fame fubject—the death-bed of the Mother of our Lord—by Martin Schön, now in the National Gallery. All the Apoftles are fuppofed to be gathered round her; to the right of the fpectator ftands St. Peter fprinkling her with holy water from the filver fprinkle in his right hand; next to this chief celebrant is St. John, the acolyte, with the holy water ftoop in his left hand, and in his right the lighted taper, which he is about to put into the hand of his adopted mother—an emblem of the lighted lamp with which each wife virgin in the Gofpel awaited the coming of the bridegroom. Behind him again, and with his back turned, is another apoftle, blowing into the halfextinguifhed thurible, which he is raifing to his mouth; the reft of the Apostles are nicely grouped around. The ground of this hood is of rich gold thread, and the figures of the scene are separately wrought and afterwards "applied." The orphreys, that are rather narrow, measuring only 5¼ inches in breadth, are of a golden web and figured, on the right hand side, with St. Mary Magdalen, carrying a box of ointment in her hands; St. Bernadin of Siena, holding a circular radiated disc inscribed with I.H.S. in his right hand, and in his left a Latin cross; St. Bicta—for so the inscription seems to read—bearing the martyr's branch of palm in her right hand, and a sword thrust through her throat; and St. Kymbertus in a cope, with a crozier in his right hand, and in his left a closed book: on the left hand orphrey, St. Elizabeth, the Queen of Hungary, with a child's article of dress in one hand, and a royal crown upon her head; St. Severinus, wearing a mitre and cope, and holding in his right hand a crozier, in his left a church; St. Ursula, with the martyr's palm in one hand, in the other a long large silver arrow, and having six of her martyred virgins at her sides; and St. John Baptist, with the "Lamb of God" on the palm of his left hand, and the forefinger of the right outstretched as pointing to it. The heads of all these figures are done in silk and "applied," but the hands and diapering of the garments, as well as the emblems, are wrought by the needle, in gold or in silk, upon the golden web-ground of these orphreys. At the lower part of the hood is "applied" a shield—no doubt the armorials of the giver of this fine cope—party per pale—*gules* two chevronels *argent*, a chief *or*—*azure* three garbs (one loft), *argent*, two and one.

8355.

CHASUBLE of Damask Cloth of Gold; the orphreys figured with arabesques in coloured silk upon a golden ground, and busts of saints embroidered in coloured silks within circles of gold. There is a shield of arms on the body of the vestment, on the left side. French, 17th century. 7 feet 3 inches by 2 feet 4 inches.

The cloth of gold is none of the richest, and may have been woven at Lyons; but the orphreys are good specimens of their time: that on the back of this vestment, 4¼ inches in width, and made in a cross, shows a female saint holding a sword in her right hand, and in her left a two-masted boat—perhaps St. Mary Magdalen, in reference to her penitence and voyage to France; St. John with a cup, and the demon serpent coming up out of it; the Empress Helen carrying a cross (?). The orphrey in front, three inches broad, gives us, in smaller circles, St. Simon the apostle with his saw; a female saint (Hedwiges?) holding a cross; and two prophets, each with a rolled-up scroll in his hand. On the back, and far apart from the orphrey, is a shield *argent* (nicely diapered), a chevron *sable* between three leaves slipped *vert*, hanging as it does on the left hand, it may be presumed there was another shield on the right, but it is gone. This chasuble, small as it is now, must have been sadly reduced across the shoulders, from its original breadth.

8356.

PIECE of Carpet, of wool and hemp; ground, red; pattern, boughs, and flowers, in blue, and the so-called pomegranate, blue with a large yellow flower in the middle; border, two stripes blue barred with yellow, one stripe yellow barred red. Spanish, 16th century. 3 feet 10 inches by 3 feet 7 inches.

In every way like the following specimen of carpeting, with its warp of hempen thread; and originally employed for the same purpose of being spread up the steps leading to the altar, but more especially upon the uppermost or last one for the celebrant to stand on.

8357.

PIECE of Carpet; ground, dark blue; pattern, a large so-called pomegranate design in light blue, spotted with flower-like circles, white and crimson (now faded). At each end it has a border in red, blue, green, white, and yellow lines. Spanish, 16th century. 9 feet 3 inches by 8 feet 6 inches.

The warp, as in the foregoing example, is of hempen thread, the woof of worsted; and this textile was woven in breadths 4 feet 3 inches wide. In all likelihood this piece of carpeting, valuable because very rare now, served as the covering for the steps that led up to the altar, and corresponded to what in some old English church inventories were called pedalia, or pede-cloths:—"Church of our Fathers," i. 268. Finer sorts were spread on high feast days upon the long form where sat the precentor with his assistant rulers of the choir, or upon the stools which they separately occupied. Ib. ii. 202.

8358.

LITURGICAL Cloth of grey linen thread, figured all over with subjects from the New Testament, angels, apostles, flowers, and monsters. Rhenish, end of the 14th century. 10 feet by 3 feet.

This curious and valuable piece, of the kind denominated "opus araneum," or spider-web, is very likely the oldest as well as one among the very finest specimens yet known of that peculiar sort of needlework. The design is divided into two lengths, one much shorter than the other, and reversed; thus evidently proving that its original use was to cover, not the altar, but the lectern, upon which the Evangeliarium, or Book of the Gospels, is put at high mass for the deacon to sing the gospel from: judging by the subjects wrought upon it, and in white, it appears to have been intended more especially for the daily high mass, chaunted in many places every morning in honour of the Blessed Virgin Mary.

Beginning at the lower part of the longer length, we see an angel, vested like a deacon, in an appareled and girded alb, playing the violin, then six apostles—St. Simon with the fuller's bat in his hand, St. Matthias with sword and book, St. James the Greater with pilgrim's bourdon or staff, St. Jude, or Thaddeus, with club and book, St. Andrew with book and saltire cross, St. Thomas with spear; then another like vested angel sounding a guitar—all of which figures are standing in a row amid oak boughs and flowery branches. Higher up, and within a large quatrefoil encircled by the words:—☩ "Magnificat: Anima: mea: Dominum;" the Visitation, or the Blessed Virgin Mary and St. Elizabeth, both with outstretched hands, one towards the other, the first as a virgin with her hair hanging down upon her shoulders, the second having her head shrouded in a hood like a married woman; they stand amid lily-bearing stems (suggested by the lesson read on that festival from Canticles ii.); in each of the north and south petals of the quatrefoil is a kneeling angel, deacon-vefted, holding in each hand a bell, which he is ringing, while in the eaft and weft petals are other like-robed angels, both incenfing with a thurible. Outfide the quatrefoil are reprefented within circles at the fouth-weft corner the Britifh St. Urfula—one of the patron faints of Cologne—ftanding with a book in one hand, and an arrow in the other; at the fouth-eaft corner St. Helen (?), with crofs and book ; at the north-weft, St. Lucy with book and pincers ; at the north-eaft, a virgin martyr, with a book and a branch of palm. At each of the angles, in the corners between the petals, is an open crown. Above ftands in the middle a double-handled vafe, between two wyverns, jeffant oak branches. Over this fpecies of heraldic border is another large quatrefoil arranged in pre-cifely the fame manner : the angels—two with bells, two with thuribles—are there, fo too are the corner crowns, within and encircled by the words ✠ Gloria : in : exc(e)l(f)is : Deo : et : in : terr(a), we have the Affumption of the Bleffed Virgin Mary, after this manner: feated upon a throne is our Lord in majefty, that is, crowned and hold-ing the mund or ball furmounted by a crofs in His left hand ; with His right He is giving His bleffing to His mother, who is feated alfo on the fame throne, crowned, with her hair about her fhoulders, and with hands upraifed to Him as in the act of prayer. At the top, to the left, is St. Catherine, with a fword in one hand, a wheel armed with fpikes in the other ; to the right, St. Dorothy, with a blooming branch in one hand and in the other a bafket—made like a cup with foot and ftem—full of flowers ; below, St. Barbara, with tower and palm-branch, in the left fide; on the other, St. Mary Magdalen, with an ointment box and palm. Here the defign is reverfed, and very properly fo, as other-wife it would be, when thrown over the lectern, upfide down ; and curioufly enough, juft at this place there is a large hole, caufed, as is clear, by this part of the needlework being worn away from the con-tinual rubbing of fome bofs or ornament at the top of the folding lec-tern, which moft likely was wrought in iron. This fhorter length of the defign—that portion which hung behind—begins with the double-handled vafe and two wyverns, and has but one quatrefoil arranged like the other two in the front part : within the circle infcribed ✠ Ecce : ancilla : Domini : fiat : michi—we fee the Annunciation ; kneeling before a low reading defk, with an open book upon it, is the Bleffed Virgin Mary, with the Holy Ghoft under the form of a nimbed dove coming down from heaven, fignified by the nebulæ or clouds, upon her ; and turning about with arms wide apart, as if in wonderment, fhe is liftening to Gabriel on his knees and fpeaking his meffage in those words:—ave : gracia : ple(na), traced upon the scroll, which, with both his hands, he holds before him. In the corners of the petals are, at top, to the left, a female saint, with a cross in one hand, a closed book in the other ; to the right, a female saint with palm-branch and book ; below, to the left, a female saint—St. Martina, V. M.—with book and a two-pronged and barbed fork ; on the right, a female saint with a book, and cup with a lid. As the other end began, so this ends, with a row of eight figures, of which two are angels robed as deacons, one playing the violin, the other the guitar ; then come six apostles—St. John the Evangelist exorcising the poisoned cup ; St. Bartholomew, with book in one hand and flaying knife in the other ; St. Peter, with book and key ; St. Paul, with book and sword held upwards ; St. Matthew, with sword held downwards, and book ; St. Philip, with book and cross.

The figures within the quatrefoils and of the apostles are about seven inches high ; those of the female saints—all virgins, as is shown by the hair hanging in long tresses about their shoulders—measure six inches. The spaces between are filled in with branches of five-petaled and barbed roses, and at both ends there originally hung a prettily knotted long fringe. All the female saints are dressed in gowns with very long remarkable sleeves—a fashion in woman's attire which prevailed at the end of the 14th and beginning of the 15th centuries.

The exact way in which these now very rare specimens of mediæval needlework used to be employed in the celebration of the liturgy, may be seen, by a glance, on looking at any of those engravings in which are figured a few of those old lecterns ; made either of light thin wood, or iron, or of bronze, so as they could be easily folded up : they were thus with readiness carried about from one part to another of the choir, or chancel, even by a boy. When set down the veil was cast over them. Some of our own archæological works afford us good examples of such lecterns ; as fine, if not finer, are those two which M. Viollet Le Duc has given in his instructive " Dictionnaire du Mobilier Français," t. i. pp. 162, 163, especially that from the Hotel de Cluny. Speaking of the coverings for such lecterns, he tells that in the treasury of Sens Cathedral there yet may be found one which is, however, according to his admeasurements, much smaller every way than this piece of curious needlework before us. Whether the one now at Sens be of the 10th or 11th century assigned it, far too early date to our thinking, it cannot, to judge from the coloured plate given by M. Viollet Le Duc, be put for a moment in competition with the present one, as an art-work done by the needle. In our own mediæval records notices of such lecterns may be sometimes found; in the choir of Cobham College, Kent, A.D. 1479, there was such an article of church furniture, "Church of our Fathers," ii. 201, and doubtless it was usually covered with a veil.

8359.

CHASUBLE of Silk Damask, green and fawn-coloured, freckled in white with small flowers, inscriptions, and other ornaments; the pattern, in bands, consists of a large fan-like flower-bearing plant, and a double-handled vase, from which shoots up the thin stem of a tree between two hunting leopards collared, and addorsed, with an Arabic inscription beneath the vase, both plant and vase occurring alternately; these bands are separated by a narrower set of bands divided into squares enclosing birds of prey alternately gardant segeant. Syrian, late 13th century. 9 feet 5 inches by 4 feet.

This stuff betrays a few lingering traditions of the Persian style of design, and some people will see in the little tree between those hunting leopards the "hom," or sacred tree of the olden belief of that country. The material of it is thin and poor, and in width it measures twenty-one inches. The characters under the vase holding the leopards and "hom," are but an imitation of Arabic, and hence we may presume that it was woven by Jewish or Christian workmen for the European market, and to make it pass better, as if coming from Persia, inscribed as best they knew how, with Arabic letters, or imitations of that alphabet.

8360.

BACK of a Chasuble, blue silk wrought all over with beasts and birds in gold beneath trees. The orphrey of crimson silk is embroidered with flowers and armorial shields. The blue silk, Italian, 14th century; the orphrey, German, 15th century. 3 feet 8¾ inches by 2 feet 5 inches.

The birds that are shown on this blue-grounded piece of rather shining silk are peahens, standing on green turf sprinkled with white flowers, and three very much larger flowers stand high above their heads; the beasts are leopards, with their skin well spotted, and they seem to be, as it were, scenting and scratching the ground. The orphrey, crofs-fhaped, and 5¼ inches wide, is overfpread with gracefully intertwined rose-branches, the leaves of which are of gold shaded green, and the flowers in silver, seeded and barbed. It is blazoned all over with armorial bearings, seemingly of two houses, of which the first is a shield, tincture gone, charged with a lion rampant *or*, langued and armed *gules*; the second, a shield, barry of twelve, *gules* and *or*, with a lion rampant, *argent*, langued and armed *azure*, in the dexter canton. There are three of each of these shields, and all six are worked on canvas, and afterwards sewed on. On the upright stem of the cross may be read in places the name of " Lodewich Fretie," the individual who bore those arms and gave the chafuble.

8361.

ALMATIC of blue silk damasked with gold; the pattern consists of alternate rows of oxen, and pelican-like birds amid flowers and foliage. North Italian, late 14th century. 7 feet 7¾ inches by 4 feet.

A rather showy piece, and very effective in its pattern, though the gold about the thread with which the design is brought out is sparingly employed, so that it looks more yellow than metallic. The sleeves now but eleven inches long, are slit quite up, and were very likely shortened when the slitting was inflicted on them, and that, within the last hundred years, in compliance with the somewhat modern practice that took its rise in France.

8388.

IECE of Embroidery of our Lord upon His mother's lap. Florentine, 15th century. 8¼ inches by 5½ inches.

The Blessed Virgin Mary is robed in the usual crimson tunic, and sky-blue flowing mantle, and bearing, as is customary in the Italian schools of art, a golden star figured on her left shoulder. Sitting upon a tasseled cushion, and holding a little bird in His left hand, we have our Lord quite naked, with His crossed nimb about His head. Those who bring to mind that lovely picture of Raphael's, the so-called "Madonna del Cardellino," or our Lady of the gold-finch, will see that such an idea was an old one when that prince of painters lived. This piece of needlework was originally wrought for the purpose of being applied, and shows on the back proofs that, in its last use, it had been pasted on to some vestment or altar-frontal.

8561.

SMALL Piece of Silk; ground, purple; pattern, boughs of green leaves twining amid rosettes, green, some with crimson, some with yellow centres. Sicilian, late 14th century. 6¼ inches by 3 inches.

Good in material and pretty in design, though the colours are not happily contrasted.

8562.

PIECE of Silk; ground, purple; pattern, circles inclosing, some a tree which separates beasts and birds, some a long stripe which seemingly separates birds, all in yellow. Syrian, 14th century. 1 foot 1¼ inches by 7¼ inches.

The piece is so faded that with much difficulty its design can be traced, but enough is discernible to show the Persian feelings in it. No doubt the beasts are the cheetah or spotted hunting leopard addorsed and separated by the traditional "hom," and the birds over them, put face to face, but parted by the "hom," are eagles.

8563.

PIECE of Yellow Silk; pattern, a broad oval, filled in and surrounded with floriations. Florentine, 15th century. 11 inches by 7¾ inches.

The once elaborate design, now indiscernible, was brought out not by another coloured silk but by the gearing of the loom; some one, very recently, has tried to show it by tracing it out in lead-pencil.

8564.

IECE of White Silk; pattern, within circles, two birds addorsed, regardant, and separated by a tree. Syrian, 14th century. 12¼ inches by 9 inches.

The satin-like appearance and the creamy tone of this piece make it very pleasing, and in it we find, as in No. 8562, the same Persian influences; here, too, we have the mystic "hom," put in, no doubt, by Christian hands.

8565.

IECE of Silk Tissue; ground, red; pattern, embroidery in various-coloured silks, gold thread, and coloured small beads. German, 14th century. 3¾ inches by 3¾ inches.

In most of its characters this end of a stole is just like those attached to the fine specimen noticed under No. 8588.

8566.

IECE of Silk Damask; ground, red; pattern, squares filled in alternately with a pair of animals and flower-like ornaments. Syrian, 13th century. 7 inches by 2 inches.

The old Persian tradition of the "hom" may be seen here dividing the two addorsed regardant lionesses, and the whole design is done with neatness.

8567.

IECE of Silk Damask; ground, red; pattern, two popinjays divided by a bowl or cup looking much like a crescent moon, in an octagonal frame-work, all yellow. Spanish, 13th century. 8¼ inches by 6 inches.

This stuff is of very light material, which has, however, kept its colour very well.

8568.

PIECE of Gold Tissue, embroidered with the needle; ground, gold; pattern, the Archangel Gabriel, with his head, hands, folds of his dress, and lines in his wings done by needle in different coloured silks. Italian, 14th century. 8¼ inches by 5 inches.

This beautiful and rare kind of textile, combined with needlework, merits the particular attention of those occupied with embroidery. The loom has done its part well; not so well, however, he or she who had to fill in the lines, especially the spaces for the hands and head, on which the features of the face are rather poorly marked.

8569.

TWO Portions (joined together) of Gold Tissue; ground, gold; pattern, in various-coloured silks, of birds, beasts, monsters, and foliage. English or French, 13th century. 13 inches by 2 inches.

Among the monsters, we have the usual heraldic ones that so often occur upon the textiles of that period; but the recurrence of the unmistakable form of the fleurs-de-lis, though sometimes coloured green, persuades us that this piece, entirely the produce of the loom, came from French, very likely Parisian hands, and was wrought for female use, as a band or fillet to confine the hair about the forehead, just as we see must have been the fashion in England at the time from the marked way in which that attire is shown in the illuminations of MSS. and sepulchral effigies of our Plantagenet epoch. Our countryman, John Garland, tells us, as we noticed in our Introduction, that women-weavers, in their time, wove such golden tissues, not only for ecclesiastical, but secular uses; and these two pieces seem to belong to the latter class.

8570.

PORTION of an Orphrey; ground, crimson silk; pattern, foliage with fruit and flowers in gold. German, 14th century. 9¼ inches by 3¼ inches.

F F

So sparingly was the gold twined about the yellow thread, and of such a debased amalgamation that it has almost entirely disappeared, or where it remains has turned black.

8571.

PORTION of Gold Tissue, figured with birds and beasts in gold upon a crimson ground. French or English, late 12th century. 9 inches by 2¼ inches.

When new this textile must have been very pretty; but so fugitive was its original crimson, that now it looks a lightish brown. Within circles, divided by a tree made to look like a floriated cross, stands a lion regardant, and upon the transverse limbs of the cross, as upon the boughs of a tree, are perched two doves; while the spandrils or spaces between the circles are filled in with fleurs-de-lis growing out of leafed stalks. Though, in after times, it may have been applied to church use, it seems, like the specimen under No. 8569, to have been at first intended for female dress, either as a girdle or head attire.

8572.

TWO Portions of Embroidery (joined together), the one showing, on a reddish purple silk ground, figures of birds and animals within circles, all embroidered in gold; the other, a similar ground and pattern within lozenges. German, 14th century. 2 feet 1¾ inches by 2 inches.

The figures are heraldic monsters with the exception of the three birds, and are all done with great freedom and spirit; like the preceding piece, this looks as if it had originally been wrought for a lady's girdle. The present two portions seem from the first to have formed parts of the same ornament, and to have been worked by the same needle.

8573.

SMALL Fragment of Red Silk, having a narrow border of purple with lozenge pattern, in gold. English or French, 13th century. 2 inches by ¾ inch.

Alike, in its original use, to the foregoing pieces.

8574.

WO Fragments (joined together) of Purple Silk, much faded, with a cotton woof. Byzantine, 12th century. 2¼ inches by 1¼ inches

8575.

WO Fragments (joined together) of Silk and Gold Tissue; ground, light crimson, now quite faded, bordered green; pattern, an interlacing strap-work, in gold. English or French, 13th century. 2 inches by 2 inches.

Like, for use, to the other similar specimens.

8576.

ERY small Fragment of Gold Tissue on a red ground. 13th century. 1¾ inches by ½ inch.

This cloth of gold must have been showy from its richness.

8577, 8577 A.

WO small Pieces of Silk, Tyrian purple. Byzantine, 12th century. Each 1¼ inches square.

8578, 8578 A.

TWO Rosettes, in small gold thread on deep purple silk, bordered by an edging of much lighter purple. 14th century. 1½ inches square; 1 inch square.

8579.

PIECE of Silk and Linen Damafk; ground, green; pattern, a monfter animal within a circle ftudded with full moons, and a fmaller circle holding a crefcent-moon ftudded in like manner. Syrian, 13th century. 1 foot 8¼ inches by 1 foot 2 inches.

This bold and effective defign is fomewhat curious, exhibiting, as it does, a novel fort of monfter which is made up of a dog's head and fore-paws, wings erect, and a broad turned-up bufhy tail freckled with fquares, in each of which is an ornament affecting fometimes the fhape of an L, fometimes of an F, at others of an A. Around the neck of this imaginary beaft is a collar which, as well as the root of the wing, fhows imitations of Arabic characters.

8580.

PORTION of Gold Embroidery; ground, dark blue filk; pattern, large griffins in gold. Early 13th century. 1 foot 4½ inches by 12½ inches.

Pity it is that we have fuch a fmall part, and that fo mutilated, of what muft have been fuch a fine fpecimen of the needle. Though the whole pattern may not be made out, enough remains to fhow that the griffins, which were langued *gules*, ftood in pairs and rampant, both figured with two-forked tails ending in trefoils, all worked in rich gold thread.

8581.

PORTION of an Orphrey; ground, crimfon filk; pattern, ftars of eight points, within fquares, both embroidered in gold. 14th century. 5½ inches by 2 inches.

This is one of the very few fpecimens which have pure gold, or perhaps only filver-gilt wire, without any admixture of thread in it, employed in the ftars and narrow oblong ornaments in the embroidery,

Needlework, and Dresses.

the wire itself being stitched to its grounding by thin linen thread. The large and small squares, as well as the borders, are executed in gold-twisted thread, very poor of its kind. The glittering effect of the pure metal-wire is very telling.

8582.

IECE of Silk Damask; ground, crimson; pattern, conventional peacocks and foliage, in yellow. Syrian, 13th century. 13 inches by 9¾ inches.

A good design bestowed upon very thin materials.

8583.

ORTION of Gold Tissue; ground, light crimson, now quite faded, edged green; pattern, a diaper of interlacing strap-work. English or French, 13th century. 2¼ inches by 1¼ inches.

8584.

ORTION of Gold Tissue; ground, green, edged crimson; pattern, lozenge-shaped diaper in gold. English or French, 13th century. 7¼ inches by 1 inch.

8585.

ORTION of Gold Tissue; ground, green, now quite faded; pattern, in gold, almost all worn away, a lozenge diaper. English or French, 13th century. 5 inches by 1¼ inches.

This, as well as the other two pieces immediately preceding, were woven by female hands for the binding of the hair.

8586.

FRAGMENT of Silk Tissue; ground, purple; pattern, small squares, green and black, enclosing a black disk voided in the middle. Byzantine (?), 12th century. 7 inches by 2 inches.

This stuff, which was thin in its new state, is now very tattered and its colours dimmed.

8587.

FRAGMENT of Silk Tissue; ground, purple; pattern, a rosette within a lozenge, with a floral border. Italian, 14th century. 4 inches by 2 inches.

8588.

STOLE of Gold Tissue, figured with small beasts, birds, and floriated ornaments, bordered on one side by a blue stripe edged with white and charged with ornamentation in gold, on the other, by a green one of a like character, as well as by two Latin inscriptions. The ends, four inches long, are of crimson silk, ornamented with seed-pearls, small red, blue, gold, yellow, and green beads, pieces of giltsilver, and have a fringe three inches long, red and green. Sicilian, 13th century. 6 feet by $3\frac{1}{4}$ inches.

As a piece of textile showing how the weavers of the middle ages could, when they needed, gear the loom for an intricacy of pattern in animals as well as inscriptions, this rich cloth of gold is a valuable specimen. Among the ornaments on the middle band we find doves, harts, the letter M floriated, winged lions, crosses floriated, crosses sprouting out on two sides with fleurs-de-lis, four-legged monsters, some like winged lions, some biting their tails, doves in pairs upholding a cross, &c; and above and below these, divided from them by gracefully ornamented bars, one blue the other green, may be read this inscription,—"O spes divina, via tuta, potens medicina ✠ Porrige subsidium, O Sancta Maria, corp. (*sic*) consortem sancte fortis patrone ministram. ✠ Effice Corneli meeritis (*sic*) prece regna meri. ✠ O celi porta, nova spes mor. (*sic*) protege, salva, benedic, sanctifica famulum tuum Alebertum crucis per sinnaculum (*sic*) morbos averte corporis et anime. Hoc contra signum nullum stet periculum. ✠ O clemen. (*sic*) Domina spes defe'erantibus una."

The ends of this stole, German work of the 14th century, widen like most others of the period, and in their original state seem to have been studded with small precious stones, the sockets for which are very discernible amid the beads; and in each centre must have been let in a tiny illumination, as one still is there showing the Blessed Virgin Mary with our Lord, as a child, in her arms; and this appears to have been covered with glass. Amid the beads are yet a few thick silver-gilt spangles wrought like six-petaled flowers. As a stole, the present one is very short, owing, no doubt, to a scanty length of the gold tissue; in fact, it might easily be taken for a long maniple. When it is remembered that the Suabian house of Hohenstaufen reigned in Sicily for many years, till overthrown in the person of the young Conradin, at the battle of Tagliacozzo, by the French Charles of Anjou, A.D. 1268, we can easily account for Sicilian textiles of all sorts finding their way, during the period, into Germany. In his "Geschichte der Liturgischen Gewänder des Mittelalters," 4 Lieferung, pt. xviii. fig. 3, Dr. Bock has given a figure of this stole.

8589.

PIECE of Silk and Linen Tissue; ground, yellow, with a band of crimson; pattern, crowned kings on horseback amid foliage, each holding on his wrist a hawk, and having a small dog on the crupper of his saddle. Sicilian, early 13th century. 1 foot 4⅜ inches by 7 inches.

From a small piece to the left, figured with what looks like an English bloodhound or talbot, it would seem that we have not the full design in the pattern of this curious stuff, which speaks so loudly of the feudalism of mediæval Italy and other continental countries. Seldom was a king then figured without his crown, besides carrying his hawk on hand and being followed by his dogs, like any other lord of the land.

The little hound behind him is somewhat singular. To us it appears curious that such an elaborate and princely design, meant evidently for the hangings of some palace, should have been done in the rather mean materials which we find. Parts seem to have been woven in gold thread; but so thin and debased was the metal that it is now quite black, and the linen warp far outweighs the thin silken woof.

8590.

PIECE of Silk Tissue; ground, green; pattern, a so-called pomegranate of elaborate form, amid flowers of white and light purple, now faded, both largely wrought in gold. Spanish, 15th century. 1 foot 11 inches by 1 foot 2 inches.

Not only is the design of the pattern very effective, but the gold, in which the far larger part of it is done, looks bright and rather rich; yet, by examining it with a powerful glass, we may discover an ingenious, not to say trickish, way for imitating gold-covered thread. Skins of thin vellum were gilt, and not very thickly; these were cut into very narrow filament-like shreds, and in this form—that is, flat with the shining side facing the eye—afterwards woven into the pattern as if they were thread, a trick in trade which the Spaniards learned from the Moors.

The warp is of a poor kind of silk not unlike jute, and the woof is partly of cotton, partly linen thread, so that with its mock gold filaments we have a showy textile out of cheap materials; a valuable specimen of the same sort of stuff from a Saracenic loom will be found under No. 8639, &c.

8591, 8591 A.

TWO Pieces of Silk Tissue; ground, a bright green; pattern, not complete, but showing a well-managed ornamentation, consisting of the so-called pomegranate with two giraffes below, the heads of which are in gold, now so

Needlework, and Dresses. 225

faded as to look a purplish black. Sicilian, early 14th century.
7½ inches by 4¾ inches; 4¾ inches by 4¼ inches.

This is a specimen interesting for several reasons. When new and fresh, this stuff must have been very pleasing; the elaborate design of its pattern, done in a cheerful spring-like tone of green upon a ground of a much lighter shade of the same colour, makes it welcome to the eye. The giraffes, tripping and addorsed, with their long necks and parded skins, have something like a housing on their backs. From such a quadruped being figured on this stuff, he who drew the design must have lived in Africa, or have heard of the animal from the Moors; he must have been a Christian, too, for green being Mohammed's own colour, and even still limited, in its use, to his descendants, no Saracenic loom would have figured this stuff with a forbidden form of an animal. Yet, withal, there may be seen upon it strong traces of Saracenic feeling in its pattern. That singular ornament, made up of long zero-like forms placed four together in three rows, which we find upon other examples in this curious collection (No. 8596, &c), seems distinctive of some particular locality; so that we may presume this fine textile to have been wrought at the royal manufactory of Palermo, where the giraffe might have been well known, where Saracenic art-traditions a long time lingered; and people cared nothing for the prohibition of figuring any created form, or of wearing green in their garments, or hanging their walls with silks dyed green; in some specimens the zero-like ornamentation takes the shape of our letter U; moreover the large feathers in the bird's long tail are sometimes so figured.

8592.

IECE of Silk Damask; ground, red; pattern, the castle of Castile and fleur-de-lis, both in yellow. Spanish, 13th century. 10 inches by 6¼ inches.

Though of poor and somewhat flimsy silk, this stuff is not without some merit, as it shows how exact were the workmen of those days to be guided by rule in the choice of colour; for instance, the tinctures here are correct, so far that metal *or* is put upon colour *gules*. It was woven in stripes marked by narrow blue lines.

G G

8593.

PORTION of some Liturgic Ornament (?); ground, deep blue; pattern, fleurs-de-lis embroidered in gold. French, 14th century. 7 inches by 3¼ inches.

Whether this fragment once formed a part of maniple, stole, or orphrey for chasuble, cope, dalmatic, or tunicle, it is impossible to say; heraldically it is quite correct in its tincture, and that is its only merit.

8594.

PIECE of Silk Damask; ground, fawn-colour; pattern, birds and beasts amid foliage, all in green. Sicilian, early 14th century. 10¼ inches by 4 inches.

Though every part of the design in the pattern of this charming stuff is rather small, the whole is admirably clear and well rendered, and we see a pair of hawks perched, a pair of lions passant, a pair of stags tripping, a pair of birds (heads reversed), a pair of monster-birds (perhaps wyverns), and a pair of eagles (much defaced) with wings displayed. The lions are particularly well drawn.

8595.

FRAGMENT of Silk Tissue; ground, crimson and gold, with three white and green narrow stripes running down the middle, and an inscription on each side the stripes. Spanish, 14th century. 7 inches by 6 inches.

The warp is of thick cotton thread, the woof of silk and gold. Though very much broken, the inscription is Latin, and gives but a very few entire words, such as "et tui amoris in eis," with these fragments, "—tus. Re— —le tuoru—." From this, however, we are warranted in thinking this textile to have been wrought, not for any vestment—for it is too thick, except for an orphrey—but rather for hangings about the chancel at Whitsuntide. See Introduction, § 5.

8596.

IECE of Silk Damafk; ground, light crimfon; pattern, in deep brown, vine-leaves within an ellipfis which has on the outer edge a crocket-like ornamentation, and on both fides a clufter as if of the letter U, arranged four in a row, one row above the other. Sicilian, 14th century. 8½ inches by 6 inches.

As we faw in Nos. 8591, 8591 A, fo here we fee that very curious and not ufual ornamentation, in the former inftances like an O or zero, in the prefent one like another letter, U. The fame crifpinefs in the foliage may be obferved here as there; and in all likelihood both filks iffued from the fame city, perhaps from the fame loom, but at different periods, as the one before us does not come up, by any means, in beauty with thofe fragments at Nos. 8591, 8591 A. In fome inftances the feathers in a bird's tail are made in the fhape of our capital letter U.

8597.

IECE of Silk Damafk; ground, blackifh purple; pattern, conventional foliage in greyifh purple. Italian, 14th century. 1 foot 8 inches by 1 foot 6 inches.

The foliage, fo free and bold, is quite of an architectural character, and fhows a leaning to that peculiar fcroll-form fo generally to be feen on Greek fictile vafes. Perhaps this ftuff was wrought at Reggio in South Italy; but evidently for fecular, not ecclefiaftical ufe.

8598.

IECE of Silk Damafk; ground, purple; pattern, large monfter birds, and, within ovals, fmaller beafts, all in gold thread, relieved with green filk. Sicilian, 14th century. 2 feet 4 inches by 10 inches.

The defign is bold and very effective, and confifts of an oval bordered very much in the Saracenic ftyle, within which are two leopards addorfed rampant regardant. Above this oval ftand two wyverns with heads averted and langued green or *vert*. This alternates with another oval enclofing two dog-like creatures rampant addorfed regardant; above this two imaginary birds, well crefted, langued *vert*, with heads averted, and feem to be of the cockatoo family. From the fhape of this piece, as we now have it, no doubt its laft ufe was for a chafuble, but of a very recent make and period; and fadly cut away at its fides.

8599.

PIECE of Silk Damafk; ground, green; pattern, in light purple or violet, an ellipfis filled in with Saracenic ornamentation, having below two fplit pomegranates in gold, and above, two giraffes, which alternate with a pair of long-necked gold-headed birds that are flanked by an ornament made up of letters like U. Sicilian, 14th century. 1 foot 10¼ inches by 2 feet 2 inches.

Though this fpecimen has been fadly ill-ufed by time, and made out of feveral fhreds, it evidently came from the hands that defigned and wrought other pieces (Nos. 8591, 8591 A, 8596) in this collection. Upon this, as upon them, we have the fame elements in the pattern— the ellipfis, the giraffes, and that fingular kind of ornamentation, a fort of letter U or flattened O, not put in for any imaginary beauty of form, but to indicate either place or manufacturer, being a fymbol which we have yet to learn how to read and underftand. That in time we fhall be able to find out its meanings there can be little or no doubt.

Though of fo pleafing and elaborate a defign, the ftuff, in its materials, is none of the richeft.

8600.

PIECE of Silk Damafk; ground, yellow; the pattern, in violet, an ellipfis filled in with Saracenic ornamentation. Sicilian, 14th century. 10 inches by 2¼ inches.

There can be little doubt that this inferior textile, fhowing, as it does, the fame feelings in its pattern, came from Palermo.

8601.

PIECE of Silk Damaſk; ground, yellow; pattern, a broad ſtripe of gold with narrow ſtripes, two in green, two in blue, and yellow bands charged with birds and flowers in gold. Spaniſh, late 14th century. 13 inches by 8 inches.

The narrow ſtripes running down the broad one, and conſtituting its deſign, are ornamented with ſquare knots of three interlacings and a ſaltire of St. Andrew's croſs alternatingly. The bands diſplay birds of the waterfowl genus—a kind of creſted wild-duck—very gracefully figured as pecking at flowers, one of which ſeems of the water-lily tribe.

Here, as at No. 8590, we have the ſame ſubſtitution for gold thread, of gilt vellum cut into thread-like filaments, and ſo woven up with the ſilk and cotton of which the warp and woof are compoſed. This, like its ſiſter ſpecimen, ſo ſhowy, is juſt as poor in material; and, from its thinneſs, it may have ſerved not ſo much for an article of dreſs as for hangings in churches and ſtate apartments.

8602, 8602 A, B, C, D, E.

SIX Fragments of Silk Damaſk; ground, fawn-colour; pattern, a floriated ellipſis encloſing a pair of eagles, with foliage between the elliptical figures. Sicilian, 14th century. Dimenſions, all ſmall and various.

In many reſpects theſe fragments of the ſame piece of tiſſue cloſely reſemble the fine ſtuff under No. 8594; the ground, fawn-colour, is the ſame; the ſame too—green, and of the ſame pleaſing tone—is the colour of its pattern, which, however, gives us the peculiarity of a knot of two interlacings plentifully ſtrewed amid the foliage. It is ſlightly freckled, too, with white.

8603.

PIECE of Silk Damaſk; ground, fawn-colour; pattern, birds in pairs amid foliage (all green) and flowers, ſome blue, ſome gold, now faded black. Italian, 14th century. 18 inches by 12¾ inches.

Not a ſatisfactory deſign, as the birds are in green and hard to be diſtinguiſhed from the heavy foliage in which they are placed. The materials, too, are poor and thin, the warp being cotton.

8604.

FRAGMENT of Silk Damaſk; ground, deep fawn-colour; pattern, birds pecking at a flower-ſtem amid foliage, all yellow, occaſionally ſhaded deep green. Sicilian, 14th century. 6½ inches by 4¾ inches.

As far as it goes, the deſign is neat and flowing, with the peculiarity of the deep green, now almoſt blue, ſhadings both in the birds and foliage. The warp is fine cotton, and the whole ſpeaks of a Sicilian origin.

8605.

PIECE of Damaſk; ground, light purple; pattern, in yellow, a net-like broad ribbon, within the meſhes of which are eight-petaled conventional flowers. Italian, 14th century.

The texture of the ſpecimen is ſomewhat thin, but the tones of its two harmonious colours are good, and its pattern, in all its parts, extremely agreeable; upon thoſe broad ribbon lines of the net, the branches, ſprouting out into trefoils, are gracefully made to twine; and an inclination to figure a crowned M on every petal of the flower inſide the meſhes is very diſcernible. Poſſibly Reggio, ſouth of Naples, is the town where this ſhowy ſtuff was wrought, ſerviceable alike for ſacred and ſecular employment.

SILK DAMASK
Damas. 14th century

8606.

IECE of Silk Damask; ground, black; pattern, not easily discernible, though evidently elaborate. Italian, 14th century. 10 inches by 6¼ inches.

So much has damp injured this piece that its original black has become almost brown, and its pattern is well nigh gone. In its fresh state, however, the design, traces of which show it to have been sketched in the country and about the time mentioned, was thrown up satisfactorily, for it was woven in cotton from the silken ground of the piece.

8607.

IECE of Silk Damask; ground, fawn-colour; pattern, trefoils and vine-leaves, in green. Sicilian, 14th century. 8¾ inches by 4½ inches.

Like all the other specimens of this kind, the present one is pleasing in its combination of those favourite colours— fawn and light green— as well as being remarkable for the elegance with which the foliage is made to twine about its surface; the materials, too, are thick and lasting.

8608.

FRAGMENT of Silk Damask; ground, dark blue; pattern (very imperfect in the specimen), an ellipsis filled in with ornamentation and topped by a floriation, out of which issue birds' necks and heads, all in lighter blue, edged with white, and two conventional wild animals in gold, but now black with tarnish. Sicilian, 14th century. 6 inches by 6 inches.

8609.

PIECE of Silk Damask; ground, fawn-colour; pattern, wreaths of white flowers, green boughs bearing white flowers, forming part of a design in which an ellipsis in green constitutes a leading portion; and a broad band figured with scroll-work and an Arabic sentence, all in gold. Sicilian, 13th century. 1 foot 5¾ inches by 5¾ inches.

Probably in the sample before us we behold a work from the royal looms or "tiraz"—silk-house—of Palermo, when Sicily was under the sway of France, in the person of a prince belonging to the house of Anjou. In the first place, we have the fawn—a tone of the murrey colour of our old English writers—and the light joyous green; in the second place, the ellipsis was there, though our specimen is too small to show it all. Those narrow borders that edge the large golden lettered band present us with a row of golden half-moons and blue fleurs-de-lis on one side; on the other, a row of golden half-moons and blue crosscrosslets: on the band itself we find, alternating with foliage, an oblong square, within which is written a short sentence in Arabic—a kindly word, a wish of health and happiness to the wearer—such as was, and still is, the custom among the Arabs. Sure is it that this textile, if wrought by Saracenic hands, was done under a Christian prince, and that prince a Frenchman.

8610.

PIECE of Silk Damask; ground, fawn-colour; pattern, birds and dogs in green. Sicilian, 14th century. 1 foot 4½ inches by 10¼ inches.

Like so many other specimens of the Palermitan loom, both in colours and design, this piece is rather poor in its silk, which is harsh and somewhat thin. The birds are a swan ruffling up its feathers at the presence of an eagle perched just overhead, amid branches and foliage in which the trefoil abounds.

8611.

IECE of Silk Damaſk; ground, red; pattern, foliage in green, wild dogs in blue, gold, and white. South Italian, 14th century. 15 inches by 12½ inches.

The wild dogs are ſegeant face to face, in pairs; one blue, the other gold; one white, the other gold: and below are flowers blue, gold, and white, alternating like the animals. The warp is cotton, the woof ſilk, and altogether the ſtuff is coarſe.

8612.

RAGMENTS of Silk Damaſk; ground, black; pattern, a tower ſurrounded by water and a figure holding a hawk, and hawks perched, in pairs, on trees. Italian, 15th century. 9 inches by 5½ inches; 9 inches by 4¼ inches.

Pity that this curious piece is ſo fragmental and decayed that its ſingular deſign cannot, as in another ſpecimen of the very ſame tiſſue, all be made out. Whether it be man or woman ſtanding on high outſide the tower with a bird at reſt on the wriſt is here hard to ſay. The caſtle is well ſhown, with its moat, and its draw-bridges—for it has more than one—all down. Like No. 8606, it ſhows its pattern by the difference of material in the warp and woof. All over it has been thickly ſprinkled with thin gilt trefoils that were not ſewed but glued on; many have fallen off, and thoſe remaining have turned black. See No. 7065.

8613.

IECE of Silk Damaſk; ground, black; pattern, in gold thread, birds amid foliage. Italian, 14th century. 14 inches by 7¼ inches.

The bold and facile pattern of this piece is very conſpicuous, with its eagles ſtooping upon long-necked birds perched on waving boughs; to much beauty in deſign it adds, moreover, richneſs in material.

8614.

PIECE of Silk Damask; ground, light brown; pattern, the same colour, palmettes and rosettes, with Arabic sentences repeated. Attached is a piece of green silk wrought with gold. Sicilian, 14th century. 16¼ inches by 15½ inches.

A quiet but rich stuff, and especially noticeable for its Arabic or imitated Arabic inscriptions, one within the rosettes, the other all round the inner border of the palmettes or elliptical ornamentations. The cloth of gold is plain.

8615.

PIECE of Linen, block-printed in a pattern composed of birds and foliage. Flemish, late 14th century. 1 foot 9 inches by 3 inches.

Of this kind of block-printed linen, with its graceful design in black upon a white ground, there are other good examples (Nos. 7027 and 8303) in this collection. From the marks of use upon its canvas lining, this long narrow strip would seem to have once served as an apparel to an amice in some poor church.

8616.

PORTIONS of Crimson Silk, brocaded in gold; the pattern, angels holding crescents beneath crowns, from which come rays of glory, and hunting leopards seizing on gazelles. Italian, end of 14th century. 2 feet 8¾ inches by 2 feet.

This rich stuff betrays in its design an odd mixture of Asiatic and European feeling; we have the eastern hunting lion spotted and collared blue, pouncing on the gazelle or antelope, which is collared too; so far we have the imitation, but without lettering, of a Persian or Asiatic pattern. With this we find European, or at least Christian, angels, clothed in white, but with such curious nebule-nimbs about their heads as to make their brows look horned, more like spirits of evil than of good. The open crowns are thoroughly after a western design; and the head and shoulders of a winged figure, to the left, show that we have not the entire design before us. From the graceful way in which the figures are made to float, as well as from several little things about the scrolls, we may safely conclude that the designer of the pattern lived in upper Italy, and that this costly and elegant brocade was wrought at Lucca. Of the Oriental elements of this pattern we have said a few words at No. 8288.

8617.

STOLE of deep purple silk, brocaded in gold and crimson; pattern, a long flower-bearing stem, and large flowers. Italian, early 15th century. 9 feet 6 inches by 4 inches.

Like all the old stoles, this is so long as almost to reach down to the feet, and is rather broader than usual, but does not widen at the ends, which have a long green fringe. The stuff is of a rich texture, and the pattern good.

8618.

PART of a Linen Cloth, embroidered with sacred subjects, and inscribed with the names, in Latin, of the Evangelists. German, end of the 14th century. 6 feet by 4 feet.

Unfortunately, this curious and very valuable sample of Rhenish needlework is far from being complete, and has lost a good part of its original composition on its edges, but much more lamentably on the right hand side. Not for a moment can we think it to have been an altar-cloth properly so-called, that is, for spreading out over the table itself of the altar; but, in all likelihood, it was used as a reredos or ornament over but behind the altar, as a covering for the wall. Another beautiful specimen of the same kind has been already noticed under

No. 8358, for throwing over the deacon's and subdeacon's lectern at high mass; and, from the fact that, in both instances, the subjects figured are in especial honour of the B. V. Mary, it would seem that, in many German churches, and following a very ancient tradition that the Blessed Virgin wrought during all her girlhood days ornaments for the Temple of Jerusalem with her needle, the custom was to have for the "Mary Mass," and for altars dedicated under her name, as many liturgical appliances as might be of this sort of white needlework, and done by maidens' hands.

In the centre we have the coronation of the B. V. Mary, executed after the ordinary fashion, with her hair falling down her shoulders, and a crown upon her head; she is sitting with arms uplifted in prayer, upon a Gothic throne, by her Divine Son, who, while holding the mund in His left, is blessing His mother with raised right hand; overhead is hovering an angel with a thurible; at each of the four corners is an Evangelist represented, not only by his usual emblem, but announced by his name in Latin. At first sight the angel, the emblem of St. Matthew might be taken for Gabriel announcing the Incarnation to the B. V. Mary. Above and around are circles formed of the Northern Kraken, four in number, put in orb, and running round an elaborately floriated Greek cross, symbolizing the victory of Christianity over heathenism. In many places, within a gracefully twining wreath of trefoil leaves and roses barbed, is the letter G, very probably the initial of the fair hand who wrought and gave this beautiful work to our Lady's altar; and the spaces between the subjects are filled in with well-managed branches of the oak bearing acorns. To the left is seen a hind or countryman hooded, carrying, hung down from a long club borne on his shoulder, a dead hare; and further on, still to the left, an old man who with a lance is trying to slay an unicorn that is running at full speed to a maiden who is sitting with her hair hanging about her shoulders, and stroking the forehead of the animal with her left hand. The symbolism of this curious group, not often to be met with, significative of the mystery of the Incarnation, is thus explained by the Anglo-Norman poet, Phillippe de Thaun, who wrote his valuable " Bestiary " in England for the instruction of his patroness, Adelaide of Louvaine, Queen to our Henry I :—" Monoceros is an animal which has one horn on its head; it is caught by means of a virgin: now hear in what manner. When a man intends to hunt it and to take and ensnare it, he goes to the forest where is its repair, there he places a virgin with her breast uncovered, and by its smell the monoceros perceives it; then it comes to the virgin and kisses her breast, falls asleep on her lap, and so comes to its death: the man arrives immediately, and kills it in its sleep, or takes it alive and does as he likes with it. . . . A beast of this description signifies Jesus Christ; one God he is and shall be, and was and will continue so; he placed himself in the virgin, and took flesh for man's sake: a virgin she is and will be, and will always remain. This animal in truth signifies God; know that the virgin signifies St. Marye; by her breast we understand similarly Holy Church; and then by the kiss it ought to signify that a man when he sleeps is in semblance of death; God slept as a man, who suffered death on the cross, and His destruction was our redemption, and His labour our repose," &c.—" Popular Treatises on Science written during the Middle Ages, &c, and edited for the Historical Society of Science by T. Wright," pp. 81, 82.

The figure of the countryman carrying off the hare is brought forward in illustration. As the rough coarse clown, prowling about the lands of his lord, wilily entraps the hare in his hidden snares, so does the devil, by allurements to sin, strive to catch the soul of man. These interesting symbolisms end the left-hand portion of the reredos. Going to the right, we find that part torn and injured in such a way that it is evidently shorn of its due portions, and much of the original so completely gone that we are unable to hazard a conjecture about the subject which was figured there.

8619.

PIECE of Silk Damask; ground, rose-coloured; pattern, peacocks, eagles, a small nondescript animal, and a lyre-shaped ornament, all in green, touched with white. Italian, late 14th century. 11 inches by 10½ inches.

A curious design, in which the birds are boldly and freely drawn. Each horn of the lyre-shaped ornament ends, bending outwardly with what to herald's eyes seems to be two wings conjoined erect.

8620.

PIECE of Silk and Gold Damask; ground, dark blue, in some places faded; pattern, a band charged with squares in gold, every alternate one inscribed with the same short Arabic word, lions in gold beneath a tree in light blue shaded white, and cockatoos in gold. Syrian, 14th century. 19 inches by 13¼ inches.

So strong is the likeness between this and the stuff at No. 8359, both in the texture of the silk and the treatment of the beasts and birds, that we are led to suppose them to have come from the same identical workshop. That tree-like ornament, under which the shaggy long-tailed lion with down-bent head is creeping, seems the traditionary form of the Persians' "hom." The gold is, in most parts, very brilliant, owing to the broadness of the metal wrapped round the linen thread that holds it; and, altogether, this is a rich specimen of the Syrian loom.

8621.

PIECE of Silk Damask; ground, fawn-colour; pattern, foliage in green, flowers, some white, some in gold, and lions in gold. Sicilian, late 14th century. 22½ inches by 10 inches.

The warp is of linen, and the silken woof is thin; so sparingly was the gold bestowed, that it has almost entirely faded; altogether, this specimen shows a good design wasted upon very poor materials. In the expanding part of the foliage there seems to be a slight remembrance of the fleur-de-lis pattern, and the lions are sejant addorsed regardant.

8622, 8623.

TWO Portions of Silk Damask; in both, the ground, fawn-colour; the pattern, in the one, ramified foliage, amid which two lions sejant regardant, in gold; in the other, two eagles at rest regardant, in green, divided by a large green conventional flower, including another such flower in gold. Sicilian, 14th century. 11 inches by 5¼ inches; 9¼ inches by 4¾ inches.

Very likely from the same loom as No. 8621, and every way corresponding to it.

SILK DAMASK

8624.

IECE of Silk Damafk; ground, pale brown; pattern, in a lighter tone, ftags and funbeams, and below eagles within hexagonal compartments. Sicilian, late 14th century. 18 inches by 14 inches.

The ftags, well attired, are in pairs, couchant, chained, with heads upturned to funbeams darting down on them, with fpots like rain coming amid thefe rays; beneath thefe ftags are eagles. The material is very thin and poor for fuch a pleafing defign. In a much richer material part of this fame pattern is to be feen at No. 1310.

8625.

IECE of very fine Linen. Oriental. 2 feet 4 inches by 1 foot 5 inches.

This is another of thofe remarkably delicate textiles for which Egypt of old was, and India for ages has been, fo celebrated. A fine fpecimen has been already noticed at No. 8230; but to indicate the country or the period of either would be but hazarding a conjecture. Surplices were often made of fuch fine tranfparent linen, as is fhown by illuminated MSS. See "Church of our Fathers," t. ii. p. 20.

8626.

IECE of Silk Damafk; ground, fawn-colour; pattern, flowers and birds, both in green. Italian, end of 14th century. 11 inches by 8½ inches.

The birds are in two pairs, one at reft, the other on the wing darting down; between them is an ornament fomewhat heart-fhaped, around which runs an infcription of imitated Arabic. Moft likely this filk is of Sicilian work.

8627.

PIECE of Silk Damaſk; ground, dark blue; pattern, lozenge-ſhaped compartments, filled in with quadrangular deſigns varying alternately. Spaniſh, late 14th century. 10¼ inches by 8 inches.

There is a Mooriſh influence in the deſign, which leads to the ſuppoſition that this ſtuff was wrought ſomewhere in the South of Spain.

8628, 8628 A.

TWO Fragments of Silk Damaſk; ground, light yellow; pattern, flowers and birds, with the letters A and M crowned, all in pale red. Italian, late 14th century. 6 inches by 5 inches; 6 inches by 3½ inches.

A very pleaſing deſign, in nicely toned colours, and evidently wrought for hangings, or perhaps curtains, about the altar of the B. V. Mary, as we have the whole ſprinkled with the crowned letters A M, ſignificative of " Ave Maria."

8629.

FRAGMENT of Silk Damaſk; ground, purple; pattern, four green hares in a park walled, with conventional flowers, yellow. Italian, late 14th century. 5 inches by 4¾ inches.

The colours, both of the ground and deſign, of this piece are much faded, ſo that it becomes hard, at firſt ſight, to make out the pattern, eſpecially the four green hares tripping within a park, which, inſtead of being ſhown with pales, has a wall round it.

8630.

FRAGMENT of Silk Damask; ground, red; pattern, foliage and flowers in green, with animals, alternately in gold and dark blue. Italian, late 14th century. 5 inches by 4 inches.

Though the materials be thin, the design is interesting and displays taste. The animals, seemingly fawns, are lodged, but so sparingly was the gold bestowed upon its cotton thread that it has almost entirely disappeared from the would-be golden deer.

8631.

FRAGMENT of Silk Damask; ground, deep purple; pattern, a circle inclosing a heart-shaped floral ornament, in red, with an indistinct ornament, once gold. South of Spain, 14th century. $6\frac{1}{4}$ inches by $5\frac{1}{2}$ inches.

The colours of what may have been a rich stuff, as well as the brightness of the gold, are much dulled.

8632.

PIECE of Silk Damask; ground, pale yellow; pattern, vine-leaves and grapes, with the letter A, all in light purple. Italian, late 14th century. $11\frac{3}{4}$ inches by 3 inches.

One of those cheerful designs which are to be found in this collection; and had the specimen been larger, very likely an M would have been shown under the A.

8633.

PIECE of Silk Damask; ground, purple; pattern, within interlacing strapwork forming a square, two parrots addorsed alternating with two dogs addorsed, all yellow, with ornamentations of small circles and flowers, once gold, but now so tarnished that they look black. Sicilian, 14th century. 5¼ inches by 5 inches.

One of those specimens which will be sought by those who want examples of stuffs figured with animals. This stuff is shewn in Dr. Bock's "Deſſinateur pour Etoffes," &c. 3 Livraiſon.

8634.

PIECE of Silk Damaſk; ground, fawn and green; pattern, ſmall ſquares encloſing leaves, birds, and beaſts alternately. Italian, 14th century. 7¼ inches by 3 inches.

Though ſmall, the pattern is good and comes from either a Sicilian or a Reggio loom. Lions, and ſtags with branching horns, eagles, parrots, and undecipherable birds, in braces with necks croſſing one another, are to be found upon it; among the foliage the vine-leaf prevails.

8635.

ALTAR Frontal of Linen, embroidered with the filfot in white thread freckled with ſpots in blue and green ſilk, and lozenge-ſhaped ornaments in blue, green, and crimſon ſilk. German, 14th century. 3 feet 10 inches ſquare.

There can be little doubt but this piece of needlework was originally meant for an altar frontal, and its curious but coarſer lining, may have been wrought for the ſame ſeparate but diſtinct purpoſe. The filfot or gammadion, a favourite object upon veſtments, is its chief adornment, while its lining, a work of a century later, is worked with a palm-like deſign in thick linen thread. At a later time, it ſeems to have been employed as a covering to the table itſelf of the altar, and is plentifully ſprinkled with ſpots of wax-droppings.

8636.

PIECE of Linen Cloth, embroidered with filfots, ſome in white, ſome in blue ſilk. German, 14th century. 1 foot 11 inches by 9 inches.

Needlework, and Dresses. 243

This handsome piece of napery was evidently woven for the service of the church, and may have been intended either for frontals to hang in front of the altar, or as curtains to be suspended away from, but yet close to, the altar-table on the north and south sides. The favourite gammadion appears both in the pattern of the loom-work and in the embroideries wrought by hand, sometimes in blue, sometimes in white silk, upon it.

8637.

PIECE of Silk and Gold Damask; ground, green; pattern, flower-bearing stems, in gold, amid foliated tracery of a deep green tone, all enclosed by a golden elliptical border. Italian, early 15th century. 11½ inches by 7¼ inches.

This rich and pleasing stuff is most likely from the loom of some workshop in Lucca and was manufactured for secular purposes, and deserves attention not only for the goodness of its materials, but for the beauty of its design.

8638.

PIECE of Thread and Silk Damask; ground, purple slightly mixed with crimson; pattern, vine-branches bearing grapes and tendrils all in green, amid which are wyverns in gold, langued green. South Italian, 15th century. 1 foot 1 inch by 9¾ inches.

The warp is of thread, and the woof of silk. Such was the poverty of the gold thread in the wyverns, that it has almost entirely dropped off or turned black. This specimen shows how, sometimes, a rich pattern was thrown away upon mean materials. Its uses seem to have been secular.

8639.

PIECE of Silk Damask; ground, gold; pattern, a circle showing, in its lower half, a crescent moon and an eight-petaled flower, in the round centre of which is an Arabic inscription, all in black, and the spaces filled in with a

Saracenic scroll in light blue, light green, and crimson (now faded). Moresco-Spanish, 14th century. 1 foot 1¾ inches by 5¾ inches.

This unmistakeable specimen of a Saracenic loom would seem to have been wrought somewhere in the south of Spain, may be at Granada, Seville, or Cordova.

As a sample of its kind it is valuable, showing, as it does, that the same feelings which manifested themselves upon Moorish ornamentation for architecture were displayed in the patterns of textiles among that people. The fraud, so to say, of gilt shreds of parchment for threads covered with gold is exemplified here; and hence we may gather that the Spaniards of the mediæval period learned this trick from their Saracenic teachers in the arts of the loom. As in No. 8590, &c, so here, the gold ground is wrought, not in thread twined with gold foil, but with gilt vellum cut into very narrow filaments, and worked into the warp so as to lie quite flat.

8640.

PIECE of Silk Damask; ground, light blue; pattern, a circle elaborately filled in with a wreath of leaves edged with a hoop of fleur-de-lis, and enclosed in an oblong garland made up of boughs and flowers, in a slightly deeper tone of the same blue. Italian, early 15th century. 1 foot by 8¼ inches.

So very like in design to No. 8637, that we may presume it to have been wrought at Lucca.

8641.

PART of an Orphrey; ground, once crimson, but now faded to a light brown colour; pattern, quatrefoils, with angles between the leaves, embroidered with male saints in various colours upon a golden ground. Each quatrefoil is separated by a knot of three interlacings, and the sides filled in with a pair of popinjays, gold and green, and two boughs of the oak bearing acorns, alternately. On both fides runs a border formed of a fcroll of vine-leaves, done alternately in gold and filver, upon a green filk ground. North Italian, 15th century. 2 feet 7 inches by 5⅓ inches.

The whole of this elaborate piece of needlework has been done with much care, and in rich materials; but as the faints have no peculiar emblems given them, their identification is beyond hope. Whether for cope or chafuble—for it might have ferved for either veftment—this embroidery muft have been very effective, from the bold raifed nature of much of its ornamentation.

8642, 8642 A.

TWO Pieces of Silk Damafk; ground, green and fawn; pattern, intertwining branches of the vine, with bunches of grapes. Sicilian, 14th century. 9¾ inches by 4½ inches; 6 inches by 4 inches.

Another of thofe graceful green and fawn-coloured filks almoft identical in pattern with others we have feen from the fame country.

8643.

PIECE of Network; ground, reticulated pale brown filk; pattern, a fort of lozenge, in green and in brown filk, hand-embroidered. German, 14th century. 7 inches by 5 inches.

From the circular fhape of this piece it feems to have been a portion of female attire, moft likely for the fhoulders. One of its ornaments looks very like a modification of one form of the heraldic mill-rind, with the angular ftructure.

8644.

PORTION of an Orphrey; ground, gold; pattern, a fhield of arms, and an infcription in purple letters, repeated. German, 15th century. 1 foot 9 inches by 2¼ inches.

This specimen of the German loom may have been woven at Cologne, probably for the narrow orphreys of a whole set of vestments given to the church by some Duchess of Cleves, of the name of Elizabeth Vancleve, since, to such a lady, the blazon and the inscription point. The shield is party per pale *gules*, an escarbuncle *or*, and *purpure*, a lion rampant *argent*, barred *gules*, ducally crowned and armed *or*.

8645.

PIECE of Linen; ground, light brown; pattern, small blue squares or lozenges, separated into broad bands by narrow stripes, once ornamented with green lozenges and bordered all along by red lines. German, 15th century. 1 foot by 7 inches.

The warp and woof are linen thread; the green of the narrow stripes, from the small remains, appears to have been woollen.

8646.

FRAGMENT of a Piece of Silk and Gold Embroidery on Linen; ground, as it now looks, yellow; pattern, interlacing strapwork, forming spaces charged with the armorial bearings of England, and other blazons, rudely worked. 14th century. 5 inches by 3¼ inches.

So faded are the silks, and so tarnished the gold thread used for the embroidery of this piece, that, at first sight, the tinctures of the blazon are not discernible. In the centre we have the three golden libards or lions of England, and the silk of the ground or field, on narrow examination, we find to have been scarlet or *gules*; immediately below is a shield quarterly, 1 and 4 *or*, a lion rampant *gules*, 2 and 3 *sable*, a lion rampant *or*; immediately above, a shield *gules*, with three pales *azure* (?), each charged with what are seemingly tall crosses (St. Anthony's) *or*; above, the shield of England; but to the right hand, on a field barry of twelve *azure* and *or*, a lion rampant *gules*; below this shield, another, on a field *or*, two bars *sable*; these two shields alternate on the other side. The strapwork all about is fretty *or*, on a field *gules*.

8647.

IECE of Silk and Gold Damaſk; ground, crimſon, ſprinkled with gold ſtars; pattern, the Annunciation. Italian, 14th century. 1 foot 1¼ inches by 8 inches.

In this admirable ſpecimen of the Florentine loom we have ſhown us the B. V. Mary not quite bare-headed, but partly hooded and nimbed, as queen-like ſhe ſits on a throne, with her arms meetly folded on her breaſt, the while ſhe liſtens to the words of the angel who is on his knees before her, and uplifting his hand in the act of ſpeaking a benediction, while in his left he holds the lily-branch, correctly—which is not always ſo in art works—blooming with three, and only three, full-blown flowers. Above the archangel the Holy Ghoſt is coming down from heaven in ſhape of a dove, from whoſe beak dart forth long rays of light toward the head of St. Mary. The greater part of the ſubject is wrought in gold; the faces, the hands, and flowers are white, and a very ſmall portion of the draperies blue. The drawing of the figures is quite after the Umbrian ſchool, and, therefore, not merely good, but beautiful. In his "Geſchichte der Liturgiſchen Gewänder des Mittelalters," 1 Lieferung, pl. xiii. Dr. Bock has figured it.

8648.

N Embroidered Figure of St. Urſula, within a Gothic niche, which with much of the drapery, was done in gold, on a ground now brown. Rheniſh, 14th century. 8¾ inches by 3¾ inches.

So ſadly has the whole of this embroidery ſuffered, apparently from damp, that the tints of its ſilk are gone, and the gold about it all become black. That this is but one of ſeveral figures in an orphrey is very likely; it gives us the ſaint with the palm-branch of martyrdom in one hand, a book in the other, and an arrow ſticking in her neck, the inſtrument of her death; being of blood royal, ſhe wears a crown; emblem of heaven and paradiſe, the ground ſhe treads is all flowery.

8649.

IECE of Woollen Carpet; ground, red; pattern, a green quatrefoil bearing three white animals. Spanish, late 14th century. 1 foot 11 inches by 1 foot 1 inch.

A moſt unmiſtakeable piece of mediæval carpeting; the lively tone of its red is yet bright. The quatrefoils are quite of the period, and look like four-petaled roſes barbed, that is, with the angular projection between the petals. So unlion-like are the animals, that we may not take them as the blazon of the Kingdom of Leon.

8650.

IECE of Silk Damaſk; ground, crimſon; pattern, the ſo-called artichoke in yellow and green, lined white, and foliage of green lined white. Spaniſh, 15th century. 1 foot 9 inches by 1 foot 4¼ inches.

A good example of this ſhowy pattern, once ſo much in favour, and of which the materials are very good and ſubſtantial; much of the yellow portions of the deſign was in gold thread, the metal of which has, however, almoſt all gone. From the quantity of glue ſtill ſticking to the hind part of this ſilk, its laſt deſtination would ſeem to have been the covering of ſome ſtate room.

8651.

HE "Vernicle," embroidered in ſilk, and now ſewed on a large piece of linen. Flemiſh, middle of 15th century. 9¼ inches by 7¼ inches; the linen, 2 feet 10¼ inches by 2 feet 9 inches.

To the readers of old Engliſh literature, eſpecially of Chaucer, the term of "Vernicle" will not be unknown, as expreſſing the repreſentation of our Saviour's face, which He is ſaid to have left upon a napkin handed Him to wipe His brows, by one of thoſe pious women who crowded after Him on His road to Calvary. It is noticed, too, in the "Church of our Fathers," t. iii. p. 438. This piece of needle-work ſeems to have been cut off from another, and ſewed, at a very much later period, to the large piece of linen to which it is now attached; for the purpose of being put up either in a private chapel, or over some very small altar in a church, as a sort of reredos; or, perhaps, it may have originally been one of the apparels on an alb: never, however, on an amice, being much too large for such a purpose. One singularity in the subject is the appearance of crimson tassels, one at each corner of the napkin figured with our Lord's likeness, which is kept with great care still, at Rome, among the principal relics in St. Peter's, where it is shown in a solemn manner on Easter Monday. It is one of those representations of a sacred subject called by the Greeks ἀχειροποίητος, that is, "not made by hands," or, not the work of man, as was noticed in the Introduction to the present Catalogue.

8652.

LINEN Towel, with thread embroidery; pattern, lozenges, some enclosing flowers, others, lozenges. German, 15th century. 3 feet 11 inches by 1 foot 6¼ inches.

Most likely this small piece of linen was meant to be a covering for a table, or may be the chest of drawers in the vestry, and upon which the vestments for the day were laid out for the celebrating priest to put on. In the pattern there is evidently a strong liking for the gammadion—a kind of figuration constructed out of modifications of the Greek letter gamma. In England the gammadion became known as the "filfot," and seems to have been looked upon as a symbol for the name Francis or Frances, and is of frequent occurrence in our national monuments—especially in needlework—belonging to the 14th and 15th centuries. From the presence of that large eight-petaled flower in this cloth we are somewhat warranted in thinking that the same hand that wrought the fine and curious frontal, No. 8709, worked this, and that her baptismal name was Frances.

8653—8661 A.

TEN Fragments of Narrow Laces for edgings to liturgical garments, woven, some in gold, some in silk, and some in worsted. 8658 is a specimen of parti-coloured fringe; 8659 shows a two-legged monster as part of its design;

and in 8661 and 8661 A we find a knot much like the one to which Montagu gives the names of Wake and Ormond, in his "Guide to the Study of Heraldry," p. 52.

8662.

THE Napkin for a Crozier, of fine linen ornamented with two narrow perpendicular ftrips of embroidery of a lozenge pattern in various-coloured worfteds, and having, at top, a cap-fhaped finifhing made of a piece of green raifed velvet, which is figured with a bird, like a peacock, perched juft by a well, into which it is looking. At each corner of this cap is a fmall parti-coloured taffel, and, at the top, the fhort narrow loop by which it hung from the upper part of the crozier-ftaff. German, 15th century. 2 feet 2¼ inches by 1 foot 8¼ inches.

This is another of thofe liturgical ornaments, valuable, becaufe fo rare, of which we have fpoken under No. 8279 A. But in the fpecimen before us we find it in much diminifhed form—half only of its ufual fize. The defign of the raifed velvet, in its cap, is as unufual as curious.

8663.

LINEN Cloth, embroidered in coloured filks with facred emblems and hagiological fubjects, and infcribed with names amid trees and flowers. German, 15th century. 1 foot 1¾ inches by 4 inches.

In all likelihood this needlework was meant as the covering for a table in the veftry of fome church, or oratory in fome lady's room. On the left is figured St. George flaying the dragon; next, the pelican in its piety, above which is the "vernicle," and over this the word "Emont," with a ducal coronet above it. Then the names "Ihs," "Maria," and, above them, the word "Eva" crowned. In the middle of the cloth is a crofs with all the emblems of the Paffion around it, as well as a ftar and crefcent. Then an animal fpotted like a panther and chained to a tree; this is followed by the name

"Meltinich;" laft of all we find the name "Amelia," and beneath, a half-figure of a woman having long hair with a large comb in her right hand, altogether refembling a mermaid. At bottom runs a narrow parti-coloured thread fringe.

8664.

RONTLET to an Altar-Cloth, embroidered in coloured filks upon fine linen, with flower-bearing trees and a fhield of the Paffion, along with faints' names, &c. German, 16th century. 1 foot 1¼ inches by 4 inches.

The fhield in the middle is charged with a chalice and confecrated hoft, and four wounds (hands and feet) of our Lord. Under one tree occur the names "Jhefus," "Maria;" under another, "Andreas," "Anna." From amid the grafs on the ground fpring up tufts of daifies.

8665.

IECE of Embroidery, done upon fine linen in coloured filks and gold thread. German, middle of the 15th century. 7¼ inches fquare.

The fubject of this piece is the death of the Bleffed Virgin Mary, figured according to the traditional manner much followed by the mediæval fchools of art in moft parts of Chriftendom. It is, however, to be regretted that this embroidery has been at fome time mutilated; in its original ftate it may have, perhaps, ferved as an apparel to an alb, and occupied the place of one of thofe to be feen at No. 8710.

8666.

RAGMENT of thin Silk Damafk; pattern, a lozenge-fhaped diaper; colour, a much faded crimfon. Oriental, 13th century. 8¼ inches by 4¼ inches.

Though fmall, the pattern is pretty, and much refembles a ftuff of filk and gold very lately found in the tomb of one of the Archbifhops of York, in that cathedral.

8667.

PORTION of an Orphrey, wrought partly in the loom, partly by the needle, and figured with an angel-like youth holding before him an armorial shield, as he stands within a Gothic niche, with an inscription below his feet. German, very late 15th century. 10¾ inches by 5¼ inches.

This instructive piece deserves the attention of those who study embroidery. The loom was geared in such a manner that the spaces for the head, face, neck, and hands were left quite empty, so that they might be filled in by the needle. But this was not all the hand had to do; the architectural features of the canopy, its shading in red, the nimb, and nicely floriated diapering all over the angel's golden alb, were put in by the needle.

The inscription, woven in, reads " Johā vā geyē," and the piece is figured in Dr. Bock's "Geschichte der Liturgischen Gewänder des Mittelalters," 2 Lieferung, pl. xv.

8668.

PART of an Orphrey, mostly loom-woven, and figured with the Crucifixion, on one side of which stands the Blessed Virgin Mary, on the other, St. John the Evangelist. German, late 15th century. 12¾ inches by 5 inches.

Like the preceding piece, the greater part is woven, even the body itself of our Lord, so that in His figure, as in those of His mother and the beloved disciple, the only embroidered portions are the head and face, besides those blood-spots all over His person, the tricklings from His five wounds, and the crossed nimb about His head.

8669.

PORTION of a Maniple, in much faded tawny silk; pattern, a rose-like floriation. Flemish, 16th century. 1 foot 10½ inches by 3¼ inches.

Though peculiar, the pattern in the design of this silken stuff is very pretty; the piece of parti-coloured silken fringe that edges the end of this maniple is older than the textile to which it is sewed.

EMBROIDERY, SILK & GOLD

Under a Gothic canopy &c — German late 15th century

8670.

THE hind Orphrey for a Chasuble, with embroidered figures applied upon a ground red and gold. The figures are a knight bareheaded and kneeling in prayer, with his helmet and shield before him, St. Catherine of Alexandria, and St. Anthony of Egypt reading a book. German, middle of the 15th century. 2 feet 11 inches by 5¼ inches.

The figures are well done, and all show the varieties of process then brought into use; they were worked on canvas, of which the portions for the face and hands were left untouched, saving by the few slight stitches required for indicating the hair and features of the countenance and indications of the fingers. Some of the dress was cut out of woven cloth of gold and sewed on; other parts worked with the needle, as were such accessories as books, instruments of martyrdom, and other such emblems. The knight, probably the giver of the chasuble, is meant to be indicated by his blazon, which is a shield *or* charged with eight *torteaux* in orle, and this is surmounted by a golden helmet with mantling, and a crest, consisting of golden horns fringed with four *torteaux* each. The ground upon which the embroideries are set is rich, and woven with golden wheel-like circles with wavy, not straight, spokes upon a bright red field.

8671.

FRAGMENT of an Orphrey, woven in gold and coloured silks; pattern, intertwining brambles of the wild rose, bearing flowers seeded and barbed. German, beginning of the 16th century. 7¾ inches by 4½ inches.

Though the ground is, or rather was, of gold, so sparingly was the precious metal bestowed upon the thread, that it has been almost entirely worn away. The same may be said of the very narrow tape with which, on one of its edges, it is still bordered.

8672.

PART of an Orphrey, embroidered upon linen, in coloured filks, and figured with St. Anthony and a virgin martyr-faint, both ftanding beneath Gothic canopies. Rhenifh, late 15th century. 1 foot 9 inches by 3¾ inches.

Notwithftanding the embroidery be fomewhat coarfe, like much of the fame kind of work at the period, it is fo far valuable as it inftructs us how three methods were practifed together on one piece. The canvas ground was left bare at the faces and hands, fo that the features of the one and the joints of the other might be fhown by appropriate ftitches in filk. Pieces of golden web, cut to the right fize, were applied for the upper garments of the figures, and the folds fhaded by hand in red filk, and the borders of the robe edged with a fmall cording, while all the reft of the work was filled in with needlework. The clofely fitting fcull-cap, but more efpecially the ftaff ending in a tau-crofs, indicate St. Anthony, but the female faint cannot be identified; her long hair flowing about her fhoulders fignifies that fhe was a virgin, and the green palm-branch in her right hand indicates that fhe underwent martyrdom.

8673.

PIECE of Raifed Velvet; ground, yellowifh pink, the raifed velvet, bright crimfon; pattern, a large compound floriation within a circle formed by fmall hooked lines having flowers at the cufps, and the round itfelf fpringing out of a fomewhat fmaller floriation. Flemifh, 16th century. 2 feet 3 inches by 1 foot 1¾ inches.

8674.

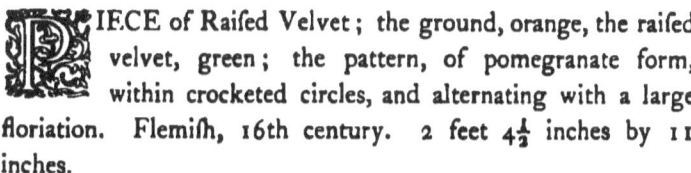IECE of Raised Velvet; the ground, orange, the raised velvet, green; the pattern, of pomegranate form, within crocketed circles, and alternating with a large floriation. Flemish, 16th century. 2 feet 4½ inches by 11 inches.

The raised pattern, from its rich pile, stands up well, and was hung upon walls, or employed for curtains and other household appliances, for which such stuffs were generally produced.

8675.

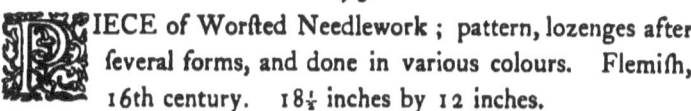IECE of Worsted Needlework; pattern, lozenges after several forms, and done in various colours. Flemish, 16th century. 18¼ inches by 12 inches.

Worked after the same fashion, and with the same materials, that our ladies at this day employ upon their Berlin wool work.

8676.

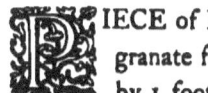IECE of Linen Damask; pattern, artichoke and pomegranate forms. Flemish, 16th century. 1 foot 3 inches by 1 foot 1¾ inches.

The design is carefully elaborated; and the piece itself is evidence of the beauty of old Flemish napery.

8677.

 SMALL Cloth for an Oratory, of fine linen, embroidered with sprigs of flowers in their proper colours, in silk, and with I. H. S. in red gothic letters, within a thorn-like wreath in green. Flemish, 16th century. 2 feet 6 inches by 1 foot 10 inches.

That this cloth has been cut down is evident; the sacred monogram is not in the middle, and the higher row of flowers is shortened. Though hemmed with tape on one side, and edged on two sides by very narrow strong lace, and on the fourth or front border by a broader lace, its last use was as a covering for some sort of table, not an altar properly so called; it is by far very much too small for any such purpose. In all likelihood, this cloth was made to overspread the top of a praying desk, or some little table strewed with devotional objects in a bed-room or private oratory.

8678.

PORTION of Worsted Embroidery upon light brown linen; the pattern, a scroll of flowers and foliage in colours German, late 16th century. 1 foot 5¾ inches by 4¼ inches.

The design is made to run along well, and the colours are nicely contrasted.

8679.

PIECE of Silk Damask, of a light red and straw colour; pattern, two varieties of the pomegranate mixed with large artichokes and small crowns, and separated by thick branches, which are purpled with broad ivy-like leaves. Italian, 16th century. 2 feet 10 inches by 1 foot 11 inches.

A bold pattern, remarkable for the originality of some parts of its design.

8680, 8680 A.

TWO Pieces of Raised Velvet, green and gold; pattern, a modification of the favourite pomegranate and its accompanying intertwining foliage; very large and incomplete. Florentine, early 16th century. 2 feet 1 inch by 9¾ inches; 1 foot 3 inches by 10½ inches.

Needlework, and Dresses. 257

These two pieces give us specimens of those gorgeous stuffs so often sent forth to the world from the looms of Tuscany, and afford, in portions of the design, samples of velvet raised upon velvet so very rarely to be found. The little short loops, or spots, of gold thread, with which the velvet is in some parts freckled, ought not to go unnoticed.

8681.

PIECE of Embroidery, wrought with a running pattern of leaves and flowers in coloured threads upon a golden ground, now much tarnished. German, 16th century. 1 foot 6 inches by $4\frac{1}{4}$ inches.

Embroidery in thread is of somewhat rare occurrence.

8682.

PART of a Web for church use, wrought in thread and silk upon a golden ground, now much faded. The pattern, trees bearing white flowers, bunches of white lilies, wheels with stars, and the words "Jhesus, Maria." Cologne, late 15th century. 6 feet by 5 inches.

That it once formed a frontlet or border to the front edge of an altar-cloth is very likely, not only from the spots of wax with which it is in some parts sprinkled, but more especially from the way in which its pattern is wrought, so as to be properly seen when stretched out horizontally.

8683, 8684.

TWO Specimens of Web for church use; woven in silks, upon a golden ground; the first with the sacred name "Jhesus," and a tree bearing white and red flowers, with daisies at its foot, and the name "Maria," beneath which is a garland of white and red flowers twined about the letter M; the second, with a round ornament, having red and gold stars upon a tawny white ground between each of its eight radii, and underneath the sacred name, in dark blue silk. German, late 15th century. 1 foot 7½ inches by 2¼ inches; 7 inches by 3¼ inches.

Like several other examples of the same kind to be found in this collection, and wrought for the same liturgical purposes.

8685.

IECE of Raised Velvet, dark blue; pattern, one of the several varieties of the pomegranate. Italian, 16th century. 1 foot 3¼ inches by 1 foot 3 inches.

Rich neither in material nor design, this velvet may have been wrought not for ecclesiastical but personal use.

8686.

IECE of Silk Damask, purple; pattern, the pomegranate. Italian. 2 feet 5 inches by 11¾ inches.

Like the preceding, meant for personal use, but exhibiting a much more elaborate design, and the variety of the corn-flower (centaurea) springing forth all round the pomegranate, which itself grows out of a fleur-de-lis crown.

8687.

IECE of Embroidery, on canvas; ground, figured with St. John the Baptist and St. John the Evangelist. Rhenish, 16th century. 1 foot 4 inches square.

To the left is seen St. John the Baptist, clothed in a long garment of camel-hair and his loins girt with a light-blue girdle, preaching in the wilderness on the banks of the Jordan. In his left hand he holds a clasped book, upon which rests the "Lamb of God," and just over, a flag, the white field of which is ensigned with a red cross; his upraised right hand, with the first two fingers elevated as in the act of blessing, is pointed to the lamb. To the right we have St. John the Evangelift, holding a cup in one hand, while with the other he makes the poifonous drug in it harmlefs by a bleffing.

The grounding has been filled in moftly with golden thread, but of fo poor a quality that the thin metal on it is fcarcely difcernible. In both figures the whole of the perfon, the flefhes, as well as clothing, are all done in woven white filk cut out, fhaded, and featured in colours by the brufh, with fome little needlework here and there upon the garments and acceffories. The figures of the faints are "applied;" and one cannot but admire the effect which a few ftitches of rich green filk produce upon the canvas ground, while a piece of applied filk, flightly fhaded by the brufh, is an admirable imitation of a rocky cliff. The two tall trees and green garlands between them are telling in their warm tones. Altogether this is a precious fpecimen of applied work, and merits attention. It feems to have been the middle piece of a banner ufed for proceffions, and may have once belonged to fome church at Cologne dedicated to the two SS. John.

8688

ORTION of an Orphrey, crimfon fatin, embroidered with flowers in coloured filk and gold thread. 17th century. 1 foot 3½ inches by 2 inches.

From what liturgical veftment this was taken it would be hard to guefs, but there is no likelihood that it ever ornamented a mitre. The yellow flowers, of the compofite kind, and heart's-eafes are very nicely done, whether the work of an Italian, French, or German hand. They have much about them that fpeaks of France.

8689.

IECE of Raifed Velvet, brown, with floriated pattern in gold thread. North Italy, early 16th century. 1 foot 1½ inches by 6¼ inches.

Moft likely from the looms of Lucca, and with a pretty diapering in the gold ground where it is bare of the velvet pile.

8690.

PIECE of Green Velvet, spangled with gold, and embroidered with three armorial shields in gold thread and coloured silks. German, 17th century. 10 inches by 9¾ inches.

All the shields are very German, especially in their crests. The shield on the right hand will attract notice by its anomaly; on a field *azure* it gives a rose *gules* barbed *green*, or colour upon colour; the crest, too, is a curiosity, at least in English blazon, displaying an Elector's cap with very tall bullrushes, five in number, and coloured proper, issuing from between the ermine and the crimson velvet.

8691.

LINEN Napkin, for liturgic use, embroidered, in coloured silks, with conventional flowers. German, end of the 16th century. 2 feet ½ inch by 1 foot 11 inches.

This is another of those liturgical rarities—Corpus Christi cloths—of which we have spoken at No. 8342, under the name of Sindons, or Pyx-cloths. Such appliances were employed for mantling the pyx or ciborium when shut up in the tabernacle—that little temple-like erection on the table, or rather step, on the wall-side of the altar—when the custom ceased of keeping the pyx hanging up beneath a canopy.

8692.

HOOD of a Cope, silk damask, red and yellow, with the subject of the Assumption of the Blessed Virgin Mary woven in it. Florentine, late 15th century. 1 foot 5 inches by 1 foot 4½ inches.

Uprising from her grave, and amid rays of glory and an oblong or elliptic aureole, the Virgin Mary is being wafted to heaven by four angels, who are not, as of yore, vested in long close albs like deacons, but in flowing garments so slit up as to show their naked arms, bare legs, and lower thighs. Upon the empty tomb, from out of which are springing up lilies, is written "Affunta eft;" and at one corner kneels the apoftle St. Thomas who, with head uplifted and both his arms outftretched, is receiving from the mother of our Lord her girdle, which fhe is holding in her hands and about to let drop down to him. "La Madonna della cintola"—this fubject—may often be met with in Italian, more efpecially Florentine, art of the middle ages, and is clofely linked with the hiftory of the fine old church of Prato, as we gather from Vafari, in his "Vite dei Pittori," t. i. p. 279, Firenze, 1846; and the Englifh tranflation, t. ii. p. 75.

8693.

LINEN Napkin, for liturgic ufe, embroidered in white, brown, and blue thread, with figures of our Lord and the twelve Apoftles. German, 4 feet 8 inches by 1 foot 4½ inches.

Like the valuable fpecimen of the needle defcribed at No. 8358, the example before us ferved the purpofe of covering the lectern in the chancel at the celebration of the liturgy.

As in the ufual reprefentations of the Jeffe-tree, the buft of each of the thirteen figures is made to reft within a circular branch upon its tip, where it fprouts out like a wide flower. At the top of this tree we behold our Lord with His right hand uplifted in the act of benediction, His left refted upon a mund, and, about His head a fcroll infcribed "Pax F(V)obis." To the right is St. Peter—fo infcribed—holding a key; to the left, St. John, as a beardlefs youth—infcribed "S. Johnis;" then St. Anderus (Andrew), with a crofs faltirewife; and St. Jacob (James), with his pilgrim's ftaff in hand, and on his large flouched hat turned up in front he has two pilgrim-ftaves in faltire; St. Jacobi (James the Lefs), with fuller's bat; St. Simonus (Simon), beardlefs, with a long knife or fword jagged or toothed like a faw; St. Thomas, with his fpear; St. Bartlyme (Bartholomew), with the flaying knife; St. Judas Tadvs (Jude or Thaddeus), with a knotted club; St. Matheus (Matthew), with a hatchet, and beardlefs; St. Philippe, with a crofs bottony, and beardlefs; St. Mathias, with a halbert. At bottom is marked, in blue ink, 1574; but it may be fairly doubted if this date be the true one for this embroidery, of which the ftyle looks at leaft fifty years older.

8694.

RAGMENT of Silk and Cotton Tissue, green, with small flower pattern. Italian, late 16th cetury. 6¼ inches by 4¼ inches.

A pleasing specimen, rich in material, and bright in its tones, very likely from the South of Italy.

8695.

IECE of Silk Damask, crimson and yellow; pattern, scroll and foliage. French, end of 16th century. 1 foot 7¾ inches by 1 foot 9 inches.

This piece, intended for household use, is not without effect in its design. Though the warp is silk, in the woof there is linen thread, though not easily perceived.

8696.

IECE of Fine Linen, with broad border of flowers in coloured silks. Syrian (?), 15th century. 12¼ inches by 1 foot 7 inches.

This very fine linen has all the appearance of having been wrought in some country on the eastern shores of the Mediterranean, and reminds us of those thin textures for which India was, and yet is, so celebrated. The embroidery, too, is but a timid imitation of flowers, and is so worked as to be equally good on both sides. To all appearance it is the end of a woman's scarf.

8697.

IECE of Needlework in coloured worsteds, upon a canvas ground; pattern, zig-zag lozenges, containing tulips and other liliacious flowers. German, middle of 16th century. 1 foot 4¾ inches by 1 foot 1 inch.

Seemingly, this is but a small piece of a foot-cloth for the upper step of an altar.

8698.

LINEN Damask Napkin; pattern, scrolls enclosing a pomegranate ornamentation; border, at two sides, rich lace. Flemish, 16th century. 4 feet 3 inches by 2 feet 3¼ inches.

This napkin probably served for carrying to the altar the Sunday "holy loaf," as it was called in England, the use of which is still kept up in France, and known there as the "pain benit." For an account of this ancient rite, see the "Church of our Fathers," i. 135.

8699.

SMALL Bag, silk and linen thread, embroidered in quadrangular pattern. German, 15th century. 3¼ inches square.

Very like the one under No. 8313. It may have been used as a reliquary, or, what is more probable, for carrying the rosary-beads of some lady. Concerning the form of prayer itself, see the "Church of our Fathers," t. iii. p. 320.

8700.

PIECE of Embroidery, upon an older piece of white silk, brocaded in gold, three armorial shields in their proper tinctures, all within a golden wreath. German, late 16th century. 4 inches square.

8701.

PIECE of Black Raised Velvet, with small flower pattern. Italian, 16th century. 1 foot by 7 inches.

A pleasing example of the Genoese loom.

8702.

PIECE of Damaſk, ſilk and linen, tawny and yellow; pattern, a modification of the pomegranate within oblong curves, and other floriations. Florentine, 16th century. 2 feet 11¼ inches by 1 foot 1¼ inches.

Of a large bold deſign, though not rich in material.

8703.

PIECE of Damaſk, ſilk and linen, tawny and yellow; pattern, a ſlight variation of the foregoing, No. 8702. Florentine, 16th century. 3 feet 4 inches by 9¼ inches.

So much alike are theſe two ſpecimens, that at firſt ſight they look parts of the ſame ſtuff; a near and cloſe inſpection ſhows, however, that for one or other there was a ſlight alteration in the gearing of the loom. Both may have originally been crimſon and yellow: if ſo, the firſt colour has ſadly faded. From the ſhape of this piece, its laſt uſe muſt have been for a chaſuble, but of a very recent period, judging from its actual ſhape.

8704.

CHASUBLE, cloth of gold, diapered with a deep-piled blue velvet, ſo as to ſhow the favourite artichoke pattern after two forms, with embroidered orphreys and armorial ſhields. Flemiſh, very late 15th century. 4 feet 4¼ inches by 3 feet 10¾ inches.

This chaſuble, rare, becauſe not cut-down, has been lately but properly repaired. The back orphrey, in the form of a croſs, is figured with the Crucifixion, the B. V. Mary fainting and upheld by St. John; a ſhield *gules*, with chalice *or*, and hoſt *argent*, at top; another ſhield at bottom, *gules*, a column *argent*, twined with cords *or*; the front orphrey is figured with the B. V. Mary crowned, and carrying our infant Lord in her arms; beneath her, the words inſcribed in blue, "Salve Regina;" lower down, St. John the Evangeliſt bleſſing a golden chalice,

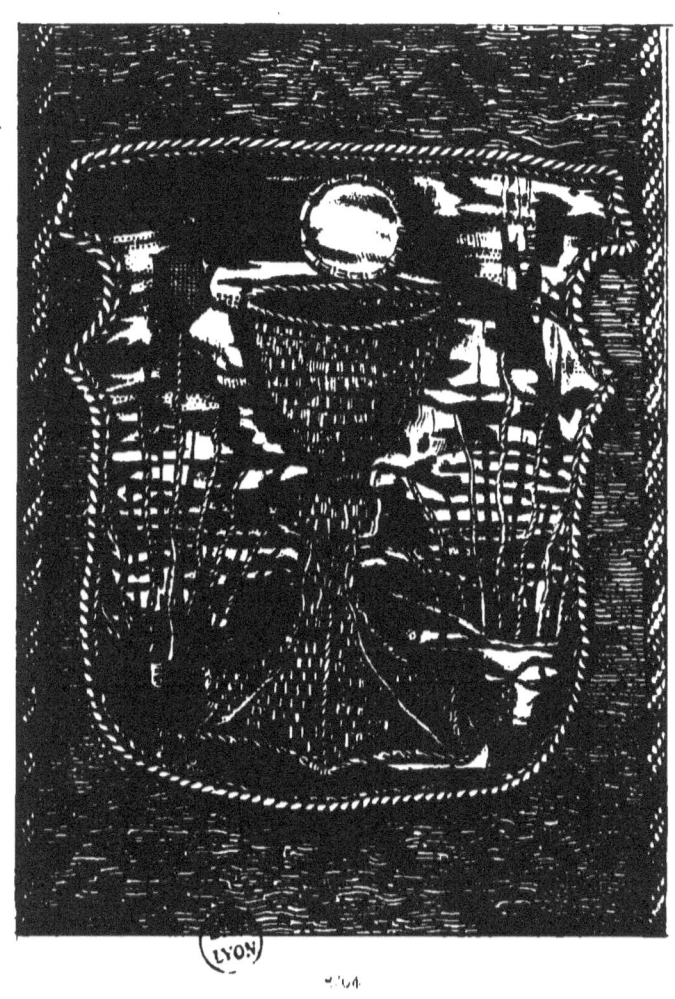

PART OF THE ORPHREY OF A CHASUBLE
French 13th Century

out of which is coming a dragon, and having the infcription at his feet, "Sanctus Iohannes." Lower ftill, St. Catherine with a book in her right hand, and in the left a fword refting on a wheel.

The front orphrey is done in applied work; the back orphrey confifts of a web with a ground of gold, figured with green flower-bearing boughs, and having fpaces left for the heads and hands to be filled in with needlework. The fhield of arms *or*, with a chief *azure*, charged with three fquare buckles *argent*, we may prefume to be the blazon of the giver of this gorgeous veftment.

8705.

FRONTLET to an Altar-Cloth of diapered linen. The frontlet itfelf is the broad border of purple cloth on which is figured a Latin infcription within wreaths of flowers done in white linen. German, late 15th century. 10 feet 9 inches by 6½ inches; the linen, 9 inches.

This is another liturgical appliance, once fo common everywhere, and fo often mentioned in Englifh ecclefiaftical documents, which has now become a very great rarity. From the fhred of the altar-cloth itfelf to which it is fewed, that linen, with its fine diapering and its two blue ftripes, diapered, too, and vertically woven in, muft have been of a coftly kind, and large enough to overfpread the whole table of the altar, fo that this blue frontlet fell down in front. The Latin infcription, each word parted by a wreath, from four parts of which fhoot fprigs of flowers, reads thus :—"O Gloriofum lumen ec(c)lefiarum funde preces pro falute populorum." The letters, as well as all the floral ornamentation of this fhort prayer, are wrought in pieces of linen ftitched on with red thread; and below is a worfted parti-coloured fringe, 1¼ inches deep. For the ufe of the frontlet in England, during the mediæval period, the reader may confult the "Church of our Fathers," i. 238.

8706.

AN Altar-Frontal in very dark brown coarfe cloth, on which are applied armorial fhields, and the ground is filled in with flower-bearing branches, in worfted and

M M

filk. German, beginning of 16th century. 7 feet 8 inches by 4 feet 1 inch.

Though of so late a period, this altar-frontal can teach those studious of such appliances how readily and effectively such works may be wrought. The whole is divided into eight squares; in the middle of each is put a shield alternating with another in its blazon, the first being *or*, three hearts *gules*, two and one, between three bendlets *sable*; the second, *argent*, an eagle *sable* on an arched bough raguly *azure* in the dexter base. The ramifications twining all over the ground are done in light brown broad worsted threads stitched on with white thread; and the flowers, all seeded and barbed, some white, some yellow, as if in accordance with the tints of the two shields, are done in silk. At bottom this frontal has been edged with a deep fringe, parti-coloured white and black.

8707.

CHASUBLE, blue cut velvet; pattern, one of the pomegranate forms, with orphreys. German, late 15th century. 9 feet 5 inches by 4 feet 9 inches.

To the liturgical student fond of vestments in their largest, most majestic shapes, this chasuble will afford great satisfaction, as it is one of the few known that have not been cut down. The front orphrey is a piece of narrow poor web, once of gold, but not much worn; the hind orphrey is a long cross, raguly or knotted, with our Lord nailed to it; above is the Eternal Father wearing an imperial crown of gold lined crimson, and in the act of blessing, between whom and our Saviour is the Holy Ghost in shape of a silver dove with outspread wings. At foot is the group of the Blessed Virgin Mary fainting, and hindered from falling by St. John.

8708.

THE Blue Linen Lining of a Dalmatic, with the parti-coloured fringe bordering the front of the vestment, and some other fragments. 4 feet 1¼ inches by 5 feet 7 inches. The silk Sicilian, 14th century.

The silk is much like the specimen fully described under No. 8263.

8709.

ALTAR-FRONTAL of grey linen, figured in needlework, with flowers, stars, and heraldic animals, on alternating squares of plain linen and net-work. German, 15th century. 9 feet 5¼ inches by 4 feet 2½ inches.

This important piece of stitchery was never meant for a covering to the table or upper part of the altar; it served as a frontal to it, and was hung before, and at each corner of the altar so as to cover it and its two sides down to the ground. From all its ornaments having an armorial feeling about them, this elaborate piece of needle-work would seem to have been wrought by the hands of some noble lady, who took the blazon of her house for its adornment. At the lower part, in the middle, is a shield of arms *argent*, charged with two bars once *gules*; high above, a star of eight points voided *gules*; below, a fleur-de-lis barred *argent* and *gules*; at each of the four corners of the square a manelefs lion rampant barred *argent* and *gules*. To the right, on the same level, a square filled in with fleurs-de-lis; then a square with birds and beasts unknown to English heraldry: the birds, natant, have heads of the deer kind, horned, and the beasts a beaked head with a single arched horn coming out of the forehead with the point of the bow in front; both birds and beasts are paled *argent* and *gules*. On the next square are stars of eight points, and flowers with eight petals, within quatrefoils all *argent*, upon a field (the netting) *gules*. The last square is separated into three pales each charged with a flower-like ornament alternately *argent* and *gules*. Above this square is another of net *gules*, charged with four flowers *argent*; and, going to the left, we have a square showing two bears combatant barred *argent* and *gules*; still to the left, birds at rest, and stars alternating *argent* upon a square of net *gules*. Next to this a large antelope tripping paled *argent* and *gules*; then a square having lions rampant within lozenges with a four-petaled flower at every point, all *argent*, on a field (of net) *gules*. Following this is a large dog, maned and rampant barred *argent* and *gules*; to this succeeds a square of net *gules* charged with lozenges, having over each point a mascle, and within them stars of eight points all *argent*. The last square to the left on this middle row is charged with a heart-shaped ornament voided in the form of a fleur-de-lis, and put in three piles of four with flowers between. The only other square differing from those just noticed are the two charged with an animal of the deer kind, with antlers quite straight. The narrow borders at the sides are not the least curious parts of this interesting specimen; that on the left hand is made up of a dog running after a bearded antelope, which is confronted by a griffin so repeated as to fill up the whole line. The border on the right hand is made up of the beast with the one horn.

8710.

ALB of White Linen appareled at the cuffs, and before and behind at the feet, with crimson and gold stuff figured with animals and floriations of the looms of Palermo. Sicilian, 14th century. 5 feet 7 inches long, 4 feet across the shoulders, without the sleeves.

For those curious in liturgical appliances this fine alb of the mediæval period will be a valuable object of study, though perhaps not for imitation in the way in which it is widened at the waist. Its large opening at the neck—1 foot $4\frac{1}{4}$ inches—is somewhat scalloped, but without any slit down the front, or gatherings, or band. On each shoulder, running down 1 foot $3\frac{1}{4}$ inches, is a narrow piece of crochet-work inscribed in red letters with the names "JESUS," "MARIA." The full sleeves, from 1 foot 6 inches wide, are gradually narrowed to $6\frac{1}{4}$ inches at the end of the apparels at the cuffs, which are 4 inches deep and edged with green linen tape. At the waist, where it is 3 feet 10 inches, it is made, by means of gatherings upon a gusset embroidered with a cross-crosslet in red thread, to widen itself into 6 feet, or 12 feet all round. Down the middle, before and behind, as far as the apparels, is let in a narrow piece of crochet-work like that upon the shoulders, but uninscribed. The two apparels at the feet—one before, the other behind—vary in their dimensions, one measuring 1 foot 1 inch by 1 foot $1\frac{1}{4}$ inches, the other, which is made up of fragments, 1 foot by $11\frac{1}{4}$ inches. Very elaborate and freely designed is the heraldic pattern on the rich stuff which forms the apparels. The ground is of silk, now faded, but once a bright crimson; the figures, all in gold, are an eagle in demi-vol, langued, with a ducal crown, not upon, but over its head; above this is a mass of clouds with pencils of sun-rays darting from beneath them all around; higher up again, a collared hart lodged, with its park fet between two large bell-fhaped feeded drooping flowers, beneath each of which is a dog collared and courant. For Englifh antiquaries, it may be interefting to know that upon the mantle and kirtle in the monumental effigy of King Richard II, in Weftminfter Abbey, the hart as well as the cloud with rays form the pattern on thofe royal garments, and are well fhown in the valuable but unfinifhed " Monumental Effigies of Great Britain," by the late brothers Hollis. This alb is figured, but not well with regard to the apparels, by Dr. Bock, in his " Gefchichte der Liturgifchen Gewänder des Mittelalters," 4 Lieferung, pl. iii. fig. 1.

8711.

CHASUBLE, Cloth of, now tawny, once crimfon, filk; pattern, animals amid floriations. Sicilian, 14th century. 4 feet 5 inches by 3 feet 6 inches.

Made of precifely the fame rich and beautiful ftuff employed in the apparels of the alb juft noticed, No. 8710, the elaborate defign of which is here feen in all its perfectnefs. The chafuble itfelf has been much cut away from its firft large fhape.

8712.

PART of a large Piece of Needlework, done upon linen in coloured worfteds, figured with a king and queen feated together on a Gothic throne, and a young princefs fitting at the queen's feet. All about are infcriptions. German (?), 15th century. 5 feet 6¼ inches by 3 feet 10 inches.

Wofully cut as this large work has been, enough remains to make it very interefting. The king,—whofe broad-toed fhoes, as well as the very little dog at his feet, will not efcape notice,—holds a royal fceptre in his left hand, and around his head runs a fcroll bearing this infcription, " Inclitus Rex Alfridus ex ytalia Pacis amator." About the head of the queen, which is wimpled, the fcroll is written with, " Pia Hildefwit Fundatrix Peniten (?), Aº. Mº. XIIº." Below the princefs, whofe hair, as that of a maiden, falls all about her fhoulders, and whofe diadem is not a royal one, nor jewelled like those worn by the king and queen, runs a scroll bearing these words, " Albergissa Abbatissa." Just under the king, on a broad band, comes—" o. dāpnacionis (damnationis) in &." At top, on a broad bright crimson ground, in large yellow letters, we read—" v (ex voto?) hoc opus completum ē (est)." From droppings of wax still upon it, this curious piece of needlework must have been used somewhere about an altar—very likely as a sort of reredos; and from the inscription, it would seem to have been wrought as an ex voto offering.

8713.

IECE of Needlework, in silk, upon linen, figured with St. Bartholomew and St. Paul, each standing beneath a round arch. German, early 12th century. 2 feet 8 inches by 1 foot 6 inches.

The linen upon which this venerable specimen of embroidery is done shows a very fine texture; but the silk in which the whole is wrought is of such an inferior quality that, at first sight, though soft to the touch, it looks like the better sort of untwisted cotton thread. Such parts of the design as were meant to be white are left uncovered upon the linen, and the shading is indicated by brown lines. As such early examples are scarce, this is a great curiosity. Dr. Bock has figured it in his " Geschichte der Liturgischen Gewänder des Mittelalters," 2 Lieferung, pl. viii.

8942.

ERSIAN Tunic, crimson satin, embroidered in various-coloured silks after shawl-patterns, with a double-mouthed long pocket in front. 4 feet by 3 feet.

8973.

IECE of Embroidered Silk; ground, blue silk; pattern, flowers in coloured flos-silks and gold thread, and broad band figured with wood-nymphs, syrens, boys,

Needlework, and Dresses. 271

and an animal half a fish and half a lion. Italian, 17th century. 6 feet ¼ inch by 3 feet 1¼ inches.

No doubt this embroidery served as domestic decoration. It may have been employed as the front to a lady's dressing-table.

8975.

OUNTERPANE; ground, thread net, embroidered with foliage and flowers in various silks. Italian, 16th century. 8 feet by 7 feet 10 inches.

The flos-silks used are of a bright colour, and the whole was worked in narrow slips sewed together in places with yellow silk; in other parts the joinings were covered by a narrow silk lace of a pleasing design.

8976.

RONTAL to an Altar; ground, crimson; pattern, sacred subjects and saints, some in gold, some in yellow silk. Venetian, early 16th century. 6 feet 6 inches by 2 feet 3½ inches.

This frontal is made out of pieces of woven orphreys, and by the way in which those pieces are put together we know that they must have been taken from old vestments, some of which had been much used. It is composed of nine stripes or pales of broad orphrey-web; and allowing for the two end pales being brought round the ends of the altar when hung there, it would then present seven stripes or pales to the eye. Looking at it thus, we find the first pale of crimson silk, figured in yellow silk, with the B. V. Mary holding our Lord as an infant on her lap, with the mund or terraqueous globe surmounted by a cross in His right hand, amid a strap-like foliation; the next pale of crimson silk is figured in gold, with a saint-bishop vested in alb, stole crossed over his breast, and cope, and wearing jewelled gloves, with his pastoral staff in his right hand. The third pale, in yellow silk upon a crimson ground, presents us our Lord's tomb, with soldiers watching it, and our

Lord Himself uprising, with His right hand giving a blessing, and in His left a banner, and by His side cherubic heads. The fourth pale at top gives us the B. V. Mary and our infant Saviour in her arms, very much worn away, and beneath, St. Peter with his keys, in gold upon crimson. The other pales are but repetitions of the foregoing. Altogether, this frontal, thread-bare as it is in places, is well worth the attention of those who interest themselves in the history of Venetian design, and the art of weaving.

8977.

HOOD to a Cope; ground, two shades of yellow silk; subject, the Assumption of the Blessed Virgin Mary. Venetian, 16th century. 1 foot 4 inches by 1 foot 3½ inches.

Within an oval, upheld by four angels, and radiant with glory, and having a cherubic head beneath her, the B. V. Mary is rising heavenward from her tomb, out of which lilies are springing, and by it St. Thomas on his knees is reaching out his hand to catch the girdle dropped down to him. On an oval upon the face of the tomb is witten "Assunta est," like what is shown in other pieces in this collection.

8978.

PIECE of Silk Orphrey Web; ground, crimson; pattern, the Coronation, in heaven, of the Blessed Virgin Mary, in yellow. Venetian, 16th century. 1 foot 7¼ inches by 10¾ inches.

This design, though treated after the tradition of the Italian schools, has one peculiarity. On the royal diadem which our Lord, who wears, as Great High Priest of the new law, a triple-crowned tiara, is putting on the head of His mother a large star is conspicuously shown; one of the titles of St. Mary is "stella maris," star of the sea, which would not be forgotten by a seafaring people like the Venetians.

8979.

TISSUE of Crimson Silk and Gold Thread; pattern, the Blessed Virgin Mary in glory, amid cherubic heads, and having two angels, one on each side, standing on clouds. Venetian, 16th century. 1 foot 4 inches by 1 foot.

The subject, a favourite one of the time, is the Assumption of the B. V. Mary, and the tissue was woven entirely for the adornment of liturgical furniture.

9047.

CUSHION, elaborately wrought by the needle on fine canvas, and figured with animals, armorial bearings, flowers, and love-knots, as well as with the letters I and R royally crowned. Scotch, 17th century. 11 inches by 8 inches.

We have on the first large pane a rose tree, bearing one red rose seeded *or*, barbed *vert*, and at its foot, but separating them, two unicorns *argent*, outlined and horned in silver thread; above them, and separated by the red rose, two lions passant, face to face, langued and outlined in gold thread; above the flower a royal crown *or*, and two small knots *or*, and at each side a white rose slipped; over each unicorn a gold knot, and a strawberry proper. Beneath this larger shield are three small ones: the first, fretty *or*, and *vert* (but so managed that the field takes the shape of strawberry leaves), charged with four true-love-knots *or*, and in chief *vert*, a strawberry branch or wire *or*, bearing one fruit proper, and one flower *argent*; the second shield gives us, on a field *azure*, and within an orle of circles linked together on four sides by golden bands, and charged with strawberry fruit, and leaf, and flower proper, and alternating, a plume of Prince of Wales's feathers *argent*, with the quill of the middle feather marked red or *gules*, at each of the four corners there is a true-love-knot in gold; the third small shield is a series of circles outlined in gold, and filled in with quatrefoils outlined green; below, on a large green pane, a white rose slipped, with grapes and acorns; by its side, the capital letters, in gold, I and R, with a strawberry and leaf close by each letter, and above all, and between two love-knots, a regal crown. By the fides of this device are feveral fmall panes, exhibiting fanciful patterns of flowers, &c: but in moft of them the true-love-knot as well as the ftrawberry plant, in one combination or another, are the principal elements; and in one of the fquares or panes the ornamentation evidently affects the fhape of the capital letter S; upon the other fide, with an orle of knots of different kinds, is figured a mermaid on the fea, with a comb in one hand, and on one fide of this pane is fhown a high-born dame, whofe fan, feemingly of feathers, is very confpicuous. Underneath the mermaid are fhown, upon a field *vert*, a man with a ftaff, amid four rabbits, each with a ftrawberry-leaf in its mouth, and at each far corner a ftag. As on the other fide, fo here the larger fquares are furrounded by fmaller ones difplaying in their defign true-love-knots, ftrawberries, acorns, rofes, white and red, and in one pane the combination, in a fort of network, of the true-love-knot with the letter S, is very ftriking. In Scotland feveral noble families, whether they fpell their name Frafer or Frazer, ufe, as a canting charge in their blazon, the frafier or ftrawberry, leafed, flowered, and fructed proper; the buck, too, comes in upon or about their armorial fhields. And this may have been worked by a member of that family.

9047 A.

SILK Damafk; ground, white; pattern, wreaths of flowers and fruits, in net-work, each mefh filled in with two peacocks beneath a large bunch of red centaurea, or corn-flowers. Sicilian, late 15th century. 2 feet 3¼ inches by 1 foot 8 inches.

The garlands of the mefhes, made out of boughs of oak bearing red and blue acorns, have, at foot, two eagles red and blue; at top, two green parrots beneath a bunch of pomegranates, the fruit of which is red and cracked, fhowing its blue feed ready to fall out. The cornflower is fpread forth like a fan. This ftuff fhows the mark of Spanifh rule over the two Sicilies.

9182.

THE Syon Monaftery Cope; ground, green, with crimfon interlacing barbed quatrefoils enclofing figures of our Lord, the Bleffed Virgin Mary, the Apoftles, with winged cherubim ftanding on wheels in the intervening fpaces, and the orphrey, morfe, and hem wrought with armorial bearings, the whole done in gold, filver, and various-coloured filks. Englifh needlework, 13th century. 9 feet 7 inches by 4 feet 8 inches.

This handfome cope, fo very remarkable on account of its comparative perfect prefervation, is one of the moft beautiful among the feveral liturgic veftments of the olden period anywhere to be now found in chriftendom. If by all lovers of mediæval antiquity it will be looked upon as fo valuable a fpecimen in art of its kind and time, for every Englifhman it ought to have a double intereft, fhowing, as it does, fuch a fplendid and inftructive example of the "Opus Anglicum," or Englifh work, which won for itfelf fo wide a fame, and was fo eagerly fought after throughout the whole of Europe during the middle ages.

Beginning with the middle of this cope, we have, at the lowermoft part, St. Michael overcoming Satan; fuggefted by thofe verfes of St. John, "And there was a great battle in heaven, Michael and his angels fought with the dragon, and the dragon fought and his angels; . . . . and that great dragon was caft out, that old ferpent, who is called the Devil and Satan," &c.—Rev. xii. 7, 9, to which may be added the words of the Englifh Golden Legend: "The fourth victorye is that that tharchaungell Mychaell fhal have of Antecryft whan he fhall flee hym. Than Michaell the grete prynce fhall aryfe, as it is fayd Danielis xii, He fhall aryfe for them that ben chofen as an helper and a protectour and fhall ftrongely ftande ayenft Antecryft . . . . and at the laft he (Antichrift) fhall mount upon the mount of Olyvete, and whan he fhall be . . . entred in to that place where our Lorde afcended Mychaell fhall come and fhall flee hym, of whiche victorye is underftonden after faynt Gregorye that whyche is fayd in thapocalipfis, the batayll is made in heven," (fol. cclxx. b.). As he tramples upon the writhing demon, the archangel, barefoot, and clad in golden garments, and wearing wings of gold and filver feathers, thrufts down his throat and out through his neck a lance, the fhaft of which is tipped with a golden crofs crofslet, while from his left arm he lets down an azure shield blazoned with a silver cross. The next quatrefoil above this one is filled in with the Crucifixion. Here the Blessed Virgin Mary is arrayed in a green tunic, and a golden mantle lined with vair or costly white fur, and her head is kerchiefed, and her uplifted hands are sorrowfully clasped; St. John—whose dress is all of gold—with a mournful look, is on the left, at the foot of the cross upon which the Saviour, wrought all in silver—a most unusual thing,—with a cloth of gold wrapped about His loins, is fastened by three, not four, nails. The way in which the ribs are shown and the chest thrown up in the person of our Lord is quite after old English feelings on the subject. In the book of sermons called the "Festival" it is said, with strong emphasis, how "Cristes body was drawen on the crosse as a skyn of parchement on a harow, so that all hys bonys myght be tolde," fol. xxxiii. In the highest quatrefoil of all is figured the Redeemer uprisen, crowned as a king and seated on a cushioned throne. Resting upon His knee, and steadied by His left hand, is the mund or ball representing the earth—the world. Curiously enough, this mund is distinguished into three parts, of which the larger one—an upper horizontal hemicycle—is coloured crimson (now faded to a brownish tint), but the lower hemicycle is divided vertically in two, of which one portion is coloured green, the other white or silvered. The likelihood is, that such markings were meant to show the then only known three parts of our globe; for if the elements were hereon intended, there would have been four quarters—fire, water, earth, and heaven; instead, too, of the upper half being crimsoned, it would have been tinted, like the heavens, blue. Furthermore, the symbolism of those days would put, as we here see, this mund under the sovereign hand of the Saviour, as setting forth the Psalmist's words, " The earth is the Lord's, and the fulness thereof, the world and all that dwell therein;" while its round shape—itself the emblem of endlessness—must naturally bring to mind that everlasting Being—the Alpha and the Omega spoken of in the Apocalypse—the beginning and the end, Who is and Who was, and Who is to come—the Almighty. Stretching forth His right arm, with His thumb and first two fingers upraised—emblem of one God in three persons—He is giving His blessing to His mother. Clothed in a green tunic, over which falls a golden mantle lined with vair or white fur, she is seated on the throne beside Him, with hands upraised in prayer. It ought not to be overlooked, that while the Blessed Virgin Mary wears ornamented shoes, our Lord, like His messengers, the angels and apostles, is barefoot. To show that as He had said to those whom He sent before His face, that they were to carry neither

Needlework, and Dresses.

purse, nor scrip, nor shoes, so therefore, is He Himself here and elsewhere figured shoeless. Though already in heaven, still, out of reverence towards Him, the head of His mother is kerchiefed, as it would have been were she yet on earth and present at the sacred liturgy. John Beleth, an Englishman, who, in A.D. 1162, a short century before this cope was worked, wrote a book upon the Church Ritual, lays it down as an unbending rule that, while men are to hear the Gospel bare-headed, all women, whatever be their age, rank, or condition, must never be uncovered, and if a young maiden be so her mother or any other female ought to cast a cloth of some sort over her head;—" Viri, itaque . . . aperto capite Evangelium audire debent . . . Mulieres vero debent audire Evangelium tecto et velato capite etiamsi sit virgo, propter pomum vetitum. Et si eveniat ut virgo capite sit aperto, ut velamen non habeat, necesse est, ut mater, aut quævis alia mulier capiti ejus pannum vel simile quippiam imponat." Divin. Offic. Explic. c. xxxix. p. 507.

The next two subjects now to be described are—one, that on the right hand, the death of the Blessed Virgin Mary; the other, to the left, her burial. To fully understand the traditional treatment of both, it would be well to give the words of Caxton's English translation of the "Golden Legend," from the edition " emprynted at London, in Fleteftrete at yᵉ sygne of yᵉ Sonne, by Wynkyn de Worde, in yᵉ yere of our Lorde M.CCCCXVII," a scarce and costly work not within easy reach. " We fynde in a booke sente to saynt Johan the evangelys, or elles the boke whiche is sayd to be apocryphum . . . in what maner the Assumpcyon of the blessyd vyrgyn saynt Marye was made . . . upon a daye whan all the apostles were spradde through the worlde in prechynge, the gloryous vyrgyne was gretely espryfed and enbraced wyth desyre to be wyth her sone Ihesu Cryste . . . and an aungell came tofore her with grete lyghte and salewed her honourably as the mother of his Lorde, sayenge, All hayle blessyd Marie . . . . Loo here is a bowe of palme of paradyse, lady, ... whiche thou shalte commaunde to be borne tofore thy bere, for thy soule shall be taken from thy body the thyrde daye nexte folowynge; and thy Sone abydeth thee His honourable moder . . . All the apostles shall assemble this daye to thee and shall make to thee noble exequyes at thy passynge, and in the presence of theym all thou shalte gyve up thy spyryte. For he that broughte the prophete (Habacuc) by an heer from Judee to Babylon (Daniel xiv. 35, according to the Vulgate) may without doubte sodeynly in an houre brynge the apostles to thee . . . And it happened as Saynt Johan the euangelyst preched in Ephesym the heven sodeynly thondred and a whyte cloude toke hym up and brought hym tofore the gate of the bleſſyd vyrgyne Marye at Jeruſalem (who) ſayd to hym, . . . Loo I am called of thy mayſter and my God, . . . I have herde ſaye that the Jewes have made a counſeyll and ſayd, let us abyde brethren unto the tyme that ſhe that bare Jheſu Criſt be deed, and thenne incontynente we ſhall take her body and ſhall caſte it in to the fyre and brenne it. Thou therefore take this palme and bere it tofore the bere whan ye ſhall bere my body to the ſepulcre. Than ſayd Johan, O wolde God that all my brethren the apoſtles were here that we myght make thyn exequyes covenable as it hoveth and is dygne and worthy. And as he ſayd that, all the apoſtles were ravyſſhed with cloudes from the places where they preched and were brought tofore the dore of the bleſſyd vyrgyn Mary . . . And aboute the thyrde houre of the nyght Jheſu Criſt came with ſwete melodye and ſonge with the ordre of aungelles . . . Fyrſt Jheſu Criſt began to ſaye, Come my choſen and I ſhall ſet thee in my ſete . . . come fro Lybane my ſpouſe. Come from Lybane. Come thou ſhalte be crowned. And ſhe ſayd I come, for in the begynnynge of the booke it is wryten of me that I ſholde doo thy wyll, for my ſpyryte hath joyed in thee the God of helth ; and thus in the mornynge the ſoule yſſued out of the body and fledde up in the armes of her ſone . . . And than the apoſtles toke the body honourably and layde it on the bere.—And than Peter and Paule lyfte up the bere, and Peter began to ſynge and ſaye Iſrahell is yſſued out of Egypt, and the other apoſtles folowed hym in the ſame ſonge, and our Lorde covered the bere and the apoſtles with a clowde, ſo that they were not ſeen but the voyce of them was onely herde, and the aungelles were with the apoſtles ſyngynge, and than all the people was moved with that ſwete melodye, and yſſued out of the cyte and enquyred what it was.— And than there were ſome that ſayd that Marye ſuche a woman was deed, and the dyſcyples of her ſone Jheſu Criſt bare her, and made ſuche melodye. And thenne ranne they to armes and they warned eche other ſayenge, Come and let us flee all the dyſciples and let us brenne the body of her that bare this traytoure. And whan the prynce of preſtes ſawe that he was all abaſſhed and, full of angre and wrath ſayd, Loo, here the tabernacle of hym that hath troubled us, and our lygnage, beholde what glorye he now receyveth, and in the ſaynge ſo he layde his hondes on the bere wyllynge to turne it and overthrowe it to the grounde. Than ſodeynly bothe his hondes wexed drye and cleved to the bere ſo that he henge by the hondes on the bere and was ſore tormented and wepte and brayed. And the aungelles . . . blynded all the other people that they ſawe no thynge. And the prynce of preſtes ſayd, ſaynt Peter deſpyſe not me in this trybulacyon, and I praye thee to praye for me to our Lorde.—And faynt Peter fayd to hym—Kyffe the bere and faye I byleve in God Jhefu Crift. And whan he had fo fayd he was anone all hole perfyghtly.—And thenne the apoftles bare Mary unto the monument (in the Vale of Jofaphat outfide Jerufalem) and fatte by it lyke as oure Lord had commaunded. And at the thyrde daye . . . the foule came agayne to the body of Marye and yffued gloryoufly out of the tombe, and thus was receyved in the hevenly chaumbre, and a grete company of aungelles with her; and faynt Thomas was not there; and whan he came he wolde not byleve this; and anone the gyrdell with whiche her body was gyrde came to hym fro the ayre, whiche he receyved, and therby he underftode that fhe was affumpte into heven; and all this it here to fore is fayd and called apocryphum," &c. ff. ccxvi, &c.

With this key we may eafily unlock what, otherwife, would lie hidden, not only about the coronation, but, in an efpecial manner, the death and burial, as here figured, of the Bleffed Virgin Mary; the former of thefe two is thus reprefented on the right hand fide. In her own fmall houfe by the foot of Mount Sion, at Jerufalem, is Chrift's mother on her dying bed. Four only of the apoftles—there would not have been room enough for fhowing more in the quatrefoil—are ftanding by the couch upon which fhe lies, dreffed in a filver tunic almoft wholly overfpread with a coverlet of gold; fhe is bolftered up by a deep purple golden fretted pillow. St. Peter is holding up her head, while by her fide ftands St. Paul, clad, like St. Peter, in a green tunic and a golden mantle; then St. Matthew, in a blue tunic and a mantle of gold, holding in the left hand his Gofpel, which begins with the generation of our Lord as man, and the pedigree of Mary His mother; while, in front of them, ftands John, arrayed in a fhaded light-purple tunic, youthful in look, and whofe auburn hair is in fo ftrong a contraft to the hoary locks of his brethren. On the left-hand fide we have her burial. Stretched full-length upon a bier, over which is thrown a pall of green fhot with yellow, lies the Virgin Mary, her hair hanging loofe from her head. St. Peter, known by his keys, St. Paul, by his uplifted fword, are carrying on their fhoulders one end of the bier, in front; behind, in the fame office, are St. Andrew bringing his crofs with him, and fome other apoftle as his fellow. After them walks St. Thomas, who, with both his uplifted hands, is catching the girdle as it drops to him from above, where, in the fkies, her foul, in the fhape of a little child, is feen ftanding upright with clafped hands, within a large flowing fheet held by two angels who have come from heaven to fetch it thither. Right before the funeral proceffion is a fmall Jew, who holds in one hand a scabbard, and with the other is unsheathing his weapon. By the side of the bier stand two other Jews also small in size—one, the high priest. One of them has both his arms, the priest but one, all twisted and shrunken, stretched forward on the bier, as if they wanted to upset it; while the latter holds in one of his wasted hands the green bough of the palm-tree, put into it by St. John.

With regard to St. Thomas and the girdle, this cope, if not the earliest, is among the earlier works upon which that part of the legend is figured, though after a somewhat different manner to the one followed in Italy, where, as is evident from several specimens, in this collection, it found such favour.

Below the burial, we have our Lord in the garden, signified by the two trees (John xx. 17). Still wearing a green crown of thorns, and arrayed in a golden mantle, our Lord in His left hand holds the banner of the resurrection, and with His right bestows His benediction on the kneeling Magdalene, who is wimpled, and wears a mantle of green shot yellow, over a light purple tunic. Below, but outside the quatrefoil, is a layman clad in gold upon his knees, and holding a long narrow scroll, bearing words which cannot now be satisfactorily read. Lowermost of all we see the apostle St. Philip with a book in the left hand, but upon the right, muffled in a large towel wrought in silver, three loaves of bread, done partially in gold, piled up one on the other, in reference to our Lord's words (John vi. 5), before the miracle of feeding the five thousand. At the left is St. Bartholomew holding a book in one hand, in the other the flaying knife. A little above him, St. Peter with his two keys, one gold, the other silver; and somewhat under him, to the right, is St. Andrew with his cross. On the other side of St. Michael and the dragon is St. James the Greater—sometimes called of Compostella, because he lies buried in that Spanish city—with a book in one hand, and in the other a staff, and slung from his wrist a wallet, both emblems of pilgrimage to his shrine in Galicia. In the next quatrefoil above stands St. Paul with his usual sword, emblem alike of his martyrdom, and of the Spirit, which is the word of God (Ephes. vi. 17), and a book; lower, to the right, St. Thomas with his lance of martyrdom and a book; and still further to the right, St. James the Less with a book and the club from which he received his death-stroke (Eusebius, book ii. c. 23). Just above is our Saviour clad in a golden tunic, and carrying a staff overcoming the unbelief of St. Thomas. Upon his knees that apostle feels, with his right hand held by the Redeemer, the spear-wound in His side (John xx. 27).

Needlework, and Dresses.

As at the left hand, so here, quite outside the sacred history on the cope, we have the figure of an individual probably living at the time the vestment was wrought. The dress of the other shows him to be a layman; by the shaven crown upon his head, this person must have been a cleric of some sort: but whether monk, friar, or secular we cannot tell, as his gown has become quite bare, so that we see nothing now but the lower canvas with the lines drawn in black for the shading of the folds. Like his fellow over against him, this churchman holds up a scroll bearing words which can no longer be read.

When new this cope could show, written in tall gold letters more than an inch high, an inscription now cut up and lost, as the unbroken word " Ne " on one of its shreds, and a solitary " V " on another, are all that remains of it, the first on the lower right side; the second, in the like place, to the left. Though so short, the Latin word leads us to think that it was the beginning of the anthem to the seven penitential psalms, " *Ne* reminiscaris, Domine, delicta nostra, *vel* parentum nostrorum; neque vindictam sumas de peccatis nostris," a suitable prayer for a liturgical garment, upon which the mercies of the Great Atonement are so well set forth in the Crucifixion, the overthrow of Antichrist, and the crowning of the saints in heaven.

In its original state it could give us, not, as now, only eight apostles, but their whole number. Even as yet the patches on the right-hand side afford us three of the missing heads, while another patch to the left shows us the hand with a book, belonging to the fourth. The lower part of this vestment has been sadly cut away, and reshaped with shreds from itself; and perhaps at such a time were added its present heraldic orphrey, morse, and border, perhaps some fifty years after the embroidering of the other portions of this invaluable and matchless specimen of the far-famed " Opus Anglicum," or English needlework.

The early writers throughout Christendom, Greek as well as Latin, distinguished " nine choirs" of angels, or three great hierarchies, in the upper of which were the " cherubim, or seraphim, and thrones;" in the middle one, the " dominations, virtues, and powers;" in the lower hierarchy, the " principalities, angels, and archangels." Now, while looking at the rather large number of angels figured here, we shall find that this division into three parts, each part again containing other three, has been accurately observed. Led a good way by Ezekiel (i.), but not following that prophet step by step, our mediæval draughtsmen found out for themselves a certain angel form. To this they gave a human shape having but one head, and that of a comely youth, clothing him with six wings, as Isaias told (vi. 2) of the seraphim, and in place of the calf's cloven hoofs, they made it with the feet of man; inftead of its body being full of eyes, this feature is not unoften to be perceived upon the wings, but ofteneft thofe wings themfelves are compofed of the bright-eyed feathers borrowed from the peacock's tail.

Thofe eight angels ftanding upon wheels, and fo placed that they are everywhere by thofe quatrefoils wherein our Lord's perfon comes, may be taken to reprefent the upper hierarchy of the angelic hoft; thofe other angels—and two of them only are entire—not upon wheels, and far away from our Lord, one of the perfect ones under St. Peter, the other under St. Paul, no doubt belong to the fecond hierarchy; while thofe two having but one, not three, pair of wings, the firft under the death, the other under the burial of the Virgin, both of them holding up golden crowns, one in each hand, reprefent, we may prefume, the loweft of the three hierarchies. All of them, like our Lord and His apoftles, are bare-foot. All of them have their hands uplifted in prayer.

For every lover of Englifh heraldic ftudies this cope, fo plentifully blazoned with armorial bearings, will have an efpecial value, equal to that belonging to many an ancient roll of arms. To begin with its orphrey: that broad band may, in regard to its fhields, be diftinguifhed into three parts, one that falls immediately about the neck of the cleric wearing this veftment, and the other two portions right and left. In this firft or middle piece the fhields, four in number, are of a round fhape, but, unlike the fquare ones, through both the other two fide portions, are not fet upon fquares alternately green and crimfon (faded to brown) as are the quatrefoils on the body of the cope. Taking this centre-piece firft, to the left we have—

6. Checky *azure* and *or*, a chevron *ermine*. WARWICK.

7. Quarterly 1 and 4 *gules*, a three-towered caftle *or*; 2 and 3 *argent*, a lion rampant *azure*. CASTILE AND LEON.

8. Vair *or* and *gules*, within a bordure *azure*, charged with fixteen horfe-fhoes *argent*. FERRERS.

9. *Azure*, three barnacles *or*, on a chief *ermine* a demi-lion rampant *gules*. GENEVILLE.

Thefe four fhields are round, as was faid before, and upon a green ground, having nothing befides upon it. All the reft compofing this orphrey are fquares of the diamond form, and put upon a grounding alternately crimfon and green; on the crimfon are two peacocks and two fwans in gold; on the green, four ftars of eight rays in gold voided crimfon. Now, beginning at the furthermoft left fide, we fee thefe blazons :—

1. *Ermine*, a crofs *gules* charged with five lioncels ftatant gardant *or*. EVERARD.
2. Same as 8. FERRERS.
3. *Gules*, the Holy Lamb *argent* with flag *or*, between two ftars and a crefcent *or*. BADGE OF THE KNIGHTS TEMPLARS.
4. Same as 2. FERRERS.
5. Same as 1. EVERARD.
10. Checky *azure* and *or*, a bend *gules* charged with three lioncels paffant *argent*. CLIFFORD.
11. Quarterly *argent* and *gules*; 2 and 3 fretty *or*, over all a bend *fable*. SPENCER.
12. The fame as 3, but the Lamb is *or*, the flag *argent*. BADGE OF THE KNIGHTS TEMPLARS.
13. Same as 11. SPENCER.
14. Same as 10. CLIFFORD.

Juft below the two middle fhields are four nicely-formed loops, through which might be buttoned on to the cope the moveable hood —or different hoods, according to the feftival, and figured with the fubject of the feaft—now loft. On the other edge of the orphrey, to the left, are feen other three loops, like the former, made of thick gold cord, by which was made faft the morfe that is alfo blazoned with ten coats, as follows:—

1. *Gules*, a large fix-pointed ftar *argent* voided with another ftar *azure* voided *argent* voided *gules*, between four crofs-crofflets *or*.
2. *Gules*, an eagle difplayed *or*. LIMESI or LINDSEY.
3. CASTILE AND LEON.
4. *Gules*, a fefs *argent* between three covered cups *or*. LE BOTILER.
5. CASTILE AND LEON.
6. FERRERS.
7. *Azure*, a crofs *argent* between four eagles (?) difplayed *argent* (?).
8. SPENCER.
9. Same as 2. LINDSEY.
10. GENEVILLE.

The ground is checky *azure* and *or* upon which thefe fmall fhields in the morfe are placed.

On the narrow band, at the hem, the fame alternation of green and crimfon fquares, as a ground for the fmall diamond-fhaped fhields, is obferved, as in the orphrey; and the blazons are, beginning at the left-hand fide:—

1. Barry of ten *azure* and *or* imbattled, a fefs *gules* fprinkled with four-petaled flowers feeded *azure*.

2. *Or*, charged with martlets *gules*, and a pair of bars gemelles *azure*.
3. FERRERS.
4. CASTILE AND LEON.
5. *Azure*, a crofs *or*. SHELDON.
6. *Azure*, a lion rampant *or*, within a bordure *gules* charged with eight water-bougets *argent*.
7. WARWICK.
8. SPENCER.
9. *Azure*, a bend between fix birds *or*. MONTENEY of Effex.
10. *Gules*, fprinkled with crofs-crofflets *or*, and a faltire verry potent *argent* and *azure*. CHAMPERNOUN.
11. GENEVILLE.
12. ENGLAND.
13. Checky *argent* and *azure*, on a bend *gules*, three garbs (?) or efcallop-fhells (?) *or*.
14. *Or*, on a fefs *gules* between fix fleurs-de-lis three and three *gules*, three fleurs-de-lis *or*.
15. *Gules*, a lion rampant *argent*, within a bordure *azure*, charged with eight water-bougets *or*.
16. Checky *or* and *gules*, on a bend *azure*, five horfe-fhoes *argent*.
17. Same as 1.
18. Same as 2.
19. Same as 3. FERRERS.
20. Same as 10. CHAMPERNOUN.
21. Same as 10 in the orphrey. CLIFFORD.
22. Same as 8. SPENCER.
23. *Azure*, between fix efcallop-fhells (?) three and three, a bend *or*. TYDDESWALL.
24. Same as 6.
25. Paly of ten *argent* and *azure*, on a bend *gules*, three efcallop-fhells (?) *or*. A coat of GRANDISON.
26. *Gules*, a lion rampant *or*. FITZ ALAN.
27. Barry *argent* and *azure*, a chief checky *or* and *gules*.
28. GENEVILLE.
29. Party per fefs *azure* and *or*, a crofs fufil counterchanged.
30. *Argent*, four birds *gules*, between a faltire *gules*, charged with nine bezants. HAMPDEN (?).
31. *Azure*, five fufils in feffe *or*. PERCY.
32. Same as 1, on the orphrey. EVERARD.
33. Same as 6, on the orphrey. WARWICK.

34. *Gules*, three lucies hauriant in fefs between fix crofs-crofflets *or*. LUCY.

35. Paly of ten *or* and *azure*, on a fefs *gules*, three mullets of fix points *argent*, voided with a crofs *azure*. CHAMBOWE (?).

36. Party per fefs *gules*, fretted *or*, and *ermine*. RIBBESFORD (?).

37. Same as 9.

38. *Or*, on a crofs *gules*, five efcallop-fhells *argent*. BYGOD.

39. Barry, a chief paly and the corners gyronny, *or* and *azure*, an inefcutcheon *ermine*. ROGER DE MORTIMER.

40. Same as 6.

41. Party per fefs, *argent* three eight-petaled flowers formed as it were out of a knot made crofs-wife, with two flowers at the end of each limb, and *azure* with a ftring of lozenges like a fefs *argent*, and three fleurs-de-lis (?) two and one *or*.

42. *Gules*, a fefs checky *argent* and *azure*, between twelve crofs crofflets *or*. Poffibly one of the many coats taken by LE BOTILER.

43. *Azure*, three lucies hauriant in fefs between fix crofs-crofflets *or*. LUCY.

44. *Ermine*, on a chevron *gules*, three efcallop-fhells *or*. GOLBORE or GROVE.

45. Gyronny of twelve *or* and *azure*. DE BASSINGBURN.

Befides their heraldry, fquares upon which are fhown fwans and peacocks wrought at each corner, afford, in thofe birds, objects of much curious intereft for every lover of mediæval fymbolifm under its various phafes.

In the fymbolifm of thofe times, the ftar and the crefcent, the peacock and the fwan, had, each of them, its own feveral figurative meanings. By the firft of thefe emblems was to be underftood, according to the words, in Numbers xxiv. 17, of Balaam's prophecy,—" a ftar fhall arife out of Jacob,"—our Saviour, who fays of His divine felf, Apocalypfe xxii. 16, "I am the bright and morning ftar." By inference, the ftar not only fymbolized our Lord Himfelf, but His Gofpel—Chriftianity—in contradiftinction to Mahometanifm, againft which the crufades had been but lately carried on. The ftar of Bethlehem, too, was thus alfo brought before the mind with all its affociated ideas of the Holy Land.

The crefcent moon, on the fhields with the Holy Lamb, reprefents the Church, for the reafon that fmall at firft, but getting her light from the true Sun of juftice, our Lord, fhe every day grows larger, and at the end of time, when all fhall believe in her, will at laft be in her full brightnefs. This fymbolifm is fet forth, at fome length, by Petrus

Capuanus as quoted by Dom (now Cardinal) Pitra in his valuable "Spicilegium Solefmenfe," t. ii. 66. But for an Englifh mediæval authority on the point, we may cite our own Alexander Neckam, born A.D. 1157 at St. Albans, and who had as a fofter-brother King Richard of the Lion-Heart. In his curious work, "De Naturis Rerum," not long fince printed for the firft time, and publifhed by the authority of Her Majefty's treafury, under the direction of the Mafter of the Rolls, Neckam thus writes:—" Per folem item Chriftus, verus fol jufticiæ plerumque intelligitur; per lunam autem ecclefia, vel quæcunque fidelis anima. Sicut autem luna beneficium lucis a fole mendicat, ita et fidelis anima a Chrifto qui eft lux vera. P. 53.

Not always was the peacock taken to be the unmitigated emblem of pride and foolifh vanity. Ofmont the cleric, in his "Volucraire, or Book of Birds," after noticing its fcream inftead of fong, its ferpent-like fhape of head that it carries fo haughtily, but lowers quite abafhed as it catches a glimpfe at its ugly feet, and its garifh plumage with the many bright-eyed freckles on its fan-like tail which it loves to unfold for admiration, draws thefe comparifons. As the peacock affrights us by its cry, fo does the preacher, when he thunders againft fin ftartle us into a hatred of it; if the ftep of the bird be fo full of majefty, with what fteadinefs ought a true Chriftian fearlefsly tread his narrow path. A man may perhaps find a happinefs, nay, fhow a pride in the conviction of having done a good deed, perhaps may fometimes therefore carry his head a trifle high, and, ftrutting like the peacock, parade his pious works to catch the world's applaufe; as foon as he looks into Holy Writ and there learns the weaknefs, lowlinefs, of his own origin, he too droops his head in all humility. Thofe eye-fpeckled feathers in its plumage warn him that never too often can he have his eyes wide open, and gaze inwardly upon his own heart and know its fecret workings. Thus fpoke an Anglo-Norman writer.

About the fwan an Englifhman, our Alexander Neckam, fays:— "Quid quod cygnus in ætate tenella fufco colore veftitus effe videtur, qui poftmodum in intentiffimum candorem mutatur? Sic nonnulli caligine peccatorum prius obfufcati, poftea candoris innocentiæ vefte fpirituali decorantur."—*De Naturis Rerum*, p. 101. Here our countryman hands us the key to the fymbolic appearance of the fwan upon this liturgical garment; for, as while a cygnet, its feathers are always of a dufky hue, but when the bird has grown up its plumage changes into the moft intenfely white, juft fo, fome people who are at firft darkened with the blacknefs of fin, in after days become adorned with the garb of white innocence.

Besides their ecclesiastical meanings these same symbols had belonging to thém a secular significance. Found upon a piece of stuff quite apart from that of the cope itself, and worked for the adornment of that fine vestment after a lapse of many years, made up too of an ornamentation the whole of which is heraldic and thus bringing to mind worldly knights and their blazons and its age's chivalry, it is easy to find out for it an adaptation to the chivalric notions and customs of those times. The Bethlehem star overtopping the Islam badge of the crescent moon showed forth the wishes of every one who had been or meant to be a crusader, or rather more, not merely of our men at arms but of every true believer throughout Christendom whose untiring prayers were that the Holy Land might be wrested from the iron hand of the Mahometan. At great national festivities and solemn gatherings of the aristocracy, not the young knight alone then newly girt, but the grey-haired warrior would often, in that noble presence, bind himself by vow to do some deed of daring, and swore it to heaven, and the swan, the pheasant, or the peacock as the bird of his choice, was brought with a flourish of trumpets, and amid a crowd of stately knights waiting on a bevy of fair young ladies, and set before him. This sounds odd at this time of day; not so did it in mediæval times, when those birds were looked upon with favour on account of the majestic gracefulness of their shape, or the sparkling beauty of their plumage. It must not be forgotten that this orphrey was blazoned by English hands in England, and while all the stirring doings of our first Edward were yet fresh in our people's remembrance. That king had been and fought in the Holy Land against the Saracens. At his bidding, towards the end of life, a scene remarkable even in that period of royal festive magnificence, took place, when he himself, in the year 1306, girded his son, afterwards Edward II, with the military belt in the palace of Westminster, and then sent him to bestow the same knightly honour, in the church of that abbey, upon the three hundred young sons of the nobility, who had been gathered from all parts of the kingdom to be his companions in the splendours of the day. But that grand function was brought to an end by a most curious yet interesting act; to the joyous sounds of minstrelsy came forwards a procession, bearing along a pair of swans confined in a net, the meshes of which were made of cords fashioned like reeds and wrought of gold. These birds were set in solemn pomp before the king; and there and then Edward swore by the God in heaven and the swans that he would go forth and wage war against the Scots: Matthew Westminster, p. 454. No wonder, then, that along with the star and crescent we find the knightly swan and peacock mingled in the heraldry of the higheſt families in England, wrought upon a work from Engliſh hands, during the fourteenth century. A long hundred years after this elaborate orphrey was worked we find that Dan John Lydgate, monk of Bury St. Edmund's, in his poem called " All ſtant in chaunge like a mydſomer Roſe," upon the fickleneſs of all earthly things, while ſinging of this life's fading vanities, counts among them—

" Vowis of pecok, with all ther proude chere."
MINOR POEMS, *ed. Halliwell for Percy Society*, p. 25.

To the wild but poetic legend of the ſwan and his deſcendants, we have already alluded in our Introduction.

A word or two now upon the needlework, how it was done, and a certain at preſent unuſed mechanical appliance to it after it was wrought, ſo obſervable upon this veſtment, lending its figures more effect, and giving it, as a teaching example of embroidery, much more value than any foreign piece in this numerous collection.

Looking well into this fine ſpecimen of the Engliſh needle, we find that, for the human face, all over it, the firſt ſtitches were begun in the centre of the cheek, and worked in circular, not ſtraight lines, into which, however, after the middle had been made, they fell, and were ſo carried on through the reſt of the fleſhes. After the whole figure had thus been wrought; then with a little thin iron rod ending in a ſmall bulb or ſmooth knob ſlightly heated, were preſſed down thoſe ſpots upon the faces worked in circular lines, as well as that deep wide dimple in the throat eſpecially of an aged perſon. By the hollows thus laſtingly ſunk, a play of light and ſhadow is brought out that, at a ſhort diſtance, lends to the portion ſo treated a look of being done in low relief. Upon the ſlightly-clothed perſon of our Lord this ſame proceſs is followed in a way that tells remarkably well; and the cheſt with the upper part of the pelvis in the figure of our Saviour overcoming Thomas's unbelief, ſhows a noteworthy example of the mediæval knowledge of external anatomy.

We muſt not, however, hide from ourſelves the fact that the edges, though ſo broad and blunt, given by ſuch a uſe of the hot iron to parts of an embroidery, expoſe it ſomewhat to the danger of being worn out more in thoſe than other portions which ſoon betray the damage by their thread-bare dingy look, as is the caſe in the example juſt cited.

The method for filling in the quatrefoils, as well as working much of the drapery on the figures, is remarkable for being done in a long zigzag diaper-pattern, and after the manner called in ancient inventories, "opus plumarium," from the way the ftitches overlie each other like the feathers on a bird.

The ftitchery on the armorial bearings is the fame as that now followed in fo many trifling things worked in wool.

The canvas for every part of this cope is of the very fineft fort; but oddly enough, its crimfon canvas lining is thick and coarfe. What conftituted, then, the charaƈteriftics of the "opus Anglicum," or Englifh work, in mediæval embroidery were, firft, the beginning of the ftitchery in certain parts of the human figure—the face efpecially—in circular lines winding clofe together round and round; and, in the fecond place, the finking of thofe fame portions into permanent hollows by the ufe of a hot iron.

A word or two now about the hiftory of this fine cope.

In olden days not a town, hardly a fingle parifh, throughout England, but had in it one or more pious affociations called "gilds," fome of which could fhow the nobleft amongft the layfolks, men and women, and the moft diftinguifhed of the clergy in the kingdom, fet down upon the roll of its brotherhood, which often grew up into great wealth. Each of thefe gilds had, ufually in its parifh church, a chapel, or at leaft an altar of its own, where, for its peculiar fervice, it kept one if not feveral priefts and clerics, provided, too, with every needful liturgical appliance, articles of which were frequently the fpontaneous offering of individual brothers, who fometimes clubbed together for the purpofe of thus making their joint gift more fplendid. Now it is moft remarkable that upon this cope, and quite apart from the facred ftory on it, we have two figures, that to the left, pranked out in the gay attire of fome rich layman; on the right, the other, who muft be an ecclefiaftic from the tonfure on his head; each bears an infcribed fcroll in his hand, and both are in the pofture of fuppliants making offerings. This cleric and this layman may have been akin to one another, brothers, too, of the fame gild for which they at their joint coft got this cope worked and gave to it. But where was this gild itfelf?

Among the foremoft of our provincial cities once was reckoned Coventry. Its Corpus Chrifti plays or myfteries, illuftrated by this embroidery, enjoyed fuch a wide-fpread fame that for the whole eight days of their performance, every year, they drew crowds of the higheft and the gentleft of the land far and near, as the "Pafton Letters" teftify, to fee them; its gild was of fuch repute that our nobility— lords and ladies—our kings and queens, did not think it anywife beneath their high eftate to be enrolled among its brotherhood. Befides many other authorities, we have one in that fplendid piece of English tapestry—figured with Henry VI, Cardinal Beaufort, Humphrey, Duke of Gloucester, and other courtiers, on the left or men's side, and on the women's, Queen Margaret, the Duchess of Buckingham, and other ladies, most of them on their knees, and all hearing mass—still hanging on the wall of the dining hall of St. Mary's gild, of which that king, with his queen and all his court became members; and at whose altar, as brethren, they heard their service, on some Sunday, or high festival, which they spent at Coventry. Taking this old city as a centre, with a radius of no great length, we may draw a circle on the map which will enclose Tamworth, tower and town, Chartly Castle, Warwick, Charlcote, Althorp, &c. where the once great houses of Ferrers, Beauchamp, Lucy, and Spencer held, and some of them yet hold, large estates; and from being the owners of broad lands in its neighbourhood, their lords would, in accordance with the religious feeling of those times, become brothers of the famous gild of Coventry; and on account of their high rank, find their arms emblazoned upon the vestments belonging to their fraternity. That such a pious queen as the gentle Eleanor, our First Edward's first wife, who died A. D. 1290, should have, in her lifetime, become a sister, and by her bounties made herself to be gratefully remembered after death, is very likely, so that we may with ease account for her shield—Castile and Leon—as well as for the shields of the other great families we see upon the orphrey, being wrought there as a testimonial that, while, like many others, they were members, they also had been munificent benefactors to the association. A remembrance of brotherhood for those others equally noble, but less generous in their benefactions, may be read in those smaller shields upon the narrow hem going along the lower border of this vestment. The whole of it must have taken a long, long time in the doing; and the probability is that it was worked by the nuns of some convent which stood in or near Coventry.

Upon the banks of the Thames, at Isleworth, near London, in the year 1414, Henry V. built, and munificently endowed, a monastery to be called "Syon," for nuns of St. Bridget's order. Among the earliest friends of this new house was a Master Thomas Graunt, an official in one of the ecclesiastical courts of the kingdom. In the Syon nuns' martyrologium—a valuable MS. lately bought by the British Museum— this churchman is gratefully recorded as the giver to their convent of several precious ornaments, of which this very cope seemingly is one. It was the custom for a gild, or religious body, to bestow some rich church vestment upon an ecclesiastical advocate who had befriended it by his pleadings before the tribunals, and thus to convey their thanks

Needlework, and Dresses.

to him along with his fee. After such a fashion this cope could have easily found its way, through Dr. Graunt, from Warwickshire to Middlesex. At the beginning of Elizabeth's reign it went along with the nuns as they wandered in an unbroken body through Flanders, France, and Portugal, where they halted. About sixty years ago it came back again from Lisbon to England, and has found a lasting home in the South Kensington Museum.

197.

EB for Orphreys; ground, crimson silk; design, the Assumption, in yellow silk and gold thread. Florentine, 15th century. 2 feet 2½ inches by 1 foot 2¾ inches.

The same sort of stuff frequently occurs in this collection, and the present specimen, which consists of two breadths sewed together, is the same as the one fully described in No. 4059. In its present shape it may have served as a back hanging to a little praying-desk in a bedroom.

198.

 CRIMSON Velvet Stole, with crosses and fringes of green silk. Spanish, 16th century. 6 feet 8 inches by 2¼ inches, and 5¼ inches.

The pieces of crimson velvet out of which this stole was made, not so many years ago, are of a deep warm tone of colour, and soft rich pile; both so peculiar to the looms of Spain. The velvet must have been in use for church purposes before this stole was made out of it.

1207.

 CRIMSON Velvet Stole, with crosses of poor gold lace, and fringes of crimson silk. Spanish, 16th century. 7 feet 7 inches by 3 inches, and 8 inches.

Like the foregoing stole in quality of velvet.

254-55.

WO Crimson Velvet Maniples, with crosses and fringes of green. Spanish, 16th century. 1 foot 6¼ inches by 3 inches, and 5 inches.

These were to match the like kind of stole.

524.

 CRIMSON Velvet Maniple, with crosses of gold and fringes of crimson silk. Spanish, 16th century. 1 foot 5¼ inches by 3¼ inches, and 6½ inches.

733.

 PIECE of Raised Velvet; ground, yellow silk; design, in velvet pile, pomegranates, and conventional floriations, enclosing an oval with a quatrefoil in the middle. Spanish, late 16th century. 1 foot 6 inches by 7 inches, and by 1 foot 2 inches.

This raised velvet must have been for household decoration, and may have been wrought at Almeria.

902.

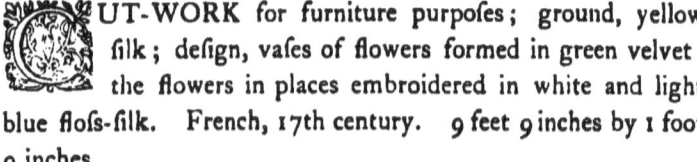UT-WORK for furniture purposes; ground, yellow silk; design, vases of flowers formed in green velvet; the flowers in places embroidered in white and light blue floss-silk. French, 17th century. 9 feet 9 inches by 1 foot 9 inches.

This specimen well shows the way in which such strips for pilasters were wrought. At first the green velvet seems the ground, which, however, is of amber yellow silk, but the velvet is so cut out and sewed on as to give the vases and their flowers the right form, and sometimes is made to come in as foliage. The flowers, mostly fleurs-de-lis and tulips, are well finished in white silk, shaded either by light blue in the first, or pink in the second instance, where, however, there are only five instead of six petals; and the whole is edged in its design with yellow silk cord.

910.

AN Altar Frontal, silk and thread; ground, yellow; design, vases and conventional artichokes, amid floriations, all in crimson silk, and trimmed at the lower side with cut-work, in a flower pattern, of various-coloured silks, edged with yellow cord. Italian, early 17th century. 6 feet by 2 feet 8¼ inches.

The silk in this stuff is small in comparison with the thread, which, however, is so well covered as to be kept quite out of sight in the pattern. The fringe, six inches in depth, is left quite open.

911.

A BED-QUILT; ground, green silk; design, in the middle the goddess Flora, around her large flowers and branches, amid which are birds (doves?), and hares climbing up the boughs, all in floss-silk of very showy colours, with a deep border of flowers, worked upon dark net. Italian, 18th century. 8 feet 3 inches by 6 feet.

Such coverlets were, as they still are, used for throwing over beds in the day-time. The flowers, both on the silk and the netting, are so embroidered as to show the same, like East Indian needlework, on both sides. The love for lively colour, not to say garishness, was such as to lead the hand that wrought this piece to render the branches of some of the parts parti-coloured in white and crimson. Other specimens of embroidered net may be seen at Nos. 623, 624, 4462.

PART THE SECOND.

Tapestry.

1296.

IECES of Tapestry Hanging, figured with poetic pastoral scenes. Flemish, perhaps wrought at Audenaerde, in the first half of the 16th century. 29 feet 4 inches by 11 feet.

Soon after the early part of the 16th century, there sprang up throughout Europe a liking for pastoral literature as seen in Virgil's eclogues: poets sung their dreams of the bliss to be found in rustic life, in which sports and pastimes, amid well-dressed revelry and music, with nought of toil or drudgery belonging to it, formed the yearly round; and in summer tide, nobles and their ladies loved to rove the woods and fields, and play at gentle shepherdism. How such frolics were carried out we learn from the tapestry before us, which, in many of its features, is near akin to those low reliefs of the same subject that adorn the walls in the court-yard of the curious and elaborately ornamented Hotel de Bourgtheroud, at Rouen.

At the left-hand side, lying on a flowery bank, is a gentleman shepherd, whose broad-toed shoes and thick cloth leggings, fastened round the knees and about the ancles, are rather conspicuous. On the brim of his large round white hat is a sort of square ticket, coloured. From his waist hangs a white satchel, bearing outside various appliances, such as countrymen want. Over him stands, with a tall spud in her hands, a youthful lady dressed in a scarlet robe, and wearing her satchel by her side, a thin gauze cap, not a hat, is on her head, and with her hand upraised she seems to be giving emphasis to what she says to her friend upon the ground.

In the middle of this piece is a group, consisting of four characters, all of whom are playing at some game of forfeits. A young lady clad in blue satin, with the usual rustic pouch slung at her side, is sitting on the flowery grass, with her hands on the shoulders of a youth at her feet, and hiding his face in her lap. Standing over him and about to strike his open palm is another youth in a blue tunic turned up with red, and holding a spud. Behind the blindfolded youth stands a young lady, whose flaxen locks fall from under a broad-brimmed crimson hat, upon her shoulders over her splendid robe, the crimson ground of which is nearly hidden by the broad diapering of gold most admirably shown upon it.

In the other corner, to the right, is a lady, kerchiefed and girded with her rustic wallet, with both hands grasping a man, who seems as if he asked forgiveness. Overhead is a swineherd leading a pig, and going towards a farm-labourer who is making faggots; further on is another clown, hard at work, with his coat thrown down by him on the ground, lopping trees; and last of all, a gentleman and lady, both clad in the costume of the first half of the sixteenth century. These groups on the high part of the canvas are evidently outside the subject of the games below, and are merely passers by. All about the field are seen grazing sheep; and to the right, a golden pheasant on the foreground is so conspicuous as to lead to the thought that it was placed there to tell, either the name of the noble house for which this beautifully-wrought and nicely-designed tapestry was made, or of the artist who worked it.

In a second, but much smaller pane of tapestry, the same subject is continued. Upon the flowery banks of a narrow streamlet sit a lady and a little boy, bathing their feet in its waters. A gentleman—a swain for the nonce—on his bended knee, holds up triumphantly one of the lady's stockings over the boy's head. Just above and striding towards her comes another gentleman-shepherd, with both his hands outstretched as if in wonderment, over whom we find a real churl in the person of a shepherd playing a set of double pipes—the old French "flahuter à deux dois"—to the no small delight of a little dog by his side. Serving as a background to this group, we have a comfortable homestead amid trees. Somewhat to the right and lower down, over a brick arch leans a lady, to whom a gaily-dreſſed man is offering money or a trinket, which he has juſt drawn forth from his open *gipcière* hanging at his girdle. Below ſits a ˌlady arrayed in a white robe, the ſkirts of which ſhe has drawn and folded back upon her lap to ſhow her ſcarlet petticoat. She is liſtening to a huntſman pranked out with a belt ſtrung with little bells; falling from his girdle hangs in front a buglehorn, and his left hand holds the leaſh of his dog with a fine collar on. Over this ſpruce youth is an unmiſtakable real field labourer with a Flemiſh *botte*, or wooden cradle, filled with chumps and ſticks, upon his back; and before him walk two dogs, one of which carries a pack or cloth over his ſhoulders. Still higher up is a windmill, toward which a man bearing a ſack is walking.

In both theſe pieces, which are fellows, and wrought for the hangings of the ſame chamber, the drawing of the figures, with the acceſſories of dreſs, ſilks, and even field-flowers, is admirable, and the grouping well managed: altogether, they are valuable links in the chain for the ſtudy and illuſtration of the ancient art of tapeſtry.

1297.

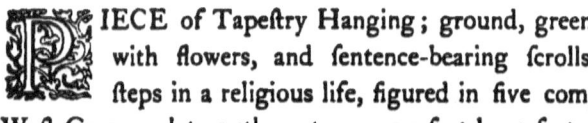IECE of Tapeſtry Hanging; ground, green ſprinkled with flowers, and ſentence-bearing ſcrolls; deſign, ſteps in a religious life, figured in five compartments. Weſt German, late 15th century. 12 feet by 2 feet 10 inches.

1. A young well-born maiden, with a narrow wreath about her unveiled head, and dreſſed in pink, is ſaying her prayers kneeling on the flowery green ground, with theſe words traced on the ſcrolls twined gracefully above her,—" Das wir Maria kindt in trew mage werden ſo . . . . t ich myn gnade . . . . n af erden ;" " Let us become like to Mary's child, (ſo) we ſhall deſerve mercy on earth."

2. Seated on a chair, with a book upon his lap, is an eccleſiaſtic, in a white habit and black ſcapular. To this prieſt the ſame young lady is making confeſſion of her ſins; and the ſcrolls about this group ſay,— " Vicht di ſunde mit ernſt ſonder ſpot ſo findeſtic Godez trew gnadt ;" " Fight againſt ſin with earneſtneſs and without feigning; you will find the true mercy of God."—" Her myn ſunde vil ich ach dagen uff das mir Gots trew moge behagen ;" " Lord, I will mourn over my ſin, in order that the truth of God may comfort me."

3. The same youthful maiden is bending over a wooden table, upon which lies a human heart that she is handling; and the inscriptions about her tell us the meaning of this action of hers, thus,—" Sol ich myn fund hi leschen so musz ich ich mÿ hertz im blude wesche;" "To cleanse away my sin here, I must wash my heart in the blood."

4. We here see an altar; upon its table are a small rood or crucifix with S. Mary and S. John, two candlesticks, having prickets for the wax-lights, the outspread corporal cloth, upon which stands the chalice, and under which, in front and not at the right side, lies the paten somewhat hidden. At the foot of this altar kneels the maiden, clad in blue, and wearing on her head a plain, closely-fitting linen cap, like that yet occasionally worn at church in Belgium, by females of the middle classes,—and the priest who is saying mass there is giving her Communion. The priest's alb is ornamented with crimson apparels on its cuffs and lower front hem, inscribed with the word "haus," house, is well rendered. The inscriptions above are, as elsewhere, mutilated, so that much of their meaning is lost; but they run thus,—" Wer he . . . versorget mich mit Gottes trew das bitten ich;" "If . . . not procure me the love of God that I pray for."—" Emphang in trewen den waren Crist dmit dyn;" " Receive with fidelity the very Christ in order . . . . "

5. A nunnery, just outside of which stands its lady-abbess, clothed in a white habit, black hood, and white linen wimple about her throat. In her right hand she bears a gold crozier, from which hangs that peculiar napkin, two of which are in this collection, Nos. 8279 A, and 8662. Behind stands an aged nun, and, as if in the passage and seen through the cloister windows, are two lay sisters, known as such by the black scapular. In front of the abbess stands the young maiden dressed in pink, with her waiting woman all in white, in attendance on her. Upon the scrolls are these sentences,—" Dez hymels ey port Godez vor (m)eyn husz disz ist;" " A gate of heaven—God's and mine house this is."—"Kom trew Christ wol. p. . eidt nym dy Kron dy dir Got hat bereit."—" Come, true Christian well . . . . take the crown which God has prepared for thee."

Though but a poor specimen of the loom, this piece gives us scraps of an obsolete dialect of the mediæval German, not Flemish, language.

1465.

PIECE of Tapestry Hanging; ground, grass and flowers; design, a German romance, divided into six compartments, each having its own inscribed scrolls, meant to describe the subject. South German, middle of the 15th century. 12 feet by 2 feet 6 inches.

In the first compartment we see a group of horsemen, of whom the first is a royal youth wearing a richly-jewelled crown and arrayed in all the fashion of those days. Following him are two grooms, over one of whose heads, but high up in the heavens, flies an eagle; and perhaps the bird may be there to indicate the name of the large walled city close by. Pacing on the flowery turf, the cavalcade is nearing a castle, at the threshold of which stand an aged king and his youthful daughter. On a scroll are the words,—" Bisg god wilkum dusig stunt(?) grosser frayd wart uns nie kunt;" "Be right welcome for a thousand hours; a greater joy we never knew." Of course the coming guest utters his acknowledgments; but the words on the scroll cannot be made out with the exception of this broken sentence,—" Heute ich unt . . .;" "To day I and . . ."

In the second compartment, in a room of the castle we behold the same royal youth, wearing, as before, his crown upon his long yellow locks, along with his three varlets. On a scroll are the words,— " Fromer dieur bestelle mir die ros ein wagge ist nun lieber;" "Pious servant, order me the horses, a carriage is preferred."

In the third compartment is shown, and very likely in his own home, the same young wouer talking, as it would seem by the scrolls, to his three waiting-men; and after one of them had said,—" Wage uñ rofz sint bereit als . . . .;" "Carriage and horses are ready as . . . ." he says,—" Wo schien gluck zu difer vart nie kein reise;" "If luck has shone on this journey, I never liked travelling better." Of the three servants, one holds three horses, while the upper groom is presenting, with both hands, to his royal young master a large something, apparently ornamented with flowers; the churl wears, hanging down from his girdle in front, an anelace or dagger, the gentleman a gay *gipcière*, but the shoes of both are very long and pointed.

In the fourth compartment the same crowned youth again is seen riding towards the castle-gate, though this time no lady fair stands at its threshold for the greeting; but instead, there stands with the old king a noble youth who, to all appearances, seems to have been beforehand, in the business of wooing and winning the young princess's heart, with the last comer. There are these words upon the scroll,—" Ich hab vor einem . . . gericht einer tuben und mich yr verpflicht;" "I have before a . . . tribunal of a dove, and have myself engaged to her;" meaning that already had he himself betrothed the king's daughter, by swearing to her his love and truth before a dove—a thing quite mediæval, like the vows of the swan, the peacock, and the pheasant, as we have noticed in the Introduction, and again while treating of the Syon Cope, at p. 28. On his side, the old king thus addresses him,— " Mich dunckt du komst uber land . . . zu der hochzeit;" "Methinks thou comest over-land . . . to see the wedding." In this, as in other inscriptions, the whole of the words cannot be made out.

The fifth compartment shows us the second and successful wooer, dressed out in the same attire as before, but now riding a well-appointed steed, and booted in the manner of those times. He is waited on by a mounted page. On a scroll are the words,—" Umb sehnlichst ich nun köme . . . . ist die ewige . . . ;" "That I most passionately now can . . . is the eternal," &c.

In the last compartment the rejected wooer is seen riding away as he came—without a bride—followed by two grooms.

Though rough in its execution, this piece of tapestry is valuable not only for its specimens of costume, like our own at the period, but especially for its inscriptions, which betray the provincialisms belonging to the south of Germany; and some of their expressions are said to be even yet in daily use about the neighbourhood of Nuremberg, to which locality we are warranted, for several reasons, in ascribing the production of this early example of the German loom.

1480.

TAPESTRY Hanging; within a narrow border of a dark green ground, ornamented with flowers mostly pink, and fruit-bearing branches of the vine, is figured a subject just outside the gates of a large walled city, and upon the flowery turf. Flemish, beginning of the 16th century. 13 feet by 11 feet 6 inches.

To all appearance the subject is taken from the Gospel of St. John, chap. 9, where the miracle is related of our Lord giving sight to the man born blind, who has juſt come back from waſhing in the pool of Siloam, and is anſwering his neighbours who had hitherto known him as the blind beggar. In front ſtands an important perſonage in a tunic of cloth of gold ſhot light blue, over which he wears a ſhorter one of fine crimſon diapered in gold, having a broad jewelled hem; of a rich gold ſtuff is his lofty turban. In his left hand he holds a long wand, ending in an arrow-ſhaped head. At the feet of this high functionary kneels the poor man bleſſed with ſight, while he is taking from him a ſomething like a ſquare glaſs bottle, and holds his coarſe hat in his hand. Near but above him ſtands a lady wearing a moſt curious head-dreſs, which is blue, with two red wings briſtling at its ſides. The reſt of her array is exactly like, in ſhape and ſtuffs, to the magnificent apparel of the firſt portly male figure, ſo as to lead us to believe that ſhe muſt be his wife, himſelf being one of the Jewiſh chief prieſts. Talking with her is another Jew ſplendidly dreſſed, and bearing a wand in one hand; and behind her we ſee a man wearing ear-rings, and a woman belonging to the lower claſs—probably the cured man's father and mother. Not far away from the prieſt, and at his back, are ſoldiers with lances, and one with a halbert, before whom ſtands a well-dreſſed, mantled and hooded Phariſee, with a rolled-up volume in his hand, and looking with a ſomewhat haughty ſcowl upon the man kneeling on the ground. Above the walls are ſeen the domes of ſeveral large buildings, of which one looks as if it were the temple of Jeruſalem; and all about the battlements are people gazing down upon the ſcene beneath them.

So Flemiſh is the Gothic ſtyle of architecture on the gates, around which are mock inſcriptions, and on the walls of the city, that we find at once that the tapeſtry muſt have been deſigned and wrought in Flanders. Though the ſhapes of the dreſſes be for the moſt part quite imaginary, ſtill the diapering on the gorgeous cloths of gold is after the ſtyle then in vogue and well rendered.

1481.

TAPESTRY Wall-hanging; ſubject, Neptune ſtilling the wind-ſtorm raiſed at Juno's requeſt by Æolus againſt the Trojan fleet on the Sicilian coaſt. Flemiſh, 17th century.

Evidently the deſigner of this tapeſtry meant to illuſtrate Virgil at the beginning of his firſt book of the Æneid. To the left hand is ſeen

Boreas with a lance, which he is aiming againſt Neptune, in one hand, while in the other he holds by a cord a rough wooden yoke, to which are tied two boys floating in the water, and each with a pair of bellows, which he is blowing. Drawn by two ſteeds comes Neptune with up-lifted trident, to ſtill the winds raiſed by the two boys; and over his head are Eurus and the weſtern wind in the ſhape of females flying in the air, one ſnapping the tall maſt of one of Æneas's ſhips, and the other pouring out broad ſtreams of water from four vaſes, one in each hand. The bellows are very like thoſe elaborately-carved ones in the Muſeum, out of Soulages collection.

1483.

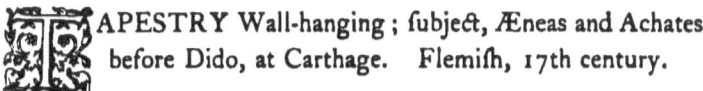APESTRY Wall-hanging; ſubject, Æneas and Achates before Dido, at Carthage. Flemiſh, 17th century.

The paſſage, in Virgil's firſt book of the Æneid, deſcriptive of Æneas, with the faithful Achates at his ſide, relating his adventures to Dido, the Carthaginian queen, is here illuſtrated. The youthful prin-ceſs, enthroned beneath a cloth of eſtate, is liſtening to the Trojan prince before her, and around are her ladies in gay coſtume, her own being of light blue ſilk damaſked with a large golden flower. As a back-ground we ſee the port filled with Æneas's ſhips, to which countrymen are driving ſheep and oxen for their crews. The women are quite of the Flemiſh type of fat beauty, and the odd head-dreſs for a man on Achates is remarkable.

1582.

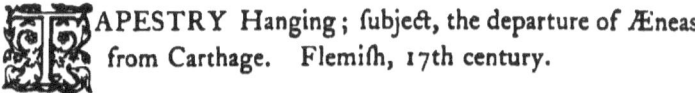APESTRY Hanging; ſubject, the departure of Æneas from Carthage. Flemiſh, 17th century.

In the foreground is Æneas taking leave of Dido, who is fainting into the arms of her waiting ladies. Behind, is a youth working as a maſon and building a wall: further back, are ſeen horſes richly capari-ſoned, upon one of which rides Dido, while Mercury comes flying down bidding Æneas to haſte him away.

1683.

APESTRY Wall-hanging; subject, Venus appearing to Æneas in a wood.

The second book of the Æneid has furnished the designer with the materials for this piece. Just as Æneas had uplifted his hand to slay Helen, Venus appears, stays his arms, and reasons with him. So says Virgil; but here we merely see Mercury coming down from the clouds, and Venus revealing herself to her son. The admirers of the beautiful in form and face will not find much to please them in the lady's person. This piece closes the history of Æneas as given in these tapestries, which came from the palace, or, as it used to be called, the King's House at Newmarket. All through, Dido is made to appear in the same kind of costume; but the dresses in general are purely imagined by the artist, without the slightest authority from the monuments of either Greek or Roman antiquity: and the architectural parts are quite in the debased classic style of the 17th century, as followed in Flanders. All these tapestries are framed in a red border, wrought at the sides with scrolls and shields, and below, with winged boys holding labels once showing inscriptions (now faded) all shot with gold, but tarnished black. Many of the female figures are slip-shod, like St. Mary Magdalen in Rubens's "Taking down from the Cross," at Antwerp.

6733.

TAPESTRY Hanging; subject, the story of Arria and Paetus, copied from a painting by Francois André Vincent, and dated 1785. The border was added afterwards. French, done at the Gobelins. 12 feet by 10 feet 6 inches. Presented by His Imperial Highness Prince Napoleon.

The subject is a startling one; being condemned to die, by the Emperor Claudius, and put an end to his life with his own hand, Paetus hesitated. Seeing this, his wife Arria snatched up the weapon and plunged it to the hilt in her own bosom, and then handing the dagger to her husband, said, "It does not pain me, Paetus."

At top, on a blue ground, is a large N in yellow, indicative of the firſt Napoleon, who, in the year 1807 preſented this fine ſpecimen of the far-famed Gobelin tapeſtry to his brother Jerome, at the time King of Weſtphalia, as a marriage gift. By the late Prince Jerome it was ſent, through his ſon, the preſent Prince Napoleon, for preſentation to this Muſeum.

2442.

APESTRY Wall-hanging; deſign, groups of richly-dreſſed ladies and gentlemen around a queen. Flemiſh, early 16th century.

Apparently the crowded ſcene before us is meant to illuſtrate ſome ſymbolic ſubject. In the midſt of them all ſtands a queen, whoſe hands are claſped. Before her kneels a man who reſpectfully bares his head the while he outſtretches to the princeſs a written paper. Behind ſtands a magnificent chair. Further back is a nicely-ſhown interior of a room having its cupboard loaded with vaſes ſtanding on the ſhelves; there ſit three ladies in earneſt talk. All about are groups of richly-clothed men and women, each of whoſe dreſſes is worthy of notice.

2443.

APESTRY; ſubject, a landſcape, the foreground ſtrewed with human and animals' bones, and a living figure ſitting among rocks. French, early 17th century.

This is one of a ſhort ſeries of tapeſtries ſetting forth, but ſometimes laughing at, the ideas of the ancient cynics. Before us here we have a wild dell clothed in trees on one ſide, on the other piled with rocks capped, in ſome places, by ruins. Seated on a ſtone, with a book held in his hand, is Diogenes in meditation, with human bones, animal ſkulls, and monſter things about him. The work is well done, and ſhows how perfect was the loom that wrought it. On a blue tablet at top runs this inſcription,—" Diogenes deriſor omnium in fine defigitur."

2807.

APESTRY; fubject, the vifit of Alexander the Great to Diogenes in his tub. French, early 17th century.

The fcene is well laid out, peopled with many figures, and its ftory neatly told. Above, in the ufual place, is this infcription,—" Senfit Alexander teftā quum vidit in illā magnum habitatorem, quanto felicior hic, qui nil cuperet (*quàm*) qui totum fibi pofceret orbem."

3818.

APESTRY; fubject, a beautifully-wooded fcene with a ftream running down the middle of it, and acrofs which two men, one on each fide, are talking. French, early 17th century.

On one fide ftands Dionyfius; on the other, and holding a bunch of vegetables, which he is about to wafh in the brook, is Diogenes, who was not remarkable for his perfonal cleanlinefs. Dionyfius, it would feem, has been twitting him upon that fubject, and gets for anfwer that his very prefence taints with dirt Diogenes himfelf, and the waters in which he is about to wafh his pot-herbs: " Sordet mihi Dionyfius lavanti olera," as the Latin infcription reads above.

4331.

APESTRY Wall-hanging; defign, a wooded fcene in the background; in the foreground, Diogenes and a man. French, early 17th century.

Before a large tub, lying on its fide, is ftretched out Diogenes, pointing his finger to his curious dwelling, with his head looking towards a wayfarer, to whom he feems to fay thofe words traced on the blue label at the top,—" Qui domum ambit hanc (anne?) me fepeliat." This appears to have been drawn from his lips by the man going by, who is pointing towards the gaping mouth of the tub.

4650.

APESTRY; subject, a gate-way built of rough stone, over which a female is tracing an inscription, of which are written in large capital letters these words:—

"Nihil hic ingrediatur mali."

Besides this, we find these sentences also:—
"Diogenes Cynicus subscribit;" and, "Spado sceleratus scripsit."

In these five pieces of tapestry, which were evidently employed for hanging the walls in some especial hall, we cannot but admire the ease and freedom of their whole design, and be struck especially by the beauty of their wild, yet charming landscapes, which are so well brought out by the weaver-artist who wrought them.

7926.

APESTRY; subject, the Holy Family, after Raphael. Presented by His Imperial Majesty the Emperor Napoleon III.

No words are necessary to call the observer's attention to this admirable specimen of the French loom. Of the many fine pieces sent forth by the manufactory of the Gobelins, this may easily take a place among the very finest; and, at first sight, many people might be led to think that it was the work of the pencil, and not of machinery. About it there is a warmth and depth of mellow colouring which has partly fled from the original, through time and, may be, want of care. Those who have seen the pictures at the Louvre must well remember the grand and precious original of which this is such a successful copy.

189.

TAPESTRY Wall-hanging; defign, our Lord giving the power of the keys to St. Peter, after Raphael's cartoon. Englifh (probably from Soho), 17th century. 17 feet 1 inch by 12 feet.

The point of time chofen by the great Roman painter is that indicated by St. Matthew, xvi. 18, 19; for St. Peter holds the keys promifed him by his divine Mafter, at whofe feet he alone, of all the apoftles, is kneeling. Behind our Lord is a large flock of fheep, as explanatory of the paftoral power beftowed, after His uprifing from the grave, by our Saviour upon St. Peter more efpecially, to feed the fheep as well as lambs in His flock, as we read in St. John, xxi. 16, 17: both fubjects are naturally connected.

By the many engravings, but, more particularly, the fine photographs of the original cartoon, once at Hampton Court, now in this Mufeum, this fubject is well known. In this efpecial piece, the colouring, being fo badly graduated and garifh, is by no means as good as in the earlier one, ftill to be feen in the Gallery of the Tapeftries at the Vatican. Here, the tone of our Lord's drapery is not diftinguifhable from the ftony hue of the wool upon the fheep behind Him.

8225.

PANEL of Tapeftry; ground, light blue; defign, bunches of flowers upon a white panel. 2 feet 11¾ inches by 2 feet 3½ inches. Aubuffon, prefent century. Prefented by Meffrs. Requillart, Rouffel, and Chocqueel.

After Paris with the Gobelins, and the city of Beauvais, there is no town in France which produces fuch fine tapeftries as Aubuffon, the carpets of which are much admired.

7927 to 7930.

FOUR Pieces of Tapeſtry; ground, light blue; deſign, flowers. French, preſent century. Preſented by His Imperial Majeſty the Emperor Napoleon III.

Beauvais, which produced theſe beautiful ſpecimens, has long been famous for the works of the loom; and the preſent lovely figures of ſuch well-drawn, nicely-coloured flowers are worthy of that city's reputation.

594.

TAPESTRY Wall-hanging; ſubject, Eſther about to venture into the preſence of Ahaſuerus. From the Soulages Collection. Flemiſh, firſt half of the 16th century. Height 13 feet, breadth 11 feet 6 inches.

The hiſtory, as here ſhown us, of a moſt eventful achievement, is at top diſtributed into four groups, each made up of figures rather ſmall in ſtature; and at bottom, into other five cluſters, in which all the perſonages aſſume a proportion little ſhort of life-ſize.

Beginning with thoſe higher compartments on the piece, we find in the two at the left-hand ſide the commencement of this Scriptural record. The mighty Ahaſuerus is preſented to us in the ſecond of thoſe two groups there, as ſeated amid trees, and robed as would have been a ſovereign prince during the firſt half of the ſixteenth century. All about his head and neck the Perſian king wears, wrapped in looſe folds, a linen cloth, over which he has a large ſcarlet hat with an ornament for a crown, made up of ſmall ſilver ſhield-ſhaped plates, marked with wedge-like ſtripes of a light blue colour, or heraldically, *argent*, five piles *azure* meeting at the baſe; over his ſhoulders falls an unſpotted ermine cape jagged all about its edge ſo as to look as if meant for a nebulée border. Upon the left breaſt of this ſort of mantle is ſewed a little crimſon ſhield-ſhaped badge marked in white ſeemingly with the letter A, not having, however, the ſtroke through it, but above, the ſign of contraction daſhed. He wears a blue tabard, is girt with a ſword, and holds in his left hand a tall wand, that golden ſceptre which, if not outstretched in token of clemency towards the man or woman who had the hardihood to come unbidden to his presence, signified that such a bold intruder, were she the queen herself, must be put to death. Having nobles and guards about him, this monarch of one hundred and twenty-seven provinces is handing to Haman, one of those three princes before him, a written document from which hang two royal seals: this is that terrible decree, which, out of spite towards Mordecai, and hatred for the Jewish race, Haman had won from his partial master Ahasuerus, for the slaughter, on a certain day, of every Hebrew within the Persian empire.

Yet further to the left is another group, wherein we observe some of the richly-attired functionaries of the empire. A bareheaded old man, a royal messenger, who holds up his left hand as if to indicate he had come from the court of Ahasuerus, delivers to one of the nobles there this original decree to be copied out and sent in all directions through the kingdom.

Looking still at top, but to the far right, we have in the background, amid the trees, a large house, from out of the midst of which stands up a tall red beam, the gibbet, fifty cubits high, got ready by Haman at his wife's and friends' suggestion for hanging on it Mordecai. In this foreground we behold Haman clad in a blue mantle and a rich golden chain about his neck: to the man standing respectfully before him, cap in hand, Haman gives the written order duly authenticated by the two imperial seals upon it, for the execution of Mordecai. Immediately to the left of this scene we are presented with the inside view of a fine chamber hung with tapestry, and ornamented with tall vases, two of which are on a shelf close by a lattice-window. In the middle of this room is a group of three women: one of them, Esther, richly clad, is seated and wringing her hands in great grief, as if she had learned the fell death awaiting her uncle, and the slaughter already decreed of all her nation: two of her gentlewomen are with her, wailing, like their queen-mistress, the coming catastrophe.

Right in the centre of the piece, and occupying its most conspicuous position, we behold the tall stately figure of a beautiful young queen, splendidly arrayed, and wearing over the rich caul upon her head a royal diadem. She seems to have just arisen from the magnificent throne or rather faldstool close behind her. With both her hands clasped in supplication, she is followed in her upward course by her train of attendants—two ladies and a nobleman—all gaily dressed, threading their way through as they ascend from the hall below crowded with courtiers, men and women gossiping together in little knots, and set off in fashionable dress. While bending her steps, Esther looks towards the spot where Ahasuerus is sitting. At this moment an oldish man steps forward, clad after a beseeming fashion: in one hand he holds his red cap, while with the other hand he is stretching out, for Esther's acceptance, his inscribed roll. This person must be Mordecai, thus shown as instructing and encouraging his niece-queen Esther in the hazardous work of saving her people's lives, at the same time that he furnishes her with a copy of the decree for their utter annihilation.

This inner court of the King's house where Esther is now standing over against the hall in which Ahasuerus sits upon his throne is crowded with courtiers, all remarkable for the elegance and costliness of their dress. In a circle of three great personages to the right, one of those high-born dames has brought with her her guitar, made in the form of the calabash, to help on by her music the expected mirth and revelry of the day.

In those several instances in which the royal decree is figured with the imperial seals hanging from it, the impression stamped upon the wax seems, no doubt, to be taken as the cipher of Ahasuerus, a large A, but without the stroke through it.

One remarkable feature among the ornaments of dress assumed by almost all the great personages in this piece of tapestry is the large-linked, heavy golden chain about the neck, worn as much by ladies as by gentlemen. The caps of the men are mostly square.

The elaborately-adorned, closely-fitting, round-shaped caul worn by the women in this court of Ahasuerus is in strict accordance with the female fashion abroad at the beginning of the sixteenth century; while here, in England, the gable-headed coif found more favour than the round with our countrywomen. Then, however, as now, ladies loved long trains to their gowns; and the men's shoes had that peculiar broad toe so conspicuously marked in Hans Holbein's cartoon for a picture of our Henry VIII. belonging to the Duke of Devonshire, and exhibited among the National Portraits on loan to the South Kensington Museum, A. D. 1866.

8979.

TAPESTRY Hanging; subject, the three Fates with a young lady lying dead at their feet. Flemish, early 16th century.

With a grove of blooming trees behind them, and upon a lawn, everywhere sprinkled with many kinds of flowers, stand the Fates. Each of the weird sisters may be individually known by her proper name written in white letters near her head. Beginning from the right side of the piece, we have the spinster Clotho, who is figured as a youthful maiden; amid the boughs of a tree just above her is seen a long-billed bird of the snipe-kind; she is gaily dressed in a yellow kirtle, elaborately diapered after a flowery pattern done in green, over which she wears a gown of deep crimson velvet, while from her girdled waist falls a large golden chain ending in a gold pomander. In her left hand she holds a distaff, keeping at the same time between her fingers the thread which she has but just done spinning. Next to Clotho stands Lachesis, almost as young in look; she is not quite so sprightly but yet as elegantly clad as her sister with the distaff; billing and cooing above this feigned manager of individual destiny we behold a pair of turtle-doves; this second of the Fates is clad in robes of a light pink tone nicely and artistically diapered, and with her left hand she takes from Clotho the thread just spun and with her right passes it on to Atropos. This the last, and the most dreaded of the fatal three, looks older than the other two, and is arrayed more matronly. Clothed in deep blue, Atropos wears a large full white kerchief, which, as its name implies, not only covers her head, but falls well down from her shoulders half-way to her broad girdle, upon which is flung a string of beads for prayer—a rosary. Atropos, whose imaginary office was to cut with knife, or scissors, or a pair of shears, the thread of life, uses no such an instrument here; for with her hands she has broken the life-cord, and the spindle, around which it had been wound, lies thrown upon the flowery turf close by the head of the victim of the Fates. At the feet of these three sisters lies, stretched out in all her fullest length, a youthful lady dead. She wears a kerchief on her head, and over her richly-diapered pink gown she has a light crimson mantle thickly powdered with small golden crescents. Her bed seems made of early summer flowers; and alongside of her, and as if just fallen from her outstretched right hand, lies the tall stalk, snapped short off near the lower end, of a blooming white lily. At one side, but lower down, is the half-figure of a monkey; some way to the right, but on the same level, sits in quiet security a large brown hare; while between these two animals, from out a hole in the ground, as if they snuffed their future prey in the dead body, are creeping a weasel and a stoat, just after a large toad that has crawled out before them.

This piece of tapestry, valuable alike for its artistic excellence and its good preservation, has a more than common interest about it. In all likelihood it gives us the hiftory, nay, perhaps affords us the very portraiture of fome high-born, beautiful young lady, well known and admired in her day. A little fomething at leaft may be gathered from its fymbolifm. By the heathen mythological diftribution of functions among the poetic Parcæ, or Fates, to the fecond of thefe three fifters, to Lachefis, was it given to decide the efpecial deftiny of each mortal the hour that fhe or he was born. Now in the inftance before us a pair of turtle-doves, love's emblem, is confpicuoufly fhown above the head of Lachefis. As this young lady's life-thread flipped through her fingers Lachefis has touched it, quickened it fo that the child for whom it is being fpun fhall have a heart all maidenly, but foft to the impreffions of the gentle paffion—love. She has been wooed and made a bride, for fhe has on the married woman's kerchief. That lily-ftem with its opening buds and full-blown flowers at top is the emblem of a fpotlefs whitenefs, an unftained innocence ; the ftalk is broken, but the flowers on it are un-withered. What fitter tokens of a bride's unlooked-for death, the very morning of her marriage? But that monkey-emblem of mifchief, evil, moral uglinefs, and in particular of lubricity—perhaps may mean us to underftand the worthleffnefs of wanton, profligate men. As the harmlefs unfufpecting hare is eafily fnared and taken in a toil, fo fhe might have been caught, but may have been fpared, by early death, a life of mifery. Thofe loathfome things coming from out the ground warn men that all of us muft one day or another become the prey of the grave, and that youth, and innocence, and beauty will be its food.

THE BROOKE COLLECTION.

542. '64.

CHRISTENING Ribbon, white filk with filver gimp edge. Englifh, 18th century. Length 6 feet 9 inches, width 2¼ inches. Prefented by the Rev. R. Brooke.

858, 858 B. '64.

COURT Suit, coat and knee-breeches, of cherry-coloured Genoa velvet, white fatin lining, waiftcoat white fatin embroidered in coloured filks and filver. Englifh, dated 1772. Length of coat 3 feet 2½ inches, length of breeches 2 feet, length of waiftcoat 2 feet 5 inches. Prefented by the Rev. R. Brooke.

859, 859 B. '64.

DRESS Suit, coat, waiftcoat, and knee-breeches, of pink filk brocade with a diapered flower pattern. Englifh, date about 1770. Length of coat 3 feet 2½ inches, length of waiftcoat 2 feet 6 inches, length of breeches 2 feet 4 inches. Prefented by the Rev. R. Brooke.

Needlework and Dresses.

860. '64.
APRON, white silk, with raised floral embroidery. English, date about 1720. Length 2 feet 0½ inch, width 2 feet 9¼ inches. Presented by the Rev. R. Brooke.

861. '64.
APRON, yellow silk, with raised floral embroidery, in colours, bordered with silk lace. English, date about 1720. Length 2 feet 1 inch, width 2 feet 10 inches. Presented by the Rev. R. Brooke.

862. '64.
APRON, white silk, with coloured floral embroidery and silver cord. English, date about 1720. Length 1 foot 7½ inches, width 3 feet. Presented by the Rev. R. Brooke.

863. '64.
APRON, white silk, with purple floral embroidery and gold cord. English, date about 1720. Length 1 foot 9 inches, width 3 feet 2 inches. Presented by the Rev. R. Brooke.

864. '64.
PORTION of Embroidery, flowers in coloured silks (chiefly orange) on linen ground covered with stitched scroll pattern. English, 18th century. Length 1 foot 10¼ inches, width 1 foot 6 inches. Presented by the Rev. R. Brooke.

865. '64.
PORTION of Embroidery, flowers in coloured silks (chiefly orange) on linen ground covered with stitched scroll pattern. English, 18th century. Length 1 foot 1½ inches, width 1 foot 6 inches. Presented by the Rev. R. Brooke.

866. '64.

PORTION of Embroidery, flowers in coloured filks (chiefly orange) on linen ground covered with ftitched fcroll pattern. Englifh, 18th century. Length 2 feet 2¾ inches, width 2 feet. Prefented by the Rev. R. Brooke.

867. '64.

PIECE of Brocade, crimfon fatin with cut velvet floral pattern; bordered with filver gimp and fpangles. French, date about 1770. Length 3 feet 5¼ inches, width 3 feet 2 inches. Prefented by the Rev. R. Brooke.

868. '64.

PIECE of Brocade, crimfon fatin with cut velvet floral pattern; bordered with filver gimp and fpangles. French, date about 1770. Length 6 feet, width 3 feet 2 inches. Prefented by the Rev. R. Brooke.

869. '64.

MANTILLA, yellow filk and black lace. Englifh, date about 1770. Length, as worn, 5 feet, width of fkirt 3 feet. Prefented by the Rev. R. Brooke.

870. '64.

BODDICE, yellow filk. Englifh, date about 1770. Height 12½ inches, width 2 feet 4½ inches. Prefented by the Rev. R. Brooke.

Needlework and Dresses.

871. '64.

TABLE-COVER, pink silk edged with silver gimp. English, 18th century. Length 3 feet 5 inches, width 3 feet. Presented by the Rev. R. Brooke.

872. '64.

PIECE of Silk, pink ribbed, lined with pink sarsnet. English, 18th century. Length 3 feet 4 inches, width 4 feet. Presented by the Rev. R. Brooke.

873. '64.

SILK Fringe, green and yellow. English, date about 1740. Length 8 feet 1 inch, depth 3½ inches. Presented by the Rev. R. Brooke.

874. '64.

COUNTERPANE, white linen embroidered with running pattern; in centre a scroll ornament with cipher and scroll border, all in yellow silk. English, 17th century. Length 7 feet 8 inches, width 6 feet 11 inches. Presented by the Rev. R. Brooke.

875. '64.

CUSHION-COVER, white linen embroidered with running pattern and scroll ornament, yellow silk; cipher in centre. English, 17th century. Length 2 feet 1 inch, width 1 foot 5¼ inches. Presented by the Rev. R. Brooke.

876. '64.

CUSHION-COVER, white linen embroidered with running pattern and scroll ornament, yellow silk; cipher in centre. English, 17th century. Length 1 foot 8¼ inches, width 1 foot 3½ inches. Presented by the Rev. R. Brooke.

877. '64.

CUSHION-COVER, white linen embroidered with running pattern and scroll ornament, yellow silk; cipher in centre. English, 17th century. Length 1 foot 5½ inches, width 1 foot 2 inches. Presented by the Rev. R. Brooke.

878. '64.

PIECE of Brocade, white silk and gold in narrow stripes. French (?), 18th century. Length 10 feet 4 inches, width 2 feet 2 inches. Presented by the Rev. R. Brooke.

879. '64.

TABLE-COVER, crimson Genoa velvet with broad border of silver gimp, Indian (Delhi) work. Length 5 feet 2 inches, width 5 feet 2 inches. Presented by the Rev. R. Brooke.

880. '64.

SADDLE-CLOTH, dark blue Genoa velvet, ornamented with broad bands of flowered gold lace; trappings for the horse of H. Osbaldeston, Esq., High Sheriff of Yorkshire, A.D. 1772-3. Length 4 feet 5 inches, width 1 foot 8½ inches. Presented by the Rev. R. Brooke.

881, 881 A. '64.

PAIR of Holsters for Pistols, dark blue Genoa velvet, ornamented with broad bands of flowered gold lace; trappings for the horse of H. Osbaldeston, Esq., High Sheriff of Yorkshire, A.D. 1772-3. Length 1 foot 9 inches, width 1 foot 6¾ inches. Presented by the Rev. R. Brooke.

882. '64.

SADDLE-CLOTH, scarlet cloth with border of gold lace, used by the attendants of the High Sheriff of Yorkshire, A.D. 1772-3. Length 3 feet 8 inches, width 1 foot 6 inches. Presented by the Rev. R. Brooke.

883. '64.

SADDLE-CLOTH, scarlet cloth with border of gold lace, used by the attendants of the High Sheriff of Yorkshire, A.D. 1772-3. Length 3 feet 10½ inches, width 1 foot 6¾ inches. Presented by the Rev. R. Brooke.

884. '64.

SADDLE-CLOTH, scarlet cloth, with border of gold lace, used by the attendants of the High Sheriff of Yorkshire, A.D. 1772-3. Length 3 feet 10 inches, width 1 foot 6¾ inches. Presented by the Rev. R. Brooke.

885. '64.

PAIR of Pistol Holsters, scarlet cloth bordered with gold lace, used by the attendants of the High Sheriff of Yorkshire, A.D. 1772-3. Length 12 inches. Presented by the Rev. R. Brooke.

886, 886 A. '64.

AIR of Piſtol Holſters, ſcarlet cloth bordered with gold lace, uſed by the attendants of the High Sheriff of Yorkſhire, A.D. 1772-3. Length 12 inches. Preſented by the Rev. R. Brooke.

887, 887 A. '64.

AIR of Piſtol Holſters, ſcarlet cloth bordered with gold lace, uſed by the attendants of the High Sheriff of Yorkſhire, A.D. 1772-3. Length 12 inches. Preſented by the Rev. R. Brooke.

888. '64.

RESS Silk Brocade, white ground with pattern of flowers in various colours. French(?), early 18th century. Length 4 feet 7 inches, width 8 feet 4 inches. Preſented by the Rev. R. Brooke.

889. '64.

ADY'S Shoe, pink prunella, with high heel. Engliſh, date about 1765. Length 9⅛ inches. Preſented by the Rev. R. Brooke.

890 '64.

RENADIER'S Cap, ſcarlet and white cloth and crimſon velvet, with ſilver and gold embroidery, and gold ſpangles. Engliſh, date about 1770. Height 14 inches. Preſented by the Rev. R. Brooke.

891. '64.

ADY'S Workbag, made from the bark of a tree, bordered with green and white. Engliſh(?), 18th century. Length 2 feet, width 1 foot 1 inch. Preſented by the Rev. R. Brooke.

892. '64.

PIECE of Silk Embroidery in frame, white satin ground, on which are worked in high relief King Ahasuerus, Queen Esther, various animals, fruits, and other objects, in coloured silk and gold cord. English, early 18th century. Height 1 foot 1 inch, width 1 foot 7 inches. Presented by the Rev. R. Brooke.

893. '64.

WAISTCOAT, white ribbed silk embroidered with flowers in various colours, silver cord, and spangles. English, date about 1770. Length 2 feet 3 inches. Presented by the Rev. R. Brooke.

894. '64.

WAISTCOAT, crimson satin, with floral brocade border in various colours. English, date about 1770. Length 2 feet 7 inches. Presented by the Rev. R. Brooke.

895. '64.

WAISTCOAT, blue and white striped silk brocade with flower spot pattern. English, date about 1770. Length 2 feet 2¼ inches. Presented by the Rev. R. Brooke.

896. '64.

SKIRT of a Lady's Dress, white silk printed with flowers in various colours. French(?), 18th century. Height 3 feet 6 inches, width 9 feet 8 inches. Presented by the Rev. R. Brooke.

897. '64.

PIECE of Silk, white silk printed with flowers in various colours. French(?), 18th century. Height 3 feet, width 2 feet. Presented by the Rev. R. Brooke.

898. '64.

KERCHIEF, yellow silk gauze with floral pattern, border of pink and yellow silk lace. French(?), 18th century. Length 4 feet 3 inches, width 3 feet. Presented by the Rev. R. Brooke.

899. '64.

TRIMMING of a Dress, chocolate silk gauze, embroidered with flowers in various colours. English, 18th century. Length 5 feet, width 12 inches. Presented by the Rev. R. Brooke.

900. '64.

CHRISTENING Suit, viz. cap, bib, mittens, and dress (in two pieces), old point lace. Flemish(?), 18th century; worn in 1773. Length of dress 1 foot 11 inches, width 1 foot 3½ inches. Presented by the Rev. R. Brooke.

919. '64.

RETICULE, silk embroidery of various colours, with yellow satin neck. English, 18th century. Length 9 inches, width 6 inches. Presented by the Rev. R. Brooke.

932. '64.

SWORD-BELT, black silk web; part of a Volunteer uniform. English, early present century. Length 3 feet 5 inches. Presented by the Rev. R. Brooke.

933. '64.

SWORD-BELT, pale blue silk web, with steel clasps; part of a Volunteer uniform. English, early 18th century. Length 3 feet 8 inches. Presented by the Rev. R. Brooke.

934. '64.

SWORD-BELT, black leather, gilt metal mounts; part of a Volunteer uniform. English, 18th century. Length 2 feet 11 inches. Presented by the Rev. R. Brooke.

935. '64.

BADGE for a Cap Front, crown, cipher, and motto in steel on scarlet cloth; part of a Volunteer uniform. English, 18th century. Height $4\frac{7}{8}$ inches, width 5 inches. Presented by the Rev. R. Brooke.

966. '64.

BAG, or Purse, links of silver filagree. Modern Genoese. Length $5\frac{3}{4}$ inches. Presented by the Rev. R. Brooke.

978. '64.

SCREEN; white silk gauze painted with flowers and birds with a vase in centre. Modern Chinese. Length 12 feet 8 inches, height 2 feet $6\frac{1}{4}$ inches. Presented by the Rev. R. Brooke.

979. '64.

SCREEN, white silk gauze, painted with flower-sprigs, insects, and a basket hanging from a tree. Modern Chinese. Length 12 feet 10 inches, width 2 feet 5 inches. Presented by the Rev. R. Brooke.

980. '64.

SCREEN, white silk gauze, painted with flowers and birds. Modern Chinese. Height 3 feet 6½ inches, width 4 feet 8¼ inches. Presented by the Rev. R. Brooke.

981. '64.

PIECE of Embroidery, white satin ground with pattern of leaves and flowers highly relieved in coloured silks and gold cord. English, 18th century. Length 1 foot 10 inches, width 1 foot 1½ inches. Presented by the Rev. R. Brooke.

982, 982 D. '64.

FIVE Funeral Banners, silk, emblazoned with armorial shields. English, 18th century. Length 1 foot 9¼ inches, width 1 foot 4⅝ inches. Presented by the Rev. R. Brooke.

983. '64.

FUNERAL Banner, calico, emblazoned with armorial shields. English, 18th century. Length 1 foot 2 inches, width 1 foot 4 inches. Presented by the Rev. R. Brooke.

983 A. '64

FUNERAL Banner, calico. Englifh, 18th century. Length 1 foot 2 inches, width 1 foot 1 inch. Prefented by the Rev. R. Brooke.

LENT BY HER MAJESTY AND THE BOARD OF WORKS.

APESTRY; ground crimfon, diapered with foliage; defign, within a broad arch, a white panel, figured with Diana, and about her flowers, birds, and animals, dead and alive. At the right corner, on the lower hem, is infcribed, " Neilfon, ex. 1786." French, from the Gobelin factory.

Diana holds by a long blue ribbon a greyhound; below, are other two hounds and two little naked boys, of whom one is about to dart an arrow; the other, to fhoot one from a bow at Diana herfelf, who, with her fhadow caft upon a cloud, is holding her favourite dog by its blue ftring: at her feet lie her own bow and arrows. This piece is gracioufly lent by Her Majefty, and is a favourable fpecimen of the Gobelins royal manufactory, over which the Neilfons, father and fon, prefided, from A. D. 1749 till 1788. Moft likely this piece was wrought by the elder Neilfon, who, as well as his fon, worked with the "baffe liffe," or low horizontal frame, as diftinguifhed from the "haute liffe," or high vertical one.

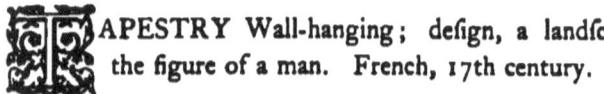APESTRY Wall-hanging; defign, a landfcape with the figure of a man. French, 17th century.

The landfcape is fomewhat wild, but nicely rendered. In the foreground, fitting on a ftone, we have a youth with both his hands upon a claffic-fhaped vafe, ftanding between his feet. In the background are seen a few goats; and further on still, a building with pillars, very likely a well. This fancy piece is surrounded by a border figured with ornamentation, and though it be small and made to fit some panel in a room, is a good specimen of its time, and seems to have come from the same hands that designed and wrought the Diogenes pieces.

TAPESTRY; design, within a crimson border ornamented, in white, with scroll-work after a classic character, a large mythologic, perhaps Bacchanal subject. French, 17th century.

Upheld by pilasters and columns wreathed with branches of the vine, we see a wide entablature coloured crimson and blue, figured with tripods, vases, and other fanciful arabesque ornamentation, and amid these, heathen gods and goddesses, centaurs, birds, and groups of satyrs. Below, and between the pilasters and columns, a male figure is playing the double pipe, women are carrying fruits in dishes, another is dancing, and some high personages feasting at a table, with some men looking on. Lowermost of all is another scene, in which we have little naked boys, satyrs carrying grapes, and an ass laden with them, and other satyrs pouring into vases the red wine which they are getting from a fountain brim full of it. A border of a crimson ground figured in places with full-faced heads, and all over with small figures, the draperies of which are shaded in gold now quite black, and arabesques after a classic form, goes round the whole piece, which is fellow to another showing the labours of Hercules, in this collection. In the tapestry before us, all the subjects are so Bacchanalian that we must suppose that the designer meant to set forth the ways of the god of wine. Like the drawing in the Hercules piece, the drawing here is good; but the piece itself is in a somewhat bad condition.

TAPESTRY Wall-hanging; subject, the labours of Hercules. Flemish, late 17th century. 21 feet 6 inches by 16 feet.

This large piece is divided into three broad horizontal bands; on the first of these, upon a dark blue ground, amid arabesques and monsters after classic models, are observable the infant Hercules strangling the two serpents; in the middle, a female holding two ropes, and about her little boys carrying tall reeds, which at top expand into a cup full of fire, as she stands upright upon a pedestal over a door-way, in the tympanum of which, within a round hollow, is the bust of a man having a wine-jug on one side, and a dish filled with fire on the other; still further to the right, there is, within an oval, a child reading at a three-legged desk, and seated on the bending bough of a tree, at the foot of which is a book, and a comic mask. On the second band, the ground of which is light blue, within the doorway, coloured green, stands Hercules crofs-legged, bearing in his right hand his club, and with the left upholding the lion-skin mantle. To the right, Hercules is seen wrestling; next, Hercules fighting the Nemean lion with his club; and then the hero shooting with his bow and arrows the Stymphalian birds, half human in their shape: to the left, Hercules is beheld strangling with his own hands the Nemean lion; then he is seen with this dead beast upon his shoulders as he carries it to Eurystheus; and lastly, he is shown loaded with a blue globe, marked with the signs of the zodiac, upon his back. On the third band, which is crimson, we find Hercules, leading by a chain the many-headed Cerberus from the lower world, having along with him Athena, who is seen with clasped hands, and Theseus, who is clad in armour with a reversed dart in his hand; in front lies a dead man. The middle of this band is filled in with architectural scroll-work, upon which are seated two half-bust winged figures, one male, the other female, and hanging between them a shield figured with the rape of Europa. After this central piece we come to the scene on the journey into exile of Hercules and his wife Deianira: the centaur Nessus is carrying the lady in his arms over the river Evenus, and while doing so insults her, whereupon Hercules lets fly an arrow, on hearing his wife's screams, and shoots Nessus to the heart. The whole is enclosed within a border of a crimson ground, figured with arabesques and heads of a classic character. The third band has a hermes or terminal post at each end; and, curiously enough, in the top band, and resting on the foliations, are four nests of the pelican, billing its breast and feeding its young ones with its blood; besides this we see in places two lions rampant, and regularly langued *gules*, being caressed by a sort of harpy: all of which would lead us to think that in the bird and the animals we have the armorial charge upon the shield, and its supporters, of the noble, but now unknown, owner for whom this piece of tapestry was originally wrought. Its fellow-piece, figured not so much with the triumphs as the festive joys of Bacchus, is in this collection.

TAPESTRY Wall-hanging; ground, white; subject, the young Bacchus on a cloud, with a cup of wine in one hand, and the thyrsus-staff in the other; and all about, his symbols. French, or Gobelin, 18th century.

Within a rather broad panelled arch, wine-red in its tone, is figured the young Bacchus with a couple of Thyrsus-staves, crossed saltire-wise above him: below, is a fountain with an animal's face, from the mouth of which runs red wine, and by it two little satyrs playing with tigers, into whose open maws they are squeezing the juice of the purple grape. Within a tablet in the higher part are figured two letters M. M. seemingly the ciphers of the individual for whom this piece was woven.

TAPESTRY Wall-hanging; ground, white; subject, Venus surrounded by her emblems. French, or Gobelin, 18th century.

This is a fellowpiece to the foregoing one, and arranged in the same manner. Riding on a cloud, Venus holds a small dart, and leans upon a swan, with a Cupid by her feet. Like the other piece, it has the cipher M. M.

TAPESTRY Wall-hanging; ground, mostly white; subject, shepherds and shepherdesses sacrificing to Pan. French, or Gobelin, 18th century.

This large fine piece has a very cheerful tone, and the background is so managed as to be very lightsome in its skies, and hills, and water. In many parts of the costumes, and the vegetation, the colouring is warm without being dauby or garish.

TAPESTRY Wall-hanging; subject, Melchizedek bringing bread and wine to Abram after his victory. Flemish, late 17th century.

On a tablet at the top of the piece is this inscription:—" Sodomâ expugnatâ Lot capitur. Abram illum recepit. Rex Melchizedek victori Abram offert panem et vinum." As the reader will easily bring to mind, the subject as well as the inscription are borrowed from the fourteenth chapter of Genesis. Supposing that Sodom, after the overthrow by Abram's night attack of the four kings, had been retaken, and his nephew Lot and his substance freed from the hands of the four conquered princes, the artist has chosen that point of time in the story, when Melchizedek, the King of Salem and the Priest of the Most High, went out to meet Abram as he was coming from the slaughter; and bringing forth bread and wine, blessed him.

The two principal personages occupy the centre of the foreground. Crowned as a king and wearing a costly sword, Melchizedek comes forth with outstretched right hand to welcome Abram, from whom he is separated by a highly ornamented tall vase full of wine. Behind this King of Salem one of his own serving men, who carries on his shoulders a basket full of food, is coming down the wide staircase from which his royal master has just issued, while outside a doorway, under an upper portico in the same palace, stand two men gazing on the scene below them. On the other side of the vase, Abram, holding a long staff in his right hand, is stepping forwards toward Melchizedek, whom he salutes with his lowered left hand, and behind him a second servant of Melchizedek has just set upon the ground a large hamper full of flat loaves of bread. A little higher in the piece, and somewhat to the left of this domestic, a group of soldiers are quenching their thirst gathered about an open tun of wine, which they drink out of a wide bowl; hastening towards the same spot, as if from an archway, flows a stream of other military men. Amid the far-off landscape may be seen banners flying, and beneath them all the turmoils of a battle raging at its height. To the right, the standard-bearers and some of the vanquished are seen in headlong flight.

The deep golden-grounded border is parted at bottom by classic monstrous hermæ, male and female, each wearing a pair of wings by its ears. The spaces between these grotesques are filled in with female figures, moftly fymbolizing vices. "Violentia" is figured by a youthful woman, who, with a fheathed fword by her fide, is driving before her a captive young man, whom fhe holds by the cords which tie his hands behind him, and whom fhe hurries onwards by the blows from a thick ftaff that fhe wields in her uplifted right hand. "Depredatio," with her fingers ending at their tips in long fharp ravenous nails, is riding aftride a lion. "Gratitudo" is a gentle young maiden, who is feated with a bird in her lap, a ftork, which fhe feems to be fondling. "Pugna," or brawling, is fhown by two middle-aged women of the lower clafs. With their difhevelled hair hanging all about their fhoulders, they are in the height of a fight, and the woman with a bunch of keys hanging from her girdle has overcome the other, and is tugging at one of her long locks. "Tyrannis" is an old haggifh female with dog-like feet, and fhe brandifhes a fword; almoft every one of the other women on the border has, curioufly enough, one foot refembling that of an animal. In feveral parts of the compofition befides the border, in the warp and for fhading, golden thread has been woven in, but fo fcantily employed, and the gold itfelf of fuch a debafed bad quality, that the metal from being tarnifhed to quite a dull black tone is hardly difcernible.

The coftume, like the fcenery and buildings, has nothing of an oriental character about it, but is fafhioned after an imagined claffic model.

APESTRY Wall-hanging; fubject, the Progrefs of Avarice. Flemifh, middle of the 17th century.

Up above within the border of this large piece is a tablet bearing this infcription :—

"Semper eget fitiens mediis ceu Tantalus undis
Inter anhelatas femper avarus opes."

Beginning at the top left hand of the fubject reprefented, we fee a murky fort of vapour ftreaked by a flafh of red lightning. Amid this brownifh darknefs, peopled with horrid little phantoms and fmall fantaftic fprites, we difcover a diminutive figure of Death wielding a long-handled curioufly-headed fcythe.

Juft below is a man pointing with his right hand up to Death, and with his left hand to a little harpy before him; behind him ftands a figure with two heads, one a woman's, the other a man's, set together Janufwife. Lower down; and of a much larger fize, are three male figures, one a youth well clad, were it not for his ragged pantaloons, the next an old man wearing fandals and bearing in his right hand what looks like a reliquary glazed and coloured red, while in his left he holds two unfolded fcrolls, the upper one of which is illuminated with a building like a caftle, by the fide of which ftands a man, over whofe head is the tau or T, with a bell hanging under it—the fymbols of St. Anthony of Egypt.

Befide the laft perfonage ftands the figure of a monk-like form, clafping in both hands a pair of beads or rofary. Next we have, half leaning from out her feat placed upon a car, and bending over an open cheft, into which fhe is dropping golden pieces of money from her claw-like fingers, a female form with hideous wings and vulture feet, fuch as harpies have. The chariot drawn by a wyvern-like animal, with its fiery long tongue thruft out, has knocked down an elderly man, who, from the tonfure on his grey head, would feem to be a prieft, and its wheel is going to crufh a youth upon the ground, while the wyvern's outftretched claws are about to gripe a ghaftly cut-off head. Hanging on the mouldings of this car are empty money-bags, crumpled-up deeds, and a wide-open account book. Alongfide of this fiendifh hag trips a flaunting courtier; before her rides Midas with afs's ears to his bloated face, unkempt locks falling down its fides, a royal diadem upon his head, and a withered branch in his hand; and, as if bound to her chariot, walks a king, having with him his queen. Before, but on one fide, paces another crowned prince on horfeback, while full in front rides a third king carrying in his arms a naked woman.

Laft of all and heading, as it were, this progrefs of Avarice, fits a female figure fidewife on a horfe, which fhe has juft reined up. In her right hand fhe bears a red ftandard emblazoned with a monkey on all fours, fharp clawed, and fomething which may be meant for gold pieces.

Flying down from the fkies comes an angel, who, with his out-ftretched right hand, feems to ftay the march of the frightful woman in the chariot with her kingly rout, and forbid its onward progrefs.

In the far-off landfcape we difcover a group of foldiers, near whom lies ftretched out on the ground a dead body, upon which an angel gazes. Far to the right we find an open building, intended, may be, for a church; near it are two military men in armour; infide, a third feems holding out his hand as if he were leaving his offerings on the altar there. Outfide, and not far from this fame building, may be feen other four men, two of them pilgrims, of whom one kneeling before another looks as if he were making his confeffion.

The broad border to this large piece is defigned with elaborate care. At each of the two lower corners it is figured with the one fame fubject, which confifts in a group of three naked winged boys or angels; of thefe one holds a fhort-ftemmed cup or chalice, from out of which rifes a hoft or large round altar bread, fhowing marked on it our Lord hanging upon the crofs, between the B. V. Mary and St. John Evangelift; a fecond angel kneeling has in his hands an uplifted crown of thorns, while lying behind him are two books; and the third angel fhows us a tablet written with the Greek letters A Ω. All the reft of this frame-work is filled in with flowers, fruits, birds, and fnakes. Of the flowers the moft frequent are the fritillary, the rofe, the lily, the amaryllis, poppies, white campanulas, large daifies, fleurs-de-lis, and corn-flowers. Among the fruits we fee the pomegranate, of which fome are fplit, pears, Indian corn, apples, plums, and figs. The birds are moftly parrots, woodpeckers, ftorks, cocks, doves, and fome other birds of the fmaller kinds. In places may be difcovered a knot of fnakes coiled about a garland made of yellow leaves.

The allegory of the piece is read with eafe. The progrefs of Avarice is headed by Wickednefs, who carries aloft her blood-ftained flag, emblazoned with the monkey, the emblem of moral uglinefs and mifchief. Hard upon the heels of Wickednefs comes a lecherous potentate, the type of immorality. The crowned heads, whether mounted or on foot, that come next have for their brother-companion Midas, the emblem of the fenfual mifer's greed of gold, to remind us how kings, nay queens too, fometimes thirft for their fubjects' wealth to gratify their evil wifhes; and the gay young man behind them, coming by the chariot's fide, perfonates thofe courtiers who are recklefs of what they do to help their royal mafters in their love for lucre. Next we are told what harpy-avarice will not waver to execute while led on by wicked fovereigns. Look at thofe about and beneath her chariot: from them we learn that fhe beggars the nobility, and leaves them to walk through the world in rags; fhe deftroys churches, and, when lacking other means for her fell purpofe, will fhed innocent blood and behead her opponents. But here below, Avarice and thofe who lead her on, though they be kings and queens, will have their day: Time will bring them to a ftand. The rifled altar will be ornamented again, the rites of worfhip reftored, and hofpitals reopened. While an angel from heaven ftops the progrefs of Avarice, high up in the eaftern fky a thunder-ftorm is gathering; and on earth a man, whilft pointing with one hand to grim Death, armed with his scythe, amid a cloud of loathsome winged things flitting around him, with the other that same person warns a harpy that her sister harpy Avarice will soon be overtaken; and just as the heathen Januslike figure close by—emblem of the past, and of a certain future—he also tells her of that just retribution which, by the hands of Death and in another world, will be dealt out to herself and all this miscreant company.

It would seem that this piece was wrought to stigmatize the memory of some of those many wanton acts of spoliation perpetrated in France and Belgium during the latter years of the 16th and the beginning of the 17th centuries. Perhaps the clue to the history and import of this fine specimen of the Flemish loom may be found all about the person of that old man, who carries in one hand a reliquary so conspicuously painted red, and in the other two parchment scrolls, upon one of which we find a sort of sketch of some particular spot, with an important edifice on it. By its size and look it seems to be some great hospital, and from the presence there of a man having above his head the letter tau or T and a bell hanging to it, we are given to understand that this building belonged to some brotherhood of St. Anthony, in the service of the sick ; and that its suffering inmates were principally those afflicted with erysipelas, a disease then, and even yet, called abroad St. Anthony's fire, once so pestilential that it often swept away thousands everywhere. Near Vienne, in the South of France, stood a richly-endowed hospital, founded A. D. 1095, chiefly for those suffering under this direful malady. This house belonged to and was administered by Canons Regular of St. Anthony. The town where it stood was Didier-la-Mothe, better known as Bourg S. Antoine. During the troubled times in France this great wealthy hospital, here fitly represented like a town of itself, by those lofty walls and that tall wide gateway, had been plundered: hence, one of its brothers is shown upbraiding Avarice for her evil doings, of which those sad tokens of moneyless purses, well-searched rent-books, and ransacked title-deeds are still dangling on her car. If not all, most, at least, of the persons here figured are meant, as is probable, to be characterized as the likenesses of the very individual victims and the victimizers portrayed upon this tapestry.

TAPESTRY Wall-hanging; fubject, Abraham's upper fervant meeting Rebecca at the fpring of water. Flemifh, late 17th century.

At top, in the middle of the broad border, a tablet gives us the following infcription:—Cumque perveniffet (fervus?) ad fontem et fibi (aquam?) petiiffet et Batuelis filia Rebecca ex hydria potum dediffet et camelis hauftis et filio Abrahe eam fore conjugem oraculo cognovit.

In the twenty-fourth chapter of Genefis we read how Abraham in his old age fent his eldeft fervant unto his own country and kindred, thence to bring back a wife for his fon Ifaac; and how that man, at his mafter's beheft, immediately took ten camels, carrying fomething of all his lord's goods with him, and went on to Mefopotamia, to the city of Nahor; and how, when he had reached that place, and had made a halt without the town near a well of water, in the evening, at the time that women were wont to come out to draw water, he befought Heaven that the maid to whom he fhould fay, "Let down thy pitcher, I pray thee, that I may drink, and fhe fhall fay, Drink, and I will give thy camels drink alfo—let the fame be fhe that Thou haft appointed for thy fervant Ifaac." This faithful fteward had not yet ended thefe words within himfelf, and behold Rebecca came out, the daughter of Bathuel the fon of Milcha, wife to Nahor, the brother of Abraham, and fpoke and did as this fervant had wifhed: and then he gave her golden earrings and bracelets.

As was fitting, the whole fcene is laid in the open air, amid a charming landfcape fcattered all over with buildings. To the left, in the foreground, we behold a maid with a pitcher getting water out of a large fquare tank, ready, as it feems, for a fecond ferving-woman to carry off, and who is coming back with another pitcher empty to be again refilled. In the middle ground a young woman, who carries a large pot of water on her head, is clambering over a wooden fence, and going towards an arch or bridge leading to a houfe.

Right in the centre of the piece ftands Rebecca, with one foot refting on a flab of veined marble, on which is placed a richly ornamented vafe; and from out another like veffel, which fhe holds up in both her hands, fhe is giving drink to the fteward Eliezer, who is refpectfully bending forwards while carrying to his lips this fame pitcher to flake his thirft. A kind of fhort fword, or anelace, dangles from his girdle, and a long ftout ftaff lies by his feet upon the ground. Two tall trees with vines twining about them overshadow the spot. In the distance stand several camels burdened; but behind him, some of his men, having unloaded one or two of those beasts, are opening certain gaily ornamented trunks, and looking out, no doubt, the bracelets and earrings to be afterwards given to Rebecca. In the background are fine large buildings, fortifications, a castle, and a palace-like erection conspicuous for its tall tower and cupola, besides the walls of a little town.

The piece is framed with a very elaborately designed broad border, containing accessories which show a strong leaning towards the ornamentation that grew out of the classicism that burst forth at the end of the fifteenth century all over Europe.

On the lower band, standing one at each side of a short pedestal, or rather low dado, are, back to back, two bearded grotesques, each of which is made up of a human head and face having three goats' horns growing out of the forehead, and of a wyvern's body, holding aloft in one of its claws a tall tapering torch. Further on comes a series of spaces peopled with emblematic personages, and separated from one another by two little naked winged boys standing on a highly elaborate zocle, and with the left hand swinging by a cord, at each end of which hang from a ring, and done up in bunches, fruits and flowers. In the first space is "Prudentia," bearing in her right hand a long-handled convex mirror, in her left, a human skull; in the second space, upon a sort of throne, sits "Sollicitudo," upholding in her right hand an oblong square time-piece, while on her left, with her elbow propped up by one arm of her chair, she leans her head as if buried in deep thought; in the third space sits "Animi-(Probitas)" with both her arms outstretched, as if reprovingly; in the fourth space we have "Ceres," the heathen goddess of corn: crowned with a wreath of the centaurea flowers, she carries ears of wheat in her right hand, in her left, a round flat loaf of bread; in the fifth space, "Liberalitas," who, from the emblems in her hands, must have been meant to personify not generosity but freedom, for in her right hand she shows us a hawk's jesses, with the bells and their bewits, and on her left wrist, or, as it should be phrased, the "fist," the hawk itself without jesses, bells, lunes, or tyrrits on—in fact quite free.

At the left side of the upright portion of the border, stands first, within an architectural niche, "Circumspectio," or Wariness, who, while she gathers up with her right hand her flowing garments from hindering her footsteps, with her left, holds an anchor upright, and carries on her wrist a hawk with two heads, one looking behind, the other before, fit token of keen-sightedness, which, from a knowledge of the past, strives to learn wisdom for the future. Higher up "Adjuratio" is standing, with her right hand outstretched afar, as if in warning of the awfulness of the act, and her left hand held upon her bosom in earnest of the truth of what she utters, whilst all about her head, as if enlightened from heaven, shines a nimb of glory. Last of all on this side, we have " Bonus zelus," or Right-Earnestness, in the figure of a stout, hale husbandman, who is about clasping within his right arm two straight uprooted saplings, evidently apple-trees, by the fruit hanging from the wisp which binds them at their middle height.

Going to the right-hand strip, we find, at the lower end, occupying her niche, " Pudicitias," (sic), figured as a young maiden, who holds upon her breast with her left arm a little lamb, which, with her uplifted right hand, and the first two fingers put out according to the Latin rite, she seems to be blessing. In his own niche, and just overhead, we see " Requisicio," or Hot-wishfulness, who is shown to us under the guise of a young knight, girt with an anelace, which hangs in front of him : in the hollow of his left outstretched hand he carries a heart—very likely as his own—all on fire. The last of this very curious series is " Diligentia," as a matronly woman, who, with one hand keeping the ample folds of her gown from falling about her feet, carries the branch of a vine in the other hand.

From the quantities of dulled and blackish spaces all over the border-ground, and amid the draperies upon the figures in this tapestry, it is evident that much gold thread was woven into it, so that when fresh from the loom it must have had a splendour and a richness of which at present we can image to ourselves but a very faint idea. Though the glitter of its golden material is gone for ever, its artistic beauty cannot ever fade. Much gracefulness in the attitudes, several happy foreshortenings, and a great deal of good drawing all about this design, show that the man who made the cartoon must have deeply studied the great masters of Italy, and, in an especial manner, those belonging to the Roman school : unfortunately, like all of them, he too had forgot to learn what was the real Oriental costume, and followed a classic style in dress, which, as he has given it, is often very incorrect.

TAPESTRY Wall-hanging ; subject, Tobit, the father, sending his son to the city of Rages for the recovery of the moneys lent to Gabael. Flemish, late 17th century.

Sitting in the open air, we see first the elder Tobit. Well stricken in years, and blind, he is leaning his right hand upon a staff; in his left hand he holds a folded document—the note-of-hand figned by Gabael. Thinking that he muſt die in a ſhort time, he has called to his ſide his well-beloved child the young Tobias, and after having given him the moſt wholeſome counſel for his religious and moral behaviour through life, ſpeaks of his own burial, and how he wiſhes that when his wife Sarah's days are done, the boy ſhould lay his mother's body by his father's in the grave. As an ending to this difcourſe, the elder Tobias ſaid, "'I ſignify this to thee, that I committed ten talents to Gabael—at Rages in Media. Seek thee a man which may go with thee, whiles I yet live—and go and receive the money."

Then Tobias going forth, found a beautiful young man, ſtanding girded, and as it were ready to walk; and not knowing that he was an angel of God, he ſaluted him and ſaid: "Canſt thou go with me to Rages, and knoweſt thou thoſe places well?" To whom the angel ſaid: "I will go with thee, and I know the way well." Then Tobias going in told all theſe things to his father; and all things being ready, Tobias bade his father and his mother farewell, and he and the angel ſet out both together; and when they were departed, his mother began to weep; and Tobias went forward, and the dog followed him.—Book of Tobit, chapters iv. v.

Seated, and leaning his right hand upon his ſtaff, the old man is outſtretching with his left to his ſtarting ſon the note-of-hand to Gabael, behind him ſtands his wife Sarah weeping; before him is his ſon, who, leaning his long travelling ſtaff againſt his ſhoulder, with his left hand is about to take the important document from his father, at the ſame time that he turns himſelf half round and points with his right hand to the angel behind him, as if to comfort his father in the knowledge that he is to have ſuch a good companion for his guide. The angel, who carries a traveller's ſtaff in his left hand, holds out his right towards the young man, as telling his father and mother how carefully he would lead him to Rages, and bring him ſafely home again. Laſt of all, and ſtanding beneath a tree we find a ſaddled aſs with a large gaily ornamented pilgrim's wooden bottle for water hanging by its ſide, and the aſs's head is turned round as if looking on the faithful dog that is lying on the ground ready to follow his young maſter on the way. Magnificent buildings ariſe as a background to the ſpot where we ſee old Tobit ſeated, and ſtanding behind him his weeping wife Sarah. On the threſhold of their own fine houſe behind them there ſtands in a niche the ſtatue of Moſes, who is figured with the two horns upon his forehead, as repreſenting the light that ſhone about his face, and darted all around it in rays like horns, as he came from Sinai a ſecond time with tables of the law: his left hand leans upon those two tables that stand beside him; and on his right arm lies a long scroll.

The borders all about the piece are made up of wreathed boughs of foliage, from out of which peep forth fruits and flowers. The left-hand strip shows a peacock perched upon the stem of a vine, and little boys are shooting blunt-headed arrows at it: on the strip to the right, other little boys are disporting themselves amid the branches, playing music, one beating a drum, a second blowing the flute, others clambering up amid the roses, fruits and flowers; one little fellow, conspicuous for his dress, is waving a flag in great delight: on the lower border children are at their gambols with equally graceful energy. At every one of the four corners is a large circle, wrought in imitation of bronze, all in gold, but now so faded that the smallest lustre from the metal is lacking. They were figured by the means of outlines done in brown silk, each with a subject drawn from the Book of Tobit. In the circle, at the upper left-hand corner, we observe the young Tobias going out from his father to seek, as he had bidden him, for some trusty guide to Gabael's house; in the lower round of the same side the wished-for companion, Raphael in his angel shape, has been brought in, and is speaking with the blind old man. Looking at the circle on the upper right-hand of the border we see the same Tobit giving comfort to his sorrowing wife Sarah, just as both have been left by their son gone on his journey.

Gold-covered thread has been much employed all about this fine specimen of tapestry; but, like too many other instances of misapplied economy in material, this exhibits nothing but blotches of dirty brownish black in those laces which should have shone with gold.

.

TAPESTRY Wall-hanging; ground, rather white; subject, a feast. French, or Gobelin, 18th century. Lent by the Board of Works.

Within a large stone hall, roughly built and festooned, is spread a long well-provided table, at which the guests, male and female, are sitting: in the foreground are the servants, some of whom are shown in very daring but successful foreshortenings, reminding us somewhat, on the whole, of one of Paolo Veronese's banquets, though here we behold a rustic building in a garden, not an architectural hall in a Venetian palace.

APESTRY Wall-hanging; ground, moſtly white; ſubject, Cupid among the ruſtics. French, or Gobelin, 18th century. Lent by the Board of Works.

Amid the ruins of an Ionic temple in the foreground we have a ſhepherd and his dog faſt aſleep, while a winged youthful genius is hovering juſt above, and ſcattering very plentifully poppy-flowers all about the ſpot. Behind, a young little Cupid, ſeated on a cloud, is ſurrounded by a crowd of ruſtics, men and women, thronging, as it were, to hear him. As in the other fellow-piece to this, the colouring is cheerful and very pleaſing, in parts ſo ſoft and well graduated in their tones, and ſo remarkable for their foreſhortenings. From their large ſize they muſt have been intended for ſome great hall, and ſeemingly were all wrought for the ſame ſpacious room.

APESTRY Hangings for Pilaſters; ground, brown; deſign, arabeſques done in red, blue, and yellow. French, early 18th century. Lent by the Board of Works.

Theſe two pieces ſeem to have been eſpecially wrought to cover ſome pilaſters in a hall, and not to border any larger production of the loom.

INDEX I.

BRAM and MELCHISE-
DECH figured, 88, 328.
ABRAHAM's fervant meet-
ing Rebecca at the well,
333.
Adderbury Church, Oxon, monfter
fculptures outfide of, 157.
AHASUERUS and ESTHER, figured, 307.
Alhambra, 55.
Alb, apparels for, 65, 146, 199.
—— fine mediæval one, 268.
Algerine embroidery, 18.
Almeria, its fine filks, 63.
Altar, cere cloth for, 160.
Altar-cloths, 60, 62, 73, 79, 265.
Altar-curtains, 51, 201.
Altar-frontals, 14, 31, 87, 101, 265, 266, 267.
Altar-frontlets, 62, 265.
Amices, 185, 195.
Amice, apparel for, 34, 186, &c.
ANASTASIUS BIBLIOTHECARIUS, quoted, 155, 161.
Angels, nine choirs of, 22, 281.
Animals, fee Zoology.
Anjou, Royal Houfe of, 32.
ANN of Bohemia, Richard II.'s queen, 53.
Annunciation of the B.V. Mary, figured, 2, 186, 247.
ANTHONY, S., figured, 253, 254.
—— Canons Regular of, 332.
—— fire of, or eryfipelas, 332; hof-
pital for the cure of it at *Bourg S.
Antoine* in the fouth of France, 332.
Apparels for Albs, 65, 146, 149, 181, 199, 268.
—— for amices, 34, 185, 187, 195, 234.

Apparels for dalmatics and tunicles, 206.
Apocalypfe quoted, 288.
Applied or cut-work, 2, 17, 20, 21, 77, 81, 146, 199, 215, 265.
Arabic infcriptions, real, 179, 232, 238, 243.
—— pretended, 25, 29, 45, 53, 76, 122, 125, 137, 138, 146, 177, 181, 213, 220, 234.
Araneum opus, 162.
Architectural defign on ftuffs, 10, 32, 33, 108, 131, 150, 233, 252.
Armorial bearings of—
 BRANDENBURG, 63.
 BASSINGBURN, DE, 285.
 Bohemia, 63.
 BOTILER, LE, 283, 285.
 BYGOD, 285.
 CHAMBOWE (?), 285.
 CHAMPERNOUN, 284.
 Caftile and Leon, 282.
 Cleves, 22, 246.
 CLIFFORD, 283.
 England, 246, 284.
 EVERARD, 283.
 France, 84.
 FERRERS, 282.
 FRETIE, 214.
 FITTON, 148.
 FITZ ALAN, 284.
 GRANDISON, one of the coats, 284.
 GENEVILLE, 282.
 GOLBORE or GROVE, 285.
 HAMPDEN (?), 284.
 Knights Templar's badge, 283.
 LIMESI or LINDSEY, 283.
 LUCY, 285.
 MARCK, DE LA, 22.
 MONTENEY of *Effex*, 284.

Armorial bearings *continued*.
  MORTIMER, ROGER DE, 285.
  PANDOLFINI, 143.
  PERCY, 284.
  RIBBESFORD (?), 285.
  SHELDON, 284.
  SPENCER, 283.
  THORNELL of *Suffolk*, 148.
  TYDESWALL, 284.
  WARWICK, 282.
Assumption of the B. V. Mary figured, 89, 272, 273, 276, 278.
Atonement, symbol of, 30.
Aubusson tapestry and carpets, 306.
Audenaerde famous for its tapestry, 294.
Avarice personified, and progress of, figured, 329.
ἀχειροποίητος, what, 249.

Bags, liturgical, 188, 263; Persian travelling, 83.
Balaam's prophecy quoted from Numbers, xxiv. 17, 285.
Balm cloth, 19, 20.
Bamberg cathedral, stuffs there, 153.
Banners for church processions, 259.
Bath, old English vestments found hidden in a house at, 88.
Bayeux, so-called tapestry, piece of, 6.
Beads, embroidery in, 169.
—— making of, at Venice, 169.
—— or rosary, for prayers, 263.
Beasts, see Zoology.
Beauvais tapestry, 307.
Bed-quilts, 20, 86, 104, 293; hangings, 107.
BELETH, JOHN, quoted, 277.
BERNARD, ST., chasuble of, 159.
Birds, see Zoology.
Bishops' liturgical stockings, 56.
Bissus or Byssus, what, 25, 152, 175, 239.
BLACK PRINCE, 129.
Blessing, the liturgical, how given in the Latin rite, 187; figured as given with the left or wrong hand, 71.
BLICKIN VON LICHTENBERG, ANNA, 94.
Block printing on linen, 118, 120, 183, 184, 234.
—— on diaper, 61.
—— on silk, 31.

BOCK, Rev. Dr., quoted, 25, 26, 29, 34, 45, 49, 52, 55, 58, 60, 89, 122, 123, 151, 152, 155, 158, 162, 165, 169, 175, 184, 187, 207, 223, 242, 247, 252, 264, 270.
Bohemia, arms of, 63; ANN of, 63.
Bordering, or Lace, 160.
Borsa, the Italian, gibeciere or pouch, 3.
Boots or legging, like stockings, worn by bishops while pontificating, 56.
Botany—
  Flowers:
    Artichoke, bloom of, 64, 137.
    Bignonia, or trumpet flower, 75.
    Centaurea, or corn flower, 47, 49, 53, 62, 89, 99, 258.
    Fleur de lis, 5, 27, 29, 32, 35, 59, 91, 110, 116, 130, 138, 162, 167, 196, 226.
    Frittilary, 66.
    Foxglove, or digitalis, 66.
    Honeysuckle, 73.
    Heartsease, or pansey, 259.
    Ivy, 132.
    Lily, 69, 89, 110, 115, 257, 310.
    Penstemon, 66.
    Pinks, 115.
    Pomegranate, 11, 12, 13, 14, 20, 66.
    Rose, 20, 34, 47, 59, 61, 107, 188, 193, 195.
    Trefoil, 137.
    Tulips, 42, 62.
  Fruits, &c.:
    Acorns, 115, 202, 245.
    Apples (?), 137.
    Arbutus unedo, or strawberry tree, 110.
    Artichoke, 36, 47, 60, 62, 64, 65, 66, 69, 70, 72, 73, 80, 114, 115, 116, 118, 129, 130, 134, 145, 152, 192, 256.
    Grapes, 49, 69, 74, 75, 163, 241, 245.
    Mulberry, 65,
    Oranges (?), 137.
    Pomegranate, 7, 48, 50, 66, 73, 91, 114, 115, 128, 134, 191, 192, 193, 197, 199, 228, 256, 258.
    Strawberry, 110.
    Wheat-ears, 90, 113, 137, 177.

Index I. 341

Botany *continued*.
  Trees:
    The Homa, hom, or sacred tree of the Persians, 84, 140, 154, 213, 215, 216, 238.
    Oak-leaves, 202, 245.
    Vine, 163, 245.
Box for corporals, 112, 193, 194.
—— for reservation of the consecrated Host, from Maundy Thursday till Good Friday, 112.
Brandenberg, arms of, 63.
Brocades, 8, 9, 10, 12, 15, 19, 20, 29, 114, 116, 117, 122, 126, &c.
BROOKE, the Collection, 312.
Bouchier Knot, 168.
Bourgtheroud, Hotel de, at Rouen, 294.
Boy-bishop, 85.
Bugles, 169.
Burse, or corporal-case, 144, 145, 194.
Byssus, see Bissus.
Byzantine stuffs, 155, 159, 160, 161, 219, 222.

C, the letter, interlaced, 5, 38.
Cairo, 57.
Canvas, what kind of stuff meant by the word in old inventories, 185.
Cap, scull, 16; of estate or state, 86.
CAPUANUS, PETRUS, quoted, 286.
Carpet, 66, 83, 209, 248; see Pedalia, or Pede-cloth.
CAXTON, his translation of the "Legenda Aurea," quoted, 275, 277.
Cendal, 163.
Cere-cloth, for laying immediately over the altar-stone, 160.
Chairs, seat-covers for, 110.
Charles I.'s scull cap, 16.
Chasubles, 1, 5, 13, 21, 76, 81, 82, 88, 142, 208, 213, 264, 266, 269.
Chaucer quoted, 64.
Cheetahs, see Zoology.
Chinese silks, &c. 1, 8, 11, 12, 16, 75.
Choirs, nine, of angels, 22, 281.
"Church of our Fathers," quoted, 19, 34, 36, 46, 85, 103, 170, 174, 181, 186, 194, 196, 202, 203, 205, 206, 210, 239, 248, 265.
Clare, Margaret de, Countess of Cornwall, 6.
CLEVES, princely house of, 246.

CLEVES, its armorial bearings, 22.
Cloth, Corpus Christi, what, 202, 260.
—— for crozier, 174, 250.
—— for lectern, 210, &c.
—— for pyx, 202, 260.
—— of estate, 107.
—— of gold or lama d'oro, 204, 208.
Cluny, Hotel de, at Paris, 212.
Cobham college and church, Kent, iron lectern once at, 213.
Cobweb stuff, so-called, 162.
Collars of Orders—St. Michael, 84; The Holy Ghost, 84.
Cologne, 61, 187; painting in cathedral 187; woven stuffs for church use, see orphreys of web.
—— embroidery, 61, 66, 67, 246.
Colours, murrey, once such a favourite in England, 9.
—— pink or gules, and green, somewhat peculiar to Parlermitan looms, 165, 170, 178, &c.
—— those used in the Latin as well as the Greek rite, 172; black in services for the dead, 197.
Copes, 2, 15, 80, 207, 275.
—— hoods of, 67, 144, 198; in England, how shaped, 41.
Coral beads, 169.
Cornelimunster, abbey of, 26; sudary of our Lord there, 26.
Coronation of the B. V. Mary figured, 236, 272, 280.
Corporals or square pieces of altar linen, 144, 145, 194, 195.
—— cases for keeping, 112, 144, 145, 194; see Burse.
Corpus Christi cloths, 202, 260.
Costume, mediæval, 78.
Counterpane, 271.
Coventry, its famous gild, 289, &c.
Coverlets, 20, &c.
Cracowes or pointed shoes, so called, 53.
Cradle-coverlets, 4, 13, 66, 67, 100, 103, 104, 110.
Crape, 126.
Creeping to the cross, ceremony of, on Good Friday, 174.
Crescent moon and star, symbolical of our Lord and His church, 285.
Crocet work, 18, 72.

Cross, St. Andrew's, 161, 229; the so-called Y cross, 82.
—— cramponnée, 161; flory, 161; foliated, 218; pommée, 140.
—— filfod, 161.
—— gammadion, 161.
—— Greek, figured on stuffs, 160.
—— creeping to, ceremony of, 174.
Crown, supposed, of King Edward the Confessor, 153.
—— of St. Edgitha, 153.
Crozier, napkin for, 174, 250.
Crucifixion figured, 6, 30, 82, 83, 142, 276.
—— with four nails, 30.
—— old English manner of figuring, 276.
Crystal balls, 206.
CURETON, Dr., quoted, 179.
Curtains, 7, 12, 13, 15.
—— for the altar, 51, 201.
Cushions, 4, 59, 111, 142, 174, 273.
—— used in the liturgy, 59, 174.
Cut-purse, what meant by the expression, 3.
Cut-work, 22, 76, 141, 189, 199, 259, 292; see Applied work.
Cyrillian alphabet, the, 172.

Daisies, the symbolism of, 149, see Botany—Flowers.
Dalmaticks, 76, 143, 206, 214, 266.
Dalmatics, apparels on, 206.
Damask, Chinese, 75.
Damasks, figured with pictorial subjects, 165, 184, &c., see "Stuffs historiated."
Damask in linen, 73, 201, 203, 238.
—— in linen and woollen, 202.
—— in silk, 10, 11, 13, 15, 25, 41, 42, 43, 47, 48, 49, 50, 52, 55, 56, 57, 62, 67, 72, 73, 74, 81, 113, 114, 115, 116, 121, 124, 125, 126, 127, 128, 129, 130, 131, 133, 136, 137, 138, 139, 140, 152, 154, 155, 156, 159, 160, 162, 163, 168, 190, 191, 196, 197, 202, 203, 204, 205, 206, 213, 215, 216, 221, 224, 225, 226, 227, 228, 229, 233, 234, 237, 238, 239, 240, 241, 244, 245, 251, 256, 274.

Damask in silk and cotton, 60, 166, 167, 230, 231, 262.
—— in silk and gold, 46, 47, 52, 53, 54, 56, 57, 60, 63, 64, 65, 66, 113, 129, 130, 132, 134, 137, 138, 139, 146, 151, 159, 162, 164, 165, 166, 167, 168, 170, 177, 178, 179, 180, 181, 183, 184, 191, 193, 201, 213, 224, 225, 227, 228, 233, 234, 235, 237, 238, 241, 243, 247, 273.
—— in silk and hemp, 164.
—— in silk and linen, 74, 130, 136, 154, 166, 204, 243, 262, 264.
—— in silk and silver, 161, 177, 183.
—— in silk, wool, linen, thread, and gold, 129.
DANIEL, the book of, quoted, 227.
Design, architectural, upon stuffs, 10, 32, 33, 108, 131, 150, 233, 252.
Didier-la-Mothe or *Bourg S. Antoine* hospital at for those struck with S. Anthony's fire or erysipelas, 332.
DIOGENES, subjects, in tapestry, from the life of, 303, &c.
Door-curtains, 7, 12, 13, 15.
Dorneck, a coarser kind of damask so called, 129.
Dory, John, the fish so called, 151.
Dove, emblem of the Holy Ghost, 58.
Dragon, the five-clawed Chinese, 1.
Dress, Lady's, 14, 18, and the Brooke Collection, 313, &c.
Duc, M. VIOLLET LE, quoted, 212.
DUGDALE's St. Paul's, quoted, 151.
Durham, Anglo-Saxon embroidered vestments kept in the cathedral library at, 205.

Eagle, double-headed, 26, 28, 37, 86.
—— German, of Charles V. of Spain, 7.
Edward I., how he knighted his son, 287; and swore by the swans that he would wage war against Scotland. *Ib.*
Egyptian gauze, 57; linen, 25; silk, 56; taffeta, 57.
Elephant, 45.
—— and Castle, 170.

Index I.

Embroidery, Chinese, 7, 12, 16.
—— English, 5, 6, 16, 88, 147, 275, 283.
—— Flemish, 119, 144, 198, 248.
—— Florentine, 58, 91, 111, 120, 142, 214.
—— French, 85, 110, 219, 226.
—— German, 51, 53, 58, 59, 60, 66, 103, 108, 119, 120, 139, 140, 150, 153, 156, 158, 165, 166, 186, 187, 189, 190, 196, 206, 207, 216, 218, 249, 250, 252, 253, 254, 257, 258, 269.
—— Indian, 86, 262.
—— Italian, 71, 145, 199, 271.
—— Persian, 270.
—— Sicilian, 149.
—— Spanish, 65, 82, 204.
—— Syrian, 262.
—— Venetian, 168.
—— in quilting, 14, 16, &c.
—— in waving lines, 59.
—— done in beads, 44, 169, 190.
—— as cut-work and applied, 146, 189, 199, 248.
—— in gold wire, 220.
—— in gold and silver wire, 150.
—— done in solid silver gilt wire, 150, 220.
—— in pearls and precious stones, 199.
—— with goldsmith's work amid it, 168, 169, 186, 199, 223, 233.
—— in silk, 2, 3, 4, 5, 6, 7, 12, 13, 16, 34, 103, 117, 120, 133, 144, 153, 155, 156, 166, 168, 181, 217, 252, 271, 273, 275.
—— on linen in silk, 29, 58, 60, 65, 119, 186, 187, 189, 258, 262.
—— on linen in thread, 31, 51, 120.
—— done in thread, 19, 20, 53, 58.
—— done in worsted, 140, 256, 262, 269.
—— figured with birds, 16, 158.
—— historic, 7, 91, 147, 150, 269, 273.
—— flowers, 4, 5, 11, 12, 13, 16, 121, 199, 213.
—— figured with saints, 2, 6, 56, 58, 88, 111, 116, 144, 145, 146, 147, 149, 151, 165, 186, 187, 189, 190, 198, 207, 217, 244, 248, 250, 254, 258.
English chintz, 84.
—— conventional flowers in embroidery, 88.
—— purse, 106.
—— quilting, 16, &c.
—— tapestry, 306.
—— textiles in a ribbon-like shape, 24, 33, 38, 161, 217, 218, 219, 221.
—— embroidery, 5, 6, 16, 88, 147, 275, 283; and "The Brooke Collection," 312, &c., passim.
—— silks, "The Brooke Collection," passim, 312.
—— velvet, "The Brooke Collection," passim, 312.
—— small hand-loom woven strips for stoles, &c., 24, 33, 38, 217, 218, 219, 221.
Erysipelas, or St. Anthony's fire, hospital for, in France, 332.
ESTHER and AHASUERUS, figured in tapestry, 307.
Eucharist, how borne to the sick and dying, 188.
—— reservation of, 194, 203.
EUSEBIUS, quoted, 280.
Evangelists' symbols, 149.
EZECHIEL, quoted, 281.

Fan, the liturgic, 60.
Fates, the three, figured, 309.
Fenrir, the Scandinavian fabled water-wolf, 151.
Festival, the old English so-called book, quoted, 147, 276.
Filfod, or Full-foot, 161, 174, 242, 249.
Fish, figured, 151.
FITTON, arms of the family of, 148.
Flemish embroidery, 3, 117, 248, 255.
—— linen, damask, or napery, 34, 61, 73, 75, 124, 203, 205, 255, 263.
—— linen, block-printed, 118, 120, 234.
—— napery, 34, 75, 124, 255.
—— silk damask, 190, 191, 197, 252.
—— tapestry, 294, 299, 300, 301, 302, 303, 307, 328, 329, 330, 335.

Flemish velvet, 254, 255, 264.
Florentine embroidery, 58, 91, 111, 120, 142, 214.
—— silk, damasked, 202, 215, figured with angels, 36, 133.
—— silk and linen, 264.
—— velvets, plain, 12, 142.
—— velvets, with gold, 85, 144, 145.
—— velvets, raised, 18, 82, 144, 145.
—— web for orphreys, 89, 136, 142, 260, 291.
Flowers, see Botany.
——, the English conventional, in embroidery, 88.
Foot-cloths, 140, 263.
Frames for enamels, 34, 85.
FRASER, or FRAZER, Scotch family of, 274.
French cloth of gold, 204, 208.
—— cut-work, 81, 292.
—— embroidery, 5, 7, 14, 19, 21, 29, 107, 205, 226.
—— gloves, 105.
—— heraldry, 14, 29, 130.
—— lace (gold), 131.
—— lectern-veil, 141.
—— purses, 89, 106.
—— quilting, 13, 104.
—— satin, 8, 14, 21, 104.
—— silk, brocaded, 9, 15, 105.
—— silk, damasked, 13, 204, 205, 206.
—— tapestry, 302, 303, 304.
—— velvet, 14, 106.
—— webs, 29, 130.
FRETIE, LODEWICH, 214.
Fringe of gold, 145; of silk, 252, 266.
Frontals to altars, 14, 31, 87, 101, 265, 266, 267, 293.
Frontlets, 62, 251, 257, 265.

G, the letter as an initial (for Gabriela?), 236.
Gabriel the archangel, how figured, 186, 217.
Gammadion, 34, 60, 127, 174, 175, 185, 242, 249.
GARLAND, JOHN, noticed, 38, 162, 217.
Gauze, 57.
GRISPITZHEIM, HENRY VON, 94; his armorials, 93.
Genoa brocade, 114, 134.

Genoa damask, 115, 116, 201.
—— silk, 12.
—— velvet, 3, 18, 62, 90, 107, 110, 145, 192, 199, 200, 263.
—— velvet raised, 18, 62, 107, 134.
Geography of textiles, &c.; see Index II.
German embroidery, 18, 21, 34, 35, 42, 51, 58, 61, 92, 99, 100, 101, 103, 104, 116, 133, 144, 153, 158, 165, 185, 187, 207, 246, 249, 252, 253, 261, 263.
—— embroidery on linen in silk, 29, 55, 59, 60, 62, 109, 133, 139, 174, 186, 187, 196, 242, 250, 261, 266, 267, 270.
—— embroidery on linen in thread, 31, 35, 60, 79, 235, 267.
—— embroidery in thread, 18, 31, 42, 92, 99.
—— embroidery in worsted, 66, 79, 108, 246, 266, 269.
—— napery, 190.
—— netting, 175, 245, 267.
—— silk and linen, 192, 270.
—— tapestry, 296, 298.
—— velvet, 260.
—— webs, 61, 62, 63, 64, 69, 80, 82, 116, 117, 118, 119, 174, 175, 252, 253.
Gianitore, a fish, and what, 151.
Gibeciere, 3.
Gilds, English, 289.
—— their Corpus Christi plays, 289.
—— at Coventry, 289.
—— their members, 289.
—— their vestments, 289.
Gilt parchment, 140, 224, 229, 244.
—— vellum; see gilt parchment.
Gimp, 102.
GIOTTO, 186.
—— and his school of painting, 186.
Girdles, 57, 126, 205, 218, 219.
Girdle at Prato, of the B. V. Mary, 261, 272, 280, 282.
GLOVER, ROBERT, Somerset herald, quoted, 148.
Gloves, ladies', 105.
Gobelins tapestry, 302, 305.
Golden Legend, Caxton's English translation quoted, 275, 277.
Goldsmith's work found upon em-

Index I. 345

broidery and textiles; see Silversmith's work.
Good Friday's celebration, 113.
Good Friday rite among the Greeks, 113, 173.
—— rite among the Latins, 113, 174.
Grail, or Grayle, the liturgic book, what, 34.
Granada textiles, 26, 27, 60, 65, 73, 128, 161, 166.
GRAUNT, Master Thomas, 289.
Greek, alb, chitonion, 171.
—— dalmatic or stoicharion, 171.
—— ritual noticed, 113, 124, 126, 171, 191, 205.
—— stoicharion or dalmatic, 171.
—— textiles, 27, 28, 33, 36, 123, 124, 126, 127.
—— mixed with cotton, 27, 126, 219.
——, thread, 33, 123.
Green, colour of, 57, 281.
Gregory's (St.), " Pity," what, 34.

HABACUC, 277.
HAMAN, fall of, figured, 308.
HAMPDEN, arms of (?) 287.
Hand, in benediction, 54.
Hangings of velvet, 17, 18, 107.
—— for walls, wrought of cut-work, and figured with the romance of Sir Guy, of Warwick, and the Northumbrian "worm" or dragon, 77.
Hare, its symbolic meaning, 237.
Harts, lodged, 43.
HENRY II, emperor of Germany, 153; tunic of, 153, 154.
Heraldry, 14, 19, 22, 28, 32, 37, 38, 39, 40, 63, 73, 76, 84, 93, 103, 104, 108, 128, 130, 143, 148, 175, 177, 181, 183, 196, 203, 204, 205, 207, 209, 214, 246, 253, 260, 263, 264, 266, 267, 269, 273, 282, 283, &c.
" Hierurgia," the work so entitled, quoted, 171, 185, 196, 203, 205.
HOLLIS, the brothers', "Monumental Effigies of Great Britain," quoted, 269.
Holosericus, what, 155.
Holy loaf, what, 263.

Hom, or Homa, the Persian sacred tree, 84, 140, 154, 213, 216, 238.
Hood, the, upon English copes, how shaped, 41.
Hoods of copes, 2, 3, 41, 144, 198, 260, 272.
Ωρολογιον, or Horologion, one of the Greek ritual books quoted, 172.
Hotel de Bourgtheroud at Rouen, 294.
HOHENSTAUFEN, House of, 29, 38.
Housing, 204.
HUNSDON, Lord, gave silk stockings to Queen Elizabeth, 200.

Illuminated MSS., gauze between leaves of, 57.
Incarnation, mystery of, how symbolized, 236.
Indian embroidery, 14.
Initials—
Two C's interlaced, 5, 38.
G, 236.
L and K, 73.
R, 52.
V, four V's put crosswise, 28.
Inscriptions, 206, 214, 223, 226, 250, 257, 265, 269, 270, 273.
Inscriptions in Arabic, see Arabic.
—— in German, 93, 256, 296.
—— in Greek (Cyrillian letters), 172.
—— in Latin, 31, 62, 66, 80, 82, 89, 111, 119, 148, 166, 176, 187, 201, 206, 210, 211, 223, 226, 257, 264, 265, 269, 305, 329.
——, mediæval, German, 296, 298.
ISAIAS quoted, 281.
Italian altar-frontals, 87, 101, 293.
—— bed-quilt, 293.
—— cut-work applied, 17, 20, 293.
—— silk damask, 11, 13, 15, 25, 33, 46, 56, 58, 60, 73, 74, 81, 115, 129, 130, 136, 162, 163, 165, 196, 206, 227, 230, 233, 239, 240, 242, 256, 258.
—— damask, in silk brocaded with gold, 13, 46, 56, 58, 60, 117, 162, 165, 170, 176, 213, 233, 235.
—— silk, damasked in gold, 177, 181, 183, 241.
—— in silver, 183.

Y Y

Italian silk, damasked in silk and cotton, 37, 60, 181, 230, 262.
—— in silk and hemp, 164.
—— in silk and linen, 37, 124, 130, 176, 204, 243.
—— embroidery, 4, 12, 34, 58, 87, 91, 101, 120, 121, 244, 293.
—— fringe, 293.
—— lace, (silk), 271.
—— net-work, 3, 4, 101, 162.
—— quilting, 14.
—— satin, 14.
—— velvet in silk, 9, 17, 62, 70, 72, 88.
—— velvet in silk, raised, 62, 80, 87, 89, 185, 194, 258.
—— velvet in worsted, 12.
—— web, 221.

James I, 273.
JAMESON, Mrs. quoted, 198.
Jerusalem, the two stars, symbols of, 55.
John Dory, fish so called, 151.
Jubinal's work on tapestry noticed, 86.

KENNEDY, Margaret, one of the ladies in waiting on Mary Queen of Scots at her beheading, 203.
Keys, St. Peter's, one gold, the other silver, 6.
KNIGHT's History of England quoted, 203.
Knot, the Bouchier, 168.
—— the Wake and Ormonde, 250.
Knots, 160, 229, 244.
——, petty, 120, 146.
——, love, 123, 157.
Kraken, the Scandinavian fabled sea-monster, 236.

Lace, old English, 6.
—— gold, 6, 131, 160, 197, 249.
—— nuns', so called, 73.
—— open-worked, 13.
—— silk, 241, 271.
—— silk, and velvet, 85.
——, worsted, 249.
——, woollen and linen, for carriage-trimmings, 191.
Lama d'oro, or cloth of gold, 204.

Lamb, Holy, 58.
Languages, see "Inscriptions."
Languages—
    German mediæval, 296, 298.
Latin rite, 187.
Lappet of a mitre, 51.
Lap-cloths, bishop's, 19, 20.
Lavabo cloths, 203.
Leather gilt, and used as edging, 65, 78.
Lectern cloths or veils, 20, 141, 145, 210, 261.
Legend, the English Golden, quoted, 275, 277.
——, the Golden, translated by Caxton, quoted, 278, 284, 285.
Λειτουργία των προηγιασμενων, 113.
Lent, and Passion-tide, liturgic colours for, 36, 133.
Lenten vestments, 133.
"Letters," the "Paston," noticed, 289.
Linen, or byssus, 25, 152, 175, 239.
—— diaper, 61.
——, embroidered, 29, 65, 71, 181, 185, 190, 235, 242, 246, 249, 250, 251, 255, 256.
—— and gold tissue, 169.
——, printed, 118, 120, 183, 184, 234.
—— and woollen, 246.
Lion, the symbol of Christ, 156.
Liturgical appliances, of rare occurrence in public collections, 99, 112, 120, 142, 171, 174, 184, 186, 188, 196, 202, 205, 210, 242, 243, 250, 263.
Loaf, see Holy Loaf.
—— holy, what, 263.
LOKE, the Scandinavian god, 151.
Lombardy, once famous for its opus araneum, or cobweb weaving, 162.
London wrought stuffs, 161.
Lord, our, how figured on the cross, 276.
Louvre, museum of, silks in, 44.
Love knots, 157.
Lucca damasked silks, 15, 50, 65, 145, 163, 235, 244.
—— damasked silk, brocaded in gold, 243.
—— velvets, 62, 72, 192, 259.
LYDGATE quoted, 288.

Lyons, damasked silk, 19, 20, 91, 105.
———, brocaded in gold and silver, 91.
———, in silver, 19.

M, the letter figured on stuffs, 156, 166, 182, 222, 230, 241.
Madonna del Cardellino, 215.
—— della Cintola, subject of, how treated in the Italian schools, 267.
Magdalen College, Oxford, and its builder Waneflete's fine liturgical shoes, 46.
"Man of Sorrows," our Lord as the, 34.
MANDEVILLE, Sir John's, travels, quoted, 178.
Maniples, 35, 38, 45, 46, 53, 88, 116, 121, 138, 156, 252, 292.
MARCK, DE LA, armorial bearings of the House of, 22.
Marguerite, La, what the flower signifies, 149.
MARTIN'S (Pere), learned and valuable work—"Melanges d'Archéologie," quoted, 44, 130.
Mary, the B. V., her assumption, how figured on the Syon cope, 276.
—— on Florentine textiles, 291. See "Assumption."
———, B. V., the death and burial of, how figured on the Syon cope, 277.
———, St., of Egypt, her legend figured, 54.
—— Queen of Scots, and the cloth over her face when she was beheaded, 203.
Mass of the Presanctified, 113.
Matilda, the Norman William's queen, and the Bayeux so-called tapestry, 7.
Maundy Thursday, mass on, 112, 194.
Melchizedek and Abram, figured, 88, 328.
Memling and his school of painting, 198.
MERCŒUR, House of, 30.
Michael the archangel, how figured, overcoming Satan, 30, 275.
Midgard, the Scandinavian fabled serpent, 151.
Milan, famed for its looms, 162.

Milanese embroidery, 3.
—— lace, 197.
—— net-work, 200.
—— steel-work, 3.
—— velvet raised, 7.
Missal-cushion, 142.
Missal, the Roman, quoted, 142.
—— the Salisbury, quoted, 284.
Mitre, lappets of, 51, 85.
Monstrance for liturgical use, what, 184.
Moon, crescent, 220, 243.
—— crescent, symbolism of, 288.
—— figured in pictures of the Crucifixion, 30.
Moorish tissue, 123.
Moresque, Spanish, 51, 55, 121, 124, 125, 152, 160, 180, 240, 244.
Moslem use, stuffs for, 57, 61.
Mund or ball, so called, 276.
—— how anciently divided, 276.
Munich, the Maximilian museum at, 153, 154.
Murano and its manufacture of beads, 169.
Murrey-colour liked in the mediæval period by the English, 9.
Musical instruments, mediæval, 23, 157.
Mythology, Scandinavian, 150.

Napery—
  Flemish, 34, 61, 73, 75, 124, 203, 205, 255, 263.
  German, 62.
Napkins for crozier, 174, 250.
—— embroidered, 99, 100, 101, 261.
Napkin of linen, 35.
—— for pyx, 202, 260.
Neapolitan embroidery, 13.
—— silk, 13.
NECKAM, ALEXANDER, quoted, 286.
Needlework, 79, 99, 100, 101, 262.
—— old English, the admired "opus Anglicum," 147, 275, 281, 288.
—— old English, how to be known, 288.
Net-work, 3, 4, 61, 101, 107, 175, 200, 245.
Newburg, near Vienna, robes at, 38.
Newmarket, king's house at, 302; tapestries from, 302.
Nineveh sculptures, 25, 122.
Numbers, Book of, quoted, 288.

Nuns' lace, 73.
Nuremberg, old tapestry wrought at, 298.
Nursery rhymes, old English, 103.

O, the, or zero form of ornamentation, 225, 227, 228.
OAKDEN, RALF, Esq., gift of old English embroidered apparels, 147.
Odilia, a French lady-embroideress, 30.
Opus Anglicum, 275, 281, 288.
—— Araneum, 162, 210.
—— Plumarium, 288, 289.
Oriental damasked silk, 25, 128, 132, 136, 140, 154, 155, 160, 251.
—— brocaded in gold, 25, 133, 137, 138, 151, 156.
—— modern damasked silk, 21.
—— brocaded in gold and silver, 21.
—— very fine linen, or byssus, 239.
Orphreys, embroidered, 1, 6, 21, 29, 55, 68, 76, 82, 117, 120, 143, 145, 168, 189, 244, 245, 247, 252, 253, 254, 259, 265.
—— of web, or woven stuff for the purpose, 28, 33, 61, 62, 68, 80, 83, 89, 112, 116, 118, 119, 136, 143, 161, 174, 175, 191, 201, 207, 208, 252, 253, 265, 291.
Orphrey web, Venetian, 71, 112, 271, 272.
ORVIETO, altar-frontal from, 101.
OSMONT's "Volucraire," or Book on Birds, 286.
Ostrich-feathers figured, 19, 129.

Palermo, stuffs woven at, 38, 44, 45, 53, 130, 131, 139, 150, 163, 165, 170, 228, 232.
—— its "Tiraz," or silk-house, 232.
Pallæ or palls, what, 194, 196.
—— or liturgical palls, 196.
Palls for casting over tombs in churches, 56.
Palm-branch carried by St. John Evangelist at the burial of the B. V. Mary, 278.
—— held by the Jew as figured on the Syon cope, 280.
PANDOLFINI, armorials of the family of, 143.

Paper, gilt and stamped out like flowers pasted on silken stuffs, 43.
Papyonns, or cheetahs, 154, 178.
Parchment, gilt, 140, 224, 229, 244.
—— gilt and woven into silken stuffs, 132, 140, 224, 229, 244; the trade trick learned from the Moors by the southern Spaniards, 244.
Parrots; see Zoology—Birds.
"Paston Letters" noticed, 289.
Pastoral amusements, 295, &c.
—— literature, 294.
Paul's, S. cathedral, London, vestments once belonging to, 151.
Peacock, oaths sworn by the, 287.
—— symbolism of the, 286, &c.
Pedalia or Pede-cloths, 209, 210, 263.
Persian carpeting, 83.
—— damask, silk brocaded in gold, 133.
—— damask, silk and worsted, 84.
—— embroidery, 270.
—— satin, 270.
—— tunic, 270.
Peter's, St., fish, 151.
Pin, an old one (?), 254.
PITRA, Dom, now Cardinal, quoted, 286.
Pity, the so-called, of St. Gregory, what, 34, 194.
Plumarium Opus, what, 288, 289.
Pomegranate; see Botany—Fruits.
—— ensign of Queen Catherine of Arragon, 134.
—— ensign of Spain, especially of Granada, 7.
—— symbolic meaning of, 13.
Polystauria or stuffs figured all over with the sign of the cross, 161.
Porphyreticum, what, 155.
Pouch, 3.
Prato, church of, 261.
Presanctified, mass of, 113.
Printing by block, on silk, 31, &c.; see Block printing.
Psalms, Book of, quoted, 281.
Purses, 3, 89, 106.
—— liturgical, 188, 263.
Pyx cloth, 202, 260.

Quilting, 14, 16.
—— English, 16.
Quilts, 4, 5, 13, 14, 16, 86, 104, 293.

Index I. 349

R, the letter, wrought upon a silken stuff, 52.
Rain-drops, shower of, 52, 54, 239, &c.
RAINE, Mr., his St. Cuthbert, noticed, 205.
RAPHAEL's Madonna del Cardellino, 215.
REBECCA meeting ABRAHAM's servant at the well, figured in tapestry, 333.
Relics, bag for, 42.
Reredos of embroidered linen, 53, 235.
Resurrection, how figured on woven stuffs, 113, 272.
—— of our Lord, how embroidered upon the Syon cope, 276.
Rhenish cut or applied work, 21, 258.
—— embroidery, 2, 52, 247, 258.
Ribbon, green silk and gold thread, 121.
RICHARD II.'s monumental effigy in Westminster Abbey, 269.
Rite, Greek, noticed, 113, 124, 126, 171, 191, 205.
—— Latin, 113, 124, 172, 187, 188, 191, 194, 205.
Rock crystal, balls of, used on vestments, 206.
Romance, the, of Sir Guy of Warwick, figured, 77.
Rosary-beads, 263.
Rose of England, 134.
—— red and white, 188.
ROVERE DELLA, family of, 115.
Ruthenic work, 171.

Saddle-bags, 84.
Saddle-cloth, 204.
—— Saints, figured
S. Andrew, Apostle, 158, 279.
S. Ann, mother of the B. V. Mary, 147, &c.
S. Anthony of Egypt, 253, 254.
S. Bartholomew, Apostle, 270.
S. Bernard, 198.
S. Bernard's life, 198.
St. Blase, 38.
S. Catherine of Alexandria, 253.
S. Christina, and her life, 142.
S. Dorothy, 211.
Santa Francesca Romana, and her life, 92.

S. James, Apostle, called of Compostella, 280.
S. James the Less, Apostle, 280.
S. Jerome, 142.
S. John, Evangelist, 142, 145, 276, &c.
S. Kilian or Kuln, 187.
S. Louis, King of France, 144.
S. Lucy, 142, 211.
S. Mark, Evangelist, 111.
S. Mary, B. V., 148, 210, 211, 236, 251, 260, 272, 273, 276, 279.
St. Mary of Egypt, 54.
S. Mary Magdalen, 30, 209, 211, 280.
S. Michael, Archangel, 30, 275.
S. Odilia, 187.
S. Onuphrius, hermit, 2.
S. Paul, Apostle, 146, 278, 279.
S. Peter, Apostle, 145, 149, 278, 279.
S. Philip, Apostle, 149, 280.
S. Simon, Apostle, 149, 210.
S. Stephen, stoning of, 6, 38.
S. Thomas, Apostle, 279, 280; see "Girdle at Prato."
S. Ubaldo, 102.
S. Ursula, 211, 247.
Saints' tombs, 56.
Salisbury rite, noticed, 34, 36.
SAMPSON slaying the lion, figured, 123.
Saracenic damask, 127, 178, 244.
Sashes, 21.
Satin, 8, 9, 13, 14, 16, 20, 110, 113.
—— French, 110.
—— Italian, 113.
Scandinavian mythology, 150.
Scarf, 18.
—— liturgical, 105.
SCHÖN MARTIN, 207.
School, Umbrian, of painting, 184, 186.
—— of Umbria for painting, 247; and its beauty, 247.
Sclaves, 172.
Scotch embroidery, 273.
SCOTT, SIR WALTER, quoted, 3.
Scull-cap, 16.
SHAW's "Dresses and Decorations of the Middle Ages," quoted, 86.
Shoe, liturgical, 46.
Shower of rain-drops, figured, 54, 239.
Sicilian stuffs, 28, 29, 32, 37, 38, 39, 40, 41, 43, 44, 45, 46, 47, 48, 49, 50, 51, 52, 53, 76, 115, 127, 130,

132, 137, 139, 146, 150, 154, 156, 158, 159, 163, 164, 165, 167, 168, 169, 178, 179, 180, 215, 222, 223, 224, 225, 226, 227, 228, 229, 230, 231, 234, 238, 239, 242, 245, 266, 268, 269, 274.
Sicilian cendal, 163.
—— damasks, figured with beasts and flowers, 47, 50, 51, 52, 53, 127, 130, 137, 139, 146, 150, 164, 166, 178, 179, 269.
—— damasks in silk, 32, 53, 76, 115, 132, 137, 156, 159, 163, 168, 169, 180, 215, 226, 227, 239, 245, 274
—— damasks in silk, brocaded in gold, 28, 29, 37, 38, 39, 40, 41, 43, 45, 46, 47, 50, 51, 52, 53, 126, 130, 139, 146, 150, 159, 164, 165, 167, 168, 224, 227, 228, 231, 232, 234, 238, 242, 266, 268, 269.
—— damasks, silk and cotton, 41, 44, 230.
—— damasks, silk and cotton, brocaded in gold, 39, 45, 48.
—— damasks, in silk and thread, 154, 223.
—— damasks, silk and thread, brocaded in gold, 48, 49, 238.
—— damasks in linen thread, brocaded in gold, 169.
—— damask or tapestry, silk, cotton, and wool, 158.
—— embroidery, 149, 158, 159.
—— lace, silk, and gold, 160, 161.
—— taffeta, 75, 121.
—— tissue or web, 222.
Silk-house, or Tiraz, at Palermo, 232.
Silk gauze, 57.
Silks, block-printed, 31.
Silk mixed with cotton, 5, 24, 26, 27, 33, 37, 39, 41, 42, 43, 44, 47, 60, 126, 152, 181, 219, 226.
—— mixed with linen, 27, 33, 37, 122, 123, 124, 176, 192, 220, 223.
—— worsted, 84, 114; see Damask.
—— net-work, 200.
Silversmith's work amid embroidery, 168, 169, 186, 199, 223, 233.
Sindon, the Greek liturgical embroidery, so-called, 170.
—— or pyx-cloth of the old English ritual, 202, 260.

Sorrows, Man of, our Lord figured as, 34.
—— the B. V. Mary, of, 69.
SOTHENER, MASTER STEPHEN, and his fine picture in Cologne cathedral, 187.
Spangles, 186, 190, 223.
Spanish carpeting, 209, 248.
—— crocet work, 20.
—— damasked silk, 36, 48, 67, 72, 73, 74, 115, 121, 126, 128, 129, 168, 182, 216, 224, 225, 240, 248.
Spanish damasks, brocaded in gold, 50, 62, 66, 116, 132, 193, 229.
————, in silver, 177.
—— embroidery, 65, 81, 204.
Spanish-Moresco stuffs, 51, 121, 124, 125, 152, 160, 180, 241, 244.
—— net work, 20.
—— stuffs, cotton and linen, 224.
————, linen, and gilt parchment, 140, 224.
————, silk and cotton, 26, 47, 166.
————, linen, 122, 166.
—— of wool and hemp, 209.
—— of wool and thread, 114.
—— taffetas, 47.
—— velvets, 81, 135, 189, 207, 291, 292.
SPENSER quoted, 64.
Spicilegium Solefmense quoted, 286.
Spider, figured, 182.
Star and Crescent, their symbolism, 285.
Star, symbolism of, 55, 272, 285.
Stauracin, 124, 127, 160, 161.
"Stella Maris," or "Star of the Sea," one of the old symbolical attributes of the B. V. Mary, 272.
State cap, 86.
Stauracina, what, 124, 161.
Stenciled satin, 113.
Stichery of a fine kind, 4, 7, 19.
Stockings, silk, one of the first pair made in England, given to Queen Elizabeth, and now belonging to the Marquis of Salisbury, 200.
Stoles, 24, 44, 58, 138, 185, 222, 235.
——, 58, 121, 191.
Stones, precious, used, 81, 82, 199.
STOTHARD, MRS., 7.

Index I.

Strap-shaped ornamentation on textiles, as well as in bookbindings, 201.
Stuffs, loom-wrought, with history-pieces, 271, 272.
Stuffs, &c.,
  Of the Adoration of the Magi or three Kings, 186.
  Of Angels, 142, 143.
  —— holding crescents, 234.
  ——— a monstrance, 184.
  Of Angels swinging thuribles, and carrying crowns of thorns and crosses in their hands, 36.
  Of the Annunciation, 247.
  Of the Assumption of the B. V. Mary, 272, 273.
Stuffs figured with—
  Beasts, 5, 25, 32, 41, 42, 43, &c.
  Birds, 26, 28, 29, 32, 37, 41, 42.
  Men and beasts, 122.
  With a Chinese subject, 75.
  Of the coronation in heaven of the B. V. Mary, 272.
  Of Emblems of the Passion, 133.
  Figured with flowers and fruits, 11, 13, 15, 41, 42.
  Of a king on horse-back, with hawk on hand, &c., 223.
  Of a man or woman with hawk on wrist, 233.
  Of the B. V. Mary, with our Lord as a child in her arms, or on her lap, 63, 71, 271, 272.
  Of St. Mary of Egypt, 54.
  Of St. Peter, apostle, 136.
  Of the resurrection.
  Of Sampson overcoming the lion, 122.
  Of women gathering dates, 165.
Subdeacon's liturgical veil worn over the shoulders, 144.
Sudary of our Lord, 26.
Sun-beams and rain-drops figured, 54, 239.
Sun and moon figured in art-works of the Crucifixion, 30.
Surplices, 239.
—— of transparent linen, 239.
Symbolism, 149, 236, 237, 272, 276, 285, 311, 329, 330, 331, 332.
Syon Nunnery, beautiful cope once belonging to, 275.

Syrian crape drapered with a pattern, 126.
—— stuffs, 125, 127, 139, 213, 215, 216, 221.
—— damask in silk and cotton, 24, 152.
—— damask, silk and gold, 122, 178, 180, 238.
—— damask, silk and linen thread, 42, 136, 220.

Table-covers, 16, 19, 92, 108, 141.
Taffeta, 47.
—— Egyptian, 56, 57.
—— Sicilian, 75, 121.
Tangier stuff, 123.
Tapestry, 6, 158, 294, &c.
Tapestry—
  English, 306.
  Flemish, 294, 299, 300, 301, 302, 303, 307, 328, 329, 333.
  French, 302, 303, 304, 305, 306, 307, 309.
  German, 296, 298.
Tassels on dalmatics, 206.
TAYLOR's "Glory of Regality," quoted, 153.
Tetuan stuff, 123.
THAUN, PHILIPPE DE, quoted, 236.
The Three Wise Men, clothed and crowned as kings going to Bethlehem, 148.
THORNELL of Suffolk, arms of, 148.
Thread embroidery, 19, 20, 53, 58.
Throne-room in Roman princely houses, 87, 107.
Tiles, glazed for paving, 183.
Tiraz or silk-house at Palermo, 232.
TOBIT, the elder, sending his son to Rages, figured, 335.
Toca, what, 204.
Tombs in churches, palls for throwing over, 56.
Trimming for carriages, 191.
—— vestments, 193.
Tunicle, 143.
Turkish net, 61.
Tyrian purple, so called, 155, 159, 160, 219.

The U form of ornamentation, 227, 228.

Unicorn, hunting of the, 53, 236.
Umbrian school of painting, 184, 186, 247.
V, the letter, put crofs-wife, 28.
Vallombrofa, book from the monaftery at, 87.
Varnicle or Vernicle, 198, 248.
Vafari, quoted, 261.
Veil for lectern, 20, 141, 145, 212, 261.
Veil or fcarf worn over his fhoulders by the fubdeacon, 144, 145.
Velvet, brocaded in gold, 62, 65, 85, 107, 134, 135, 144, 185, 189, 193, 198, 259.
Velvet, cut and applied, 17, 20.
—— embroidered, 198, 200, 204.
—— figured, 17, 62, 135, 192, 193, 207.
—— freckled with golden loops, 257.
——, pile upon pile, 1, 257.
——, plain, 2, 3. 9, 14, 143, 199, 204, 206.
——, raifed, 4, 18, 62, 65, 69, 70, 72, 80, 82, 87, 89, 90, 107, 110, 134, 135, 144, 145, 185, 193, 200, 254, 256, 257, 258, 263.
——, Englifh, fee Brooke Collection, 312, &c.
—— Flemifh, 254, 255, 264.
—— Florentine, 17, 18, 82, 85, 142, 144, 145, 198, 256, 257.
—— French, 14, 89, 106.
—— Genoa, 3, 18, 62, 90, 107, 110, 134, 145, 192, 199, 200, 263.
—— Italian, 65, 89, 90, 199.
—— Lucca, 62, 72, 192, 198, 259.
—— Spanifh, 81, 135, 189.
Venetian beads, 169.
—— damafk, 54, &c.
—— embroidery, 44, 168.
—— embroidery in beads, 169.
—— lace, 141.
—— table-covers, 141.
—— webs, 71, 112, 271, 272.
Veftments often blazoned with armorial bearing of thofe who gave them, 22, 148, 214, 282.
——, Englifh, 41, 146, 275.
VINCENT, FRANCOIS ANDRE, 302.

VIOLLET, LE DUC, quoted, 212.
VIRGILIUS, fubjects from, figured in tapeftry, 300, 301, 302.

WALLER's braffes, noticed, 181.
WANEFLETE's, BP., liturgical fhoes, 46.
Warwick, Sir Guy of, and the Northumbrian dragon, figured, 79.
Webs, 28, 33, 61, 62, 63, 64, 71, 80, 112, 116, 117, 118, 119, 136, 143, 161, 174, 175, 191, 201, 217, 221, 222, 223, 257, 261, 271, 272, 291.
Wire of pure metal gold, or filver, 220.
Wife men or Magi, adoration of, figured, 3.
Wire, pure metal, 220.
Witfuntide, ftuff for, in the ritual, 226.
Witfunday, how fignified, 2.
Worfley, The, fepulchral brafs, 181.
Worfted and thread, 114.
—— work, 61, 79.
WYDEROYD, Paftor S. Jacobi Colon, 189.

Y, the crofs fo called, 81. 82.
York, cloth of gold, found in a grave at the cathedral of, 251.
Ypres, 34, 61, 73, 75.

Zoology—
  Beafts:
    Antelopes, 46, 47, 52, 234.
    Boars, wild, 180.
    Cheetahs, or papyonns, 74, 136, 137, 154, 178, 215, 234.
    Deer, 108, 226, 242.
    Dogs, 33, 42, 45, 50, 52, 124, 138, 155, 165, 168, 180, 223, 233, 241, 336.
    Elephant, 45; and caftle, 170.
    Gazelles, 179, 234.
    Giraffes, 225, 228.
    Hares, 240, 310.
    Harts, 41, 42, 43, 51, 118.
    Hounds, 49, 76, 167.
    Leopards, 154, 163, 164, 214.
    Lions, 27, 30, 33, 42, 49, 57, 111, 122, 131, 137, 138, 146, 165, 177, 183, 218.
    Monkey, 108, 310.
    Oxen, 214.
    Panther, 250.

Index I.

Zoology *continued*.
  Beasts:
    Papyonns; see cheetah.
    Squirrels, 58.
    Stags, 53, 99, 166, 180.
    Talbot, or English blood-hound, 223.
    Toad, 310.
    Weasel, or stoat, 310.
    Wolf, 158.
  Beasts, emblematic, 198, 156, 163, 311.
  Beasts, heraldic, 5, 40, 41, 46, 47, 52, 53, 58, 59, 60, 156, 161, 217, 218, 228, 246, 267.
    Elephant and Castle, 170.
    Griffins, 5, 29, 32, 40, 47, 49, 130, 131, 154, 155.
    Leopard, noued, 164.
    Libbards, 240.
    Lion, noued, 165.
    Lioncels, 5.
    Wyverns, 40, 47, 131, 133, 158, 159, 163, 168, 228.
  Beasts, monsters, 3, 25, 30, 40, 41, 42, 99, 106, 150, 155, 157, 158, 160, 177, 181, 217, 218, 222, 226, 251.
    Kraken, 236.
    Mermaid, 251.
    Midgard Serpent, 151.
    Satyr, 3.
    Sphinxes, 181.
    The Wolf Fenrir, 151.
  Beasts, symbolical:
    Hare, of man's soul, 237, 311.
    Lion, of Christ, 156.
    Monkey, of mischief and lubricity, 311.
    Monoceros or unicorn, of Christ as God-man, 237.

Zoology *continued*.
  Birds:
    Cocks, 39.
    Cockatoos, 133, 228.
    Cranes, 164.
    Doves, 124, 218, 310; symbol of love, 311.
    Ducks, wild, 229.
    Eagles, 7, 25, 26, 40, 43, 50, 51, 76, 81, 129, 137, 138, 158, 163, 164, 178, 180, 183, 229, 232, 233.
    Hawks, 155, 166, 223, 226, 233.
    Hoopoes, 45, 137, 146.
    Owls, 3.
    Parrots, 119, 131, 139, 140, 154, 159, 166, 168, 241, 242, 244.
    Peacocks, 154, 250.
    Pelican, 214.
    Pheasants, 60.
    Swans, 49, 166, 179, 232.
    Wild ducks, 229.
  Birds, heraldic, or monster things with wings:
    Dragon, 1.
    Eagle, double-headed, 7, 37, 86.
    Griffins, 5, 29, 32, 40, 47, 49, 131.
    Harpies, 329, 330.
    Wyverns, 40, 47, 131, 158, 159, 163, 168, 228, 330.
  Fish, 151.
  ———, St. Peter's, the Italian Gianitore, or our John Dory, 151.
  Insects:
    Butterflies, 16, 44, 66.
    Spider, 182.
  Shells, 7.
  Snakes, 177.

INDEX II.

GEOGRAPHY OF TEXTILES.

EUROPE.

ENGLAND:
 Chintz.
 Embroidery.
 Quilting.
 Satins.
 Silks.
 Tapeſtry.
 Velvets.
 Webs, ribbon-like.

FLANDERS:
 Embroidery.
 Lace.
 Linen, block-printed.
 Linen, damaſked.
 Napery.
 Silk, damaſked.
 Tapeſtry.
 Velvets.

FRANCE:
 Cloth of gold.
 Embroidery.
 Lace in gold.
 Quilting.
 Silks, brocaded.
 Silks, damaſked.
 Tapeſtry.
 Velvets.
 Webs.

GERMANY:
 Cologne, and other Rheniſh towns:
  Embroidery in ſilk, in thread, in worſted.
  Napery.
  Silk and linen.
  Tapeſtry.
  Velvet.
  Webs in ſilk, in ſilk and linen.

GREECE:
 Silks.
 Silks mixed with cotton.
 Silks mixed with linen thread.
 Byzantine ſtuffs hiſtoried.

ITALY:
 Florence:
  Embroidery.
  Silks, damaſked.
  Silks, hiſtoried.
  Silks mixed with linen.
  Velvets, pile upon pile.
  Velvets, plain.
  Velvets wrought with gold.
  Velvets raiſed.
  Webs, hiſtoried.
 Genoa:
  Silks, brocaded in gold.
  Silks, damaſked.
  Velvets, plain.
 Italian Textiles, &c.:
  Applied or cut-work.
  Embroidery.
  Fringe.
  Lace.
  Quilting.
  Satins.
  Satins, brocaded in gold and ſilver.
  Silks, brocaded in gold.
  Silks, damaſked.
  Silks mixed with cotton.
  ———— with hemp.
  ———— with flax.
  Velvets raiſed.
  Velvets of ſilk.
  Velvets of worſted.
  Webs

Lombardy:
  Cob-web weaving.
  Lace.
Lucca:
  Silks, brocaded in gold.
  Silks, damasked.
  Velvets.
Milan:
  Embroidery.
  Lace.
  Velvets.
  Velvets, raised.
Naples:
  Embroidery.
  Silks.
Reggio:
  Silks, damasked.
Sicily:
  Cendal.
  Damasks in linen, brocaded in gold.
  Embroidery.
  Lace in silk and gold.
  Silks, brocaded in gold.
  Silks, damasked.
  Silks mixed with cotton.
  Silks mixed with cotton and wool.
  Silks mixed with flaxen thread.
  Silk taffeta.
  Silk webs.
Venice:
  Embroidery.
  Embroidery in beads.
  Laces in gold.
  Silks, damasked.
SPAIN:
  Carpeting.
  Crocet-work.
  Embroidery.
  Silks, brocaded in gold and silver.
  Silks, damasked.
  Silks mixed with gilt parchment.
  Silks mixed with cotton and linen
    thread.
  Silks mixed with linen thread.
  Silks mixed with linen thread, and
    gilt parchments.

SPAIN *continued.*
  Stuffs of wool and hemp.
  Stuffs of wool and thread.
  Taffetas.
  Velvets.

ASIA.
CHINA:
  Embroidery.
  Satins.
  Silks.
  Silks, damasked.
INDIA:
  Embroidery.
  Linen.
PERSIA:
  Carpeting.
  Embroidery.
  Satins.
  Silks.
  Silks, brocaded in gold.
  Silks, damasked.
  Silks mixed with wool.
SYRIA:
  Crape.
  Silks, brocaded in gold.
  Silks, damasked.
  Silks mixed with cotton.
  Silks mixed with linen.

AFRICA.
ALGIERS:
  Embroidery.
  Fine linen.
EGYPT:
  Byssus or very fine linen.
  Gauze.
  Silks.
  Silks mixed with cotton.
  Taffetas.
MOROCCO:
  Tangier:
    Silks.
  Tetuan:
    Silks.

www.ingramcontent.com/pod-product-compliance
Lightning Source LLC
Chambersburg PA
CBHW031933290426
44108CB00011B/536